THE BLUE GUIDES

Albania
Austria
Belgium and Luxembourg
China
Cyprus
Czechoslovakia
Denmark
Egypt

FRANCE
France
Paris and Versailles
Burgundy
Normandy
South West France
Corsica

GERMANY
Berlin and Eastern Germany
Western Germany

GREECE
Greece
Athens and environs
Crete

HOLLAND
Holland
Amsterdam

Hungary
Ireland

ITALY
Northern Italy
Southern Italy
Florence
Rome and environs
Venice
Tuscany
Umbria
Sicily

Jerusalem
Malta and Gozo
Morocco
Moscow and Leningrad
Portugal

SPAIN
Spain
Barcelona

Switzerland

TURKEY
Turkey
Istanbul

UK
England
Scotland
Wales
London
Museums and Galleries
  of London
Oxford and Cambridge
Country Houses of England
Gardens of England
Literary Britain and Ireland
Victorian Architecture in
  Britain
Churches and Chapels
  of Northern England
Churches and Chapels
  of Southern England
Channel Islands

USA
New York
Boston and Cambridge

Jugendstil house in Eisenach

BLUE GUIDE

Berlin and Eastern Germany

Anne Massey

A&C Black
London

WW Norton
New York

First edition 1994

Published by A & C Black (Publishers) Ltd
35 Bedford Row, London WC1R 4JH

A CIP catalogue record of this book is available from the British Library.

ISBN   0–7136–3871–0   914.310 4879 MAS

Published in the United States of America by
WW Norton and Company Inc,
500 Fifth Avenue, New York, NY 10110

Published simultaneously in Canada by
Penguin Books Canada Limited
10 Alcorn Avenue, Toronto, Ontario M4V 3BE

ISBN   0–393–31197–X   USA

The author and the publishers have done their best to ensure the accuracy of all the
information in Blue Guide Berlin and Eastern Germany; however, they can accept no
responsibility for any loss, injury or inconvenience sustained by any traveller as a result
of information or advice contained in the guide.

For permission to reproduce the illustrations in this book the publishers would like to
thank: Archiv für Kunst und Geschichte, Berlin: pages 53, 57, 151, 155, 157, 293, 313,
331, 333; Sächsische Landesbibliothek, Dresden: pages 30, 36, 104, 115, 167, 197, 217,
239, 277, 297, 323; Bildarchiv Foto Marburg: pages 99, 163, 285; Barnaby's Picture
Library, London: pages 49 (R. Gardner), 71 (Landesbildstelle Berlin), 171 (Hubertus
Kanus); Tony Mott: pages 997, 291; Anne Massey: page 2.

Regional map and town plans by Terence Crump.

Map of the Berlin S and U Bahn network reproduced by kind permission of Berliner
Verkehrs-Betriebe.

Anne Massey studied the History of Modern Art, Design and Film at the
University of Northumbria where she was awarded a PhD in 1985. She has
lectured and written extensively on art and design, and her book *Interior
Design of the Twentieth Century* is published by Thames and Hudson. She
has worked and researched in Germany over the past five years, witnessing
the re-unification of Germany. Based at Southampton Institute of Higher
Education, she was Reader in Design History and Head of the Research
Centre for Consumer Culture and is now Head of the Media Division.

The publishers invite readers to write in with their comments, suggestions
and corrections for the next edition of the guide. Writers of the most
informative letters will be awarded a free Blue Guide of their choice.

Printed in Great Britain by The Bath Press, Avon.

Introduction

This is the first Blue Guide to concentrate exclusively on Berlin and eastern Germany. It was conceived before the events of 1989 brought this area of Europe to international attention. With the demise of the Berlin Wall and the Unification of East and West Germany the need for a guide to the forgotten treasures of the former GDR became even more apparent. A visit to eastern Germany at present is special as history is quite patently in the making. Many historic buildings were neglected during Communist rule, but their untouched state increases their fascination. The lack of commercial exploitation over the last fifty years also adds to the charm of the eastern Länder. Therefore, do not expect pristine buildings and fast moving, efficient roads or service. Instead, expect to be thrilled and enchanted by the wealth of architectural and art gems to be discovered.

Since 1990 eastern Germany has been divided into six *Länder* (or regions) which provide the structure of this book. The areas were divided on the basis of historical precedent and so each district has its own distinct cultural heritage and geographical features. Bearing in mind that Germany became a nation only in 1871, the identities of Freistat Sachsen (Saxony) and Thüringen (Thuringia) are far more individual than those of the separate counties of, for example, Great Britain. The northern Baltic coastline is particularly scenic, with the Island of Rügen of special interest. The remainder of the *Land* of Mecklenburg-Vorpommern (Mecklenburg-Pomerania), which covers the northern region of the country, is comparatively untouched, scattered with lakes and arable farmland. A key feature of this district is the brick Gothic architecture—also to be found in Brandenburg to the south. Brandenburg, the biggest of the new *Länder*, borders onto Poland, and the highlight must be its capital, Potsdam. Some of the finest Rococo and Neo-Classical architecture and interior decoration in Europe is situated in the Sanssouci park at Potsdam. This *Land* also boasts the quaint Spreewald region with its waterbourne way of life. Berlin is a separate Bundesland, situated right in the middle of Brandenburg. The main fascination here is the lingering effect of the Berlin Wall. It was here that East and West, Communist and Capitalist, actually interfaced, as Berlin was sliced in half by the Iron Curtain. Out on a limb for so long, the city is being restored to its former glory and will host the State Parliament by the turn of the century. The great art and archaeological collections of the former Prussian state are of key importance, and a visit to the Pergamon and Dahlem Museums should not be missed.

To the south of Brandenburg is the picturesque state of Freistat Sachsen, known as Saxon Switzerland because of its mountainous scenery. Here are the incredible palaces and collections of the former Saxon nobility at Dresden and Meissen, home of Europe's finest porcelain. The musical capital, Leipzig, is also situated in Freistat Sachsen. To the west is Thüringen, with its atmospheric wooded hills and centre of the German Enlightenment, Weimar. To the north is Sachsen-Anhalt which features the Harz mountain range with the unspoilt, medieval villages of Quedlinburg and Halberstadt. Here also is the home of the German Reformation, Wittenberg and one of the most glorious medieval cathedrals in Europe—Naumburg.

Eastern Germany has only recently opened up for the independent traveller and I can only hope that you, armed with this guide, will derive as much pleasure and satisfaction from your visit as I have over the last five years.

Acknowledgements

I would like to express my thanks to the many people who have helped in the writing of this book. First and foremost, Sarah Martin, who wrote and researched the chapter on Mecklenburg–Vorpommern and much of the section on Brandenburg; without her continual support and stalwart efforts the guide would never have been written. Many thanks also to Agatha Suess and Silva Giesen at the German National Tourist Office, London and the individual tourist offices throughout eastern Germany. I am grateful to P & O European Ferries and Lufthansa for travel facilities and Maritim Hotels for accommodation. Thanks also to the Research Committee at Southampton Institute of Higher Education for invaluable support and to my agent, Caroline Davidson, for endless encouragement and inspiration. May I also express my gratitude to Gemma Davies of A & C Black for her patience and enthusiasm.

Note on Blue Guides

The Blue Guide series began in 1915 when Muirhead Guide-Books Limited published 'Blue Guide London and its Environs'. Findlay and James Muirhead already had experience of guidebook publishing: before the First World War they had been the editors of the English editions of the German Baedekers, and by 1915 they had acquired the copyright of most of the famous 'Red' Handbooks from John Murray.

An agreement made with the French publishing house Hachette et Cie in 1917 led to the translation of Muirhead's London guide, which became the first 'Guide Blue'—Hachette had previously published the blue-covered 'Guides Joannes'. Subsequently, Hachette's 'Guide Bleu Paris et ses Environs' was adapted and published in London by Muirhead. The collaboration between the two publishing houses continued until 1933.

In 1933 Ernest Benn Limited took over the Blue Guides, appointing Russell Muirhead, Findlay Muirhead's son, editor in 1934. The Muirhead's connection with the Blue Guides ended in 1963 when Stuart Rossiter, who had been working on the Guides since 1954, became house editor, revising and compile several of the books himself.

The Blue Guides are now published by A & C Black, who acquired Ernest Benn in 1984, so continuing the tradition of guidebook publishing which began in 1826 with 'Black's Economical Tourist of Scotland'. The Blue Guide series continues to grow: there are now more than 50 titles in print with revised editions appearing regularly and many new Blue Guides in preparation.

'Blue Guides' is a registered trade mark.

CONTENTS

Introduction 5
Acknowledgements 6
A Note on Blue Guides 6

Background Information
Historical Introduction 11
Brief Chronology 15
Art, Design and Architecture in eastern Germany 17
Glossary of Architectural and German terms 21
Select Bibliography 22

Practical Information
Planning your trip 23
Arriving in eastern Germany 25
Food and drink 26
Travelling around Germany 26
General Information 27
Useful words 29

I Berlin
Introduction 31
Tourist Information 31
Arriving in Berlin 31
Getting around the city 32
Festivals 33
History 34

Route 1 Essential Berlin 39
2 City Centre Museums: East and West Museum Island 58
The Tiergarten Museums and Galleries 64
3 The Charlottenburg Palace, Park and Environs 67
4 Down at the Dahlem 73
The Dahlem Museum Complex 74
The Botanischer Garten 80
Grunewald 81
5 Alternative Berlin 83
6 Köpenick and the Museum of Applied Art 90

II Brandenburg
7 The Park Sanssouci at Potsdam 93
8 Potsdam Town Tour 101
9 Palaces on the Havel 106
10 The Spreewald: from Berlin to Lübben, Lübbenau and Cottbus 110
A. Lübben 111
B. Lübbenau 113
C. Cottbus 114
11 Berlin to Eberswalde and Chorin 118
A. Eberswalde 118
B. The Monastery of Chorin 120

Route 12 Berlin to Frankfurt an der Oder and Neuzelle 123
          A. Frankfurt an der Oder 123
          B. The Monastery of Neuzelle 130
       13 Prenzlau 132
       14 Brandenburg 135

III Freistat Sachsen
       15 Dresden 143
          A. From the main railway station to the Albertinum 145
          B. The Albertinum 148
          C. The Palace Quarter 153
          D. The Zwinger 157
          E. The Neustadt 160
          F. The Weisser Hirsch 161
       16 From Dresden to Pirna via Pillnitz 162
          A. The Palaces and Gardens of Pillnitz 162
          B. The Kunsthandwerkmuseum Schloss Pillnitz 164
          C. Pirna 166
       17 From Dresden to Leipzig via Radebeul,
           Schloss Moritzburg and Meissen 168
          A. Radebeul 169
          B. Schloss Moritzburg 170
          C. Meissen 173
       18 Leipzig 177
          A. Town Tour 180
          B. Beyond the Ring 185
          C. South of the City: the Volkerschlachtdenkmal and
              surrounds 187
       19 Upper Lustia: from Dresden to Zittau via Bautzen
           and Görlitz 188
          A. Bautzen 188
          B. Görlitz 191
          C. Zittau 193
       20 From Leipzig to Zwickau via Colditz and Chemnitz 195
          A. Colditz 195
          B. Chemnitz 198
          C. Zwickau 200
       21 From Zwickau to Dresden via Augustusburg
           and Freiberg 201
          A. Augustusburg 202
          B. Freiberg 202

IV Mecklenburg-Vorpommern
       22 Schwerin 205
          A. The Old Centre 206
          B. Schloss Schwerin 210
          C. The environs of Schwerin 213
       23 From Schwerin to Güstrow 213
       24 From Schwerin to Neustrelitz 220
       25 From Neustrelitz to Neubrandenburg 223
       26 Wismar and the Island of Poel 226
       27 The Baltic Coast: from Wismar to Rostock 232
       28 Rostock 235

Route 29   The Baltic Coast from Rostock to Stralsund   243
     30   Stralsund   244
     31   The Island of Rügen   251
     32   Hiddensee   256
     33   From Stralsund to Griefswald, Eldena and the Island of
        Usedom   257
     34   From Schwerin to Neustadt Glewe   263

V   Saxony-Anhalt
     35   Magdeburg   266
     36   The Harz Mountains   271
        A.   Halberstadt   271
        B.   Wernigerode   273
        C.   Quedlinburg   275
     37   From Halle to Naumburg   278
        A.   Halle   278
        B.   Merseburg   282
        C.   Naumburg   283
     38   From Wittenburg to Dessau   286
        A.   Lutherstadt Wittenburg   286
        B.   Wörlitz   289
        C.   Dessau   291
     39   The Altmarkt Region   294
        A.   Stendal   294
        B.   Tangermünde   295

VI   Thüringen
     40   From western Germany to the Thüringian Forest   298
        A.   Schmalkalden   299
        B.   Suhl   301
        C.   Ilmenau   302
        D.   Arnstadt   302
     41   Eisenach and the Wartburg Castle   305
        A.   Eisenach Town Centre   306
        B.   The Wartburg Castle   310
     42   Erfurt   312
     43   From Eisenach to Weimar via Gotha   318
        A.   Gotha town centre   320
        B.   Schloss Friedenstein and Grounds   321
     44   Weimar   326
        A.   Town Tour   328
        B.   Park an der Ilm and the Schloss Belvedere   335
        C.   From the Marktplatz to the Goethe-Schiller Crypt   336
        D.   From the Kegelplaz to the Tierfurt Park and Schloss   338
     45   From Weimar to Mühlhausen via Ettersberg, Sondershausen
        and Nordhausen   340
        A.   Ettersberg   340
        B.   Sondershausen   341
        C.   Nordhausen   341
        D.   Mühlhausen   342
     46   From Weimar to Gera via Dornburg, Tautenburg
        and Jena   344

Route 47   Gera   349
        48   From Gera to Kohnen-Sahlis via Altenburg and
              Windischleuba   352
              A.   Altenburg   353
              B.   Windischleuba   355
        49   From Weimar to Grosskockberg, Rudolstadt, Saalfeld and
              the Schloss Schwartzburg   356
              A.   Rudolstadt   357
              B.   Saalfeld   358
Index   361

Maps and plans

Regional map   *inside the front and back covers*
Berlin S and U Bahn   *at the end of the book*

Berlin   40–5
Brandenburg   137
Dresden   146–7
Eisenach   307
Gera   351
Gotha   319
Halle   279
Leipzig   178–9
Magdeburg   267
Naumburg   284
Potsdam   102
Rostock   237
Schwerin   207
Weimar   327

Historical Introduction

From Pre-history to the Holy Roman Empire

Germany has no natural frontiers. It lies in the centre of Europe and has been affected by the myriad of political, social and economic upheavals which have taken place in the continent throughout history. What we now know as Germany has been inhabited since prehistoric times. Evidence of stone, bronze and iron age civilisations have been discovered in the area. Only the southern and western parts of Germany were occupied by the Romans, with the northern area inhabited by the Germanic tribes, described in some detail by Tacitus (AD 55–116) in *Germania*. After the fall of the Roman Empire in the 5C the western parts of Germany were settled by newly Christianised Germans. From the 6C onwards monasteries were established throughout the western region with the majority of the population living as serfs under feudal rule. Germany was first given shape by the Emperor Charlemagne, King of France from 771, who also reigned over what are now the Netherlands, Belgium, Switzerland, the Lombardy region of Italy and Germany as far as the river Elbe. Charlemagne introduced Christianity to the heathen Saxons, strengthening existing bishoprics and instigating new ones. Following the death of Charlemagne's successor, Louis the Pious, in 840 the newly revived Roman Empire was split three ways under the Treaty of Verdun in 843. The first German king was Conrad I, Duke of Franconia, whose son Duke Henry of Saxony was elected to succeed him in 919. From this date until the death of Henry III in 956 Germany developed into the Holy Roman Empire of the German Nation. In 936 the Saxon, Otto I, was crowned king at Charlemagne's former capital, Aachen, to mark his role as successor to the great Emperor. Otto I played off the feuding duchies against the church, enjoying total control over the latter. The archbishops, bishops and abbots provided valuable military strength for the king. Henry I and Otto I used this military power to push the eastern frontiers of Germany back, cutting into Magyar territory. The conquered areas were forcibly converted to western Christianity from the traditional, eastern Byzantine form. In 962 Otto was crowned as Emperor by the Pope in Rome, and the uneasy union of Roman empire and German monarchy survived until 1806.

Turbulence and Chivalry in the High Middle Ages

When Conrad II was elected king in place of the childless Henry II in 1024, a period of great unrest began which would last throughout the high Middle Ages until the mid 12C. It is certainly true that palaces and cathedrals were founded during this era, particularly at Magdeburg, but there was also a series of civil wars and revolutions. There was the Saxon revolt of 1073–75 and the election of Pretender Duke Rudolf of Swabia in 1077. The Salians struggled to reign until 1125 when King Henry V died to be succeeded by Duke Lothar of Supplinburg. There then followed the reign of the Hohenstaufen line including the famous Frederick I or Barbarossa, whose epic battles during his reign of 1152–90 are now legend. The small territories ruled by princes consolidated their power during this period which was also marked by economic growth through trade and farming. Craft production began in this period with the significant foundation of guilds. The expansion east continued, with the Slav territories from the River Elbe colonised during 1150–1300. This period also witnessed a burgeoning court culture with its own code of chivalry, revived in the 19C as Germany's golden age. The Knights of the Teutonic Order led the colonisation of eastern Slav land throughout the 13C, laying the foundation of the state of Prussia.

From the Late Middle Ages to the Reformation

The number of towns in Germany increased tenfold during the 13C. The disparate nature of German rule meant that individual towns acquired power and prestige without one, single capital emerging. There were Landesstädte, governed by a local bishop or duke and Reichsstädte, responsible only to the Emperor. Towns formed themselves into powerful Leagues, the most relevant to eastern Germany being the Hanseatic League, formed in the mid 14C and led by the northern port of Lübeck. Meanwhile the Hohenstaufen line has died out to be replaced by Emperor Charles IV, whose royal court was situated at Prague. The Holy Roman Empire was becoming increasingly diffuse, with the Imperial assemblies formed by the Emperor, princes, ecclesiastical heads and knights and local assemblies where the relevant duke met with local nobles. From 1356, the Golden Bull established the method for electing the ruler of the Holy Roman Empire, with a group of seven forming the electoral college. This comprised the Archbishops of Cologne, Mainz and Trier plus the King of Bohemia, Duke of Saxony, Margrave of Brandenburg and the Count of the Rhine. By the beginning of the 16C there was a confusing array of Imperial Free Cities, ecclesiastical principalities and countless minor knights and lord-ships. When Emperor Charles V was crowned in 1519 the Reformation was gathering force in eastern Germany, following Martin Luther's nailing of the 95 theses to the door of the Castle Church in Wittenberg. This was the conventional method of publicising one's theological arguments, much like the academic journals of today. Luther, then a professor at the local university, criticised the established church for its corruption and the practice, known as indulgences, of buying pardon for your sins. News of Luther's radical message spread quickly as the theses were printed and Luther preached throughout Germany. At the Imperial Diet of Worms in 1521 Luther refused to denounce his beliefs in front of Charles V and the German heads of state. From here he was forced into hiding at the Wartburg Castle in Eisenach, where he composed hymns and began translating the New Testament into everyday German. The advent of printing aided the spread of the Protestant message, which gathered pace during 1521–24.

Further unrest was caused by the **German Peasants' War** of 1524–26, whereby an uprising of a new prosperous group of working people and clerics spread from south-west Germany into the areas of Thuringia and Saxony which was then quashed by the German princes. Luther himself did not support the Revolt, but the ideals of the Reformation, that each individual was responsible for his or her own salvation, certainly contrib-uted towards its outbreak. Several German rulers converted to the Protes-tant faith as a way of establishing their independence from the powerful church. From 1417 the Hohenzollern family had controlled the frontier territory (march) of Brandenburg and in 1525 Albrecht von Hohenzollern became the first ruler of Prussia, having denounced the Catholic Church and converted to Protestantism. Imperial cities to adopt the Reformation included Erfurt, Zwickau, Magdeburg and Augsburg. The League of Schmalkalden was founded in 1531, bringing together the Protestant forces of six princes and 10 cities. During the Schmalkaldic War of 1546 Charles V attempted to vanquish the Protestant threat and, with support from the

Pope, almost captured Wittenberg. However, internal disputes weakened Charles's attack and in 1548 the tolerant Augusburg Interim was agreed, formalised at the 1555 Peace of Augsburg.

The **Thirty Years War**, which lasted from 1618–48, had a devastating effect on Germany. The origins lie in the unsuccessful Peace of Augsburg and the weakening of the Holy Roman Empire. The Imperial Diet had ceased to function in 1608 when the Protestant supporters left and founded the Protestant Union. The war broke out as a result of a revolt by Bohemian nobles in which the Catholic Emperor, Ferdinand II fought against west and north German Protestants who were supported by Sweden and France against the powerful Catholic Habsburgs. The fighting ruined many towns and cities, reducing the population from 21 to 13 million. The Treaty of Westphalia of 1648 created 300 separate seats of government within Germany.

The Creation of the German State

From this weak position it seemed that a fully united German nation could never materialise. However, it was through the rise of the powerful state of Prussia that a unified Germany was to emerge in 1871. The state of Prussia was an amalgam of the Electorate of Brandenburg, the Duchy of Prussia and a myriad of smaller principalities. After Prince Albrecht had founded the Protestant Prussia, the kingdom was further strengthened by Hohenzollern princess Anne's marriage to the Electoral Prince of Brandenburg, forming the core of the future all-powerful, Prussian state. The kingdom gathered strength in the 18C under the rule of Frederick the Great, who annexed part of Poland and Austria to enlarge his kingdom. The Napoleonic wars of the early 18C swept away many of the smaller principalities and although Berlin, the capital of Prussia, was occupied, the long term benefit to Prussia was the annihilation of the Holy Roman Empire, leaving the leadership of the German states open. The 1815 Congress of Vienna reduced the number of German states down from over 200 to 39. The 1848 revolution which swept through Europe failed to have any long-term effect on Germany and its liberal ideals were soon supplanted by a return to traditional values. The unification of Germany was realised by the Brandenburg count Otto von Bismarck, chancellor of Prussia. He achieved unity through three carefully orchestrated wars, the first with Denmark in 1864, the second with Austria in 1866 and the last with France in 1870. Building on these military victories and sense of unity the Empire of Germany was proclaimed in the Hall of Mirrors in Versailles in 1871 with King William I declared Kaiser. His son, Frederick III reigned only for a few months in 1888, before being succeeded by his son.

Kaiser William II ascended to the throne in 1888, spreading German interests abroad with the annexation of four African territories into the German Empire. William II also built up the German navy, which threatened British supremacy and was one of the contributing factors in the outbreak of the First World War. Industrial expansion was another major feature of William II's rule, with factories erected at a rapid rate, railways built throughout Germany and the growth of urban slums. The First World War broke out in 1914 over the assassination of the Austrian heir to the throne in Sarajevo and the neutrality of Belgium. Although the Germans entered in high spirits, buoyed by their militaristic past, they were to emerge the losers challenged by the combined might of America, Britain and France. The Treaty of Versailles added humiliation to Germany's defeat, heaping heavy financial reparations on Germany, depriving her of her colonies and creating the Polish corridor to Danzig from East Prussia. The Treaty was unjust in placing the entire blame for the war on Germany and the harshness of the terms fuelled the resentment which led to the rise of Hitler.

The Weimar Republic and the Rise of Hitler

Kaiser William abdicated and fled to Holland after the First World War, leaving the stage clear for the establishment of a Republic. The Weimar Republic, so called because it was founded in the Thuringian town of Weimar, was declared in 1919. There followed a period of adventure and experiment in the arts with decadence emerging, particularly in Berlin, in the early 1930s. The Wall Street Crash of 1929 triggered widespread unemployment in Germany and general disillusionment with the seemingly ineffectual Weimar Republic led to the rise of Hitler to power. Following the unsuccessful Putsch of 1923 Hitler used various bully-boy tactics to seize power. In 1930 the Nazis gained 107 of the 491 Reichstag seats with a gain of 44 per cent of the votes in 1933. Hitler expoited the discontent of the German people following the Treaty of Versailles and in 1936, having been established as Chancellor, took control of the Rhineland in contravention of the Treaty. Hitler also rearmed, which again violated the Treaty. In March 1938 he annexed Austria and parts of Czechoslovakia. By 1939 he had control over the whole of Czechoslovakia and Poland, which instigated the outbreak of the Second World War. German aggression led to the occupation of Belgium, Holland and France and it was only the intervention of America which saved the opposing forces. Germany was soundly defeated in 1945, partly because Hitler refused to acknowledge that his great Third Reich was destroyed. Suicide saved him from the ultimate humiliation.

Post-war Germany

After the war, the map of Europe was virtually redrawn with Germany itself divided into West and East. A large portion of East Germany was handed over to Poland to compensate for Soviet expansion. Germany was controlled by the four Allies—France, Britain, America and Russia—with increasing tension emerging between Communist and Capitalist regimes. Border controls were strictly enforced from 1949 by the Soviet authorities who controlled the GDR (German Democratic Republic) to prevent the drain of skilled professionals escaping to the West. Life in post-war East Germany was grim. Soviet-style propaganda dominated the media and the arts. Although full employment was enjoyed, industry was outdated, following asset-stripping by Russia, and any form of opposition to the system was repressed. The secret police or Stasi built up a network of spies where family members would even spy on one another. Only the party faithful enjoyed the privileges of good education or decent food. The East Germans could not travel outside the Communist Bloc and holidays were spent in Russia or Yugoslavia. Travel for westerners within East Germany was also restricted with only organised parties allowed to tour, led by an official guide who was usually a party supporter. It appeared that nothing could break the powerful rule of Communism so the events of 1989, when the Iron Curtain quickly disintegrated, sent out shock waves throughout the world.

Die Wende

As Mikhail Gorbachev introduced more relaxed policies in Russia the GDR regime became even more entrenched in dogma. In February 1989 Chris Gueffroy was shot trying to cross the Berlin wall, thankfully the last victim of GDR harsh policies to die in this way. The relaxation of travel restrictions between Hungary and Austria meant many East Germans could escape to the West, with thousands crossing during August and September 1989. Open demonstrations against the government took place and the New Forum acted as a talking shop for opponents of Stalinist style rule. The GDR authorities responded by replacing Erich Honecker with Egon Krenz, who expressed a desire to open up discussions with the burgeoning opposition. On 4 November there was a massive demonstration in East Berlin which was followed by the resignation of the existing regime, to be replaced by a more liberal government headed by Hans Modrow. The Berlin Wall was opened up on the night of 9 November 1989 with suprisingly little ceremony but by the next day a full-scale street party was taking place around the Brandenburg Gate as West and East Germans, seperated for over forty years, openly embraced without a dry eye to be seen. Germany was formally re-united on 3 October 1990 in a strategy masterminded by West Germany's Chancellor, Helmut Kohl.

This re-unification of Germany, known as **Die Wende** or the turning point, has not been without its problems. It has drained the resources of the previously economically successful west Germans who now must pay higher taxes to finance the unification programme. The gap between the east and west is social, political and economic and will take well into the next century to disappear. The east lags so far behind as far as industry and housing goes that a certain resentment has grown over the colonial attitude of the west. It should not be forgotten that much popular discontent in the GDR was based on a naive image of life in the west, fuelled by television programmes such as Dallas. It is now hard for eastern Germans to come to terms with the fact that they will not be driving around in plush Mercedes or own houses with a swimming pool. However, the stage is set for the growth of Germany into a leading European and world nation once more, no longer needlessly divided into two separate lands, at the mercy of Cold War foreign policy.

Brief Chronology

1000–100 BC	Germanic tribes settled in northern and central Europe
AD 9–300	German lands as far as Elbe becomes part of Roman Empire
378	Goths defeat Romans at Battle of Adrianople: decline of Roman Empire
768–814	Reign of Charlemagne and consolidation of Frankish Kingdom
800	Charlemagne crowned Emperor of the Romans
843	Charlemagne's empire divided three ways, with the eastern Frankish Kingdom to be nucleus of future Germany

936–973	Reign of Otto I Crowned Emperor by Pope John XII, Holy Roman Empire established
1056–1105	Reign of Henry IV
1122	Concordat of Worms
1152–1190	Reign of Frederick Barborossa of Hohenstaufen dynasty
1254–1273	Feuding nobles terrorise the country over imperial succession
1273	Election of Rudolf I, first Hapsburg emperor
1356	Golden Bull of Emperor Charles IV regulates imperial succession
1415	Frederick I of Hohenzollern family appointed Elector of Brandenburg
1517	Reformation begins, Martin Luther nails his 95 Theses to Witttenberg church door
1519–1558	Reign of Charles V
1521	Diet of Worms chaired by Charles V denounces Luther, forced into hiding at Wartburg Castle
1546–1547	Schmalkaldic War:Protestant princes and free cities defeated by Catholic forces led by Charles V
1555	Peace of Augsburg introduces some degree of religious tolerance
1618–1648	Thirty Years War settled by Peace of Westphalia
1701	Frederick I of Prussia proclaims his duchy a kingdom
1713–1740	Reign of Frederick William I of Prussia
1740–1786	Reign of Frederick William II (Frederick the Great) of Prussia
1740–1748	War of the Austrian Succession with the victor, Prussia, gaining new territory
1756–1763	Seven Years War with Prussia the victor over Austria
1795	Prussia defeated by France
1797–1840	Reign of Frederick William III of Prussia
1803–1815	Napoleonic Wars
1806	Francis I of Austria defeated by Napoleon, relinquishes title of Holy Roman Emperor and the Empire is dissolved
1807	Prussia defeated by Napoleon, Berlin occupied by French
1813	Prussia member of anti-Napoleon coalition
1815	Napoleon defeated
1840–1861	Reign of Frederick William IV of Prussia
1848	Revolutions in Germany with little long-term impact
1861–1871	Reign of William I of Prussia
1862–1890	Chancellor Otto von Bismarck in office
1864	Prussia and Austria victorious over Denmark
1866	Allies split. Prussia continues and defeats Austria
1871	Prussia wins Franco-Prussian war. William I of Prussia declared Kaiser (Emperor) of united Germany
1888–1918	Reign of Kaiser William II
1914–1918	First World War
1918	Kaiser abdicates
1919–1934	Weimar Republic

1933–1945	Nazi Third Reich
1945	Allied rule: Germany divided into four zones of occupation
1948–1949	Berlin Blockade
1949	Establishment of Federal Republic (West Germany) and Democratic Republic (East Germany)
1961	Berlin Wall erected
1989	Freedom of travel for East Germans introduced
1990	Germany is Reunified

Art, Design and Architecture in eastern Germany

The Romanesque

The Romanesque period in eastern Germany lasted from the mid 10C to the early 13C, the Gothic taking longer to make an impact here than in other parts of Europe. There is a rich heritage of Romanesque architecture and art in this area as the kings and bishops tended to establish themselves here. For example, at Quedlinburg Henry the Fowler founded his royal capital and his wife, Mathilde a powerful abbey. The Stiftskirche St Servatius is a quintessential example of German Romanesque architecture, with the richly carved capitals crowning square stone pillars in the majestically simple interior. There are similar examples at Magdeburg, founded by Otto the Great, and Halberstadt. In terms of secular building, the earliest surviving example is the Wartburg Castle near Eisenach which dates from the 12C and has the same solid stone construction, round arches and intricately carved capitals. A powerful simplicity can also be found in the sculpture of the period, sometimes unusually executed in stucco as, for example, at Halberstadt. The high point of late Romanesque sculpture is the statues of the founders in Naumburg Cathedral. Worked by an unknown master in the workshops there, the purity of the facial expressions and realism of the image is outstanding.

Brick Gothic Architecture

One characteristic movement in the architecture of Mecklenburg-Vorpommern and Brandenburg is the early and unusual use of brick in the construction of churches, town halls, town gates and monastery buildings. The bricks were made locally and were highly adaptable, perfect for erecting high-ceilinged naves and gates with decorative detail moulded in the bricks themselves. This form of building construction was introduced into north Germany from Holland and Lombardy and began to make an impact from the 12C onwards. Early examples include the Nikolaikirche at Brandenburg and the Premonstratensian church at Jerichow. In tandem with the use of brick came the impact of the Gothic from France to the Rhine via southern Germany. However, the graceful French Gothic is rarely to be found in eastern Germany. The cathedrals of Halberstadt and Magdeburg are rare examples of this form of Gothic, showing the use of a skeleton structure with soaring buttresses infilled with minor detail. Gothic architecture in eastern Germany is more solid and pragmatic, limited in part by the continued use of brick. The majority of churches were Hallenkirchen or hall churches, in which the nave and aisles are of the same height. During the later period of brick Gothic, the pillars of the nave merged into the ribbed vaulting without the conventional break of a capital. The enrichment of the church interiors came from the carved, wooden rood screen, stalls and altars. Metalwork was frequently used for the font and elaborate candle-holders.

Although there are fine examples of monasteries built in brick at, for example, Chorin, most of the building was civic in origin, showing the great pride of the German towns as they gathered strength through trade and craftwork. The majority of churches, for example the Marienkirche at Lübeck, were built by the emerging class of wealthy burghers. This is why the choirs were so modest in size, as little room was needed for the clergy. It also explains why the town gates, town halls and churches were so similar in style and so pragmatic in design.

The German Renaissance

Just as the French Gothic made only a muted impact in Germany, so the Italian Renaissance had only a moderate effect on art and architecture in Germany during 1520 to 1640. Renaissance decorative details, for example classical motifs, were incorporated onto the facades of buildings but their basic structure and plan remained unchanged. In terms of painting and the graphic arts the influence was more prominent. Albrecht Dürer (1471–1528) was an important catalyst in the assimilation of Renaissance art in Germany. Beginning his career as a goldsmith, he travelled to Venice in 1494 and became acquainted with humanist thought as well as seeing the work of Mantegna. Returning to Nuremberg in 1495 he embarked on his outstanding artistic career, producing portraits, religious works and engravings. Returning to Venice in 1505–07 he became convinced of the new status of the artist, a Renaissance concept, whereby he was elevated above the level of mere craftsman to be accorded God-given, creative powers. This also accorded with the emphasis on the individual instigated by the Reformation. The greatest artist of the Reformation was Lucas Cranach the Elder (1472–1553), the Saxon court painter who operated from his Apothecary's shop in Wittenberg. His clear, delineated images of the leading lights of the Reformation are mingled with images of Jesus and the Apostles in the triptychs he painted. Cranach was also one of the first artists in the western world to paint full-length portraits, as in the two paintings of Duke Henry the Pious and Duchess Anna of Mecklenburg in the Old Masters Gallery at Dresden. Cranach's workshops were controlled after his death by his son, Lucas Cranach the Younger (1515–86).

The Baroque and Rococo in Germany

During the 17C Dutch painting was to dominate east German artists, while the influence of the Italian Baroque can be best seen in the architecture of Berlin. Architects Johann Arnold Nering (1659–95) and Andreas Schlüter (1664–1714) designed the Schloss and Arsenal for this new, royal capital. The sculptural properties of these two buildings are as important as the architectural design. Indeed, Schlüter originally trained as a sculptor and travelled to Italy to study the work of Michelangelo. The 21 masks of the dying warriors which he created for the Arsenal are emotional and fluid portraits in the Baroque tradition. Schlüter also revealed the inspiration of the Italian Baroque in his equestrian sculpture of Frederick I which stands before the Charlottenburg Palace in Berlin. Schlüter was court architect during 1698–1707 and was responsible for the first phase of the Charlottenburg Palace, which he built in Roman Baroque style. The other great centre for the Baroque in east Germany was Dresden. It was here that Matthaeus Daniel Pöppelmann (1662–1736) designed the great Zwinger Palace during 1711–22, a sculptural, playful building designed for holding great events and fêtes rather than functioning as a residence. Dresden was also the fountainhead of the Rococo in east Germany with the creation of Meissen porcelain, a perfect vehicle for this delicate and fanciful form of ornament; the factory was founded in 1710.

The Classical Ideal

The excesses of buildings like the Zwinger were soon to lose their appeal as the Classical ideals of Roman and Greek culture were revived first in France and England followed by Germany during the mid 18C. The discoveries of archeologist Johann Joachim Winkelmann (1717–68) and his highly influential book, *Thoughts on the Imitation of Greek Works of Art* (Dresden, 1755) called on artists to imitate the 'noble simplicity and calm grandeur' of ancient antiquity. A new, more scientific philosophy of art was created by Johann Wolfgang von Goethe (1749–1832) which instigated a unique Neo-Classical epoch in Germany. Centred around the sedate Thuringian town of Weimar, a revival of interest in Greek and Roman art and architecture swept through Germany. This was apparent in the painting of Raphael Mengs (1728–79) and the architecture of Karl Friedrich Schinkel (1781–1841) who reshaped the face of Berlin in Classical form in the early 19C. The processional route of Unter den Linden was classicised with the addition of buildings like the Neue Wache and the area around the Lustgarten given a facelift with the building of the Alte Museum.

German Romanticism

Whilst Schinkel is best known for his classically inspired architecture, he was also an earnest admirer of the German Gothic. He was instrumental in preserving the ruined monastery at Chorin and used Gothic forms in the design of the Werdersche Kirche in Berlin. This hankering after a golden past was very much part of the Romantic movement which inspired German culture throughout the 19C. In painting, Caspar David Friedrich (1774–1840) was the key exponent. His canvases convey an aura of mysticism as lonely figures, most often seen from behind, look out across a deserted landscape. Finding spiritual values in nature typified the work of the Romantic artists. The Nazarenes, so called because they drew inspiration from the Catholic religion in Rome, lived a simple monastic life and returned to the works of pre-Renaissance simplicity for inspiration. Their leader, Johann Friedrich Overbeck (1789–1869), remained in Italy but the other Nazarenes, including Peter von Cornelius (1783–1867) and William Schadow (1788–1862) returned to Germany to exert a powerful influence. The 19C wall paintings at the Wartburg Castle by Moritz von Schwind (1804–71) are influenced by the Nazarene approach. The more realist approach of French painting of the mid 19C and the genre painting of the British school also influenced art in Germany in the work of Eduard Meyerheim (1808–79), Max Liebermann (1847–1935) and Ludwig Knaus (1829–1910).

Industrialisation and Modernism

Germany was quick to harness the discoveries of the Industrial Revolution and establish itself as a leading European, industrial nation. Following the Unification of Germany in 1871, design theorists were particularly important in the adoption of design standards, desperately needed for uniting the disparate railway systems. Factory buildings were simple and functional and the work of Peter Behrens (1868–1940) for the electrical giant, A.E.G., was of leading importance for the establishment of Modern architecture in Europe. The stripped-down, Classical forms were pioneering for the early 20C. Through the Deutscher Werkbund, established in 1907 as a semiofficial organisation, German designers and industry worked together closely and established themselves as world leaders in the production of rational, functional design. The decorative style of Art Nouveau was adapted for German purposes as Jugendstil (New Style) and was always more geometric and solid than the delicate work of French designers like Lalique.

Germany was also to establish a lead in avant-garde painting with the Expressionist movement. Artists formed themselves into the group known as **Die Brücke** (The Bridge) in Dresden in 1905. This included Ernst Ludwig Kirchner (1890–1938), Erich Heckel (1883–1970) and Karl Schmidt-Rottluff (1884–1976) who produced violently emotional canvases, with images crudely and boldy painted in bright colours. Trying to communicate more than merely a representation of visual reality, the Expressionists attempted to paint the spirit and emotion of humanity and nature. A group with similar ideals, **Der Blaue Reiter** (The Blue Rider) formed in Munich in 1912 with Russian-born artist Wassily Kandinsky (1866–1944) and Franz Marc (1880–1916) as the chief exponents. The movement disintegrated after the First World War to be replaced by the far more worldly Dada and Neue Sachlichkeit which both lampooned and criticised the German establishment during the time of the Weimar Republic. Dada had been founded in neutral Zürich during the First World War, but enjoyed a second stage in Berlin with the political collages of Hannan Hoch (1889–1978) and Kurt Schwitters (1887–1948). The Neue Sachlichkeit (New Objectivity) emerged in the 1920s in the work of Otto Dix (1891–1969) who portrayed the corruption of officialdom in all too gruesome detail.

The oppositional nature of Modernist culture was to find particular resonance at the **Bauhaus**, a school of art and design which was run from 1919 by Walter Gropius in Weimar in the old Ducal Academy of Art. Avant-garde artists from throughout Europe gravitated to the school as the centre of experiment and Modernism. This was to alienate the reactionary inhabitants of Weimar and the school moved to the more sympathetic environment of Dessau in 1926. The school was housed in one of the first Modernist pieces of architecture in the world, designed by Walter Gropius with a flat roof and bold display of new construction techniques. Artists and designers of international reputations such as Kandinsky, Oskar Schlemmer (1888–1943) and Paul Klee (1879–1940) taught at the school which was eventually closed down by the Nazis in 1933 as part of their drive against modern 'degenerate' art. During the later 1930s most modern artists, architects and designers fled Nazi persecution and found refuge in Britain, France or America. Under Hitler's regime a traditional architecture, whether classical or 'Volk', and representational art, were encouraged.

After the war, Modernism continued to dominate architecture, design and art in the West. However, in the East only an official **Socialist Realism** was tolerated. The huge busts of Marx and emblems of Russian Communism erected during this era will not stand the test of time. Eastern Germany is currently undergoing a wave of exhibitions devoted to post-war American and West German painting which leaves many inhabitants, unfamiliar with modern art, at something of a loss. The joy and pain of re-unification has inspired artists to produce some exciting pieces of work, most notably Hans Haacke's German Pavilion at the Venice Biennale, in which he took a sledgehammer to the building—erected during Nazi rule—shattering the floor. Visitors walk on the crumbled masonry which symbolises the break up of the split, Cold War Germany and the tremendous effort now needed to rebuild the nation in architectural as well as social, political and economic terms.

Glossary of architectural and German terms

Altstadt, old part of the town
Bahnhof, station
Bau, building
Berg, mountain or hill
Brücke, bridge
Brunnen, fountain
Burg, fortress or castle
Denkmal, memorial, monument
Dom, cathedral, not necessarily a bishopric in Germany
Dorf, village
Fachwerkhaus, half-timbered house
Festung, fortress
Hallenkirche, church in which the nave and aisles are of the same height
Hof, courtyard
Insel, island
Jagdschloss, hunting lodge
Jugendstil, German form of Art Nouveau prevalent in the early 20C
Kapelle, chapel
Kirche, church (the name is usually added to the beginning, e.g. Marien-kirche is the Church of St Mary)
Kloster, monastery or convent
Markt, market or market square, usually at the town centre
Palast, residential part of a castle
Pfarrkirche, parish church
Platz, square
Rathaus, town hall
Ratskeller, cellar beneath the Rathaus where food and drink is available
Retable, altarpiece
Rundgang, way round
Saal, hall
Sammlung, collection
Schloss, castle, palace or stately home
See, lake
Stadt, town

Stucco, decorative plaster work
Tor, gateway
Turm, tower
Viertel, district or quarter of a town
Vorburg, outer part of a fortress or castle
Wald, forest

Select Bibliography

John Ardagh, *Germany and the Germans*, Penguin, 1988.

Michael Farr, *Berlin! Berlin!*, Kyle Cathie Ltd, 1992.

Michael Farr, *Vanishing Borders: The Rediscovery of Eastern Germany, Poland and Bohemia*, Penguin, 1993.

Mary Fullbrook, *A Concise History of Germany*, Cambridge University Press, 1990.

Peter Gay, *Weimar Culture: The Outsider as Insider*, Peregrine, 1988.

John Heskett, *Design in Germany 1870–1918*, Trefoil, 1986.

Erich Hubala, *Baroque and Rococo*, Herbert, 1989.

Christopher Isherwood, *Goodbye to Berlin*, London, Methuen, first published 1939.

Rory Maclean, *Stalin's Nose: Across the Face of Europe*, Flamingo, 1993.

Ingelore Menzhausen, *Early Meissen Porcelain in Dresden*, Thames and Hudson, 1990.

Alan Palmer, *Frederick the Great*, Weidenfeld and Nicolson, 1974.

William Vaughan, *German Romantic Painting*, Yale University Press, 1980.

David Watkin and Tilman Mellinghoff, *German Architecture and the Classical Ideal 1740–1840*, Thames and Hudson, 1988.

Frank Whitford, *The Bauhaus*, Thames and Hudson, 1984.

Christa Wolff, *A Model Childhood*, Virago, 1988.

PRACTICAL INFORMATION

Planning your trip

Germany enjoys a similar climate to Britain, with temperatures an average of 22 degrees centigrade (70 fahrenheit) in the summer and -5°C (23°F) to 12°C (54°F) in the winter. At present the crowds in eastern Germany are not too much of a problem so travel between spring and late summer is probably ideal, ensuring that everything will be open and boat tours will be running. Nationals of EC countries in possession of a valid passport do not need a visa. Holders of American and Canadian passports do not need a visa, providing their stay does not exceed three months.

The German Tourist Board

General information including maps, glossy brochures on various towns and regions and camping is obtainable from the German National Tourist Office, Nightingale House, 65 Curzon Street, London W1Y 7PE (tel. 071 495 6129) in Britain and 747 Third Avenue, 33rd Floor, New York, NY 10017 (tel. 212 3083300) for America and Canada. Do not expect the same service as for former West Germany as the Tourist Board has only quite recently merged with the former GDR's Berolina Travel. Through the Tourist Office you can order the German Hotel Guide.

Disabled Travellers

Access for disabled travellers in Berlin is very good with over 50 per cent of buildings and underground stations accessible by wheelchair. The major sites in former West Berlin are excellent, particularly the Dahlem. For more information contact RADAR at 25 Mortimer Street, London W1M 8AB (tel. 071 637 5400) and the Behindertendienst (Disabled Service) at Joachim-staler Strasse 15, Berlin (tel. 880033) which organises special bus tours. In general the comparative lack of crowds in the east means that you can get closer by car to major attractions. However public toilets are frequently situated down difficult stairs with no special disabled facilities.

Getting to eastern Germany by air

The best destination to fly to to start your tour of eastern Germany is Berlin, with a flight time of 1 hour 55 minutes from London. Air France, American Airlines, British Airways, Delta, KLM, Olympic Airways, United Airlines and TWA all fly into Berlin. The most efficient service to Berlin's Tegel Airport as well as Leipzig and Dresden is operated by the German state airline, Lufthansa, 10 Old Bond Street, London W1X 4EN (tel. 0345 737747). Currently Lufthansa offer special Youth Prices on these flights for under 25s. Flights as yet are not directly to Leipzig or Dresden and passengers must change in Frankfurt or Düsseldorf. Flying to Berlin is more expensive, with charter flights more difficult to come by, than to, say, Frankfurt. Travellers from America and Canada will probably find that flying to Frankfurt then changing for Berlin is the best option. Other agencies to contact are The German Travel Centre, tel. 071 379 5212 and GTF Tours, tel. 071 792 1260.

Tour operators which organise travel and accommodation in eastern

Germany include GTF Tours (see above), Regent Holidays Ltd, tel. 0272 211711, and Moswin Tours Ltd, tel. 0533 719922.

Getting to eastern Germany by rail

There are excellent rail connections to eastern Germany from throughout Europe and if you are a student or under the age of 26 or over 60 the Eurotrain option is very economical with return from London to Berlin at around £110, Dresden £131 and Leipzig £130. Eurotrain are at 52 Grosvenor Gardens, London SW1W OAG, in front of Victoria Railway station (tel. 071 730 3402). InterRail has now been replaced by the Domino scheme. Most routes leave from Victoria via the Dover-to-Ostend ferry. Operated in Germany by the east German Deutsche Reichsbahn (DR) and west German Deutsche Bundesbahn (DB) it costs £119 for three days, £133 for five days and £198 for ten days (which need not run consecutively) with a £40 reduction for under 26s.

Getting to eastern Germany by bus

This is a fairly inconvenient and comparatively expensive way to travel to Berlin with a journey time of around 26 hours and return fare of approximately £90. Contact Eurolines, 52 Grosvenor Gardens, London SW1W 0AG (tel. 071 730 0202) for coaches which depart from Victoria Station.

Getting to eastern Germany by car

Connections from the various European ports to the former GDR are excellent. You may opt to drive down from Ostend or Zeebrugge in Belgium or the Hook of Holland via Antwerp and through western Germany. To cover the distance in comfort you will need to stop off overnight, perhaps in the Osnabrück area where there is a good campsite and plentiful accommodation. Do not underestimate the length of the drive—it is over 1000km from London to Berlin.

Getting to eastern Germany by sea

P & O European Ferries run crossings from Felixstowe to Zeebrugge which take approximately five hours 45 minutes. Foot passengers pay around £48 for a standard return; a car with up to five passengers pay from £64 for a five day return or from £125 for a standard return (of six days and more). Contact P & O European Ferries at Channel House, Channel View Road, Dover, Kent, CT17 9TJ (tel. 0304 203388). Other ferry companies to cross the channel from Britain include Sealink, Charter House, Park Street, Ashford, Kent TN24 8EX (tel. 0233 647047); Hoverspeed, Maybrook House, Queens Gardens, Dover, Kent, CT17 9UQ (tel. 0304 240241); Sally Lines, 81 Piccadilly, London W1V OJH (tel. 071 409 2240). North Sea Ferries operate the Hull to Zeebrugge or Rotterdam lines for around £94 return for foot passengers and a further £114 to take a car; lower fares apply for senior citizens and under 25s. The only company to sail directly to Germany is Scandinavian Seaways from Harwich or Newcastle to Hamburg. During the peak season the passenger fare is £102 single and a further £120 return for the car or £430 for a special four-in-a-car return. There are many special reductions including a 50 per cent reduction for students, children aged 4–15 and those aged over 60 as well as the Seapex Return, bookable 21 days in advance with a 20 per cent saving. Crossing time is 20 hours but this option does save a lot of driving once the continent is reached. Scandinavian Seaways can also book accommodation for you in Germany. Contact them at Scandinavia House, Parkeston Quay, Harwich, Essex, CO12 4QG (tel. 0255 240240, lines open seven days a week).

Currency

The newly united Germany now operates one single currency which is based on the Deutschmark (DM) which is broken down into 100 Pfennigs. Take a combination of cash and travellers cheques. Credit cards are an option in the main cities of Berlin, Dresden and Leipzig but otherwise cash is preferable. Beware that in the smaller towns of eastern Germany it is often difficult to cash travellers cheques without a full passport. There are no restrictions on how much money you may take into the country. Money may generally be changed in banks or at railway stations.

Arriving in eastern Germany

Accommodation

Accommodation is not as plentiful as in western Europe or the United States. Eastern Germany was geared up for a tourist trade which consisted simply of organised parties staying in rather soulless, four-star hotels run by the state-owned Interhotel organisation. Many of these have now been bought by the German company of Maritim Hotels, who now own the Grand Hotel and Hotel Metropol, Berlin; Hotel International, Magdeburg; Hotel Stadt Halle, Halle; Hotel Astoria, Leipzig; Hotel Bellevue, Dresden and Hotel Gera, Gera. All these hotels are of a high standard and are centrally placed with rooms ranging from DM200 to DM515 for singles and DM300 to DM500 for doubles (not including breakfast) per night. For reservations and information call 071 937 8033 or in America toll-free on 1 800 843 3311 and 1 800 268 1133 in Canada. Further down the scale, modest hotel rooms are at a premium as tourists vie with business travellers from the west for rooms. Lists are available from the local tourist information offices, as are details of pensions and rooms in private houses. The latter are more plentiful and very reasonable at DM10 to DM30 per night for bed and breakfast. Local tourist information offices will also book you into a hotel, guesthouse or bed-and-breakfast accommodation if you write to them three weeks in advance. The German National Tourist office can supply sample booking forms. There is a reasonable supply of youth hostels and campsites. These are affordable at DM12 per night for a car and family. The shower and toilet facilities may be rather old-fashioned but the sites are sometimes situated near a lake with swimming or in a wood. During the summers of 1992 and 1993 there was no problem with sites being full in eastern Germany. A list of campsites is available from the German Tourist Board and more details can be found in *DDR Privatplätze für Camping und Wohnmobile*, published by Alexandra Verlag.

Food and drink

Unification seems to have had little effect on the poor standard of food and drink generally available in eastern Germany. There is no problem in Berlin, with its plentiful supply of Italian, Chinese and Indonesian restaurants. Traditional German food tends to revolve around the *Schwein* (pig) in any shape or form—the word also means good luck in German! Best value are the *wurst* (sausages) which are available in the restaurants but also from Imbiss or snack bars, with chips. Look out for eastern European restaurants, particularly Hungarian, which offer tasty varieties of the basic goulash. Fresh vegetables, fruit and dairy products still seem in rather limited supply. Vegetarians will find eastern Germany difficult and it may be advisable to take dried fruit or cereal bars to aid survival. Some foodstore chains from the west are now opening in eastern Germany including MacDonalds and the excellent Pollo, which specialises in chicken. Look out also for bakers' shops which often sell good sandwiches, snacks and cakes. On the drinks front the picture is a little cheerier. The beers available in eastern Germany are excellent, and whether locally brewed or from the west, there is usually a wide range available at reasonable prices. The white wine is generally very good. Teas and coffees can often be rather strange with fresh milk never an option and curious alternatives offered. Soft drinks, like anywhere else in Europe, are fairly pricy but are usually served cool.

Travelling around eastern Germany

By rail

This is a sensible option as the prices are reasonable and the connections good. If you are travelling in certain areas, the Regional Pass restricted to large areas, defined partly by the various Länder, represent good value at £49 for five days and £75 for ten days, full price. The family pass is £89 for five days and £134 for ten days. For instance, Dresden, Leipzig and the whole of Saxony are included in Region 110 and Berlin, Dresden and Leipzig in Region 115. Contact German Rail at 18 Conduit Street, London W1R 9TD or DER Travel Service (tel. 071 408 0111). Note that some of the rolling stock is rather antiquated and journey times may be slow. Narrow-gauge steam railways form part of the DR network with lovely examples on the Island of Rügen, the Harz mountains and Thuringia.

By bus

Buses are recommended only as an option when the journey is not served by the extensive rail network. Some coaches are operating longer routes—details are available from the local tourist offices. Note that rail passes are not valid on other modes of transport.

By car

Travelling around eastern Germany by car is often like stepping back in time. The motorways are the roads built by Hitler in the 1930s and are being gradually updated. However, if a motorway is marked it is often a dual carriageway. For example, the E70 leading across the former border from Bad Hersfeld to Eisenach has an average speed of 95 kmph with only two lanes. The battered roads are also crowded so allow plenty of time to make connections. In the towns the road surfaces are frequently poor, with cobbles being fairly common. Motorcyclists in particular should beware of the deep potholes in many of the roads. Road signs also need some improvement, so do go armed with a decent map and be aware that petrol stations are less common than in the west. Whilst driving in cities watch out for the speeding trams as they have right of way. Look out also for the *Grüner Pfeil* (green arrow) which is often attached to the main traffic light, indicating that if the main light is on red and you are turning right you may do so if nothing is coming from the left. For breakdowns the AA and RAC have a reciprocal arrangement with the ADAC (Allgemeiner Deutscher Automobileclub) whereby efforts will be made to solve the problem at the roadside. (If this fails ADAC will tow you to the nearest garage where you will need to pay for parts and labour.) Contact the ADAC (tel. 19211) from the orange emergency telephone boxes at the roadside and ask for Stassenwachthilfe (Road Patrol Assistance). The service is excellent in the west but slower in the east, garages are also few and far between, particularly for non-German makes. GTF Tours at 182–186 Kensington Church Street, London W8 4DP (tel. 071 792 1260) offer some excellent fly-drive or self-drive packages in their Go-As-You-Please programme. This may include car-hire, flights, rail travel and accommodation using the Wundercheck system of vouchers: prices are around £424 per person in twin accommodation with £27 per day supplement for car hire. Tabar Holidays (126 Sunbridge Road, Bradford, West Yorkshire, BD1 2SX, tel. 0274 393480) run the German Only range of holidays which includes tailor-made options.

For private cars without a trailer the speed limit outside built-up areas is 100km/ph; within built-up areas it is 50km/ph. There is a standard speed limit of 130km/ph on motorways. Rear and front seat safety belts must be worn while travelling. Children under 12 years of age must not travel in front seats of cars which have rear seats, unless they are fitted with a special safety device. The maximum permitted blood alcohol level is 80mg/100ml.

Drivers with licences issued in the USA, Canada or Australia must carry a translation of the licence. The Police, accident and emergency number is 110.

Maps

For general touring around Germany the Michelin *Deutschland* (No. 984) is fine. For more detailed coverage of each of the Lander the maps published by RV Verlag are excellent and on sale at main railway stations and bookshops. Maps of each town are readily available from Tourist Information locally.

General Information

Opening Hours

Opening hours in Germany are fairly restricted, with shops allowed to open only until 18.30 during the week and 14.00 on Saturdays, apart from the first Saturday of the month known as the *Langer Samstag* (longer Saturday), and during the four weeks leading up to Christmas. Shops rarely open on Sundays apart from those at railway stations and chemists working to a strict rota. There is late opening until 20.30 on Thursdays. Bank hours are officially Mon–Fri 09.00–12.00 and 13.30–15.30 with late opening on Thursdays until 18.00. Museums and historic houses are often closed on Mondays but opening times vary greatly throughout the east. Opening times have been given wherever possible but these are bound to change with unification.

Public holidays and special events

New Year's Day, Epiphany (6 Jan) Good Friday, Easter Monday, Labour Day (1 May), Ascension Day, Whit Monday and Day of German Unity (3 October), Day of Prayer and National Repentance (variable date in November), Christmas Day and Boxing Day are all public holidays in eastern Germany. Special events include the Dresden Music Festival from the last week in May to mid-June, the Handel Festival in Halle in mid-June and the Schumann Festival in Zwickau. During December Christmas fairs or markets are held throughout Germany with events in Lübeck, Dresden, Leipzig, Weimar and Erfurt during the first three weeks of December. Full details can be found in the German Tourist Board's annual publication *Forthcoming Events*, which also includes details of temporary exhibitions, important concerts and trade fairs.

Newspapers and magazines

In eastern Germany, English newspapers are scarce outside Berlin. In Berlin a good source of information in English is *Checkpoint*, published monthly at DM5 by Checkpoint Berlin Verlag GmbH, Nauheimer Strasse 27, 1000 Berlin 14197 (tel. 030 821 6096) with newsy features and up-to-date information on exhibitions and opening times.

Telephones

The telephone system has recently been re-united but this has not been without its difficulties. Codes are in the process of being changed and information given here is as up-to-date as possible. The dialling code from Germany to Britain is 00 44, and 001 to Canada and America. You then use the local code without the first 0, followed by the number. In Germany the operator is on 03, 001188 is international directory enquiries, 115 Ambulance, 112 Fire and 110 Police. Phone cards can be purchased from any post office.

Addresses

Note that all addresses have been given in the German form where the street number comes after the name of the street and the postcode before the town. Street names have been radically altered since the *Wende* with many Karl Marx Strasses no longer in existence. The new names have been given wherever possible but confusion may reign for some time.

Public toilets

These tend to be rather antiquated but clean. About DM1 is expected and there is often an attendant on duty who often decorates the environment with cheery magazine cuttings.

Useful Words

Do bear in mind that Russian, not English, was the second language taught in schools in the former GDR, so outside Berlin it is rare to find English spoken fluently. If your knowledge of German is scanty take a good phrase book, and try attending classes before you leave or use a tape and book-learning package such as the BBC's *Deutsche Direkt*. Useful words to know include:

Ja *yes*

Nein *no*

Bitte *please*

Danke *thank you*

Danke Schön *thank you very much*

Wo? *where?*

Wann? *when?*

Wieviel? *how much?*

Hier *here*

Jetzt *now*

Später *later*

Geöffnet *open*

Geschlossen *closed*

Gross *big*

Klein *small*

Gut *good*

Schlecht *bad*

Heiss *hot*

Kalt *cold*

Mit *with*

Tag *day*

Nacht *night*

Woche *week*

Wochende *weekend*

Montag *Monday*

Dienstag *Tuesday*

Mittwoch *Wednesday*

Donnerstag *Thursday*

Freitag *Friday*

Samstag *Saturday*

Sonntag *Sunday*

Januar *January*

Februar *February*

März *March*

April *April*

Mai *May*

Juni *June*

Juli *July*

August *August*

September *September*

Oktober *October*

November *November*

Dezember *December*

Feiertag *public holiday*

1 eins

2 zwei

3 drei

4 vier

5 fünf

6 sechs

7 sieben

8 acht

9 neun

10 zehn

11 elf

12 zwölf

13 dreizehn

14 vierzehn

15 fünfzehn

16 sechszehn

17 siebzehn

18 achtzehn

19 neunzehn

20 zwanzig

21 einundzwanzig

22 zweiundzwanzig

30 dreissig

40 vierzig

50 fünfzig

60 sechzig

70 siebzig

80 achtzig

90 neunzig

100 hundert

Dürer's drawing of his mother, in the Kupferstichkabinett, Altes Museum, Berlin

I BERLIN

Introduction

BERLIN (3.41 million inhabitants) is probably one of the most exciting and intriguing European cities to visit at the present time. The wealth of art collections and rich heritage of museums would make it special enough but there is the additional interest in seeing history in the making. The Berlin Wall, which stood at the interface of West and East, has now gone, although traces remain. The lively culture which developed in the heady days of post-war Berlin still prevails. The great Baroque architecture of Andreas Schlüter and the grand, Neo-Classical vistas of Karl Friedrich Schinkel can be enjoyed in the city, which also makes an excellent touring base for the Schloss Sanssouci at Potsdam, 19C palaces around the Havel and the Spreewald region (see section II).

Tourist Information

Verkehrsamt Berlin (Berlin Tourist Information), 105 Martin-Luther-Strasse, Berlin 10825. Tel. 21234. Opening times: 09.00–15.00 daily.
Tourist Information, Europa-Center, 45 Budapester Strasser, Berlin. Tel. 262 60 31. Opening times: 08.00–22.30 Mon–Sat, Sun 09.00–21.00.
Verkehrsamt im Bahnhof Zoo (Tourist Information in Zoo Station—actually just opposite the main entrance. Tel. 313 9063/4). Opening times: 08.00–23.00 Mon–Sat.
Verkehrsamt im Flughafen Tegel (Tourist Information at Tegel Airport. Tel. 4101 3145). Opening times: 08.00–22.30 daily.
Berlin Information, Information Centre at the Radio Tower, 1 Panorama-strasse, Berlin 10179. Tel. 212 4675 or 212 4512. Opening times: Mon 13.00–18.00, Tues–Fri 08.00–18.00, Sat and Sun 10.00–18.00.
Fraueninfothek, 47 Dirchenstrasse, Berlin 10179. Tel. 282 3980). Opening times: 10.00–20.00 Tues–Sat. Information for women and accommodation booking service—write four weeks in advance.

Tegel Airport Information Tel. 41 01 23 06.
Tempelhof Airport Information Tel. 690 96 05.
Schönefeld Airport Information Tel. 678 70.

Arriving in Berlin

Arriving by air. International flights normally arrive at Tegel Airport, situated in the north-west of the city. A frequent bus service, line 109, takes about 15 minutes to the Zooligischer Garten where connections to the rest of Berlin via U-Bahn or S-Bahn can be made (see below). Alternatively, a taxi to the centre of town costs about 25DM.

Arriving by rail. This will normally be at the Zoo Station (Hauptbahnhof Zoologischer Garten, Hardenbergplatz) right in the centre of Berlin with excellent connections anywhere in the city. (Information tel. 19419).

Arriving by coach. Buses arrive at the Central Bus Station, Messedamm, 1/19 just opposite the Radio Tower where the U-1 line takes you from the Kaiserdamm station to the town centre (direction Schlesisches Tor). (Information tel. 18028).

Arriving by car. Berlin is served by an efficent ring road but, as in most city centres, it is impossible to find parking in the centre. There are privately run car parks (Parkhaus) in the city centre which are open 24 hours. Parkhaus am Zoo in Budapester Strasse and Parkhaus Europa Center in Nürnberger Strasse are centrally placed.

Getting around the city

The public transport system in Berlin is clean, efficient and reliable and run by BVG (Berliner-Verkhers-Betriebe). It is also good value, particularly if you buy the Berlin Ticket, which allows 24-hour travel on any of the modes of transport listed below with one child aged 6–14 travelling for no extra charge. Make sure you stamp the ticket in the machine before making your way to the platform to indicate when your 24-hour period begins. A normal adult ticket costs 2.70DM and lasts for two hours. (See the map of the system at the back of the book.)

U-Bahn (Untergrundbahn: Underground Railway). Probably the most convenient and simplest method of travel around the city. There are nine lines in all which cover the city, and specific stations are given for the tours which follow. Note that tickets may be bought at the yellow machines at the entrances to the stations, which often take notes as well as change and which have clear instructions in English. Make sure the train is travelling in the right direction by checking its final destination, given on the platform and on the front of the trains. Trains run from around 04.00 to 01.00 and many of the routes and stations are interesting in themselves, for example the U1 line from Zoo to Schlesisches Tor which runs above street level (see Route 4).

S-Bahn (Schnellbahnnetz–Express Railway). This is Berlin's urban rail system which is quick and efficient, covering a similar area to the U-Bahn plus further afield to destinations such as Babelsberg and Köpenick. The service was severely curtailed during the time of the Berlin Wall but the lines that had been closed are now all open once more. For example, the stretch between Blankenfelde and Lichtenrade on the S2's southern extremity re-opened in 1992 when 5.7km of track was replaced.

Regionalbahn (Regional Railway). These trains service areas at the extremity of the city and may be useful for reaching Potsdam. Most leave from Friedrichstrasse station.

Buses. Berlin's network of buses is clean, efficent and fast. The bus-stops are signposted with a green 'H' and provide clear information about destinations. Pay the driver at the front, and exit by the middle door, making sure to press the red button when you wish to alight. The Berlin Ticket bought at the U-Bahn stations may be used on the buses, but the drivers themselves sell only singles. The No. 100, which runs from the Zoo to Alexanderplatz 24 hours a day, passes many of the major sights covered in Route 1, Essential Berlin. Buses run from 04.30 to 01.00 with Nightline Buses running from 01.00–04.00.

Trams. Tram services still run in former East Berlin and there are plans to extend services to the Zoo station.

Taxis. The yellow Mercedes run by Berlin's taxi service may be hailed easily on the street. Reasonably priced at 3.40DM minimum rising by 1.93DM per kilometre between 06.00 and 23.00 and by 2.10DM after 23.00. There are taxi ranks at the airports, Zoo station, Alexanderplatz and Savignyplatz. Taxis can be ordered by phone on 6902 or 26 10 26. After 20.00, if you are disabled or female, the stationmaster at the U-Bahn station will call you a taxi via the Taxi-Ruf-System.

On Foot. Berlin is a pleasant city to walk around although the distance between sites is often considerable. A combination of public transport and walking is probably the best method of getting around. Be careful not to walk in the bicycle lanes, marked with red, or you will be tinkled at loudly! Also, the Germans strictly observe the pedestrian lights, so do not jaywalk.

Disabled Visitors. Parts of Berlin are reasonably accessible with a wheelchair, particularly the Dahlem Museum complex which has brilliant facilities, and roughly 50 per cent of the U-Bahn stations are equipped for wheelchairs. The area around the Brandenburg Gate and the East in general will present problems. The Behindertendienst (Disabled Service) at Joachimstaler Strasser 15 (tel. 880033) organises bus tours and in Britain RADAR at 25 Mortimer Street, London W1M 8AB (tel. 071 637 5400) can offer information on holidays for the disabled.

By Boat. It may come as a suprise to learn that Berlin is surrounded by lakes and traversed by canals and rivers. It is possible to explore these waterways by boat: ferries run from Wannsee S-Bahn station to Spandau or across the Wannsee itself. During April to October the firm of Stern und Kreisschiffahrt (Sachtlebenstrasse 60 near S1 Zehlendorf, tel. 8100040) run a four-hour cruise which covers all the lakes to the west of Berlin plus lots of seasonal specials.

Festivals

Berlin plays host to important classical music festivals during the summer months, including the Berlin Philharmonic Orchestra at the Waldbühne, an open-air stadium, in late June and the Bach Days Berlin during the last two weeks of July. Held in various churches, concert halls and even the Sanssouci palace at Potsdam, this is a popular festival. For information contact VDMK, Kaiserdamm 31 (tel. 301 55 18). The Jazzfest Berlin takes place in the autumn (tel. 254890 for details) and the famous Berlin International Film Festival takes place during mid February.

For general news on events in English the monthly **Checkpoint** magazine is useful at 5DM from most newsagents, including the airport, complete with a public transport map and street map.

History

The history of Berlin is inextricably linked with the history of Germany as a whole, as it acted as the capital city of Germany between 1871 and 1945. It is based on two towns—Berlin and Cölln—which were granted municipal charters by the Saxons in the 12C when the Slavs were expelled from the territory. Founded on marshland around Museuminsel and Fischerinsel, the two towns assumed separate identities although both were ruled by the Ascanian family who were the Margraves of Brandenburg throughout the 13C, joining the Hanseatic League in 1369. After a period of fragmentation, when the Dukes of Pomerania and the von Quitzow brothers attempted to capture the territory, Berlin came under the rule of Friedrich Hohenzollern, the Burgrave of Nuremburg, who then became the first Elector of Brandenburg (1415–40), allowing him the right to vote in the election of the Holy Roman Emperor. He was then superseded by his brother, Friedrich II (1440–70). To symbolise Hohenzollern supremacy a chain was placed around the neck of the black bear—the city's emblem. The Hohenzollerns moved their court here and built a Renaissance schloss which was finished by 1540, raising the profile of Berlin-Cölln as the capital of the Mark of Brandenburg. The Reformation made an impact on Berlin during the reign of Elector Joachim II Hector (1535–71) who converted to Protestantism. The town suffered badly during the Thirty Years War, when it was continually under attack by the Swedes. Post-war reconstruction began under the rule of Elector Frederick William of Brandenburg (1640–88) and the building of new fortifications, royal and civic buildings earned Friedrich the name of the Great Elector. He was influenced by Dutch concepts of town planning and architecture and established the Lustgarten by the Schloss.

A tolerant attitude to immigration was adopted and Berlin's cosmopolitan population began to grow with Viennese Jews and Catholics from Southern Germany settling here in the 17C. The Huguenots, who also found refuge here from persecution in their native France, included important crafts-workers and traders, almost 5000 in all. Berlin also grew as a trading centre with the Friedrich Wilhelm Canal which linked the Spree and the Oder running through the town from east to west. The Great Elector was succeeded in 1688 by his son, Friedrich III, who then became Frederick I (1688–1713), King of Prussia, bringing more prestige to the town. It was during this period of expansion that the Zeughaus (now the Museum für Deutsche Geschichte) and the Friedrichstadt and Charlottenberg districts were founded. In 1709 the two towns of Berlin and Cölln were finally united.

Frederick I was succeeded by his warlike son, Frederick William I (1713–40)—the Soldier King. Culture took a back seat during his reign as parade grounds and drills took precedence over the arts, and Berlin developed into a garrison town; the Pariser Platz, just by the Brandenburg Gate, was established as a parade ground by Frederick and the Friedrichstrasse was founded to link Berlin with the Tempelhof parade ground.

Berlin was established as a great cultural capital under the rule of Frederick I's son, Frederick II, better known as Frederick the Great or Der alte Fritz (1740–86). Although Frederick established his residence at nearby Potsdam, his interest in the French Enlightenment and in Classical culture had a long-lasting impact on Berlin. Unter den Linden was developed during the 18C with prestigious new buildings like the Altes Bibliothek being built as well as the Schloss Bellevue in the Tiergarten. Berlin was left virtually bankrupt by the reign of Frederick the Great, with his constant warring particularly the Seven Year War which began in 1756. The stage seemed to be set for the ascendancy of Prussia over the other German states, but during the reign of Frederick William II (1786–97) Prussia slid into decline. He was succeeded by Frederick William III (1797–1840) during whose reign the city enjoyed an international reputation as a centre for Romanticism, though her political might was not so impressive. This culminated in the Napoleonic occupation of Berlin from 1806 when the jubilant victors paraded down Unter den Linden and entered Berlin through the Brandenburg Gate.

Following the defeat of Napoleon at Leipzig in 1813 the reactionary Biedermeier era dawned with Prussia extending her borders once more. This was the era in which Neo-Classical Berlin was constructed with Karl Friedrich Schinkel's brilliant designs for the Neue Wache and the Altes Museum changing the face of the city. Industrialisation also began to make an impact on Berlin with the growth of railways, factories and working-class housing in the form of tenement blocks. The revolutionary fervour of 1848 affected Berlin as it did most other European cities, but no ground was gained by the protestors and King Frederick William IV (1840–61) quickly reassumed his power. He eventually went insane and was replaced by his brother, Prince William (1861–88) whose reign was dominated by his Chancellor, Otto Von Bismarck, and the unification of Germany in 1871. Wilhelm II was now a Kaiser and Berlin was growing at a dramatic rate. The period is known as the Gründerzeit (Foundation Years) and is characterised by flamboyant architecture and grandiose design. This is the period when the Reichstag, the Berliner Dom and Kaiser-Wilhelm Memorial Church were built. Berlin's population almost doubled from 820,000 in 1871 to nearly two million in 1890. Under the rule of Kaiser Wilhelm II (1888–1918) Berlin enjoyed more expansion with the population doubling once again by 1914. Berlin joined in the nationalistic celebrations at the outbreak of World War I and, like the rest of Germany, grew disillusioned as the War dragged on. Berlin was the focus for Socialist opposition in 1917 when the Independent Socialist Party (USPD) was formed which combined forces with the International Group, later the Spartacists, of Rosa Luxemburg and Karl Liebknecht. Following the defeat of Germany general unrest culminated in the November Revolution in Berlin, where the population took to the streets inspired by the example of the Russian Revolution. Kaiser Wilhelm II abdicated and the Social Democratic Party (SPD), the announced the foundation of a German Republic with their leader, Friedrich Ebert, at the head.

However, Ebert was not radical enough for the Spartacists who led an uprising in January 1919 which was brutally crushed by the old imperial guard, the Freikorps, with the blessing of Ebert. Luxemburg and Liebknecht were tortured and murdered by the Freikorps, their bodies tossed into the Landwehr Canal. A new Weimar Republic was voted into power with Ebert as president and the seat of power moved from Imperialistic Berlin to Weimar. During the inter-war years Berlin became a vibrant centre for avant-garde culture with the Dada movement shifting its headquarters here from Zurich in 1919. Jazz made an impact in the cafés of the

'Die Ideologen' by Max Beckmann in the Print Collection of the Altes Museum. © DACS 1994

Ku'damm and Berlin earned a reputation for being the most tolerant city in Europe with transvestite clubs and a general rejection of outmoded conventions. This is the Berlin portrayed by the British author Christopher Isherwood, and satirised by the artists George Grosz and John Heartfield. Max Rheinhardt dominated Berlin's lively theatrical scene and Bertold Brecht's *Dreigroschen Oper* (Threepenny Opera) opened in Berlin. This was also the heyday of Berlin cabaret and a general atmosphere of decadence prevailed.

With the rise of the National Socialists (Nazis) in Germany an era of violence in Berlin dawned with confrontations between left-wing Berliners and the SA becoming a regular feature of city life. Anti-semitic violence erupted and the Wall Street crash of 1929 and ensuing economic collapse brought power to the Nazis in 1933. The Reichstag Fire of February 1933 was manipulated to aggravate anti-Communist feeling and known anti-Nazis were soon fleeing the city. Kandinsky, Brecht and Kurt Weill all fled and the notorious *Buchverbrennung* (book burnings) began outside the Old Library. Berlin became the capital of the Nazi Reich, staging innumerable processions plus the 1936 Olympics. Hitler had great plans for Berlin, which he pored over with architect Albert Speer, constructing models and conceiving the name of Germania to replace that of Berlin. Progress was halted with the onset of the Second World War, though at first Berlin suffered little as Nazi aggression secured more and more territory for Germany. However, from 1943 onwards, bombing raids by British and American aircraft totally demoralised the city. Having expected a quick end to the War, Berliners watched stunned and distressed as their city suffered enormous damage, the streets filled with rubble and between 50,000 and 80,000 inhabitants were killed. Defeat was all too obvious even to the Nazis on 27 January 1945 as the Russians crossed the River Oder only 100 miles from Berlin. However, Hitler refused to hear any suggestion of surrender and ill-equipped troops were sent to defend the Third Reich. Berlin was turned into a fortress but constant Allied bombing and Russian fire to the east made the task almost impossible. By 20 April the Soviet troops were at the Berlin borders, outnumbering those trying to defend the territory. On 25 April Berlin was completely encircled by the Russians who had joined forces with the Americans advancing from the west. The situation became so hopeless that on 30 April Hitler and his mistress Eva Braun committed suicide, having married the day before. Had he surrendered earlier some of the terrible damage to Berlin could have been averted and many civilian lives spared. For example, many were drowned when the canal locks were blown up by German troops to halt the Soviet advance, leading to flooding of the U-Bahn tunnels where families were sheltering.

When surrender eventually came on 8 May 1945, Berlin was occupied by a 2,000,000 strong force which placed a terrible strain on the virtually non-existent services and supply of food. Rationing was well below subsistence level and only basic survival was possible. In July 1945, British, American and French troops arrived to occupy the western part of the city. The Potsdam Conference of 17 July to 3 August settled the post-war fate of Germany as the Allies met. Conditions in Berlin deteriorated as the severely cold winter of 1946–47 and the shortage of food and fuel created a crisis in the city. Wolves were seen scavenging amongst the ruins and citizens froze to death on trains. Conflict between Russia and the American, French and British occupying forces came to a head in June 1948 when the Russians cut off power, road and rail links to the west, triggering the Berlin Blockade. With the Berlin Airlift of 26 June 1948 Berliners in the western zone were supplied with rations brought in by American and British planes until the following spring. The Russians then abandoned the Blockade and their claims for Berlin as the capital of their sector. The Federal Republic of Germany was founded in May 1949 and the German Democratic Republic in October of the same year, and West and East Berlin were formally divided. The capital of West Germany moved to Bonn and West Berlin became a Land (state) of the new Republic. Movement between East and West was still easy at this time and Berlin became the spy capital of Europe with the American CIA and Russian KGB operating within the same city. West Germany's 'economic miracle' began to gather pace during the 1950s with West Berlin quite obviously benefitting, much to the chagrin of the East. This led to a mass migration of Germans from the East to the West, particularly those with much valued skills. Negotiations between the superpowers failed and on 13 August 1961 the border between West and East was sealed by 40,000 East German troops. The Berlin Wall was then built—essentially two walls with a central *Sperrgebeit* (forbidden zone) between them and watchtowers guarded by troops with orders to shoot any would-be escapees.

Movement between West and East was difficult throughout the succeeding years—right up until 1989. During the 1960s Berlin became an important centre for youth rebellion, focussed around the Free University, with the added attraction of no conscription for Berlin residents. Student protests were met with heavy-handed treatment (a peaceful demonstration against a visit by the Shah of Iran led to one student being shot on 2 June 1967). The *Alternative Liste* was founded by Green pressure groups, and leftwing supporters and delegates were elected to the Berlin Senate for the first time in 1981. The alternative lifestyle became a fact of life in the Schöneburg and Kreuzburg districts of West Berlin with a proliferation of squats. There seemed to be little sign of the Cold War abating during the 1980s. I myself was in the GDR and East Berlin during the August of 1989 and whilst there was talk of the *'Neues Forum'* in the East the Berlin Wall seemed as permanent as ever as I stood beside border guards, looking to the West but unable to enter, on my Group Visa, without the whole group. As I gave my English address to the East German guide she looked at me with a wry smile, indicating that she would never be able to travel beyond the Communist Bloc.

Barely three months later, back in Britain, I could hardly believe the television news reports of 9 November as jubilant Berliners climbed on top of the Brandenburg Gate and surged through the former border crossings, drinking champagne and celebrating the demise of the Wall. The following January, the greatest new year's eve party in Europe followed to herald the new era. Now that the euphoria has declined and West Berliners no longer embrace East Berliners on sight the long, hard job of unifying the city is well underway. The U-Bahn and S-Bahn systems are almost one whole network again, more international flights leave from Berlin and building development is taking place on almost every street corner. With the centre of government moving from Bonn to Berlin by the end of the century and the highly convincing bid for the year 2000 Olympic Games the future looks rosy. A visit to Berlin is guaranteed to be special, particularly at this point in time, when history is definitely still in the making.

1

Essential Berlin

This walk takes one full day at the very least—you may prefer to spread it over two days and allow for a more leisurely pace. The walk includes the major sights of this fascinating city. A powerful sense of history in the making as well as the historic past of the German nation is central to the tour. Some of the finest architecture in Berlin, including work by Schinkel, is to be seen, as well as some of the worst at Alexanderplatz in former East Berlin.

Begin at the **Bahnhof Zoologischer Garten**, an incredibly busy spot as the station is the major intersection for buses, U-Bahns and S-Bahns as well as providing connections to western Germany and beyond. Before 1989 this was Berlin's only mainline station, where illegal currency dealing took place, and an air of intrigue and slight seediness still prevails.

From the station it is worth paying a visit to the ***Zoologischer Garten Berlin** (Berlin Zoological Garden) particularly if you have children in tow as it offers a welcome oasis in this busy city and has a lovely Pets' Corner. From the station cross Hardenbergplatz east and the main entrance is situated beyond the MacDonald's Restaurant to the north (opening times: April–Sept 09.00–18.00, 1–15 October 09.00–17.30, 16 October–28 February 09.00–16.45).

The Zoo is situated in a large, leafy and well-planned park with an abundance of cafés and restaurants, the focus of Berlin's social life before the War. The animals are not caged in but restricted by the subtle use of moats. The Zoo was one of the first in the world, opening in the Tiergarten in 1844, and much of the 19C flavour has been preserved. The Arabian style Zebra House which stands beside the bridge crossing the Landwehr-Kanal is still intact, complete with Jugendstil tiles around its white domed tower. The Aquarium situated to the south has an amazing collection of exotic snakes, lizards and sealife matched by the exotic building. A life-size statue of a fierce iguana greets visitors whilst carved insects grace the doorway. Designed by Oskar Heinroth in typically German Art Nouveau style, it opened in 1913.

From the main entrance of the Zoo proceed south down Hardenbergplatz and right down Hardenbergstrasse to the Breitscheidplatz. This is one of the busiest traffic intersections in Berlin, with five major roads radiating from here including the main shopping street—the Ku'damm (Kurfürstendamm) to the south-west. In the centre stands the controversial **Kaiser-Wilhelm-Gedächtniskirche** (Kaiser William Memorial Church; opening times: daily 09.00–19.30).

The Neo-Romanesque original, designed by Franz Schwechten and built in 1891–95, was badly damaged by bombing during the Second World War. Of the original, only the ruined west tower and part of the nave remains, with the craggy, burnt-out tower losing 55m of its original height. The church earned its controversial reputation when unsympathetic additions were made in 1959–61 by Egon Eiermann in uncompromisingly modern

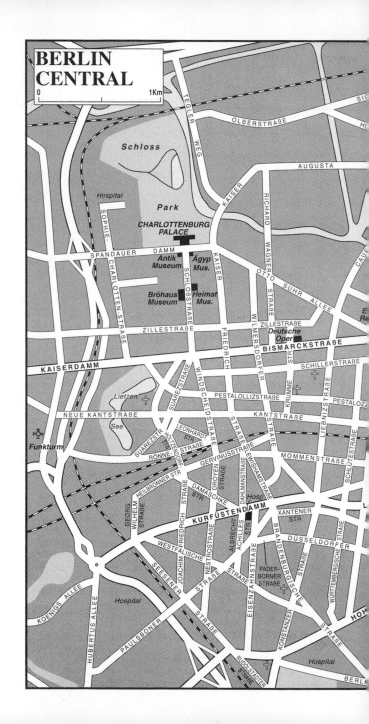

BERLIN CENTRAL

0   1Km

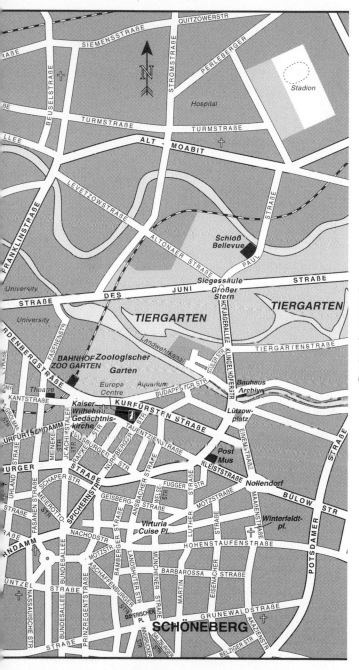

Continued on page 42

QUITZOWERSTR

SIEMENSSTRAßE

STRAßE

BEUSELSTRAßE

STROMSTRAßE

PERLEBERGER

Stadion

Hospital

N

TURMSTRAßE

TURMSTRAßE

ALT - MOABIT

FRANKLINSTRAßE

LEVETZOWSTRAßE

ALTONAER STRAßE

PAUL STRAßE

Schloß Bellevue

University

STRAßE DES JUNI

Siegessäule Großer Stern

STRAßE

TIERGARTEN

University

TIERGARTEN

HOFJÄGERALLEE

Landwehrkanal

TIERGARTENSTRAßE

FASENENSTR

HARDENBERGSTRAße

BAHNHOF Zoologischer
ZOO GARTEN Garten

KLINGELHOFERSTR

STULERSTR

Theatre

Europa Centre

Aquarium

Bauhaus Archive

KANTSTRAßE

BUDAPESTER STR

Kaiser
Wilhelm
Gedächtnis-
kirche

KURFÜRSTEN STRAße

Lützow-
platz

KURFÜRSTENDAMM

JOACHIMSTALER

RANKESTR

NÜRNBERGER STR

TAUENTZIENSTRAßE

EINEM STRAßE

STRAßE

MENEKE STR

RANKE STR

AUGSBURGER STR

Post
Mus

STRAßE

BURGER STRAßE

KLEISTSTRAßE

Nollendorf

BÜLOW STR

UHLANDSTRAßE

FASANEN STRAßE

SCHAPER STR

MEIEROTTO

SPICHERNSTR

ANSBACHER STRAße

FUGGER STR

WELSE STR

LUTHER STRAßE

MOTZSTRAßE

MAAßEN STRAßE

POTSDAMER STRAßE

GEISBERG STRAßE

Virturia
Cuise Pl.

Winterfeldt-
pl.

NACHODSTR

MOTZSTR

MÜNCHENER STR

EISENACHER STRAßE

HOHENSTAUFENSTRAßE

HNDAMM

BUNDESALLEE

BUNDESALLEE

LANDSHUTER STR

BAMBERGER STRAßE

ASCHAFFENBURGER STR

BARBAROSSA STRAßE

NASSAUISCHE STR

UNTZEL STRAßE

PRINZREGENTSTRAßE

BAYERISCHER PL.

MARTIN LUTHER STR

MÜNCHENER STR

GRUNEWALDSTRAßE

ANZAISTR

SCHÖNEBERG

STRAßE

WALDECKER STR

INSBRUCKER STR

BELZIGER STR

42

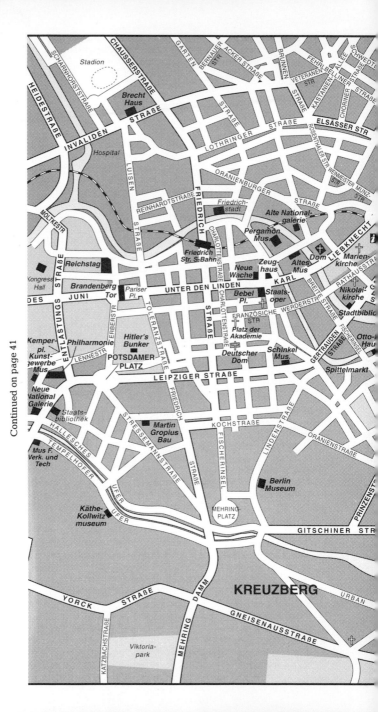

Continued on page 41

Stadion

Brecht
Haus

SCHARNHORSTRAßE

HEIDESTRAßE

CHAUSSERSTRAßE

STRAßE

INVALIDEN

MOLTKESTR

Hospital

LUISEN STRAßE

REINHARDTSTRAßE

CHARLOTTENSTRAßE

FRIEDRICH STRAßE

Friedrich
Str. S-Bahn

GARTEN STRAßE

BERNAUER STRAßE

ACKER STRAßE

BRUNNEN STRAßE

VETERANEN STR

BELLINER STR

FEHRLBELLINER STRAßE

KASTANIEN ALLE

CHORINER STRAßE

SCHWEDT

ELSÄSSER STR

LOTHRINGER STRAßE

ORANIENBURGER STRAßE

ROSENTHALER STR

WEINMEISTER STR

MUNZ STR

STRAßE

Friedrich-
stadt

Alte National-
galerie

Pergamon
Mus.

Altes
Mus.

Dom

Marien-
kirche

LIEBKNECHT

RATHAUSSTR

Nikolai-
kirche

Stadtbiblio

Otto-
Hau

Spittelmarkt

Reichstag

Kongress
Hall

DES

JUNI

ENTLASTUNGS STRAßE

Brandenberg
Tor

Pariser
Pl.

EBERSTR

Hitler's
Bunker

Kemper-
pl.
Kunst-
gewerbe
Mus

Philharmonie

LENNESTR

POTSDAMER
PLATZ

Neue
National
Galerie

Staats-
bibliothek

STRESSEMANNSTRAßE

Martin
Gropius
Bau

HALLESCHES

TEMPELHOFER UFER

Mus F.
Verk. und
Tech

Käthe-
Kollwitz
museum

UFER

Neue
Wache

Zeug-
haus

Staats-
oper

Bebel
Pl.

KARL

BREIT STR

WERDERSTR

FRANZÖSISCHE STR

Platz der
Akademie

Deutscher
Dom

Schinkel
Mus.

TOLERANZSTRAßE

CHARLOTTENSTRAßE

UNTER DEN LINDEN

LEIPZIGER STRAßE

FRIEDRICH STRAßE

KOCHSTRAßE

FISCHERINSEL

GERTRAUDEN STRAßE

FISCHERINSEL

LINDENSTRAßE

ORANIENSTRAßE

Berlin
Museum

MEHRING-
PLATZ

GITSCHINER STR

PRINZENST

KREUZBERG

URBAN

YORCK STRAßE

KATZBACHSTRAßE

MEHRING DAMM

GNEISENAUSTRAßE

Viktoria-
park

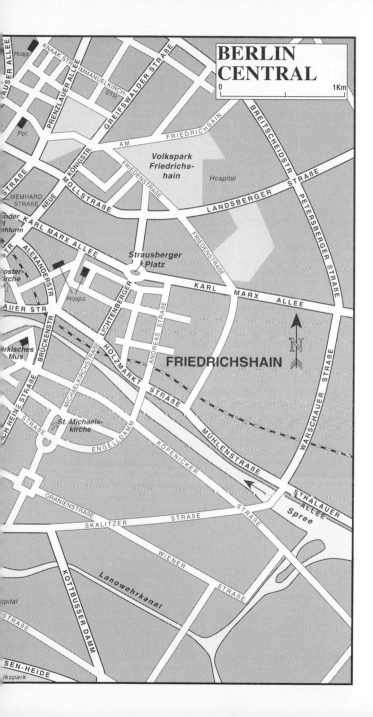

BERLIN CENTRAL

0   1Km

TO HAMBURG & ROSTOCK

BERLIN GENERAL

0   4km

HERMSDORF

Berliner Forst Tegel

RUPPINER CHAUSSEE

HEILIGINESESTRAßE

SCHÖNWALDER ALLEE

NIEDERNEUENDORFER ALLEE

Havel

KAROLINENSTRAßE

WAIDMANNSLUSTER DAMM

ORANIENBURGER

ROEU

EICHBORNDAMM

HOLZHAUSER ALLEE

Huboldt Schloß

Berliner Forst Spandau

Tegeler See

BERNAUER STRAßE

SEIDELSTR

SCHARNWEBER STRß

BEINICH DORF

MÜLLER

SE

GARTENFELDER STR

BERNAUER STR

Flughafen Tegel

FALKENSEER CHAUSSEE

SCHÖNWALDER STR

Spandauer Zitadelle

NONNENDAMMALLEE

SPANDAU

BRUNSBÜTTELER DAMM

WILHELMSTRAßE

St *Spree*
Nicolai

CHARLOTTENBURGER CHAUSSEE

SPANDAUER DAMM

CHARLOTTENBURG

HEERSTRAßE

GATOWER STR

Olympia Stadion

HEERSTRAßE

BISMARCKSTRAßE

POTSDAMER CHAUSSEE

TO HAMBURG & LÜBECK

KLADOWER DAMM

HAVEL CHAUSSEE

Berliner Forst Grunewald

KOENIGSALLEE

KURFÜRSTENDAMM

HOHENZOLLERN DAMM

WILMERS

SCHÖ

Havel Wannsee

ONKEL-TOM STR

HÜTTEN ALLEE

KONIGIN - LUISE

ARGENTISCHE ALLEE

CLAY ALLEE

ALLEE

DAHLEM

Mus Dahlem

FABECKSTR

STRAßE

Botanischer Garten

STRAßE

STEGLI

ZEHLENDORF

SPANISCHE ALLEE

POTSDAMER CHAUSSEE

POTSDAMER STR

BERLINER

TELTOWER DAMM

DRAKESTRAßE

HINDENBURGDAMM

OSTPREUßENDAMM

KAISER

TO POTSDAM

KÖNIGSTRAßE

GOERZALLEE

OSTPREUßENDAMM

TELTOW

N

TO HALLE & LEIPZIG

TO DRESL

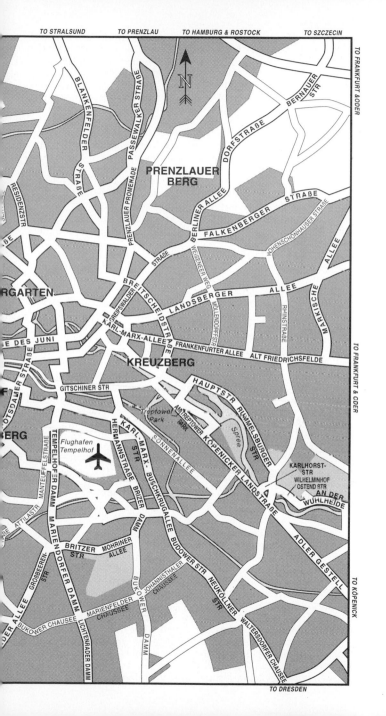

style. It was formally opened in 1895 to celebrate the military achievements of Kaiser Wilhelm I and the original mosaics, commemorating various battles of this warlike leader, may be seen in the Memorial Hall which was installed inside the ruined tower in 1987. Here photographs of war-torn Berlin and remnants of the original nave may be seen (opening times: Tues–Sat 10.00–18.00, Sun 11.00–18.00). The two glass and concrete towers added by Eiermann in the early 1960s frame the Neo-Romanesque ruin in a modernist gesture which is now difficult to appreciate. The octagonal, flat-roofed tower to the west houses the new church whilst a smaller chapel, seating 110, is situated in the base of the taller tower to the east. The bland network of grilles on the exterior is better seen from the interior, where the abstract richness of the Chartres glass can be fully appreciated. The church acts as a centre for the city's less fortunate visitors and inhabitants, and various down-and-outs tend to congregate here.

Continue north-east up Budapester Strasse which skirts the Zoo with its Art Nouveau reliefs of various dinosaurs and glimpses of the aquarium. Further north the street is lined with various travel agents, and the Hotel Berlin Hilton is on the left. Designed by Pereira and Luckman in elegant, international modernist style, this chic hotel opened in 1958. Opposite is the highly recommended Moncee Italian restaurant serving authentic pizza and pasta. Continue north-east across the Landwehrkanal which connects the Upper Spree with the Lower Spree and was constructed in 1845–50 to designs by Peter Joseph Lenné.

Head north up Stüler Strasse to the busy 'Schnellstrasse' which links the Grosse Stern in the north with the Lützowplatz in the south. Note the **Siegessäule** (Victory Column), an important Berlin landmark, to the left. This towering column of almost 70m was erected in 1873 to commemorate victories over Denmark in 1864, Austria in 1866 and France in 1870–71. At the base of the column is a square plinth of Swedish granite decorated with panels celebrating military victory; inside the colonnade above are mosaics by Anton von Werner depicting the unification of Germany. The sandstone column itself is adorned with gilded gun-barrels captured from the ene-mies. Stone eagles support the upper platform, which is commanded by a 8m high, newly-gilded figure of the goddess Victory holding a laurel wreath and sceptre with Iron Cross. There is a spiral staircase of some 285 steps which may be climbed to reach the observation platform with panoramic views of the city including the Brandenburg Gate and Reichstag (opening times: April–Nov, Tues–Sun 09.00–18.00, Mon 13.00–18.00). It should be noted that the Victory Column originally stood in front of the Reichstag and was moved to its present position by the Nazis in 1938.

Cross the busy Hofjäger Allee to reach Tiergarten Strasse and continue east. On your left is the verdant *Tiergarten, used as a hunting ground by the Prussian Electors from the 16C. The grounds were landscaped in the 19C by Lenné in the fashionably informal, English style with newly planted trees and artificial lakes. Devastated by bombing at the end of the Second World War, the trees were used for firewood and the land for growing food by the desperate Berliners. No evidence of this destruction now remains and the park has been totally revitalised with the planting of over one million new trees and shrubs since 1949. Before the War Tiergarten Strasse was the location of many Embassies; although most were destroyed by bombing, the former Japanese Embassy has survived at Nos 24–28 and now houses the Japanese-German Centre of Berlin whilst at Nos 30–31 in the former Krupp headquarters is the Jesuit Canisius College. Further east on the right is a statue devoted to Wagner by Eberlein of 1903, one of many statues of important individuals erected in the Tiergarten during the reigns of Wilhelm I and II. The many miles of paths may be explored at your leisure in the park and other statues admired, including that of Queen Luise by Encke (1880) which stands on Luise Island to the north-east.

As you continue east on Tiergarten Strasse the **Kulturforum** (Culture Forum) lies to the right. This is a complex of important museums and the Philharmonic Hall was developed by the modernist architect, Hans Scharoun, from the early 1960s onwards. The area between the Landwehr Canal, the Brandenburg Gate and Kemperplatz was totally flattened during the war and the West German authorities decided to develop the expansive site as a cultural centre (see Route 2).

Cross Kemper Platz and take Bellevue Strasse to reach POTSDAMER PLATZ, the hub of the city and Berlin's equivalent to Piccadilly Circus before the war, being the first public place in Europe to be lit by electricity (as well as the first to boast a traffic light). The area was then controlled by East Germany and lay in no man's land, covered by barbed wire and armed with land mines to prevent East Germans escaping to the West. Two walls ran south from the Brandenburg Gate, encasing this strip of land. From September 1989 until recently this area was a wasteland where weeds sprouted out of the broken pavements and tramlines suddenly stopped. However, from 1994 the valuable city centre site is to be developed by Sony and Daimler-Benz as office and sales space in new, controversial plans. Turn left down Erbert Strasse which has been newly paved and lined with saplings in a brave attempt to erase the memories of the sinister no man's land which lay here. To the left is the eastern border of the Tiergarten where a detour will bring you to the Gotthold Ephraim Lessing Monument, erected by his great-grand-nephew Otto Lessing in 1890 and further north, near the Goldfish Pond, to a group of *Löwen* (Lions) by A. Wolff (1872).

To the right of Erbert Strasse, in the former no man's land, is the entrance to the Potsdamer Platz station, now reopened after it was suddenly closed and bricked up by the GDR authorities in August 1961 to prevent the migration of Germans from East to West. Further north and to the right is a seemingly inocuous bump in the barren landscape. This was **Hitler's Bunker** where he spent his last days in 1945, retreating from imminent invasion by Soviet and American troops. Here he committed suicide on 30 April with Eva Braun, after needlessly prolonging the war.

Further north is the ****Brandenburger Tor** (Brandenburg Gate), the perennial symbol of the city of Berlin. Originally built in 1789–91 from sandstone it was inspired by the Acropolis at Athens. It was designed by Carl Langhans to replace one of 18 Baroque city gates which were set into Berlin's ramparts. It had pride of place as it stood at the head of Unter den Linden, the royal procession route from the palace which led to Brandenburg. The gate is a monumental 26m high and stretches 65.5m in width. Six massive Doric columns form the main structure of the gate on each side, creating five passageways with the central space of 5.65m originally built for royal carriages now used by everyday traffic, including an escalating number of sight-seeing buses. The two buildings on either side originally housed the toll-collectors.

The columns support an architrave above which is a frieze of metopes and triglyphs with a projecting cornice. The whole structure is crowned by a Quadriga (four-horsed chariot) in copper by Gottfried Schadow and was originally intended to represent the Greek goddess of peace, Eireni. However, after only 15 years the meaning of the 'Gate of Peace' was totally transformed by Napoleon's triumphal entrance through it in 1806. When the conquering emperor left, he took the Quadriga with him as a war trophy and stored it in the Orangery of the Louvre. Following his defeat in 1813 the statue was transported back to Berlin with great pomp and ceremony. Eireni was transformed into Nike, the goddess of Victory, and to underline this shift of meaning Schinkel redesigned the shaft which the goddess held aloft over the new, Neo-Classical Berlin. The shaft was now surmounted by an iron cross, a garland of oak leaves and the warlike Prussian eagle. The gate was an important focus for celebration following the defeat of France by Prussia in 1870. It was also used by the Nazis for propaganda in the 1930s including a torch-lit procession by storm troopers in 1933 to celebrate Hitler's acquisition of power. Sadly, in 1945, the gate lay in ruins like much of the surrounding area to be apportioned to the East German zone. Throughout the 1950s arguments raged over the replacement of the Quadriga as the GDR authorities declined the West's offer of casts made from the original in 1942. New symbols were considered, including a Soviet style model nuclear family. Eventually, in 1958, a compromise was reached and the Quadriga was replaced but without the militaristic iron cross and Prussian eagle. Further restoration was completed in December 1989 when the iron cross and eagle were again installed. The Brandenburg Gate has become the symbol of the fall of the Berlin Wall, playing host to celebrations in October 1990.

From the Brandenburg Gate it is a short walk north to the ***Reichstags-gebäude** (Reichstag Building), which stands majestically overlooking the Platz der Republik. Built to house the Imperial Parliament for the new state of Germany created in 1871, the Neo-Renaissance headquarters were constructed between 1884–94. The architect was Paul Wallot and the inscription,'*Dem Deutsche Volke*' above the portico was designed by modern architect, Peter Behrens. The building is familiar in most people's minds as the site of the Reichstag Fire, a mysterious event in 1933 during which the building was set ablaze. The fire was blamed on the Communists and the Nazis were able to seize more power and suspend basic freedoms as a result. The building was badly damaged during the Second World War and partial restoration took place during the 1960s. However, the main dome, blown up in 1957, has so far not been replaced and the rich ornamentation which decorated the exterior is also sadly missing. It is possible to visit the interior with its small cafeteria on the ground floor and multi-media exhibition *Fragen an die deutsche Geschichte* (questions on German history) on the first floor (opening times: Tues–Sun 10.00–17.00). This traces the beginnings of the German state from 1800 onwards with photographic, film and reconstructions of various key events. It is also possible to view the main Plenarsaal (Plenary Chamber) where the Bundestag (Federal Parliament) met from 1963 onwards following its restoration by Paul Baumgarten. Presently it is planned that the national government will sit here when it leaves Bonn around the year 2000.

From the Reichstag return to the Brandenburg Gate and continue east through one of its archways to reach the PARISER PLATZ, originally constructed in 1734. This was a prestigious square, where the 19C French Embassy once stood to the north and the Palais Blücher, used as the American Embassy, to the south, but after the Second World War it stood in no man's land, protected by East German border guards. Following the fall of the Berlin Wall it was a lively focus for street hawkers selling GDR

The Brandenburg Gate, originally built in 1789–91 and inspired by the Acropolis at Athens

militaria, sausages and cold beer. The buzz has now been replaced by a humdrum road which carries taxis and tourist buses through the Brandenburg Gate.

Continue east to the grandest boulevard in Berlin—**··Unter den Linden** which stretches a magnificent 1.5km from here to the Schlossbrücke in the east of Berlin. The road originated as a track to the Grunewald hunting grounds and was planted with walnut and lime trees in the 17C by Friederich Wilhelm and connected his palace with the Tiergarten. In the 18C Karl Friedrich Schinkel layed out the centre of the city with Unter den Linden as the focal point and main east–west axis. When Hitler came to power he used Unter den Linden for his military displays, destroying the trees which gave the boulevard its name (Under the Lime Trees) to make way for flags and pillars. The trees were replanted after the Second World War, to restore the street's soft, shaded ambience.

The first building on the right after crossing Otto-Grotewohl-Strasse is the former East German Ministry for Education followed by the monstrous former **Soviet Embassy**, designed by Russian architect, A.P. Strijewski and built by the Germans. The Embassy contains some 320 sumptuously decorated rooms, and occupies the site of the former luxurious Hotel Bristol and Archbishop's Palace. Continue east crossing Glinkastrasse noting the administrative offices of the Comic Opera and the Grand Hotel, opened in 1987, to the right. This leads to the the famous intersection with FRIEDRICHSTRASSE, so busy that the city's first traffic warden was installed here in 1902, complete with whistle. Three renowned cafés once stood here: the Café Kranzler (now situated in the Ku'damm), Café Bauer (inside the Grand Hotel) and Café Victoria (now to be found in the Hotel Unter den Linden). This section of Friedrichstrasse is now undergoing substantial development with the new FriedrichstadtPassagen (Friedrichstadt Passages) shopping mall due to open in here March 1995. For the meantime, major building work marrs the site but the projected buildings look promising.

To the north and left down Friedrichstrasse are the Friedrichstrasse U-Bahn and S-Bahn stations which connect with most of the city's main lines. If you have decided that your legs will take no more, this would be a good point at which to stop and continue the walk another day. Alternatively, if your energy reserves are not fully depleted, continue east up Unter den Linden, crossing Charlottenstrasse. On the left is the **Deutsche Staatsbibliothek** (German State Library) designed by Ernst von Ihne and built in sandstone in imperial, Neo-Baroque style between 1903 and 1914. Until 1945 this was the Prussian State Library, whose 3,820,000 volumes were distributed to 30 locations during the war. Since renamed the German State Library, its collection was based on part of the Prussian Library, with over one half of this forming the basis of the West's new State Library of Prussian Cultural Heritage in the Culture Forum (see Route 2). The German State Library now holds over six million volumes. The 105m wide façade is adorned with allegorical figures and portico with Corinthian columns. The library is open to the public, although mainly inhabited by University students, and has a fairly good café (opening times: Mon–Fri 09.00–21.00, Sat 12.00–17.00).

Continue east to the splendid equestrian statue in the centre of Unter den Linden. The great Romantic sculptor, Daniel Christian Rauch, laboured for 11 years (1840–51) over this creation. It is the biggest and best known work by Rauch and is known as **Der Alte Fritz** (Old Fritz). It represents Frederick the Great astride Conde, his favourite steed, resplendent in coronation cloak and three-cornered hat. The base is decorated with life-size statues of great men of letters and military might from Frederick's reign, while tablets above depict scenes from the king's life. The statue was politically unacceptable during GDR times and was moved to Sanssouci in Potsdam in 1950, but it returned to its original position in 1980. The building behind the statue is **Humboldt University**, founded in 1806 by the writer Wilhelm von Humboldt the writer and known as the Friedrich-Wilhlem-Universität before 1949. The Neo-Classical building by Johann Boumass dates from 1748–66, based on plans by Knobelsdorff as a residence for Frederick the Great but occupied by his brother, Prince Heinrich. The main façade is graced by six columns surmounted by six figures of Greek goddesses. The two northern wings were designed by Ludwig Hoffmann and added in 1913–19. The gardens are scattered with monuments to the great and the good including the brothers Grimm, physicist Hermann von Helmholtz and Einstein. Facing Unter den Linden are marble statues of Wilhelm von Humboldt in deep thought by Paul Otto, dated 1883 and his brother Alexander von Humboldt by R. Begas from the same year. The university was the largest in former East Germany, with some 13,000 students. However, unification has led to cut-backs and uncertainty in higher education generally and some doubt hangs over the future of the university as funds become concentrated in the west.

Opposite the university is the historic BEBELPLATZ, known as the Opernplatz until 1952 when it was renamed after the Socialist leader,

August Bebel. The square was planned by Frederick the Great with his architect Knobelsdorff in an attempt to emulate the great squares in Rome, and was originally known as the Forum Fridericianum. The square is best known as the site where the dreadful Nazi book-burning of May 1933 took place. Overlooking Bebelplatz on the west side is the **Alte Königliche Bibliotek** (Old Royal Library) built in 1774–86 by G.F. Boumann following plans by G.C. Unger who had emulated the Hofburburg in Vienna. This explains the comparatively fluid styling of the building, with its curved façade—earning it the nickname Kommode (Chest of Drawers). The Prussian State Library was housed here until 1914, when it moved to the new building on Unter den Linden, now the German State Library. The Old Royal Library was used by the University and was burnt out in 1945 to be immaculately restored, remaining part of the University. On the south-east corner of Bebelplatz is **Hedwigskirche** (St Hedwig's Cathedral; open daily, 10.00–17.00) built under the patronage of Frederick the Great. Begun in 1747, the architects and builders struggled with the technical challenge of building such a large dome, and it was not successfully completed until the late 19C. It was burnt down in an air raid in March 1943 to be restored with the former lanterns replaced by a simple cross. The only Catholic church in the city until 1854, its original design was by Jean Legeay and consists of a circular ground plan, a huge dome, visible for miles around, and portico modelled on the Parthenon complete with six Ionic columns. The decoration in the pediment carved by Nikolaus Geiger shows the Adoration of the Kings, dating from 1895. Inside little of the original interior remains; double columns support a new concrete dome.

Continue south from the Hedwigskirche and west down Französische Strasse taking the next left to reach the ****PLATZ DER AKADEMIE**, formerly the Gendarmenmarkt. Four impressive pieces of architecture line the pedestrianised square. Dominating the Platz is the suprisingly simple **Schauspielhaus** designed by Schinkel in 1819–21 to replace the original which had burned down in 1817. Schinkel built his masterpiece on the foundations of the National Theatre and retained six of the 18C pillars for the portico. Largely inspired by Greek forms, the main façade facing east has the six Ionic columns salvaged by Schinkel and the portico is reached by means of an imperial flight of steps. Now home to the Berlin Symphony Orchestra, this building, along with its neighbours in the square was left in ruins after the War and restoration did not begin until the 1980s. The interior now only contains a concert hall whereas Schinkel designed a central auditorium flanked by offices, workrooms and double-storey concert hall to the other side.

The exterior has been faithfully restored and in front of the main steps stands a splendid statue of Schiller by Reinhold Begas dating from 1871. The seated poet is surrounded by the four Muses representing Drama, Poetry, History and Philosophy. The statue was removed by the Nazis in 1936 and was returned from Charlottenburg by the western authorities only in 1986, to be fully restored in 1989. The bronze statues on either side of the main entrance are by Frederick Tieck showing genii riding a lion on the right and panther on the left. Tieck also created the Children of Niobe sandstone sculpture in the tympanum which crowns the portico. Behind this, on the main façade, rises a bronze sculpture of Apollo riding in a chariot, drawn by mythical griffins—also by Tieck with the assistance of Rauch. The sculpture which surmounts the western façade represents Pegasus whilst those on the northern and southern tympana, both by Tieck, show Bacchus with Ariadne and Orpheus with Eurydice respectively. Apart from the classically inspired sculpture, the exterior generally is plain without being stark. The plentiful fenestration is divided by plain pilasters. The Schauspielhaus opened on 26 May 1821 with Goethe's *Iphigenie auf Tauris* to a rapturous audience, charmed by the stage set which Schinkel had designed showing the Gendarmenmerkt where the building stood. The Schauspielhaus was reopened in 1984 as a concert hall.

The **Deutscher Dom** (German Church) stands on the south side of the square and the **Französischer Dom** (French Church) to the north. Both were built at the behest of Frederick the Great in imitation of the Santa Maria in Montesanto and the Santa Maria dei Miracoli in Rome. Designed by Carl von Gontard they were erected during 1780–85 as decorative additions to the civic perspective. The Deutscher Dom was intended for the city's Lutheran community, and was built onto a simple chapel dating from 1701–08. The great Neo-Classical tower is crowned by a 7m high, gilded sculpture of Virtue. Similarly, the Französischer Dom was built onto a chapel intended for the great surge of Huguenot immigrants who were welcomed into Berlin following the revocation of the Edict of Nantes. Both churches were severely damaged during the Second World War but skilful restoration of the Französischer Dom was completed by the late 1980s. It is worth visiting the interior of the Französischer Dom as stairs lead to the 40m high viewing balustrade on the dome where splendid views can be enjoyed, including a close-up of Apollo on the roof of the Schauspielhaus to the south. (Opening times: daily 10.00–18.00.) Note that there is a wine bar at 20m and on the ground floor the Huguenot Museum which tells the story of the Huguenots in Berlin and Brandenburg from their welcome in 1685 with Friedrich Wilhelm's Edict of Potsdam (opening times: Tues–Thurs, Sat and Sun 10.00–17.00, closed Mon and Fri). By the turn of the century, 6000 Huguenots lived in Berlin, making up one third of the population and contributing greatly to the craft and culture of the city. The tower contains a five-octave carillon which is rung at 12.00, 15.00 and 19.00 with concerts on Tuesdays at 14.00 and Saturday at 15.00.

On the eastern side of the Platz is the **Akademie der Wissenschaften** (Academy of Sciences) housed in the building of the former Preussische Staatsbank, erected in 1901. The Academy was founded in 1700 by Friedrich III as the Brandenburg Society of Sciences, resurrected in 1946, and renamed the Academy of Sciences in 1972, providing a focus for some 40 different institutes concerned with research.

Return to Bebelplatz and then Unter den Linden. The building on the eastern side of Bebelplatz, opposite the Old Royal Library is the *Deutsche Staatsoper (German State Opera), with its main façade facing onto Unter den Linden. It was originally built in 1740–43 by Knobelsdorff in the form of a Corinthian temple as the first public opera house in Prussia. Alterations were made by Langhans in 1788 to form a galleried theatre and further changes were made by his son, Carl Ferdinand, in 1844 following a fire. During the early 20C it enjoyed an international reputation but the destruction of the Second World War forced closure until 1955 with further modernisation taking place in 1986. The pediment relief, cast in zinc, dates from 1844 and represents the Muses and the Arts. Nestling in the recesses are monuments of Greek dramatists including Sophocles, and perched on the cornices are statues of Apollo and the Muses. Beside the German State Opera is the Operncafé (Opera Café)—a restaurant and disco combined—housed in the restored **Prinzessinnenpalais**. Built in 1733 and 1811 this long, two-storey Baroque building has a more recent terrace added to its

The Deutsche Staatsoper, originally designed by Knobelsdorff in 1740–43. Its main façade faces onto Unter den Linden

front. It originally formed one wing of the Palais Unter den Linden founded in 1633 and was known as the Princesses' Palace because the three daughters of Friedrich Wilhelm III lived here until they were married.

If time permits, a detour south and then east down Oberwallstrasse brings you to the **Friedrichwerdersche Kirche** on the left at Am Werderscher-Markt (opening times: daily 10.00–18.00). This twin-towered church is important as it houses a display devoted to the life and work of its architect, Schinkel. Designed and built during 1821–30, it is also a rare example of Gothic Revival architecture by this renowned Classical designer. Schinkel was inspired by English Gothic church design which he knew from his visit to England and published engravings. The church is built from traditional German Gothic materials including red brick with moulded, terracotta detailing. Less traditional are the cast-iron doors crafted by Friedrick Tieck on Schinkel's designs. A striking terracotta statue of St Michael crowns the double doorway with its two pointed arches. The interior is quite impressive with five cross-ribbed vaults which rest on ribbed piers with painted star ribs. A gallery runs round the interior, supported on arcades of pointed arches in wood. This simple interior perfectly complements the collection of Neo-Classical sculpture on display. (Opening times: Tues–Sun 10.00–18.00.)

Return to Bebelplatz noting the grandiose building opposite the Schinkel church. Designed by Fascist architect Heinrich Wolff in 1931–38 Hitler's central bank, it was transformed into the Communists' Central Committee building in 1959; its future is yet to be decided. Return to Unter den Linden and continue east for a fine view of the first and best of Schinkel's buildings in Berlin, the *Neue Wache (New Guard House) which faces the Opera House.

Built during 1816–18 in the form of a Roman Castrum, the Neue Wache replaced the Königswache and was used as a base for the guards of the Palace opposite. This small but classically elegant structure has a Doric portico with six columns. Above each column is a carved classical figure by Schadow and the relief decorating the pediment is by August Kiss, dating from 1842. In 1931 Hindenburg used the building as a monument to those who fell in the First World War. Heinrich Tessenow designed the dark, still interior lined with limestone with a round, open skylight. After the Second World War the Neue Wache was made into the Monument to the Victims of Fascism and Militarism, with soldiers of the People's Army stationed outside, who changed guard with goose-stepping precision daily until 1990. What is most striking are the all too obvious remnants of war damage which remain—most notably shrapnel damage. The building is now undergoing total restoration and the eternal flame is barely visible through the plastic sheeting. Work is due to be finished by 1994.

Continue north from the Neue Wache to the **Museum für Deutsche Geschichte** (German Historical Museum, opening times: Thurs–Tues 10.00–18.00), housed in the massive *Zeughaus or former arsenal.

Despite its blackened state, this is one of the best surviving Baroque buildings in Berlin. Begun in 1695 it was built on a square layout to designs by Arnold Nering and completed by French architect Jean de Bodt in 1706. This solid building was used to store weapons until 1875, when it was converted into a museum of military equipment which opened to the public in 1880. As part of the adaptation the central courtyard was roofed over with glass. The two-storey building is rather severe but this impression is softened by the effective sculpture which decorates the exterior. This includes Andreas Schlüter's trophies on the roof balustrade and classical helmets adorning the keystones of the windows. In the courtyard the windows and portals are decorated with 22 haunting Heads of Dying Warriors, also by Schlüter. The four sculptures by the main entrance represent arithmetic, geometry, mechanics and pyrotechnics, and are by French artist Hulot. On top of the roof are various sculptural groups including a warlike Mars. A good terrace café is situated to the east of the building but the boat trips which leave from the same terrace are not recommended, unless you are interested in the movement of scrap metal by barge or how polluted the River Spree is.

The Museum of German History opened here in 1952 and was a dreary affair, showing a biased Marxist account of the German nation over a tedious 7700 sq m. This chance to experience Communist dogma has thankfully now disappeared, as the museum closed throughout 1990–93 for a total overhaul. It has reopened as the German Historical Museum, where the authorities have tackled the problem of retelling German history by means of temporary exhibitions with, for example, an examination of Cold War propaganda from both sides in *Deutschland im Kalten Krieg*, covering eight galleries on the second floor with a rich mixture of posters and pamphlets showing the depiction of evil—be it a Red Army soldier or American capitalist. The Arsenal will form part of the government's buildings when the move from Bonn takes places in 2000.

The Zeughaus borders onto the River Spree, which encircles Museuminsel (Museum Island, see Route 3). Cross the SCHLOSSBRÜCKE (known as the Marx-Engels-Brücke in GDR times). The bridge was designed by Schinkel and built in 1822–24. The cast-iron balustrades are decorated with charming dolphins and sea-horses framed by Greek key borders. The glorious statues which decorate the bridge were returned only in 1981, having been kept in storage in the west since the Second World War. The eight groups of sculptures in marble were made by pupils of Rauch between 1845 and 1857 and represent the life of a Greek warrior.

On the left of the eastern end of the bridge is the splendid **Berliner Dom**, the restoration of which is almost complete. This Neo-Baroque edifice was built during 1894–1905 by Julius Rachsdorff for Kaiser Wilhelm II, replacing that built by Frederick the Great. The massive, central dome is flanked by two smaller cupolas. During the Second World War the central lantern was bombed and sent plunging into the crypt. Restoration work initially concentrated on the exterior but from 1984 work on the interior has been underway. Ascending the main flight of steps to the west facing the Zeughaus the Museum area and balcony are reached via the marbled staircase. (Opening times: Mon–Sat 10.00–18.00, Sun 12.00–17.00.) At the top is a photographic exhibition of churches in eastern Germany including Halberstadt as well as an historic exhibition devoted to the Dom itself. Continue through a small doorway on the left to a small gallery where the whole, splendid interior can be enjoyed. Restoration is still underway but one cannot help but be impressed by the glinting new gilding and the sparkling white stone amid the roar of electric drills. The great organ has been totally restored and is visible beyond the scaffolding. The fabulous pulpit, designed by Andreas Schlüter, has been newly gilded and the soaring dome is truly impressive. The altar is framed by marble and gilt Corinthian columns. Still closed to the public is the crypt with its fascinating collection of over one hundred coffins, including the 16C tomb of Elector Johann Cicero in bronze and the sarcophagi of Frederick I and Queen Sophie Charlotte, designed by Schlüter.

On the opposite side of the bridge stands the modern Communist status symbol, the **Palast der Republik** (Palace of the Republic), with its bronze reflective glass and vast interiors. It was built during the 1970s by Erich Honecker as both the government headquarters and an entertainment and leisure complex for all. It is closed now due to asbestos scares and the general discreditation of Communism, and the Bonn authorities wish to demolish the entire building. However, east Berliners are resistant to the idea, as this is where the east German MPs agreed to vote for unification. Arguments now rage about the Palace's demolition, with Professor Heinz Graffunder who headed the collective responsible for its design arguing for its restoration rather than destruction. During the summer of 1993 the entire building was cloaked by Parisian artist, Catherine Feff, with a canvas carrying an image of the old Schloss which was demolished in 1951 to make way for the Palace. The Schloss was the residence of the Hohenzollerns, the Margraves and Electors of Brandenburg as well as the Kaisers of Germany from 1470 until 1918. The main Baroque Schloss was initially designed by Andreas Schlüter in 1698 with later additions, including the West Wing added in 1845–53. It is a tragedy that such an historic building, already damaged during the War, should be totally destroyed. The same may perhaps one day be said of the Palace of the Republic.

Continue north up Karl-Liebknecht-Strasse. On the left is the Palast Hotel, one of the few places where westerners could stay before 1989. Directly opposite, down Spandaustrasse E is the pedestrianised Postrasse which leads to the ***Nikolaiviertal** (Nicholas Quarter). Modelled on the medieval city quarter during the 1980s, the narrow cobbled streets seem rather sham. One of the few buildings of any genuine architectural interest is the **Nikolaikirche**—an aisled hall church and the oldest church in the city. The bases of the two towers date back to c 1230 and the choir to 1380. Badly damaged during the Second World War it was virtually rebuilt during 1956–58 (opening times: Sun and Mon 10.00–17.00, Thurs and Sat 10.00–18.00, Fri 10.00–16.00). The exhibition inside is of passing interest, showing the early development of Berlin by means of maps and models.

South of the Nikolaikirche overlooking the River Spree is the **Ephraim-palais on Mühlendaum**. On this site originally stood the premises of Frederick the Great's jeweller, Veital Heine Ephraim. The Rococo building was demolished by the Nazis in 1935 to be replaced by a new road. Some relics of the façade were preserved in the Spandau Citadel and have formed the basis of this recreation. Inside is a museum devoted to the history of Berlin from the 17C to the 19C (opening times: Mon 10.00–16.00, Tues–Sun 10.00–17.00, Wed and Sat 10.00–18.00).

Continue north-west up Postrasse to the **Knoblauchhaus** which houses an exhibition outlining the development of the German Enlightenment (opening times: Wed and Sat 10.00–18.00, Thurs and Sun 10.00–17.00, Fri 10.00–16.00). To the right of this, across the square, is the **Handwerk-museum** devoted to local arts and crafts (opening times: Mon 10.00–17.00, Tues and Wed 09.00–17.00, Sat and Sun 10.00–18.00). Directly north across Spandauer Strasse is the distinctive **Rotes Rathaus** (Red Town Hall). Designed by Hermann Friedrich Waesemann in 1859, it was built in quasi-Venetian Gothic red brick with terracotta decorations. The City Council for East Berlin met here until 1948.

Cross Rathausstrasse west to reach the Neuer Markt and the impressive **Neptunbrunnen** (Neptune Fountain). Created by Reinhold Begas in 1891, it originally stood in the Schlossplatz, until its removal here in 1945. The fountain consists of playful sea creatures and the god Neptune surrounded by four female figures who represent the four major rivers of Germany: Rhine, Elbe, Oder and Weichsel. Continue north-west to the **Marienkirche** on the left. A parish church has stood on this spot since at least 1292 and this comparatively contemporary building is based on the design by Langhans dating from 1789–90; the distinctive steeple combines Gothic and Classical forms. The interior was restored during the late 1980s and is definitely worth a look (opening times: daily 10.00–18.00). From the main entrance, head to the north-western corner to see the Baroque pulpit designed by Schlüter, dating from 1703, with the Epitaph to the Röbel family and Monument to Prediger Roloff behind. Note also the bronze 15C font in the Choir with inscriptions in Low German. The best known artefact within the church is the Dance of Death mural painting on the wall at the opposite end of the nave. This 15C mural depicts 14 separate scenes which attest to the destruction of death, with rhymes in Low German. The 22.6m long painting was covered by distemper in 1730 and re-discovered only in 1860 by August Stüler.

Continue north to ALEXANDERPLATZ, the busy hub of East Berlin, named after Tsar Alexander I in 1805 and providing the title of Alfred Döblin's famous 1929 novel. Döblin would not recognise the square today as it was totally reconstructed in anonymous, Modernist style in the late 1960s. The Zentrum department store was the biggest to be built in the GDR and the Brunnen der Völkerfreundschaft (Fountain of Friendship between Peoples) in the centre was constructed in 1969. East Germany's former Chief Architect stated in 1968 that the pedestrianised square was 'representative of all the merits of our socialist system' and perhaps he was right!

The chief attraction of Alexanderplatz is the ***Fernsehturm** (Television Tower), one of Berlin's major landmarks. A trip to the observation platform at 207m is a perfect way to conclude the tour. The lift whisks you up to the viewing platform which affords a 360 degree view of Berlin, including the route just covered. The Dom, Schauspielhaus and Brandenburg Gate are all perfectly visible on a clear day. The central flight of steps takes you up to the revolving restaurant—the **Telé Café**—which is fairly reasonable in price and a real treat. The floor revolves once every 30 minutes and a full three course meal, breakfast (including cornflakes) or snack can be enjoyed (opening times: 09.00–midnight).

The Altes Museum, 1823–30, designed by Schinkel, and one of the most important works of German classicism

2

City Centre Museums: east and west

When the city of Berlin was divided, the rich and varied collections of the museums were simply allocated according to where they were stored during the Second World War. This arbitrary division led to the splintering of entire collections across both sides of the East/West border and it is useful to bear this in mind when visiting Berlin's museums. This particular walk takes in some of the best of these including the world famous Museum Island and the Culture Forum in the Tiergarten. Obviously tastes and levels of interest vary, but this walk should occupy one day at the least, while those with special interest in, for example, Egyptian culture, may wish to spend longer at Museum Island.

With the division of Berlin after the war, Museum Island fell into the Soviet sector and so became accessible only to inhabitants of the Eastern Bloc and Western tourists on day trips from the 'other side' or in officially approved, organised parties. The West retaliated by building two important museums, a library and a symphony concert hall in the Tiergarten, not far from the Brandenburg Gate. This duplication is now the cause of some difficulty, as the museums all fall under the control of the Staatliche Museen Preussischer Kulturbesitz Berlin. It is therefore anticipated that major changes will be made to the location of collections and opening times.

Museum Island

*MUSEUM ISLAND, which lay in former East Berlin, is now full of visitors from the West, eager to enjoy the great cultural heritage of the Prussian state, and the level of admissions has never been greater. The Island lies in the centre of the River Spree near the Dom and the Schlossbrücke. The nearest U-Bahn station is Friedrichstrasse. One could easily luxuriate in this cultural feast by spending one full day here alone—there is so much to see and enjoy in such a compact site. This is where Berlin's oldest museums are situated, originally founded in the 1820s by Friedrich Wilhelm III and built on a marshy piece of waste land. The museums were designed to serve a new, culturally aware middle-class and display the Prussian collection recently returned from Paris, where it had been displayed by Napoleon as war booty. Schinkel was responsible for the current layout of the area—planning the Schlossbrücke to lead to the Lustgarten. The Lustgarten is the area now known as Marx-Engels-Platz which lies between Museum Island, the Cathedral, the Palace of the Republic and the former East German Ministry of Foreign Affairs. The Lustgarten was originally planned by Johann Georg of Brandenburg in 1573 as part kitchen garden and part formal garden for the Palace. This was levelled in 1715 to create a military parade ground and converted into a prestigious public space by Schinkel in the 19C.

The *Altes Museum which faces onto Marx-Engels-Platz was specifically planned by Schinkel to complement the Royal Palace opposite. The

Museum was built between 1823 and 1830 and is one of the most important works of German classicism. The imposing façade complete with a majestic row of 18 Ionic columns which rise the full, double-storey height of the building, faces squarely onto the Lustgarten. Cross the Marx-Engels-Platz and approach the main entrance noting the sculpture to the left; Albert Wolff's *Youth* (1858) and on the right *Amazon on Horseback Fighting a Tiger* by August Kiss (1842). This was one of the first purpose-built museums in Europe, erected at a similar time and for similar reasons as the British Museum in London. Standing majestically in front of the main façade is a huge granite bowl, made by Christian Gottlieb Cantian and installed here in 1831. It was originally intended to stand in the central rotunda but its 6.9m diameter was too large. Note how the central flight of stairs is precisely one third the total width of the façade, displaying Schinkel's adhesion to classical systems of proportion. Once the main steps have been climbed, look back through the colonnade onto the former Lustgarten, a view Schinkel deliberately created—regarding the layout of the grounds with lawns, trees and fountains as the best public space in the city.

The Altes Museum was originally built to house the Prussian state's Egyptian collection, assembled by various explorers including Carl Richard Lepsius who exchanged Prussian porcelain for ancient treasures in the mid 19C. Before the Second World War visitors could tour the Altes Museum, which then housed Classical sculpture, and gain direct entry to the neighbouring Neues Museum, so badly damaged during the war that it still remains closed. A further passageway connected with the Pergamon Museum with its displays of Greek and Roman architecture. Today it is best, if you intend to visit all the museums on the Island, to buy a Daily Pass. In the GDR era, under the control of the Ministry of Culture, the Altes Museum was used to display 20C painting, graphic arts from the 15C to the present day and a fine collection of drawings. The Museum is now used only for temporary shows, but the experience of the interior itself at least matches a visit to the exhibitions (opening times: Tues–Sun 10.00–18.00).

The main surprise when entering the building is the central ROTUNDA, based on the Roman Pantheon. There is no hint of this from the exterior and so this perfectly proportioned, grandiose space seems to come from nowhere. The rotunda is lit from above and 20 Corinthian columns support the first floor gallery, decorated by niches containing antique sculptures which are Roman copies of Greek originals. Doors lead from the gallery to the exhibitions beyond. The coffered ceiling is decorated with gilded signs of the zodiac.

The Altes Museum was severely damaged during the war and reopened after renovation in 1966. The ground floor housed the 20C painting collection which included rather pallid examples of official GDR art including the work of Albert Eberd. In the East Wing was the Kupferstichkabinett (Print Collection) which is now to be rehoused in a new location in Matthäikirchplatz in the Tiergarten by the end of 1993. Recent temporary exhibitions have included 'The Etruscans and Europe' showing their contemporary impact and subsequent influence.

Leave the Altes Museum by the side entrance facing the cathedral to the east and continue north to the massive colonnade which stands in front of the far less pure *Alte National Galerie (Old National Gallery, opening times: Wed–Sun, 09.00–17.00). This was designed by a pupil of Schinkel, Friedrich August Stüler, and built in 1865–76 to house the expanding art collection, boosted by a special bequest to the State from J.H.W. Wagener,

Royal Swedish Consul and wealthy Berlin businessman, in 1861, consisting of 262 works. During the late 19C, under the directorship of Hugo von Tschudi, an adventurous purchasing programme was undertaken with works by leading Impressionists and Post-Impressionists entering the collection. His successor, Ludwig Justi, amassed a fine collection of German Expressionist art as well as work by Munch and Van Gogh. Modern art of this ilk did not accord well with Nazi propaganda and so Justi was dismissed in 1933 and 435 works were sent to the Degenerate Art exhibition of 1937 in Munich whilst other works were auctioned off or simply destroyed. The museum closed in 1939 and the collection went into storage at Wiesbaden and Celle. The Gallery suffered after the war, with 630 works from its collection providing the basis for the New National Gallery in the Tiergarten. The red sandstone building is strikingly ornate in comparison to Schinkel's monumental Altes Museum. The main inspiration was a Corinthian temple, raised on a massive base with imposing flight of steps leading to the main entrance. The bronze statue in front shows Frederick Wilhelm IV on horseback by Alexander Calandrelli (1886).

The ENTRANCE HALL is graced by two sculptures by Gottfried Schadow. The marble sarcophogus of the Count of the Brandenburg March is a touching epitaph to the son of Friedrich Wilhelm II and Crown Princess Luise who died in 1791, aged nine. The tomb originally stood in the nearby Dorotheanstadt Church which was demolished in 1965. Also in the vestibule is a charming statue of Crown Princess Luise with her sister Princess Friederike, also by Schadow; the work was completed in 1795 but did not earn Royal approval. The main GROUND FLOOR gallery contains 19C German painting including important work by realist Adolph von Menzel, whose *Das Eisenwalzwerk* (The Iron Rolling Mill) was purchased in 1875, the year of its completion, by the National Gallery. It accurately records the grit and hardship of industrial labour. Other significant works by Menzel include sketches for *Frederick the Great's Flute Concert* and the *Round Table at Sanssouci*, the original paintings being lost during the War. Other significant work includes paintings by Aronold Böcklin and Raphael Mengs. The MIDDLE FLOOR is presently occupied by the work of the German Expressionists Karl Schmidt-Rottluff, Emil Nolde and Oskar Kokoschka. The latter's *Pariser Platz* (1926) depicts the area around the Brandenburg Gate before the war. There is also a smattering of French, modernist work including Degas's *Conversation*, two still lifes and one landscape by Cézanne and Raoul Dufy's *Harbour*. Examples of Neue Sachlichkeit work by Otto Dix and expressive sculpture by Barlach and Käthe Kollwitz are also worth looking out for.

The building to the west of the Old National Gallery is the **Neues Museum** (New Museum) which is still undergoing extensive rebuilding and restoration following war damage. Set to open at the turn of the century it was designed by Stüler and originally built in 1843–55. The exterior was comparatively stark but the interior was deliciously ornate. It housed the Egyptian Museum until the Second World War and plans are now afoot to return the exhibits from the Egyptian Museum in Charlottenburg and Egyptian Museum in the Bode to their pre-war home.

Return to the Bodestrasse and head west, crossing the river and turning right up Kupfergraben. Take the next bridge right which leads to the **••Pergamon Museum** (opening times: daily 09.00–17.00, Mon and Tues, Dept. of Antiquities and Western Asian Museum only). Designed by August Mensel and built by Ludwig Hoffman in 1909–30, this is the newest building on the Island. It was built specifically to house one of Berlin's star attractions, the Pergamon Altar. The winged, classical structure of the museum's outline plan with its huge flight of steps mirrors the shape of the world famous altar which was brought to Berlin in 1902. The museum offers the opportunity to walk through architectural spaces from around the world from both ancient and more modern times. Such flagrant colonialism is now rather questionable and negotiations are currently underway for the return of the Pergamon Altar to its original site at Bergama in Turkey.

After entering via the main, central steps pass through the entrance straight ahead, paying admittance on the left. A full text in English is available from the information desk. Continue up the central steps to the prize of the museum, the **Pergamon Altar**, which forms part of the DEPART-MENT OF ANTIQUITIES (Antikensammlung). The huge altar, raised on a platform and softly illuminated by the natural light which filters through from above, was one of the wonders of the ancient world. This monumental piece of architecture was originally built in 164–156 BC and dedicated to Zeus and Athena. It was excavated by Carl Humann in 1878–80 and is one of the best surviving examples of Greek sculpture in the world. The marble altar has been meticulously reconstructed with an undecorated plinth supporting the 2.3m high and 120m long frieze, surmounted by a project-ing, finely toothed cornice. A colonnade of Ionic columns graces the entire upper level.

Most intriguing is the frieze, perfectly carved in high relief on the theme of the battle of the gods and giants. Over 100 figures are shown in physical combat, with the defeated giants sporting gruesome expressions of suffer-ing. The most famous image from the altar is of the winged giant Alkyoneus being painfully siezed by the scalp by Athena, sapping him of strength by raising him from the earth below. A detailed description of the frieze's intricate symbolism and narrative threads can be found on the excellent taped guides for hire at the information desk.

More treats wait in the next room to the right which is devoted to Roman architecture including the 16.68m high **Market Gateway** from Miletus. Built c 120 AD under Emperor Hadrian, it is a stunning example of original, Roman building excavated during 1903–05 and brought, in a myriad of pieces and fragments, to Berlin where it was reconstructed. The carved acanthus frieze and the capitals of the Composite columns are particularly fine. Note also the mosaic pavement in the centre of the room dating from 2C AD decorated with Orpheus and various mythical beasts.

Continue through the Market Gate to the SOUTH WING which houses the **Vorderasiatisches Museum** (Near-Eastern Museum) and includes architecture, sculpture and jewellery from Babylon, Iran and Assyria. Most striking is the Ishtar Gate, built in 6 BC under the patronage of Nebuchad-nezzar II as part of Babylon's city wall in honour of the Babylonian female god of Ishtar. The sheer scale of the monument is quite awesome, as is the strong cobalt blue of the glazed bricks and the stylised bulls and dragons which decorate it. There follows a reconstruction of the Babylonian Proces-sional Way and a section of the façade of the Throne Room, also originating from Babylon. The three rooms to the right of the Processional Way contain smaller but significant archaeological finds from Assyria, Babylonia and Sumer to the left. The final room contains fascinating objects excavated at Tell Halaf in northern Mesopotamia and northern Syria. This includes the gigantic basalt sculpture of a bird from c 900 BC and many examples of Hittite artefacts. The reconstructed Lion Gate from the Citadel of Sinjerli is decorated with four large basalt lions around the door frame, believed to be magical guardians against evil spirits.

The NORTH WING on the other side of the Pergamon Altar contains more from the Department of Antiquities, notably Hellenistic architecture and excellent original Greek and Roman sculpture. In the first room there are reconstructions and authentic examples of Greek architecture including the propylon of the Temple of Athena and the prototype for all Ionic architecture, the Athena Temple at Priene, represented by two columns with entablatures. The remainder of the rooms concentrate on sculpture with the emphasis on representations of the human body over a 1000 year period beginning with 7C BC. In the first gallery are some fine examples of *kouroi*, statues of youths plus figures of women including the Berlin Goddess. This 1.93m marble statue is remarkable in that much of its original paint is still intact as it was buried in a vault, encased in lead until the early 20C when it was excavated. In the following room there are splendid examples of early, Classical Greek sculpture arranged thematically around tombs, statues and friezes. Further rooms document the progression of ancient sculpture from the late Classical to Hellenistic periods. The North Wing ends with Roman art created for official and private purposes. The 41cm high green schist bust of Julius Caesar is a particularly fine example of secular portraiture from the Republic Period, c 1C AD.

The UPPER FLOOR of the North Wing contains more items from the Department of Antiquities and the **Far East Collection** (Ostasiatische Sammlung) which includes Chinese ceramics, enamelwork, lacquerware and jade plus Japanese textiles and woodcuts. This section also houses the **Islamic Museum** (Islamisches Museum). Its most important exhibit is another chunk of architecture, this time the façade of the Jordan desert castle of Mshatta, dating from the 8C and donated by Sultan Abdul Hamid of Turkey to the German Kaiser Wilhelm II in 1903. This is exquisitely decorated with flat, abstract patterns which are deeply incised or even totally cut out.

From the Pergamon Museum cross the Pergamon Brücke and turn right to reach the last museum on the Island, the *•Bode*, by means of the Monbijoubrücke (opening times: Wed–Sun 09.00–17.00). This Neo-Baroque building fits neatly into the northern tip of the Museum Insel and is roughly triangular in outline plan. Built during 1898–1904 to designs by Ernst von Ihne it was known originally as the Emperor Frederick Museum, and was renamed the Bode in 1956 after the Director of the Berlin Museums from 1906 to 1920, Wilhelm von Bode, who was instrumental in building up the collections as they exist today. Several collections share space under the ornate roof of the Bode: the Egyptian Museum, the Papyrus Collection, the Early Christian and Byzantine Collection, the Sculpture Collection, the Picture Gallery, the Museum of Prehistory, the Children's Gallery and the Cabinet of Coins and Medals. The collections were much depleted after the Second World War and substantial parts came under the control of the West, providing the basis for the Dahlem Museum complex (see Route 4).

Enter by means of the domed LARGE HALL decorated by four carved, sandstone figures by Schülter in 1712 for the now demolished Haus Kameke in Berlin. The BASILICA leading on from here contains 18C German sculpture and the domed area beyond, houses bronze works by Adriaen de Vries. The 12 rooms to the right or east contain the extensive **Egyptian collection**, spanning the 5C BC to the 3C AD. The collection had been kept in the Neues Museum before the War and items not destroyed during the fire there were transported to Russia for safekeeping in 1945–46. In 1959 the artefacts were returned to go on display in the current location of the Bode. Eventually it is hoped that this collection and that currently housed in Charlottenburg may be reunited like Germany itself. However, for the time being only a fraction of the collection is on view due to space restrictions at the Bode. The rooms are layed out in roughly chronological progression beginning with early pottery and sculptures including the 52cm statue of a baboon from c 3000 BC. The Egyptian Cult of the Dead is inescapably highlighted with many fragments of tombs, sculpture used to mark the funerary route to the temple and objects made specifically for the tomb itself. Perhaps most fascinating of all are the coffins themselves, including the Inner Coffin and bottom case from Western Thebes from the 8C BC and the bronze coffin of a holy cat c 500 BC. Also of special note is the comprehensive Papyrus collection, part of which is displayed in Room eleven and consists of some 30,000 items. This not only contains Egyptian material, for example Amunemwiya's *Guide to the Netherworld*, from 13 BC, but Greek, Latin and Hebrew texts.

To the left of the central axis to the north is the **Early Christian and Byzantine Collection** (Frühchristlich-byzantinische Sammlung). This display, housed in four rooms, traces the development of carving in wood and stone in the Mediterranean countries from 3C–19C with the accent on the early Christian era. The collection grew from the acquisition of the treasures amassed by the Venetian, Pajaro in 1840. The best-known piece on display is the Apse Mosaic created from glass and marble fragments and taken from the Church of San Michele in Afrisco, Ravenna. Heavily restored after severe damage in the Second World War, it depicts Jesus holding an open Bible with the quote taken from the Gospel of St John on the two pages. Another mosaic gem from the Byzantine era is the small icon, one of many produced in workshops in Constantinople and sent as gifts to the west at the end of the 13C. This particular example measures 36.5 x 30cm and was originally kept in Sicily where the wooden frame was probably added with various holy relics inserted. The crucified Christ is portrayed in minute pieces of gold and coloured glass.

Further east from the Early Christian and Byzantine collection is the **Sculpture Collection**, again much depleted after the Second World War when many former exhibits went to the Dahlem complex. However, what remains is of special interest, ranging from German Late Gothic, to Dutch and Flemish Renaissance and the Italian Renaissance. The Late Gothic section is best viewed with the Dahlem display (see Route 4) fresh in the mind as there are even parts of the same sculptures in the two museums. For example, the Gothic Triumphal Cross from the Moritzkirche at Naumburg (c 1230) has a missing virgin which is housed at the Dahlem. Further gems include Hans Krumper's 17C *Baptism of Christ* and Nicholaus Gerhaert of Leyden's 16C *St Anne, the Virgin and Child*. A further highlight is Donatello's fine *Relief of the Madonna* with other work of note from the Italian Renaissance by Antonio Rossellino and Adrian de Vries.

The **Picture Gallery** occupies most of the UPPER FLOOR, spanning German, Italian and Dutch painting from the 15C to the 18C, with examples of English and French art from the 17C and 18C. Although this collection warrants a visit, it is disappointing when compared to the Dahlem. Some highlights include Rubens' *Christ Giving Peter the Keys to Heaven* and Vasari's *Sts Paul and John Blessing the Poor*. Also on this floor is the Children's Gallery and **Cabinet of Coins and Medals**. The latter collection consists of some half a million items including coins, medals and examples of paper money from Greek times to the present. Most of the vast collection is kept in storage but the Greek examples are on public display and are particularly special.

It is possible to continue on foot to the Tiergarten to see the Neue Nationalgalerie and Kunstgewerbemuseum if time and energy permit. However, you may prefer to tackle the next section on a different day.

The Tiergarten Museums and Galleries

From Museum Island the Tiergarten may be reached on foot, taking c 30 minutes by heading W down Unter den Linden, through the Brandenburg Gate then west down STRASSE DES 17 JUNI. This is one of Berlin's main boulevards and key east–west axis. Originally called the Charlottenburger Chaussee it was renamed in 1953 after the popular rising of the East Berliners. The broad road connects the Grosser Stern in the West with the Brandenburg Gate in the East and was widened by Hitler in 1937 to enhance its potential as a ceremonial route. Note the **Sowjetisches Ehrenmal** (Soviet War Memorial) after 100m from the Brandenburg Gate on the right. Made from the marble of Hitler's Reichskanzlei (Chancellory of the Reich) this monument was erected in 1945–46 in Soviet-controlled territory. It was built in the form of a gate of honour with a bronze figure of a Soviet soldier on the top. However, the real Red Army guard which was stationed here until recently have now gone following Unification.

Take the first left down Entlastungsstrasse to reach the **Kulturforum**, the name given to this area where two museums, one gallery and the Philharmonic Hall are currently situated. The layout of the Kulturforum was designed by German Expressionist architect Hans Scharoun, who also designed the first building of note, the *Philharmonie** (Philharmonic Hall). Built in 1960–63, this extraordinary building does not conform to the pattern of orthodox Modernism seen throughout both East and West Berlin. The building has an undulating, asymmetrical shape. The concrete roof curves almost like a tent—a welcome departure from the usual flat roof. The fluid lines of the exterior fully express the organic layout of the interior. The metallic gold-clad exterior is punctuated at irregular intervals by assorted, round windows and the undulating walls are interspersed at irregular intervals by sloping, glass roofs. The Concert Hall seats 2000 and is pentagonal in shape: the audience sits around the orchestra rather than in front of it. The rising nine terraces of the Concert Hall are reminiscent of a vineyard. Tickets are like gold dust and should be booked at least two months in advance to avoid disappointment. (Box Office opening times: Mon–Fri, 15.30–18.00, Sat and Sun 11.00–14.00; there are guided tours of the building normally daily at 09.00 (tel. 269251 to confirm).)

The **Musikinstrumenten Museum** (opening times: Tues–Fri 09.00–17.00, Sat and Sun 10.00–17.00) is directly connected to the Philharmonie in a white, angular building also by Scharoun and completed by Edgar Wisniewski in 1984. It contains the city's formidable collection of musical instruments which was founded in 1888. The exhibits include European instruments from the 16C to the 20C. There is a nice contrast between the two church organs and the 1929 Wurlitzer (concerts at 12.00 each Sat). The building also houses a comprehensive reference library on the subject of music, a photographic archive and a café in the basement.

Across Potsdamer Strasse south-east is another Scharoun building, the **Staatsbibliothek** (State Library) built in 1967–68. This is one of the largest and most efficent libraries in Europe. Purpose-built for the collection of the Prussian National Library which moved here after the Second World War, the 38,000 sq m building currently holds four million volumes and 3000 newspapers and periodicals. Special collections include the Manuscript Department which holds the 9C Psalter of Ludwig the German, a Music Department with original manuscripts and the Map Collection.

Back across Potsdamer Strasse, to the west of the State Library is the *Neue Nationalgalerie (New National Gallery). The ultra-modernist building in glass and steel was designed by former Bauhaus director, Mies van der Rohe, and built in 1965–68. The elegant building consists of a 65m x 65m glass box which houses the main collection of 19C and 20C painting plus temporary exhibitions. More paintings are displayed in the basement area and steps lead from the north and south ends of the Gallery up to a sculpture display on the roof of the basement. A separate staircase leads up to the main entrance. (Opening times: Tues–Fri 09.00–17.00, Sat and Sun 10.00–17.00.)

The main collection was acquired after the Second World War from the Alte Nationalgalerie, due to the location of wartime evacuation. This includes fine examples of Adolph von Menzel's realist work, including the intimate *The Balcony Room* (1845) which depicts the breeze blowing a muslin curtain away from a French window in a deserted but atmospheric room. This was Menzel's unfinished painting of his own apartment at 18 Schöneberger Strasse in Kreuzberg, just near the Anhalter Bahnhof. By contrast, *The Flute Concert* (1852) is a large-scale illustration of Frederick the Great in the informal, candle-lit atmosphere of Sanssouci. The French Impressionists are well represented with Claude Monet's early *St Germain l'Auxerrois* (1866), the later and more informal *Summer* (1874) and Auguste Renoir's *Summertime* (1868). There are also important examples of German and Austrian Expressionist works and the highly emotional portrait of Adolf Loos by Oskar Kokoschka from 1909 painted in blues, browns and skin tones comes as a direct contrast to the violent colours of Emil Nolde, Erich Heckel and Karl Schmidt-Rottluff's work. Of special interest is the work of the best German Expressionist artist, Ernst Ludwig Kirchner; his *Belle Alliance Square* (1914) depicts a busy intersection at the southern end of Friedrichstrasse which is now Mehringplatz and has been totally rebuilt with only the Column of Victory still extant from 1914. The urban scene of Berlin which inspired many important modernist artists including Kirchner is also in evidence in the work of George Grosz, whose *Pillars of Society* (1926) represents the decay and corruption of Weimar Germany. Note also the avant-garde work by other Europeans like the Surrealist paintings of Salvador Dalí, René Magritte and Max Ernst. As is the convention in most collections of modern art, the exhibition concludes with American Abstract Expressionism and canvases by Rothko and Frank Stella. Outside there is an impressive display of post-war sculpture, complemented by the clear lines of the modernist building. Of particular note is Henry Moore's bronze *Archer* on the northern side. The New National Gallery is also a lively centre for temporary exhibitons, concerts and performances, so check for details on arrival.

Behind the New National Gallery is the **Matthäikirche**, which looks rather forlorn amongst the modern architecture of the Kulturforum. Built in 1846 in red and white brick, it was designed by August Stüler. Formerly the Parish Church for the district, the building is now closed.

Cross the Matthäikirchestrasse heading west to conclude the tour at the ****Kunstgewerbemuseum** (Museum of Applied Arts, opening times: Tues– Fri 09.00–17.00, Sat and Sun 10.00–17.00). This is one of the most recent additions to the Kulturforum, designed by Rolf Gutbrod and built in 1984– 85 to house the stunning collection of design and applied art which has been amassed since its foundation in 1867. It is heartening to see what are normally considered the 'lesser arts' displayed with a level of care and attention to detail that is normally reserved for painting. There is certainly nothing to rival this museum in Paris or London. During 1921–44 the museum was housed in Berlin's City Palace and known as the Schloss- museum. A temporary location had to be found after the War and so it was moved to the Palace at Köpenick to be returned to the middle of Berlin with the opening of this splendid new museum in May 1985.

This is one of the best laid out and logically planned of all Germany's museums. The world class collection features artefacts from the Middle Ages to the Renaissance on the Ground Floor, Renaissance to Art Deco on the spacious Upper Floor and an exciting display of 20C design on the Lower Floor. The main entrance leads directly to the MEZZANINE LEVEL with information desk and sales kiosk. The pleasant cafeteria, complete with balcony, is tucked away in the far, north-east corner. From here it is possible to enjoy a leisurely view of Scharoun's Philharmonic Hall. Some minor parts of the collection are on view here, including a small display devoted to the history of the museum with interesting documentary photo- graphs of the former Berlin Palace with parts of the collection installed in lavishly decorated rooms. Other displays show examples of glass, ceramics and interior furnishings. Head down the main, central staircase to reach the GROUND FLOOR and beginning at ROOM 1, enjoy the richly jewelled and beautifully crafted artefacts from the Middle Ages. Highlights of this comprehensive collection include various crucifixes, altars and other eccle- siastical objects from the 12C–14C. These mainly originate from the Cathe- dral of St Blasius in Brunswick and are known as the Guelph Treasures as they were presented by the Royal house of Guelphs and acquired by the Museum in 1874. Star exhibit must be the Tragaltar (Portable Altar) by Eilbertus of Cologne, c 1150, richly decorated in gold and depicting Biblical figures. ROOM 2 is devoted to decoration from the Renaissance with a superb collection of Majolica ceramics and Venetian glass with outstanding Flemish tapestries. ROOM 3 features another highlight from the museum's collection, the Lüneburg silver. This consists of 32 gold-plated silver dishes and jugs, many crafted in the form of lions, made between 1472 and 1599. Most striking is the Reliquary, a silver casket made in 1443 with a crystal held at the top between two angels. This is where the Lüneburg townsfolk laid their hands when swearing their civic oath. Other gold and silver objects from Nuremburg and Augsburg are equally beautiful, including the Imperial Goblet by Wenzel Jamnitzer of 1565 and the Elephant Fountain by his nephew Christoph Jamnitzer, dating from 1600. ROOM 8 on this floor is reserved for special exhibitions. Proceed back up the main staircase, past the Mezzanine and on to the UPPER FLOOR.

ROOM 4 holds precious objects from beyond the Renaissance to the Baroque. The display begins with gold and silver contents of the former

Pommerssche Kunstschrank; this ebony cabinet was tragically destroyed by fire during the War. Interesting early scientific instruments, German stoneware and glass from the 17C and 18C, including a lidded goblet in gilded ruby glass, crafted at Potsdam in 1720, are displayed. The Baroque heaviness of some exhibits in this room, particularly the furniture, contrasts with the delicacy of the Meissen porcelain and Chinoiserie furnishings in ROOM 5. Note the porcelain model of the Prinzessinnengruppe by Schadow which stands in the Old National Gallery. The Chinesen Kabinett (Chinese Cabinet) is a completely reconstructed room taken from the Palazzo Graveri in Turin where it was decorated by Christian Mattheus Wehrlin in 1765. ROOM 6 continues the story of the decorative arts with an extensive display of Rococo, Neo-Classical, Biedermeier and Art Nouveau pieces from Germany, France and Britain. The best of William de Morgan, Christopher Dresser, Emile Gallé and Lalique is displayed with contemporary German design. The two Carlo Bugatti pieces from 1885 are particularly rare examples of this eccentric Italian designer's work. The development of 20C design up to the 1930s is well covered in ROOM 7 with the Art Deco glass and ceramics perfectly complemented by two Paul Poiret dresses from 1919 and 1923. The furniture designed by Eckart Muthesius for the Maharajah of Indone during the 1930s is a lavish example of the Moderne.

Continue now to the BASEMENT for a display of 20C product and furniture design in ROOMS 9, 10 and 11. It is particularly gratifying to see mass-produced objects treated with the same solemnity in a museum as unique, precious items from the past. Furniture by Bauhaus designer Mies van der Rohe is of special note, the Foen metal hair dryer and work by post-modern, Italian designers such as Mario Botta bring the collection right up to the 1980s.

The walk concludes here and transport to the rest of the city may be found via U-Bahnhof Kurfurstenstrasse south of the Kulturforum or buses 24, 29, 48 or 83.

3

The Charlottenburg Palace, park and environs

This full day visit takes in one of the best examples of 18C architecture still standing in Berlin, the Charlottenburg Palace with its lovely grounds including a Garden House by Schinkel. The nearby Egyptian Museum, Museum of Greek and Roman Antiquities and Bröhan Museum are also included plus a detour out to the Olympic district.

The Charlottenburg district lies to the west of the city centre and may be reached by means of the U1 underground to Sophie-Charlotte-Platz, U7 to Richard-Wagner-Platz or buses 54 and 74.

History. The district owes its name to Electress Sophie Charlotte, wife of Elector Friedrich III, who charged Johann Arnold Nering with building a country house during 1695–99 near to the village of Lützow. When Nering died he was replaced by Martin

Grünberg and then Johann Eosander Göthe. Grünberg added the two side wings and Göthe was responsible for the grand façade, the 50m high central dome, and the Orangery, inspired by his visit to Versailles in 1701. Sophie Charlotte held cultivated gatherings at the Schloss, where music and philosophy were earnestly discussed. Upon her death King Friedrich I gave the area the name of Charlottenburg in 1705 in memory of his wife. Later additions to the Palace include the eastern New Wing, built in 1740–46 with its two magnificent banqueting halls designed by Georg Wenzeslaus von Knobelsdorff for Friedrich the Great, who used it for family occasions including the celebration of the engagement of the Crown Prince to Sophie Dorothea. However, he came to prefer his new palace at Potsdam. During 1788–90 Carl Gotthard Langhans designed the palace theatre which was grafted onto the west end of the Orangery for Friedrick Wilhelm II who used the Palace as a summer residence. Queen Luise and Friedrich Wilhelm IV were later residents. The palace was badly damaged by fire bombs in 1943, but great efforts have been made at restoration which began with the exterior.

The **••Charlottenburg Palace** (opening times: Tues–Fri 09.00–17.00, Sat and Sun 10.00–17.00) has a massive, broad façade stretching some 505m in total. The main entrance to the courtyard is framed by two identical replicas of the Borghese Wrestler. The central courtyard is dominated by a regal bronze statue of Frederick the Great by the Baroque sculptor Andreas Schlüter, dating from 1698. Originally located on the Lange Brücke near the City Palace, it was moved by barge at the outbreak of the Second World War. The barge unfortunately sank and it was not until 1950 that the statue was rescued from the Tegeler See and successfully renovated.

Enter beneath the huge cupola, crowned by a gilded statue of Fortune. A single ticket covers the Royal Apartments and the New Wing with Art Gallery. Unfortunately, the oldest section of the palace may be viewed only by means of a guided tour in German. The ticket hall is housed in the circular vestibule which lies beneath the cupola.

All the interiors were restored during 1950–66 with various degrees of skill. The floor of the vestibule is particularly pretty, designed in the form of a rosette in grey and red Swedish marble. Adjacent is the picturesque **Oval Hall** (ROOM 116), which projects into the lovely grounds to the north of the palace, seen through three arched French windows.

The tour continues into the EAST WING, part of the early building dating from the early 18C. In the **Antechamber** (ROOM 117), very little of the original remains; the plaster ceiling was totally reconstructed in 1971 and the painted panelling replaced by 18C tapestries. The adjoining **Chamber with Mirrors** (ROOM 118) suffered a similar fate. The room does contain a fine portrait of the Charlottenburg's founder, Queen Sophie Charlotte, by Wilhelm Weidemann. The **Eosander extension** is then entered with notable carved oak panelling in the appropriately named **Oak Gallery** (ROOM 120). The highlight of this room is the grand sculpture crowning the portrait of Friedrich I, with a spiral scroll bearing the initials FR.

The tour then proceeds through the various bedrooms and antechambers which make up the WEST WING including **Friedrich I's Study** (ROOM 99) and **Bedchamber** (ROOM 96). A concealed door to the left leads to a luxurious sunken marble bath with bronze taps shaped like dolphins (ROOM 97). The tour then proceeds to the most impressive room in the West Wing, the **Porcelain Chamber** (ROOM 95), the climax of the western envilade. This room was purpose-built to display a magnificent porcelain collection, and every inch of the four walls is covered with porcelain or mirrors. The ceiling painting of Aurora and Apollo by Anthonie de Coxie (1706) was recently restored and the majority of porcelain on display was not part of the original collection. Note the carved dragons, Chinamen and Buddhas which decorate the window frames. South from here is the **Chapel** (ROOM 94) with a Royal Box of special note. The chapel was designed by Eosander in 1704–06 in Baroque style. Divided from the main chapel by means of sash windows on the north side, the Royal Box has an elaborate canopy hanging over the entrance, supported by carved cherubs and a Prussian eagle which blend into the ceiling painting above.

The remainder of the building may be viewed unescorted and starts by ascending the **Great Staircase**, just to the west of the vestibule. Built by Eosander in 1704, it is one of the first cantilevered staircases in Germany and leads to the UPPER LEVEL of the Nering building. Originally decorated in 1700, the rooms were totally remodelled in 1841 when Friedrich Wilhelm IV and his wife Elisabeth moved here. There was severe damage in 1943 and restoration is still underway. It is interesting to note that the circular hall just to the right of the staircase (ROOM 210) perfectly matches the circular vestibule below. The **Oval Hall** (ROOM 211) to the north emulates the oval chamber below; windows overlooking the garden are mirrored in the opposite wall to give the impression of sitting in a garden pavilion.

The remainder of the Palace interior, known as the NEW WING, was designed by Knobelsdorff and built during 1740–46. The Neo-Classical interior decoration of the GROUND LEVEL of the New Wing comes as a welcome contrast to the heavy, dark Baroque of the original palace. There are also some fine examples of 19C painting, for example, the **Room with Works From the Napoleonic Era** (ROOM 309) includes Jacques Louis David's *Napoleon as Counsel, Crossing the St Bernhard Pass* (1800) as well as some good Schinkel-designed arm-chairs from c 1825. The taste for the Etruscan style is very much in evidence in ROOM 318 with good quality, authentic ceiling painting by Johann Gottfried Niedlich and Fuseli engravings of scenes from Shakespeare decorating the walls.

The UPPER LEVEL of the New Wing contains the charming bedroom of Queen Luise, reminiscent of Malmaison in Paris. The walls are covered in white, pleated voile over red paper. Some original furniture remains in situ including a Schinkel-designed bed and table in pear wood with a matching, pyramid shaped clock. Continue to the two best rooms in the entire Palace—the **White Hall** (ROOM 362) and the **Golden Gallery** (ROOM 363) both decorated by Knobelsdorff and J.A. Nahl in gorgeous Rococo style in 1740–44. The White Hall occupies the broadest part of the wing and has a concave ceiling. Only the plasterwork over the doors is original and the ceiling is particularly disappointing, as it was impossible to reconstruct the original. The newly restored, 42m long Golden Gallery is far more lavish with brand new gilding everywhere. This was used by Frederick the Great as a Dining Room and Throne Room. The mirrors are pure Rococo with frothy waves and sprawling candelabra covering all the wall surfaces.

The **Concert Room** at the eastern end of the New Wing is also largely reconstructed but has a good display of original artwork including Antoine Watteau's *Tradesign for the Art Dealer Gersaint* (1720) bought by Frederick the Great, who was an admirer of the Watteau School, in 1745.

The ***Gallery of Romanticism** (Galerie der Romantik, opening times: Tues–Fri 09.00–17.00, Sat and Sun 10.00–17.00) is also located in the New Wing and specialises in 19C painting including work by German Romantic artists, particularly Caspar David Friedrich, the Nazarenes and Biedermeier painters. This is possibly one of the foremost collections of Friedrich's work in the world. Some of the best examples are on display in the first three rooms of the Gallery. This includes the virtually abstract *Monk at the Seashore* (1808–10), the deeply symbolic *Oaktree in the Snow* (1829) and intimate *Woman at the Window* (1822). A visit to the Gallery is rewarding in that the comparatively small quantity of art is balanced out by its first-class quality. It is also and interesting opportunity to see the work of Friedrich in the context of such great contemporaries as Karl Friedrich Schinkel and Johann Friedrich Overbeck in a 19C building.

From the Gallery it is a short walk to the **Kleine Orangerie**, situated by the end of the West Wing, where refreshments may be taken on the terrace. The **Museum of Prehistory** is situated in the West Wing in the **Langhaus Theatre** building. Much of this collection was lost during the War but the display has since been augmented by new acquisitions. The GROUND FLOOR concentrates on hunting and farming in the Palaeolithic, Mesolithic and Neolithic Ages whilst the UPPER FLOOR focuses on the Bronze and Iron Ages, including the original tomb chamber of Seddin.

The GROUNDS of the Charlottenburg Palace are also well worth exploring, particularly as they include work by Schinkel. Pleasantly bordered on the east by the River Spree, the grounds were planned out in formal Baroque style by Simeon Godeau in 1697 when building of the Palace began. Typically, most of this was reworked in the early 19C in the informal, English landscape style by Peter Joseph Lenné. In the post-war years the park just to the north of the Palace has been converted back to Baroque style with formal flower beds.

Start by heading north behind the Gallery of Romanticism to find the Italianate ***Schinkel Pavilion**, designed by this great Classical architect in 1824 for Friedrich Wilhelm II and his second wife, Princess Liegnitz (opening times: Tues–Sun, 10.00–17.00). The design was based on the Villa Reale Chiatamone in Naples where the King had stayed in 1822. This almost perfectly square, petite garden house measures 18m x 16.4m. The flat roof and white rendering emphasise its cubic proportions. The balcony on the upper floor gracefully encircles the entire building with small loggias allowing access onto the two longer sides via three French windows. On the shorter sides there are three windows, the outer two being blind.

The interior of the building was also designed by Schinkel in Empire style and this has been skilfully renovated. It closely follows the symmetrical design of the exterior in plan. There are eight perfectly proportioned square rooms on each floor, served by a central staircase. The most mpressive room in terms of interior decoration is the **Gartensaal** (Garden Room) which spans two of the room spaces on the ground floor. Here there is a semicircular seat inspired by the Tomb of Marmor at Pompeii, adroitly placed to enjoy the full prospect west across the park. The wall behind the seat is covered in a deep blue textile embroidered with gold stars, whilst the remainder of the walls are decorated with marbled paint. The Pompeii-inpired furniture was also designed by Schinkel and aquatints by Friedrich of Berlin are on show. Upstairs there is a good collection of Schinkel drawings and paintings which belie the Romantic vision of Classicism which so inspired his work.

Continue north from the Schinkel Pavilion, enjoying the pleasant walk through the grounds with the artificial lake with real ducks on your left and River Spree to the right. On the northern fringe of the grounds, tucked away in the trees, in the classical **Belvedere** folly, designed by Carl Gotthard Langhans as a tea house in 1788, the same year as he designed the theatre.

Schloss Charlottenburg

The building is three storeys high, crowned by a domed, copper roof. Inside there is a comprehensive display of Berlin porcelain. Huge vases feature vignettes of Sanssouci as well as the Belvedere itself. There are many examples of Chinoiserie and plates designed by Neo-Classical artist Angelica Kauffman in the display cabinets. The spiral staircase leads to the FIRST FLOOR with examples of earlier, 18C work inspired by Watteau and Boucher. On the SECOND FLOOR are examples of the Wegely-Manufaktur based at Berlin from the mid 18C. Exhibits include a beautiful coffee service packed conveniently in a trunk and the Glatl coffee service of 1768 featuring romantic imagery of ruined buildings. Enjoy the views across the park from the top storey of the Belvedere before descending the spiral staircase and continuing south across the footbridge.

Cross the little island to reach the second bridge and turn right, continuing west to reach the *Mausoleum (opening times: May–Sept 10.00–18.00, April and Oct 10.00–17.00; closed Nov–March). The approach is lined with fir trees and the strictly Classical building, designed by Heinrich, stands before you. Commissioned by Frederick William III as a tomb for Queen Luise it was built in 1810 with further extensions in 1841 and 1889. Ascend the eight steps which lead to the small portico with four granite Doric columns. The severe Classical style is matched by the chilly atmosphere and temperature inside the Mausoleum. The drama of the entrance is created by the sarcophagus of Queen Luise being raised on a platform, lit from above and framed by four Ionic columns. A bronze lamp hangs from the coffered ceiling of the Vorhalle (vestibule) with four angels bearing candleholders suspended from long chains. The finely carved sarcophagus of Queen Luise was created by Romantic sculptor, Christian Rauch during 1812–13 and it established his reputation as a leading German artist. The figure of the young, sleeping Queen in simple, Roman-style dress is a triumph of 19C sculpture. Rauch also created the marble statue of the King in 1841–46 and the two marble candalabra; carved to the designs of Schinkel, with the help of F. Tieck, they represent the Fates and the Hours. Beyond the tomb of Queen Luise are the tombs of Prince Albrecht (d. 1872), Princess Liegnitz (d. 1873) and Empress Augusta (d. 1890). On the northern wall is an apse with a fresco by Carl Gottfried Pfannschmidt.

From the Mausoleum head south back to the Palace, skirt round the west wing and out of the main gate. It is a short walk from here south across the Spandauer Damm to four enticing museums covering modern design, Egyptian treasures, local history and Greek and Roman art. The *Ägyptisches Museum (Egyptian Museum) faces the Schloss Charlottenburg to the right (opening times: Mon–Thurs 09.00–17.00, Sat and Sun 10.00–17.00). It is housed in the eastern part of the Stüler Building, the former barracks of the Gardes du Corps who were attached to the Schloss, designed by Stüler in 1850. The Museum was opened in 1966, building on some key parts of the collection of the Egyptian Museum in East Berlin which had fallen into western hands after the war. The star exhibit is the bust of Egyptian Queen Nefertiti dating from 1350 BC—displayed in splendid isolation in a first-floor room. The main entrance leads to the Rotunda, the circular space with stairs beneath the central lantern. Beyond this is the Kalabscha Gate, donated by the Egyptian authorities to Germany in gratitude for the archaeological help given whilst constructing the Aswan High Dam. The former Royal Stables, with their 19C cast-iron pillars, house the Cultural History Collection which includes fascinating items from everyday life including tomb furnishings, bronze figures, mummy masks and coffins. The Four Shafts Room (Vierschäftesaal) houses a display devoted to the Cult of the Dead and includes a double coffin from the Ptolemaic Period. This collection is scheduled to be returned to Museum Island when the New Museum is completed.

From the Egyptian Museum turn left down Schlossstrasser to the more modest Heimat Museum (opening times: Tues–Fri 10.00–17.00, Sun 11.00–17.00). Note the bronze statue of Prince Albert, brother of Emperor William I, created by Eugen Boermel in 1872 which stands at the top of the street. The Heimat Museum specialises in the local history of the Charlottenburg district with photographs of the Weimar period and wartime damage on show.

Cross Schlossstrasse west and almost directly opposite is the *Bröhan Museum (opening times: Tues–Sun 10.00–18.00, Thurs 10.00–20.00), housed in the former infantry barracks. This impressive museum of 20C art and design was donated to the city of Berlin by Karl H. Bröhan in 1982. The museum is fascinating as it contains entire room settings by particular Art Nouveau and Art Deco designers. Turn left into ROOM 2 to discover the Salon Hector Guimard, taken in its entirety from the Castle Henriette in Sèvres and complemented by Hagemeister paintings and lustre glass by Loetz. Rooms by Louis Majorelle, Bruno Paul and Edgar Brandt follow on the Ground Floor. In the Suite Ruhlmann, which spans ROOMS 10–13, are displayed a bed, chair and desk originally shown at the 1925 Paris Exposition des Arts. Apart from the attractive room settings there are discreet displays of 20C porcelain in the Fanlight Room and a beautiful range of silver and Art Deco enamelwork in **Room 15**. Upstairs there are further delights including **Room 22** devoted to the Wiener Werkstätte with an elegant 1903 chair by Josef Hoffman and good examples of silver.

From the luxurious 20C exhibits of the Bröhan it is a short walk north up Schlossstrasse to the last of the museums in this district, the **Antikenmuseum** (Museum of Greek and Roman Antiquities; opening times Tues–Fri 09.00–17.00) with its notable collection of Roman silver treasures, excavated at Hildesheim. The collection was founded as an Antiquarium in 1830 and was formerly held in the Bode Museum. After the Second World War part of the collection of Minoan, Byzantine and Roman objects came to the western sector and the museum, housed in the western part of the Stüler building, was opened in 1960. The Treasure Chamber in the basement houses the Hildesheim Treasure, dating from the era of Emperor Augustus. Look out in the basement for the Egyptian mummy portraits and the Scythia Gold Treasure.

West from the Schloss Charlottenburg is the **Olympic Stadium**, built by Hitler for the 1936 Olympics (nearest U-Bahnhof is Olympia-Stadion). This immense concrete structure in official, Neo-Classical style is still in use today, seating 85,000 spectators. West is the **Glockenturm**, a bell-tower which was rebuilt after war damage. It is possible to climb the tower for the lovely views of the surrounding Grunewald to the south and the natural amphitheatre of the Waldbühne, to the north-west. From the Stadium, proceed south down Reichsportfeld and to the right, up Heilsberger Allee, is a multi-storey block designed by Le Corbusier. Too large to form part of the Interbau building competition of 1957 in Hansa, it was erected here. It is strikingly similar to the Unité d'Habitation in Marseille by the same architect.

Continue east to the **Georg Kolbe Museum** in Sensburger Allee (opening times: Tues–Sun 10.00–17.00) which celebrates the life and work of this great German sculptor who died in 1947. His former house and studio are much as he left them with fine examples of his bronze figures, sketches and drawings on show. If you continue south to Heerstrasse, then right and east you will reach the **Funkturm**, the Television Tower which used to broadcast to East Germany and which now serves the police and local taxis. Built in 1928 it is of historic interest, and houses a small Museum of Radio and Broadcasting (opening times: Tues–Sat 10.00–18.00, Sun 10.00–16.00) but far more popular is the 138m high observation tower. There is also a fairly pricey but high quality restaurant half-way up the tower which you may care to visit to round off the tour.

4

Down at the Dahlem

It is a good idea to take the U-Bahn to the Dahlem complex as some of the stations on the U2 route are quite remarkable. Built from 1902 onwards their architecture has been well preserved with Jugendstil storks, for example, decorating glazed brick stations with lovely Art Nouveau lettering. The Wittenbergplatz station at the start of the U2 line has been restored to 1920s style with authentic posters. The Dahlem-Dorf (Dahlem Village) station itself was built in 1913 to resemble a half-timbered thatched cottage, thus reinforcing the bucolic atmosphere of the Dahlem area.

First mentioned in 1275, the village of **Dahlem**, which lies to the south-west of Berlin, was developed in the early 20C as the site for important scientific institutions without damaging the rustic nature of the area. Dahlem became well known after the Second World War as the location of the Freie Universität Berlin (Free University of Berlin) which was founded in 1948 in protest at academic restrictions imposed at the Humboldt University in East Berlin. The **Dahlem Museum** complex houses some of the best parts of the State Museum's collections with world class displays of pre-19C European painting and sculpture plus Indian, Oriental and Islamic Art all on one site.

The Dahlem Museum complex

Follow the signs from the station by crossing Saargemstrasse heading south for approximately two minutes to reach the chic, Modernist block which houses the vast collection on Lansstrasse (opening times: Tues–Fri 09.00–17.00, Sat and Sun 10.00–17.00, closed Mon). The kernel of the museum building survived the Second World War and dates from 1912–16. Designed by Bruno Paul as the centre for Asiatic Art, it underwent major rebuilding in the 1960s to house the augmented sculpture and paintings galleries.

Ascend the steps to the left of the building passing through the spacious vestibule, with cloakroom and ticket office, to the bookshop. A full catalogue of the Picture Gallery is available here but little else in English. As you tour round the various collections fact sheets (Führungsblätter), some in English, are strategically placed in the rooms and may be purchased for about 25 pfennigs. From the bookshop head left to the ***Museum für Indische Kunst** (Museum of Indian Art) a vast, rectangular space divided into nine exhibition areas which follows a circular route. The collection was formed in 1963 from the Ethnological Museum and moved into this new space in 1971. Arranged according to geographic region of origin, the exquisite pieces are displayed in simple glass cases against dark grey walls and picked out by spotlights.

In the first and second rooms are artefacts from the **Indian subcontinent** dating from the prehistoric Mohenjo Daro period and covering the three religions of Buddhism, Jainism and Hinduism. Of particular interest are the ceramic objects and fertility symbols, with later work created in bronze from the 8C to the 18C. The third room to the right is long and narrow, containing dramatic work delicately carved in wood, ivory and jade dating from the 10C to the 19C. The 18C Haustempel (House Temple) with intricately carved, wooden reliefs of the Buddha and elephants is 270cm tall and leads into the miniature painting section with fascinating depictions of court life only 13cm high.

The next section contains the art of **Nepal and Tibet** with figures in wood and bronze, textile paintings and metal objects decorated with semi-precious stones. The stairs in the top right-hand corner of this section lead up to the gallery of **South-east Asian art**. Here are 10C to 13C works taken from Buddhist temples in Burma, ceramics and bronze objects from the prehistoric era of Ban Chiang (2000–200 BC) in Thailand and bronze effigies of the Buddha.

Back down the stairs on the GROUND FLOOR continue through the Nepal and Tibet area to reach the **Turfan Sammlung** (Turfan Collection) gleaned from four expeditions to Buddhist cave temples in Central Asia during 1902–14. Turfan Art flourished during the 5C to 11C in the Tarim basin on the Silk Road to China. The displays of sculpture, murals, textile painting and illuminated manuscripts are of special interest. In the centre of the section is the **Tempelraum** (Temple Room) where an entire, open-air temple has been reconstructed.

From the Museum for Indian Art continue straight ahead to the ***Museum für Völkerkunde** (Museum of Ethnography) which is divided into different geographic sections: America, Oceania, Africa, East Asia and South Asia. The origins of the extensive collection can be traced back to the Royal Prussian Kunstkammer (Royal Prussian Chamber of Art) which was transformed into the Ethnographical Collection in 1829. The Berlin Museum of Ethnography was in turn founded on this collection in 1873 with its own building opening in 1886 in the Kreuzberg district. This was destroyed during the War and the entire collection of some 338,000 items was allocated to the Dahlem. Only a fraction of the collection is on show and plans are afoot to build a new Museum for Western Art, releasing space for Ethnography at the Dahlem. The first two rooms (the second is off to the left) contain part of the American Archaeology collection with artefacts from pre-Columbian Mexico and Peru. The highlight must be the collection of gold ornaments and other objects from Peru, Costa-Rica and Colombia. Also of special note are the stone stelae and sculptures from Guatemala.

Continue straight ahead again to reach the more interesting **Südsee** (Oceanic) display. One cannot fail to be amazed by the collection of boats, original dwellings and Polynesian feather objects. The collection continues onto the first floor via a staircase in the top, left-hand corner. Although this part of the Dahlem is fascinating, be careful not to dally too long if your time is limited as the picture and sculpture collections are of equal, if not greater, merit.

To reach the **Skulpturengalerie** (Sculpture Gallery) return to the American Archaeology section then back to the main vestibule, then head north to the beginning of the display. The Sculpture Gallery is situated on two floors in a horseshoe-shaped area and covers work from the Early Christian-Byzantine era to 19C Romantics. The collection, like the Ethnography Collection, dates back to the Royal Prussian Kunstammer. Renaissance and Baroque artefacts were moved to the Altes Museum when it opened in 1830 to be displayed alongside Greek and Roman examples. The Sculpture Collection grew under the Directorship of Wilhelm von Bode from 1872 to be displayed at the Kaiser Friedrich Museum (now the Bode Museum) in 1904. Many of the Italian examples were destroyed during the War whilst two thirds were evacuated to West Germany, providing the basis for the current Dahlem show with over 100 new acquisitions made in the early, post-war years. This is a comprehensive display of West European sculpture up to the 19C and is laid out chronologically.

The GROUND FLOOR space is dedicated to the **Frühchristliche-Byzantinische Sammlung** (Early Christian and Byzantine Collection) starting with a 167cm high, marble sculpture representing the spirit of Christ from

3C AD and carved in Constantinople. The carved ivory artworks which follow are outstanding, including a carved panel 18.4cm high representing Christ entering Jerusalem and dating from 10C, and the diptych of Christ and Mary created in 6C Constantinople. The display of Byzantine and Russian icons is also of note, including the Byzantine mosaic icon *Christ the Father of Mercy* dating from the first half of the 12C. There follow some fine examples of ecclesiastical carved, wooden figures from the 13C to the 15C. From the exit ascend by the steps to the left to reach the UPPER FLOOR and the Riemenschneider saal (Riemenschneider Room). This chiefly contains work by the great 15C Würzburg sculptor, Tilman Riemenschneider, who created carved, wooden figures of the Evangelists for the **Münnerstädt Altar** in 1490–91. The realistically carved figures in red limewood are reminiscent of the style of Dürer who was working at roughly the same time. There are fine examples of German sculpture from the Baroque and Rococo periods, with the massive Holy Knights by Martin Zürn (1638–39) a particular point of interest. The Kunstkammer is adjacent to this space and contains 16C to 18C work which formed part of this important Royal collection, in glass cabinets. Look out for the sculpture of Friedrich Wilhelm on horseback, vanquishing a squirming serpent with a spear, by Johann Gottfried Leygebe (1680).

Return to the Riemenschneider Room and then enter the **Italienische Sammlung** (Italian collection) which occupies the U-shaped gallery space. This is one of the most extensive displays of Renaissance sculpture outside Italy. One of the earliest exhibits is the painted Madonna by the Presbyter Martinus dating from 1199. Of the many fine examples of Renaissance sculpture, the *Angel with Tambourine* (1429) in bronze and the marble relief of the *Madonna Pazzi* (c 1420) by Donatello are of an outstanding quality. A prime collection of lively, Baroque sculptures follow, including the huge, 258cm high *Diana* by Bernardino Cametti (1717–20) in marble and Bernini's *Putto on a Dolphin* (1618–19). The display concludes with a graceful, Neo-Classical dancing figure by Antonio Canova (1809–12). Pass through the Kunstkammer and Riemenschneider Room once more to reach the main landing of the Upper Floor where the 19C examples are shown. Reinhold Begas's *Amor and Psyche* (1857) is a romantic version of this classical myth where a winged Amor stoops over a sleeping Psyche.

At this point you may well be in need of sustenance and the café, situated in the basement, is highly recommended although the menu is rather limited. Descend by means of the stairs leading from the 19C sculpture display. Weather permitting, it is well worth sitting on the terrace outside to admire the splendid Indian, ceremonial gate—the **East Gateway of the Stupa of Sanchi**. This is a stone copy of the east gateway to an ancient Indian monument, created by order of Napoleon III in 1865. The rich surface decoration represents the life of the Buddha, although he is not represented in human form. The wheel, tree, throne and stupa symbolise his life on the three lintels and four panels between the architraves.

Ascend to the GROUND FLOOR and enter the **٭٭Gemäldergalerie** (Picture Gallery) by means of the second room of the American Archaeology display.

Again the beginnings of this splendid collection date back to the Kunstkammer and in particular the taste of Frederick the Great for 18C French painting. Augmented by the purchase of the Giustiniani and Solly collections, the pictures were displayed at the Altes Museum from 1830 and then moved to the Kaiser Friedrich Museum in 1904. Built up by the systematic purchasing policy of Wilhelm von Bode between 1872 to

1929 the collection suffered some devastating losses during the Second World War when the Friedrichshain air raid shelter was burnt out. Thankfully, many of the paintings were safely stored in mines in West Germany; these were installed in the Dahlem from 1950 onwards.

Entering the gallery via the American Archaeology display brings you into Section A, devoted to **13C–16C Italian painting**. The first room features important work by the great Venetian artist, Giovanni Bellini, including *The Dead Christ Supported by Two Mourning Angels* (c 1480–85) and *The Resurrection* (1475–79). This leads to a collection of earlier Italian painting beginning with Giotto's *The Death of the Virgin* (c 1310) which depicts the dead Mary in the arms of an apostle with Jesus standing over her, holding a small child symbolising her soul.

Continue left, and round the next corner are some key examples of the work of Florentine painter Fra Filippo Lippi. *The Virgin Adoring the Child* (c 1459) is quite breathtaking; the graceful Mary delicately kneels before the baby Jesus who lies sleeping on the flower-covered ground. Originally painted for the Medici Chapel in Florence it was subsequently transferred to the Palazzo delle Signoria, sold by the Riccardi family and acquired by the Prussian authorities in 1821 as part of the Solly collection.

This room also contains a fantastic array of work by Botticelli, including *The Virgin and Child Enthroned with the Two Johns* (1485). Mary looks down tenderly at the baby Jesus with John the Baptist to the left and John the Evangelist to the right against a lush background of three arbors made up of palm leaves and branches of myrtle and cypress. There follows a fine collection of Raphael Madonnas including *The Virgin and Child with the Infant St John* (1505), one of the first Madonnas the artist painted on his arrival in Florence in 1504 when the influence of Leonardo da Vinci was most pronounced. This section concludes with the far more sensual work of Titian and Correggio. Titian's *Venus with the Organ Player* (1550–52) depicts a languorous Venus, lying naked on a swathe of velvet with a small dog and Amor to the right and clothed organ player, closely resembling King Philip II, to the right. The painting is thought to be a celebration of the sense of sight over sound, as the male figure has ceased to play and gazes adoringly at Venus. Correggio's *Leda and the Swan* (c 1532) was painted for the Duke of Mantua and depicts the myth of the seduction of Leda by Jupiter in the form of a swan. The voluptuous nude Leda is painted holding the swan's phallic neck against her chest.

Continue back through the early Italian painting rooms to reach Section B, **German Medieval and Renaissance Painting, 13C–16C**. Of course this is a real visual feast, with the highly influential work of Albrecht Dürer in ROOM 138 and his one time pupil, Hans Baldung in ROOM 136. Note the early forms of secular portraiture which was so important for both these Reformation artists' work, including Baldung's *Portrait of the Count of Löwenstein* (1513) amd Dürer's *Portrait of Jacob Muffel* (1526). Far more polished portraits by Holbein follow on to the left in ROOM 133 complemented by the work of Lucas Cranach the Elder, whose depictions of scenes from the Bible had a massive influence on German art until the end of the 16C.

Retrace your steps and head into Section C, dedicated to **Early Netherlands Painting, 15C–16C** which covers the work of Van Eyck, Bruegel and Bosch. Return to the Cranach section, then proceed into Section D and the marvellous collection of **18C British and French paintings**. Starting in ROOM 32, there are four paintings by Antoine Watteau with *The Dance* (c 1719) probably the most notable, with four children and a dog acting out a *fête galante* against a soft landscape. This work is strongly contrasted by the two works by Jean Baptiste Simeon Chardin: *The Draughtsman* (1737) and *Still Life With Dead Pheasant and Hunting Bag* (1760) with characteristic manipulation of light and dark orchestrated against stark backgrounds. ROOM 131 contains a quite surprising display of 18C English Romantic painting, with Thomas Lawrence, Joshua Reynolds and Thomas Gainsborough well represented. The work of Neo-Classical artists including the German, Anton Raphael Mengs who spent much of his later career in Rome are grouped together in ROOM 130. Giovanni Paolo Panini's views of 18C Rome reveal its importance during the 18C as the centre for a revival of interest in classical culture.

Ascend to the FIRST FLOOR by means of the main, central staircase back through the Early German section where the Arnimallee Entrance is situated. This brings you into the **Flemish and Dutch Baroque** Section E. In the large-scale ROOM 240, with plenty of welcome seating, there is a full range of 17C painting. Jacob Jordaens's *The Rape of Europa* (c 1615–16) by the entrance is a full-blown, Baroque evocation of the myth of Jupiter's metamorphosis into a white bull to seduce Europa, surrounded in this case by voluptuous female nudes. The paintings by Petrus Paulus Rubens are of special note and earn pride of place in the centre of the room. *Andromeda* (c 1638) and *Perseus and Andromeda* (c 1622) represent the same classical myth in characteristic, loose brush-strokes and warm, golden lighting. One of his greatest achievements, *St Sebastian* (c 1616–17), measures 200cm x 128cm and represents the earnest martyr, bound to a tree and pierced by arrows. The work was probably influenced by Andrea Mantegna's treatment of the same subject, which Rubens saw during his trip to Italy. Look out also for the matching pair of paintings by Anthony van Dyck, *Portraits of Genoese Couple* (c 1622–26) by the door which leads to ROOM 241. A further feast of Rubens's work takes up most of this room, with the tender *Child with a Bird* (c 1624–25) of special appeal. Note also Jan Brueghel's *Bouquet of Flowers* (c 1619–20), a prime example of the Flemish, 17C still-life genre. ROOM 242 adjacent concentrates on Dutch painting of the same period. Here is a comprehensive collection of interior scenes which contributed to the Golden Age of Dutch Art. One of Pieter de Hooch's most important works, *The Mother* (c 1661–63) shows a perfectly painted Dutch period interior where a mother sits, lacing her bodice and looking down at a crib. Willem Kalf's *Still Life with a Chinese Porcelain Bowl* (1662) is a minutely observed piece of work in the great Dutch tradition of still lifes established during the 17C. Other artists of note represented in this room include Vermeer and Gerard Dou. The display of Dutch painting continues in ROOM 243 with two good examples of a church interiors by Emanuel de Witte and Pieter Jansz Saenredam.

Return to ROOM 240 and then turn left into ROOM 245 which marks the beginning of the important collection of **17C and 18C paintings from Spain, Italy, France and Germany**. ROOM 245 houses the powerfully Realist *A Couple of Old Peasants Eating* (c 1620) by Georges de La Tour and ROOMS 246 and 244 contain more 17C works. Moving onto ROOM 247 there are two striking paintings around the theme of Amor. Caravaggio's *Amor Victorious* (1602) shows a playful young boy, representing Amor, standing precariously on a pile of objects representing the liberal arts including the newly invented violin. The version by Giovanni Baglione, *Heavenly Amor Conquering Earthly Amor* (c 1602–3) was painted at virtually the same time as Caravaggio's work for the same patron, Cardinal Giustiniani, and it shows a clothed, adult Amor standing over the naked Earthly Amor. There are more French 17C examples in the next space, ROOM 248 in which hang no less than three works by Nicolaus Poussin, the most important French painter of classical subjects of the 1600s. His *The Infant Jupiter Nurtured by the Goat Amalthea* (c 1639) illustrates the Greek myth of Jupiter being sent to the island of Crete, where he was cared for by nymphs, to protect him from his father Saturn. The classical inspiration is also very much in evidence in the work of Claude Lorraine, seen here in *Italian Coastal Landscape in the Morning Light* (1642). ROOMS 249 and 250 include more classically-inspired works, including that of German artist Johann Liss who spent most of his life in Rome and Venice. ROOM 251 contains some masterly works from 18C Venice, not least Tiepolo's *The Martyrdom of St Agatha* (c 1750) and Sebastiano Ricci's *Bathsheba in her Bath* (c 1725). ROOM 252 is dominated by the huge Canaletto, *The Campo di Rialto* (c 1758–63) painted after he returned from England. The final room in this section, ROOM 253 contains some fine Baroque paintings from Italy.

It is now necessary to retrace your steps back to ROOM 240 to conclude your tour of the Gallery with the best it has to offer—the collection of Rembrandts. Beginning at ROOM 239, with its small array of early Dutch painting, ROOM 238 includes a fine cross-section of the work of Frans Hals. *Malle Babe* (c 1629–30) is incredibly lifelike, depicting an old crone drinking beer from a tankard, with an owl perched on her shoulder. ROOM 237, with some gems of 17C landscape painting by Esaias van de Velde and Jacob van Ruisdael, is followed by ROOM 236 with prime examples of **Rembrandt**'s work. First on the left, *The Man with the Golden Helmet* (c 1650–55) was formerly attributed to Rembrandt but the fantastic way in which the gold shimmers through the use of heavy impasto is considered by some experts to be uncharacteristic of the artist; it is therefore thought that it could be the work of the Rembrandt School, although this does not detract from its visual appeal. Rembrandt's *Self-Portrait with a Velvet Beret and a Fur Collar* (1634) shows a confident, successful young artist during the year he married Saskia van Uylenburgh. Further gems include *Portrait of Hendrickje Stoffels* (1659) and *The Mennonite Preacher Anslo and his Wife* (1641). One of Rembrandt's earliest works, *The Parable of the Rich Man* (1627) is shown in ROOM 235 with ten other fine examples. To the left of the exit to ROOM 234 is his version of *Susanna and the Elders* (1647) in which the two sinister elders lurk against a dark background whilst Susanna shimmers with light and looks out appealingly at the viewer. Rembrandt based his painting on Pieter Lastman's version of the myth, painted in 1614 and shown here. The last room contains later 17C, mainly landscape, Dutch painting.

Exit from ROOM 234 to find yourself once more in the Baroque section of the Sculpture Gallery. Head out to the main landing from where the **Museum für Islamische Kunst** (Museum for Islamic Art) can be reached. Founded in 1904 by Bode the collection was split as a result of the Second World War, and the majority is now to be found at the Pergamon on Museum Island. This portion of the Dahlem contains sculpture and decorative art from the 8C to the 18C with leading examples of carpets, miniature painting and textiles.

Adjacent is the **Museum für Ostasiatische Kunst** (Museum of East Asian Art) which opened in 1970 and covers woodcuts, sculptures and lacquer-work from China, Korea and Japan. Most interesting are the 6C–9C Chinese bronze mirrors and the 17C throne of a Chinese Emperor. The

°Kupferstichkabinett (Print and Engraving Cabinet) is situated near the Arnimallee entrance. This important collection comprises mainly German but also other European wood cuts, etchings, engravings and lithographs from the 15C–20C. It was founded at the suggestion of Wilhelm von Humboldt in 1831 and housed in the New Museum at Museum Island from 1848 until the Second World War. Most of the collection was evacuated to West Germany and installed at the Dahlem in 1957. Highlights include drawings and prints by Dürer, Grünewald, Holbein and Rubens. The woodcut illustrated books from the 15C and 16C are particularly fine. Items from the collection not on display may be seen in the **Studiensaal des Kupferstichkabinett** (Visitors' Room of the Collection of Prints and Drawings, opening times: Tues–Fri, 09.00–16.00).

From the main Dahlem site it is a fairly short walk to the **Museum für Deutsche Volkskunde** (Museum of German Ethnology), simply turn right from the main Lansstrasse exit then left down Luisestrasse and first right down Im Winkel. This Museum (opening times: Tues–Fri 09.00–17.00, Sat and Sun 10.00–17.00) concentrates on the popular culture of German-speaking people in central Europe from 16C to the present day. The collection was founded in 1889 by the doctor, Rudolf Virchow, and assimilated into the Berlin State Museum Group in 1904. The museum suffered extensive damage during the War and remained closed until 1979 when it reopened in the building formerly used for the storage of Secret State Archives from 1925 onwards. The museum has an interesting display of folk craft and culture including some good examples of rustic painted furniture, earthenware and costume on the GROUND FLOOR. The objects are divided into interesting themes including 'Country Furniture Based on City Models' and 'Yesterday's Fashions, Today's Costumes'. The FIRST FLOOR is devoted to domestic tasks including food preservation and storage, spinning and weaving with an extensive display of embroidery. On the SECOND FLOOR is an unusual exhibition of 'The Gospel in Homes Around the World' showing religious customs as carried out in domestic settings, including a Devotional Nook from early 20C Russia.

The Botanischer Garten

There are a variety of other sites of interest which may be visited from this point. Ten minutes' walk east down Arnimallee and Königin-Luise-Strasse brings you to the **Botanischer Garten** (Botanical Garden, opening times: daily, Nov–Feb 09.00–16.00; Mar and Oct 09.00–17.00; April and Sept 09.00–19.00; May–Aug 09.00–21.00).

These beautiful grounds cover some 42 hectares and originated in the kitchen garden of the Royal Palace in the Lustgarten. The garden was then moved to the Kleist Park in Schönburg but space again became a problem and so the garden was moved once more to its present site in 1896. During 1899 to 1910 German Botanist Adolf Engler created a botanic garden in the same mode as Kew Gardens, London, with a huge glass Tropical House 25m in height. There is an historic Electoral Garden which contains plant types originating in the 17C and a special garden for the blind which concentrates on touch and scent. Beside the southern entrance, there is a good restaurant Unter den Eichen (Under the Oaks), which is open throughout the summer. The Botanisches Museum (Botanical Museum) is situated east of the Königin-Luise-Strasse (opening times: Tues, Thurs–Sun 10.00–17.00, Wed 10.00–19.00). This houses a herbarium of over two million plants and a specialist library. There are displays of poisonous and edible fungi, an Egyptian Department and various interactive exhibits.

Grunewald

Alternatively, you may wish to explore the Grunewald area with the Brücke Museum and Jagdschloss Grunewald by heading west down König-Luise-Strasse. On the right after the Dahlem-Dorf station is the Dorfaue (Village Green) overlooked by the **Gutshaus Dahlem** (Dahlem House). This mansion house was built by Cuno Hans von Wilmersdorff in 1680 on the site of an old farmhouse. Most interesting is the baroque façade which faces onto the courtyard and bears the Wilmerstorf/Hake Alliance coat of arms in its triangular gable. Inside is a modest museum which recounts the history of the Dahlem estate (opening times: Mon and Wed–Sun 10.00–18.00). Of special note is the ground-floor **chapel**, Gothic in origin which has a fine stellate vaulted ceiling.

Adjacent to the Dahlem House is the brick Gothic **Annenkirche** (opening times: Mon, Wed and Sat 14.00–17.00). Dating from 1220, this was the village church of Dahlem with the late Gothic chancel added in the 15C. The tower was built on in 1781 and was used as a relay station for Berlin's first optical telegraph line which ran to Koblenz from 1832 to 1892. Inside, the Baroque pulpit decorated with rustic painting is worth looking at. Note the 17C strap vaulting in the nave and cross-rib vaulting in the chancel. The traces of 14C mural painting in the nave, illustrating scenes from the life of St Anne, were uncovered in 1893. The tombs of the local ruler, Cuno Hans Wilmersdorff (d. 1720) and his wife (d. 1711) are also situated here.

Continue west down König-Luise-Strasse until you reach the end, then turn right and continue north up Clay-Allee then first left down Pückler-strasse. If the walk seems a little daunting (30 minutes to the Jagdschloss), take the number 60 bus which stops at the Clay-Allee/Pückler Strasse intersection. From here walk west into the Grunewald Forest and turn first left down Fohlenweg and first right to Bussardsteig where the **Brücke Museum** can be found at No. 9 (opening times: Mon, Wed–Sun 11.00–17.00). This specialist museum was built in 1967 and designed by Werner Düttmann as a memorial to the Brücke group of artists, which was formed in Dresden in 1905 and created the first Expressionist art in Germany. One of the movement's founding artists, Karl Schmidt-Rottluff, was largely responsible for the foundation of the museum, donating 74 of his own paintings to the collection and initiating fund-raising events. Key work by other members of Die Brücke are also on display, namely Erich Heckel, Emil Nolde and Ernst Kirchner, Otto Mueller and Max Pechstein. Work by other German artists to be associated with the Group, including Emil Nolde and Emy Röder, may also be seen. It is gratifying that these Expressionists should have such a museum devoted to them, given the vandalism carried out by the Nazis against their work in the 1930s and 1940s.

From the Brücke Museum continue west down Pücklerstrasse for 20 minutes to the **Jagdschloss Grunewald** (Grunewald Hunting Lodge) on the banks of the Grunewaldsee (opening times: April–Sept, Tues–Sun 10.00–

13.00, 13.30–18.00, Mar and Oct 10.00–17.00, Nov–Feb 10.00–16.00). This 16C Hunting Lodge, built for Elector Joachim II by Caspar Theyss, was initially called 'Zum grünen Wald' (Green Wood) and the name was eventually adopted for Berlin's largest forest. Covering some 32 sq km east of the River Havel, the Grunewald is a popular weekend destination for Berlin cyclists, swimmers and picnickers. Wild deer populate the forest which consists of oak, beech and pine trees. The land was only opened up to the public at the beginning of the 20C and was formerly a royal hunting reserve with the Hunting Lodge as the focal point. Construction of the plain, Renaissance style building began in 1542 with various alteration made subsequently. The present appearance of the building dates back to changes made by Frederick I of Prussia at the beginning of the 18C. Further adaptations include the addition of a service courtyard and store-rooms for the hunting equipment in the reign of Frederick the Great. Only the vestibule and staircase tower survive from the original building. The house was opened as a museum in 1949 and much restored in the early 1960s. The FIRST FLOOR has retained the atmosphere of a hunting lodge with its plain but sturdy furnishings. The Central Salon contains some notable paintings including a portrait of Joachim II by Lucas Cranach the Younger, depictions of the Royal Hunt by Abraham Begeyn (1690) and some large, 18C paintings of animals. There are more works of art on the FIRST FLOOR with examples of Dutch and Flemish 17C works including a Rubens portrait of Caesar. In the right wing is a good Cranach the Elder depiction of Adam and Eve. On the SECOND FLOOR may be found further Dutch paintings plus a series of rooms decorated and furnished in German 18C and 19C style.

From the Jagdschloss it is possible to explore the forest further by continuing west on Hutton Weg then north up Königs-Allee to reach the Grunewald S-Bahn station on the left up Fontanestrasse. Alternatively, further south down Clay Allee (named after General Lucius D. Clay, Supreme Commander in the US Zone of Germany during 1947–49), is the **University district**. Indeed, it is impossible to avoid American connections in this part of Berlin, with the US Headquarters on the corner of Clay-Allee and Saargem Strasse. The Freie Universität Berlin (Free University of Berlin) can be found by continuing south down Clay-Allee and bearing left down Gary-Strasse. The University was founded in the American sector with the main building constructed in 1952–54 from funds donated by the Henry Ford Foundation. Student accommodation was built by means of a grant from the US State Department and the John F. Kennedy Institute was founded in 1963. Kennedy was awarded an honorary doctorate by the University when he visited Berlin in 1963. Scene of much student unrest during 1968 and 1988, the campus is still lively today. Return to central Berlin via the Thielplatz U2 station.

5

Alternative Berlin

During the 1920s and 1930s Berlin was an international centre for avant-garde culture and the bohemian lifestyle. The creation or enjoyment of modern art, Hollywood films and jazz was totally banned by the Nazis, only to resurface with a vengeance after the war. Berlin became and important centre for modern architecture, acting as a showcase for both eastern and western authorities. The bohemian lifestyle was reincarnated in West Berlin which became a hive of anarchist and general youth rebellion. Modern art was officially encouraged by the West German government and Berlin also provided a haven for those wishing to avoid conscription. The alternative lifestyle took hold here to the same degree as in Amsterdam and Ibiza. Divided arbitrarily into East and West, the global Cold War scenario was played out in miniature in the city. The absurdity of this situation gave more credibility to those on the fringes of normal society. With the demise of the Wall this special atmosphere has been largely lost as Berlin becomes a western European city like any other. Buses trundle over the former Death Strip and Wasser Taxis cruise along the River Spree where so many escape attempts met with a tragic end.

This tour takes in some of the less well known Berlin sites which relate to the city's unique 20C heritage, beginning with Brecht's House to the north of Friedrichstrasse, moving on to the groovy district of Kreuzberg, the strictly modern Bauhaus archives and concludes with the arty square of Savignyplatz for well-earned repast!

Take the U-Bahn or S-Bahn to **Friedrichstrasse station**, the principal railway station in Berlin before the War and quickly reasserting its importance since the *Wende*. During the Cold War this was the only border crossing which everybody could use—whether East German, foreigner or West German—to enter East Berlin by public transport. Passes were issued here and trains were searched by border guards. Thankfully, this has all now disappeared but the station retains a haunting atmosphere. Opposite the station is the Metropol Theater, home of the musical revue and built in the late 19C.

Turn left from the station and head north over the River Spree by means of the 19C wrought-iron WEIDENDAMMBRÜCKE and you are in the centre of Berlin's Theatre District. To the left is Bertolt-Brecht-Platz and the **Theater am Schiffbauerbamm**, built during 1891–92 and where the Berliner Ensemble have been based since 1954 (opening times: Mon–Sat 11.00–18.30, Sun 15.00–18.30). A life-size statue of Brecht, created by Fritz Cremer in 1988 to mark the 90th anniversary of his birth, stands at the entrance. Inside the theatre has a well preserved, Jugendstil foyer. To the north is the **Deutscher Theater**, built during 1849–50 to designs by Eduard Titz; the Renaissance Revival interior, added in 1872, has been lovingly restored. This is where Max Reinhardt worked as a Director from 1905 to 1933 and the theatre currently presents modern and classic German plays as well as productions of international works (opening times: Mon–Sat,

12.00–18.30, Sun 15.00–18.30). The Kammerspiele, adjacent to the main building, was added in 1906.

Continue north, and on the right is the **Friedrichstadt-Palast**, a huge cabaret venue which began its life as Berlin's first market hall in 1868 and was used as a circus during the late 19C. Alterations were made by the great Expressionist architect Hans Poelzig, in 1919, to create a Schauspielhaus for Max Reinhardt, with a fantastic stalactite-effect ceiling which was unfortunately altered in 1937. Continue north to the intersection with ORANIENBURGER STRASSE, the centre of Berlin's Jewish community until the Holocaust. The **Synagogue** on Oranienburger Strasse was attacked and gutted during the Nazi's Kristallnacht of 8 and 9 November 1938. Further damaged during the War, this fine 19C building is now in the process of restoration, complete with newly-gilded dome, and will reopen in 1995. It was designed in exotic Moorish style by Eduard Knoblauch and F.A. Stüler and officially opened in 1886 at a ceremony attended by the Prussian King and other important dignitaries. Just past the Synagogue—to the left down Grosser-Hamburger-Strasse and on the right—is the site of the former Jewish Cemetery which was destroyed by the Nazis, and beside it a simple yet harrowing memorial to the 55,000 Berlin Jews who left from this collection point for Auschwitz and Theresienstadt.

Return to Friedrichstrasse, noting the various squats and the alternative arts centre, Tacheles, housed in a disused department store near the end of Orangienburger Strasse. In Auguststrasse opposite is the trendy VeB OZ bar with a scrap Trabi adapted into a couch. Note also that this area is a popular parade ground for a growing number of prostitutes after dark.

Continue up Friedrichstrasse and cross Wilhelm-Pieck-Strasse north to enter CHAUSSEESTRASSE. On the left is the fascinating **Dorotheenstädtischer und Friedrichswerdersche Friedhof** (Dorotheenstadt and French Cemeteries, opening times: dawn to dusk daily). This is one of the most important burial grounds in Berlin: first opened in 1762, it contains the graves of Hegel, Schinkel (with a monument designed by himself), Rauch, Schadow and Ernst Litfass who invented the Litfass-Säule (advertisement column) situated here. The grave of Heinrich Mann is marked by an urn with bronze bust on his headstone, and that of Brecht by a boulder.

At No. 121 Chausseestrasse, a plaque marks the place where German revolutionary, Karl Liebknecht, founded the Communist Spartacus League. At No. 125 is the former **house of Bertolt Brecht** and Helene Weigel (opening times: by booked guided tour only (tel. 282 99 16 to book an English speaking guide); Tues–Fri 10.00–11.30 every 30 minutes, Thurs 10.00–11.30 and 17.00–18.30, Sat 09.30–13.30 every 30 minutes except at 12.00). The tours are restricted to a maximum of eight and are cosy affairs. Enter by means of the gate to the left and the door to the right in the courtyard. The house is modest but has been kept exactly as Brecht knew it. After returning from exile in America in 1948 the avant-garde playwright settled here in the new Communist state until his death in 1954. It is fascinating to see the interior of his home with its sturdy, second-hand furniture (which Brecht chose deliberately in preference to new), bare floorboards and Chinese wall decorations. Also on view to the visitor are his intriguing collection of books and stark bedroom. The premises also house the Brecht and Weigel Archives, accessible by appointment. In the basement is the Cellar Restaurant, open during the evenings only.

If the fancy should take you, further north up Chausseestrasse and left into Invalidenstrasse is the **Museum für Naturkunde** (Museum of Natural History, opening times: Tues–Sun, 09.30–17.00). The largest museum of its kind in Germany and one of the five biggest in the world, this massive collection was mainly assembled during the 19C and early 20C and displayed in this Neo-Renaissance building from 1889 onwards. The museum is in many ways comparable to the Natural History Museum in London, down to its reconstructed dinosaur skeletons.

It is a 15-minute walk south down Chausseestrasse from the Brecht house, and along Invalidenstrasse heading east, to the **Prenzlauer Berg** district; take the S-Bahn to Alexanderplatz then the U2 to Eberswalder Strasse. Developed in the 19C with cheap, working-class housing in tenement blocks, it escaped war damage to become the home of East Berlin's artists and radicals. The area is now being slowly revamped but still retains something of the atmosphere of dissent.

Continue east down Invalidenstrasse until it merges into Veteranenstrasse. Pass the Zionskirche on the left and continue east to reach Schönhauser Allee at the Senefelderplatz U-Bahn station. From here continue north up Kollwitzstrasse to reach KOLLWITZ PLATZ with its pleasant cafés and reasonable restaurants. The square is decorated with a bronze statue of the artist, Käthe Kollwitz. Leading off to the north from Kollwitz Platz is the immaculately restored HUSEMANNSTRASSE. It was manicured to celebrate the 750th anniversary of Berlin in 1987, the concept being to recreate the charm of turn-of-the-century Berlin. There are some rather twee antique shops here, food shops and, at No. 1 the popular Restauration 1900 restaurant. At No. 8 is the idiosyncratic **Friseurmuseum** (Hairdressing Museum, opening times: Tues–Thur 10.00–17.00, Sat and Sun 10.00–17.00), a rare museum devoted to hair and its styling. Turn-of-the-century barber's equipment is moderately interesting and the decorations made from old hair positively disgusting. At No. 12 is the **Museum Berliner Arbeiterleben um 1900** (Museum of Berlin Working-Class Life around 1900, opening times. Tues–Thurs 10.00–17.00, Fri 10.00–15.00, Sat 10.00–18.00). This shows an ordinary home as lived in with the family sleeping in one room, heated by a coal-burning stove. The paraphernalia of everyday life is much in evidence, with books, toys and sewing littered around.

Return to Friedrichstrasse and travel by the U6 line two stops down to the Kochstrasse station. You are now in the west of the **Kreuzberg** district—the home of punks, Turks and activists and a rich assortment of Europe's 'others'. Turks (known as Gastarbeiter or guest-workers) were actively encouraged to settle in West Berlin to replace the thousands of East Berlin workers lost when the Wall was erected. The area is bounded to the west by the Tiergarten and Schöneberg districts and to the south by the Tempelhof and Neukölln; the north was bounded by the Berlin Wall. It was entirely run down during the Cold War years, but attempts are now being made to gentrify the area, although this programme seems to be moving rather slowly.

Head north up Friedrichstrasse to No. 44 and the **Museum Haus am Checkpoint Charlie** (Checkpoint Charlie Museum, opening times: 09.00–22.00). Set up by Human Rights activists when the Berlin Wall was erected in 1961, this poignant museum houses a photographic display on the history of the Wall, documents the various escape attempts and celebrates the non-violent struggle for Civil Rights from Gandhi to Lech Walesa along with various contemporary artists' interpretation of the Wall. There is also a popular café here.

From the Museum walk west down Zimmerstrasse and cross Wilhelmstrasse. On the right is the former **Nazi Air Ministry**, used subsequently for the GDR cabinet offices and now the headquarters of the Treuhandanstalt— the organisation faced with the unenviable task of privatising eastern German industry. Turn left down Wilhelmstrasse and take the next right down Anhalter Strasse where the ruins of the **Anhalter Bahnhof** stand. It is difficult to believe that this was once one of Europe's busiest railway stations. Designed by Franz Schwechten, architect of the Emperor William Memorial Church, in grand Neo-Renaissance style, it was blown up, amid great protest, in 1961, and only the portico remains standing. Once it was Berlin's Gateway to the south handling 40,000 passengers per day, but only two S-Bahn lines stop here now.

Continue west down Anhalter Strasse and right into Stresemannstrasse to reach the *Martin-Gropius-Bau (opening times: Tues–Sun 10.00–20.00). This beautifully decorated, red stone building housed the Museum of Arts and Crafts until 1921 when the collection moved to the city Schloss. It was designed by Martin Gropius, the uncle of modern architect Walter Gropius, between 1877 and 1881. Badly damaged during the Second World War, the building has now been restored to its former glory and houses an important collection of 20C German art as well as hosting large, touring exhibitions. The permanent exhibition in the **Berlinische Galerie: Museum für Moderne Kunst, Photographie und Architektur** (Berlin Gallery: Museum for Modern Art, Photography and Architecture) on the first floor recalls the fast-moving, decadent Berlin of the inter-war years which has now all but faded from memory. The gallery was founded in 1975 and has been on show here since 1986. The enthralling exhibition traces the history of art in Berlin from 1870 to the present day in a broad range of some 500 paintings, drawings, sculptures, photomontages and photographs. Here are excellent examples of the Berliner Sezession artists who painted realist images in the late 19C and included Max Liebermann and Lesser Ury, whose *Leipziger Strasse* (1898) portrays the new electric street lights of Berlin in evocative detail. There are good examples of Dada art from the 1920s, with rare photomontages by Hannah Höch and Raoul Hausmann contrasted with the Neue Sachlichkeit artists, Otto Dix and George Grosz, who painted in sometimes shocking graphic detail. The Berlin Gallery is also rich in post-war art, particularly the Neo-Expressionist work of K.H. Hödicke and Rainer Fetting which is now fêted in contemporary art circles the world over. The Martin-Gropius-Bau also houses a specialist modern art library (opening times: Mon–Fri 10.00–12.00 and 14.00–16.00) and important archive (open by appointment only). On the ground floor is a restaurant and terrace café. The Jewish section of the Berlin Museum may also be found here with an exhibition documenting 'Jews in Berlin'.

The area behind the Martin-Gropius-Bau was the site of the SS headquarters from where Nazi opponents were tortured, interrogated and watched. This is commemorated in the exhibition to the east of the Martin-Gropius-Bau, entitled the **Topographie des Terrors** (Topography of Terror, opening times: daily, 10.00–18.00). The dreadful acts of cruelty carried out on this site are documented in a photographic exhibition and the Gestapo cellars beneath, used for the interrogation of important prisoners, can be visited.

From here it is a 15-minute walk to the *Museum für Verkehr und Technik (MVT) (Museum of Transport and Technology, opening times: Tues–Fri 09.00–17.30, Sat and Sun 09.00–18.00) which can also be reached on the No. 29 bus. The museum is situated in Trebbiner Strasse, south-east of Anhalter Bahnhof down Schöneberger Strasse, across the Landwehrkanal and right down Tempelhofer Strasse. This large, new museum is eyecatching from quite a distance thanks to a bright mural by Klaus Büscher (1982) on the gable-end wall facing the canal, depicting the layout of the museum in whimsical style. The museum opened in 1983 in the old market buildings which date from 1908; the Transport Hall opened in 1985 and the Locomotive Shed in 1987, with a second following the year after. This is a massive undertaking on behalf of the state and demonstrates its commitment to preserving the history of technology which played such an important role in the development of Germany. The MVT builds on the tradition of museums of technology, and in particular the Transport and Building Museum which opened in Berlin's Hamburger Railway Station in 1906 and was handed over to the West Berlin authorities by the East in 1984. The museum holds a collection of some 25,000 objects of which only 20 per cent are currently on show.

Enter by means of the Trebbinerstrasse through a connecting passage to the horse ramp—steps originally used by horses. On the GROUND FLOOR are exhibitions illustrating the history of street traffic, the production of household appliances (including vacuum cleaners), suitcase manufacture and textiles. There is also an excellent bookshop and restaurant on this floor. On the FIRST FLOOR are more modern exhibits relating to automation and computing technology, air traffic control and research and development. The SECOND FLOOR is devoted to the history of type and printing with paper technology, typewriters and printing presses exhibited. The Library (opening times: Tues–Thurs 13.00–18.00) and the Archives (open by appointment only) are situated on the FOURTH FLOOR.

A connecting passage leads from the first floor of the main Museum to the LOCOMOTIVE SHEDS. The First Locomotive Shed (Part I) has examples of steam trains from 1835–80 and (Part II) examples from 1880–1920. The tour then continues into the Housing Block with a cafeteria in a dining-car. The ground and first floors show hydraulic engineering and shipping, including a diorama of 'The Electoral Shipyard in Havelberg' and lovely hand-crafted models of ships. There is more on the history of shipping on the second floor together with an interesting display of scientific instruments. The third floor shows the history of photography and sterophotography. Finally, the Second Locomotive Shed charts the history of rail transport from 1920 to the present day. Outside, in the open-air park, there are windmills and a solar heating plant. It is hoped to extend the museum further into the area once occupied by the Anhalter Goods Station.

From the MVT walk east along the side of the canal, crossing at the Zossenerbrücke, and head north up Lindenstrasse—a ten-minute walk which may be avoided by taking the U1 line from Gleisdreieck one stop to Hallesches Tor which drops you near the bottom of Lindenstrasse. Continue north up Lindenstrasse to reach the **Berlin Museum** at No. 14 (opening times: Tues–Sun 10.00–22.00). This substantial museum is housed in the former **Kammergericht** (Supreme Court) building, designed by Philip Gerlach and built during 1734–35. The Baroque edifice was created for Friedrich Wilhelm I to house the judicial and administrative officials who were previously based at the palace. The building was left in ruins after the war but marvellously restored to house the Berlin Museum which opened its doors to the public in 1969. At the time of writing the museum was still open with the following range of exhibits, but there are plans to close the Berlin Museum down in the autumn of 1993 and place the most important exhibits in the Märkisches Museum and the rest in storage whilst a new museum is built, to open around the year 2000.

Note the bust of the Emperor Justinian, statues of Justice and Charity and the Prussian coat of arms above the main portal, which brings you into the Great Hall and an exhibition on the history of the Berlin Wall with two actual examples, now a rare sight in Berlin as most fragments have been spirited away by souvenir collectors. The museum tells the story of Berlin from the mid 17C to recent times by means of art work, period interiors and photographs. Starting with Room 1 to the left, the display follows a chronological order on the ground floor. ROOM 7 at the end of the northern wing contains the Alt-Berliner Weissbier Stube (Old Berlin White Beer Room) which sells traditional, Berlin refreshments. On the upper floor are some interesting examples of 19C portraits in ROOM 15 and reconstructions of bourgeois interiors dating from 1815 to 1920. On the top floor is a display of Berlin fashion from 18C to the present day and various toys, including dolls' houses.

Proceed north up Lindenstrasse, noting the new Lindenmarkthalle opposite the Berlin Museum which houses Berlin's flower market. After approximately ten minutes the Spittelmarkt is reached; continue east up Gertrauden Strasse and then left up BRÜDER STRASSE. This gently curving street once led directly to the Schloss and is named after a Dominican friary which once existed in the Lustgarten area. At No. 13 is the Nicolai-Körner-Haus, 18C residence and bookshop of author and publisher Christoph Friedrich Nicolai. Built in 1710 and altered in 1787 it is now occupied by the National Monuments Board but housed lively soirées during Nicolai's time with guests including Moses Mendelssohn, Gottfried Schadow, writer Anna Luise Karsch and graphic artist Daniel Chodowiecki. At No. 33 is the former residence of sculptor Andreas Schlüter and No. 10 is the Gelgenhaus (Gallows House) dating from 1680. Once the deanery of St Petri, it is known as the Gallows House because a young maid was hanged here for pilfering a silver spoon which was later discovered by its owner to have been trodden into the ground by a goat.

Return to the Spittelmarkt and head east down Wall Strasse to reach the GDR's equivalent to the Berlin Museum, the *Märkisches Museum (Brandenburg Museum), situated on the southern banks of the River Spree near the Köllnischer Park (opening times: Wed–Fri 09.00–17.00, Sat 09.00–18.00, Sun 10.00–18.00). The museum documents the history of both the city and the Brandenburg Marches from Pre-History to the 20C and is thus more extensive than the Berlin Museum. It also has a longer pedigree, having been founded as the Brandenburg Provincial Museum in 1874 and moving into these purpose-built premises in 1908. Designed by Ludwig Hoffman, the building is inspired by the Brick Gothic style so characteristic of the Brandenburg region. The square tower is based on the Wittstocker Bishop's Palace near Potsdam. At the entrance stands a 1905 copy of the 1474 Brandenburg Roland statue. On the ground floor the history of the region from the earliest times to 1815 is chronicled with arrowheads from Biesdorf, dating from c 9000 BC, and a model of a medieval Slav fortress. On the mezzanine floor is an exhibition of the Berlin Theatre 1740–1933 with portraits of well-known actors, authentic posters, set designs and photographs. On the first floor is an unusual display of tombstone carving plus information on Berlin from 1815 onwards. The second floor houses indigenous examples of decorative art with wrought-iron, stoneware, the Royal Porcelain Manufactory, pewter and musical boxes. Also on this floor are examples of 19C and 20C Berlin painting and sculpture.

To the south of the museum is the Köllnischer Park with a bear-pit housing two of Berlin's city symbols. To the west is Inselstrasse, where at No. 7 is a section of the museum devoted to the circus, cabaret and variety. A stunning collection of some 9000 circus posters dating back to 1782 forms the backbone of this special collection.

For those with a keen interest in early 20C art there is the **Otto Nagel Haus Gallery** situated at Nos 16–18 Markisches Ufer to the north of the Markisches Museum (opening times: Mon–Thurs and Sun 09.00–17.00). The two 18C houses have housed a museum dedicated to revolutionary art since 1982. The work of Otto Nagel, Käthe Kollwitz and Max Linger borrowed from the National Gallery are sympathetically hung in this unusual museum. There is also a small café situated on the ground floor.

To reach the **Bauhaus-Archiv-Museum für Gestaltung** (Bauhaus Archive Museum of Form, opening times: Wed–Mon 10.00–17.00) on Klingehöferstrasse in the southern part of the Tiergarten, take the U-Bahn to Wittenbergplatz on the U2 and U3 lines. From the Märkisches Museum station this entails travelling two stops west to Stadtmitte on U2, then one stop south to Hallesches Tor on U6 and six stops west on U3. Head south-east down Wittenbergplatz and then north-east up An Der Urania and Schillstrasse to reach this simple, white modern building with its distinctive curved roof lights. The archive was founded by the great historian of the Bauhaus, Hans Wingler, in 1960 in Darmstadt. The collection moved to Berlin in 1971 and into these splendid premsies in 1979. Specially designed by the first Bauhaus Director, Walter Gropius, this is an example of modern architecture at its best where no expense has been spared. The main attraction is the permanent exhibition devoted to this great school and cradle of modernism, which existed between 1919 and 1933. The great advantage of this collection is that the textiles, silver, ceramics, drawings, paintings and furniture are seen together and not in isolation as in most museums. It is thus easier to get a flavour of what the school was about in all areas of art and design. Highlights include tubular steel furniture by Marcel Breuer and metalwork by Marianne Brandt. There is also a specialist library and archive here with an important collection relating not only to the German Bauhaus of inter-war years but to its post-war successors in Ulm and Chicago (opening times: Mon–Fri 09.00–13.00). The bookshop has some excellent publications in English whilst the café serves good coffee.

The northern fringe of the Tiergarten includes some important examples of 18C and modernist post-war architecture which do not measure up to the Bauhaus Archive building but which you may think worthy of a detour. Head north up Klingelhöferstrasse then Hofjägerallee to the Grosser Stern. Take the Spreeweg to the right and continue north-east. On the left is the **Schloss Bellevue**, official Berlin residence of the President of Germany and therefore inaccessible to the public. This is a great shame as the gilded interiors, created for the brother of Frederick the Great in 1785, are quite stunning. The Schloss was designed by Michael Philipp Baumann in the form of a French Baroque château. Behind the palace to the north is an English Garden, laid out in the 19C and restored after the war with help from various British cities and the Shropshire Horticultural Society; this may be visited when the President is not in residence.

Turn right down the John-Foster-Dulles Alle to the astonishing **Kongresshalle**. Known locally as the 'pregnant oyster' because of its odd shape, this hall was built by the US Allied Command as a gift to the Berliners in 1957 as part of the International Architecture fair. However, the experimental structure of the building caused it to collapse in 1980. Happily it is now restored to its former glory for conferences and exhibitions. Just past the Kongresshalle is the Carillon, a gift from Daimler-Benz to the city in 1987, which consists of a steel and concrete tower sporting 68 bells which ring at 12.00 and 18.00. In front stands a Henry Moore sculpture set off by an attractive pond.

To reach the **Käthe-Kollwitz-Museum** to the west of the Tiergarten, take the U3 west from Wittenbergplatz two stops to Uhlandstrasse. From the station head south down Fasanenstrasse to No. 24 and the elegant, three-storey town house which contains the museum (opening times: Wed–Mon, 11.00–18.00). The museum opened in 1986 and houses an impressive display of this Expressionist artist's work. Her self-portraits and graphic art representing the great themes of death, birth and childhood belie the troubled life which she led, losing her son Peter in the First World War. The work seems somewhat incongruous, placed in this smart, private gallery when Kollwitz herself was a committed Socialist. She died in Moritzburg, near Dresden where there is a similar and equally touching exhibition devoted to her life.

To round off the tour you may wish to explore the arty square of SAVIGNYPLATZ by heading north, noting the Literaturhaus Berlin at No. 23 Uhlandstrasse with its well-stocked bookshop, cosy café and art gallery. Cross the Ku'damm and continue north up Fasanenstrasse to the **Jüdisches Gemeindehaus** (Jewish Community Centre) at Nos 79–80. Once one of the finest synagogues in Berlin, the Byzantine structure was burnt to the ground in the Reichskristallnacht in 1938. The Community Centre was built after the War, incorporating relics of the synagogue in its structure. Continue north to reach Kantstrasse with its many bars, restaurants and bargain shops. Turn left to reach Savignyplatz, whose grassed centre and surrounding bistros are a lively spot day or night. Zwiebelfisch at No. 7 on the corner has a warm atmosphere and offers reasonably priced, traditional German food.

6

Köpenick and the Museum of Applied Art

If you grow tired of the city, a day out to Köpenick south-east of the centre offers an appealing alternative. This is the largest and most pleasant suburb of Berlin, boasting a vast lake, the Grosser Müggelsee, with beach and woodlands. To reach the Schloss Köpenick by car take the Köpenicker Strasse heading south-east which branches off from the Brückenstrasse, just behind the Märkisches Museum.

Continue down this road in a south-easterly direction for approximately 15km and turn left down Schneller Strasse and Oberspree to reach Köpenick itself. Continue across the bridge and north up Lindenstrasse, bearing north-east up Bahnhofstrasse to reach the S-Bahn station from where the tour begins. To reach the area by public transport take the S-Bahn from Friedrichstrasse or Alexanderplatz as far as Ostkreuz and then change to the S3 line and travel five stops to Köpenick.

KÖPENICK is the largest borough of Berlin and has a long history, dating back to the Bronze Age. By the mid 12C Jaczo de Copnic was Prince of the town and it received its first documentary mention in 1240 when the Burg Koppenick on the island to the south was described. The town was founded on the northern tip of an island with fishing as the mainstay of the population; the Müggelspree river comes in from the east and the wider Dahme to the south. Indeed, the name of the town derives from the Slav *copanic* meaning place on a river. The Altstadt (Old Town) is connected to the mainland by means of four bridges. Elector Joachim II built a hunting lodge here in the 16C on the site of the ruined Burg Koppenick and Köpenick became a royal retreat. During the 19C Köpenick felt the impact of the Industrial Revolution with several large factories being built here, including that of AEG, and a radical urban culture developed. Opposition to Hitler was strong here, and was savagely quashed during the Köpenicker Blutwoche (Kopenick Week of Blood) during which time 91 opponents of Nazism were killed and almost 500 imprisoned. Formerly placed in the eastern zone, the area is now a popular weekend retreat for all Berliners with plentiful watersports, walking and beach recreation on offer.

Next to the S-Bahn station is the **Köpenick Local History Museum** (opening times: Tues 09.00–18.00) which outlines the beginnings of the town. Continue south down Bahnhof Strasse, a detour to the right, down Linden Strasse then An der Wühlheide leads to the **Pioneerpark Ernst Thälmann** in the Wühlheide Woods with various children's rides including the popular narrow-gauge railway, the Pioniereisenbahn. To the south and west of the park in the Oberschöneweide area are factories and workers' housing designed by Peter Behrens for AEG at the beginning of the century. Continue south-east down Lindenstrasse across the Dammbrücke to reach the **Altstadt** sited on the peninsula at the confluence of the rivers Spree and Dahme. Just past the bridge, boats once run by the state owned company of *Weisse Flotte* (now by Stern und Kreisschiffahrt, tel. 2727181 for details) leave for tours of Müggelsee and beyond. To the left is the Gothic Revival Rathaus, a brick building erected in 1903–05 and designed by Hans Schütte. There is an impressive variety of cafés, shops and restaurants in the Altstadt, which retains much of its medieval ambience and is currently undergoing restoration. Continue south to reach the Schlossinsel where the **Schloss Köpenick** is situated. Built on the site of a Slav fortress in the 16C by Elector Joachim II as a hunting lodge in Renaissance style, the building was occupied by King Gustavus Adolphus of Sweden during the Thirty Years War. The lodge was then completely rebuilt for Prince Friedrich, the Great Elector's son, during 1677–82, to the Baroque designs of Rutger van Langevelt. It was in the Wappensaal on the first floor that Prince Friedrich was put on trial with his friend, Lieutenant von Katte, for attempting to escape to England from his authoritarian father. The Lieutenant was beheaded for his part in the crime in front of the Prince.

During more peaceful times the Schloss was occupied by a teacher-training college, between 1849–1926, and since 1963 has housed the **Kunstgewerbemuseum** (Museum of Applied Art, opening times: Wed–Sun, 10.00–18.00). The objects on show are part of the Berlin Schloss Museum collection, founded in 1867, which is now displayed in the Tiergarten Museum of Applied Art (see Route 2). The furniture, ceramics and metalwork date from the past 900 years and are effectively shown in the authentic Baroque interiors of the Schloss. On the ground floor are examples of gold jewellery, once worn by Empress Gisela c 1000 AD. Gothic decorative art includes the front panel from a wooden chest originating from Lower Saxony and dated c 1300. On the first floor is a reconstructed oak-panelled room dating from Renaissance times with an impressive coffered ceiling. On the second floor are some remnants from the interior of the Berlin Palace. These include an elaborate sofa from c 1690 and a large collection of Baroque tableware from the Rittersaal (Knight's Chamber) in silver, gold and brass by the Augusburg Brothers Brill dated c 1690. There are also good examples of Biedermeier furniture, Jugendstil decorative arts and Moderne work from the 1920s and 1930s. Attached to the Schloss is the Schlosskapelle (Palace Chapel), built in 1684 by Johann Arnold Nering, where concerts are held during summer weekends.

From the Schloss head east to the **Kietz** district, incorporated into Köpenick in 1898. Kietz was an ancient Slav fishing settlement, founded over 1000 years ago. The bijou fishermen's cottages are now being renovated and the district boasts some interesting antique shops and art galleries. The lake of **Grosser Müggelsee** is c 5km east from here and may be explored on foot, stopping off at the Müggelberge, south-east of the lake, with its observation tower and restaurant. Alternatively, bus No. 27 will take you there from Köpenick itself; the lake may also be reached by boat from Dammbrücke in Köpenick.

For further ideas for day trips from Berlin please consult Chapter II on Brandenburg, which includes Potsdam, the Spreewald, the Monastery of Chorin and Brandenburg.

7

The Park Sanssouci at Potsdam

Tourist Information: Friedrich–Ebert–Strasse 5, 14467 Potsdam. Tel. 21100.
Opening times: Mon–Fri 9.00–20.00, Sat and Sun 9.00–18.00.

To reach the Park Sanssouci from Berlin take the S-Bahn line S3 to
Potsdam–Stadt and change to line R3 or R4 and travel two stops to
Wildpark. By road take the Berliner Ring travelling south-west and exit
at Potsdam North. Continue west down Königstrasse, across the
Glienicker Brücke, south-west down Berliner Strasse, left down Friedrich-Ebert-Strasse turning left before the Lange Brücke up Breite
Strasse and finally, by bearing left at the quasi-mosque pump works
(see Potsdam tour), you reach the entrance to the park via Geschwister-Scholl-Strasse. Turn right up Am Neuen Palais and parking can
be found on the left, just before the Neues Palais.

POTSDAM, the capital of the Land of Brandenburg, lies to the south-west
of Berlin, surrounded by the various waterways of the Havel. As Berlin's
own version of Versailles, it is one of the most popular tourist destinations
in Germany. In the Park Sanssouci there are two important palaces to see
plus smaller buildings of equal architectural merit, including one rare
example of authentic interior decoration by Schinkel. A visit to Sanssouci
is a must for anyone travelling to eastern Germany and equals Dresden in
terms of architectural and historic interest.

History. Potsdam celebrated its 1000-year anniversary in 1993 and owes much of its
great past to the Hohenzollern dynasty. First settlements date back to Slavonic
colonisation in the 8C, the town received its first documentary mention in 993 and
received its charter in 1317. The Hohenzollern family ruled Brandenburg from 1417
and in 1525 Albrecht von Hohenzollern, grand Master of the Teutonic Knights, became
the first Duke of a joint Brandenburg/Prussian state—later to be shortened to Prussia
and eventually to form the dominant state in the unification of Germany. However, it
was only after the Thirty Years War (1618–48) that Potsdam came to prominence when
the Elector Frederick William (1620–88), who ruled from 1640–88, paid off the town's
debts (it had been pawned to noble families) and established it as his second residence
in 1660. The 17C plague had reduced the population from 1782 to 711 and Frederick
William encouraged growth and trade in the town with his Edict of Potsdam of 1685
guaranteeing persecuted Huguenots sanctuary and freedom of worship. This led to
20,000 French Protestants settling in Potsdam, bringing their expertise with them.

King Frederick I, who reigned 1688–1713, built up a royal court in Berlin rather than
to Potsdam but under Frederick William I (reigned 1713–40) Potsdam developed into
a royal residence with burgeoning textile and munitions industries. Potsdam also
became a garrison town under this 'Soldier King' with his favourite Lange Kerls, an
elite corps of tall grenadiers, and the Royal Guards and other troops billeted there. All
house owners had to accommodate two, four or six soldiers and at a certain time each
night the corporals inspected the streets and the soldiers saluted at the windows to
indicate their presence. By the end of his reign 80 per cent of state revenues were
spent on the peacetime army.

Frederick William's son had a tough childhood at the hands of this military fanatic.
He was accused of being effeminate because he hid in a thicket to read a novel rather

than chase deer, wanted to wear gloves whilst riding in the depths of winter and used to leap from a bolting horse. He was a sensitive, caring boy, interested in reading and culture, who suffered psychological damage at the hands of his brutal father.

The Francophile Frederick II or Frederick the Great (ruled 1740–86) came to the throne in 1740 and made Potsdam his permanent summer residence. The palace of Sanssouci was built between 1745–47 as a Rococo retreat for the King where he could indulge in French dinner conversation, music recitals and writing. He also added the Orangery, later called the Neue Kammer in 1747, followed by the Neptune Grotto (1751–57), the Chinese Teahouse (1757), the Art Gallery (1755–64), the Neues Palais (1756–63), the Drachenhaus (1770) and Belvedere (1770–72). The growth of Potsdam mirrors the growth in stature of Prussia as an important European state.

Through the Seven Years War Frederick II defended the new acquisition of Silesia from Austria against Russia, Austria and France. Prussia emerged as a major force after this war. Frederick II also orchestrated the takeover of Poland by Prussia, Russia and Austria in 1786 which connected Brandenburg with East Prussia to make up one complete tract of land across central and northern Germany.

When King Frederick William III ascended to the throne in 1797 Prussia had been neutral for two years in the Napoleonic Wars. However, the Prussian army were not the force they once were and had become badly disciplined and slovenly, so they were crushed by Napoleon's forces who occupied Potsdam from 24 October 1806 until they were driven out by the Russians in 1813. In 1838 the first railway line in Prussia was built between Berlin and Potsdam and the town became a popular destination for day-trippers from Berlin.

King Frederick William III added the Schloss Charlottenhof, the Roman Baths (1836) and the Orangery Palace (1860) to the Potsdam complex. In 1840 King Frederick Willhelm IV came to the throne—rather unbalanced and inconsistent, he was later certified insane. His reign saw the rapid expansion of the Prussian economy and industry and he was succeeded in 1861 by William I who was crowned as the first Emperor of Germany in 1871. He died at the ripe old age of 91 in 1888 and his son, Frederick III succeeded him, only to die of cancer of the throat in the same year. He was succeeded by his son, William II, then aged 30. His reign was marked by increased industrialisation and internal conflicts which could not be resolved, leading to his abdication in 1918 when the Emperor fled to Holland. He bought a small estate there and lived the life of an English country squire until his death in 1941. The land and buildings of Sanssouci became public property in 1927. In April 1945 Potsdam was liberated by the Russian army and the Potsdam Agreement between America, Russia and Great Britain was signed at Cecilienhof on 2 August 1945. Potsdam was designated capital of Brandenburg in the Soviet Occupied Zone and grew into one of the largest Soviet bases in the GDR. The Palaces and their grounds were a popular destination throughout the post-war, Communist era with coachloads of Eastern Bloc visitors making their way there as well as parties of westerners. With unification, travel to Potsdam is much simpler and its proximity to Berlin makes it a popular destination.

From the railway station Wildpark head north up Am Neuen Palais, one of the more recent buildings in the parkland. The grounds cover 3 sq km and lie to the west of the town centre itself. Work began on the layout of the grounds in 1744 and was continued by Peter Joseph Lenné from 1816 during the reigns of Frederick William III and IV. The **Neues Palais** (New Palace) was built during 1763–69, after the Seven Years War in heavy, late Baroque style by Johann Buring and C. von Gontard. It was originally destined to be a guest-house with Frederick II staying in Sanssouci, which lies 2km to the east. The Neues Palais was later used by Wilhelm II as a summer residence until his abdication in 1918 and much of the interior decoration dates from the turn of the century.

The main façade is truly impressive, consisting of a huge central dome towering over the main entrance, framed by Corinthinan pilasters alternating with French windows which continue across the three storey frontage. The entire façade, which is some 213m long including the three lower wings on either side, is richly decorated with carved sandstone. The balustrade across the top is surmounted by various sandstone statues created by the Raentz Brothers and J.C. Wohler the Elder. The overall impression is one of total grandiosity, summed up by Frederick II who (described it as a *fanfaronnade* (piece of conceit) to celebrate Prussia's enhanced prestige following the Seven Years War. Inside the palace is equally impressive (opening times; daily all year with the exception of the second and fourth Monday of each month: April–Sept 09.00–17.00, Oct 09.00–16.00, Nov–Jan 09.00–15.00, Feb–March 09.00–16.00). Most striking is the *GROTTEN-SAAL (Grotto Hall) on the ground floor facing the park. This piece of Rococo fantasy was initiated in the 18C with simple decorations of glass, shells, corals and minerals. During the late 19C more ostentatious semi-precious stones and fossils were added and this stunning room now houses 20,000 different fragments. The floor is decoratively patterned with multi-coloured marbles laid out in squares and scrolls. The ceiling is decorated with fabulous squirming serpents and shell mosaics. Each of the four corners houses a niche with delicate, Rococo staute surmounted by a shell design. The walls are decorated with six broad bands of stones and shells. Look in particular at the south-west corner of the Grottensaal, to the left of the main entrance, where different coloured minerals glisten, including quartz crystals. The effect is further enhanced by splendid chandeliers and Rococo wall sconces.

To the south of the Grottensaal are interiors from the time of Frederick II (Rooms 4–13) and the 19C north drawing rooms and bedrooms including those used by Prince Heinrich (Rooms 24–34). Also not to missed is the MARMORSAAL (Marble Hall) on the first floor which served as a banqueting hall. Most striking is the 16m high ceiling, decorated with a painting by Pedrozzi. The walls repeat the decoration of the exterior of the palace with Corinthian pilasters and statues lining the huge room. The room is named after the white Carrara marble which covers the floor and walls, (complemented by red jasper and sumptuous gilding. Note the view from the window which takes in the main avenue, linking the west to the east of the park and ending with the 18C Obelisk. The Schlosstheater (Palace Theatre) is housed in the southern wing on the first floor. Built in 1766–68 to designs by Johann Christian Hoppenhaupt, the theatre seats an audience of 300. The theatre was inspired by the designs of ancient amphitheatres, with its rising tiers of seats and boxes above. The carved and gilded palm trees on either side of the arched stage are pure Rococo fantasy. The theatre was restored during 1989–90 and is currently hosts productions by the Hans Otto Theatre company. Also note that the South Wing houses a cafeteria on the ground floor.

The strange building to the west of the Neues Palais is the **Communs**, designed by Karl von Gontard during 1766–69 as accommodation for servants and courtiers. The central colonnade is flanked by two Palladian villas, one which housed the kitchens and were connected to the Palace by tunnels, and one with quarters for the court. Like the Neues Palais opposite, the structure is decorated with statues to create an ostentatious effect. From the Neues Palais continue south-east to reach the far more pleasing **Charlottenhof Palace** on the southern fringe of the Park, designed by K.F. Schinkel in 1826 as the summer residence for Crown Prince Frederick William. The name was derived from the previous occupant Charlotte von Gentzkow, whose 18C house was converted. The property had been bought by Frederick William III in 1825 as a present for the Crown Prince. The designs were based on the Roman villa, particularly the Villa Albani known in Germany through the publications of French interior decorators Percier and Fontaine. Parts of the 18C building were retained, including the tall windows and window bays of the upper storey, but the addition of a Doric portico to the east with Roman style terrace finished off with semi-circular stone seat by Schinkel, transports the visitor back to the days of ancient Rome. A pitched roof connects east and west façades whilst the two wings have flat roofs. The interior of the Charlottenhof Palace may be visited only by a guided tour; with luck, this may be in English, but in any case it is well worth viewing Schinkel's apogee as an interior decorator. (Opening times: 09.00–1700 between mid-May and mid-October, closed on the fourth Monday of each month.)

The VESTIBULE is the most impressive room in the Palace, two storeys in height with walls marbled in pale grey. Gracing the entrance is a bronze fountain, designed by Schinkel for the Gewerbe-Institut but moved here in 1843. The two staircases run up either side of the vestibule with graceful brass and wood banisters to reach the first floor landing. The white walls of the upper section are divided by blue and green stripes into simple rectangles. The top of the wall is decorated with a frieze with winged figures connected with garlands, inspired by Percier and Fontaine's designs for Malmaison in Paris. Upstairs eight rooms, designed on a small, intimate scale can be visited, including the CROWN PRINCESS'S WRITING ROOM (Room 5) which shows an extraordinary sense of colour. The walls were papered and painted in pink, the ceiling in white and the skirting boards, door frames and window frames in apple green. Schinkel also designed the silvered wood writing desk with its classical columns for legs. Beside the writing room is the Princess's living-room with the hall beyond—Room 7, the SPEISESAAL. This is the largest room in the Palace with its white walls decorated with coloured engravings after Raphael. The tour then moves on to the ROTES ECKKABINETT (red corner room), Room 9, with rich wallpaper and 19C, gouache landscapes, which gives access to the pergola in the garden. The tour concludes with the remarkable tent room or WOHNZIMMER DER HOFDAMEN (Room 11), furnished in 1830 for the ladies-in-waiting, it is directly inspired by Malmaison. The room is lined with matching blue-and-white striped paper and fabric with folding iron furniture to evoke the popular campaign look. By contrast, Room 4, the SCHLAFZIMMER (Crown Prince's Bedroom) is decorated in plain, emerald green with gilded, Empire style candelabra and bedposts.

From the Charlottenhof Palace proceed north by the side of the **Maschinenteich** (Machine Pond) where the mechanisms for feeding water to the rest of the Park once stood (dismantled in 1923). An island stands in the centre of the pond, graced by a statue of Mercury. The **Romanische Bade**r (Roman Baths), a collection of small buildings beyond, conjure up a fantasy world of classical civilisation and were created by Schinkel's pupil, L. Persius during 1829–35 around his mentor's plans. The baths have never been used to wash, simply to transport the visitor into a different time zone. (opening times: mid-May to mid-Oct, daily 09.00–17.00, closed third Monday of every month.) The Court Gardener's House was built in the style of an Italian farmhouse with its low-pitched roofs and pergolas. To the left is the later Gardener's Assistant's House in similar style and behind are the Roman Baths, built in the style of Roman houses as seen at Herculaneum rather than being authentic copies of Roman thermal baths. The view directly into the Baths from the arcaded hall in the courtyard is quite spellbinding. Two dark grey, marble pillars frame the green, antique bath lit from the sides and surrounded by red and black walls. In front of the bath

Schloss Sanssouci, Potsdam

stands a statue of the Dying Gaul with another of Bacchus to the left and one of Apollo to the right. Beyond the atrium is a blue, semi-circular niche occupied by a romantic statue of a youth and girl by Werner Henschel.

Continue north to reach the Okonomieweg and turn right to reach the **Chinesiches Teehaus** (Chinese Teahouse) built in 1754–57 by J.G. Büring in fashionable, Chinoiserie taste. This round pavilion is exotically decorated with gilded figures including, on the roof, a cross-legged mandarin complete with sunshade. Each of the three porches are decorated with columns in the form of palm trees with groups of Chinese figures at the base. Chinese musicians decorate the remainder of the wall space. The Chinoiserie scupltures were created by Benckert and Heymueller and the interior houses a porcelain collection. (Opening times: mid-May to mid-Oct 09.00–17.00, closed second Monday of every month.) Continue east down

Okonomieweg until the Grosse Fontane (Great Fountain) appears on your left and the prospect of the **••Schloss Sanssouci** opens up before you.

This single-storey Rococo building was designed by the architect, Prussian aristocrat and close friend of Frederick, Georg Wenzeslaus von Knobelsdorff (1699–1753) and based upon plans by Frederick the Great himself. Knobelsdorf had travelled to Italy for Frederick in the late 1730s. Upon Frederick's succession to the throne in 1740 he was sent to Dresden and Paris to prepare himself for more ambitious projects. Upon his return he added a wing to Monbijou for the Queen Mother (1740–42) and a wing to Charlottenburg for the King (1742–46) with remarkable Rococo interiors. In 1741 he was appointed Surveyor General of Royal Palaces and Parks, Director in Chief of all buildings in the Royal Provinces, and a member of the Prussian Council of Ministers. He began work on the Stadtschloss at Potsdam, which was subsequently destroyed, and began on Sanssouci in 1745. However, he quarrelled with the King in 1746 and he was dismissed, ending his architectural career; he died seven years later.

'Sans souci' means 'without a care' and this is how the King intended to use his summer palace. The words 'Sans Souci' were inscribed over the dining room doors. The terraces were built on the hillside first—six in all, sited 3.5m apart, and planted with vines. The climate was too cold for vines and the plan was abandoned. A broad flight of 144 steps was built separating the west from the east terraces. Frederick the Great so adored the palace that he decreed that he should be buried here, at the top of the terrace on the right-hand side. His son disregarded the King's wishes, however, and he was buried in Potsdam's Garrison Church. However, in a great symbolic gesture in 1991 his body was finally moved to his beloved Sanssouci with great pomp and ceremony, signalling that the new Germany was not forgetting its historic past. In the centre of the south front is an oval dining room with long, elegant glass doors through which guests could step onto the terrace. Guests were usually male, apart from Frederick's sister Wilhelmina, and included the great French philosopher Voltaire. He travelled to Berlin in June 1750 with the promise of free lodging and generous pension. He was accommodated at Sanssouci but refused to compromise and be the tame intellectual that Frederick had in mind. He found the discussion of military affairs boring and the King's own writing far from perfect and eventually left in March 1753. They kept up their correspondence but remained geographically apart.

The main entrance to Sanssouci Palace is at the opposite side to the terraces, around the back of the Palace with the ticket office to the west. Admission is by guided tour only, but these are available periodically in English. (Opening times: April–Sept 09.00–17.00, Oct 09.00, Nov–Jan 09.00–15.00, Feb–March 09.00–16.00, closed first and third Monday of each month.) Enter the colonnaded courtyard with its sweeping arms which screen the entrance. The first room on the tour is the VESTIBUL (Vestibule) with floor clad in cream, Silesian marble, gilded Corinthian capitals and pilasters crowned by a painted ceiling by J. Harper (1746).

Proceed west into the eastern wing or KUCHENFLUGEL and the Kleine Galerie (Small Gallery), a long passageway which acted as a showcase for painting and sculpture. The decoration of the space is typically Rococo with gilded, stucco embellishments virtually dripping down the wall. The ceiling was painted in five parts by J.G. Glume in 1747 and depicts playful putti distributing flowers. The patterned floor is of oak and linden wood. Works of art on display do not really measure up to the interior decoration, with

The Concert Room, Schloss Sanssouci, Potsdam

18C porcelain, paintings by followers of Watteau and 18C copies of Roman busts. The gallery was originally decorated with work by Watteau which were evacuated to the west and are now in the Charlottenburg Palace.

The King's personal apartments are located in the eastern wing of the palace including a library at the end of the Kleine Galerie without one German book. The room is circular in plan with cedar wood panelling and bookcases built into the wall. Sensuous, animated gilded decoration covers almost every surface of the room. Adjacent to the Library is the ALKOVEN (Alcove), formerly a bedroom, which contains the chair in which Frederick II died. Neighbouring this is a reconstructed bedroom with fine bronze statue of Frederick II with his beloved greyhounds by Schadow dating from 1821.

The KONZERTZIMMER (Concert Room) is possibly one of the finest examples of the German Rococo with fantastic asymmetrical, gilded mirror and picture frames. The paintings are by Frederick II's French court painter A. Pense. They were inspired by the *Metamorphoses* by Roman poet Ovid and include representations of Pygmalion and Galathea, Vertumnus and Pomona and Bacchus and Ariadne.

The EMPFANGSZIMMER (Reception Room) lies between the Concert Room and Vestibule with ceiling painting by Pense. To the south of the

Vestibule is the Marmorsaal (Marble Hall) an oval-shaped room which leads directly onto the terrace. This grand, public room is decorated with eight pairs of Corinthian columns in white Carrara marble with gilded capitals. The floor is patterned with inlay of various coloured marble. Look out for the stucco-work figures at the base of the painted cupola which represent architecture, music, painting, sculpture and astronomy.

Guests were accommodated in the west wing and joined the King for the main meal at noon and in the evening for conversation and music. The three main guest rooms in the **Damenflugel** were all restored in the early 1970s. Most unusual is the fourth guest room, the Voltairezimmer (Voltaire Room) named after the French philosopher who visited Potsdam but did not stay in this particular room. The restored Rococo decorations consist of stucco and wrought iron garlands of flowers on the walls and ceilings with curious carved monkeys, storks and parrots in relief.

Return to the terrace and continue south down the left-hand side to reach the **Neptune Grotto**, designed by Knobelsdorff to enhance the beauty of the garden. The classical arch is decorated with shells on either side and crowned with a statue of Neptune by J.P. Benckert. Designed originally as a garden folly, it was converted into a fountain during the 19C.

To the north-west of the Grotto and east of the main palace is the **Bilder Galerie** (Picture Gallery) which houses a collection of 17C paintings including work by Rubens, van Dyck, Reni, Caravaggio and others. Designed by J.G. Buering and erected during 1755–64, it was the first purpose-built art gallery in Germany. (Opening times: mid-May to mid-Oct 09.00–1700, closed on fourth Monday of each month.) It is well worth visiting the Gallery for the interior alone. The long, single-storey building is divided into two wings by a central dome. The west wing contains some fine, 17C Italian painting including Carlo Maratta's *The Discovery of Romulus and Remus* (1692) and Caravaggio's powerful *Doubting Thomas* (c 1600). The east wing contains work by Rubens, including *The Crowning of Diana* (1625), and Van Dyck.

Further to the south-west is the main entrance to the Park graced by the 20m high **Obelisk**, erected in 1748 at the easternmost point of the grounds. A path leads from the Obelisk with its decorative hieroglyphics to the main portal with two groups of Corinthian columns which stand in the centre of a curved, stone balustrade decorated with statues of Classical gods and goddesses including Pomona and Flora.

On the opposite side of the Schloss stands the equivalent to the Art Gallery, the **Neue Kammern** (New Chambers). Originally built as an orangery in 1747 to designs by Knobelsdorff, it was converted into a guest-house during 1771–74 by G.C. Unger. Like the Art Gallery it is a long, single-storey building divided by a central dome. The slender windows look out over the gardens below. Badly damaged during the war, the building underwent extensive restoration by Polish craftsmen during the 1980s. It is now newly opened with extensive fresh gilding and wall painting. (Opening times: April–Sept 09.00–17.00, Oct 09.00–16.00, Nov–Jan 09.00–15.00, Feb–March 09.00–16.00, closed Fridays.) Of special note are the oval Buffet Room and Ovid Gallery decorated with gilded reliefs from Roman mythology. The effect is heightened by the shimmering scrolls and garlands of flowers which decorate the white walls. Just west of the New Chambers is the pleasant **Sizilianischer Garten** (Sicilian Garden) layed out in 1857 by Lenné in the informal, Mediterranean style with orange trees and palms flourishing in this sheltered spot.

Continue north across the Maulbeerallee to the **Orangery** which was built between 1851 and 1862 on the instructions of Frederick Wilhelm IV who wanted Sanssouci to look like Rome. Its design is reminiscent of an Italian Renaissance palace with its two towers linked by a colonnade. Building work was overseen by two of Schinkel's pupils, F.A. Stueler and L.F. Hesse and the original plans were by Persius. (Opening times: mid-May to mid-Oct 09.00–17.00 daily, closed fourth Thursday of each month.) The Raphael room in the centre of the building contains 47 copies of paintings by the artist, whilst the five well-appointed guest rooms are lavishly decorated in various, 19C revival styles. The Orangery was built as a guest house for notable visitors including Tsar Nicholas I of Russia and Charlotte, sister of Frederick William IV.

A walk further north-west is rewarded with the remarkable sight of the **Drachenhaus** (Dragon House) built in 1770 by C. von Gontard in the form of a Chinese pagoda, based partly on Chambers's version of this exotic building form at Kew Gardens. The building was intended as accommodation for the head of the vineyard and now serves as a thoroughly acceptable restaurant (opening times: daily from 12.00). Note the 16 gilded dragons which decorate the curved roof and give this strange building its name. Further north up the Klausberg is the classical **Belvedere**; bombed out during the War it was fully restored for the 1000 year celebrations.

From this point it is a short walk south to the Neues Palais and the Wildpark railway station or car park.

8

Potsdam town tour

143,000 inhabitants.

Tourist Information: See Route 7, The Park Sanssouci.

Although Potsdam is best known for Sanssouci and the other palaces and follies within the palace grounds, there is much to see in the actual town of Potsdam itself. Having recently celebrated 1000 years of existence, much effort and funding has been poured into the renovation of key buildings before and after unification.

Potsdam Stadt railway station can be reached easily from Berlin on the S3 line or by road via the Berliner Ring. From the station head north over the Lange Bridge, built in 1825, past the luxury Hotel Potsdam where boats leave during the summer to tour the Havel. Continue north on to the Friedrich Ebert Strasse, where the Tourist Information Office is situated, and take the first right down the Heinrich Rau Allee; the ALTER MARKT (Old Market) on the left. This was the heart of the 18C town where the Stadtpalais once stood.

The ***Nikolaikirche** (St Nicholas Church) was designed by Schinkel and Persius and built between 1830 and 1837 on the site of a Baroque original

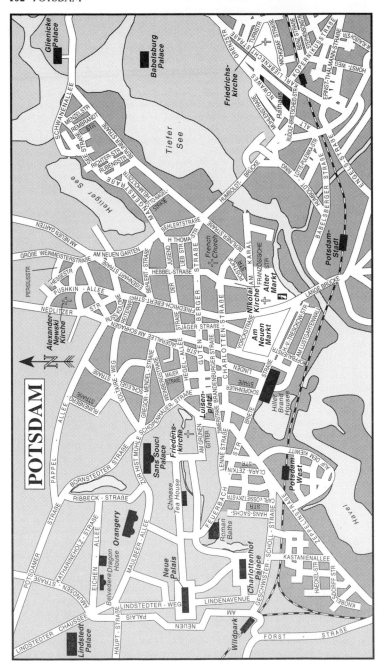

which had been destroyed by fire. Badly damaged during Allied bombing of 1945, the Nikolaikirche has been painstakingly restored and is one of the most important domed buildings in Germany. The church was originally built without the dome, as King Frederick William III wanted the building to be in the form of a basilica. It was only after the King's death that Schinkel's plans to build an elegant dome could be realised and work began in 1843 under the direction of Persius as Schinkel had also died. The exterior was finished in 1847, the interior in 1849 and the church was eventually dedicated in 1850. The dome is centrally placed, framed by four corner towers surmounted by winged angels. The dome is made up of four tiers beginning with a stepped section followed by a circle of Corinithian columns which support a squatter circle of Corinthian pilasters. The tall dome rests on this layer, topped by a lantern and angel. The interior has been extensively restored and the paintings of scenes from the New Testament which decorate the interior of the dome are quite breathtaking. The church is now used for recitals and concerts.

The former **Rathaus** (Town Hall) is on the eastern side of the square and is now the Hans Marchwitz arts centre with restaurant, wine bar and dance bar. Built between 1753 and 1755 in Baroque style, it boasts Corinthian columns with statues representing the virtues of the town burghers above, sculpted by Johann Gottlied Heymuller. The tower on top is surmounted by a gilded statue of Atlas carrying the world. Beside the Town Hall, connected by a 1960s addition, is the **Knobelsdorffhaus** built in 1750. Badly damaged during the war, this former burgher house is now part of the arts centre. The 16m high obelisk in the centre of the square was also designed by Knobelsdorff and erected during 1753–55. This version was resurrected in 1978–79.

Return to the Heinrich Rau Alle, cross the Friedrich Ebert Strasse into Breite Strasse (formerly Wilhelm-Kulz-Strasse). On your right is the National Film Archive/Museum, housed in the **Marstall** (Royal Stables), designed by Knobelsdorff in Baroque style in 1746. The characteristic sculptures of horses which adorn the skyline were created by Friedrich Christian Glume. The museum celebrates the history of German film-making from 1895 to 1980 (opening times: Tues–Sun 10.00–17.00). The German film industry was born in the Babelsberg district of Potsdam and the UFA film company (formerly the Babelsberg film company) launched many stars including Greta Garbo.

Adjacent to the Marstall, set back slightly from Breite Strasse in Am Neuen Markt is the **Portal des Langen Stalls** (Portal of the Long Stable) built in 1781 by Unger as an addition to the single-storey drill building. The Garnisonskirche (Garrison Church) once stood to the left of the Portal. Built in 1731–35 it was bombed out in April 1945 and the ruined remains were demolished in 1968. This great Baroque edifice was the final resting place of important members of the Hohenzollern family including Frederick William I and his son Frederick II. On Dortustrasse, at Nos 30–34, is an imposing Neo-Baroque building, originally erected in 1907 to house the government's audit office, and now housing the Theodor Fontane Archives.

Further west along Breite Strasse in a fine Neo-Classical building at Nos 8–12, is the **Potsdam Museum** (opening times: Tues–Sun 10.00–17.00) which charts local history from 993 to 1900 as well as the natural history of the region. Opposite are the Baroque **Hiller-Brandt Houses**, named after the 18C owners and inspired by Inigo Jones's Whitehall Palace in London. Built in 1769 they now house the 20C section of the Potsdam Museum.

The Nikolaikirche, Potsdam, designed by Schinkel and Persius and built in 1830–37

Behind the Hiller-Brandt Houses is the **Kiezstrasse**, with some well restored 18C town houses. Further west down Breite Strasse is the remarkable **Moschee** (Mosque) built in 1841–42 by Persius to house the palace's waterworks. This fake mosque is richly decorated with coloured brick, the steam-driven pump is disguised as a minaret and the steam engine itself, which ran until 1894, is situated in the Dome Room. This intriguing piece of industrial history may be visited (opening times: Wed–Sun 10.00–17.00).

Turn right up Zeppelinstrasse to reach the **Brandenburger Tor** (Brandenburg Gate) in the Luisenplatz Platz. Built in 1770 in the style of a Roman triumphal arch, it was designed by Carl von Gothard and Georg Christian Unger as a celebration of victory in the Seven Years War. This is one of the three recently restored town gates and it opens out to the east into a pedestrian zone in Brandenburger Strasse, with good cafés and take-away snack shops.

From the Brandenburg Gate continue north up Schopenhauer Strasse and on the second left you will find the **Friedenskirche** (Church of Peace) begun in 1842 and finished in 1854 by Ludwig Persius. Inspired by St Clements Church in Rome it houses the Byzantine Aspis mosaic dating from 1108. Originally from San Cipriano on Murano island near Venice, it was brought to Potsdam in 1834 and installed as a feature of the church. Also of note within the church is the last work by Romantic sculptor, Christian Daniel Rauch, *Moses with Aaron and Hur.* The Church displays Frederick William's passion for Italian culture and is a good example of the Rund-bogenstil, a term which the Germans used to describe the revival of Romanesque, round arches. To the west of the Church lies the Marly Garden, designed by Lenné at the same time.

Rejoin Schopenhauer Strasse and cross east to Hegel Allee. On the left is the **Jagetor** (Hunter's Gate), the second of the town gates built in 1733 and surmounted by a dying stag being attacked by hunting dogs. At the bottom of Hegel Allee is the **Nauener Tor** (Nauen Gate), another of the restored town gates designed by Johann Gottfried Büring in 1755 in a Romantic Gothic style. Two round, castellated towers with pointed, arched windows stand at either side of the pointed archway. Turn right into Friedrich-Ebert-Strasse and on the first left is the **Hollandisches Viertel** (Dutch Quarter). Between 1737 and 1742, 134 houses were built in a Dutch style to house immigrant Dutch workers. Construction Work was directed by the Dutch architect Johann Boumann. The area has been spruced up and there are some presentable examples of the red-brick gabled houses in Mittelstrasse.

Continue north for approx 15 minutes up Friedrich Ebert Strasse until you reach the **Alexandrovka Settlement**, built in 1826 for 12 Russian musicians stranded by the Napoleonic Wars. The two storey wooden houses are in Russian style with steeply sloping roofs, and Cyrillic script decorates the doorways. Further north on the Kapellenberg Hill is the **Alexander-Newski-Kirche** of 1829. This Russian Othodox Church, specially built for the new settlers to plans sent from Petersburg and adapted by Schinkel, has a distinctive onion-domed tower. The entrancing interior is decorated with Russian icons. From this point you are not far from the **Neuer Garten** (see Route 9, Palaces on the Havel) or you may choose to return to the train station by walking south down Friedrich-Ebert-Strasse and crossing the Lange Brücke. Further south from the station is the Telegraphenberg (Telegraph Hill), reached via Albert Einstein Strasse, where the **Einstein Tower** stands. Designed by Hans Poelzig in 1920, this important piece of Expressionist design, with its sweeping forms, foreshadows the Stream-lined style of the 1930s.

9

Palaces on the Havel

Sanssouci marked the beginning of a spate of building summer palaces and landscaping around Potsdam. Subsequent areas were developed including the Neuer Garten, to the north-east of Potsdam town centre, Babelsburg to the east, Glienicke on the east bank of the Havel and Pfaueninsel (Peacock Island) situated in the Havel itself. The tour may be covered by car and boat or train and boat and conjures up a picture of the life of the Prussian Royal Family in more recent times. Beginning at the Neuer Garten, take the S3 from Berlin to Potsdam-Stadt station and walk or take a bus to the Neuer Garten by crossing the Lange Brücke heading north up Friedrich-Ebert-Strasse and bearing right up Eisenhart Strasse. By car follow the same route and parking is situated at the top of Eisenhart Strasse.

The **Neuer Garten** contains two significant palaces plus some curious follies. Named the New Garden to distinguish it from Sanssouci, the land was bought by Frederick William II when he was Crown Prince and the grounds landscaped by Johann A. Eyserbeck the Younger in Romantic style. This work was then revised by Lenné during 1817–25. The **Marmorpalais** (Marble Palace) commissioned by Frederick William II when he came to the throne, is reached by heading north-east for approx 200m along the signposted footpath from the main gates. This brings you past the 18C Dutch style porter's lodge, adjoining guest house and servants quarters— the Kavalierhauser and Damenhaus—to the Planetarium and the Orangery on the left. The ORANGERY was designed by Langhans and built during 1791–92 with amazing Egyptian decoration, the eastern façade is crowned by a sphinx.

The Marble Palace itself lies to the north of the Orangery. This two-storey, Neo-Classical building based on a square villa plan was begun in 1787 and completed in 1792. Unusually, the palace is constructed out of grey-white Silesian marble and red brick. Designed by Carl von Gontard with interiors by K.G. Langhans, the palace housed an Army Museum until 1990 and renovation work is now underway to restore the building to its former glory. Picturesquely located on the banks of the Heiliger See, and surrounded by greenery, the palace was a perfect summer retreat for Frederick William II. It was enlarged in the mid 19C with the addition of the two single-storey wings. The kitchen is uniquely concealed behind the façade of a mock ruin on the southern banks of the lake, linked to the Palace by an underground passage. Continue north to the **Pyramide**, a grey marble pyramid constructed to house the Palace's cold store. Further north by the banks of the Lake is the **Rotes Haus** (Red House) built for use by the gardeners.

From here its a short walk north to the chief attraction of the Park, the **Cecilienhof Palace**; built in mock-Tudor style during 1913–17, it hosted the Potsdam Conference in 1945. Designed for Princess Cecilie and her husband Crown Prince Wilhelm by P. Schultze-Naumberg it was the last Prussian Royal Palace to be built. The erstwhile Crown Prince moved back into the Palace in 1923 and lived there until 1945. Although the theme of the Potsdam Conference and the signing of the Potsdam Agreement tends to dominate a visit to the Schloss, the use of mock-Tudor for the design of a German Palace is of equal interest, particularly as the building was completed during the First World War. The English Arts and Crafts movement did have a significant influence on German design in the early 20C, with Hermann Muthesius visiting England as a cultural attaché and writing the influential book, *Das Englische Haus* published in Germany in 1907. (Opening times: daily 09.00–16.15, closed second and fourth Monday of each month.) Enter the grassy courtyard and note the plethora of chimneys which dominate the skyline—55 in all, though only three actually work. Of key interest inside is the Konferenzsaal (Conference Room) where the Potsdam Agreement was signed by Stalin, Churchill and Truman. It is preserved as it was in 1945 as are the three delegation suites which can also be visited. The English baronial style also permeates the interiors, with oak-panelled rooms, decorative plaster ceilings and mock Tudor furniture. The remainder of the Palace is now an expensive hotel with restaurant to match.

To reach **Babelsburg** return to the Potsdam-Stadt station, and bus F will take you from Ceclienhof to the town centre—travel one stop on the S3 to Babelsberg. By road follow Am Neue Garten and Behlertstrasse south then bear left onto Rudolf-Breitscheid Strasse. Note the Babelsberg Town Hall, built in 1898–99, on the left.

It is possible to make a detour at this point and visit the old Babelsberg Film Studios, now the **Babelsberg Studio TV and Film Experience** (opening times: daily 10.00–18.00, last admission 15.00). To do so by road continue east on the Rudolf-Breitscheid Strasse and bear right down Stahnsdorfer Strasse then right down August Bebel Strasse. You should then alight at Griebnitzsee and take bus 693. Turned into a film studio in 1911, this former factory was taken over by the legendary Ufa production company in 1921 to make such film classics as *The Blue Angel*, *Nosferatu* and *The Cabinet of Dr Calligari*. Under Nazi rule the studios were forced by Joseph Goebbels to produce ugly propaganda films and Germany's leading film-making talent fled to America, including Fritz Lang, Billy Wilder, Marlene Dietrich and Josef von Sternberg. During the post-war era, the studios were nationalised and renamed Deutsche Film AG (DEFA) producing Communist propaganda for the state. With heavy subsidies and over-manning Babelsberg grew into the biggest film studio in Europe covering some 430,000 sq m with about 2450 full-time employees. Following unification the work-force has been drastically cut, as in all former East German industry. The studios are now owned by a French company and public tours began in 1991. A visit here is billed as an entire, one day experience; visitors may mingle with actors, dress up in the extensive wardrobe collection, be professionally made-up and tour behind the scenes including one of the extensive prop warehouses.

From the studios head north up August-Bebel-Strasse, across Rudolf-Breitscheid Strasse to reach Karl-Marx Strasse to see some of the more luxurious villas built for the early film-makers and later occupied by select members of the Stasi. The street overlooks the Grienbnitzsee and borders onto the **Park Babelsberg**. The Park was laid out by the ubiquitous Lenné in 1832 and refined by Prince Hermann von Puckler-Muskau in 1843. Straight ahead, 2km distant in a westerly direction, just past the bridge which crosses to Glienicke, is the **Schloss Babelsberg** (opening times: summer only, Tues–Sun 09.00–17.00). Designed by Schinkel and built during 1834–49 in Gothic Revival style, it was the summer residence of

Prince William and his wife, the Anglophile Princess Augusta von Sachsen-Weimar. The Princess brought the English influence of Humphry Repton to bear on the designs. This explains why the building looks like an English medieval castle with turrets, castellated roof line, towers and Gothic windows. Upon Schinkel's death in 1841 Persius and then Heinrich Strack supervised the building work adding the more ornamental western section. Although Schinkel created designs for the individual rooms, the royal couple personalised the space with reproduction antiques, ornaments and souvenirs. King (later Emperor) William used Babelsberg as his summer residence until his death in 1888. The Schloss now houses a Museum of Pre- and Early History.

By continuing south along the banks of the Tiefer See the **Kleine Palais** may be reached; now used as a café it was built in 1841–42 by Gebhard to accommodate the ladies-in-waiting. Further south in the Park is the Gothic Revival **Flatow Tower**, erected in 1853–56 and modelled on the Eschenheim Gate Tower in Frankfurt am Main. From the Babelsberg Palace, head east to cross the water by means of the wooden bridge to the island of Wannsee. You are now in the Kleine Glienicke area which was also developed by the Prussian Royal Family for their summer use. On the left is the **Glienicke Hunting Lodge**, built for Frederick the Great in 1682–83 and converted to Neo-Baroque style in 1859. It is presently in use as a youth centre. Continue north up the hill to join König Strasse, the main road from Berlin to Potsdam. Turn left to reach the famous GLIENICKER BRÜCKE. Erected in 1908–09 from iron with sandstone piers the centre of the bridge marked the border between East Germany and West Berlin from 1961 until 1989. Here important spies were exchanged during the Cold War. It was the first East–West border to be opened up and now provides an important road link between Berlin and Potsdam.

Five minutes walk north of the bridge is the **Glienicke Palace and Park**. Work on the grounds for Prince Hardenberg began in 1816 under Lenné. Following the Prince's death in 1822 the plot was acquired for Prince Karl August, eldest of Frederick William's four sons, in 1824. It was Lenné who completed the marvellous grounds, but it was Schinkel whose inventive architecture brings the entire area to life.

The main entrance to the palace is graced by a classically inspired fountain, positioned here in 1840 and framed by two majestic lions who spout water from the top of Roman pedestals. To the right is the Stibadium, a covered, semi-circular seat which affords fine views across the Havel to Potsdam beyond. The two-storey, Italianate Schloss was designed by Schinkel in 1826 with flat roof, simple geometric shape and green shutters. The main façade is fairly severe, with sparse decoration restricted to the four central pillars. The courtyard to the rear of the building is far more informal in Italian style with a central fountain. The building was greatly improved in 1832 with the addition of a tower on the Cavalier Wing which connected the Schloss with the stables. Further delights to make up the Glienicke ensemble of buildings includes the **Grosse Neugrierde** (Great Curiosity), a circular garden pavilion used for viewing the woods of the Neuer Garten across the waters of the Havel. Access to the Schloss is limited at present, but plans are afoot to restore the building and create a new Museum.

From Glienicke it is possible, it time permits, to visit the last of the Hohenzollern's summer retreats at **Pfaueninsel** (Peacock Island). To do so head east down König Strasse then follow Nikolskoer Weg north-east. The

No. 66 bus travels along this route to the ferry landing point for Peacock Island past the Nikolskoe, a log cabin built by Frederick William II in 1819 for Prince Nicholas of Russia to woo his daughter, Charlotte. The cabin was recently rebuilt following a fire and is now a reasonable restaurant, the Blockhaus Nikolskoe (closed Thurs). Behind is the **Kirche St Peter und Paul** (Church of Peter and Paul) designed by August Stuler and built in 1834 with a Russian Orthodox inspiration. Boats run regularly from the ferry stage to Peacock Island and the journey takes only about two minutes. Note that no cars are allowed and picnicking is forbidden as the 1 sq km island has been a nature reserve since 1924.

The island was bought by Frederick William II in 1793 as a retreat for himself and his mistress, Countess Lichenau. Frederick William III and Queen Luise were also frequent visitors, introducing the peacocks which give the small island its name. The chief attraction is the **Lustschloss**, a large garden folly designed to look like a medieval ruin with two towers connected by an open-air footbridge. This was originally built in wood but was replaced in 1807 by an iron replica. There is a fascinating museum inside with beautifully crafted, late 18C interiors (opening times: April Sept Tues–Sun, 10.00–17.00; Oct 10.00–16.00, closed Nov–March). Of special note are the spiral staircase and Neo-Classical Grand Hall situated on the top floor. Elsewhere on the island there is a memorial temple devoted to Queen Luise, a dairy farm built in 1795 in the form of a mock ruin and in the centre the Kavalierhaus designed by Schinkel. This building was erected during 1824–26 and is interesting as it incorporates a Gothic façade brought from Danzig. The **Schweizerhaus** (Swiss Cottage) to the south of the island was also designed by Schinkel in 1830. Although the island is of great interest, and could easily occupy an entire afternoon, bear in mind the time of the last ferry back to the mainland!

From the ferry landing point it is possible to reconnect with the König Strasse heading east for Berlin or take bus No. 66 to the Wannsee S-Bahn station for trains to Berlin or Potsdam. This is not the only excursion which may be taken by boat. As Potsdam is virtually surrounded by water other interesting destinations may be visited including Caputh, with a summer house once owned by Albert Einstein; Geltow, with a summer villa designed by Van de Velde; Petzow with a further palace designed by Schinkel, and Sacrow with the Heiland Church. Boats leave from the Lange Brücke in Potsdam. Contact Tourist Information for details (tel. 21527). In addition, several travel companies run coach-boat trips from opposite the Gedachtniskirche on the Kurfurstendamm to Potsdam and the surrounding area. These include Berliner Baren Stadtrundfahrt (BBS, tel. 213 40 77), Berolina (tel. 882 20 91) and Bus-Verhehr Berlin (BVB, tel. 885 98 80); prices average around 50DM.

10

The Spreewald: from Berlin to Cottbus

Berlin to—50km Lübben—8km Lübbenau—35km Cottbus.

The largest but most sparsely populated region in eastern Germany is the SPREEWALD. An area of great natural beauty preserved by UNESCO as a Biosphärenreservat (Biosphere Reserve), the Spreewald is only some 50km south-east of Berlin and easily accessible by motorway. Take the E36 south from the Berliner Ring. After c 50km take the A87 heading east for 8km to reach Lübben, centre of the Spreewald. Trains run regularly to Lübben from Berlin-Lichtenberg with a journey time of just over one hour. Although so close to Berlin, the waterborne way of life of the Sorbs (Slavs) in their time-warp village has been preserved and this is best observed by boat. As an alternative to driving or taking the train, several Berlin based companies run one-day coach and bus tours to the area, costing around 55DM (see end of Route 9, Palaces on the Havel, for details of the companies). The tour ends at Cottbus, the second largest town in Brandenburg, which boasts an immaculate Jugendstil theatre.

The **Spreewald** is a labyrinth of tributaries of the River Spree and myriad lakes formed by glacial deposits at the end of the Ice Age. The Lower Spreewald, north of Lübben, was originally covered entirely by woods, but from the Middle Ages onwards settlers survived on fishing and slowly began to clear the forest, turning it into a vast water meadow. With better drainage systems, market gardening began to provide a source of income, supplying the burgeoning city of Berlin. No roads were built as the people moved about by means of wooden flat-bottomed punts and even today this is the most practical means of transport. The original settlers were mainly Slavs (Sorbs), who moved into a much greater area in 6C, but were gradually driven east form the 10C onwards. They still predominate in the region, despite persecution under the Nazis, and have retained their language (Wendish), Sorbish culture and indigenous folk costumes. Since 1945 they have been recognised as a national minority and their language is now taught in schools.

In the 18C the area was recognised as being one of outstanding beauty and, from the late 19C, tourism began as artists and the intelligentsia from Berlin were attracted to the area by its tranquil scenery and simple lifestyle. Tourism has developed so that now there are tremendous crowds in high season, yet the woods remain the habitat of many rare birds.

A. Lübben

14,300 inhabitants.

Tourist Information Office: Fremdenverkehrsverein, on the first floor of 14 Lindenstrasse, 15907 Lübben. Tel. 0 35 46-24 33/30 90.

Lübben is situated on a sandy hill at a fork in the River Spree, right in the centre of the Spreewald, between the leafy Unterspreewald to the north and the picturesque Oberspreewald to the south, so makes an excellent base for exploration. Boat tours of the Spreewald start from the harbour here.

History. The town began as a Slav fishing village in 6C, when the Sorbs, one of the Wendish tribes of Slavs, began to settle here. At the turn of 11C they were forcibly Christianised, although they retained their language and way of life. The town received its first documentary mention in 1150. The Schloss was built as an island fortress and during the Middle Ages it guarded the crossing point of several important trade routes including that from Leipzig to Frankfurt on the Oder. This strategic position had severe disadvantages for the town: Lübben was often affected by political struggles, fell prey to Wallenstein's troops during the Thirty Years War and was destroyed again by the French during the Napoleonic Wars. In the 17C and 18C about 500 weavers worked in the town and there is still a flourishing textile industry today. Lübben was seat of the Saxon rulers of the Niederlausitz (the south-east of the March of Brandenburg) and from time to time residence town of the Elector of Saxony until 1815, when Lübben became part of Prussia. At the very end of the Second World War 80 per cent of the old town was destroyed in a desperate, last-ditch defence. The best-known visitor in recent times in Raisa Gorbachov, who visited the president of Lübben's Lions Club in 1991.

If you wish to explore the Spreewald by boat, head directly to the mooring places at the harbour to take a seat for a punt-ride (Kahnfahrt) along the channels of the Spreewald. It may be best to telephone the Tourist Information Office in advance about reservations to avoid disappointment. While you are waiting, enjoy a Kaffee und Kuchen overlooking the water at the Strandcafé. A short boat ride lasts around two hours and a four-hour trip will include an hour's stop for refreshment. Full day trips are also available and to travel independently you can hire a canoe or a bicycle.

If you have time to spare in Lübben some interesting sights can be seen on foot. If you start from the railway station , straight opposite is a path that leads through a leafy quarter with turn-of-the-century villas into the heart of a 200-acre wood, the Hain. Beside the path a sign commemorates the spot where a statue of the oak-tree goddess, Liuba, stood until the mid 19C. Liuba was the Slav goddess of love and fear as is well illustrated in the myth of the Sorb princess who begged Liuba to re-unite her with her betrothed, promising her best diadem in return. On the way home her golden coach, together with the princess, sank into a bottomless morass. At the same time an arrow hit her lover on the battlefield, so they were re-united by Liuba—in death.

Alternatively, begin at the Tourist Information Office, and, turning right, cross the car park, and go along a path and over the bridge by the River Spree and harbour. Continue to the ochre-coloured **Schloss**, built in 1684 on the site of an earlier castle, with interesting Renaissance gable (1679–82) on the east side and stucco work round the windows.

To enjoy the faded glory of the main façade, make your way round to the garden overlooking the river. The splendid main portal, watched over by a

Bohemian lion, is on the town side. The Schloss is linked by an overhead passageway to the oldest section of the castle, the solid square 12C **Wehrturm** (Defence Tower). It is well worth a visit for the spectacular painted Wappensaal (Chamber of Coats of Arms) on the second floor, which is not to be missed if you are interested in the history of the Niederlausitz. In medieval times the Stände—the local aristocracy and patricians—came here to pay homage to the ruling prince of the area. At that time the chamber was smaller; it was extended in 1784 with the addition of an extra storey. Round the chamber are three alcoves, for the different degrees of nobility: two steps up to the prince's platform, one step for a Graf (Count) and no steps for the remainder.

After the Congress of Vienna, when the Niederlausitz passed from Saxony to Brandenburg the Wappensaal was neglected until it was decided to paint the room for the celebrations to mark the centenary of Brandenburg rule. 116 colourful coats of arms are shown—all for the Standesherren (noblemen) of Niederlausitz. The red bull on the silver ground is the arms of Niederlausitz, an area that has moved in and out of Saxony and Brandenburg, but whose aristocratic families have always remained close to the centre of politics. The Lynar family, from the Schloss in Lübbenau, were active in the plot against Hitler of 20 July 1941 and, in recognition, their Schloss was returned to them after the *Wende*. In 1945 the tower was badly damaged and only part of the town wall escaped destruction. The chandelier is Bohemian. Round the edge of the ceiling runs a border of the lion's head of Bohemia. Keep looking up and you will see symbols of the bounty of the Spreewald: onions and corn, fruit, vegetables, fish and flax (the blue linen apron is a hallmark of the Spreewalders). Returning down the stairs from the chamber notice the carved stone female heads, each with a different *Haube* (headdress) to indicate her village of origin. On the floor below, a very romantic Registry Office has a vaulted ceiling painted with an intertwining Slav pattern. The deep windows are set in walls 2.5m thick.

Continue to the **Paul Gerhard Kirche**; the name was changed from Nikolaikirche in 1930 to honour the well-known Lutheran hymn-writer, Paul Gerhard. Archdeacon here for many years (1669–76), he had been forced to leave Berlin following a theological dispute and is buried in front of the altar. In front of the church is a statue of him erected in 1907 to commemorate the 300th anniversary of his birth. The church is a late Gothic brick hall church with nave and two aisles, built between 1494 and 1550. The interior furnishings are late Renaissance. The stained glass windows echo the hymns by Paul Gerhardt. The church is constructed at a level significantly lower than the main street. During the Thirty Years War Wallenstein's troops destroyed the town as did Napoleon's over a century later. After each disaster the citizens rebuilt the roads and ruined buildings on top of the rubble, thus raising the level and the main street became known as the Hohestrasse, literally high street. Cross the main square diagonally to the only remaining part of the late 15C brick town wall. A round tower and a Wiekhaus (Watch House) overlooking the River Spree remain.

Turn left and walk along the side of the Spree until you come to the wide Breitstasse on the right. This was built as a boulevard in the 19C when Lübben had ambitions to become a spa. At the end is a Postmeilensäule (milestone) from 1735 that gives the distance for post coach journeys in hours rather than miles—Berlin being 12 hours away. Beyond the Breitstrasse stretches the Hain, ancient woodland worshipped by the Sorbs and much treasured by the locals. Turn left at the end of Breitstrasse to take a short cut through the modern housing estate to return to the Tourist Information Office.

From Lübben take the B115 south for c 8km to reach the smaller neighbouring town of Lübbenau.

B. Lübbenau

23,000 inhabitants.

Tourist Information Office: Fremdenverkehrsamt, Ehm-Welk-Strasse 15, 03222 Lübbenau. Tel. 22 63.

Only metres to the south-west of the town is a devastated moonscape of brown coal open cast mining, but **Lübbenau** itself lies right on the edge of one of the loveliest and most rural parts of the Oberer Spreewald with its picturesque villages. Trains run every couple of hours from Berlin-Lichtenberg to Lübben and on to Lübbenau.

History. Lübbenau grew up round the base of a Slav stronghold, was then colonised by German settlers, ans was first documented as Castrum Lubbenowe in 1301. The town prospered modestly by brewing beer, weaving linen and processing the vegetables grown in the Spreewald. With the rail link to Berlin in 19C tourism began to flourish. In the late 1950s prosperity came with the industrialisation linked to the GDR energy policy of open-cast mining and the concomitant power stations.

The heart of Lübbenau's Altstadt is the triangular market place. At the east end is the **Stadtkirche St Nikolai**, built between 1738 and 1741, spacious and galleried inside. The Baroque furnishings which adorn the interior are impressive, the most important aspect being the tombstone of M.C. Lynar (d 1768), created by Gottfried Knöffler from Dresden.

The **Schloss**, home of the Courts of Lynar until 1945, stands on the site of an earlier island-fortress. In 1600 it was altered to a Renaissance style building and in 1817–20 a Neo-Classical façade, designed by Karl Benjamin Siegel from Leipzig, was added. The substantial Schlosspark was laid out in 1820 in the fashionable, English landscape style. Exhibitions are held in the Orangery (1820) and the nearby Baroque former Court of Justice. Built in 1745–48 it now houses the **Spreewaldmuseum** (opening times: May–Oct, Tues–Sun 09.00–17.00) with a colourful collection of traditional costumes and displays on the last 300 years of local history, explaining the unique evolution of the Spreewald. The section devoted to transport in the Spreewald includes the narrow-gauge train which ran between Cottbus and Lübbenau from 1899 to 1970.

The bridge to the west of the market place leads to the local **Kahnfährhafen** (Punt Harbour), where punts for tourists have been available for hire since 1908. From here it is a pleasant half hour's walk (1.5m) along the banks of the River Spree to the entrancing village of Lehde and the **Spreewald-Freilandmuseum** (Spreewald Open-Air Museum).

Lehde is regarded as the Venice of the Spreewald. Theodor Fontane wrote: 'One cannot imagine anything sweeter that Lehde, that is made up of as many islands as houses…it is a rural Venice in a pocket-sized edition'. (*Journeys through the March of Brandenburg*, 1882.) Charming indeed, it was first discovered by artists at the turn-of-the-century and ever since been a popular day's excursion from Berlin. The village is now under a conservation order. The rustic log houses, which date from the 18C to the 20C, were built of timber for economy and convenience. Lehde has been linked to the mainland since 1926, but some outlying farms still have no access to a road. The Freilandmuseum has a fascinating collection of reconstructed houses from all over Spreewald, many with original furnishings, to give an idea of the Sorb way of life.

A good 3km walk or cycle ride further on east from the Freilandmuseum, to the south of the River Spree, along a foot and cycle path shaded by birch trees, is Leipe, another village typical of the Spreewald. The track continues to the village of **Burg** (c 8km), with its log houses, painted white and thatched. The Dorfkirche (1799–1804) is an early Classical building. The remains of a Bronze Age fortress lie beneath the Schlossberg.

From Lübbenau continue south-east on the B115 through Vetschau and Kilkwitz for 35km to reach Cottbus. Trains run from Lübbenau to Cottbus whilst the journey from Berlin direct takes 1 hour 45 minutes.

C.   Cottbus

123,000 inhabitants.

Tourist Information: Berliner Strasse 1a, 03046 Cottbus. Tel. 0355/24254. Opening times: Mon–Fri, 09.00–12.00 and 14.00–17.00.

Cottbus was once a small provincial town, as can be seen from 18C houses round the modest town square, but it is now the second largest town in Brandenburg. The rare Jugendstil theatre is quite striking, the well-run Apothecary's Museum also of interest and the delightful landscaped gardens of Schloss Branitz to the south-east of the town should not be missed.

History. A stronghold guarding the crossing of the River Spree was the base for a first Slav settlement. Slavs made up the bulk of the Cottbus population in the early years of the town, which has remained bilingual with a high proportion of Sorbs. The town was first mentioned in 1156 as the Castle of Chotibuz, which defended the crossing of the River Spree at the intersection of two important long distance trade routes. A market settlement quickly grew up, was granted a town charter in 1226 and prospered, thanks to the favourable position; by 13C the town had expanded with the influx of German settlers. The main trade route was the Salzstrasse (Salt Way) from Halle through to Frankfurt on the Oder and further east. Linen and wool, from local flax and sheep, were produced in Cottbus and made up part of the load for the traders returning towards Halle.

Several severe fires burnt almost the entire stock of medieval houses and in September 1600, 477 houses were lost, and only nine saved; in 1671, 333 houses were lost (the one street that was saved—Klosterstrasse—was lost to modern development in the GDR period). Eventually the Elector of Brandenburg decreed that roofs should in future be tiled rather than thatched. With the additional hardships of the Thirty Years War, the town suffered badly during the 17C. However, after the Revocation of the Edict of Nantes in 1685 some 200,000 Huguenots left France for fear of religious persecution; Brandenburg-Prussia, recovering from the devastation of the Thirty Years War, was one of the countries to welcome them. By 29 October 1685 Elector Fredrick William passed the Edict of Potsdam offering Brandenburg-Prussia as a haven of religious freedom. In 1701 sixty Huguenots from 13 families arrived in Cottbus. They brought with them silk worms to set up a silk industry, tobacco plants and expertise in stocking-making and tanning and the town began to prosper once more.

The cloth industry expanded to reach its zenith in the 1930s with a total of 57 cloth factories. After the Second World War the Russians dismantled the machinery and for the next 45 years, until unification, industry was based on brown coal, reputed to have the lowest sulphur content of Europe. During the expansion of the open-cast mines, 128 villages, with a total population of 21,000 have been removed and relocated to make way for the mining. The result is an ugly moonscape. Since the *Wende* attempts have been made to reduce the reliance on brown coal and environmental improvement schemes have begun.

The Jugendstil Theatre, Cottbus

The train station is located in the south-west suburbs. To save yourself a long and arduous walk, take tram No. 1 to Stadtpromenade then proceed east down Markstrasse to reach the **Tourist Information** in the old part of the town. From the Tourist Information Office turn left, heading east, passing the Rathaus, rebuilt after World War II, and continuing alongside a covered arcade. Above the pillars are the signs of the guilds and trades important to the city, such as a spinning wheel for cloth, and the Baumkuchen cake, the local bakers' speciality. At the end of the Berliner-strasse is part of the old town wall. To the left is a half-timbered house, which was built into the main structure of the wall in the 19C. During the same era a passage was broken through the wall, known as **Lindenpforte** (Lime Tree Gate) or **Judentor** (Jews' Gate) because of the synagogue nearby. The remaining section of the wall were restored in 1934 and again more recently. Through the archway turn left, following the line of the wall and noting the Socialist Realist mosaic of tiles, which celebrates the theme links between the Spreewald with the GDR energy policy. A little further along another mosaic shows Spreewalders in traditional costume displaying their wares, including fruit and vegetables from the Spreewald nursery gardens. The earth bulwarks of the medieval defence system ran along here until they were removed in the GDR time to make way for the tramlines. Cross the busy road via the pedestrian overpass and continue west along the August-Bebel-Strasse. On the right is the **Stadtmuseum** (opening times: Tue–Fri 08.30–17.00, Sat and Sun 14.00–18.00, with exhibitions of the town's history, including interesting historic photographs.

Continue to the Schillerplatz where, on the far side of the square, the splendid **Jugendstil Theatre** can be found. Designed by Bernhard Sehring in 1908 it is a successful synthesis of architecture, interior design and craft so typical of the Art Nouveau style. The exterior is decorated with geometric, classicised urns and figures carved from stone. The smooth, cream rendering highlights the undulating forms of the building with the gently protruding bays seen on three sides of the Theatre. The slender proportions of the windows and the stark constrast between dark and light are certainly reminiscent of the work of Glasgow architect, Charles Rennie Mackintosh who influenced designers in Austria and Germany at this time. The interior is more polished than those by Mackintosh, who created a handcrafted look; these gleaming white pillars, punctuated with broad bands of reflective brass and the geometric ceiling decorations point forward to Art Deco. The theatre is still used for performances today, following extensive restoration in 1986.

Turn left along the wide Karl-Liebknecht-Strasse and continue east until you come to the 31m high **Spremberger Turm** (Spremberg Tower) on your left, a bastion and town gate up to the 19C. In 1811, 10m were removed from the dilapidated top, and crenellations added by Schinkel, using brick from an old city gate. Note the wrought-iron work of the door and the crabs, the city's heraldic symbol, creeping round the keyholes. Sprembergerstrasse is a pedestrian zone which leads south from the market, and before the Second World War was an elegant shopping street. Half-way down the street on the right is the Baroque **Schlosskirche**; built between 1714 and 1717 it was originally a medieval Katharinenkapelle (1419) that burnt down in 1600. The Huguenot families who came to the town in 1701 made such a great contribution to the prosperity of Cottbus that, in appreciation, the town gave them this site for a church in their own district. The distinctive tower was added in 1870. It became known as the Schlosskirche because the vicar also preached in the Schloss. Since 1989 it has been used also as a soup kitchen.

Turn right from Sprembergerstrasse into Mühlenstrasse and on the left are modern decorative tiles depicting local trades. Continue east along Mühlenstrasse to Am Spree Ufer. The large building on the left, at the bottom of a steep slope, is the former Stasi prison, which was notorious, together with Bauzen, as the worst in GDR. Over a small bridge is Am Amsteich, where the old half-timbered houses were used by tanners, with a store below and open balconies above for drying the leather.

Return to Am Spree Ufer, then turn left into Goethestrasse, making your way round the Schlossberg, where legend has it that Henry I, en route to his campaign in Poland, ordered a fortress to be built in AD 930. Turn left into Sandowerstrasse, where you will see ahead of you another section of the city wall. Just in front of the wall is the stylish **Tuchmacherbrunnen** (Cloth Makers' Fountain) donated by the Cloth Makers' Guild in the 1930s. Round the sides, reliefs show the various stages of cloth making from sheep's wool through spinning and weaving. Just within the wall is the oldest part of town, with a weekly market.

Continue west down Sandowerstrasse, and ahead is the end of the Oberkirche. Opposite the church is an ochre and brown house, the Lierschaus, where the Prince of Pückler's personal physician lived. According to the Prince's wishes his heart, liver and lungs were removed and buried in the Wasserpyramid in the park at Schloss Branitz. The rest of Pücklers body was pickled by the physician.

The **Oberkirche** or **Nikolaikirche** is the largest in the Niederlausitz, and is a brick Gothic hall and church with nave and two aisles. The main body of the building is 13C, but the west tower with its elegant tracery of four storeys of blind windows is 15C. The great height of the nave is impressive; before the Reformation there were 41 altars in the church, giving a measure of its importance. It has suffered severe damage three times: in 1468 by lightning; in 1600 by fire; and in 1945 through war. The altar (1661) by Andreas Schultze, was walled around during the war and has survived in all its Baroque splendour. In 1988 the tower was reconstructed, and in the porch can be seen a reconstructed model of the Baroque steeple.

From the Nikolaikirche continue south-west to the ALTMARKT, where the fountain shows women selling vegetables and Baumkuchen from Spreewald, with the history of the town round the base. There is also a green-painted Weinstube with shuttered windows and an ancient Apotheke, now a fascinating and clearly laid-out **Apothecary's Museum** where the smell of the herbs and potions pervades the vaulted rooms. The future of the museum is uncertain following unification. At the end of the Altmark continue for a few metres to reach the Tourist Information Office on the left. If time permits turn right from the Altmarkt into Wendenstrasse and then north into Klosterstrasse you are now on the edge of the **Wendisches Viertel** (Sorbs' Quarter). Diagonally opposite is the 13C Franciskanerkirche, also called the Klosterkirche (it is likely to be closed—check with the Tourist Information Office), that has been very well restored by Polish workers. On some feast days a Sorb service is held. The street level is 1m higher than the interior of the church because of the accumulated rubble from the fires over the years. Several pews have stories from the Bible in German and Wendish painted on the back. Behind the church is an attractive old square, the Klosterplatz. The building with an overhanging upper storey is now a Youth Hostel.

On the south-east perimeter of Cottbus some 4km from the centre lie the lovely landscaped gardens of **Schloss Branitz**. The Schloss and Park can be reached from the Cottbus orbital road, the Stadtring, or by means of a narrow-gauge steam railway from Bahnhof Freundschaft, alighting at Bahnhof Zoo.

The park was designed by the flamboyant Prince Hermann von Pückler-Muskau (1785–1871) who completely transformed the flat terrain with artificial lakes and streams and planted fully grown native trees (30 or more years old) using labourers from the local prison during 1846–71. Soil from the excavation was heaped into the famous grass pyramids (a legacy of Pückler's travels to the Orient). The Wasserpyramide, set in its own lake, was destined to be the burial place for Pückler and his wife, Countess Lucie von Pappenheim. Schloss Branitz, now the **Fürst-Pückler-Museum** (opening times: Nov–Mar, Tues–Sun 10.00–17.00; Apr–Oct, Tues–Sun 10.00–18.00) was built in 1772 in a restrained Baroque style and is engulfed in scaffolding for restoration at the time of writing. Gottfried Semper added the terrace and pergola on the east side of the house in 1850. The interior was richly decorated by Pückler at the same time and can be seen almost unchanged since his day, with many of his acquisitions from the Middle East. A display devoted to the history of Cottbus may also be found here.

From Cottbus return to Berlin by means of the E36 motorway.

11

From Berlin to Eberswalde and Chorin

Berlin—30km Eberswalde—8km the Monastery of Chorin.

A. Eberswalde

52,000 inhabitants with Finow.

Tourist Information Office: Pavillion am Markt, 16225 Eberswalde. Tel. 03334 23168.

From Berlin take the Berliner Ring, leaving on the Parkow junction onto the A114. Take the A2 east and connect with the E28 to Finow. Eberswalde is 6km to the east on the A167. A regular train service operates from Berlin.

Hugging the tree-lined banks of the river Finow, **Eberswalde** was a thriving industrial centre as far back as the 16C when the first copper and paper mills were founded used water power. Highest quality writing paper—including the British Monarch's personal watermark—is still made here to a technique introduced by the Dutch under Frederick II. Succeeding generations have built settlements in a ribbon development along the river banks so there is no conventional town centre. Badly damaged during the Second World War, few of the old buldings remain and tourists tend to stay here as a base for visiting the nearby Abbey of Chorin.

The tour starts at the Tourist Information Office in the centre of the leafy main square and market place. Walk south up a slope to the most important sight in the town, the **Pfarrkirche St Maria Magdalene** (Parish Church of St Mary Magdalene). The church is a High Gothic brick basilica, begun c 1240 on the site of an earlier church and finished in 1307. It was found during the rule of the Askanian Margraves of Brandenburg and appears disproportionately large for the size of the town, so may have been a court chapel as Albrecht III had a castle nearby. The church was damaged by a great town fire in 1499 and the rebuilding of 1501 to 1503 was clearly influenced by the architecture of the Monastery of Chorin. For instance, the apse is an unusual shape being a 7/12 polygon (ie seven sides out of a 12-sided circle). The church was again much altered 1874–76, both internally and externally, with the addition of splendid cross-ribbed vaulting.

The church is famous for the squat, *terracotta figures depicting scenes from the Old and New Testaments that decorate the main west portal and the north entrance. They are amongst the most interesting of their kind to be found in brick Gothic churches, with their naive forms and dramatic gestures. Although eroded by wind and rain many can still be clearly identified: Mary holds the Christ child in her arms; an angel with sweeping wings aloft; on the west portal Abraham is about to sacrifice Isaac; on the north portal is the parable of Wise and Foolish Virgins.

The interior and furnishings are in Gothic Revival style dating from the 1870s, apart from the 13C bronze FONT which was donated by Margrave Johann II—note that in place of the usual biblical scenes there are twelve coats of arms representing the Askanier family. Fonts were often made from cast metal in medieval north Germany as stone was scarce locally. The size of the basin indicates that baptism by total immersion was still the practice. The large RETABLE (1606), with as many tiers as a wedding cake, is in the transitional style between Renaissance and Baroque. The central scene is of the Crucifixion, below it the Last Supper and above it the Resurrection, then a triangular gable with a face of the sun, symbol of the Holy Trinity. Higher still is the Ascension. The altarpiece is crowned by Christ on his throne, above the globe, with sword and scales in hand to judge the quick and the dead.

Leaving the church and with your back to the west entrance walk straight ahead to the Neo-Classical former town school building built in 1830 which is now the **Heimatmuseum** (opening times: Tues–Fri 08.00–12.00 and 14.00–17.00, Sun 14.00 17.00). The star of the show is a case containing Bronze Age gold vessels, copies of part of the greatest treasure trove in Germany, discovered in 1913 and now believed to be in Moscow. Well displayed collections concentrate on the town and regional history showing the stages of industrialisation. On the grassy bank outside the museum sits a powerful Amazon astride a bronze horse dating from 1909 and created by Franz von Stuck. The statue once adorned the garden of Goehring's Villa Catrinhall, on Grosser Döllnsee, a traditional Hallenhaus. Not far away stands the large cracked bronze church bell known as Barbara. It was crafted in 1518 by the Lübeck bell-founder Heinrich von Kempen.

Walking back round the church, diagonally opposite the east end is a half-timbered building, on the corner of Salomon-Goldschmidt Strasse, a former tobacco warehouse. In the late 17C the influx of Huguenots brought with them many skills including the cultivation of tobacco plants. Continue downhill to the flat market place (Tue and Fri are market days), where the oldest building of interest is the **Löwenapotheke**; built in 1703 with the present façade added in 1836, it still operates as a chemist's. It takes its name from the cast-iron lion *couchant* statue on the fountain opposite. This lion, by Christian Daniel Rauch, dates from 1836 and replaces earlier versions (1729 and 1736).

Eberswalde has always suffered from problems of subsidence due to the sandy soil, and the old Rathaus has collapsed. The new Rathaus was built in 1905–07 in Renaissance Revival style. To the left is the **Alte Rathaus**, built as a dwelling in 1775—note the town coat of arms over the door, added in

1866. Cross the road to An der Friedensbrücke. At the corner of Stein-strasse, is the half-timbered **Adlerapotheke**, the oldest house in the town, now undergoing extensive restoration. It was built as a Junkerhaus in 1663, just outside the old town wall. Later it became an apothecary, with a wooden gallery that overlooks the court. Rococo paintings on the ceiling inside are being restored.

Now cross the main road and head east to Bollwerk Strasse. To the south there are gaps left by war damage and desolate disused textile factories. More pleasant is the view to the north. Cross the Semmelbrücke to the canal basin (known as the Stadt-Schleuse) of the **Finow canal** with its historic locks. In the summer, steamer trips (3 to 4 hours) will take you to join the Hohenzollern canal and then to the Niederfinow ships' lift. The Finow canal flows the length of the town and links the rivers Havel and Oder. Using the natural course of the Finow the first stage began in 1605–20 with 11 locks built between Liebenwalde and Eberswalde and the canal covering nearly 40km in length. Work continued in stages during the 18C. The Finow canal encouraged an industrial ribbon development along its banks. By 1911 the canal was carrying so much ship traffic that another solution had to be found—the Oder-Havel canal, which lies 2km north of the town. This is perhaps a good place to end the tour, but there is more to see if you have time.

Keep straight on down Ammonstrasse and across to Friedrich Ebertstrasse. Turn left and then right to Schicklerstrasse where you will see the **Alte Forstakademie**, the former School of Forestry, with the eagle of Brandenburg above the door. This is now a Technical College for Forestry. The area opposite was once two swampy lakes, filled in to make one of Eberswalde's many parks. A pleasant half-hour's walk west from here would bring you to the **Forstbotanischer Garten** (Arboritum) and further still to the **Tierpark** (Zoo). For a diversion before relaxing in the park, continue a short way down Schicklerstrasse to take a look at the small single storey houses built for immigrant workers, the knife- and scissor-smiths who came from Ruhla and Schmal-kalden at the instigation of Frederick II.

B.   The Monastery of Chorin

Leave Eberswalde to the north, by the B2 towards Chorin which is sign-posted Angermünde. About 1km along the road is the **St Georgs Kapelle**. It was built in the 14C in the tradition of hospices dedicated to St George, patron saint of the sick. The chapels were usually sited outside the town walls for fear of infection. The main hospice buildings were razed during the Thirty Years War, and all that remains is this small brick Gothic chapel, first mentioned in 1359, with a slender tower inset to the west and three sided apse to the east. It makes an enchanting setting for Liederabende, chamber music and the chilly candlelit concerts held at Christmas. Con-tinue on the B2 about 7km north towards Angermünde, just after the village of Sandkrug the stately ruins of the monastery of Chorin come into view, glowing red against the surrounding forest.

There are also good train connections from Berlin, on the Stralsund line; alighting at Bahnhof Chorin, it is then half an hour's walk to the monastery. Buses go from Eberswalde and in the summer months there are day excursions from Berlin; check locally with tourist information. From June to August concerts are held during the '*Choriner Musiksommer*'. Tickets and information may be obtained from Geschäftsstelle 'Choriner Musik-sommer', Alfred-Moeller-Strasse 1, 16225 Eberswalde (tel. 03 73 71 or 03334 65416, open Mon–Fri 10.00–13.00); and in Berlin from Theaterkasse Zehlendorf, Teltower Damm 22, 14169 Berlin 37 (tel. 030 801 1652, open Mon–Fri).

The **••Abbey Church** and **Monastery Buildings of Chorin** are a top tourist attraction in Brandenburg, helped by its easy access from Berlin (opening times: daily April–Oct 09.00–18.00; Nov–March 09.00–16.00). A magical time to visit the abbey in its isolated silvan setting is on a winter's afternoon with snow blowing through the clerestory windows of the deserted church.

History. Chorin was founded following the expansion of the Cistercian order by St Bernhard. The Cistercians followed the central Benedictine tenet of *ora et labora* (prayer and work) and lived from the work of their hands, isolated from the world. One of the monks' tasks was to found new monasteries or daughter-houses through a well-organised system of affiliation. This coincided with the great landowners' desire to make pious bequests and endowments—often motivated by a wish to reduce their term in Purgatory as well as by a desire to see their lands brought under cultivation, for the Cistercians were the best agronomists of the Middle Ages. Personal poverty was one of the bases of their rule, but this did not preclude owning land and stock. Combined with the ideal of hard work, this meant that soon orchards blossomed and vineyards flourished around Chorin and vast acres were cultivated for the growing of crops. The monks were helped in their manual labour by lay-brothers or *conversi* (Konversen), men from the peasant classes glad to find work in these undeveloped lands.

By the time Chorin was founded in 1258 the frontiers of Christian colonisation of Germany had moved even further eastwards. The first Cistercian monastery in the March of Brandenburg was Lehnin, founded in 1183 by the Margrave Otto I. When the Askanian Margraves of Brandenburg had secured their position in the centre of the province they moved further north-east. The brothers Otto III and Johann I, joint Margraves, divided the Askanian lands in 1258 and in the same year the monastery of Mariensee-Chorin was built on the island of Pehlitzwerder in Parstoinsee, where ruins can still be seen. In September 1273 it was moved to its present site at Chorin. The construction of this monastery took 60 years, and it was intended as a mausoleum for the Askanian line, but the last of them was long since dead by the time building was finished (the line died out in 1319), although Waldemar, the last Askanian Margrave and six members of his family were buried in the monastery church (efforts to locate his grave have been in vain). Chorin had, however, been well endowed by the Askanians. When the house of Hohenzollern took the reins of Brandenburg in 1412 Chorin possessed nearly 3000 acres of land, 23 lakes and 11 mills.

Chorin had no daughter houses, for by the time it was finished the greatest days of the Cistercians in Brandenburg were over. In 1542 the monastery was secularised and the estates became crown land, with the estate offices in the former conventual buildings. Any older monks who remained received a pension from the Margrave. During the Thirty Years War Chorin was plundered but not damaged. In 1654 the Abbey was transferred to the Forestry Commission and although evangelical services were held up to 1662 the monastery was neglected and fell into disrepair. Parts of the buildings were treated as a brick quarry, particularly the missing chapels on the transepts and those remaining used to house cattle.

Karl Friedrich Schinkel recognised the architectural value of the ruins in 1810, driven by his romantic admiration of medieval German culture. By 1828 he had persuaded the King of Prussia to intervene and restore the building. Work began to save the historic ruin and has continued spasmodically ever since. Fortunately repairs were carried out sympathetically, following the lines of the original building, and Chorin has escaped the substantial changes suffered by Lehnin in the late 19C. Since re-unification much work has been carried out and the ruins are beginning to look quite spruce.

The abbey and its buildings were constructed from red brick with granite used for the base of the church, to create an impermeable layer between the porous brick and rain splashing back from the earth. Today the granite base is not always visible as the level has sunk in places. Parts of the outbuildings are also granite. Brick was chosen as it could be produced locally as opposed to the more expensive dressed stone. Clay, sand and water were there in abundance and the monks themselves provided the workforce. The clay was overwintered in pits, then in spring 'kneaded' with shovels and feet, then mixed with sand as necessary and water in a proportion of two parts clay to one part water. The material was then thrown by hand into wooden box moulds. The brick was turned out and smoothed by hand, often leaving finger prints, and fired. A skilled worker could produce 500 to 600 bricks per day. In addition to the standard bricks others of special shapes were produced for decorative effects. Note also at Chorin that the colours of the bricks vary considerably, according to the mineral content of the clay used. This has been helpful in dating the various building stages. The glowing red part of the building is the oldest, including the east end of the church to the fourth bay of the nave; the pinkish part includes the west section of the church, the Fürstensaal.

From the road walk round the east end of the church, along the north side and past the magnificent west façade to the entrance. This towering façade was the last part of the monastery to be built with incredibly ornate brickwork. The ensemble of church and monastic quarters gives an accurate impression of the layout of a medieval monastery. The Klosterkirche straight ahead is in pure early Gothic style and opens out to the cloisters to the east. This makes a perfect setting for the summer concerts.

From Chorin return to Eberswalde and follow the A167 west for 8km to reach Finow, linked as Eberswalde-Finow until 1993. Join the E28 to return to Berlin. Alternatively, the surrounding Biosphere Reserve could be explored as well as the early 20C Ship's Lift at Niederfinow.

Just past the main junction with the E28 take the B198 heading north to Eichhorst. A wooden sign with a stylised black owl marks the boundary of the **Biosphärenreservat Schorfheide-Chorin** (Biosphere Reserve Schorfheide-Chorin), which covers a triangular shaped area of lakes, forest and farmland of some 1292 sq km and is the second largest protected area in Germany. It stretches from Warnitz in the north almost to Bad Freienwalde in the south, east to Angermünde and west virtually to Templin. The aim is to maintain the delicate balance between an ecologically sensitive land use by agriculture and forest, the massive numbers of tourists who descend each summer and the conservation of threatened species and their habitats.

The northern part of the reserve was frontier territory for the Margraves of Brandenburg, first the Askanians and then Hohenzollerns. Hunting was their passion and has continued to be the sport of the rulers of Brandenburg through the centuries, even during the Third Reich and again with the leaders of the GDR. The best way to enjoy the reserve is on foot along the many well-marked paths following a map obtainable from the Tourist Information Office at Eberswalde.

Driving north on the B198 you approach the middle of the Schorfheide and the clear, deep waters of the romantic Werbellinsee which is 50m deep and 11.5km long. This tranquil lake can be glimpsed through the trees as the road winds along to the shore. Further north to the left a narrow road leads through a dense beech forest to the **Schloss Hubertusstock**. Named after St Hubert, the patron saint of hunting, the chalet was originally built as a hunting lodge for the Askanian ruling family in 1250. It was rebuilt in 1850 in its present form and has been used by German leaders including Hermann Göring and Erich Honecker. It is currently an hotel, open to the public for stylish refreshments.

Continue south on the minor road towards Britz. Once out of the woods the road is lined with sycamore trees, so typical of the many Brandenburg *Allees*. This avenue was planted originally by Frederick II with fruit trees, which were replaced by woodland species at the turn of the century. Join the B2, still heading south, and after 2km turn east towards the tiny farming community of Niederfinow and continue for another 5km to the **Niederfinow ship's lift** (signs direct you to the car park). Alternatively, take the train from Eberswalde to Niederfinow and then take a bus or walk the 2km heading north after crossing the bridge. The ship's lift is a fascinating piece of industrial history. It is a vast mechanical device built in 1927–34 to bypass a stairway of locks on the Oder-Havel-Elbe canal. The lift is wide enough to carry the broad barges, loaded with coal and gravel which arrive from Poland. It is 94m long, 27m wide and 60m high and the steel trough is raised and lowered by an electrially powered motor. The best vantage point from which to watch this amazing, ten-minute operation, is the upper canal level, reached by means of the steps on the west side of the road (allow one hour).

12

From Berlin to Frankfurt an der Oder and Neuzelle

Berlin—80km Frankfurt an der Oder—32km Monastery of Neuzelle.

From Berlin take the Berliner Ring and then the E36 towards Cottbus to connect with the E30 straight to Frankfurt an der Oder.

A.   Frankfurt an der Oder

87,500 inhabitants.

Tourist Information: Karl-Marx-Strasse 8a, 15230 Frankfurt (Oder). Tel. 32 52 16. Opening times: Mon–Fri 09.00–18.30, Sat 10.00–13.30.

Frankfurt an der Oder, situated right on the border with Poland, is a clean and airy modern town with wide tree-lined boulevards. Its medieval treasures saved from the rubble of the Second World War are worth a journey in their own right and the highest standard of music can be heard in the glorious Gothic concert hall.

History. The history of the town has always been closely linked to Frankfurt's position on the river as the best crossing point in northern Germany, just before the River Oder branches. Slav tribes already had a small trading post when German settlers from west of the Elbe appreciated the potential of a site at the intersection of long-distance trade routes. Frankfurt was founded in 1225, and quickly prospered from the heavy merchants' caravans that passed through. The River Oder connected central Europe by ship to the Baltic and the rich fishing grounds of Schonen, on the south coast of Sweden. Crossing has always been by boat or bridge. Frankfurt (Ford of the Franks) imported its name, along with the earliest German colonialists in and around Frankfurt-am-Main. In fact the river banks are steep, particularly on the west side. The early crossings were cumbersome but the system was rationalised when Margrave Johann I, who granted a civic charter in 1253, instructed the Rat to build a wooden bridge at the town's expense—this wooden bridge was south of the Friedenskirche, the oldest part of the town.

There was a tremendous surge in trade when the town obtained Niederlagsrecht (which meant that the merchants travelling through had to stop and display their wares for sale for three days) as raw materials came from the east including wood, skins, honey and copper. Finished products and luxuries were brought from the west, including cloth from Flanders and lace from Brabant. The north–south trade in salted herrings from Schonen became a lucrative near-monopoly. In return loads of grain were sent to Scandinavia, especially Norway. Artistic influences too flowed into Frankfurt. The volume of trade brought great wealth, displayed in the town's architecture, but unfortunately the entire medieval housing stock was destroyed in April 1945. Miraculously, in the centre of the rubble, the Gothic town hall and the Marien-kirche remained standing.

By 1368 Frankfurt had joined the Hanseatic League and the 14C and 15C were the heyday of the city's fortunes, reflected in architectural glories such as the south façade of the Rathaus, the ambulatory (1367) and the north chapel portal (c 1375) of the Marienkirche, and treasures like the gilt candlestick (1375) and the bronze font (1374) (now in the Gertraudenkirche). Great fairs (*Warenmesse*) were held three times a year from 1335 onwards, in spring, summer and late autumn. Industrialisation in other parts of Europe brought with it competition. While Leipzig adapted to the times and evolved its famous fair to a *Müstermesse*, where samples were shown rather than goods sold, Frankfurt did not, and soon lost ground—the final fair was held c 1885. In recent years, however, fairs have been successfully revived; this time in the format of specialist trade fairs.

In the early 16C the University of Frankfurt 'Viadrina' (1506–1811) was founded; Alexander von Humbolt is amongst the famous alumni. Frankfurt became a garrison town and administrative centre.

The overland trade routes became railway lines and until 1945 the railway industry played a significant role in the economy. In January 1945 Hitler declared the town a *Festung* (fortress) and most of the people were evacuated, so there was no-one to fight the fire that raged through the town in the final days of World War II. Within the town wall, of the 750 old dwellings, only five survived. Rebuilding began in 1951, but was hampered by a shortage of materials and funds.

Before the *Wende*, Frankfurt's main industry was making microchips for domestic appliances, with 70 per cent used for the domestic market. The 8200-strong workforce has now been cut to 800. Attempts at diversification are being made, but the unemployment level, as in many parts of eastern Germany, is very high.

The station is situated to the south of the town centre; head north up Klenkseberg and Gubenrstrasse into Karl-Marx Strasse where the **Tourist Information Office** is situated. From here turn left and continue south down Karl-Marx-Strasse (which will doubtless soon have a change of name), past the 89m high Oderturm (Oder tower), built in 1976 as a hotel with a 23rd-floor café that was very popular with the locals. It has now been bought by former west Germans for use as offices. The splendid Gothic Revival Post Office (1899–1902) further south echoes the heritage of north German brick Gothic.

Turn left into the **Gertraudengarten**; on the left is the former hospice of the Heilig Geist (Holy Spirit), originally built in the 14C. The site is now occupied by a long, low, cream and pink Neo-Classical building dating from

1787 and designed by Friedrich Knoblauch, which was recently restored. Until the *Wende* it was used as an old people's home, and it is now the Haus der Künste (House of the Arts). In the Gertraud Gardens, on the left of the path, is a memorial to Frankfurt's most famous literary figure, Heinrich von Kleist. The bronze statue dates from 1910 and was designed by Gottlieb Elster, cast by the Berlin court foundry of Martin and Pilzing and represents the soldier-poet half reclining, laurel crowned, lyre in hand. This is an idealised portrait and a small relief above the inscription is based on the only known likeness of Kleist. This is based on a miniature by August Kruger to be found in the Kleist Museum; the relief at the back of the pedestal depicts the finale of Kleist's play *The Prince of Homburg* and the side reliefs are from *Zerbrochenen Krug* and *Katchen von Heilbronn*. To the left of the path is a relief portrait of a kinsman, the poet Ewald Christian von Kleist (d. 1759); to its left is an urn with muses by Johann Gottfried Schadow as a memorial to Professor Darries.

Continue south to the **St Gertraudkirche** (opening times: summer only, open daily 10.00–12.00). The church provides an unusual contrast between the Gothic Revival exterior and the clear, light interior acting as a backcloth to the glittering treasures brought from the ruined Marienkirche. In 1368 a chapel was built on this site by the Gewandschneiderinnung (Tailors' Guild). Located outside the city walls, this was a *Gertraudenkappelle*, whose function was to care for benighted travellers to the town. In 1432 the chapel was damaged during Hussite riots. After the Reformation, in 1539, it became the parish church for the suburb of Guben. In 1631 it was destroyed by Swedish troops during the Thirty Years War and a new church was built in 1662. After the Tailors' Guild was dissolved in the mid 19C the church was enlarged and rebuilt in 1868 as a Gothic Revival basilica with balconies. The church was converted in 1980, being divided into an upper section as the church and a lower section a library and vicarage. The ceiling was put in at the former balcony height. Part of the library of the Marienkirche was stored in the crypt during the Second World War so 600 of the oldest books were saved and are now housed here, including a large Bible with a hand written frontispiece and dedication by Luther and Philip Melanchton and a 1471 edition of Thomas Aquinas, hand-copied with illuminations.

The highlights of a visit to the church, indeed to the city, are three great church furnishings, all from the Marienkirche. The towering *seven branched gilded bronze candlestick (Leuchter)* was made by an unknown master in 1376. It is 5m high and 4.20m wide. The seven candles represent the seven gifts of the spirit (Isaiah 11). The form is unusual and the decoration exceptionally rich. Four eagles of Brandenburg dangle from the undulating cross-pieces, suggesting that the piece might have been donated by the Great Elector. The fierce eagles supporting the work may well be symbols of imperial power, as a compliment to Karl IV, Holy Roman Emperor in Prague at the time. The benefactor must certainly have been extremely wealthy to afford a work of this stature. The figures on the stem depict scenes from the New Testament. The narrative ascends from the root of Jesse at the foot through the birth of Jesus attended by the Three Kings, to the Crucifixion and Descent from the Cross, with the gift of the Holy Spirit at Whitsun at the top. The Last Supper is clearly portrayed at about 2m up. There is no better example in Germany: the Leuchter to be found in Braunschweig is as large but not so complex.

In the south aisle is a High Gothic bronze *FONT (*Taufe*) dating from 1376, by Master Arnoldus. It is 4.7m high and its great size, intricate workmanship and expressive figures rank it amongst the great Gothic bronze works. Forty-four panels of reliefs show scenes from the Old and New Testament in great detail, with touches such as the fish and the knives in the Last Supper on the south side. The artist's sense of humour is apparent in the figure of the the shepherd on the hillside, who doffs his cap at the angel's appearence. At the base, the six feet represent the symbols of the four evangelists: the angel of St John (which appears three times); the lion of St Mark; the bull of St Luke and the eagle of St Matthew.

The *Marienaltar (Altarpiece of St Mary) (1489) by a master from Nürnberg, is one of the largest in north Germany. The centre-piece is a large carving of the Holy Mother and Child, flanked by two saints with Polish connections, Hedwig on the right and Adelbert on the left. The folding panels have 16 paintings of scenes from the New Testament; one of the most appealing is that of three rather clothes-conscious kings bearing sumptuous gifts. Note their Gothic shoes—similar examples may be seen in the Museum Viadrina. The altar used to belong to the Marienkirche; in 1943 it was walled in to protect it from damage, and in 1980 it was placed here. The organ (1879) is one of the earliest to be made by the Sauer factory.

Leaving the church veer right through the gardens to Gartenstrasse, which becomes Grosse Oder Strasse.

The Europa University was founded recently, to fill the gap left by the demise of the University Viadrina (1506–1811). It opened in October 1992, with many students coming from Poland and other Eastern European countries. On your left is the long university building, whose sumptuous Neo-Classical portico faces onto Scharrnstrasse, built between 1898–1903, in Neo-Baroque style with elements of Jugendstil. It is the former seat of the Royal Prussian Government of the district. Ahead of you is the polygonal choir of the east end of the Marienkirche. The bell (1426) in the churchyard is dedicated to Mary; almost opposite is a plaque on the wall to commemorate the birthplace of Heinrich von Kleist (1777–1811).

Grosse Oder Strasse widens to an open space as it reaches Bischofstrasse. Turn right towards the River Oder. You can see clearly how the river splits here, and desolate marshland stretches away on the other side. By the river bank is the large **Friedensglocke** (Bell of Peace) which was placed here in 1953. Since then it has been rung once a year on 1 September as a solemn warning against war. It was also rung in January 1993, when a chain of candles were lit as a protest against the outbreaks of racial violence. The elegant blue-and-white late Baroque building, with its ogee attic windows, is known as the **Kleisthaus**; it is the former Garrison School (1777) and was designed by the Frankfurt architect Friedrich Knoblauch. It was funded by Prince Leopold of Braunschweig, a nephew of Frederick the Great, as a school for the children of the private soldiers of the Prussian Army. It was a school for 100 years and in 1969 the **Kleist-Museum and Gedänkstätte** (opening times: Tues–Sun 10.00–17.00, Closed Mon) moved here from its small premises in the City Library. Heinrich von Kleist (1777–1811) was a Romantic writer and philosopher, active in politics at the time of the Wars of Liberation. He was a contemporary of Goethe and Schiller, although Kleist wrote for only ten years, from 1801 to his death by suicide in 1811. He is best known for his dramatic works, including *The Broken Jug* of 1811, *Prince of Homburg* and *Penthesilea*. His stories are more easily accessible to the English reader, and are written with an almost clinical objectivity.

The Marquise von O (Penguin) and *Six German Romantic Tales* (Angel) are available in paperback. The Kleist-Gedänkstätte (memorial and research institute, the equivalent of a literary museum such as Dickens' House), has a tripartite function: it organises guided tours of the museum and events for pensioners and children; houses collections of books, theatrical material, film and press clippings; and it carries out research and produces publications. The first floor museum is well worth a tour, even for those unacquainted with the oeuvre of Kleist, for the authentic furniture and room settings in this rare gem of a Baroque house. The furniture is Neo-Classical, from Kleist's time (although he never lived here) dating from c 1810–20.

Coming out of the Kleisthaus you see opposite one of the many warehouses on the river, where barges (*Kahnen*) were unloaded and goods stored. From the museum either walk straight ahead to the Rathaus (see below), or continue walking north, parallel to the river along the Faberstrasse until you come out into Carl Philip Emanuel Bach Strasse. Straight ahead is the **Viadrina Museum** (opening times: Wed–Fri and Sun 10.00–17.00). The name comes from the Roman *via Drina*, river way. The building used to be known locally as the Kurfürstichen Haus (Electors' House) and is now referred to as the Königliche Haus. When the sons of the local Junkers or the Electors of Brandenburg studied at the university they needed their own residence; it became a '*königlich*' house in 1701 when the Prussian rulers were elevated to royalty. Badly damaged in the Thirty Years War, it was rebuilt in 1675 by a Dutch master, Cornelius Ryckwaert, in Baroque style, with the addition of the section facing the river. Because the land was marshy, oak piles were used as foundations, as for many houses here. It was restored in 1986, but the traffic of 30,000 visitors affected the plaster ceilings (1680–90, by Italian masters), so at the time of writing it is under reconstruction. By autumn 1993 the whole of the ground floor should re-open with an exhibition on the town's history. Meanwhile just the hall and one room have a few exhibits, amongst which are two medieval finds: a wooden herring barrel, c 1m long, in which the herrings were transported, and a goods barrel (*Warenfass*), which is twice as large. A showcase in the main room has a fascinating display of leather shoes, c 13C–16C.

From the Museum turn right down Carl Philip Emanuel Bach Strasse, left into Oderstrasse and turning right again you will be in front of the town hall. This **Rathaus** is one of the largest and oldest and most beautiful still standing in Germany and the ornamental blind tracery of its show gable can be compared to the best church gables as part of an illustrious period of late Gothic brick architecture. It was built in 1253 as a Hall of Trade, on two storeys with a Gerichtszimmer (Court of Justice) and Ratszimmer (Council Chamber) all under one roof. In the 14C the building was extended to the south and acquired its Prunkfaçade of filigree tracery and rose windows, each 4m in diameter. The gold herring swinging from the top of the gable symbolised the virtual monopoly of Frankfurt in the herring trade and the wealth derived from this. The Y-shaped metal rods are believed to denote Frankfurt's membership of the Hanseatic League (Frankfurt was an major inland port). The coats of arms were added between the rose windows and are those of Brandenburg on the left, with the cockerel of Frankfurt on the right. The Renaissance-style west façade and the tower date from 1609. Thaddeus Paglion enlarged the former Gothic windows, added the vaulting in the large first floor chamber (*Saal*), which can be reached via the new section of the town hall, built during 1911–13, and where there is now a reasonable canteen for a quick lunch (enquire at the reception). The Galerie der Junge Kunst on ground floor of the old Rathaus, with its 17C vaulting painted white, makes a superb setting for a modern art collection from the former GDR. The Ratskeller restaurant serves good Brandenburg food in the medieval cellars including local specialities. The Rathaus was damaged during the Second World War, but the ruins were repaired for Frankfurt's 725th anniversary in 1978.

On the west side of the town hall there is a large space, used for stalls on market days. When the rubble was cleared during construction of new houses here, excavation work brought to light foundations, believed to have been those of a second building of the same dimensions as the old Rathaus, possibly another hall for trade needed during the busy years of the 15C.

Further south the **Marienkirche**, despite its ruined state, is one of the largest and most impressive churches in the March of Brandenburg. It was badly damaged by fire in April 1945 and those sections which can be salvaged are now being repaired, but areas such as the roof which were totally destroyed are being replaced with simple modern materials. The design is a brick Gothic hall church with nave and four aisles and a large double ambulatory, in the style of the Peter Parler churches of South Germany and Prague. It is 77m long and 45m wide but began as a smaller early Gothic building c 1253, and from this the columns of the nave remain—they have now been cleared of their plaster coating and the soft red of the original brick work has been exposed, as well as carved heads high up on the consoles of some of the columns. The first building must have been impressive for it aroused the envy of the Bishop of Lebus who invoked a papal edict (Bannflucht), causing a lapse in trade 1326–54. When the ban was lifted the ensuing prosperity was reflected in the enlargement of the Marienkirche by the addition in 1376 of the polygonal chapel on the north side of the transept with a hauntingly beautiful sandstone sculptured *portal influenced by the Peter Parler school of the same era as the candlestick and font in the Gertraudenkirche. In the centre is Christ giving his blessing; Mary and Child, the Three Kings and angels are below. To the left is Moses and to the right David. Above the doorway are three medallions, inserted in recognition of Kaiser Karl IV in 1373; at the top the two-headed German Reichs eagle, to the left the Bohemian lion (for the Emperor) and on the right the eagle of The March of Brandenburg. Outside these, at the same level or above, showing more than a touch of impudence, are the arms of the leading main Frankfurt patrician families. The huge empty space of the interior, almost entirely roofless, is used for concerts in the summer.

Cross the church to the sacristy, known as the **Michael Praetoriussaal**. (Michael Praetorius, 1571–1621, musician and composer, was chief organist here at the age of 15.) The Sacristy was built in 1522. In the late 1970s, when the town assumed responsibility for the church, the dividing wall in the sacristy was removed to make one large chamber. During the work the original, bright, colours were discovered, and these have been used for the rest of the decoration. They make a striking contrast to the muted red and grey of the main body of the church, and are thought to be Provençal. Nine to twelve coats of paint were stripped to reveal the original tones. Look in the vault of the central north bay where a patch of the original colours can be seen. The exterior of the church is not as harmonious as the interior; the west front in particular suffered from the loss of the south tower in 1826.

This is a good place to finish a short tour of Frankfurt as you can now turn left to return to Karl-Marx-Strasse and the Tourist Information Office is almost immediately on your right. The Konzert-Halle is well worth visiting, but check that you can get inside. You may prefer to book a seat for a concert through Tourist Information.

If you wish to extend your tour, from the north portal of the Marienkirche cross diagonally right to Grosse Scharrnstrasse, one of the main streets in medieval times. Frankfurt had narrow, dark streets before the war, and when rebuilding the city it was decided to create a city with light, leafy, wide streets instead. The brave attempt was misjudged; the blocks were too far detached from each other and the centre appeared more like a suburb. Remedial action was taken by in-filling the city centre instead of creating more satellite villages. Along Grosse Scharrnstrasse imaginative touches relieve the basic drabness; under the arcades are interesting modern murals, decorative tiles, mansards and balconies, trees, tubs of plants and pavement cafés.

Turn right into Kleine Oderstrasse, which then becomes Brücktorstrasse, and right again to reach the River Oder. From 1253 until 1895 there was a wooden bridge over the river at the end of Brücktorstrasse. The stone bridge, a little further downstream, was blown up by the Nazis in 1945, but in 1951 rebuilt on the old stone foundations. Turn left and walk along the river bank. The border with Poland runs down the middle of the river and you can walk over the bridge to Poland.

The last stop on the tour is the *Konzerthalle Carl Philipp Emanuel Bach**. On a visit to Frankfurt an der Oder do try to go to a concert in this lovely hall, converted from a Franciscan monastery church. The main part of the building is a brick Gothic hall church begun c 1270 as a monastery and completed in 1525. The later work includes the curving pattern of the Renaissance tracery on the west gable and the wonderfully decorated ceiling (1524) where the pattern of the liernes of the stellar vaulting (61m high) is picked out in rust and ochre, the original colours. In the 1970s it was restored by Polish experts.

After the Reformation it was used by the University and also served as the garrison church. The monastery buildings fell into disrepair and eventually only the church itself was left. The town then took it over in the 1960s and the church became a concert house. In 1988 the site of the former cloisters was used to provide excellent facilities for the Frankfurt Philharmonia and visiting orchestras. The City of Birmingham Symphony Orchestra played here in 1968 and a well-heeled audience from the communist hierarchy enjoyed Elgar's *Enigma Variations*. For concert-goers there is little sense of being in a church, as the audience is seated with its back to the altar, facing the sleek steel grey 1975 organ, Opus 2015 from the Sauer organ factory in Frankfurt. With its 4000 pipes and 50 registers, its tone is particularly suited to Romantic music. In the former choir, now used for chamber music, is the earliest known Sauer organ in Germany, Opus 107 (1866). The concert hall is named after Carl Philipp Emanuel Bach (1714–88), the fifth child of J.S. Bach, who studied law at Frankfurt University during 1734–38. Despite his father's wishes, he became a musician and worked for King Frederick II of Prussia.

The best view of the Konzerthalle is from the Polish side of the river and gives a clear picture of the structure of the church, with its wide hall roof and much smaller choir.

Behind the Franciskanerkirche, a little to the south, rise the twin towers of the **Friedenskirche** (Church of Peace), formerly known as the Nikolai-kirche. St Nicholas was the patron saint of merchants and sailors and this is the oldest part of town; the church itself was started between 1225 and 1235. After the Reformation the Franciscan church became the parish church and the Elector agreed that the Nikolaikirche should become a grain store. The west front and the twin towers were rebuilt in Gothic Revival style in 1881–93. It is closed for the present for restoration.

A pleasant spot to stroll is the **Lenné Park** to the south-west of the church, created in 1835–45 by Joseph Lenné as only the second burghers' park in Germany. Its site is part of the old medieval defence system. Water now flows in the former moat, shaded by carefully sited trees. At the north end of the park is a section of an ancient brick wall, a memorial to the Viadrina University of Frankfurt (1506–1811). There is an excellent example of Jugendstil architecture nearby in Am Kleistpark. Part of the street is made up of turquoise-and-red 1902 Jugendstil apartment blocks. To the left are two Gründerzeit houses, then there is a sudden return to post-war archi-tecture. The fires swept through the inner city as far as this in 1945.

B.   The Monastery of Neuzelle

Leave Frankfurt by the B112 heading south to Eisenhüttenstadt and con-tinue to Gubin, from where the 75m high slender onion-shaped dome, and the solid bulk of the Neuzelle monastery church can be seen, dominating the river plain. From the station at Neuzelle there is a good 20 minutes' walk through the small village of Neuzelle to the monastery. To a visitor accustomed to stark clear lines of north German brick Gothic, the vibrancy and colour of the High Baroque ****Monastery of Neuzelle** comes as a refreshing contrast. (Opening times: Mon, Tue, Thur 11.00–11.30, 15.00–15.30; Wed, Fri, Sat, Sun, tours at 11.00 and 14.30) The monastery is open separately, with a guided tour at 15.00. The doors are closed once the tour begins.

History. Neuzelle (*nova cella*) was the last of the great Cistercian monasteries of Mecklenburg-Pomerania and The March of Brandenburg to be secularised when, in 1817, Niederlausitz became part of Prussia. It was founded on a spur overlooking the valley of the River Oder by Margrave Heinrich of Meissen, and the church was built between 1280–1330. In the decade after the end of the Thirty Years War the monastery took on a new lease of life, to demonstrate the victory of the Catholic forces and the triumph of the Counter-Reformation in Bohemian lands. Its heyday was the 18C when it took on the aspect of a princely residence, with Orangery etc. Despite changes in the 19C, including the addition of a storey to the conventual buildings which obscured the fine north aspect of the church, Neuzelle is a large and impressive Baroque complex and unique amidst more sober architecture of north German brick Gothic.

From the main village street turn east down the drive. To your right is the Klosterteich pond where you can walk under the chestnut trees. On the left is the 400-year-old Klosterbrauerei that brews an excellent beer by tradi-tional methods. (Tours available for groups of eight or more—contact the Tourist Office, Neuzelle, tel. 0336 5216102.) The majestic entrance gate to the monastery, built in 1736, is decorated with a relief of the Supper at Emmaeus—the Risen Christ as yet unrecognised. This leads into a large courtyard. To the left is the entrance for a tour of the monastery (also a small shop and fledgling Tourist Information unit). To the right, the south side of the square is formed of a long, low set of utilitarian buildings. Straight ahead to the east is the church, originally built as a seven-bay hall church with nave and two aisles but now full-blown Baroque. The church retained its red brick exterior until 1730, when the first external elements of the transformation into Bohemian Baroque were introduced, including the clock annexe in front of the medieval tower and the figures of angels and putti above the portal.

The rounded windows, replacing the Gothic originals, were the only structural alteration to the church at this time. The most significant change came during 1736–39 when the buttresses of the, by now, plastered build-ing, were turned into Classical pilasters and the east end of the church was extended to make more space for the new high altar. The Baroque archi-tecture was completed with the addition of the hexagonal Josephkapelle, with a copper dome and high lantern, in the centre of the south side.

It was, however, in the **interior** of the church that the transformation began, under Abbot Bernhard von Schrattenbach (1641–1660) in whose coded portrait the architect is shown as one of the soldiers guarding the tomb at the scene of the Resurrection—on his shield is Abbot's coat of arms and initials. As you enter the church the sense of light and movement are overwhelming, as a vibrant whirl of stucco, gilt and frescoes surrounds you. The metamorphosis started as the columns and vaulting of the medieval building vanished behind stucco-work. Slender octagonal pillars became huge columns festooned with fruit and flowers, the capitals of those in the nave embodying the figures of the Twelve Apostles. The former vaulting was embellished with stucco to make frames for the frescoes on the ceiling. The cycle of frescoes (1654–58) are by the Italian Johannes Vanet. The central line of frescoes down the ceiling of the aisle are scenes from the life of Jesus—their typology follows an old medieval tradition and is balanced by scenes from the Old Testament: for example, the burial of Jesus, in the central third bay, corresponds to Daniel in the Lion's den in the south aisle and in the north Joseph, sunk in a well in Egypt. Both Daniel and Joseph are in mortal peril, but survive. This analogy paves the way for the Resur-rection of Christ in the next bay. Further scenes from the life of Christ are shown in the frescoes in the aisles.

The extension to the east end of the church meant that two more panels of frescoes were added in 1740 depicting musical angels praising God, and the *Decree of the Redemption* by Georg Neunherz, who was then based in Prague. Warmer, brighter colours and a looser style of painting distinguish them from the earlier works. Neunherz employs some amusing puns to sign his work in places, such as a heart with the number nine or the Nine of Hearts card.

Skilful use of perspective leads the eye to the High Altar where barley-sugar columns of red and blue-grey faux marble are mixed with a predica-tory programme of statues. Over the altar table, the focal point, is the young man at Emmaeus, who did not know Christ at the entrance to the monastery, but now recognizes the risen Lord as the bread is broken. To the sides stand Peter and Paul, Popes Clement and Gregory and the Holy warriors Florian and Georg, demonstrating the missionary, teaching and faith-defending elements of the Church. The dark picture behind is The Ascension of the Virgin Mary. High above is a choir of angels and the Holy Trinity sur-rounded by the rays of the sun. In the centre of the sun—a yellow-glazed window in the outer wall—is the dove of the Holy Spirit and, above it, God the Father and Christ.

The highly ornate altars were introduced at the base of the columns of the nave in the mid-18C, at the same time as the richly carved pulpit (1728) with statues of the four Evangelists. The cupola of Josephskapelle (1740) is painted with scenes from Joseph in Egypt and St Joseph. The restrained Neo-Classical organ, its case carved by Andreas Nerse (1806), is in contrast to the rest of the church.

Leaving the monastery church to the south-east is the Neo-Classical evangelical parish church of the Holy Cross (1728–34); however, if you wish to join in the tour of the monastery buildings, in the process of restoration, you must go there immediately after your tour of the church.

13

Prenzlau

Berlin to—68km Prenzlau.

From Berlin take the A2 and E28 north. Continue for c 50km to the Prenzlau turn-off and proceed for 14km north-west on the A198. There are efficient train links from Berlin which run via Eberswalde. Prenzlau is situated near Neubrandenburg in Mecklenburg-Vorpommern and so could be combined with a visit to this region (see Route 25).

PRENZLAU (24,000 inhabitants) boasts one of the most important brick Gothic churches, the Marienkirche, in northern Germany; the highly decorative east gable is the showpiece of the town. The town enjoys a superb setting on the banks of the wild and unspoilt Lake Uckersee. The deserted undulating landscape which surrounds Prenzlau is punctuated by clumps of rushes, birch trees and the occasional church on the horizon. Sadly, the town centre was almost totally destroyed during the Second World War, leaving only the fine churches and part of the medieval defence system intact. Prenzlau is the commercial centre for the Uckermark, the area in the north-east of the Mark of Brandenburg, which shares its eastern border with Poland.

Tourist Information: Lanser Markt 12, 17292 Prenzlau. Tel. 2791.

History. The first German merchants settled here in the 12C, near the St Nikolaikirche. They were close to a Slav fortified village, on the hill above the lake, on a site safe from floods and easily defensible. A town charter, under Pomeranian rule and Magdeburg law, was granted in 1234, when the town was laid out in a regular checkerboard pattern, which was retained when rebuilding after war damage. Another small settlement was established to the north-east of the town near to where the Jakobikirche now stands. Between these villages, a third settlement followed, on the route to the crossing point of the River Ucker by the Marienkirche. In 1250 Prenzlau came under the rule of the Askanian Margraves of Brandenburg, and at the same time the final medieval settlement was founded to the west of the main street on the shore of the lake. This became the Neustadt, and a Franciscan monastery was founded on the same site. The settlements gradually merged together and in 1287 an all-embracing city wall was built. Prenzlau was well placed for trade, at the intersection of ancient routes, and the medieval years were those of greatest prosperity for the town, as can still be seen from the splendour of the churches. Despite the strong defence system the town suffered badly during the Thirty Years War and was grateful to the Great Elector Frederick William for the transfusion of skills and enterprise that came with 150 Huguenot refugees in 1687. A garrison of Prussian soldiers enlivened a town that has remained the agricultural and administrative centre for the Uckermark. The short distance to Berlin by train and wonderful countryside make it a potential commuter town, although this is a concept new to eastern Germany.

Start outside the Tourist Information Office at the bottom of the market place, almost opposite the Marienkirche. The view from the centre of the **Langer Markt** is a celebrated townscape; looking down towards the lake is a cameo of four medieval towers—the twin towered Marienkirche, a little lower down the Mitteltorturm, and to its right the slender steeple of the Heiliggeistkirche.

The ***Marienkirche** (visits daily at 14.00, entrance via chapel on south side, otherwise enquire at the Tourist Information Office) is one of the major works of north German brick Gothic architecture and stunningly beautiful. It was burnt out when the Russians set fire to the city in 1945 and reconstruction is now under way. The houses around were bombed, so the church stands in isolation. The church was built by wealthy merchants as the Stadtkirche (Town Church) and was far larger and more impressive than a town of this standing warranted, but the merchants wanted to display not just their wealth but their power. The hall church construction was chosen as the ideal for burghers who were politically independent. Prenzlau relished its position between the rulers of Brandenburg and Pomerania and had more freedom than many towns. The main body of the church is a large hall, 56m long and 26m wide, with a nave and two aisles. Building began in 1325 and finished just 14 years later in 1340, following the demolition of most of an earlier church. Only the massive west tower remains from the first building: it is fortress-like, made of dour granite boulders that do not lend themselves to embellishment, and is in perfect harmony with a larger-than-life bronze statue (1903) of Martin Luther that stands to the west, with the inscription '*Ein fester Burg is unser gott, ein guter Wahr und Waffen*', the first line of the famous hymn 'A mighty fortress is our God'. The brick upper storeys are decorated with blind windows and topped by twin towers. Above the great west portal is an unglazed rose window. Visits to the tower, daily at 14.00, are via an open galleried way inside the church.

The monumental ***East Gable** is the highpoint of a visit to Prenzlau. Construction was difficult as the gable forms a separate skin beyond the main body of the church (as does the east gable of the Marienkirche in Neubrandenburg some 50km away). The weight is supported by the walls and buttresses of foreshortened apses at the end of the nave and aisles. The effect is of a lace veil of intricate tracery of red-and-black glazed bricks over a pale, plain wall behind. Further delicate, decorative brickwork is seen in the rows of gables interspersed by pinnacles at the top of the walls along the north and south sides of the church. The main entrance is via the 14C Christophskapelle where a photographic exhibition explains the stages of the reconstruction work. Once finished the church may be used as a museum for ecclesiastical works of art. The interior is awe-inspiring in its austerity and vast, empty space, dominated by the soft red of the twelve main pillars which measure 17m to the capitals.

Coming out of the Marienkirche turn right and walk downhill, leaving the Markt, into Marktberg, passing the **Heiligegeistkirche**, an early 14C hospice chapel on your right. Severe damage by fire in 1945 destroyed not only much of the church, but also priceless exhibits from the town museum that was housed here 1899–1945. Straight ahead is the late 15C **Mitteltorturm** (Middle Gate Tower), one of the four town gates. Originally there were also 60 defence towers, in a wall 2.6km long, 9m high and 2m thick. In between the square base and circular crenellated tower is an unusual overhanging octagonal covered parapet.

Turn left into the narrow Fischerstrasse and then right down to the edge of the lake, the Unteruckersee. Continue along the promenade, the Ucker-promenade, below the old city wall, then up a path, through an arched doorway, the Wasserpforte, and come out in a bramble-covered, devastated plot of land. Then turn right along a rough track, the Uckerwiek, beside the remains of the town wall. After 500m the **Kulturhistorisches Museum** in the Dominikanerkloster is reached (opening times: Tues–Fri 10.00–12.00, 14.00–16.00; Nov–Apr Sin 14.00–16.00; May–Oct Sat and Sun 10.00–12.00, 14.00–17.00). The Museum is situated in the well-preserved cloisters of the former Dominican monastery and specialises in the history of Prenzlau and the Uckermarkt. Ecclesiastical works of art include carved figures saved from the alterpiece of the Marienkirche dating from 1512.

To reach the Nikolaikirche, the former monastery church, turn left out of the museum and walk to the square Steinturm (Stone Gate Tower) built in the 13C on a base of granite boulders. In the 14C it was first of the gates to benefit from the addition of a decorative tower on the top, increasing its height to 28m. It was fully restored in 1962 and remarkably is used as a planetarium on Friday evenings. Turn left into Steinstrasse and left again to reach the **Nikolaikirche** on your left (opening times: tours in summer 11.00–11.30, open 14.00–16.00). According to an inscription in the choir the church was started in 1275 and consecrated in 1343. It is an early brick Gothic hall church and built as the church of the adjoining Dominican monastery. Plans are afoot to re-open the door to the cloisters which can be seen at the east end of the south aisle. Built without a tower, as befitted a monastery church, it was intended as a Predigerkirche (Preacher's Church) with acoustics designed to enhance speech as opposed to music. The space to your right was the site of the former Nikolaikirche which collapsed in 1568.

Until recently the most prized of the church furnishings were the carved figures from the Marienkirche altar. Stolen from their place in the centre of the south aisle the majority were recovered on the international art market and are now secured in the Museum. Two pieces of note which remain are the carved wooden Altar (1609) which is typical of the region, with a multitude of carved figures surrounding a central crucifix. The figures at the base of the Cross are playing the German card game of Skat instead of the more usual dice. The early 15C bronze font is another treasure of the Marienkirche, decorated with symbols of the world's evils at the base in the form of a lion, a pig and an ape.

Leaving the church turn right along Heinrich-Heine-Strasse and on your right is the former barracks, a long 18C building; continuing along here brings you back to Tourist Information.

If time permits, there are two other interesting, if derelict, medieval churches close by. To reach the Franciscan church, known as the **Dreifaltigkeitskirche** (Church of the Holy Trinity) walk north past the towers of the Marienkirche along the Strasse der Jugend. Now in a rather sad state, it was built in 1234–53 as the Franciscan monastery church of St John the Evangelist and is one of the few remaining Franciscan churches in Germany. After the Reformation it became a Lutheran church in 1598 and then, following the influx of Hugenot refugees, a French and German reformed church. The last French priest in Prenzlau retired as recently as 1936. The early Gothic construction is unusual and strikingly simple: five square vaulted bays make a long narrow rectangle with no choir or chapels.

The **Jacobkirche** is situated on the corner of Baustrasse and Dr Wilhlem-Kulz-Strasse and was built in the mid 13C as a large, village church on the site of a Slav temple. It was badly damaged in the Second World War but has since been rebuilt and much altered.

14

Brandenburg

Berlin—45km Brandenburg.

By road take the Berliner Ring to link up with the A1 heading south-west out of Berlin. By train from Berlin-Zoologischer Garten the jour-ney time is $1\frac{1}{2}$ hours; it is only 50 minutes from Potsdam.

BRANDENBURG (89,000 inhabitants) comes a pleasant surprise as its historic town centre has been comparatively untouched by war damage and the rich heritage of medieval building is of particular interest. Sur-rounded by picturesque woodland and waterways, Brandenburg has three centres: the Altstadt, the Neustadt and the Dominsel divided by the River Havel and Beetzsee. The three sites remained independent of each other until the 18C.

Tourist Information: Haupstrasse 51. Tel. 227743. Opening times: Mon–Fri 09.00–19.00, Thur 09.00–20.30, first Sat in month 10.00–16.00.

History. The history of Brandenburg is closely linked with that of the Dominsel (Cathedral Island, see below). In the 12C the town started as two settlements on either side of the River Havel. At some point during 1138 and 1150 Pribislav Heinrich, the Slav prince of the Havel tribes, invited a small group of Premonstratensian monks to settle here. They founded the Gotthardtkirche which became the nucleus of the Altstadt. The first mention of the Neustadt settlement came in 1196 with the earliest settlers attracted by the main trade axis between Magdeburg, Berlin and Kiev which traversed the town. The two settlements prospered on this basis until the 15C. Both were provincial capitals of the Mark of Brandenburg, both enjoyed a high degree of autonomy and exemption from custom duties, both had the right to mint coins and were members of the Hanseatic League. After 1412, under the rule of the House of Hohenzollern, a gradual decline set in which was hastened by the ravages of the Thirty Years War. Brandenburg was already in the shadow of Berlin and Potsdam when, in 1715, King Frederick William decreed a long-overdue formal unification of the Alt- and Neu- Stadts.

Up to the 19C the mainstay of the economy was cloth and silk manufacturing but metal working and industrialisation brought an upturn in the town's fortunes. Bicycles, prams and cars were produced by the Brennaborwerke which opened in 1871 and the Lehmann toy factory, which opened ten years later, produced mechanical toys. The emphasis changed to heavy industry in the 20C with the manufacture of arms and aeroplanes, using a workforce of 12,000 from the concentration camp which existed here during the War. Erich Honecker, later to be leader of the GDR, was interned here and nearly 10,000 mentally handicapped prisoners murdered. A memorial to the dead stands in the town. By 1945 70 per cent of factory plant was destroyed or dismantled. The 1950s heralded the growth of steel production in Brandenburg, and under the

GDR regime the town produced one third of the country's steel. The population has fallen significantly since unification, largely due to collapse of steel production and lack of employment. However, a sense of optimism pervades as reconstruction work on Brandenburg's monuments begins.

The train station lies to the south-east in the Neustadt area. Head north-east up Geschw.-Scholl-Strasse and left up Friedensstrasse to reach Plauer Strasse. Here head right, noting the **Jugendstil mansion** at Nos 5–6 Plauer Strasse. Built in 1901 for local toy manufacturer, E.P. Lehmann, the decorated gables and curved window frames are strictly German Art Nouveau whilst the stylised children refer to the owner's source of wealth. The entrance on the right leads to the 19C toy factory which was nationalised in 1948 and is virtually closed now. It is open for a few hours on Wednesdays for toy sales and a private buyer is being sought to resurrect toy production in the town. Continue north up Plauer Strasse to the **Altstädischer Markt** (Old Town Market Place)—a small square dominated by the towering Gothic gable of the Rathaus and the giant figure of Roland. The **Rathaus** was founded in 1450 as a council chamber and in 1470 the long, main building was added as a trading hall. Above the pointed arch portal, the south-west façade is embellished with fine tracery, blind windows and a slender tower. The top section of the tower, with its clock and crenellations was added by Schinkel in 1826. From 1715, when the Alt and Neustadt were united, the function of the Rathaus passed to the Town Hall in the Neustadt and this building lay empty for some years. It was intermittently used for a cloth factory and Law Court but subsequently fell into disrepair. In 1929 it was restored and the plaster removed from the decorative brickwork for the 1000 year celebrations. The cellar now houses a reasonably priced restaurant.

The 5.35m high **Roland** is a prime example of this genre of statues, medieval emblems of freedom and justice. The statue is made of sandstone, and the armour dates it to around 1474. The statue has been carefully protected over the centuries, kept in safe storage during the War to be placed here in 1946. Turn right into Schusterstrasse which brings you to a second splendid façade on the north-east side of the Rathaus. Over the impressive portal, with its Gothic pointed arch, are the arms of the Alt and Neustadt. Above this are ten slim columns, that alternate with blind, rose windows decorated with tracery to form the focal point of the gable. The coats of arms of the principal guilds of the city make a frieze on the side of the building. For a diversion continue north-east along Plauer Strasse, Parduin Strasse and Mühlentor Strasse. On your left is the Rathenower Torturm and further north the **St Gotthardtkirche**, dating from c 1140 Brandenburg's oldest church. The base is Romanesque made from granite and the main structure is in the form of a late Gothic brick hall church dating from 1456. The tower is in florid Baroque, with a dome built in 1767. Inside the most interesting feature is the late 15C, Gobelin TAPESTRY depicting the legend of the unicorn and used to wrap ecclesiastical raiments. On the south side of the same chapel is a bronze FONT from c 1300 from the original stone chapel of the first nine Premonstratensian monks. Note the inscription around the rim which reads: '*Ich bin der Erste und der Letzte. Ich wasche die Sünden ab und gebe die schönen Freuden des Himmels*'. ('I am the first and the last and give the joys of heaven'). The late Renaissance, carved sandstone pulpit of 1624 was donated by benefactors from the cloth-makers' guild.

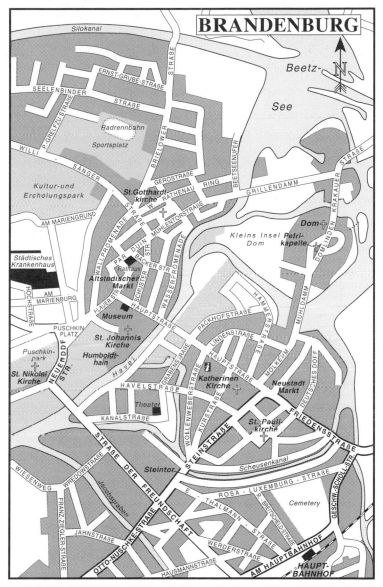

Opposite the church is the half-timbered oldest school in Brandenburg, built in 1552 and ripe for restoration. Return south to Schusterstrasse past the Rathaus and left down Hauptstrasse, the main artery of the town and where the Tourist Information Office is sited. At No. 96 is the **Museum der Stadt Brandenburg im Frey-Haus** (opening times: Tue–Fri 09.00–17.00, Sat and Sun 10.00–17.00). An imposing two-storey mansion with Baroque façade and cobbled courtyard surrounded by half-timbered building at the back, the Frey-Haus was built in 1723 for Colonel Jürgen von Massow. Much of the building material came from the former Marienkirche, demolished in 1722 on the orders of King Frederick William I. King Frederick II declared it Brandenburg's first Freihaus, freeing the owner from paying taxes. The property was subsequently occupied by other military commanders then used as workshops until it was bought by Ernst Paul Lehmann in 1912. From 1868 the Historical Society of Brandenburg had been amassing a collection of objects which had begun to overflow their first base, the Steintorturm. Lehmann therefore donated the Frey-Haus as new premises for a local history museum. Inside the ground floor is devoted to the early history of the region, including nautical history, and a miniature version of the Slav fortress on the Dominsel. On the second floor is an enchanting display of metal toys including zoo animals, lorries and knights on horseback as well as dolls' china tea sets, penny-farthing bicycles and prams.

From the museum turn left to reach the **Johanniskirche** nearby. Set back from the banks of the River Havel the ruined Gothic church with slender tower was built in the 13C as a simple hall church. Note the lovely portal and rose window. A temporary roof was erected in 1990–91 to protect the nave from further damage. Looking northwards there is an impressive view of the Baroque tower of the Gotthardtkirche. On the River Havel in the foreground are the pleasure boats which sail to Brandenburg from Berlin and Potsdam.

Continue south-east along Hauptstrasse turning left and heading north through the Neustädtischen Markt where the Rathaus der Neustadt stood from the early 14C until 1945, when it was destroyed. It is now a central parking area. Continue north up Molkenmarkt and Mühldamm to reach the Dominsel.

The **Dominsel** (Cathedral Island) is set by the idyllic River Havel. With its mellow brick Gothic cathedral, wisteria and lime trees the island seems remote from the industrial image of the town and for many centuries it was an independent entity and a centre of considerable ecclesiastical power.

History. In the 6C Slavs began to settle on the Dominsel, a small island in the middle of the River Havel, and by the mid 7C they had built a fortress, the Brennaburg, the seat of the Slav princes of the area. The German king, Heinrich I, in his campaign for expansion to the east, conquered the Brennaburg during 928–929 and forcibly converted the people. Heinrich's son, the Emperor Otto I, founded the bishopric of Brandenburg in 948 and built a cathedral from wood. This was destroyed in 983 in a Slav uprising. Two and a half centuries passed before German missionary activity again affected the area, when the Askanian prince, Albrecht the Bear, came to an agreement with Pribislav-Heinrich (1127–50), the last Slav prince of the Havel tribes. When Pribislav died in 1150, Albrecht was supposed to assume his place, but had seven stormy years before he finally became established in 1157 as the first Askanian Margrave of Brandenburg. The Dominsel remained independent until 1929, when it became part of Brandenburg.

Just past the 13C Petrikapelle is the ***Dom** itself, set in a peaceful close (opening times: Mon–Sat 10.00–12.00 and 14.00–16.00, Wed pm closed, Sun 11.00–12.00 and 14.00–16.00). In 1161 the Premonstratensian monks, who had settled at the Gotthardkirche in the Altstadt, transferred to the Dominsel. The Premonstratensians, with their simple life style, plain churches and care for the poor and the sick, did more to help the eastward expansion of Christianity than the German conquerors of the 10C. On 11 October 1165 the foundation stone of the Romanesque Dom St Peter and St Paul was laid and by 1220–40 it was completed as a Romanesque basilica. The Romanesque round-arched arcades are the main feature of the nave. The large, 12C crypt under the choir is also Romanesque. The carved sandstone capitals from 1230 are most intriguing. The double pillar in the centre of the crypt sports a carving of curiously interwoven fish and fowl, believed to signify the struggle between Slavs and the Christians. Note too the Romanesque round brick pillars at the sides and late Romanesque crucifix in the north aisle.

To the north of the choir is the chapel known as the **Bunte Kapelle** (Bright Chapel) dating from 13C to the mid 15C, with its original colourful, swirling decoration. In the 14C and 15C the cathedral was converted into a Gothic basilica, with nave and two aisles, by building five Gothic windows on top of seven bays of the existing arcades. This was to cause problems later, as the building became too heavy for its foundations on the swampy island. It was Schinkel who, as so often came to the rescue; in 1835 he introduced metal tie beams, which you can see as you look upwards in the nave. Unable to leave it at that, Schinkel also added a wide flight of steps to link the main body of the church with the elevated choir area. In 1961–65 these were removed to reveal the curving arches of the crypt and two small ambo steps and to lighten the burden on the foundations. Schinkel is to thank for the glorious blue glass in the rose window at the west end, seen at its best when the evening sun streams through.

The Gothic rebuilding also involved alterations to the choir. A five-sided polygonal shape was substituted for the Romanesque apse. The west end of the church became Gothic in style, with animal fables on the portal, including that of the fox and geese. A twin tower was planned, but a shortage of funds at the end of the 14C resulted in a temporary wooden tower until the 17C. Schinkel added the Gothic Revival steeple in 1835, as well as the crenellations where a south tower might have stood. The Baroque ORGAN dates from 1723 and was made by Prussia's most famous organ-maker, Hans Joachim Wagner. It has 2000 pipes and 33 registers, and a screen carved by Georg Glume. There is an organ concert every Wednesday evening during summer.

Of the church furnishings, the most important is the former high altar and relic shrine, the BÖHMISCHER ALTAR (Bohemian Altar) c 1375, now in the south transept and so called because at the time Brandenburg was part of Bohemia—and the work is by Bohemian artists. The seven men and seven women on the wings to the left and right are removable figurines and behind these were hidden small relics. The lower panels tell the story of Peter and Paul, patron saints of the church. In the centre the saints are attending the Crowning of Mary. The main altar, the Lehnin Altar of c 1539, was shipped by the Elector to the monastery of Lehnin. After the dissolution in 1552 it was transferred here. The subject is again the Crowning of Mary, but Peter and Paul are missing. On the left is St Benedict with his abbot's staff and in his left hand the broken jug and snake signifying his overly strict rule. In Mary Magdalen's hand is the salve used to anoint Christ's feet. On the right are Sts Bernhard of Clairvaux (founder of the Cistercian movement) and Ursula (who led 11,000 virgins to martydom).

Look up to the ceiling, where gargoyle-like spouts acted as an early-warning system to the monks and dripped when the roof had sprung a leak.

Note also the Gothic relics cupboard (1375), the carved choir stalls and the 14C sandstone font, previously lower down in the main body of the church until Schinkel had it moved. The panels on the octagonal form show scenes from the childhood of Jesus; at the base are animals symbolising the negative qualities of man, washed away by baptism: the hare stands for timidity; the fox for carnal pleasure and malice; the camel represents pride; the bear anger; the pig symbolises incontinence and the ape vanity. The altar below the rood reflects the cathedral's origins, with the patron saints: Peter, on the left, holds a key and on the right is Paul with his teacher's hat. Below, on the right, kneels a Premonstratensian monk.

The **Dommuseum** (guided tours only: Tue, Wed, Thur, and Sat 10.30 and 14.30, Sun 14.30) is entered from the north transept. The cathedral chapter of Brandenburg was, unusually, not removed after the Reformation. One of the few remaining Protestant chapters, it has retained cathedral treasures from the Middle Ages which form the basis of the museum. Of particular interest are the textiles and ecclesiastical garments, some of the earliest in Germany. The Hungertuch is outstanding, a linen embroidered cloth from late 13C with 26 scenes from the Life of Jesus and early liturgical manuscripts, including the founding document of the bishopric in AD 948.

Leaving the cathedral turn right, to circumnavigate the building. Immediately on your right, is the Gothic Revival **Ritterakademie** (Knights' Academy) built in 1705 as a school for the cathedral close which date from the 18C. (The Provost's house, the furthest to the right, used to have an overhead covered way leading to the cathedral: the remains of its Gothic doorway can be seen on the first floor, at the side of the monastery.

The monastery buildings are being restored. The removal of layers of plaster has revealed Gothic pointed arch windows. At the time of writing the refectories are being restored. The winter refectorium was the only heatable room, a Roman type hot air system being used. Continue walking to absorb the medieval atmosphere, and note the great cracks in the east end of the Dom, on the north side of the choir, due to subsidence. As you leave the tranquil close by an archway, the Domcafé is very tempting, spotlessly clean, pleasantly furnished and serving good home cooking.

Turn right and retrace your steps to the **Petrikapelle**, where Prince Pribislav is buried in an unknown grave. The church is thought to have been built by him as a Burgkapelle and certainly the lower, stone part either dates directly from his era or the stones from his chapel were used here. The building was altered in 1314–20, to become the parish church of the Domkietzer, the local fishing village (*Kietz* = fishing village). In 1520 the church acquired its current form.

Return to the Neustadt, crossing the river over Domlinden and Mühlendamm, where you pass several water-powered mills; one of these has a full-sized millwheel and a photographic exhibition of restoration work on the town.

The brick watchtower on the left to be seen as you return to the town is the **Mühlentorturm** (Mill Gate Tower), built in 1411 by Nikolaus Kraft from Stettin. This was the ancient border between the Neustadt and the Dominsel and originally a gate stood here. The look-out post, at the top of the then octagonal four-storey edifice (that once housed a prison on the ground floor), was accessible only from the parapet of the city wall.

The **Neustadt** has a bustling market every day in the Neustadt Markt, the smaller square off to the left. The parking area which forms the central square of the Neustadt, is lined by 18C and 19C town houses. On the south-east side is a well-maintained Baroque house, No. 7, with medallions to the left and right over the windows and putti over the portal. Beyond the end of the square down Steinstrasse, the 15C **Steintorturm** can be glimpsed.

Turn right into the Hauptstrasse again and on the left is the *St **Katharinenkirche**, the main parish church of the Neustadt designed by Heinrich Brunsberg from Stettin. Brunsberg was the acknowledged master of late Gothic brick architecture and unusually, a plaque in the north chapel names him and gives the date the building was begun: 1401. It is a brick Gothic hall church with nave, two aisles and an ambulatory, dedicated to Sts Katharine, Amalberga and Nicholas and is the most intricately decorated of the north German Gothic churches. At the time of building there was a strong element of competition, with the aim of creating a church more splendid than the Dom. Dark green-and-red glazed bricks on the main fabric of the building are used to great effect, but it is the decorative tracery of the gables that is most remarkable. The gable of the north chapel, the Fronleichnamskapelle (Chapel of Corpus Christi) is a high point of Gothic brick architecture. On the south side the SCHOPPENKAPPELLE DEN RATSHERRN (Chapel of the Town Jurors) runs the gamut of the artistic resources of late brick Gothic with very richly decorated gables, tracery rose windows, gablets and pinnacles ornamented with finials. The buttresses are inside the church (at first glance giving the impression of an extra aisle), as the space outside was required for the rows of terracotta saints, set in pairs under canopies of brick. Normally amongst them are Catharine and Amalberga, who have been removed for restoration at the time of writing. The original church tower collapsed one stormy night in 1582. Miraculously three pipers, employed to play hymn tunes from windows of the tower, survived. The tower was rebuilt a decade later.

During 1993 the interior of the church was undergoing restoration and scaffolding concealed much of the vaulting. However, in the choir look up to the Himmelswiese (Heavenly Fields) paintings on the vaulting. The artists were piqued—possibly because of a dispute over payment—and put hidden symbols in the painting including the fool with his belled cap a little to the right of the centre; to his right is a donkey with bagpipes and then a drummer. Above the east end of the balcony are Sts Katharine and Amalberga; behind the vaulting to the left are four heads peeping out and watching—perhaps those of the artists. The colours are the original ones. The main Katharinenalter (1474, by Gerhard Weger) cannot yet be seen but there is a 1440 bronze font in the south aisle and amongst many fine tombstones and epitaphs, the grave of Bernd von der Schulenberg with his wives and 11 children in the south-east corner is worth looking at.

Leaving the church, turn left to reach the Tourist Information Office in Hauptstrasse. If you have a little time to spare, continue south past the 15C **Plauer Torturm** (The Plauer Gate Tower), originally built to defend the city gate. Only four remain of the original nine towers along the wall and no gates are left. The tower was restored for the 1000 year celebrations in 1928/9 and the crenellated top and small steeple added, with scant regard for the tower's original aspect. The other remaining features of the medieval defence system are parts of the wall and the double moat and embankment, the Wallpromenade, which is one of the best preserved in Europe.

The park-like area to the left is the Humboldthain, named in 1869 in honour of the 100th birthday of the scientist Alexander von Humbolt, whose statue may be seen among the trees. Here the moat has been filled in to make a park below the wall, with convenient benches for a rest at the end of the tour.

From the north-west of the Plauer Torturm look up at a small hill—unusual for this flat landscape—the 79m **Marienberg**, once the site of an important pilgrims' church. The late Romanesque Marienkirche was removed in 1722 on the orders of the Prussian King Frederick William I and gives its name to the hill. At the top is a gleaming silver new tower, the Friedenswarte, 32m in height with a panoramic view and 180 steps. This is a far cry from the shrine to the Slav god Triglaw, that stood here over 1000 years ago until removed by the last Slav prince Pribislav when he was converted to Christianity.

A final diversion west across the tram lines of the Nikolaiplatz is the freshly restored **Nikolaikirche**, once the church of the long-vanished village of Luckenberg which stood outside the city gates. A Romanesque brick basilica without a transept, it is amongst the oldest examples of brick architecture in the March of Brandenburg. It was begun in 1170, and completed in early 13C with grand dimensions that have caused some doubt over its origins as a village church.

15

Dresden

520,000 inhabitants.

Tourist Information. Main Office: Prager Strasse 10/11, 01069 Dresden. Tel. (051) 495 5025 (opening hours April–Sept, Mon–Sat 09.00–20.00, Sun 09.00–13.00; Oct–March, Mon–Fri 09.00–20.00, Sat 09.00–14.00, Sun 09.00–13.00) and Branch Office: Neustädter Markt (Unterfuhrung—Pedestrian Underpass), Dresden 01097. Tel. (051) 53539 (opening hours Mon–Wed 09.00–18.00, Thurs 09.00–18.30, Fri 09.00–19.00, Sat and Sun 09.00–15.00).

Airport. Dresden-Klotzsche, Karl-Marx-Strasse, 01109 Dresden. Tel. 583141.

Railway Station. Wiener Platz.

Almost 60 per cent of former East Germany's cultural institutions (with the exception of those in East Berlin) are situated in the Land of Saxony with the finest examples to be found in its capital, **DRESDEN**.

From 1216, when Dresden was founded, it flourished into one of the most beautiful towns of 18C Europe. Located on the scenic banks of the River Elbe, Dresden is still known to Germans as the 'Florence of the North'. This is in spite of the town's virtual destruction by Anglo-American fire-bombing on the night of 13–14 February 1945. Nearly 135,000 of the town's inhabitants were killed—over twice as many as in Hiroshima—and 80 per cent of the housing destroyed in the most intense air raid of the Second World War. Most of the historic buildings were badly damaged. Worst hit was the beautiful dome of the remarkable 18C Frauenkirche, which collapsed; this was deliberately left in ruins by the GDR authorities as a dramatic reminder of the bombing, but now rigorous efforts are being made to raise funds for its restoration. A magnificent effort has been made by the people of Dresden to restore the town's chief attractions, the 18C Zwinger Palace and 19C Semper Opera House. New funds from Bonn have been injected into the city and a full renovation of its major attractions has been underway since 1989. The city now buzzes with tourists from all over the world, and its popularity as a destination for European travellers is back to early 20C levels, when it was a fashionable resort.

An important music and theatre festival is held annually from the end of May to mid-June.

History. Dresden grew as the capital of the region of Saxony during the 18C under the awesome patronage of Augustus the Strong. The region had enjoyed prosperity since the discovery of silver in the Erzgebirge (Ore Mountains) c 1168. Other findings after this included gold, tin, copper, iron and semi-precious stones such as agate, garnet, amethyst and opals. The area was ruled by the Wettin family who resided at nearby Meissen. During the 16C the family divided, one branch ruling territories outside Saxony eventually emerging as the Saxe-Coburg line in Thuringia of which Prince Albert was a member. The other line, the Albertines, ruled Saxony. The town had become the residence of the Wettins in 1464 when the Dukes Ernst and Albrecht moved there. Following the division of the Wettins, Dresden became the centre for Albertine rule in 1465. Dresden's importance as a cultural centre began in 1560 when the Elector Augustus I founded the Art Chamber on the ground floor of the Dresden Royal Castle which housed not only paintings and sculpture but also technical and scientific instruments. A strong-room was also created by Augustus I for the safe keeping of cash, documents and precious objects. The two collections were merged and form the basis of today's Green Vault.

Dresden became firmly established as a cultural centre of international importance in 1694 when Frederick August I or Augustus the Strong (1670–1733) came to the throne aged 24. He was a legendary bon-viveur and womaniser, and is rumoured to have fathered 300 children. In 1697, after converting to Catholicism, he became King of Poland and employed the best architects and craftsmen to create a Baroque capital worthy of his status as ruler of the second largest country in Europe. A huge fire in 1685 had destroyed most of the town on the north bank of the Elbe, and it was rebuilt in grand style by Augustus under the architect W.C. von Klengel—this area is still known as the Neustadt today. Augustus the Strong was also responsible for the building of Germany's most important late Baroque building, the Zwinger Palace, and brought eminent architect Matthaeus Daniel Pöppelmann (1662–1736) and Bavarian sculptor Balthasar Permoser (1651–1732) together to create this fantasy venue for festivals and other outdoor court occasions. It was also under the rule of Augustus the Strong that porcelain was discovered and the world famous Meissen factory established. Augustus the Strong had imprisoned Prussian refugee and alchemist Johann Friedrich Böttger and ordered him to manufacture gold. Böttger, though failing to achieve this impossible task, discovered in 1713 the formula for producing the first European porcelain. Although Augustus's cultural achievements were remarkable, his political career was less illustrious, and after being rescued by the Russians from Swedish attack in 1706 he acted as little more than a puppet of this huge power to the east.

Augustus the Strong was succeeded in 1733 by his son, Friedrich August II, who continued the growth of this splendid capital by adding the Catholic Hofkirche, designed by the Italian architect Gaetano Chiaveri (1689–1770) and buying the Sistine Madonna by Raphael for the State Collection. Friedrich August II also employed the young artist Bernado Bellotto—known as Canaletto—to paint 25 views of the town when he arrived in Dresden from Venice in 1747. These accurately record the beauty of Dresden in the 18C, including the magnificent skyline of the Altstadt with the dome of the Frauenkirche, and they are now on view in the Albertinum (during the temporary closure of the Gemäldegalerie Alte Meister). By 1775 the town's population was 63,000 having trebled since the end of the 17C. However, the political influence of Saxony was now on the wane. Dresden had been bombarded by Prussia in 1760 and after the Napoleonic Wars she was forced to surrender three-fifths of her territory to Prussia at the Treaty of Vienna in 1815. It was Prussia which dominated Germany throughout the 19C and into the 20C.

The cultural and commercial life of Dresden continued to flourish with the Royal Art Collections opening to the public in 1828 and Gottfried Semper, the great 19C architect, worked in Dresden during 1834 to 1849 designing the spectacular Opera House. Richard Wagner lived and worked in Dresden and from 1843 until 1849 was the Court Director of Music. *Rienzi* (1842) *The Flying Dutchman* (1843) and *Tannhauser* (1845) were all performed for the first time at the Dresden Opera. Dresden also enjoyed industrial growth during the 19C and the first long-distance railway in Germany opened in 1839 between Leipzig and Dresden. Tobacco processing was an important industry and the first factory in Germany devoted to this purpose was built here in 1862 with another 20 built by 1880. One was built in the style of a mosque, complete with mock dome and minaret, and still stands on the corner of Weisseritzer Strasse and Magdeburger Strasse. The famous Dresdner Bank was founded here in 1872 to provide much needed financial services. The company was quick to re-establish itself in the town following unification. The chemical and pharmaceutical trades also built factories, warehouses and offices in Dresden. By 1910 Dresden's population had mushroomed to 548,300—more than its present level—and it enjoyed a reputation as an important cultural centre with a large colony of English and Americans living here before the First World War.

After 1918, when Germany was declared a republic, Dresden became the capital of the Free State of Saxony and continued to be a prosperous cultural and commercial centre. When the Nazis came to power in 1933 prominent Jews and political opponents living in Dresden, including the conductor of the State Orchestra, Fritz Busch, and avant-garde artist Otto Dix were hounded out. Following the devastation of 1945 the people of Dresden were quick to begin rebuilding the town and restoring it to its former splendour. Dresden was now part of the new GDR and became one of 14 district towns; the old state of Saxony was divided into three parts from 1952 until 1990. During the post-war era the town was largely rebuilt in the monumental modernist style of the Eastern Bloc. The Opera was totally rebuilt during this period and opened on 13 February 1985 with a performance of Carl Maria von Weber's *Freischutz*. Dresden was an important centre for anti-government protest in 1989 with violent clashes between police and protesters erupting and 3000 protesters occupying the main station and attempting to board trains carrying refugees from the German Embassy in Prague to West Germany. After the collapse of the Berlin Wall and the unification of Germany a rally held at the ruined Frauenkirche to rejoice in the new future was attended by thousands of Dresden people. The first elections of the re-unified Germany were held in March 1990, and in May Dr Herbert Wagner of the CDU was voted Mayor of Dresden. In October 1990 Saxony was re-established as one of the new Länder with Dresden as its capital. The hope is now that Dresden's formidable cultural heritage will attract both tourists and investment from the West and the signs are that this coming to fruition with a large investment from Bonn for the restoration of the town.

A.   From the main railway station
to the Albertinum

From the main railway station in Wiener Platz walk north up PRAGER STRASSE. In the 1920s this was the equivalent of Berlin's Kurfürstendamm but was rebuilt as a pedestrian zone from 1969 onwards and is lined with shops and hotels in the anonymous style of official socialism. On your right at Nos 10 and 11 is the main Tourist Information office. Crossing the Dr Külz Ring, the **Neues Rathaus** (New Town Hall) is on the right. Built between 1904 and 1910 in Neo-Renaissance style and designed by Karl Roth and Edmund Brater, the sandstone building has a 98m high domed tower surmounted by a 4.9m high effigy of Hercules (Goldener Mann). He holds a horn of plenty in his left hand and proffers a protective right arm to the town. The Ratskeller is a good venue for drinks, snacks and meals. From the Town Hall cross the Sankt-Petersburger-Strasse, a busy dual carriage-way, and walk east through the Bluher Park down the Neue Herkules-Allee until you reach the **Deutsches Hygienemuseum** (German Hygiene Museum), Sat–Thurs, 09.00–18.00) on the Lingnerplatz. This is an amusing diversion, with exhibitions on the history of condoms and the famous 'Glass Lady', a model skilfully crafted showing the anatomical details of a mature woman. There are also a 'Glass Cow' and 'Glass Horse'. The building itself is interesting; erected during 1927–30 in Neo-Classical style it has some original Art Deco style light fittings. To the left of the museum is a pleasant garden, open May–Oct 07.00–20.00, Nov–April, 09.00–17.00. Retrace your steps back to the Rathaus, take Kreuzstrasse to the right of the Rathaus and head west to the ALTMARKT (Old Market).

This is the oldest square in Dresden. First documented in 1370, it was originally the centre for the town's trade and entertainment. The 18C Baroque Town Hall (designed by Johann Christoph Knoffel) once stood here. Destroyed in 1945, restoration work began in 1952 when the square was enlarged. On the east side of the square is the **Kreuzkirche** (Church of the Cross). Founded in 1200 and altered and repaired through the

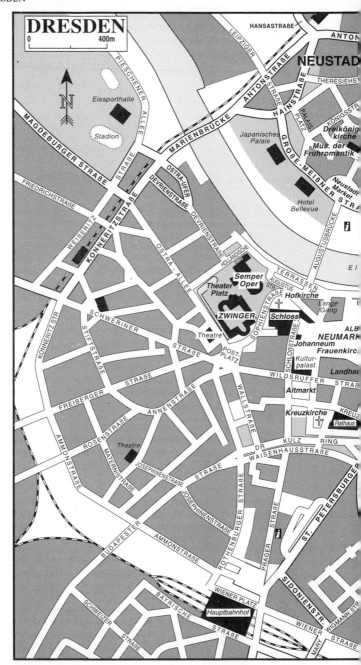

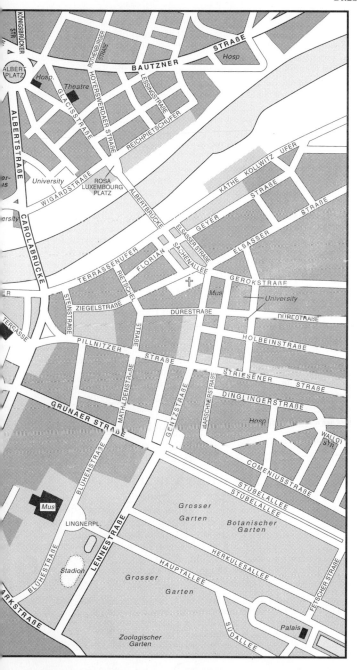

centuries, it was extensively damaged in 1945. The main body of the exterior is Baroque, with a Neo-Classical tower complete with clock. Following restoration to its 1792 state, the interior remains deliberately spartan to emphasise the massive proportions of the pillars. The church is the home of a world-class choir, specialising in 17C music, in particular the work of Dresden composer Heinrich Schutz. The church was an important meeting point during the demonstrations of the 1980s, when candlelit processions would leave from here.

Continue north across the busy main West/East road, formerly Ernst Thalmann Strasse but now renamed Wilsdruffer Strasse, to the **Kulturpalast** (Palace of Culture) built in 1969 to commemorate the 20th anniversary of the founding of the German Democratic Republic. The modern building contains a concert hall, cinema, theatre and cafés. The western façade is decorated with a mural on the theme of socialist revolution, although its future seems to be in doubt and it is presently screened with netting. Proceed east down Wilsdruffer Strasse to the only 18C building on the street, the **Landhaus** (built 1770–76; open Mon–Thurs 10.00–18.00, Sun 10.00–16.00, closed Fri). Almost entirely devastated in 1945, it has been rebuilt and the exterior painted in yellow and white. It houses an important Rococo staircase which runs through all three floors of the building. The Landhaus is now the **Museum für Geschichte der Stadt Dresden** (Museum of the Town of Dresden) and shows temporary exhibitions.

Turn left out of the Landhaus and continue up Landhaus Strasse to the NEUMARKT and the beginning of the Palace Quarter or Altstadt. The Neumarkt is dominated by the ruined **Frauenkirche**. Built during 1726–1743 from locally quarried blocks of sandstone, the church was designed by Georg Bähr as the first large Protestant church in Germany; it seated 5000 people. The mighty dome was once a powerful symbol of Dresden, rising 95m and surmounted by a graceful lantern, but it was badly damaged by bombing in 1945 and the pile of rubble which remains, overgrown by weeds, is a sad testament to the destruction of the Second World War. To the west of the ruin stands a monument to Martin Luther by Rietschel and Donndorf (1885). Also on the Neumarkt is the Dresdner Hof luxury hotel, now owned by the Hilton chain. To the east of the Neumarkt is the Albertinum.

B. The Albertinum

The Albertinum presently contains three important collections, the best to be seen in Eastern Germany outside Berlin, and warrants at least one full day. It includes three main galleries: the Alte Meister (Old Masters), the Neue Meister (New Masters) and the Grünes Gewölbe (Green Vault). Opening times: Alte Meister (Tues–Sun 10.00–18.00), Gemäldegalerie Neue Meister (Tues–Sun 09.00–17.00, Wed 09.00–18.00, closed Mon) Grünes Gewölbe (Mon–Sun 09.00–17.00, Wed 09.00–18.00, closed Thurs).

History. The Albertinum was originally the arsenal of the Electors of Saxony, built between 1559 and 1563. The building was reconstructed between 1884 and 1887 by A. Canzler in a heavy Renaissance Revival style as a sculpture museum. Only two remnants of the 16C building are in evidence: a 75m room with Tuscan pillars, now used for the sculpture collection, and two rustic style portals on the east side. The Alte Meister collection was built up during the reign of Augustus III between 1733 and

1756, when progress was halted by the Seven Years War. By then the character of the collection had been established, with a concentration on Dutch and Flemish art of the 16C and 17C as well as Italian painting from the Renaissance and Baroque periods. In 1855 the collection was moved to the purpose-built Semper Gallery where it remained until the Second World War, during which the 1240 works were kept in safe storage. More recently, the Semper Gallery has been closed for restoration and prime examples from the collection have been on display at the Albertinum. They have now been rehung in the Semper Gallery in the Zwinger Palace.

The Neue Meister collection was initiated by retired Minister of State Bernhard August von Lindenhau (1779–1854), who donated a substantial part of his pension to collecting contemporary art. In the 20C collecting continued with the help of the Dresden Museum Association and the Association of Patrons of the State Picture Gallery, and the collection is renowned for its high quality German Romantic and Expressionist works. The Grünes Gewölbe collection dates from the 15C and includes the private collections of the rulers of Saxony, reflecting the wealth of silver deposits in the nearby hills. Fine examples of gold and silver jewellery and other trinkets as well as a comprehensive coin collection are housed in the Grünes Gewölbe, so called because the original strong room was supposedly painted green. The collection grew over the centuries and was formed into a treasure chamber in Dresden Castle by Augustus the Strong during 1723–1729. The original rooms are still undergoing restoration and roughly half the collection has been on display in the Albertinum since 1959.

The **Alte Meister** collection is of a supremely high standard; a selection is currently housed on the first floor of the Albertinum. The most famous painting in the collection is the *Sistine Madonna* by Raphael. Painted c 1513 it was bought by Augustus III from the monks of the new San Sisto monastery near Milan in 1754 for an astounding 20,000 ducats—the highest price ever paid for a work of art to that date. The painting captures a young, naive Mary seemingly floating on the clouds, carrying baby Jesus in her arms. She is flanked by the figure of St Sixtus to one side and the martyr Barbara to the right. A curtain has been pulled apart to reveal the scene, as if we, the viewers, are looking onto a spiritual world, apart from everyday reality. Two cherubs at the base of the painting add a charming touch with their bored, youthful faces looking up. Many other Italian artists are represented here also: Titian, Tintoretto, Veronese, Correggio, Botticello, Carracci, and Messina, to name only a few. Other gems in the collection include the pastel *Chocolate Girl* (1743–45) by Swiss painter, Jean-Etienne Liotard and Giorgione's *Sleeping Venus* (1510). There is a wealth of 17C Dutch and Flemish art to be seen, including works by Peter Paul Rubens, Rembrandt and Vermeer. *Girl Reading a Letter at an Open Window* (1659) is entrancing—a young girl stands by an open window with a letter in her hand. Her total concentration is focussed on the piece of paper and we can only speculate about its content; is it a declaration of love or perhaps a sad farewell? This intriguing narrative is framed within a typical Dutch interior of the period, with minutely observed curtains, chair, and table decorated with a Turkey rug and bowl of fruit. Other masters from the golden age of Dutch and Flemish painting to be represented in the collection include Frans Hals, Anton van Dyck and Jacob Jordaens.

This splendid collection is complemented by an exciting range of 15C and 16C German art. There are impressive altarpieces by Albrecht Dürer and Lucas Cranach the Elder. The Dürer is an early piece, painted when the artist first established himself as a master painter in Nuremberg, and the influence of late Gothic is still in evidence. The altarpiece originally consisted of one large panel, depicting the Virgin Mary, surrounded by seven smaller scenes from the life of Christ. When the piece entered the studios of Lucas Cranach the Elder from an unknown Wittenberg church, it was sawn into separate pictures and the central image now hangs in the Alte Pinakothek in Munich. The remaining seven pictures were acquired by the Gallery in 1832 and reassembled into their original order. The *St Catherine Altar* by Lucas Cranach the Elder was painted in 1506 for the Wittenberg Castle Church, Wittenberg being the seat of the Electors of Saxony at that time and Cranach the court painter. St Catherine is represented in prayer, about to be broken on the wheel which lies before her. The left and right wings of the triptych each depict three female saints. This early piece is striking in its use of jewel-like colours and attention to detail. Cranach's remarkable skill as a portraitist is displayed in the picture *Duke Henry the Pious* (1514). This is one of the earliest German portraits not to be painted as part of an altarpiece and demonstrates the difference in attitude to the individual instigated by the Protestant Reformation. The work depicts the Duke (1473–1541), one of the Albertinum line of the House of Wettin, and his wife, Katharina of Mecklenburg, who ruled Saxony in the 16C. The carnations decorating the couple's hair signal their recent marriage and their sumptuous dress and arrogant stance signify their power and authority.

Local interest is also to be found in the splendid views of Dresden painted by Bernardo Bellotto, better known as Canaletto, who came to the city in 1747 from Venice to create a series of 25 pictures which established Dresden's image as a Baroque city. The splendour of old Dresden has been perfectly captured in these works, which include accurate representations of the Frauenkirche and Kreuzkirche. The narrow streets of Dresden are depicted, bustling with traders and shoppers. The most famous view to be painted by Bellotto is taken from the north bank of the Elbe, approximately where the aptly named Bellevue Hotel stands today. The old Elbe bridge, designed by the architect of the Zwinger Palace, Pöppelmann, is shown as well as the smart houses lining the Brühlsche Terrasse and the formidable dome of the newly completed Frauenkirche.

Before moving on to the Neue Meister it may be worth taking a break in the charming café on the first floor, where good coffee, cakes and snacks may be bought.

The **Neue Meister** collection rivals the Alte Meister in terms of world-class works and local interest. The collection is best known for its comprehensive stock of German Romantic paintings. Caspar David Friedrich's *Two Men Contemplating the Moon* (1819) is a fine example of this 19C genre. The eery quality evoked by the silvery light of the full moon is enhanced by the two male figures, their backs turned to us, who mysteriously look out into the distance. The rugged rocks on which the figures stand and the gnarled, windswept tree are similarly evocative. Two similarly haunting works by Friedrich are also in the collection, *The Cross in the Mountains* and *Cairn in the Snow*. Paintings by the Saxon illustrator Ludwig Richter in a similar style, *Crossing by the Schreckenstein* and *Bridal Procession in the Spring*, are also important works.

In complete contrast there is a representative selection of Biedermeier paintings, labelled 'bourgeois realist works' in the days of the GDR. These small-scale, domestic scenes by Carl Spitzweg and others show a contented middle class in prosperous times after the defeat of Napoleon. There are also works from the later 19C which reveal a continued preoccupation with romanticism, including work by Böcklin and Feuerbach. Some of the jewels of the collection are those by French and German Impressionists. There is

Two Men Contemplating the Moon, 1819, by Caspar David Friedrich, in the Albertinum, Dresden

Lady in Pink by Edouard Manet, works by Monet and Degas and six works by Max Liebermann. Post-Impressionism is also well represented with Gauguin's *Two Tahitian Women*, Toulouse-Lautrec's *Two Girlfriends* and a Van Gogh still life. Mention must also be made of the fine display of German Expressionism, with one branch of the movement Die Brücke, being founded in Dresden in 1905. The work of Karl Schmidt-Rottluff, Erich Heckel, Emile Nolde and Lyonel Feininger, with their stark imagery and vigorous style, is well exemplified in this collection. The post-war section is particularly interesting, as this was formed during the days of the GDR when only Socialist Realism was officially encouraged. There is therefore a lack of the abstract painting, for example, and of the conceptual art, which one would expect in a collection of this calibre. Nevertheless, Otto Dix's *War Triptych*, acquired in 1968, portrays in powerful detail the ravages of war as does *The Thousand Year Reich* by Dresden artist, Hans Grundig, who survived four years in a concentration camp.

The **Grünes Gewölbe** is the most popular of the Albertinum's attractions. The small space and the minuteness of many of the exhibits makes an early morning visit desirable. This dazzling display of precious items from the late Renaissance and Rococo eras is one of the richest in the world. The first room is devoted to silver and German semi-precious stones. The major attraction is the reconstructed silver cabinet; with Baroque curves and mirrored back, it enhances the collection of glittering objects perfectly. Exotic materials gleaned from overseas travel, such as corals, mother-of-pearl, ostrich eggs and coconut shells have been skilfully combined with silver to make intricate 16C goblets. There is a group of three 46cm high ostriches, made by Elias Geyer in Leipzig at the end of the 16C. An ostrich egg forms the body and the legs, with the wings, neck and head made from gilded silver. The head could be removed and wine drunk from the neck in the social gatherings which revolved around the drinking of alcohol. The first room also contains a delicate box for writing materials, made in gold, silver, enamel, crystal and ebony by the Nuremberg goldsmith Wenzel Jamnitzer, and dating from 1562. A larger jewellery case by the same craftsman, measuring 51cm x 53cm x 35.5cm in silver, gold, mother-of-pearl, crystal, emeralds, garnets, amethysts, topazes, coloured glass and wood, was made in 1585 and reveals the court's knowledge of Italian Renaissance culture. The figure reclining on the top of the bejewelled casket is dressed in classical Roman robes and represents philosophy; she reads a tablet inscribed in Latin which praises the sciences. Also worth noting are the small 16C bronzes by Giovanni da Bologna and Adriaen de Vries, which are situated in the first room.

Moving on to the second of the four rooms which make up the Grüne Gewölbe, the most striking exhibit is the 2m high *Amber Cabinet*. This came to Dresden in 1728 as a present from the Prussian king and is now the largest extant work in this precious material. Badly damaged during the Second World War, it was skilfully restored by Polish craftsmen. Delicate ivory sculptures dating from the 17C and precious objects of Italian and German origin, carved from lapis lazuli and rock crystal, are also well worth a close inspection. The third room contains the most popular items of the collection in the form of works by the court jeweller Johann Melchior Dinglinger and the sculptor Balthasar Permoser who contributed so much to the design of the Zwinger Palace. Enjoying pride of place in the centre of the room is the exquisite *Court of Delhi on the Birthday of the Great Moghul* created by Dinglinger and his brothers between 1701 and 1708. This miniature recreation of the Indian court of Aureng Zeb is inhabited by 137 gilded and enamelled figures. Made from gold, silver, enamel and precious stones, including 5000 diamonds, emeralds, rubies and pearls, this was the type of ostentatious display of wealth in which Augustus the Strong revelled. Other (masterpieces include the Gold Coffee Service (1701) created for Augustus the Strong for the ceremonious consumption of this newly discovered drink, and the highly decorative *Bath of Diana*. Designed in collaboration with Permoser, this delicate piece is 18cm high with Diana, carved in ivory reclining in a golden bath studded with precious stones; the bath is balanced on the antlers of a stag's head, representing the hunter, Actaeon, who glimpsed Diana bathing and as a punishment was changed into a stag and killed by his own hunting dogs. The final room holds virtually the entire Saxon crown jewels, constituting the greatest jewellery collection in Europe. Its nine sets include the Sapphire Set and the Cornelian Set made by Dinglinger's workshops for Augustus the Strong. Also on display are the 41 carat green diamond and a 648 carat sapphire, one of the biggest ever found.

After viewing such a riotously decorative collection it is something of a relief to visit the more austere *Coin Collection*, housed in the **Munzkabinett**, just off the Grünes Gewölbe. This display of some 250,000 items is impressively comprehensive, including Greek, Celtic, Roman, Byzantine, Asian, American and German coins from the Middle Ages onwards. The collection was founded by Duke George of Saxony (1500–39) and was augmented through continuous collecting of newly minted coins and the purchase of other private collections. The sculpture collection is also of some interest; it is situated on the ground floor of the Albertinum and comprises 15,000 objects. The collection was founded by Augustus the Strong when he bought 160 antique sculptures from the estate of an Italian prince as well as items from Cardinal Albani's collection. In 1782 the plaster casts of antique sculptures assembled by painter A.R. Mengs were added, and the collection continued to grow well into the twentieth century, when some modern examples were purchased. The highlights of this vast display include Edgar Degas' *Little Dancer* (1880) and Roman copies in marble of Greek masterpieces.

C. **The Palace Quarter

The most historic and architecturally significant buildings in Dresden are to be found in the Palace Quarter. Although badly bombed during World War Two, strenuous efforts have been made to restore this part of Dresden to its former royal glory. This effort has speeded up since the Wende and most of the Royal Palace, for instance, is covered in scaffolding.

Returning to the Neumarkt from the Albertinum, the impressive 19C building to the left is the former **Akademie des Bildenden Kunste** (Art School) and Saxon Art Union headquarters built in Renaissance revival style by Constantin Lipius in 1891–94. It is deserted at present but there are plans afoot to restore the building by the New Saxon Art Society which was founded in 1990. The distinctive variegated glass dome of the building, earning it the nickname of 'lemon squeezer', remains intact, surmounted by the bronze goddess of victory by Robert Henze. Head to the west of the Neumarkt to the **Stallhof** (Royal Mews), and pass through the recently restored, sturdy wooden gates to view the impressive 100m long, Tuscan arcade or **Lange Gang** (Long Walk) on the right. Built at the end of the 16C and probably designed by Giovanni Maria Nosseni, the exterior is decorated with the coats of arms of the Saxon lands and various hunting trophies. The main building, which forms the remainder of the courtyard, is the Johanneum; formerly the court stables and erected during 1586–89, it was substantially altered during 1872–75. The building now houses the Verkehrsmuseum (Transport Museum, April–Sept, Tues–Sun, 09.00–17.00, Oct–March, 10.00–17.00). This is worth a quick detour if the history of motorised transport is of interest, and there are fine views of the Stallhof from the upper floor. There is an interesting display of train carriages, including the coach used by the Saxon Royal Family, built in 1885. Early Daimler cars, a Mercedes-Benz taxi from 1932 and city trams are also on show, including a local example from 1934. There are other worthy exhibitions of the history of the bicycle, shipping and flight.

From the Stallhof turn left to experience the remarkable 102m long Fürstenzug (Procession of Princes) which flanks the south-west side of Augustusstrasse. Originally created in 1872–76 by local artist Wilhelm Walther in delicate sgraffito, the mural showed signs of damage as early as

1900. It was then transferred onto 25,000 porcelain tiles by the Meissen Porcelain factory and resurrected in 1907. The mural represents the dukes of the House of Wettin on horseback followed by various artists and scientists to make a total of 93 figures. Designed to resemble a tapestry hanging on the wall, with borders decorated with fruit and coats of arms, it offers an interesting way to familiarise oneself with the history of the Wettin house. To the right is the **Landtag** (State Parliament), designed by Paul Wallot, the architect of the Reichstag in Berlin, during 1901–03 in heavy Renaissance Revival style.

Continue north-west down Augustusstrasse to reach the Schlossplatz. To the left is the still ruined **Residenzchloss** (Royal Palace), built in 1530 with various additions through the centuries. Much of the palace was destroyed by fire in 1701 to be rebuilt during 1717–19 in a Baroque style by Augustus the Strong. The palace was again substantially renovated during 1889–1901, in Renaissance Revival style to celebrate the 800th anniversary of the House of Wettin. This magnificent building was gutted during 1945 and only a ruin remained, which was largely neglected until 1986, when the decision was taken to begin restoration work. This has been accelerated since 1990 with massive injections of cash from the West. The aim is to re-open in 2006 to mark Dresden's 800th anniversary. At present only the Spiegelzimmern (Mirror Rooms) are open to the public (Mon, Tues, and Fri–Sun 09.00–17.00, Thurs 09.00–18.00; entrance in Sophienstrasse). The 16C **Georgentor** (George Gate) faces the Elbe and was substantially restored in 1967. Originally built in the 16C in the reign of Georg der Bartige (George the Bearded), the statue decorating the Gate dates from 1901.

Directly opposite is the *Hofkirche built during 1737–55 under the direction of Italian architect Gaetano Chiaveri in splendid late Baroque style (guided tour, Mon–Thurs at 10.00, 11.00, 12.00, 14.00 and 15.00, Fri and Sat at 13.00 and 14.00, Sun at 11.45). This is the largest church in Saxony and belies the Saxon rulers' Catholic sympathies. Whilst most of the state was Protestant, Augustus the Strong found it politically expedient to convert to Catholicism in 1697 to become King of Catholic Poland. He was, however, little interested in religious affairs, and although Catholic services were held in the palace, it was not until Augustus the Strong was succeeded by his only legitimate son, Augustus III, that plans were put in motion to build a Catholic church to match the splendour of the Frauenkirche. The church is a basilica with three naves and four corner chapels. The exterior is characterised by the 83.5m high tower, which is open-tiered and divided into four storeys, crowned with a flourish by the campanile. The tower and the two balustrades which finish off each of the main storeys are decorated with 78 sandstone statues, each representing a saint and crafted by the Italian sculptor Lorenzo Matielli. The church was built at an unusual angle, facing south-west to complement the existing urban landscape by dominating the Elbe and facing the Augustusbrücke. The Hofkirche's interior is in startling white, with a Baroque sense of movement created by the undulating frieze which surmounts the Composite Roman columns and rounded windows forming the clerestory. There is a magnificent carved, late Baroque pulpit in limewood by Permoser dating from 1722 and a painting, *The Ascension of Christ*, (1751) by Anton Raphael Mengs at the high altarpice. Two other works by Mengs, *The Immaculate Conception* and *The Dream of Joseph* can be seen at the side altar. The church's organ, installed during 1750–53, was the last to be built by Gottfried Silbermann and this splendid instrument can be heard at concerts held at 4pm on Saturdays during the summer. The Saxon rulers would sit in the arcaded gallery of the church, which was connected to the Palace by means of a covered bridge. The bodies of 49 Saxon kings and the heart of Augustus the Strong are located in four vaults (Augustus' other remains are buried in the Cathedral at Kraków in Poland).

The Semper Opera House, home of the Dresden State Opera, originally designed by Gottfried Semper in 1838–41 and rebuilt by his son

Opposite the Hofkirche and facing the River Elbe is the Italienisches Dorfchen (Small Italian Village) café. It is so called because the Italian workers who came to Dresden to build the Hofkirche created a settlement on this spot. The café dates from some time later. You are now in the Theaterplatz, the prospect marred somewhat by its use as a car park and by the busy road and tramway which passes through. In the Theaterplatz is the magnificent **Semper Opera House**, now the home of the Dresden State Opera. Designed by leading architect Gottfried Semper in 1838–41 as the Hoftheater (court theatre) it was, sadly burnt down in 1869. It was rebuilt, however, under the direction of his son, Manfred Semper, between 1871 and 1878. Gottfried Semper had fled to England after the 1848 revolution and became closely involved in the circle of designers around Prince Albert. Semper contributed to the Crystal Palace exhibition, held in London's Hyde Park in 1851, and the establishment of the Victoria and Albert Museum. When the Opera House burnt down, Semper was offered the contract to rebuild it. However, he was busy with several prestigious buildings in Vienna and so delegated the task to his son. The Opera House was virtually detroyed in 1945 but was magnificently restored for reopening on 13 February 1985 to mark the 40th anniversary of the bombing.

This Renaissance Revival building has a splendid, semi-circular frontage which projects into the Theaterplatz. The separate storeys are clearly articulated on the exterior, with a rusticated finish to the ground floor, surmounted by the first floor with arched windows looking out from the sweeping bar area where the intervals are spent. The main entrance is flanked by statues of Goethe (to the left) and Schiller (to the right) by Ernst Rietschel and is surmounted by a bronze quadriga by Johannes Schilling—four lions pulling a chariot—which bear Dionysus and Ariadne. There is splendidly restored mosaic and gold-leaf decoration over the main entrance and the balcony above. The interior has been lusciously refurbished with less seating than the original after the removal of the fifth tier of seats (on safety grounds, and in order to accommodate modern luxuries such as air conditioning). Semper designed the whole of the interior of the Opera House which has been fully restored complete with Renaissance Revival ceiling painting and the stage backdrops. The main auditorium is at the front of the building, which is connected by two corridors to the workrooms where costumes and scenery are stored and the rehearsal rooms are situated. There are guided tours around the Opera House daily (check the noticeboard), except in mid-summer.

Seats for performances at the Opera may be booked at the Alstadter Wache (The Old Watch) which lies to the south, just beside the Augustusbrücke (tel. 48420/Evening Box Office 4842491). This unimposing Neo-Classical building was designed by Karl Friedrich Schinkel and built in 1930–31. The Alstadter Wache bears a striking resemblance to the Neue Wache (New Watch) in Berlin which Schinkel had designed for the Prussian King in 1817–18.The equestrian statue in front of the Opera House celebrates King John (1801–73) who made his name as a Dante scholar.

Continue north-east past the Hofkirche and up the sweeping stairs to the right of the Augustusbrücke. This broad flight of 41 steps was designed by Gottlob Friedrich Thormayer and decorated by Johannes Schilling with bronze sculptures representing times of the day: Night, Evening, Noon and Morning. The **Brühlsche Terrasse** (Brühl Terrace) affords one of the most beautiful views in Eastern Germany, overlooking the River Elbe and the hills beyond. Designed in 1738 by Count Brühl, minister of King Augustus III, as part of his private garden on the site of the old defensive ramparts, it was opened to the public in 1814 by Russian military commander, Prince Repnin, and is known as 'The Balcony of Europe'. The first building on the right is the Standehaus, built for the Saxon Landtag in 1901–03. At present this is the State Office for the Conservation of Monuments, the Museum of Mineralogy and Geology and the Museum of Zoology. Beside this is the Sekundogenitur. Built on the site of Count Brühl's library in 1897 as a small residence for the second-born prince, it is today a café, forming part of the Dresdener Hof hotel. During the warmer months it is pleasant to enjoy refreshment outside the *Café Vis-à-vis* on the terrace. A statue of the sculptor Rietschel by Schilling, dating from 1876, stands near the café.

Continue east past the Dresden Academy of Art and a bronze statue of Semper by Schilling (1892), where the stairs lead down to the Georg-Treu-Platz and an entrance to the Green Vault. The view from this part of the terrace is spectacular, particularly to the east although the views of the countryside are slightly marred by two new buildings on the opposite bank, the former Ministry of Finance (directly opposite) and (beyond the modern bridge) the General Ministry. In the north-east corner of the Terrace is the **Maurice Monument**, the oldest monument in Dresden, dating from the 16C and installed at this site in 1895. It commemorates Elector Maurice of Saxony who fell in battle against the Margrave of Brandenburg at Sievershausen in 1553. In the gardens at the end of the Brühl Terrace is the Delphinbrunnen (Dolphin Fountain), built in 1747–49 by Frenchman Pierre Coudray for Count Brühl. There are also monuments to Caspar David Friedrich and the alchemist Johann Friedrich Böttger, who invented European hard-paste porcelain, fine examples of which can be seen in the Porcelain Museum in the Zwinger.

Beneath the Brühl Terrace is the Terrassenufer and the landing stage for the Weisse Flotte (White Fleet) boats which run during April–Oct (Tel. 051/5 02 26·11). It is possible to travel by 100-year-old steamer up the Elbe to view the Sandstone Hills or down the Elbe to Meissen and Riesa.

The Zwinger Palace, built for Augustus the Strong by Matthaeus Daniel Pöppelmann in 1710–32

D.   **The Zwinger

The Zwinger contains the **Porzellansammlung** (Porcelain Museum, Sat–Thurs 09.00–17.00) Tierkundemuseum (Natural History Museum, Sat–Wed 09.00–16.00) Mathematisch-physikalischer Salon (Mathematics and Physics Collection, Fri–Wed 09.30–17.00) and Historisches Museum (Historical Museum, 09.00–17.00, closed Wed).

The **Zwinger Palace** was built in superb Baroque style for Augustus the Strong by Matthaeus Daniel Pöppelmann during 1710–32. Originally designed as a pleasure palace and setting for outdoor banquets and carnivals, the building consists of seven pavilions connected by a single storey gallery. Pöppelmann travelled extensively through Austria, Bohemia and Italy gathering information on the latest in architecture to ensure that the Zwinger was up to date. This 18C masterpiece was badly damaged during the 1945 bombing raid and restoration work is further hampered by the fact that the soft sandstone used for the construction of the building deteriorates easily when subject to modern levels of pollution.

From the Theaterplatz walk south down the side of the Zwinger and around the corner to enter through the decorative **Glockenspielpavillion**, so called because a carillon of 40 Meissen porcelain bells flank a clock which strikes every hour. Pass through this archway and into the majestic central courtyard, which measures 106 x 107m. From this central position, the layout of this pleasure palace can be fully appreciated. The Glockenspielpavillion lies to the south, the **Crown Gate** (Kronentor) to the west, Wallpavillion to the north and New Gallery to the east. The Kronentor is a two-storey triumphal arch with a dome, surmounted by a resplendent Polish royal crown guarded by eagles representing the political power of Augustus the Strong. The intertwined letters beneath the dome, ARP stand for Augustus Rex Poloniae (Augustus King of Poland), and the two musicians which line the entrance are testament to the celebrations which took place here in 1719 to celebrate the marriage of Augustus's son to Maria Joseph, daughter of the Habsburg Emperor, Joseph I. The New Gallery was added in 1847–55 to fill a gap left during the 18C when finances had run out. This wing was designed by Gottfried Semper in rather unsympathetic Neo-Classical style and, from 1993, will house the Historical Museum and Old Masters Gallery.

Proceed north to the Wallpavillion, the most intricate part of the old building, erected in 1715. Note the splendid hermae which seem to support the entire magnificent structure. The cartouche displays the joint coat of arms of Saxony and Poland and this is surmounted by a statue of Hercules shouldering a globe. Climb the stairs to reach the Nymphenbad (Nymph's Bath) to the right. This is a grotto created by the sculptor Balthasar Permoser, who worked closely with Pöppelmann in creating the splendid sculptures of shepherdesses, nymphs, fawns and vases which lavishly decorate the whole building. The charming Nymphenbad, inspired by Roman fountains which Pöppelmann had seen during a visit to Italy in 1710, consists of a waterfall with carved aquatic symbols such as seaweed, shells and fishes. The central area is surrounded by sculptures of classical figures in Roman robes. Fine views of the building and of Dresden can be glimpsed from the upper balcony on top of the Wallpavillion.

Retracing your steps to the central courtyard head out of the Glockenspielpavillion and turn right. The next staircase leads to the entrance of the **Porcelain Collection**.

After the various festivities, celebrations of the planets, balls and concerts of 1719, the Zwinger was neglected until 1728 when the palace was given a new role as a museum. Augustus had been collecting the fashionable porcelain since he came to the throne. The hard, translucent and delicate pottery was imported from Japan and China and was used in aristocratic circles for ornaments and tableware. The secret of making porcelain had eluded Europeans until a young alchemist, Johann Böttger (1682–1719), arrived in Wittenberg as a fugitive from Prussia and was immediately charged with trying to create gold. Having failed in this task he was then ordered to create the first

European porcelain. He began work in the nearby Albrechtsburg Castle only to be moved when this was invaded by the Swedes. First in the fortress of Königsberg and then in the vaults of the Brühl Terrace, Böttger laboured at his task. In 1708 he produced a high quality, reddish-brown porcelain of which fine examples from the 800 pieces in the collection are on display here. The whole operation was then moved to Meissen and mass production of this early porcelain began in earnest, employing 50 craftspeople. In 1713 Böttger succeeded in producing white porcelain from kaolin, feldspar and quartz and Meissen porcelain broke the Eastern monopoly, much to Augustus the Strong's delight. The finest examples of Meissen entered the Royal Collection and Augustus intended that they should form a prestigious display in a Japanese palace on the Neustadt side of the Elbe. However, plans were shelved when Augustus died in 1733 and the collection of Japanese, Chinese and Meissen porcelain is now housed in two well-lit rooms in the Zwinger.

Highlights of the collection include the tall Chinese *Dragoon vases*, decorated with fabulous dragons and lotus branches in underglaze cobalt blue and dating from the Wan Li period (1573–1619). These were acquired by Augustus the Strong from the ruler of Prussia in 1717 in exchange for providing troops for his dragoon regiment. Fine examples of Böttger's brown stoneware include a statuette of Augustus the Strong (1713); though only 11cm high, it portrays the arrogance and formidable stature of the king. Early white porcelain is shown, including delicate coffee pots, goblets and cups. The Meissen factory became adept at copying oriental porcelain, as the examples dating from 1720 onwards show. The tiny figurines for which Meissen is world famous were produced from the same date. Amusing statues of jesters, courting couples and harlequins were used to decorate the tables of the wealthy during the 18C, and a representative selection is on view here. More remarkable is the collection of 100 porcelain animals, created for Augustus's porcelain zoo by sculptors Kirchner and Kaendler. Splendid dinner services for over 100 guests are on display, together with a huge bouquet of flowers created entirely from porcelain. The latter was created by the French manufacturers Vincennes, with an ormolu base by the French court goldsmith, Duplessis and given as a present to Augustus III by his daughter Maria Josepha in 1749. There is also a small café adjoining the Porcelain Collection with an interesting exhibition, appropriately, on the history of coffee drinking.

If time permits, a visit to the **Mathematical and Physics Collection** is worthwhile. This is situated in the south-western pavilion and houses the royal collection of scientific instruments. The collection was installed in these rooms in 1728 and has remained here since. The first part of the exhibition is made up of over 70 globes and various historic technical instruments in the Grotto Room and Bowed Gallery. The oldest globe is Arabic and dates from 1279. On the first floor is a vast collection of clocks and watches including the magnificent 16C planetary clock created by Eberhard Beldewien and Hans Bucher for Augustus the Strong. 1.2m high, it has eight faces and tracks the paths of the five planets then known, Mercury, Venus, Mars, Jupiter and Saturn. The **Historical Museum** in the Semper Building houses arms and armoury from the Saxon Royal collection including pistols, armour, swords and the coronation robes of Augustus the Strong.

The Zwinger grounds are open 24 hours a day and are lit at night, it is worth walking through the inner courtyard in the evening when the hustle and bustle has died down and the atmosphere can be soaked up.

E. The Neustadt

Lying on the north bank of the Elbe, opposite the Altstadt, is the Neustadt, reached by crossing the Augustusbrücke (Augustus Bridge). There has been a bridge on this site since the 13C and in 1727–31 Pöppelmann built here one of the most beautiful bridges in Germany, connecting the two banks. However, its 25 arches became a hindrance as shipping developed and in 1907 the present bridge was constructed. Partially destroyed during the Second World War, it was rebuilt in 1949. A fine view of the Altstadt, complete with Semperoper and Brühl Terrace, can be glimpsed from halfway across the bridge. Beyond the Marienbrücke to the west can be seen the glass dome of the cigarette factory, Yenidze (1907) built in oriental style to resemble a mosque.

At the Neustadt end of the Augustusbrücke on the left is the **Blockhaus** (Log Cabin), so called because a wooden customs house once stood on this spot. The Baroque building has been reconstructed since the war and was originally designed by Frenchman Zacharias Longuelune in 1755 as the New Watch. It served as the Haus der Deutsch-Sowjetetischen Freundschaft (House of German-Soviet Friendship) in the days of the GDR. The Neustadt Market is reached via the pedestrian subway, where one of the Tourist Information offices is situated. The square is dominated by a magnificent statue of Augustus the Strong on horseback. Created by Ludwig Wiedemann in 1732–34 the striking gilding was added in 1965, earning it the name of Goldener Reiter (Golden Rider). Augustus the Strong had replanned this whole area after it was destroyed by fire in 1685. His original, symmetrical Baroque plan can barely be recognised as most of this district was flattened in 1945.

The street leading north from the Neustadt Market is now known by its pre-war name as the Hauptstrasse, formerly the Strasse der Befreiung (Street of the Liberation). It is a pleasant, tree-lined pedestrian zone with some remains of Baroque Dresden. No. 11 on the left remains intact and is now a popular restaurant with vaulting in the bierkeller dating from the 17C. At No. 13 is the **Museum der Fruhromantik** (Museum of Early Romanticism, Wed–Sun, 10.00–18.00), which opened in 1981. It was the home of Romantic artist Wilhelm von Kügelgen (1802–67). Leading artists Caspar David Friedrich, Kleist and Goethe visited Kügelgen here and nine rooms on the second floor are dedicated to Romanticism in art, music and literature. Of particular interest in this small museum are the authentic 18C furniture and views of Dresden by Christian Gottlob Hammer. The remainder of the Kügelgen Haus is occupied by a quality restaurant, *bierkeller*, grill and café.

From No. 13 head north up Hauptstrasse and on the next left-hand corner is the Dreikönigskirche (Church of the Three Kings), built during 1732–39 by Pöppelmann and completed by Georg Bähr. It was badly damaged in 1945 and at the time of writing was being used as the headquarters for the Saxon Parliament. Further north is a statue of Schiller by S. Werner erected in 1914. Continue north to the Albertplatz with two 19C fountains by R. Diez representing Calm Water and Stormy Waves. There is also the Artesian Well beneath a Jugendstil canopy (1906).

Take the Königsstrasse which leads south-west to the classical **Japanisches Palais**. Built for Count Flemming in 1715 by Pöppelmann, it was bought by Augustus the Strong in 1717 and altered to house the Royal collection of porcelain during 1729–41. The central courtyard is decorated in Chinoiserie style and is well worth a look. The Japanisches Palais now houses the rather dreary Museum of Prehistory and the Museum of Ethnology (Mon–Thurs 09.00–17.00, Sun 10.00–16.00). Canaletto painted one of his most famous views of Dresden from the gardens to the back of the palace adjoining the Bellevue Hotel.

Continue east down Grosse Meissner Strasse. Past the Neustadt Marktplatz is the 17C **Jägerhaus** (Hunting Lodge) which houses the Museum für Volkskunst (Folk Art Museum, Tues–Sun 10.00–17.00). The collection of 8000 objects was opened here in 1913 when the remains of the Royal Hunting Lodge were renovated and formed into a museum. The museum specialises in Saxon arts and crafts, with charming displays of Christmas decorations, hand-painted eggs and folk furniture. The museum fulfils the important role of preserving and documenting regional handicrafts.

F.   The Weisser Hirsch

The Weisser Hirsche was a famous spa resort in pre-war days. The 19C suburb can be reached by walking 5km (approx. 1 hour) upstream along the Altstadt side of the Elbe, starting from the Terrassenufer where the White Fleet are moored. Alternatively a tram can be taken, passing under the new Albertbrücke and through the Elbe Meadows with its grazing sheep. Further east of the Elbe Meadows three small castles can be viewed, built on the former vineyards.

Across the Elbe is the **Schloss Albrechtsberg** built in 1851–54 for Prince Albrecht, brother of the Prussian king Friedrich Wilhelm IV. It was designed in the tradition of Berlin classicism by Adolph Lohse, a pupil of Schinkel. During Communist rule it was used as the headquarters for the Pioneers, a children's organisation, and its future is now under discussion. Beside Schloss Albrechtsberg is the smaller **Schloss Eckberg**, built in 1859–61 by Christian Friedrich Arnold, a student of Semper, in picturesque Gothic Revival style. It is now a middle range hotel. The last of the trio of 19C royal residences is the **Schloss Lingner**, built at the same time as the Schloss Albrechtsberg by the same architect for the prince's chamberlain, Baron von Stockhausen. At the end of the 19C it was bought by Karl August Linger, who made his fortune by inventing the mouthwash 'Odol'. He bequeathed the house to the town of Dresden and it is now the Dresden Club. Continue around the bend of the river to view the **Blaues Wunder** (Blue Wonder) a magnificent bridge built here in 1891–93 and the only bridge to survive World War II intact. Painted a characteristic blue it was a great technical feat at the time it was built, hence earning the name of Blaues Wunder.

To the right of the Blaues Wunder is the 19C **Schiller Garten**, a pleasant restaurant. Crossing over the bridge, fine views of the Loschwitz slopes and the Weisser Hirsch above it can be enjoyed. This suburb was popular with artists and musicians in the 19C and early 20C and many of the houses are built in Jugendstil style. Immediately across the bridge turn left down the Schiller Strasse and the **Schillerhaus** is on your left. This is now a small museum devoted to Schiller, who stayed here as a guest of the Korner family between 1785 and 1787 (Tel. 348315 to arrange appointment to view). Here he wrote *Ode to Joy* and worked on *Don Carlos*, and various mementoes of the composer and contemporary furniture can be seen.

Turn back and enter Kornerplatz, where you can take the restored suspended railway up the hill to Weisser Hirsch. Beside the station at the top is the romantic Villa San Remo with its mini-turrets. The Luisenhof Restaurant in the Schloss is highly recommended, with its marvellous views over the Elbe valley. This is one of the best preserved Jugendstil districts in Europe and has so far escaped the impact of modern property developers.

16

From Dresden to Pirna via Pillnitz

Dresden—10km Pillnitz—7km Pirna.

This route takes in two lovely sights: the first, Pillnitz, is a castle complex in predominantly chinoiserie style featuring a good decorative arts museum and surrounded by beautiful gardens on the banks of the Elbe; the second, Pirna, is a small village tucked away from the usual tourist routes which has a visually stunning church interior.

A. The Palaces and Gardens of Pillnitz

A pleasant way to travel from Dresden to Pillnitz is by boat. The 100-year-old paddle-steamers and modern motorships of the **Weisse Flotte** (White Fleet) travel from Dresden down the Elbe to Pillnitz regularly during the summer months through what has been known as **Saxon Switzerland** since the second half of the 18C. The moorings are at the Terrassenufer, below the Brühlsche Terrasse in Dresden and from there you can take the boat heading upstream for Bad-Schandau or Schmilka. After leaving Dresden, the paddle-steamers travel past Loschwitz, then Blasewitz, soon arriving in Pillnitz (Tel. 43 72 41).

To travel to Pillnitz from Dresden by car takes you through interesting suburbs: there are vineyards to view on the hills, and also the picturesque Elbe to be seen. Leave Dresden on the A6 heading east out of the city. Travel for 4km until reaching Loschwitz, then follow the main link road for approximately 6km to Pillnitz via Wachwitz. It is also possible to reach Pillnitz from Dresden by bus.

Schloss Pillnitz, opening times: the grounds of the Pillnitz Palace are open all year round. However, the palaces are open only between May and October: the Wasserpalais Mon–Sun, 09.30–17.00, closed Tues; the Bergpalais Tues–Sun, 09.30–17.00. The Schlossschranke café-bar, which is at the entrance to the palace grounds is open nearly all year round.

History. Previously on the grounds where the present Neue Palais stands, there was a large late-Renaissance building with four wings acquired by the Wettin dynasty in 1694. It belonged to Sibylle von Neitschutz and was given to her by her lover Elector Johann Georg IV. In 1706 it was bought by Augustus the Strong, who was King of

The Bergpalais, Pillnitz, designed by Mattaeus Daniel Pöppelmann

Poland and elector of Saxony, who in turn gave it to his mistress, Countess Cosel, in 1707. After she had fallen from favour Augustus the Strong set about building a new Baroque summer palace.

The Pillnitz Palaces were built on Augustus the Strong's orders as an 'Indian' summer residence. In 1720 the first plans for a new building were made and by 1724 the Wasserpalais and Bergpalais on the river Elbe had been built by the architects Matthaeus Daniel Pöppelmann and Zacharias Longuelune. They were built in the fashionable chinoiserie style, the models for this exotic architecture being the illustrations of temples and buildings on Chinese and Japanese porcelain which Augustus the Strong collected so avidly. The wide flight of steps from the Wasserpalais down to the river is particularly impressive and were built for ease of travel by river from Dresden to the summer palace. From 1765 onwards, the palace became the permanent summer residence of the House of Wettin. Extensions to the palace were undertaken in 1788 and were completed in 1791, building work being supervised by the architect Christian Friedrich Exner, following the designs of Christian Traugott Weinlig and Johann Daniel Schade. After the old palace had been destroyed by fire in 1818, Christian Friedrich Schmidt built the Neue Palais between 1822 and 1826 in classical style. The hall in the middle wing is the only large room in Dresden that is decorated in Neo-Classical style. Christian Vogel von Vogelstein painted the murals and ceiling frescoes in this hall, in addition to those which can be seen in the Catholic chapel. Pillnitz was used by the Soviets at the end of the Second World War as an assembly point for recovered art treasures. The Museum of Arts and Crafts was established here in 1962.

The grounds surrounding Pillnitz are unique to this part of the world in that they illustrate practically the complete history of landscape gardening. The French-style **Heckengarten** (Hedge Garden), the **Lustgarten** (Pleasure Garden) and garden for courtly games including bowls were laid out during 1720–25 and the Maillebahn was added in 1766. These gardens adjoin the **Englischer Garten** (English Garden) on the hilly, south-eastern side of the palace site which was laid out c 1780. Finally, in the 19C, the landscape garden was created to fufil a more botanical and scientific aim, and was planted with rare, exotic bushes and trees. The charm of this spacious park is increased by the two pavilion buildings, the English pavilion and the Chinese pavilion, as well as the magnificent early 19C gondola in the Heckengarten, used to transport members of the Royal Family to the palace from Dresden.

If you choose to take the White Fleet you will travel east through the romantic and picturesque Elbe Sandstone Mountains. After the woody scenery along the river, you come across the picturesque bright red and ochre façades and the curved, patina green and warm blue roofs of the Indian Palace. Further on the boat glides onto the bank by the **Wasserpalais** (Water Palace). The wide steps to the Palace offers an inviting landing jetty with its two sweeping bannisters which end with two imperious stone sphinxes. The Wasserpalais faces directly onto the Elbe, with an entrance leading down to the river. The façade which faces the Elbe has amazing painted decoration on its eaves illustrating fanciful Indian and Chinese scenes. A tour could begin with a look at the contrasting historic gardens. Directly behind is the Baroque **Lustgarten** (Pleasure Garden). Behind that again is the **Bergpalais** (Mountain Palace). Both palaces were designed by Pöppelmann and they are connected by the **Neuespalais** (New Palace). This was added later and was built by Christian Friedrich Schuricht in 1822, replacing an older Renaissance building which was destroyed in the fire of 1818.

The beautiful gardens extend to the north and west of the castles. They include an Orangery dating from c 1730 which is still used to preserve palms and orange trees in the winter. The pleasure garden is a geometric, Baroque design with centrally placed fountain, which leads onto the Heckengarten between the old palaces. The Heckengarten is another formal garden, consisting of beautifully-kept hedges and paths. The Englische Garten, 100m to the north of the Heckengarten is the most informal in layout, and includes the English Pavilion (1789). The Schlossgarten (Castle Garden) lies to the north of the Bergpalais and beyond it is the Floragarten (Flora Garden), named after the statue of Flora by Wolf von Hoyer created in 1870. Further north is the Chinesischer Garten (Chinese Garden), which includes a Chinese pavilion (1804) and is a fine example of 18C chinoiserie applied to garden design. The famous Japanese Kamelienhaus (House of Camellias) contains Japanese varieties over 200 years old and the Koniferenhain (Conifer Wood).

B.   Kunsthandwerk Museum Schloss Pillnitz

Inside the **Wasserpalais** is a museum devoted to the decorative arts, which is part of the Dresden city collection. The Arts and Crafts Museum mirrors the design of the Bergpalais which it directly faces. The rooms in the Bergpalais can be viewed on the same admission ticket. Entry is gained via the Neues Palais which links the two. The collection was founded in 1876 and went on public display in 1907 in a purpose built location on the Guntzstrasse in Dresden where the School of Arts and Crafts was also housed. After the war the collection was reassembled in its original location and augmented with examples of majolica from the Porcelain Collection and furniture and glass from the Historical Museum. In 1962 the collection was moved to the Wasserpalais at Pillnitz and in 1966 more contemporary examples of art, craft and design were housed in the Bergpalais. The highlights of the Wasserpalais collection includes glassware, pewterware, Dutch and French tin-glazed earthenware, stoneware and textiles. In addition there is work in more unusual materials such as leather (in bookbinding), as well as paper (wallpaper), numerous pieces in stone and other natural materials (raffia, osier). By the end of the war many outstanding works had been destroyed or lost, for example, fifteen goblets from the 16C, 17C and 18C disappeared. In keeping with the exotic design of the Schloss Pillnitz this collection has pieces which have origins outside Europe, for example, Egyptian-Coptic, Byzantine, Indian and Peruvian fragments of textile as well as Persian tin-glazed earthenware. The oldest pieces in the collection are bronze vessels from China c 1500.

The biggest collection of the museum is the textile collection with approximately 13,000 examples; a particular strong point of the collection is the Italian cut velvet fabrics and fine silk cloths. From France there are excellent examples of brocade and silk. There are about 4000 ceramic items which are important, colourful, glazed pieces made by potters, including Italian majolica, Dutch, French and German tin-glazed earthenware and English stoneware. In the metal collection there are about 2500 items including wrought-iron, padlocks, ornamental hinges, copper-coloured pieces, brass and medallions.

There are approximately 2500 items in the collection of furniture and wood-carving. There is a large amount of Gothic work, including some sacred wood-carved figurines. The majority of the furniture is housed in the Bergpalais which forms a more interesting display. There are fine local examples, including a chest of drawers, tables, chairs, and wardrobes of the Baroque and Rococo period. Of considerable historical and artistic value are the 42 musical instruments. These include raffia, keyboard and string instruments.

There is a series of room settings arranged in chronological order with a particularly striking Jugendstil example including a glass-fronted cupboard, made c 1900 in Dresden in mahogany with brass fittings. The glass is beautifully decorated with the swirling stems and exotic flowers typical of the *fin de siècle*. Another fascinating local example of Jugendstil is the clock, designed by the leading German furniture maker Richard Riemerschmid (1868–1957) and made in the Arts and Crafts workshops established in the Dresden suburb of Hellerau at the turn of the century. More recent work includes a suprising example of Bauhaus furniture, a Marcel Breuer Modernist chair designed and made at the School just before it moved from Weimar to Dessau. The glassware collection is dominated by hollow ware. There are also some surviving enamel tankards and goblets with numerous pieces from the 19C and 20C, among them pieces by Emile Gallé.

Many of the rooms in the Bergpalais have been preserved in their original state. The **Festaal** is decorated with Chinese wall and ceiling painting, preserved from the late 19C and featuring kimono-clad figures and peacocks. The west wing of the Bergpalais features examples of 18C, Neo-Classical decoration and furniture. The **Blaues Weinlig Zimmer** (Blue Vine Room) was fully restored in 1971 and is decorated with blue-and-white striped wallpaper with classical borders, chandelier and 18C furniture. The Watteau Room, used for dining, is also quite striking painted in delicate blue and white with Watteau inspired scenes painted in Rococo panels around the room. It is also possible to explore the **Neuespalais** which has less charm than its 18C neighbours. The huge Kuppelsaal has a coffered, domed ceiling, grandiose Corinthian columns and rather pretentious wall painting. The **Schlosskapelle** (Castle Church) has clumsily placed Corinthian pilasters and overblown ceiling paintings in 19C historicist style.

The café and restaurant to the east of the palaces is pleasant enough and a trip further afield, to the north of the site up Lohmener Strasse and right into Bergweg is rewarded with the sight of the small **Weinbergkirche**, designed by Pöppelmann and built during 1723–27.

To travel from Pillnitz to Pirna it is possible to take the White Fleet boats, which sail between Dresden and Bad Schandau, stopping at various town and villages on the way. After the industrial town Heidenau, the next stop is **Pirna**. To travel by road (7km) from Pillnitz to Pirna rejoin the main link road south from Dresden, which will lead you straight into Pirna via Copitz.

If you wish to travel straight from Dresden to Pirna, take the A732 on the south side of Dresden. It is also possible to travel from Dresden to Pirna by rail.

C. Pirna

47,500 inhabitants.

Tourist Information: 31 Dohnaische Strasse. Opening times Mon–Thur 09.00–18.00 and Fri 09.00–15.00. Tel. 2897.

Pirna is a pleasant town lying on the Elbe and is known as the Gateway to Saxony Switzerland. Of particular interest is the medieval town centre with one of the most beautiful Gothic churches to be found in Saxony. The town hall (Rathaus) dating back to 1485, is situated on its own in the middle of the square and there are many well-preserved burgher houses in and around the market place.

History. Pirna developed from a Slavonic settlement on the Elbe to become a trading settlement in the 12C, and is mentioned in historic documents dating back to 1233. From 1294 until 1405 the area around Pirna belonged to the Bohemian crown, but since that time it has been part of Saxony. In the 18C and 19C sandstone extraction played a major role in the economics and trade of this area: sandstone from Pirna was used in many buildings in Germany and other countries, including the Dresden Zwinger and a castle in Copenhagen. The town was mercifully left unscathed during the Second World War and the historic ambience can be enjoyed today on a stroll around the centre.

Proceed up the main shopping street, now a pedestrianised zone, to the MARKT. Lining this picturesque square are burgher houses dating back to the 16C complete with various identification symbols to distinguish them from their neighbours before numbers for houses came into vogue. For example, No. 20 was known as the Marienhaus because a Madonna, dating from 1514, stands on the corner. There are female figures on the eaves on the second floor representing Mary. The house was used as a mint in the 17C and Napoleon stayed here in 1813. In the centre of the Markt stands the resplendent Rathaus, built in 1485 with Gothic portal and gables. The tower was added in 1718 and sports a decorative clock. To the north of the Markt is the Tourist Information office; the **Stadtkirche St Marien** (Church of St Mary) lies to the east of the Markt. (Opening times: daily 10.00–12.00 and 14.00–15.30.)

The Marienkirche, Pirna, one of the most beautifully decorated hall churches in Saxony

The Marienkirche stands on the grounds of a smaller Gothic church which was rebuilt in late Gothic style in 1466–79. It is one of the biggest hall churches in Saxony, and the dramatic vaulting with lavish decoration dating from 1544–46 is well worth seeing. The decoration was added after the church was transformed from Catholic to Protestant worship following the Reformation in 1546. The most impressive vaults can be found in the chancel, where they resemble a tree trunk *Baumstammrippen*. It is presumed that Jorg von Maulbronn was the builder of the vaulting and the plans were drawn up by Peter Ulrich (Peter of Pirna) who also worked on the Annaberger church. The present place of worship was built in 1504 around the old, 60m high tower dating from 1466–78 which was utilised whilst the rest of the old church was demolished.

The exterior of the church is simply monumental with an enormous church roof (the height of the roof truss is almost 20m) dominating the whole area. The nave is 49m long and 25m wide, with seating for 2000. The ceiling painting is dominated by green leaves and vines, and the figures of the apostles, one with the features of Luther. The sandstone pulpit dates from 1520 and the font, with its base carved with playful cherubs, from a similar date. The sandstone altar features scenes from the Old and New Testaments. The splendid organ was built in 1842 by Jahn in Dresden. Following restoration in 1979 it was enlarged to c 4000 pipes and sounds quite splendid today. Look out for the two small portals on the south side of the church decorated with dainty cloverleaves, dating from 16C. The main portal dates from 1890.

Beyond the Marienkirche and perched high above the town is the **Sonnenstein** which has had a troubled history. This 16C fortress served as a lunatic asylum from 1811 until the 1930s, when the Nazis murdered 10,000 patients here.

Other sights to look out for in Pirna include the **Klosterkirche** (Monastery) of the former Dominican order which was originally a Gothic hall church (built c 1300) with a ribbed vault. Since 1957 it has been the town's Catholic church St Heinrichskirche (church of St Heinrich). The **Stadtmuseum** is housed in a late Gothic building on the north side of the Heinrichskirche.

17

From Dresden to Leipzig via Radebeul, Moritzburg and Meissen

Dresden—8km Radebeul—10km Schloss Moritzburg—15km Meissen—58km Leipzig.

By train: from Dresden to Meissen (every 30 mins; journey time: 45 mins).

This tour takes in: Radebeul, an historic town on the fringes of Dresden; the splendid hunting lodge, now museum of the decorative arts at Moritzburg; Meissen, home of one of Europe's best known porcelain factories; and ends in Leipzig.

A. Radebeul

Follow the Leipziger Strasse to **Radebeul**, a small, attractive town approximately 8km to the north-west of Dresden, situated between the Loessnitz vineyards and the banks of the river Elbe. For many Germans, entering Radebeul is like taking a journey back into childhood, as this is the home of *Winnetou* and *Old Shatterhand*, *Sam Hawkins* and *Kara Ben Nevis*, all well loved children's stories written by Karl May. Although Radebeul possesses interesting Baroque and Renaissance buildings, it is mainly recognised for being the site of the **Karl May Museum**, situated at Karl May Strasse 5 (opening times: Tues and Sun 09.00–17.00). Karl May was a famous Saxon author who lived in the imperious Villa Shatterhand from 1896 until his death on 30 March 1912. The Villa now houses the museum in his memory. May wrote adventure stories for children, many of which were set in North America and featured the native Indians. His work is still popular even today. The museum houses an exhibition of the life and work of Karl May, in addition to some of his possessions which include oriental furniture, vessels and weapons amongst which three famous weapons are held: Henrystutzen, Silberbuechse and Baerentoeter. The Wild West and North American culture is vividly illustrated in the Villa Baerenfelt, a large log cabin out in the garden, packed full to bursting point with a unique collection of Indian objects of worship, Chiefs' robes, weapons, household objects and jewellery.

Another interesting museum worth visiting in Radebeul **Museum Haus Hofloessnitz**, is located in the Hofloessnitz Castle. (Opening times: April to November, Wed 14.00–18.00, Thurs and Fri 14.00–16.00, Sat 10.00–16.00 and Sun 14.00–17.00.) Hofloessnitz Castle is a half-timbered building which was erected as a summer residence for the Saxon Elector Johann Georg I in 1649–50. It is discreetly placed at the lower end of the Radebeul vineyards. Inside the castle, the hall on the first floor deserves a mention as it contains fascinating murals depicting exotic Brazilian birds. There is also an exhibition on the development of wine-growing in the local area, the Elbe valley. For the young at heart, Radebeul also boasts a special puppet museum, the **Marionette Theatre Collection** (opening times: closed on Mon, Fri and Sat). This special museum, situated in the Hohenhaus, originates from a private collection resulting from the joint work of Otto Link, the famous puppet show historian and Professor Doctor Arthur Kollmann, the distinguished collector and medical doctor. The two men got to know one another after the First World War and so the collection was founded. Today it consists of several thousands of items representing puppet and figure shows by different makers. The local area is especially well represented in the collection of puppets and sets of Saxon marionette theatres. Part of this interesting collection can be viewed in the permanent exhibition.

From Radebeul the road continues north to **Moritzburg**. However, it is possible to leave your car in Radebeul (at the Weisses Ross) and instead travel by means of the historic narrow gauge railway train through the vineyards to Moritzburg.

B. Schloss Moritzburg

The **Schloss Moritzburg** lies about 14km to the north-west of Dresden, surrounded by idyllic countryside dotted with small lakes, known as the Moritzburg pond district. At one time this area was one of the favourite hunting grounds of the former Saxon electors. There is a harmonious blend of culturally and historically interesting architecture with the Friedewald, a forest abundant in ponds and wildlife. The focal point of the district is Schloss Moritzburg, an impressive Baroque castle painted in ochre and white.

The Schloss houses the **Baroque Museum** (opening times: March–Oct, Tues–Sun 09.00–12.00 and 13.00–16.45, Nov and Feb, Wed–Sun 09.00–12.00 and 13.00–15.45. Guided tours every 60 minutes).

The castle was originally built by Duke Moritz of Saxony as a hunting lodge in 1542–46. However, in 1723–36 Friedrich August I, known as Augustus the Strong, king of Poland and Elector of Saxony, commissioned Pöppelmann, the builder of the Zwinger, and two Frenchmen, Zacharia Longuelune and Jean de Bodt to remodel and extend the lodge into a Baroque pleasure and hunting castle. He also had the castle grounds altered by creating an artificial lake around the castle through the merger of four smaller lakes. The Baroque hunting grounds covered a total area of 2500 hectares of lake and woodland.

The castle principally faces south, standing rather surrealistically in the centre of the artificial lake. Its main axis runs from south to north, and is a four-wing complex with four round turrets and a chapel in the western wing. The castle gardens were to be in a French style, but as a result of the death of Augustus the Strong were never fully completed. The interior of the castle, with its Baroque furnishings which have remained almost unchanged and completely preserved, was decorated by the court painter Louis de Silvestre, the interior designer Raymond Leplat and the decorator Pierre Mercier. There are notable paintings by L. Cranach and A. Thiele throughout the castle, but the sculpture of Der Schmerzesmann (Man in Pain) by B. Permoser, in the Chapel, deserves a special mention.

The tour begins in the entrance hall on the ground floor, used as a passage for carriages in the 16C–18C. One such carriage is on display in the central hall, dating from 1790. The cross vaulting of the hall is a remnant of the old 16C Renaissance building as it was when the Duke Moritz of Saxony was in residence. The splendid leather wall-coverings lend the rooms on the first floor an unusual aura: such tapestries, made of single pieces of leather are covered with silver leaf and painted with translucent warm colours and are rarely seen in situ in such quantities. On the south side of the first floor is the **Monstroesensaal** (Monstrosities Hall). Here one can see leather tapestry scenes depicting the ancient myth of the hunting goddess Diana. The scene on the western wall illustrates Diana and her brother Apollo killing all the children of Niobe. The room also contains an unusual collection of deer trophies with rare antler abnormalities. The high spot of this collection is the so-called Moritzburger 66-Ender, the antlers of a red deer which was bagged by Prince Friedrich III of Brandenburg in 1696.

The **Billiard room** is also decorated with leather tapestries. Here there are scenes depicting the *'Parforcejagd'* (a type of hunt), which was the hunting tradition of sporting heads of the household as far back as the 16C. The room contains the original billiard table dated 1700. Many of the portraits in the castle's rooms were painted by the court painter Louis de

A detail of Schloss Moritzburg, which was redesigned and extended from a hunting lodge into a castle by Matthaeus Daniel Pöppelmann in 1723–36

Silvestre. In 1715, Silvestre was called from the court of Louis XIV in France to the Saxon court. After the completion of some work in Paris he went to Dresden a year later. From 1716 onwards he carried out various orders for King Augustus II, and later for his son Augustus III. In particular Silvestre's portraits decorate the 'Quartiere' which connect the rooms. Gloriously colourful leather tapestries and chairs covered in matching coloured leather convey the first splendid impression of these 'Quartieren'. The leather chairs were made for Moritzburg in 1727–28 by Samuel Girckhoff. Some of the pieces of furniture on display are *pièces de résistance* of Saxon cabinet-making, an example of which is the Stollenschrank (gallery cupboard), crafted by the cabinet maker of Dresden, Johann Gottfried Heinrich Grahl.

The **deer trophy collection** in Moritzburg shows an extensive hunting activity and tradition which was pursued for centuries in the Friedewald. There were plans for the enclosure of a deer park going back to the 17C. Later in the 18C in the years of the renovations of Moritzburg castle, Augustus the Strong typically had his own ideas about the deer park; hand-drawn sketches and notes in his handwriting illustrate his interest in the designing of the park. The most significant part of the Moritzburg deer trophy collection is displayed in the castle dining hall. Most of the red deer trophies on display here are between 260 and 400 years old. They mainly come from healthy Saxon hunting ground or were gifts to the household from guests to the castle. Amongst them is the heaviest known red deer trophy in the world, which with 298,600 international valuation points and weighing in at 19,865 kg lies far above the present world record. A total of 22 red deer trophies of gold medal standard decorate the dining hall. Together with a further 45 significant pairs of antlers they make a spectacular sight on the walls. A single antler with a calyx formed crown has served as a welcome sign to Moritzburg castle since 1689, and can nowadays be seen in the dining hall. All the antlers are mounted on carved wooden animal heads, which were probably made by the sculptors Benjamin Thomas and Johann Christian Kirchner and date back to the 18C.

The furnishing of the museum rooms includes Baroque sculpture from France, a statue of Gegeisselten Christus created by Balthasar Permoser and placed in the castle chapel, and numerous paintings by Bottschild, Rotari, Silvestre, Fehling, Cranach and others. Since 1984, the rooms in the first floor of the hunting tower were recreated in their 1925 state. Some of the collection fell victim to the Second World War and some pieces can be found displayed in other museums. In these rooms one can see Böttger stoneware, Kaendler porcelain and pieces of different services made from Meissner, porcelain (porcelain from Meissen, which is not far from Moritzburg).

Moritzburg castle was home to noble hunting families until 1945. Prince Ernst Heinrich of Saxony carried out extensive building work on the castle between 1925 and 1935. After the completion of a state treaty between the free state of Saxony and the former *Königshaus* in 1925, in which was written the ownership relations of the former Saxon Kings and the noble families, the renovation work in the castle was begun under the direction of Dr Erwin Hensler. The parquet floor on the first floor was renewed, the attic storey was secured through an imposing steel construction, and a spacious living area was arranged in the south-east wing of the castle for Prince Ernst Heinrich and his family. The fundamental renovation work was almost totally finished in 1935. There is evidence to prove that Prince Ernst Heinrich and his family regularly stayed at Moritzburg castle in the 1920s and 30s and the family brought to the castle a large part of an expensive collection of paintings, porcelain and other valuables. The huge safe built in behind the metre thick wall of the western terrace is witness to the value of the collection. By order of the art-loving Prince Ernst Heinrich of Saxony, the 77-year-old graphic artist Käthe Kollwitz came to Moritzburg on 20 July 1944, and stayed in two small rooms in Ruedenhof nearby until her death on 22 April 1945. Since 1955, a modest exhibition of the prints and drawings of this significant German artist, which sets out her life and work, has been on show in the Moritzburg. There is a very good café-bar beside the Kollwitz exhibition. A stroll around the extensive grounds should not be missed, especially as they contain interesting garden follies.

Das Fasanenschlösschen (The Little Pheasant Palace; opening times: 15 March to 31 October daily 09.00–16.00) was erected during 1769–82 to the east of the main castle on the Great Pond (Grossteich). It is a small Rococo structure and is one of the few buildings in the Dresden area dating back to 1770 which has retained its original interior decoration and furnishing and survived the centuries without suffering any substantial war damage. Together with a miniature harbour and lighthouse, the Little Pheasant Palace forms a charming ensemble. The harbour and lighthouse were built for Augustus the Strong as a background for the naval battles he enacted here. Nowadays the Little Pheasant Palace houses an ornithological exhibition put on by the Dresden Zoological museum, and contains information on the unusual variety of species inhabiting the Moritzburg pond district. Not far from the Little Pheasant Palace is the former Electoral *Waldschenke*, which was built in 1770. Today however, it is a renowned historic restaurant decorated with partly original furnishings; it also offers accommodation and has and a large garden surrounding it.

Near to Moritzburg, and surprisingly close to a big city like Dresden is the game park. In addition, as a result of the hunting tradition of the area, the thoroughbred horse was also bred in Moritzburg. There is a publicly owned Stallion Depot (Hengstdepot), which is an internationally respected stud farm for riding horses. Each year in late summer, it stages popular stallion shows and jumping tournaments. Equally popular is the Moritzburg *Fischzug*, a fishing exhibition held on the shores of the Palace pond (Schlossteich) in the autumn. The Moritzburg ponds serve not only for the traditional carp breeding, but also offer the visitor ideal bathing and camping sites during the warmer months. Those seeking shade and stillness can find it by exploring the western nature protection area of the Friedewald.

From the Schloss Moritzburg take the A6 to Meissen which can also be reached by the regular S-Bahn trains in approximately 45 minutes, or alternatively from Dresden by a cruise down the river Elbe.

**C. Meissen

35,500 inhabitants.

Tourist Information: An der Frauenkirche 3, 01067 Meissen. Tel 4470. Opening times: Mon–Fri, 09.00–18.00, Sat (during tourist season) 10.30–14.30.

The first view of this town, best known for its delicate porcelain, is the striking silhouette comprising the Albrechtsburg castle and the filigree double-towered facing of the medieval Dom high up on the Burgberg (Castle Hill). Meissen is often crowded during the tourist season, being a popular destination for coach trips and during the height of the summer it is wise to arrive early in the morning to avoid the crowds. Meissen is basically a medieval town with numerous winding alleys, narrow passages and steps and it is therefore advisable to leave the car parked in the designated area near the river and complete your tour on foot.

History. The thousand-year-old town was historically the 'cradle of the land of Saxony'. Historical proof of the fact is clearly visible in that the cathedral, the Albrechtsburg castle and former Bishop's palace built high up on a rocky outcrop, tower over the maze of houses and alleyways down in the valley below. In 929, King Heinrich I had a border defence fort 'Misni' built in Meissen, so as to keep order over the native Slavic population. The castle as seen today was completed in 1485 when the royal seat of the Wettins transferred their residence to Dresden. The diocese of Meissen originated in 968, and the town itself was mentioned in documents as early as 1225.

For centuries the Bishops and Margraves of Meissen had great political influence and although the town did lose its political power when the royal seat moved to Dresden in 1485, it was to become renowned throughout the world thanks to the alchemist Johann Friedrich Böttger in 1710. Böttger was condemned by Augustus the Strong to live at Albrechtsburg in order to invent gold for him; instead however, he discovered the way to make 'white gold', European hard-paste or true porcelain. In 1710, the royal porcelain factory was founded in the castle. There is still a memorial to Böttger today in front of the buildings into which the oldest European porcelain factory moved in 1865.

The Thirty Years War brought terrible decay to the town and the first signs of economic recovery were further destroyed in the war of the Prussian King Friedrich II and in the Napoleonic wars. Remarkably however, Meissen suffered very little damage during the Second World War. Industrialisation made an impact on the town in the 20C and the upturn of porcelain production gave rise to growth in Meissen of exceptionally extensive industry which flourished even during the GDR regime. The town is now very popular with foreign tourists, mainly because of the links with the highly collectable porcelain, which can be bought in the shop attached to the factory.

The best place to begin your tour of the town is the MARKT (Marketplace), the centrepiece of the Bürgerstadt. Even today, the Markt is still the central point of local activity. On the northern side of the Markt is the **Rathaus**, which was built in 1472 by Arnold von Westphalen. It is a striking building with its three late Gothic decorated gables. Here you can also see one of the most beautiful houses in the town, the **Marktapotheke** (Chemist's, Markt 4), which was built in the middle of the 16C. It is also worth visiting the **Frauenkirche** (Church of Our Lady; opening times May–Sept Tues–Thurs 10.00–12.30 and 13.00–17.00) just off the Markt to the south-west, a Gothic church with a lavishly decorated interior. On the hour you can distinctly hear the chime of the porcelain carillon installed in its tower in 1929. Climbing the tower you are rewarded by a fine view of the Meissen and the Elbe beyond (opening times: May–Sept Tues–Thurs 13.00–16.00). Look out for the *Coronation of the Virgin altarpiece* dating from c 1500.

Ascend the Superintendentenstufen steps at the rear of the Frauenkirche and north up the Freiheit you reach the former monastery of St Afra. This was the site of the first parish church of Meissen, which was erected in the 11C. At the beginning of the 13C it was replaced by the new building of the Augustiner-Chorherrnstift (Augustiner Men's Choir Foundation). Here you can see the wooden pulpit (dated 1657) and the early Baroque carved altar (c 1660). The monastery was secularised in 1540 as a consequence of the Reformation. Elector Moritz of Saxony established the first Saxon 'royal school', an elite school for pupils selected on their abilities, rather than on their social standing, in its rooms. The satirist Gottlob Wilhelm Rabener, Samuel Hahnemann, the founder of homeopathy and the poets Lessing and Gellert are among the best-known former pupils of the school.

To commemorate the fact that the painter Ludwig Richter lived in Meissen from 1928 to 1936, there is a plaque on the Burglehen Freiheit 2. By crossing the SCHLOSSBRÜCKE (Castle Bridge) and going through the portal decorated with two mosaic pictures, created by Wilhelm Walther (creator of the mural Parade of Princes), you arrive at the **Burgberg** (Castle Hill). Here the splendid Meissen **Dom** (Cathedral) faces you as you approach the top of the Burgberg. (Opening times: Oct–March daily 09.00–15.30; Apr–Sept daily 09.00–16.30).

The Dom in Meissen is considered to be one of the most significant Gothic buildings to be found in Germany. It was built between the years of 1260 and 1410 on the site of a former Romanesque edifice. Work was started on the west towers at the beginning of the 14C, but sadly they were destroyed by a storm in 1413. After having been reconstructed in the 15C, they were again ruined by lightning in 1547. The towers which can be seen today, although convincingly Gothic in design, were actually erected in 1903–08 by Karl Schaefer of Karlsruhe, the winner of an architectural competition. After the Reformation the cathedral became Protestant.

The interior of the cathedral is decorated with valuable, mostly medieval furnishings. In the FURSTENKAPELLE, a small chapel built onto the west portal in c 1420, are the fine tombs of the ancestors of the erstwhile kings of Saxony dating from 15C and 16C. That of Elector Frederick the Warlike, who died in 1428, stands in the centre cast in brass surrounded by nine others from the Vischer workshop at Nuremburg. The richly decorated portal was added in the 19C and to the right is the GEORGSKAPELLE which houses the tomb of Duke George the Bearded who died in 1539 and his wife Barbara who died in 1534. There is a small Lucas Cranach altarpiece here and a striking marble relief of c 1530 above the entrance. Further into the Dom on the right is the octagonal JOHANNISKAPELLE dating from 1291 with three sculptures representing St John the Baptist, Madonna and Child and an angel. The 13C statues of the patrons and founders in the High Choir deserve a special mention. The figures are sculpted out of sandstone and have coloured settings, and are among the best 13C century sculptures to be found in central Europe. It is thought that they are most probably the work of the Naumburg Master. The triptych altarpiece shows the *Adoration of the Magi* by an unknown 16C German painter under the influence of the Dutch School. The central stained glass window in the choir dates from the 13C. Organ and choral concerts are frequently held in the cathedral.

The **Albrechtsburg** stands to the left of the Dom (opening times: Tues–Sun 09.00–17.00, last admission 16.00, closed Jan). The Albrechtsburg is a good example of the transition from a medieval fort designed to defend and protect, to a castle symbolising royal prestige. It is the most significant secular building erected in Germany towards the end of the Middle Ages. The castle was commissioned by Elector Ernst of Saxony and his brother Duke Albrecht, the rulers of the Wettin territories. It was built to the plan of Arnold von Westphalen and while the building was in progress, the heirs of the two brothers split into two opposing groups and Meissen became the seat of the Albertines. Soon after Albrechtsburg was completed, the Albertine residence was moved to Dresden. The castle did not really gain importance until the first European porcelain factory in was located here in 1710.

The Albrechtsburg has to be entered from the rear due to its grand towering position above the valley. Note the GROSSER WENDELSTEIN (Great External Staircase) which spirals up the exterior. Actually inside the castle, most of its interior is not very inviting; it has never been lived in for any length of time. In several rooms the work of 19C Romantic painters can be enjoyed with a series of heroic murals depicting the history of the House of Wettin. It is worth taking a look inside, even if just to see the eccentric vaulting which was a distinctive trait of Arnold von Westphalen; there is an incredible range of styles from one room to the next. There is also a small exhibition of 15C and 16C artwork, including prints by Dürer. The tour ends with a descent down the stone Grosser Wendelstein. Outside on the left are two very acceptable restaurants, the Domkeller and Burgkeller. The latter has an informal terrace café with fantastic views over the ancient, red-tiled rooftops of the town (open daily).

Descend the Burgberg and continue south through the Markt onto Fleischergasse to join Neugasse; this leads to Talstrasse where the **Staatliche Porzellan-Manufaktur** can be found at No. 9 (opening times: Schauhalle (Porcelain Museum) 1 March–30 Nov, Tues–Sun 08.30–16.30, last admission 16.00, closed Mon and from 12.00 on the Friday before Whitsun; Schauwerkstatt (workshop open to the public) 1 March–30 Nov, Tues–Sun 08.30–12.00 and 13.00–15.15 (last guided tour), closed on Mon and from 12.00 on the Friday before Whitsun; Visitors' Office, Tues–Fri 08.30–15.00; tel. 541, Ext. 391).

Since the middle of the 18C, Meissen porcelain has been recognised by its hallmark of the blue crossed swords, as a quintessential luxury product. All the pieces, whether items for daily use or ornamental pieces of porcelain, are created by hand using traditional methods even today. The worldwide recognition of Meissen porcelain is based on the artistry and skill of the painter and creator, and on the traditions and experiences of the last 280 years. Well over 100,000 different pieces are included in the current range and its repertoire is steadily increasing. From 6 June 1710 until 1864 Meissen porcelain was made in Albrechtsburg castle so as to keep the manufacturing process secret. A year later production was moved to the Triebisch valley, and it has remained there since.

The **Schauhalle** houses an impressive and comprehensive collection of about 3500 pieces of porcelain, following its development from 1710 up until the present day. Full dinner services from the 18C, Rococo figurines, Jugendstil and Art Deco examples are well laid out in chronological order. More disappointing are the designs from GDR times which are traditional and uninspired. This part of the Porzellanmanufaktur now contains a shop which sells lovely examples of the porcelain (before reunification it was impossible to purchase any items at the factory).

It is also possible to take a rather mechanical tour which illustrates the workshop techniques used for producing the porcelain through the individual stages. Upon entering the Porzellanmanufaktur it is wise to enquire at the kiosk when the next English tour leaves. Individual modellers and hand-painters can be seen at work and the delicate skills involved in making the porcelain fully appreciated. In the first room, you can see how the porcelain mass is produced from the three components of kaolin (china clay), feldspar and quartz. The kaolin is an indigenous raw material which is extracted from an underground mine belonging to the factory situated near by. The feldspar is imported from Scandinavia and serves as a fluxing agent, and then a small percentage of quartz is used in order to enhance the transparency of the porcelain. The information is imparted in English if you time your tour right, and played on a cassette tape over a loudspeaker. Moving onto the second room when instructed to do so by the tape, the method by which the porcelain is sent to the 'thrower', who shapes the required pieces of porcelain is shown.

In the third room, you meet the repairer, who puts the individual parts of figures together and reworks artistic details. The most famous 18C Meissen porcelain designer, was Johann Joachim Kändler who worked at the factory from 1731 until his death in 1773, and produced a huge number of porcelain figures as well as creating the major dinner and tea service designs of his time. The porcelain is painted in two stages; the first is underglaze painting which takes place after the the first baking at 900 degrees. Then, after glazing and maturing of the porcelain at 1450 degrees, on-glaze painting is carried out. In the fourth room, you can watch the underglaze painting; this can only be done with colours which are able to bear the high maturing temperature. The most famous underglaze colour used at the Meissen factory is cobalt blue, and it has been used since the 1720s. Cobalt blue was mainly used to produce the world renowned Meissen onion pattern, which was created in 1739, to resemble a Chinese prototype. After underglaze painting the piece is dipped into the glaze and then matured in gas-heated bogie kilns. Finally, if the porcelain is intended for on-glaze painting, it is then sent to the on-glaze painter. The last room demonstrates this technique, which is completed entirely unaided by machine. The painters vary the motifs so no two pieces of porcelain are alike. The colours are then baked into the porcelain in electric kilns. Finally, rims, handles and spouts are gilded using burnished gold. The piece is then baked again and to produce the desired golden gleam, the gilded surface has to be polished with an agate pencil. The process is completed by baking the porcelain for a third time at about 900 degrees in electric kilns. This tour and demonstration takes around 30 minutes and is well worthwhile even though the presentation is rather dated.

From Meissen town centre take Hochuferstrasse heading west which skirts the banks of the River Elbe to continue the journey on the A6 to Leipzig.

18

Leipzig

556,000 inhabitants.

Tourist Information: Sachsenplatz 1, 04109, Tel. 79590 and 7959326, Fax 281854. Opening times: Mon–Fri 09.00–18.00; during trade fair daily 08.00–20.00.

Leipzig Airport, PSF 1, Telex 512320, tel. 592313. Airport Leipzig-Schkeuditz tel. 313103. Aeroflot, Grimmaische Strasse 16, tel. 286025, Lufthansa, Reichsstrasse 18, tel. 273132.

Railway Stations: Hauptbahnhof (main railway station) is on the north-east side of the Ring (ringroad), tel. 7243265.

LEIPZIG is a vibrant and important commercial centre and one of the greatest publishing cities of Europe. It is best known, however, for its musical links: Johann Sebastian Bach, Mendelssohn, Schumann and Richard Wagner all lived and worked here. In addition to this, there is the production of Bluthner pianos, in a factory which was founded in 1853. Splendid historic buildings have survived including the Altes Rathaus, Alte Handelsborse (Old Trading Exchange) and Auerbach's Keller, decorated with scenes from Goethe's masterpiece. Also of interest is the fact that Lenin stayed in Leipzig; the Russian Marxist paper *Iskra* (*The Spark*) was produced in this city. Leipzig was celebrated during communist rule as a great trading centre, with the Leipzig Fair held annually and attended by an

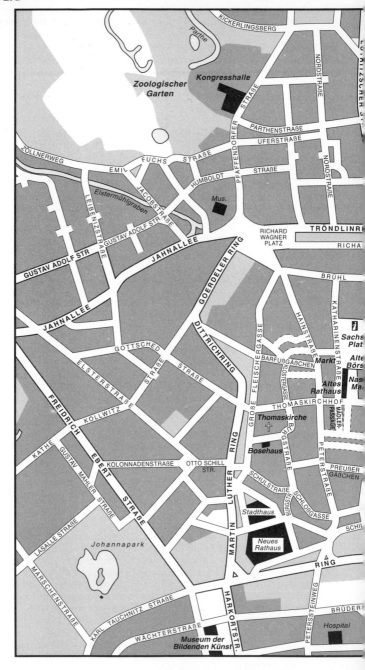

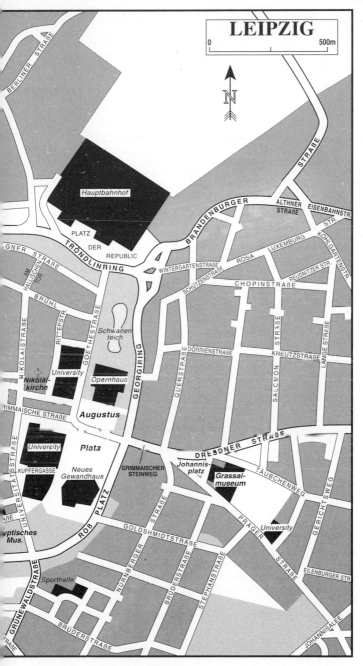

LEIPZIG

0   500m

N

Hauptbahnhof

BERLINER STRAßE

PLATZ DER REPUBLIC

TRÖNDLINRING

BRANDENBURGER

ALTHNER STRAßE

EISENBAHNSTR.

STR

GNER STRAßE

AM HALLISCHEN TOR

BRÜHL

NIKOLAISTRAßE

RITTEPSTR.

GOETHESTRAßE

Schwanen teich

WINTERGARTENSTRAßE

SCHÜTZENSTRAßE

ROSA LUXEMBURG

KOHLGARTENSTR

REUDNITZER STR.

CHOPINSTRAßE

University

Nikolai-kirche

Opernhaus

GEORGIRING

QUERSTRAßE

DÖRRIENSTRAßE

STRAßE

KREUTZSTRAßE

LANGE STRAßE

SALCMON

GRIMMAISCHE STRAßE

Augustus

UNIVERSITÄTSSTRAßE

University

Platz

KUPFERGASSE

Neues Gewandhaus

GRIMMAISCHER STEINWEG

STRAßE

DRESDNER STRAßE

Johannis-platz

Grassai-museum

TAUBCHENWEG

GERICHSWEG

ptisches Mus.

ROß PLATZ

GOLDSHMIDTSTRAßE

NÜRNBERGER STRAßE

BRUDERSTRAßE

STEPHANSTRAßE

PRAGER STRAßE

University

EILENBURGER STR

Sporthalle

GRUNEWALDSTRAßE

BRÜDERSTRAßE

JOHANNISALEE

international crowd of manufacturers, engineers and scientists from the communist bloc. This reinforced Leipzig's international links throughout the days of the GDR. The city remains a vitally important cultural centre, where the great traditions are maintained and tourism from the West is providing a growing source of trade.

History. Leipzig began as a Wendish fishing-village in the 10C, and is first mentioned as a town in 1015. It derives its name from a Slavonic castle called Libzi. In 1160 Otho the Rich, Margrave of Meissen, laid the foundations of the German town Lipzk (called Leypezik after 1456) and prohibited fairs within a five-mile radius other than those held there at Easter and Michaelmas. Leipzig's position at the intersection of many vitally important trade routes between Poland and North Germany certainly favoured its growth. The university was founded in 1409 by refugees from Prague. In 1497 and 1507 Emperor Maximilian I confirmed and extended the privileges of the Leipzig fairs. The Reformation was introduced in 1539. During the Thirty Years War Leipzig was five times besieged and captured, but its trade was only temporarily halted. In the middle of the 18C Leipzig held first place in Germany as a literary, artistic and social centre. Johann Sebastian Bach was 'cantor' at the Thomas Kirche from 1723, and Goethe studied at the university in 1765–68. Its pre-eminent position in the book trade dates from the 17C.

The Battle of Leipzig, known in Germany as the Battle of the Nations (Volkerschlacht), was fought on 16–19 October 1813. After fruitless peace negotiations at Prague in August of 1813, three armies were raised against Napoleon by the Allies (Prussia, Austria, Russia and Sweden). The main Bohemian army was commanded by Prince Schwarzenburg. In order to prevent the Allies from joining forces, Napoleon withdrew his army from Dresden to Leipzig, and the battle started on 16 August. 18 October marked the most critical phase of the battle, when the fighting intensified. By nightfall, the French had retreated to the town, which was taken by storm the following day. Napoleon fled with the rest of his army, and Germany was freed from the French.

The events of the war of liberation of 1813 in which 22,000 Russians lost their lives is commemorated in the Russian Church, which was consecrated in 1913. In that battle 300,000 Prussians, Russians, Austrians and Swedes confronted 140,000 French troops. To the south of the city there is also a 91m tall monument to the Battle of the Nations designed by Schmidt and Thema and built in 1898–1913.

During the 18C Leipzig was the focus of a literary movement under Gottsched, and it suffered greatly during the Napoleonic wars. Leipzig, as the GDR's second city assumed leadership of the *Wende*, the peaceful revolution that toppled the Communist dictatorship in 1989 and brought in the elections which led to unification a year later. Due partly to the continued importance of the Trade Fairs, with their eight-hundred-year tradition, Leipzig did not suffer under Communism the degree of isolationism experienced by so many other places behind the Iron Curtain.

A. Town Tour

The enormous **Hauptbahnhof** (main railway station) is situated at the north-eastern end of the RING (inner ring road). The ring traces the route of the old city walls and encircles the **Altstadt** where the majority of the historic buildings are situated. Apart from its unfortunate state of disrepair, the Hauptbahnhof is an important piece of early 20C railway architecture and is one of the main sights of Leipzig. It was built during 1907–15, designed by Lossow and Kuhne, and it is claimed to be one of the largest passenger train stations in the world, occupying a site that was formerly held by four small terminals and covers 1560 hectares (3855 acres). The station has two entrance halls and two levels because until centralisation was fully introduced under the Third Reich, the Prussian and Saxon authorities each ran their own separate half of the station.

From the Hauptbahnhof follow the NIKOLAISTRASSE which immediately faces the Hauptbahnhof's south entrance. This passes by the **Nikolaischule** on the left, one of the oldest schools in Germany having been founded in 1512.

The **Nikolaikirche** stands opposite, one of the two major churches in Leipzig and one of many in the city named after St Nicholas, the patron saint of merchants and traders. This church was the local rallying-point during the *Wende*. Prayers and meetings have taken place here since 1982, and the church provided one of the focal points of the revolution. Despite the fact that it looks like a sombre medieval structure from outside, the interior of the church is quite stunning. This can be attributed to the transformation undertaken by Johann Friedrich Carl Dauthe in 1784–97 which resulted in a blend of Rococo and Neo-Classical styles. The double galleried nave is particularly striking, with its brightly painted, coffered vault. This is supported by white painted Corinthian columns with capitals in the unexpected form of palm trees and painted in vivid green. The western side of the Nikolaikirche was erected in 1170 and remains one of the largest Romanesque stoneworks in Leipzig. The powerful block is 22.5m wide and 9m deep. In the 14C, the Gothic east choir and the Romanesque west wing with its octagonal tower were built. The three-naved late-Gothic hall is a result of the large-scale renovation by Benedikt Eisenburg in 1513–26. The church nave is of considerable size, being 32m long, 28m wide and 17m high; with a total length of 63m and a total width of 45m, the Nikolaikirche is the biggest church in the city.

The tower, like so many other important Leipzig buildings, goes back to the builder Hieronymus Lotter. He took charge of the construction of the middle tower in 1555 and both side towers were designed in a Renaissance style. The Baroque composition dates from 1730. With a height of 75m it dominates the main tower of the Thomaskirche by 8m. The tower holds 35 paintings by Adam Friedrich Öser, the altarpiece, the choir painting and the *trompe l'oeil* sky painting dating from 1778–87. The Gothic church fittings were all replaced in the 18C apart from the Luther pulpit which dates from 1521. Whether the reformer ever stood on the pulpit is in doubt, but thanks to the assumption that he did indeed preach from here, it was saved.

To the west of the Nikolaikirche, opposite the main door stands the **Specks Hof**, a 20C building used for the Trade Fair and containing a shopping arcade on the ground floor. Continue south to join the GRIMMAISCHE STRASSE, turning right to head west. On the south side of the Grimmaische Strasse is the famous **Auerbachs Keller**, situated in a small arcade, the Madlerpassage. Two sculptures stand at the entrance: Faust with Mephistopheles, and The Enchanted Tipplers, both of which refer to Goethe's Faust drama. Auerbachs Keller was originally built in the mid-16C but shot to international fame when Goethe set one of the major scenes of the Faust play here. Although it is always crowded, it is worth persevering to enjoy lunch or an evening meal here; the atmosphere is terrific, the food good and the interior decoration fascinating. The walls are decorated with 19C murals depicting scenes from the Faust saga. (Opening times: daily 10.00–midnight.) Return to the Grimmaische Strasse and virtually opposite is the **Alte Rathaus**, one of the most historically interesting buildings in Leipzig.

Continue west to view the entire façade of the Altes Rathaus from the vantage point of the Markt. This building was designed by Hieronymous Lotter in German Renaissance style in 1558 but virtually rebuilt in 1907 with concrete being used in the reconstruction. It is painted in cream and ochre with decorated, stepped gables, an asymmetrically placed clock tower above the main entrance, and a lengthy inscription encircling the entire building. The ground floor of the building acts as a covered arcade with shops. The upper storeys, which were the official town hall until 1905 when a new replacement was built, now accommodate the **Stadtgeschichtliche Museum** (Local History Museum; opening times: Tues–Fri 10.00–18.00, Sat and Sun 10.00–16.00). The 43m long Festsaal (festival hall) on the first floor, the former hall of justice, is impressive with its ornate chimneypieces, doorways and full-length portraits of the local mayors and Saxon Electors. The museum exhibits feature the oldest book to be printed in Leipzig: dating from 1481, it is a Latin version of the Book of Revelations. There is also a room dedicated to Felix Mendelssohn-Bartholdy, who spent the last 12 years of his life in Leipzig, composing and directing the Gewandhausorchester. Other exhibits tell the story of Leipzig's development as a city of music, books and trade.

On the north side of the Markt is another civic building by Lotter, **Die Alte Waage** (the Old Weigh House), built in 1555. Originally goods were taken here, weighed and exchanged, and duties paid to the Municipal Council. During 1661 and 1712 it was used as a post office and from 1917 until the bombing raid of 1943 it was the office where tickets could be booked for international exhibitions and music concerts. It was virtually destroyed in 1943 and only its sundial-crowned façade with stepped gables was subsequently restored during 1963–64 to be occupied by the GDR Travel Agency. On the north-western corner of the Markt is the **Barthels Hof**, a multi-purpose building used during the 18C as a base for negotiations during the Trade Fairs and the exhibition and storage of goods. It was built in Classical style in 1743 on the foundations of an earlier building, erected in 1523. A quick detour north-west down the Kleine Fleischergasse is rewarded with the sight of the historic **Zum Kaffeebaum** at No. 4 (opening times: Mon–Fri 11.00–midnight, Sat 11.00–15.00). First mentioned as a fashionable coffee house in 1694 it was where Goethe, Lessing, Liszt, Wagner and Schumann would meet with their circle of friends. A charming carved stone panel above the main entrance, depicting a Turk resplendent with turban and baggy trousers offering a cup of coffee to a delighted cherub, reminds visitors of the exotic source of the then fashionable beverage. Zum Kaffeebaum still functions as a café and inside the wood-panelled rooms there is a small memorial to Robert Schumann.

Return to the Markt and continue south noting the modern building straight ahead, the **Messehaus am Markt**, built for the Trade Fairs and bearing the familiar double M initials of the Fairs. Also on the southern edge of the Markt stands the **Königshaus**, originally built in 1610 but radically altered during 1706–07 with full restoration taking place in 1967. Eminent visitors to Leipzig including Tsar Peter the Great stayed here. Blending in with the Altes Rathaus in ochre and cream, the Baroque façade is decorated with splendid swags and a small balcony. Pass the southern edge of the Altes Rathaus and then proceed north behind it to enter the Naschmarkt and view the oldest Baroque building in Leipzig, **Die Alte Börse** (the Old Stock Exchange). This early Baroque building—noticeably symmetrical—is ascribed to the architect Johann Georg Starcke and came into being in the years 1678–87. Since the re-opening in 1963 (following reconstruction after the destruction of the Second World War), Die Alte Börse now serves as a centre for lectures and concerts. Outside the Alte Börse stands a statue of Goethe by Seffner (1903) representing the poet in his student days at Leipzig University. From the Alte Börse continue south to rejoin the Grimmaische Strasse heading west to the **Thomaskirche**.

This church is important as it was here that Johann Sebastian Bach served as *Kantor* (lead singer) during 1723–50. He composed many of his best known choral works for use in the Thomaskirche services. The church was originally part of an Augustinian monastery, founded c 1200. The monasteries played a crucial role in the development of the city's traditional role as a seat of learning. After the Reformation their manuscript collections formed the basis of the world-class University Library. Leipzig University was actually opened in the refectory of the St Thomas Cloisters in 1409. All that now remains is the Thomaskirche itself. The Romanesque Choir was rebuilt in Gothic style in 1355 and this style predominates apart from the Romanesque window on the northern side of the choir. In 1482 the entire Romanesque nave of this church was pulled down and a church in the latest Gothic style was erected, to be consecrated in the year 1496. The Baroque tower received its final form in 1702. The 17C chapel annexes and staircase tower which dominated the entire northern front of the nave were removed during a brutal 'restoration' in 1884–89, when all the Baroque ornamentation was destroyed in favour of Gothic Revival. Despite this the church's historic links with Bach and the surviving features make it well worth a visit.

The church itself is 76m long with the nave measuring 50m; it is 25m wide and 18m high. The Renaissance church galleries were constructed by Hieronymus Lotter after 1539, the year when the Reformation started. The font by Franz Doteber dates from 1614, and the Altar Cross dates from 1720. Below the south gallery are interesting tombstones, the oldest being that for a knight named Harras (d. 1451), and one for the Wiedebach family, which was erected in 1517. In the northern area of the intersection of nave and transept is a memorial to the town councillor Daniel Leicher which dates from 1612. Portraits of every superintendent of Leipzig hang in the Sanctuary which dates from 1614. The crucifix on the altar, preserved from the time of Bach, was made by Caspar Friedrich Löbelf. It is interesting to note that the stained-glass windows all date from after the 1889 restoration.

Bach himself performed in the Thomaskirche during the last 27 years of his life. After the Johanniskirche was destroyed in World War Two the remains of Bach, which had been resting there, were brought to their current home in the choir-stalls of the Thomaskirche in 1950. The organ in the west nave was built in 1889. Unfortunately the organs from Bach's time have not survived the ravages of time.

The Thomaskirche choir can normally be heard on Fridays at 18.00 and Saturdays at 13.30, and at the Sunday service at 09.30. The choir, which had 54 members in Bach's time, regard it as their very special duty to give priority to Bach's works in the weekly cantatas. Outside the church there is a monument to Bach, commissioned by Mendelssohn Brady and made by Seffner in 1908. Opposite the Bach monument at No. 16 Thomaskirchof, is the **Bosehaus**, originally built for the gold and silver merchant Georg Heinrich Bose in 1711. The Bosehaus now contains a concert hall and the **Bachmuseum** which was totally restored in 1983–85 (opening times Tues–Sun 09.00–18.00). The museum houses a vast amount of memorabilia of the great composer including a collection of musical instruments of his era. This is a peaceful museum to visit with a lovely inner courtyard, evoking the atmosphere of the 18C when Bach visited Bose here. Continue west to explore the small but charming park which lies beside the Ring. Originally laid out as a lime tree promenade in 1701, it contains a monument devoted to Plato and Dolz, the founders of Leipzig's first school.

Continue south to the Burgplatz. Here stands the imposing **Neues Rathaus**, designed by Hugo Licht and built in 1899–1905 in Renaissance Revival style on the site of the Pleissenburg castle, built by the ruling monarchs of Saxony. The Academy of Drawing, Painting and Architecture, founded here in 1764, also spawned the College of Graphic Arts and Book Design, founded in 1890. It is still in existence today and situated to the south-west of the Ring in the purpose-built premises. The original Pleissenburg castle tower was preserved and incorporated into the new structure. The massive Ratskeller seats 700 and serves modest fare. The Neues Rathaus is connected by a bridge crossing Lotterstrasse to the Stadthaus, also designed by Hugo Licht and built at the same time.

Continue east from Burgplatz to SCHILLERSTRASSE. To the right is a park opened in 1981 which features statues of the poets Christian Furchtegott Gellert and Friedrich Schiller. At the eastern end of Schillerstrasse is the mildly diverting **Ägyptisches Museum** (opening times: Tues–Fri 14.00–18.00, Sun 10.00–13.00) featuring the collection assembled by University explorers in the 19C. Crossing the Universitätsstrasse will take you into the University quarter. To the left is the modern university building which dominates the Leipzig skyline. Built in 1969 the form of a 34-storey tower with sloped roof to resemble an open book it is known locally as 'the broken tooth'. In GDR times it housed 1500 scientists and the University was attended by 6000 students in all. On the west side of the building a doorway by Schinkel has been preserved and incorporated into the modern structure. This is the only surviving part of the Augusteum, built by Schinkel for the University in 1831–36. In front of the main University building is a bronze statue by Hahnel (1883) of the great local scholar Leibniz, shown in 17C dress studying a hefty tome. The **Moritzbastei** to the south-west is the focus for student socialising and is the only remains of Lotter's city fortifications dating from 1551–53. Continue north-west to the splendid **Neues Gewandhaus**, a modern concert hall built to magnificently high standards and opened in 1981. The resident orchestra is the Gewandhausorchester, the oldest in the world and one of the finest. In the massive AUGUSTUS-PLATZ, where the Neues Gewandhaus stands, is the **Mendebrunnen**, a magnificent fountain featuring an obelisk with an inscription by Paul Heyse who was awarded the Nobel Prize for literature in the 19C. Designed by Adolf Gnauth and Jakob Ungerer and built in 1883–86, it measures 18m in height.

Opposite and across Goethestrasse is the **Oper**, standing on the northern fringe of the Augustusplatz. The former theatre was destroyed by Second World War bombing and this new Oper was built in 1960, to designs by Kunz Nierade, to seat 1636. The building is a rather bland mixture of modern and Classical elements in strong contrast to the more visually exciting Neues Gewandhaus. Behind the Oper is the Schwanenteich, a park and lake inhabited by swans. To the west of Augustusplatz is the Kroch-Hochhaus, built in 1927–28 with a carillon situated on the roof. Pass by the Kroch-Hochhaus and head west to reach the Nikolaikirche once again.

B. Beyond the Ring

Whilst the older parts of the Leipzig lie within the boundaries of the Ring, the most exciting museums can be found in the districts beyond this to the south-west and south-east.

Proceed south-west from the Neues Rathaus and cross the Ring heading south down Harkortstrasse to DIMITROFF-PLATZ. Here stands the splendid **Museum für Bildenden Kunst** (Museum of Fine Arts, opening times: Tues and Thurs 10.00–18.00, Wed 14.00–20.00, Fri 10.00–13.00, Sat and Sun 10.00 17.00) situated in the former Reichsgericht (Supreme Court of Justice). Built in grandiose Renaissance Revival style by Ludwig Hoffmann in 1888–95 its central dome, measuring 68.5m in height and crowned by a 5.5m high bronze figure of Justice by O. Lessing, is an important feature of the Leipzig skyline. The east side features a portico of six Corinthian columns. The supreme judicial body of the former German Empire was housed here until the Second World War and it is best known as the place where the trial of Georgi Dimitrov, charged with setting fire to the Reichstag, took place in 1933 in the Assembly Room on the first floor. The defendant succeeded in outwitting his accusers, the Nazi party, but the case gave Hitler the excuse to clamp down and introduce tighter controls on law and order. There was formerly a museum devoted to the former President of Bulgaria on the first floor of the Reichsgericht, giving the GDR authorities the opportunity to make political capital from the Communist Dimitrov's challenge to Fascism. This has now been renamed the **Museum des Reichsgerichts**, offering the chance to see the Assembly Room (the former propaganda is now played down). (Opening times: Mon–Fri 09.00–17.00, Sat–Sun 09.00–14.00.)

The Museum of Fine Art's collection goes back to 1837 when an Art Society was founded. The original premises in the Augustusplatz, built in 1858 by L. Lange, were enlarged by Hugo Licht in 1886. In 1952 the collection was moved to the Reichsgericht in what was supposedly a temporary measure. It occupies 32 small, fairly unsuitable exhibition rooms in the rather grim building which was designed for very different purposes. The museum is the second biggest in Saxony after that in Dresden and can show only approximately one sixth of its entire collection at any one time.

It has at its disposal over 2500 paintings, amongst which there are 380 by the Dutch Masters, 15 by Lucas Cranach and 47 by Max Klinger. The collection also includes approximately 850 sculptures, amongst which there are works by Ernst Barlach, Max Klinger, Georg Kolbe, Christian Daniel Rauch and virtually the complete oeuvre of the animal sculptor August Gaul. 55,000 illustrations, amongst which are 128 works by Albrecht Dürer, form another important part of the collection. The Museum is ordered chronologically at present, beginning with first class German works of the medieval period including *Man of Sorrows* by Master Francke. There then follows work of the German Renaissance by Lucas Cranach the elder including *Nymph at the Well*. 17C Dutch and Flemish painting is well represented with a Rembrandt *Self-Portrait* and lovely Jan van Eyck *Portrait*. The German Romantic movement is well represented by Böcklin's mysterious *Island of the Dead* and Friedrich's *The Steps of Life*. Much space is devoted to Max Klinger, who was born in Leipzig in 1857 and worked within the Romantic idiom. Sculptures by Klinger on display include the tantalising *Salome* and a bust of *Beethoven* worked in coloured marble, bronze and ivory. More recent artists are also included in the collection with a representative range of German Expressionists from Nolde, Pechstein and Schmidt-Rottluff. The sculpture rooms have examples of the work of Rodin on show. The remainder of the gloomy space is taken up with temporary exhibitions made up from other items in the collection. In the summer of 1991 there was a very pleasing exhibition entitled *Blätter und Bluten* (Leaves and Blossoms) which celebrated the tradition of flower painting with particular emphasis on Dutch masters. At the end of the exhibition is a soothing tea room with relaxing music playing and efficent service.

It is sad that such a fine collection should be housed in such an unsuitable building and that the devotion of GDR funds to the musical heritage of Leipzig led to the relative neglect of the visual arts.

Beside the Reichsgericht to the west is the **Hochschule für Graphik und Buchkunst** (College of Graphic Arts and Book Design) which was opened in 1890. Behind this is the **University Library**, built between 1887 and 1891 in Renaissance Revival style to house the magnificent collection founded in 1543. The Library was 60 per cent destroyed by bombing in the Second World War and there was little commitment to its reconstruction on the part of the GDR authorities. Opposite the library is the former site of the original Gewandhaus, a concert hall built in 1884 but totally destroyed by the bombing of 1944.

Retracing your steps north back to the Ring, head east up the ROSSPLATZ until you reach the new Post Office. Head east down Grimmaischer Steinweg into the quarter of the city devoted to bookselling and publishing. On the Johannisplatz once stood the marvellous 18C Johanniskirche, totally destroyed in the Second World War. Just beyond Johannisplatz is the **Grassaimuseum** complex which houses three interesting museums in total. The Museum originally stood to the east of the Reichsgericht in a building erected in 1893–96 by H. Licht with funds from a bequest from F.D. Grassai who died in 1880. The new museum was built during 1925–27 to plans by Carl William Zweck and Hans Voigt. The **Musikinstrumentenmuseum** (Museum of Musical Instruments, opening times Tues–Thurs 14.00–17.00, Fri and Sun 10.00–13.00, Sat 10.00–15.00) contains a comprehensive collection of 3000 musical instruments including some dating from the Middle Ages onwards but concentrating on items from the time of Bach. The **Museum für Völkerkunde** (Museum for Ethnography, opening times Tues–Fri 09.30–17.30, Sat 10.00–16.00, Sun 09.00–13.00) contains items from Asia, Africa, America and Australasia as well as Russia. Also entered by means of the inner courtyard is the **Museum für Kunsthandwerks** (Museum of Arts and Crafts, opening times Tues–Thurs 09.30–18.00, Fri 09.30–13.00, Sat and Sun 10.00–17.00). The vast collection is only partly on display but includes important examples of glass, ceramics, furniture and metalwork from the 15C to the 19C.

C. South of the city: the Volkerschlachtdenk-mal and surroundings

From Johannisplatz take the 15, 20 or 21 tram to the **Völkerschlachtdenk-mal** (Monument to the Battle of Nations, opening times daily 09.00–16.00) or follow Windmühlenstrasse south-east from the south side of the Ring. This massive, 91m tall monument was inaugurated to mark the centenary of the 1813 Battle of Nations or Battle of Leipzig which took place here and in the surrounding area, when the Russians, Prussians, Austrians and Swedes united to defeat Napoleon. The granite edifice was built in 1898–1913 on a mound of earth 24m tall with a pond spreading out before it. The monument was designed by Bruno Schmitz with sculptures by Christian Behrens and Franz Metzner. A full opportunity to enjoy the impact of this Classical and Expressionist monument is provided by the long walk to it from the car park and entrance. The sculpture at the front represents the Archangel Michael with twelve soldiers, 14m high, arranged around the dome at the top. The brute size of the blocks of granite can be appreciated at close quarters and it is worth the climb (500 steps) to the top—the view of Leipzig should not be missed. Inside there is a massive domed hall with a crypt carried by eight columns. In the upper storey are colossal figures representing courage, self-sacrifice, faith and national strength. It is interesting to speculate about the connection between Germany's increasing militarism and sense of national identity in the years leading up the First World War when this was built, and the victory over Napoleon.

Also inaugurated in 1913 and just north of the Volkerschlachtdenkmal is the **Russische Kirche** (Russian Church). Built as a memorial to the 22,000 Russian troops who fell at the Battle of Nations, it is in the style of churches in the Novgorod region of Russia with a variegated, pointed roof surmounted by a dome. Inside the church is decorated with 18C Russian icons. Further south of the Russische Kirche on Deutschen Platz is the **Deutsche Bucherei** (German Library). Built in 1913–16 for the reception and storage of every German book printed in Germany or abroad from 1 January 1913, it is the German equivalent of the British Library. The library was extended in 1934 and again in 1965 to accommodate the massive collection which now numbers over six million items. There is a huge reading room with places for 180 readers and beautiful entrance hall, complete with marble cladding and mosaics. Portrait busts of German notables decorate the entire building. Part of the library is devoted to the **Deutsches Buch und Schrift-museum** (Museum of German Books and Manuscripts, opening times, Mon–Sat 09.00–16.00) which traces the historical development of book publishing over the past 5000 years.

19

Upper Lusatia: from Dresden to Zittau via Bautzen and Görlitz

Dresden—53km Bautzen—43km Görlitz—34km Zittau—110km Dresden.

This circular route delves into the most eastern extremes of Germany. It skirts the borders with Poland and the Czech Republic and includes the scenic mountain region of Upper Lusatia.

The E40 east from Dresden will take you directly (53km) to Bautzen. For a slower but more picturesque drive, take the A6. Pass through Weissig, continue east for another 8km and turn right to reach the town of **Stolpen** where the 12C ruined Schloss can be seen, perched high on a hilltop south of the town. Enlarged in the 13C to serve the Meissen bishops in the defence against Bohemia to the south, the castle came into the Elector of Saxony's kingdom in 1559 and Augustus the Strong installed his erstwhile mistress, Countess Cosel, here in 1716. She lived an exile's existence here until her death in 1765. Her rooms in the Coselturm (Cosel Tower) are well preserved, despite attacks during the Napoleonic Wars in 1813. Thirteen rooms within the castle can be visited and a further eight in the cellars, which contain a display devoted to the history of the fort and the town as a whole. Return to the A6 and continue through Bischofswerda to Bautzen.

A. Bautzen

51,000 inhabitants.

Tourist Information: Fleischmarkt 2–4, 02625 Bautzen. Tel. 420 18.

Approaching the town the striking silhouette of the 1000 year old Ortenburg, the Michaeliskirche and the Alte Wasserkunst (Old Waterworks) perched high above the river Spree on the east bank, can be enjoyed. Bautzen is the German centre for Sorbian culture, the Sorbs having settled here in the 6C, so the road signs are in both the Sorb language—Wendish— and German (for example Bautzen is known as Budysin in Wendish).

History. Bautzen's early prosperity was founded on its geographic location at the intersection of two trade routes. Originally part of Bohemia, the Ortenburg was built by the Margrave of Meissen on the rocky plateau above the Spree valley. Bautzen grew steadily during medieval times as a town at the foot of the castle. During the 14C and 15C the town played a leading role in the Upper Lusatia League and in 1635 Bautzen became part of Saxony. The town then went into decline following major fires and war damage. In GDR times Bautzen was known as an industrial centre for the production of rolling stock but today an increasing number of tourists are enjoying the gems to be found here.

Bautzen is easily reached by train, the journey from Dresden taking one hour. From the Hauptbahnhof head north up Aussere, passing one of the main remnants of the old town wall. On the left at this point is the **Neuer**

Wasserkunst (New Waterworks) built in the 17C and new only in comparison to the 16C **Alte Wasserkunst** in the north-eastern part of the town.
Opposite and to the right is the **Deutsch-Sorbisches Theater**. Built in 1975
this is the only theatre in Germany to stage plays in Wendish. Continue
north, crossing the intersection with Lauengraben to reach the **Lauenturm**,
part of the town's medieval fortifications. Built during 1400–03, the Baroque
roof and lantern were added in 1739. Turn right down Schulstrasse to find
the **Stadtmuseum**, noting the well-preserved burgher houses at Nos 2, 6, 8
and 10. Of moderate interest, the museum situated on the Kornmarkt was
founded in 1868 and includes examples of local Gothic and Baroque
carving, prints and local arts and crafts. Right beside the Museum is the
Reichenturm, Bautzen's own leaning tower of Pisa (opening times: May–
Sept daily 09.00–17.00). Originally built as part of the town's fortifications
in 1490–92, the stone relief which decorates the tower is a portrait of
Emperor Rudolf II which was added in 1577. The ornate, Baroque roof with
lantern was added as an extra embellishment in 1715–18 and caused the
dramatic tilt. The Reichenturm is quite safe to climb, as the foundations
were strengthened after the Second World War. The climb is rewarded with
a stunning view of Bautzen which establishes your bearings for the remainder of the walk.

To the north is the **Wendischer Turm**, so called after the Sorbs who settled
in this quarter. Schinkel designed the **Kaserne** (Barracks) in Gothic Revival
style and incorporated the Turm into his plan—the building is now used for
local government offices. From the Reichenturm head west down the
pedestrianised Reichenstrasse. This leads into the historic centre of the
town at the HAUPTMARKT. Tourist Information is situated on the right and
to the left is the **Gewandhaus**, built in 1882–83 in Renaissance Revival style.
It is well worth visiting the Ratskeller, situated in the original cellars which
date back to 1472 with magnificent vaulting. On the opposite side of the
Hauptmarkt, standing in the traditional, central position right in the middle
of the market square, is the equally interesting **Rathaus**. The building was
founded in the Middle Ages, and some of these original parts are still in
evidence, most notably the Gothic tower. The main body of the present
Rathaus was built in Baroque style during 1729–32. Note the 17C burgher
houses on the west and eastern sides of the square at Nos 6, 7, and 8.

The Rathaus separates the Hauptmarkt from the Fleischmarkt, which lies
to the north. Walk behind the Rathaus to view the impressive **Petridom**,
which stands on the northern side of the Fleischmarkt. In the centre stands
a statue, dating from 1865, of Elector Johann Georg I (1585–1656), the first
Saxon ruler of the town. There are further impressive Baroque dwellings
to the right. The Petridom, or St Peter's Cathedral, is a three-naved Gothic
hall church built in various stages from 1213–1497 with a 85m high tower.
The church is remarkable in that it has served both Protestant and Catholic
worshippers since 1524. Inside the Church the two religions are clearly
divided by a wrought-iron screen. In the Catholic sector which occupies the
choir there is a fabulous high altar by G. Fossati dating from 1722–24 with
a painting by G.A. Pellegrini showing St Peter receiving his keys. Within
the choir is a quite overpowering sculpture in sandstone by Balthasar
Permoser, dating from 1714, of the Crucifixion. The Protestant sector in the
nave is comparatively modest with the Prince's Balcony and Altar dating
from the 17C.

From the Petridom continue north across An de Petrikirche to visit the
Domstift, the former Bishop's residence. Enter through the highly

decorative gateway which displays the Cathedral's coat of arms dating from 1755. The building is Baroque in style, consisting of three wings, and houses the cathedral treasure chamber (tel. 44102 to make an appointment to view). From the Domstift continue north past the **Nikolaiturm**, built as a further part of the town's fortifications in 1522, to the ruined Nikolaikirche. Founded in 1444, this Gothic church was damaged during the Thirty Years War and now serves as a cemetery. The gravestones stand in the former nave and choir, overgrown with ivy and surrounded by the walls of the church—plants sprout from the tops of the pointed arch where a roof once existed, and the romantic mood of the site is undeniable. Note the pleasing views over the Spree from the Nikolaikirche before continuing west to the best part of any visit to Bautzen—the Ortenburg.

Perched high on a rocky plateau overlooking the banks of the River Spree, the ***ORTENBURG** contains the **Schloss** and **Museum der Sorben**. The first building to be encountered on the right is the Museum für Geschichte und Kultur der Sorben (opening times: Mon, Wed and Fri–Sun, 09.30–12.30 and 13.30–16.00, Tues and Thurs, 09.30–12.30 and 13.30–17.00) housed in the Baroque wing of the Schloss Ortenburg. The display inside documents the lived culture of the Sorbs including their traditional folk costume, festivals and literature. The main body of the Schloss dates from the late 15C and is in late Gothic style; major rebuilding work took place after the Thirty Years War in 1660. The audience hall on the first floor is particularly noteworthy for its stucco ceiling, dating from 1662 by Vietti and Comotan, representing scenes from local history.

The **Schlossturm** (Castle Tower) dates from 1486 and was part of the rebuilding work undertaken by King Matthias Corninus when Laustia was a province of Hungary during 1469–90. Continue south down Oster-Rey-mann-Weg, passing another of Bautzen's old fortifications, the Mühlbastei, built in 1480, to reach the **Michaeliskirche**. Completed in 1498 from stone with a square tower, this was the Sorbs' own Protestant parish church. Opposite this is the town's landmark—the **Alte Wasserkunst**. This round, stone tower was built on the rocky banks of the River Spree in 1588 to serve the town, which it did faithfully until 1963. It is now an interesting technical museum (opening times: May–Sept 09.00–17.00 daily) with the ancient workings on display and the added bonus of a viewing platform which is worth the climb for exciting panoramas of the river and the town. Descend to the banks of the river, noting the **Hexenhauschen** (Witch's House); this was the only authentic fisherman's house to have survived intact, giving rise to rumours about the magical powers of its inhabitants. Continue south down Fischergasse, noting the picture postcard view of the Alte Wasserkunst from the Friedensbrücke. Continue south back to the railway station.

Take the E40 south-west from Bautzen and after c 8km the 561m high mountain of Czorneboh appears to the right. Pass through the village of Hochkirch and into Löbau which lies just west of the Löbauer mountain with a height of 447m. Continue east on the A6 to the extremely well preserved, historic border town of Görlitz.

B. Görlitz

80,000 inhabitants.

Tourist Information: 29 Obermarkt. Tel. 055 5391. Opening times: Mon–Fri 09.00–17.00, April–Sept, Sat 09.00–12.00).

Görlitz is the eastern most town in Germany and intriguingly had to be sliced in half after the Second World War as the Neisse River was taken as the limit of the German border. Hence the historic town centre on the west bank remained German whilst the new, eastern suburbs became Polish with the new name of Zgorzelec. Known appropriately as the town of towers, this is the largest town in Upper Lusatia.

History. Görlitz is a real melting pot; originally a Slav settlement it became part of Germany in the 13C. Görlitz flourished as a trading centre during the Middle Ages, standing as it does in control of the river and at the intersection of two trade routes from west to east between Breslau and Dresden. Textile production also flourished here from the 14C onwards. Following the Thirty Years War, Görlitz became part of Saxony to be taken over by Prussia in 1815. Industrialisation followed with Görlitz emerging as an important centre for the production of railway rolling stock. The town has been comparatively well preserved but is now in need of a massive facelift to enhance the treasures to be found here.

Trains to Görlitz take approximately two hours from Dresden or one hour from Bautzen. From the Hauptbahnhof head north to Marienplatz and the Altstadt. Just past the main post office is the **Frauenkirche**, a late Gothic hall church built during 1459–86 for the local hospital and poorhouse. Just beside the Frauenkirche is the **Centrum** department store; built in 1911–13 it is the oldest example of this building type to remain in its original condition in Germany. Built in Jugendstil mode, it is fabulously decorated with sculptures on the exterior and its fine, near original interior complete is double-storey.

Continue north to the **Dicker Turm** (Fat Tower) a remnant of the town's fortifications dating from 1305; the carved sandstone coat of arms was added in 1477, and the round, squat tower was graced with a Baroque cupola in the 17C. To the left of the Dicker Turm is the Annenkapelle, built during 1508–12. Continue north-east from the Marienplatz to the Demianiplatz where the **Kaisertrutz** stands. An imposing, cylindrical fortification, this bastion was built in 1490 and then underwent extensive rebuilding in 1850. The Kaisertrutz houses the Stadtgeschichtliche Abteilung der Städtischen Kunstsammlungen (Local History and Art Exhibition; opening times: Tues and Wed 10.00–13.00 and 14.00–18.00, Thurs–Sun 10.00–13.00 and 14.00–16.00). Inside, the original 15C tower can be seen as well as fine examples of medieval art and more recent work by local artists including Slevogt, Corinth, Royski, Uhde and Sterl.

Also worth visiting in the Demianiplatz is the **Reichenbacher Turm**, a gate-tower forming part of the 14C town walls, built in 1376 with the top added in 1782. The Turm houses the Museumsabteilung (Weapon Museum, opening times as Kaisertrutz, above). Inside the municipal collection of arms and suits of armour can be viewed and the tall tower climbed to enjoy panoramic views of the town.

Continue east to the second of the three central squares in the town, the OBERMARKT. The rectangular market place is lined with fine examples of Baroque houses. Of special interest is the façade of No. 29 on the north side which is splendidly decorated with Baroque figures and ornate pilasters dating from 1718. Walk across the square heading north-east and opposite the Tourist Information Office—situated in another fine Baroque building— is the Gothic **Dreifaltigkeitskirche**. The church was originally built as part of a Franciscan monastery; the choir dates back to 1371–81 and the remainder is 16C. The most characteristic feature of the church is its tall, spindly tower—one of the seven which make the town's skyline so attractive. Inside are a wealth of late Gothic furnishings, including the authentic monks' choir stalls, carved in 1484. Also note the wall altar depicting the Virgin Mary (1511) and high Baroque altarpice dating from 1713.

The fountain outside the Dreifaltigkeitskirche, the Rolandsbrunnen, depicts the youthful Roland bearing the Saxon coat of arms erected in 1590. Continue down Brüderstrasse noting some of the most beautiful Renaissance and Baroque townhouses preserved in the area. Outstanding is No. 8—known quite rightly as the Schönhof. Built in 1526, it was designed by Wendel Roskopf, who was responsible for rebuilding the town following a severe fire in 1525. Brüderstrasse then opens out into the best of the three squares—the UNTERMARKT. The east side is lined with picturesque, late Gothic and Renaissance houses known as the Lange Läuben. Housed in No. 4 is the exclusive Goldener Baum hotel with a highly recommended restaurant in the cellar. On the north side is the very early Ratapotheke, a dispensary dating back to 1550 with a double sundial gilding its façade. At No. 22 is the lovely Gothic doorway known colloquially as the Flüsterbogen (Whispering Arch) as the stone arch carries the merest whisper from one side to the other. Also note the Renaissance building at No. 23, dating from 1536.

The **Rathaus** occupies the western side of the square. Founded at the end of the 14C it has been extended and remodelled over the succeeding centuries. The curved flight of steps leading to the main entrance, the portal itself and the sculptured column bearing a statue of Justice all date from the 16C and are fine examples of work from the German Renaissance. The base of the tower dates from 14C, the top section from 16C and the crowning cupola from 18C. Proceed east from Untermarkt to the Städtische Kunstsammlungen (Municipal Museum; opening times as Kaisertrutz, see above) at No. 30 Neissatrasse. Housed in an impressive Baroque dwelling, the museum's collection includes indigenous arts and crafts from 16C to 19C, furniture including some Biedermeier examples and a display devoted to the town's philosopher, Jakob Böhme (1575–1624). He was an alchemist, in the medieval mode, but also an eminent naturalist and philosopher, thus providing an important link with the future and the German enlightenment. The adjacent building at No. 29 is the Biblisches Haus. Dating from 1570 the house is extensively decorated with scenes from the Bible.

Continue north to the **Pfarrkirche St Peter and St Paul**, founded in 1423–97 but extensively rebuilt following a fire in the 17C. This is one of the best examples of late Gothic ecclesiastical architecture to be found in the region. Of particular note is the massive St George crypt. The church is a five-aisled hall type with two Gothic Revival towers added in 1889–91. To the south is the oldest surviving dwelling in Görlitz, the Renthaus or Waidhaus. Proceed to the terrace in front of the house, which was built onto the old town walls, for a fine view across the River Neisse to Poland.

Continue south-west down Nikolaigraben, noting the Nikolaiturm—part of the old town fortifications dating from 1348—and then head north to the **Nikolaikirche**. Much of the present day structure dates from 1452–1520 but of more interest is the surrounding graveyard, the Nikolaifriedhof, where Jacob Böhme (amongst many other town notables) is buried with some highly decorative tombstones.

Continue west from the Nikolaikirche down Steinweg to a fascinating oddity, the **Heiliges Grab** (Holy Sepulchre). Built during 1481–1504 this was the first copy of the Holy Places of Jerusalem to be built in Europe. According to local myth, the son of the Mayor of Görlitz, Georg Emmerich, was forbidden to marry his true love as she was a member of a rival family who supported the Bohemian heretic, King Georg of Podeburg. He was sent on a pilgrimage to the Holy Land and charged Conrad Pflüger to build replicas of the key sites of Jerusalem when he himself became Mayor. It is possible to visit the Heiliges Grab (opening times Tues–Sun 11.00–13.00) complete with its two-storey Kapelle zum Heiligen Kreuz (Chapel of the Holy Cross), its Sabhaus with the beautiful statue of the Virgin Mary and its Grabkepelle—a smaller but accurate copy of the original tomb in the Holy Land. The walk concludes here but Görlitz offers more for visitors in the south-east of the town with the picturesque Stadtpark and Tierpark.

The B99 south to Zittau skirts the River Neisse and Polish border for the entire 34km, making it a fascinating drive.

C. Zittau

40,000 inhabitants.

Tourist Information: Rathausplatz 6, 02763 Zittau. Tel. 3986.

More modest in size than Görlitz, Zittau stands right next to the German borders with both Poland and the Czech Republic and is known as the Dreilandereck (Corner of Three Countries). The majority of visitors to the town come to explore the nearby Zittau mountains by means of the idiosyncratic Bimmelbahn, the narrow-gauge steam trains which leave from the Hauptbahnhof. It is 12km south by train to **Kuort Oybin**, a sleepy mountain town of some 1300 inhabitants which is overlooked by the Oybin Mountain with a ruined castle and monastery on its summit, built in the 14C but struck by lightning in the 16C. A good example of a romantic ruin, it was much visited by painters in the 19C looking for inspiration. Zittau itself makes a charming stop-off point for an hour's stroll through the streets.

History. Originally part of the kingdom of Bohemia, Zittau was founded in 1238 by Otakar I. Zittau was part of the Upper Lusatia Town League (with Görlitz, Bautzen, Löbau, Kamenz and Lauban) which was opposed to the rule of the nobility. The town's prosperity grew during the 14C and 15C and was based around textile production. Badly damaged during the Thirty Years War by Austrian troops, Zittau fell within Prussian rule following the Treaty of Vienna. Today the town still relies on textile production for economic security with tourism as an added bonus.

From the Hauptbahnhof head south down Strasse der Einheit past the Christian-Weise-Bibliothek and then south down Bautzenerstrasse to the **Johanniskirche** on the right. This Neo-Classical church was rebuilt in 1837 after plans by Schinkel. It is sometimes possible to climb the tower for fine views of the town and to establish your bearings. The church stands in Johannisplatz where the oldest dwelling in Zittau, the Dornspachhaus, is situated, dating back to 1553.

Continue south to the cobbled **Platz der Jugend** with a Roland Fountain, known alternatively as the Mars Brunnen. This fine Renaissance fountain, erected in 1585, shows the figure of Roland on a decorative pillar with the fountain at its base. The square is lined on three sides by 17C and 18C townhouses and the old dispensary. The Rathausplatz joins the Platz der Jugend to the east with the high spot, architecturally, of a visit to Zittau—the **Rathaus**. A little-known work by Schinkel and built in 1840–45 in the style of an Italian Renaissance palace, this is a suprising and unusual building, given the normal tendency to preserve the flavour of the German Renaissance or Baroque original or build a 19C Gothic Revival replacement. This building has a symmetrical façade with a certain dynamism injected through the use of turrets of varying heights at roof level. The building bears a striking resemblance to Schinkel's work at Potsdam in its Italian inspiration and clear-cut lines. Also of note on the square is the Baroque guesthouse, Zur Sonne, built in 1710, the Rococo Fürstenherberge from 1767 and the Noacksche Haus from 1689.

Continue east behind the Rathaus to the old **Marstall** or stables on August-Bebel Platz. This rectangular open space is characterised by its three impressive fountains. In the south the Samariteriunenbrunnen (Good Samaritan Fountain), the Herkulesbrunnen (Hercules Fountain) in the centre and Schwannenbrunnen (Swan Fountain) to the north. The Marstall stands in the centre. It was originally built as a warehouse for the precious commodity of salt in 1511; the Mansard roof was added in 1730 when it was converted into a stable block. The imposing building now houses the Zittau town archives.

Continue north to the Klosterplatz where the late Gothic, Franciscan **Klosterkirche St Peter and St Paul** stands. It was founded in the 13C with additions dating up to the 17C. The interior is well worth a look, particularly the 17C altar and chancel as well as the rich array of tombstones. The Stadtmuseum (Town Museum; opening times: Mon, Tues and Thurs–Sat 10.00–12.00 and 14.00–16.00, Wed 10.00–12.00 and 14.00–18.00, Sun 10.00–12.00) is also in the August-Bebel Platz, situated in the Franciscan monastery itself. On show is a pleasing collection of ceramics, glass and traditional hand crafts. In front of the museum stands the best of the town's fountains, the **Grüne Born**, and opposite is the **Heffterhaus**. This has striking stepped gables, decorated with carved sandstone scrolls and filigrees, dating from 1662. Continue north and then west along Ernest Thälmann Ring and back to the station.

From Zittau take the B178 north to Löbau, passing through the small town of Herrnhut after c 15km. Take the E40 to Bautzen and then the A6 or E40 west to Dresden.

20

From Leipzig to Zwickau via Colditz and Chemnitz

Leipzig—48km Colditz—35km Chemnitz—45km Zwickau.

This drive holds particular interest for British visitors as it includes the notorious former prisoner-of-war camp, Oflag IVC, situated in the small town of Colditz. Chemnitz is the next call on the route—the third largest town in Saxony, known as Karl-Marx-Stadt from 1953 until the local referendum of 1990 reinstated the original name. Although the town was badly damaged during World War Two bombing, some fascinating historic buildings survived intact and are undergoing restoration. The route then continues westwards to Zwickau, home of the Trabant car and birthplace of composer Robert Schumann.

From Leipzig head south on the A95 for 16km to Rötha. In this small town there is a late Renaissance castle, founded in 1668, which can be visited, plus the late Gothic Marienkirche (St Mary's Church). Continue south for a further 10km and take the B176 off to the left before reaching Borna. Pass through Bad Lausick to reach Colditz.

A. Colditz

6000 inhabitants.

Tourist Information: Rathaus, Markt 1, Colditz 04680. Tel. 34381 380.

Well off the beaten track for most European tourists—the town receives no mention in the German Baedeker guide to eastern Germany—Colditz is however something of a comparative mecca for British visitors. The famous Colditz Castle towers above the modest town, nestled by the banks of the river Mulde. Little has changed since the Second World War and it is easy to imagine the setting in which Allied prisoners made their successful and less successful bids for freedom.

History. The town began as a small settlement, based around a ford over the river Mulde, in the 12C. In 1404 Colditz was assimilated into Meissen territory and the town prospered, particularly its textile trade. Industrialisation made an early impact on Colditz with the opening of a factory for weaving as early as 1769 and for spinning cotton in 1811. More recently economic security was based on the production of ceramics, but this ceased with unification. The town is dominated by the 16C castle, built on a craggy rock, which has served as a royal residence, hunting lodge, poorhouse, lunatic asylum and prisoner-of-war camp. There are now plans to turn Colditz Castle into a major tourist attraction with luxury accommodation. If you prefer to see historic places of interest in an uncommercial atmosphere, now is the time to go.

Entering Colditz on Lausicker Strasse turn right to cross the bridge over the Zwickauer Mulde river. Take the left fork up Badergasse and then turn right into the main Markt where plentiful parking is available. If arriving by train the Bahnhof is situated in the west of the town: head south-east up Bahnhofstrasse, cross the river and head up Badergasse to reach the Markt. Trains run from Leipzig via Rochlitz.

On the southern edge of the Markt square is a good tavern, the Schloss-Café, for meals or light refreshments. The renowned and highly palatable Colditz beer may be bought at the grocer's on the east side.

The Tourist Information Office is not easy to find, situated on the first floor of the **Rathaus** on the north-east corner of the Markt. Dating from 1540, the Rathaus is an ornate Baroque building, indicative of more prosperous times when Colditz was an important commercial and regal centre. This solid building commands the corner site and is characterised by stepped gables on three sides, the façade facing the Markt being decorated with clock and small balcony beneath. Walk up the staircase on this side, through the main entrance and up the staircase for Tourist Information.

Continue north-east across Töpfergasse and up the steep, narrow street of Kirchgasse. At the top is the modest whitewashed 17C **Stadtkirche of St Egidien**. The remodelled, 18C interior has a simple altarpiece and Neo-Classical balcony. Continue east up Tiergartenstrasse to the **Städtisches Museum Colditz** (Town Museum of Colditz; opening times: Tues–Sun 10.00–16.00) housed in the 18C Johann-David-Köhler-Haus.

The Town Museum was originally situated in the Rathaus before being moved to the Castle after the First World War. However, use of the Castle as a hospital and prison expanded and so the museum was moved to its present location in 1938. Founded mainly to celebrate local arts and crafts, in particular the ceramics industry, the museum is best known today for its collection relating to the Second World War. Press the bell to gain entry— the attendant spends most of her time in a top storey flat. The charge, currently 5DM, covers entry to both the museum and guided tour of the castle itself. The museum is mainly visited by the British, as the visitor's book shows—up to 12 British parties per day come through the doors, mainly on day trips from Leipzig. Climb the stairs to the main museum display, complete with medieval torture instruments. To the right is a small room devoted to British prisoners at the Schloss with the original plaited sheets used as rope, a drawing for the wildly eccentric escape glider and an amusing set of photographs which capture wartime life at the castle complete with the successful drama club. Ingenious contraptions like wooden sewing machines to make fake uniforms, forged passes and money bear witness to the inventiveness and skill of the inmates. At the back of the museum is a room devoted to Colditz porcelain, with interesting examples from the inter-war period when Art Deco obviously had a great influence on tableware here as throughout the Western world.

From the museum it is a short walk up the hill north-west to the entrance to the Castle and the guided tour. The **Castle** was founded in 1046 as a defensive fort, well placed on the jagged rocks. Following a fire in 1504 the castle was rebuilt by August von Sachsen in 1578–91 to be used by his widow Sophie von Sachsen as her residence during 1603–22. Augustus the Strong used the castle as a hunting lodge but the splendid new palaces at Dresden proved superior and Colditz was subsequently neglected. At the beginning of the 19C the building was converted into an almshouse and in 1829 an early lunatic asylum. This use continued for over one hundred years, with the unfortunate inmates securely interned in this fortress. During 1933–34 anti-Nazi political prisoners were secured here and until

1939 it was also used as an old people's home. During the Second World War it became the notorious, reputedly escape-proof, Oflag IVC where more difficult prisoners were held. Each had at least one escape attempt behind them, and all had distinguished themselves as unlikely simply to sit the war out passively. The British, French, Polish, Dutch and Belgian officers pitted their wits against the Germans and some succeeded in escaping. This was despite the castle's impregnable position, barbed wire surrounds, spotlights and armed sentries and its position 700km from any allied border. A post-war myth of Colditz has now been established through film, television, books and even a board game. Eminent inmates included Winston Churchill's nephew, Giles Romilly.

Schloss Colditz, built by August von Sachsen in 1578–91

A sign sponsored by Smirnoff Vodka at the entrance to the castle tells of the 11 successful British and 12 successful French escapes during the War. Enter the gate of what is currently a grim psychiatric hospital and old people's home. The guided tour is in English and begins on the hour in the first courtyard or Vorburg. This area housed the German officers whilst the inner courtyard of Hauptburg, which lies beyond this, housed the prisoners in high security conditions. Note the Saxon coat of arms above the archway which leads into the Hauptburg, one symbolising August von Sachsen and the other his wife, Sophie von Sachsen. In the second courtyard the barred windows which restrained the incumbents, and still do, are all too obvious. To the left it is possible to see a cell used for solitary confinement which currently doubles as storage space for the hospital. It is also possible to see the old wine cellar where the French dug a tunnel for a mass escape. The tunnel took eight months to dig and is 44m in length. The enormity of their task is brought home when the huge stones and massive floorboards which needed to be moved are seen and the confined space in which they worked witnessed. The tunnel led into the chapel, where visitors can see the exit. The escape attempt never took place as the tunnel was discovered by the Germans. Also, in the very neglected chapel, visitors can see a small display of English, French and Canadian tins, sent by the Red Cross. Empty tins were joined end to end to pump air into the escape tunnels. The chapel is in a severely dilapidated state and has been used for storage, the needs of the hospital coming before the interests of British tourists in the GDR. The tour does not take in any other aspects of the interior and misses out the Festsaal, decorated in 1876 with plasterwork medallions of famous German writers and composers and used for the prisoners' famous amateur dramatics.

Return to the Markt by means of the steep descent down the Schlosstreppe. Take the B107 out of Colditz, crossing the bridge once more and turning left down Rochlitzen Strasse. This small road follows the Mulde as far as Rochlitz for 11km. From here take the A175 to join the A95 heading towards Chemnitz.

B. Chemnitz

300,000 inhabitants.

Tourist Information: Strasse der Nationen 3, 09111 Chemnitz. Tel. 62051. Opening times: Mon–Fri 09.00–18.00, Sat 09.00–14.00.

In direct contrast to the neglected town of Colditz, the industrial centre of Chemnitz has been largely rebuilt following war damage and was a showpiece of modern town planning for the GDR. Some interesting, older parts have survived intact including the Schlosskirche and Gothic Revival Neue Rathaus.

History. Chemnitz lies in the foothills of the Erzgebirge mountains. Its early development was triggered by its location at the intersection of two trade routes. A Benedictine monastery was founded here in 1136 and economic growth guaranteed by the textile and bleaching trades. Badly damaged during the Thirty Years War Chemnitz entered a period of decline, relieved by its growth as an industrial centre in the 19C. Factories were built at such a pace and pollution reached such levels that it was nicknamed the German Manchester. During post-war years it was renamed Karl-Marx-Stadt because of its industrial heritage and tradition of left-wing politics rather than any personal connection with Marx himself. The name has now been revoked and Chemnitz is once more Chemnitz.

Parking can be found beside Tourist Information on Strasse der Nationen in the town centre. If you are arriving at the railway station, cross Bahnhof Strasse heading north up Georgstrasse and the **Technische Universität** faces you. A smart, Renaissance Revival building, it dates from the turn of the century. To view the main façade, turn left into the **Strasse der Nationen**—the main street in Chemnitz. Directly opposite is the wooded **Schillerplatz**. Head west and left down Strasse der Nationen and on the right is the early 20C **Theaterplatz**. The **Opera House** facing directly south was built in 1906–09 in Neo-Baroque style. The church on the eastern side of the square, the **Petrikirche**, was completed at the same time but is a revival of Gothic forms. The **Museum am Theaterplatz** (Museum on the Theaterplatz) on the south-west corner was also completed in 1909 and is easily distinguished by the amazing collection of petrified tree trunks arranged outside. The 250 million-year-old Steinerner Wald is explained inside the museum, along with other natural history exhibits (opening times: Tues–Sun 09.00–18.00).

Probably of more interest are the art and design displays. Three leading Expressionist artists—Emile Nolde, Schmidt-Rottluff and Heckel—studied together at the local High School before pursuing their artistic careers in nearby Dresden with the Die Brücke manifesto appearing in 1906. Work by the artists can be seen here, with great emphasis given to Schmidt-Rottluff. Amongst the design exhibits are furniture and interiors by leading Art Nouveau Belgian designer Henry van de Velde for the Haus Esche.

Continue west down Strasse der Nationen and turn next right up Brücken Strassen. On the right is an alarming piece of socialist monumental art—a 7m high, bronze bust of Karl Marx, made in Russia and erected in 1971. Opposite is the modern conglomeration of the Hotel Congress and Stadthalle. Just to the south of this and facing the Strasse der Nationen is the **Roter Turm** with the modern Tourist Information Office beside it. This square, red brick tower is all that remains of the medieval town fortifications. It is over 800 years old and has been used throughout the centuries as a watch-tower, prison and home. Continue west, crossing Rathaus Strasse to reach the MARKT. Here stands the impressive New and Old Town Halls. The west part was built in 1496 and the east in 1907–11. The **Neues Rathaus** was designed by Möbius and the sturdy, Jugendstil exterior and interior have survived intact. The façade is decorated with a handsome, 5m statue of Roland. Inside are the splendidly painted Wandolhalle in blue and gold and the Council Hall which contains a large, allegorical painting by symbolist artist Max Klinger, dating from 1918. The **Altes Rathaus** was built in 1496–98 with several alterations over the centuries. It is predominantly late Gothic in style; facing onto the Markt is the tower with splendid Renaissance portal dating from 1559, depicting Judith and Lucretia.

On the west side of the Markt is the **Siegertsches Haus** (Siegert's House) with richly decorated Baroque façade dating from 1737–41, now the Café am Markt. Just beside it stands the 15C **Jakobikirche** (St Jacob's Church) which was heavily restored in 1913. This is a late Gothic, three-nave hall church, whose west façade was rebuilt in Jugendstil form. At the northern side of the square is the Klosterstrasse—a pedestrian arcaded walkway.

There are two buildings of note to the north of Chemnitz, the **Schlosskirche** and **Schlossbergmuseum** which can be reached by heading north from the Markt, along Theater Strasse, west up Harfmannstrasse over the river and right up Promenadenstrasse. This leads to the banks of the Schlossteich, a pleasant artificial lake. On the hill to the north overlooking the lake is the Schlosskirche (Castle Church), founded in 1136 but rebuilt in 1514–25 in late Gothic style. Most notable is the north portal of 1525—the church was originally built as part of the Benedictine Monastery in the early 12C. Inside is the painted, carved wooden group, representing the Scourging of Christ, by Hans Witten in 1515. The Schlossbergmuseum is due to reopen in 1994 and is housed in the Renaissance castle, built on the site of the monastery.

From Chemnitz return west to the E441 to Zwickau, taking the fourth exit marked Zwickau Ost after c 34km.

C. Zwickau

122,000 inhabitants.

Tourist Information: Hauptstrasse 6, 08056 Zwickau. Tel. 375 26007.

Zwickau, nestled on the banks of the river Mulde and the western most point of the Erzgebirge mountain range, is best known for the manufacture of the GDR's most popular car, the Trabant. The now trendy Trabi, for which there was a 13-year waiting list, ceased production in April 1991 leading to widespread unemployment in the town. Zwickau is currently being regenerated with the sale of the Trabant works to a private investor and a revival of interest in the history and culture of Zwickau.

History. Early prosperity was based on traditional trade routes between Halle, Leipzig and Prague. The mining of iron-ore, other minerals and later coal stimulated more growth and Zwickau became an important industrial centre in the 19C. Textiles, iron, steel and coal mining were the key industries by the 20C, the town's mines producing 2.5 million tons of coal in the inter-war period. The mines were closed in 1977 and the workforce concentrated on car production, churning out 140,000 vehicles annually.

The Hauptbahnhof lies to the west of the **Altstadt** (Old Town) where the tour begins. The old centre of Zwickau is situated around the HAUPTMARKT with the main sites of interest concentrated here. At No. 5 is the **Geburtshaus von Robert Schumann** (birthplace of Robert Schumann) which has been a museum devoted to the great, Romantic composer since 1956 (opening times: Tues–Fri 10.00–17.00, Sat and Sun 10.00–12.00). The fascinating displays inside reveal something of the musician's tortured life, shared with his wife, the great pianist, Clara Wieck. Some of the original furnishings can be seen, portraits, prints and books relating to the ill-fated pair. Also note the interesting town houses dating from the 16C at Nos 17–18 Hauptmarkt. The Gothic Revival **Rathaus** on the south side was built in 1862, masking the 15C original. The late Gothic **Gewandhaus**, built as a hall for the drapers guild, has survived rather better. Much of the original 1524 building remains, having been used as the town's theatre since 1823; note the original stepped gables.

Head to the west side of the Hauptmarkt to the **Mariendom**—one of the best examples of late Gothic architecture in Saxony. Built on the hall church model, it dates mainly from 1465–1506 and was extensively and clumsily restored in 1889–91. The nave, aisles and choir are finely decorated with flat groined vaulting. The high altar, dating from 1479, is beautifully carved in wood and gilded with a painting of Mary surrounded by eight female saints by the Nürnberg master, and Dürer's mentor Michael Wolgemut. Note also the fine choir stalls and Renaissance pulpit. The Holy Sepulchre, in graceful late Gothic and early Renaissance style and dating from 1507, is another high point as is the painted, wooden Pietà by Peter Breuer in the northern chapel.

Continue south from the Mariendom for a view of the amazing **Schiffchen Haus**, a German Renaissance dwelling built to resemble the bow of a ship. Head north back to the Markt and then north up the Otto-Grotewohl-

Strasse to see the unique **Pulverturm** (Powder Tower) the only remaining part of the town's medieval fortifications. Continue north to the **Pfarrkirche St Katharinen** (Parish Church of St Katherine), founded in 1206 as part of the Benedictine Monastery but rebuilt in the 14C as a Gothic hall church. It is well worth a look inside as the winged altarpiece by the workshops of Lucas Cranach the Elder of 1517 is truly inspiring.

Further north is the **Schloss Osterstein**, founded in the 13C with major rebuilding in 1565–85. This former royal residence of the Saxon Electors was used as a prison from the 18C until recently. Major restoration is now underway, with plans to open an upmarket hotel here in 1994. From the Schloss Osterstein head south back to the Markt then west, back in the direction of the Hauptbahnhof to the pleasant **Stadtpark**.

Head north up Crimmitschauer Strasse to Lessingstrasse where the interesting **Städtisches Museum** (Town Museum) is situated (opening times: Tues–Fri 09.00–17.00, Sat and Sun 10.00–17.00). Known as the König Albert Museum before the Second World War, the town's museum is situated in a purpose-built, Jugendstil structure. On display is sculpture from the medieval to Baroque periods including the work of local artist, Breuer. Painting and porcelain from the 17C to 20C may also be seen. The museum holds an extensive archive of first edition publications, including writing by Thomas Müntzer and Martin Luther.

North of here, on Walter-Rathenau-Strasse, is an **Automobilmuseum** (opening times: Tues and Wed 09.00–16.00, Thurs 09.00–18.00, Fri 09.00–14.00, Sat and Sun 10.00–14.00) which mirrors the Automobile Museum at Eisenach in Thuringia, only this celebrates the production of the Trabant as well as interesting examples from the early 20C including models from Audi. Those with time to spare could continue north-east up Leipziger Strasse to the park on the banks of the Mulde where the **Neue Welt** (New World) entertainment centre stands at No. 182. This is a splendid Jugendstil construction with large, beautifully decorated hall. The tour concludes here and may be linked to Route 21 which begins at Zwickau and ends in Dresden taking in Augustburg and Freiburg.

21

From Zwickau to Dresden via Augustusburg and Freiberg

Zwickau—74km Augustusburg—26km Freiberg—43km Dresden.

This route could easily be joined on to Route 20 or taken as a day trip from Dresden. It traverses some scenic parts of the region, known as the Erzebirge (Ore Mountains) a range which stretches 130km in length and 40km in width along the southern part of Saxony and into the Czech Republic. The highest mountain is the Keilberg, 1244m above sea level. The highest point culturally speaking is the cathedral in the mountain town of Freiberg with its famous Tulip Pulpit.

From Zwickau head south-east crossing the E441 motorway through picturesque Wildenfels on the banks of the River Zwickauer Mulde. At

Aue join the A169 heading north to Stollberg and then the A180 north-east to Augustusburg, which lies on the southern outskirts of Chemnitz.

A. Augustusburg

2400 inhabitants.

Tourist Information: Feriendienst Augustusburg, 11 Wilhelm-Pieck-Strasse, 09573 Augustusburg. Tel. 07291 251/2.

The **Schloss Augustusburg**, which towers above the small village, was built during 1568 to 1572 on the site of the ruined Schellenberg Castle as a hunting lodge for Augustus I—hence the name. It is possible to reach the castle by road or travel the 3km by cable-car from the train station at Erdmannsdorf. The Augustusburg is positioned picturesquely between the river Flöha and the Zschopau valley. The architect of this solid, Renaissance building was Hieronymus Lotter, builder of the Leipzig Rathaus. The hunting lodge was not used for long and fell into disrepair, later finding use as a prison with major restoration starting in 1957. The castle now functions as a youth hostel, motorcycle museum and museum of hunting and has several, well preserved interiors including the **Schlosskapelle** (Castle Chapel) which can be seen on the guided tour (open daily 09.00–17.00).

The tour features the **Brunnenhaus**, a 130m deep well and original wooden mechanism, the **Marstall** (Stables) which now house a collection of coaches used by the Saxon princes and the splendid Schlosskapelle. Completed in 1572 this galleried room contains a gilded altarpiece by the Salzburg workshops of west Schreckenfuchs, dated 1571, over which hangs a painting by Cranach the Younger depicting August I and his family. The pulpit is decorated with paintings of Christ by the same artist. The Baroque compact organ is also of interest, built in 1758 by G. Reukenitz. Further delights at the castle include the lovely Hasenhaus (Hare Wing) which can be visited independently and is decorated with a mural depicting the War of the Hares where these animals take on all too human characteristics. The room also contains a display about the fauna of the Erzebirge region. Opposite is the **Küchenhaus** (Kitchens) which now house the collection of two-stroke motorcycles, including recent racing machines.

From Augustusburg head north on the A180 to Flöha then take the A173 east through Oederan from where it is a further 14km to Freiberg.

B. Freiberg

50,000 inhabitants.

Tourist Information: Wallstrasse 24, 09599 Freiburg. Tel. 0762 3602.

History. Freiberg is a well preserved town, built on the spoils of lucrative mining of silver and other semi-precious metals. The town was mainly responsible for the creation of Saxony's wealth, celebrated so splendidly at the Green Vault in Dresden. Silver was discovered here in 1168 and a settlement soon developed, receiving its charter in 1186. The name of the town, meaning Free Mountain, also dates back to the 12C when a royal decree gave anyone the right to mine here and keep the proceeds. The town has been closely connected with mining ever since. The first book to be published on mining was written by Freiberg citizen, Rülein von Calw. The first Mining Academy in the world was founded here in 1765 with famous students including Alexander von Humboldt and Goethe. Mining declined from the 19C onwards but Freiburg remained an important centre for training and research in the subject.

The high point of any visit to Freiberg is the ****DOM**. Situated on UNTER-MARKT it is one of the earliest hall churches to be built in Saxony and its interior is quite stunning with rich carving from the 15C–18C and a world class, original Silbermann organ. The first Romanesque cathedral dating from the early 13C was burnt down in 1484. Fortunately, some fine parts of this early building remain including the GOLDENEN PFORTE (Golden Porch) dating from 1230, so called as it was originally gilded. This is built into the later Gothic structure of 1484–1501 on the south side. It was originally the main entrance to the Dom and is a beautifully preserved combination of Romanesque architecture and sculpture. The sculptures represent the Kingdom of God as revealed to humanity by Christ. Surmounting the arch in the centre are the Madonna and Child, the Adoration of the Magi lies to the left and the angel Gabriel and Joseph to the right. Below are beautifully carved figures from the Bible: Daniel, the Queen of Sheba, Solomon and John the Baptist to the left and to the right Aaron, the Church, David and St John the Evangelist.

Inside the Dom is equally enchanting. Most arresting is the TULPEN-KANZEL (Tulip Pulpit) dating from 1508–16 by Hans Witten. Carved in sandstone this amazing piece of fantasy art is in the form of an elaborate tulip with the flower forming the pulpit. Decorating the base is a carving of a miner in the role of Daniel in the Lion's Den, complete with splendid maned lion. The pulpit beside this is the Bergmannskanzel (Miner's Pulpit) carved in 1638. The ORGAN is also noteworthy, located in the western part of the gallery, the first great creation of local craftsman, Gottfried Silbermann, in 1714. The sound is absolutely delightful and it is well worth planning your tour to coincide with the weekly, evening concerts held every Thursday at 20.00 during May to September. There is a second, smaller organ, made by Silbermann in 1718–19, located nearby. The main altarpiece is decorated with a painting in Cranach style, depicting local worthies observing the Last Supper. On entering the choir note the Pietà above the door, complete with horsehair wig for extra realism.

Such was the economic importance of Freiberg that in the late 16C the Dom was chosen as the burial place for the Albertine line of the house of Wettin. In **Kurfürsten-Graft**, specially constructed in 1592 behind the high altar in what was the choir, 41 Saxon princes are entombed, beginning with Duke Henry the Pious (d. 1541) through to Elector George IV (d. 1694). The huge Renaissance sarcophagus of Elector Maurice is particularly impressive. Skilfully carved from several rare types of marble with a statue of the kneeling prince, it was designed by the Thoala brothers of Brescia and carved by A. van Zerum of Antwerp in 1563. Beside the 28 brasses inlaid into the floor there is also a tomb designed by Baroque sculptor, Balthasar Permoser for two Saxon princesses and his partner in the design of the Zwinger at Dresden, Pöppelmann, designed the royal gallery in 1726–27.

From the Dom head to the northern corner of Untermarkt where the **Bergbaumauseum** (Museum of Mining) is located in the late Gothic, 15C Domerrenhof (opening times: Tues–Sun 09.00–16.00). The former Canonry, built in 1480, has contained such a museum since 1903. This is a museum devoted mainly to mining, with several large-scale displays as well as sections devoted to the history of the town and a small collection of religious, wooden carved figures. Continue north to reach the **Mineralien-sammlung der Bergakademie** (Exhibition of Minerology) at No. 14 Brennhausgasse (opening times: April–Sept Wed and Thurs 08.00–11.00 and 14.00–16.00, Fri 08.00–11.00, Nov–March Wed and Thurs 10.00–12.00 and 14.00–16.00, Fri 10.00–12.00). This exhibition of minerals, drawn from the four corners of the globe, is one of the most important in Germany.

Continue west down Brennhausgasse to Otto-Nuschke-Platz where the Renaissance **Schloss Freudenstein** stands on the northern edge, overlooking the Kreuzteiche lake. Originally founded in 12C, the Schloss was totally rebuilt in 1566–77 in German Renaissance style. It was used by the Electors of Saxony until the 18C but has been rather neglected since, being used as a military grain store until recently. Continue south down Karl-Marx-Strasse to OBERMARKT, the second most important focal point of the old town. On the east side is the **Rathaus**, founded in 1410–16 and altered in 1470–74 in late Gothic style with subsequent additions. The Freiberg coat of arms crowns the Baroque main entrance. On the north side is the **Kaufhaus**, which now houses the Ratskeller, note the lovely Renaissance portal dating from 1545. In the centre stands an attractive fountain and statue of the town's founder, Otto der Reiche (Otto the Rich). Turn right heading west to reach the **Petrikirche**, a late Gothic hall church dating from the early 15C which also houses a Silbermann organ. Behind this to the north is the moderately interesting Naturkundemuseum (Natural History Museum).

From Freiberg take the A101 heading north through Grossschirma to connect with the E40 east to Dresden. If time permits, a detour 20km south to **Frauenstein** is rewarded with the sight of a Renaissance Schloss dating from 1585–88 with Museum and the Heimatmuseum housing an exhibition on the life of local celebrity, Gottfried Silbermann.

22

Schwerin

126,000 inhabitants.

Tourist Information: Am Markt 11, 19055 Schwerin. Tel. 812314.

Schwerin is the elegant capital of Mecklenburg-Vorpommern, in the heart of the rolling fields and woods of Mecklenburg. The city is built around seven lakes. The highlights of a visit to Schwerin are the fantastic turretted Schloss Schwerin in its island setting and the superb collection of 17C Dutch paintings in the art gallery.

Schwerin is easily accessible from England on the Harwich–Hamburg overnight ferry and the journey from Hamburg is little over an hour. Park in the large Parkplatz 2000, south of the Burgsee. There are good train connections with Berlin, Magdeburg and Rostock. The station is situated to the north-west of the town; reach the centre by heading south down Wismarsche. A good way to get an overall view of Schwerin is to take the Petermännchen open bus that drives round the city centre and through the Schlossgarten.

If you arrive by train, the route from the railway station will take you from Grunthalplatz in front of the Hauptbahnhof (1888–89). Grunthalplatz is named after the teacher Marianne Grunthal, who was hanged by the SS for speaking out in favour of an early end to World War II. Take the steep road zum Bahnhof to reach the Pfaffenteich. The Pfaffenteich (Priests' Pond) is an artificial lake, dammed for use as a millpond in medieval days. Take the ferry, sailing by the fountains, for a superb view of the old town looking towards the cathedral.

The massive white structure on the south-west bank of the Pfaffenteich is the **Arsenal**, which now houses the Innenministerium of the Mecklenburg-Vorpommern Land. It was designed by Demmler (1840–44) and was influenced by Florentine Renaissance palazzo architecture; 136m long, it makes a striking landmark with its square towers and crenellations. Follow the Pfaffenteich north-east along Arsenalstrasse, then turn right into the main shopping street, the pedestrianised Mecklenburgstrasse. Turn left into Schmiedestrasse and come out in the Alter Markt to start the tour at the Tourist Information Office.

History. Schwerin is the oldest city in Mecklenburg and its history runs parallel to that of the Schloss on the Schlossinsel. In 1160 Heinrich der Löwe of Saxony, in his campaign against the Slavs, conquered Niklot, the last free prince of the Obotrite tribe, the Wendish rulers of the area. Niklot's son, Pribislav, was converted to Christianity, married Mathilde, Heinrich's only daughter, and ruled under the Germans. From his line the Dukes of Mecklenburg are directly descended, making it one of the oldest ruling families in Europe. In 1167 Schwerin became the seat of the Bishop of Mecklenburg and a settlement was founded near the cathedral, by the Markt. In the Middle Ages Schwerin was never part of the Hanseatic League, but thrived as the administrative and ecclesiastical centre of Mecklenburg. In 1358 the Counts of Schwerin became the Dukes of Mecklenburg, with the Schloss as their residence. Town fires in

1531 and 1558 and 1661 destroyed the medieval dwellings of the city, which also suffered during occupation by imperial troops in the Thirty Years War. In 1764 Duke Frederick der Fromme (the Pious) moved the ducal residence to Ludwigslust, putting a brake on the city's fortunes. It also meant that Schwerin has virtually no Baroque buildings (apart from the Schelfkirche). In 1837 the court returned from Ludwigslust and the city as you see it today is largely 19C, designed by Georg Demmler, who created elegant, attractive streets and buildings, a fabulous Schloss and the ambience of a capital city. An attempt at industrialisation brought rapid growth in the 1950s and 1960s. Enormous blocks of flats were built to the south-east of the city, at the Grosser Dreesch, which now houses nearly half the population. In 1991, after hot competition with the much larger Rostock, Schwerin became the capital city of Mecklenburg-Pomerania.

A.   The Old Centre

The city has two focal points, the Dom and Markt in the Altstadt and Schloss Schwerin and the Alter Garten to the south-east. Start from the Tourist Information Office and walk diagonally north-west across the Markt to enter the **Dom of St Mary and St John the Evangelist** by the main entrance, in the south side. The Dom is a major work of north German brick Gothic architecture and the only surviving medieval building in Schwerin. It is built on the site of two earlier cathedrals, of which the only remaining evidence is a Romanesque doorway, the Paradiespforte (c 1230) on the south wall of the tower. The present building was conceived on a grand scale, as a brick Gothic basilica 100m long. Work began in 1280, encouraged by the stream of pilgrims visiting a relic of precious drops of the Holy Blood, brought back during the Crusades. The design of the east end of the Dom was strongly influenced by the Marienkirche in Lübeck and the cathedrals of northern France, as may be seen in the choir (1327) with ambulatory and corona of radiating chapels on a pattern of five eighths of an octagon, covered by a single roof span. The work continued in stages, until the vaulting of the nave in 1416 completed the rebuilding, apart from the late Romanesque tower. The tower was eventually demolished in 1888 and replaced by a 117.7m version in Gothic Revival style designed by Georg Daniel. Visitors can climb the tower to 50m for a panoramic view over the city, the lakes and woods around. On the north side of the cathedral are cloisters, of which only the north wing remains untouched by rebuilding schemes in the 19C.

The proportions of the interior are harmonious, with the nave 13.1m wide and 26.5m high (i.e. 1:2). The Gothic upward thrust is intensified by the slender pointed arches of the arcades and the shafts that soar up to support the vaulting, uninterrupted by capitals. The interior has pale walls and the ribs of the vaulting picked out in terracotta and green, based on the medieval colour scheme. Many of the medieval church furnishings were swept aside in early 19C enthusiasm for the Gothic Revival. The ALTARPIECE, all that remains from the Middle Ages, was displayed in a museum, until restored to its rightful position in 1948 for the cathedral's 700th anniversary. It has a fine centre-piece, carved from sandstone c 1440, probably in Lübeck, skilfully composing a succession of episodes from the Passion into one turbulent scene, starting with Christ carrying the Cross outside the Gates of Jerusalem and ending with His descent into the gaping jaws of Hell. A recent introduction is the glorious great turquoise, red and gold ROOD CROSS (1420), saved from the Marienkirche in Weimar, and

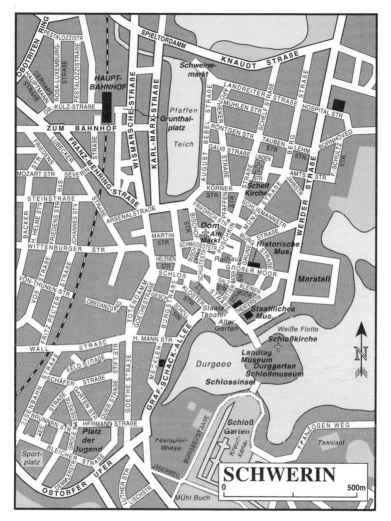

SCHWERIN

0   500m

placed here in 1990 (the figures of Joseph and Mary will be added when their restoration is completed).

In the north transept, the finely etched memorial BRASSES to four early bishops from the von Bülow family are an outstanding example of late 14C metalwork from Flanders. The large bronze font (c 1400), in the Maria Himmelfahrts-Kapelle in the north aisle to the east of the transept, is supported by eight male figures in 15C garments. The sides are divided into eight panels, each depicting two saints. The imposing late Renaissance sepulchre (1595), in the north-west chapel of the ambulatory, is by the workshop of Robert Coppens of Antwerp. Life-size effigies of the Duke Christoph of Mecklenburg and his wife are carved from white marble with their costumes portrayed in detail. The Gothic Revival organ is the largest in Mecklenburg dating from 1871, by Friedrich Ladegast.

From the Dom, walk diagonally back across the square to Rakel's, the excellent baker's shop, to the right of the Tourist Information Office. Here turn around for a splendid view of the cathedral—note the only slight differentiation in roof height and almost equal length of choir and nave. Looking from this spot, the mass of the red Gothic Dom creates a backdrop for the Neo-Classical white **Neues Gebäude** in front. Built during 1783–85 by Johann Joachim Busch (architect of Schloss Ludwigslust) for Duke Friedrich der Fromme, the Neues Gebäude is generally referred to as the 'Säulengebäude' because of its 14 Doric columns; it was intended as a market hall (Krambudengebäude) to replace what the Duke considered to be untidy and unhygienic food stalls in the open square. It now houses a permanent exhibition on the city's history, the Historisches Museum Schwerin (opening times: Tue–Sun 10.00–18.00).

On the east side of the square is the cream **Altstädtisches Rathaus**. The half-timbered crenellated façade was added to the original gabled building by Georg Demmler in 1834–35; looking at the building from behind, the original four gables are retained. Above the clock, the toy-town golden knight on his charger is a tribute to Heinrich der Löwe.

Leave the square by Puschkinstrasse, in the south-east corner. Continue south down Puschkinstrasse to Schlossstrasse, still in the central pedestrianised zone. Turn left at Schlossstrasse and immediately on your left is **Café Prague**, the best in Schwerin. Continue east, almost to the end of Schlossstrasse. The corner building on the left is a late 18C half-timbered mansion, the **Alte Palais**, a gift from Crown Prince Friedrich Ludwig to his 15-year-old Russian bride, the Tzar's daughter Princess Helena Pavlovna (d. 1803; her mausoleum is in the park at Schloss Ludwigslust). It was later used as the residential palace by the Archduke Paul Friedrich, who lived here whilst work was being carried out on the Schloss.

Opposite the Alte Palais are two large Neo-Classical buildings, built for the government of Mecklenburg. The grey building on the left was built by Georg Demmler in 1825–34 and reconstructed in 1866–67 after a fire. Demmler was greatly influenced by the Neo-Classical work of Schinkel which he had seen in Berlin. Today it is the Staatskanzlei (Provincial Treasury) of the President of Mecklenburg-Vorpommern. The yellow building, linked by a covered bridge and known colloquially as the *Beamtenlaufbahn* or 'bureaucrats' racetrack' was added in 1890–92 by Georg Daniel. Ahead the **Alter Garten** opens up—a splendid large square, where the fairytale Schloss is surrounded by the water of the lake behind. Its name (Old Garden) is rather misleading as it was first laid out as a garden in 1633. It became known as the Alter Garten during the early 18C when the gardens on the mainland to the south-east of the Schloss were laid out. Walk to the centre of the square, taking great care with the traffic which comes as something of a surprise after the pedestrian zone, to get the best view of the feast of architectural styles around.

Next to the Alte Palais, on the north side of the square, is the rather overpowering Neo-Baroque **Mecklenburg Staatstheater**, designed by Georg Daniel to replace an earlier building by Demmler which was burnt down. The theatre was finished in 1885, despite difficulties with the swampy ground that involved driving great oak posts as far as 45m deep. There is a long tradition of theatre in Schwerin, going back to spiritual plays held in the Dom in 16C and troupes of strolling players performing in the court in the 17C and 18C. In May 1753 the first German Dramatic Academy was opened here, directed by Conrad Ekhof. Theatre was encouraged by the culture-loving Duke Christian Ludwig II, but his death in 1756 brought an abrupt halt to a golden age of court dramatics, as his successor, Friedrich der Fromme, forbade any sort of gaiety. In the 19C the focus was on music, with appearances by Mendelssohn, Clara Schumman, Saint-Saëns and Brahms. Schwerin was regarded as second only to Bayreuth in productions of Wagner, with the first performance outside Bayreuth of *Die Walküre*, staged here in 1878. In the post-1945 years there was a regeneration of the lively theatrical tradition—a high point was Goethe's *Faust I and II* performed in one evening. Since unification cuts in subsidies, easier access to television and a high level of unemployment have led to a drop in attendance.

Next to the theatre, on the north-eastern side of the Alter Garten, is the ***Staatliches Museum Schwerin, Kunstsammlungen** (opening times: Tues–Sun 10.00–17.00, closed Mon). A long flight of steps leads up to the grand Neo-Classical portico, designed in 1877–82 by Hermann Willebrand, a colleague of Demmler. The museum has always been an art gallery and boasts one of the most comprehensive collections of 17C Dutch and Flemish paintings in Europe, thanks largely to Duke Christian Ludwig II (1683–1756), a connoisseur of 17C Dutch art.

Climb the steps to the main entrance on the first floor (at the time of writing there is no easy access for wheelchairs). Straight ahead is Room 4 (the building is E-shaped, with Room 4 in the centre and the main rooms leading off it). Concentrate on the rooms to the right. As you tour the main rooms of Netherlands works of art, you will find helpful fact sheets (*Führungsblätter*) in English, to read and return. ROOM 4 is devoted to the work of Caravaggists. It includes the *Portrait of an Old Man* (c 1630), doubtfully attributed to Rembrandt but certainly showing Rembrandt's characteristic use of light. Turn right into ROOM 5, a room of 17C landscapes and architectural pieces. Jacob von Ruisdael, arguably the greatest Dutch landscape painter, is represented here by the romantic scenery of Norway in *Mountain Landscape with Falls*. *Damplatz in Amsterdam* by Gerrit Berckheyde (1665) shows the mighty town hall as a symbol of the independence of Dutch towns. Continue straight through to ROOM 6 for the highlight of the museum's collection, *The Guardsman (1654, *Die Torwache*) a rare work by Carel Fabritius, who died at the age of 34. Fabritius made a dramatic change in the style of Dutch painting, with a dark central figure and a sunlit background. Two cheerful portraits by Frans Hals show a *Boy Holding a Flute* and a *Boy Drinking*. The *Girl Suffering from Love* by Jan Steen is a masterpiece of genre painting—the messenger in the background handing over a letter will do far more to relieve the maiden's distress than all the physician's potions. The *Winter Landscape* by Hendrick van Averkamp is a lively skating scene, with the 17C notion of vanitas in the dilapidated houses of the foreground, a symbol of the transience of this world. Marine paintings are also featured in this room. The left-hand corner of the room leads into the bottom of the 'E', ROOM 7, devoted to still life painting. The most important of the early still life painters are Pieter Claesz and Willem Claesz Heda. In Willem Claesz Heda's *Breakfast Table with Ham* a pewter plate, a glass, a linen cloth enhanced with a silvery gleam, become objects of serene beauty. In late 17C the paintings become more flamboyant, with gorgeous full-blown flower arrangements by Jan de Heem, in glowing, almost translucent, tones. Other celebrated flower-painters represented in this room are Jan van Huysum and his son Justus, making this display a glorious profusion of colour.

Return through Room 6, this time taking the exit into the *Kabinette rechts*, and continue past the first small room, to the third *Kabinett rechts*. Paulus Potter, one of the most celebrated Dutch animal painters, is well represented here. With five pictures, this is the third biggest collection of his work after those in Amsterdam and Leningrad. *The Milkmaid* is a jolly, bucolic scene and *The Black Horse in the Meadow* demonstrates Potter's mastery of technique. As you leave the Kabinette, in the last small room you will pass works by Gerard Dou and his school of genre-painting. To the left of the entrance hall is the Kabinette display of Flemish art, including *A Nymph pursued by Pan* by Jan Breughel the Elder. The works of art in the main rooms to the left of Room 4 are 18C–20C. You may enjoy Thomas Gainsborough's portrait of *Queen Charlotte of England*, Princess of Mecklenburg-Streliz, in ROOM 1, before leaving the art collection. Now head downstairs to the basement to see the Meissen porcelain, mainly dating back to Duke Christian Ludwig II. In the basement there is also a fine display of medieval ecclesiastical works of art and architecture and the large collection of coins and medallions.

Leaving the museum head diagonally across the Alter Garten to the bridge that will take you to the Schlossinsel (Castle Island).

B. Schloss Schwerin

At the east end of the Alter Garten rises **Schloss Schwerin** on a small island, the **Schlossinsel**, at the edge of the Schweriner See. With sparkling water all around, a silhouette of fanciful towers and turrets and a proud Slav prince on his charger guarding the entrance, the Schloss is quite enchanting.

History. The Schlossinsel, a small and solid island poised on the edge of marshy mainland, was ideal for a stronghold. In the 11C it became the island fortress Zuarin (meaning a place abounding with game) of the Slav princes of the Obotrite tribe. In 1160, attacked by Heinrich the Lion and his German forces, Prince Niklot and the Obotrite defenders, seeing the enemy's superior strength, burnt down the fort as they retreated. Because of the superb strategic site a castle was quickly rebuilt, and became the seat of the Counts of Schwerin, later the Dukes of Mecklenburg. Little is known of the history of the Schloss, until Duke Albrecht I commissioned two Renaissance style additions to the medieval castle between 1553 and 1555—the Grosses Neues Haus and the Bischofshaus, the latter was intended as a residence for his brother Magnus, the first Protestant bishop of Schwerin. The unifying motif of these two buildings is the terracotta decoration from the workshop of Statius von Düren of Lübeck. In the 19C 'improved' versions replaced many of the original tiles, some of which may still be seen in the Orangery. The castle chapel was rebuilt during 1560–63 by Johann Baptista Parr (brother of Franz Parr, architect of Schloss Güstrow) in Renaissance style, based on the revolutionary design of the Protestant chapel at Torgau. In 1855 a Gothic Revival choir was added to the chapel, the architect quite failing to appreciate that this was deliberately omitted in the original plan, which centred on the preacher's pulpit.

In the 17C Duke Adolph Friedrich I outlined a grandiose building programme, with an extraordinary design by the Dutch architect Ghert Evert Piloot. This had only got as far as the kitchen wing when it was disrupted by the Thirty Years War. The legacy of the 18C is a Baroque garden, designed by Jean Legeay 1748–56 and now a characteristic east German blend of formal and wild. When Duke Paul Friedrich returned to Schwerin after the House of Mecklenburg had been resident in Lud-wigslust for 80 years he intended to build a new palace in the Alter Garten (on the site of the museum), but by the time of his death in 1842 this had got no further than the foundations. His son Friedrich Franz II decided instead to remodel the old island castle dramatically and sent the architect Georg Demmler on a study tour of Europe. Demmler was particularly impressed by the châteaux of the Loire and based the plans for the Schloss Schwerin on Chambord. Gottfried Semper was also involved in the design, and at a later stage Stühler also, when Demmler was dismissed in 1851 for being a democrat involved in the 1848–49 Revolution. Demmler, however, was the presiding genius of the design. His great gift was to take a mixture of styles and periods, adding flamboyant dashes of his own, such as the fanciful main tower, to produce a castle of great harmony and beauty that does justice to its stunning lake setting.

The schloss was the residence of the Archdukes of Mecklenburg until 1918. Then for a long period it was used as a school for kindergarten teachers. In 1974 a major restoration began and today the schloss is home to the Landtag (provincial parliament), and the Bundesbank met here in 1992.

It is easy to walk round the outside of the castle, on the island, to get an overview of the blend of styles. The parts of the interior of the Schloss that can be visited belong to the **Schlossmuseum Schwerin** (opening times: Tues–Sun 10.00–17.00), which has its entrance at the garden door. Before you cross to the Schlossinsel look straight ahead from the centre of the Alter Garten, to the elaborate double-winged entrance (August Stühler, c 1851) with its statue of the last free Slav prince, Niklot, the direct ancestor of the House of Mecklenburg. On the bridge the groups of riders are by Christian Genschow (1874–76). Now cross to the Schlossinsel to walk round the castle in a clockwise direction. The main body of the building is Neo-Renaissance, but earlier parts remain, as Friedrich Franz wished to preserve some of the old parts of the Schloss, such as the Schlosskapelle, on the north side of the building as you look up to the right. The path round the castle, through the Burggarten, is at two levels, but at the time of writing, ongoing restoration work means access along the paths may vary. On the lower one is the strange Grotto made of boulders from the lake shore. As you move round the castle to the central, eastern aspect you pass the colonnade of the Orangery. From the upper path there is a far-reaching vista across the lake to the islands of Kaninchenwerder (Rabbit Isle) and Ziegelwerder (Goat Isle). If you wish you can leave this walk on the south side of the Schloss, to cross a small bridge into the Baroque Schlossgarten, laid out 1748–56 by Jean Legeay. Here you can stroll among the clipped box hedges or beside the canal that forms the central south-east to north-west axis, flanked by Neo-Classical statues of heroes of the antique world which are copies of the 1720 originals by Balthasar Permoser and meander through the leafy tunnels of pleached limes.

If you are not diverted, you will reach the south wing of the castle and the main entrance to the Schlossmuseum Schwerin. Much of the interior was lost in a fire in 1913 and not repaired. Further loss occurred through misuse during and after World War II. In 1974 a major restoration began and is still ongoing. The highpoints of a visit are the state rooms, on the Festetage, especially the gorgeously decorated **Thronsaal** (1855) with its historical theme. Around the entire room runs a frieze of 40 coats of arms that includes all the towns in Mecklenburg at the time of building. Between them are plaster figures symbolising the attractions of the province, such as fishing, horse-breeding and agriculture. The focus of the room is the red and gilt baldacchino over the velvet throne. The 16 columns around the room are of marble from Carrara. The heating stoves are concealed behind gilt cast iron doors with intricate reliefs. Make sure not to miss the adjoining Ahnengalerie, with its rather more restrained decoration and wood panelling making a superb setting for portraits of leading members of the House of Mecklenburg from 14C–19C. Parallel to the Ahengalerie is the Schlösser-galerie, with pictures of the castles in possession of the Mecklenburg family, including Güstrow, Ludwigslust and the Palais in Rostock. Beside these splendid official rooms, the ducal family's quarters appear more modest, although still on a vast scale. Those of the Duchess, one floor lower on the Beletage, include the charming circular-shaped BLUMENZIMMER (flower room), in the main tower, with direct access to the Burggarten. Stucco-work festoons and garlands decorate the circular ceiling, supported by Hermes, and twirling vine motifs even creep into the pattern of the parquet floor. On the Duchess's floor you will notice pictures of an imp-like figure in big boots and a high hat—this is Petermännchen, the good spirit of the castle, but always willing to play a prank.

Leaving the museum continue round the Schloss and back over the main bridge, then turn right and head north along Werderstrasse, which runs parallel to the lake. At the landing stage of the *Weisse Flotte* you can take a steamer ride round the lake (c two hours), to the beach at Zippendorf or the island of Kaninchenwerder. Walk a further 200m north along the Werderstrasse, to the four-winged Neo-Classical **Marstall** (1838–42). This is a masterpiece of Demmler's architecture and ingenuity as the marshy ground meant that huge oak piles had to be sunk to hold the foundations. The Marstall was intended for the equine element of the ducal court, with stables, a coach house building and an indoor manège. Part is now used as a small theatre and the rest by the Ministries of Welfare and Culture.

All of this eastern corner of Schwerin was once marshy ground, hence the name, GROSSER MOOR, of the street on your left, opposite the Marstall. Turn into this street. In 17C the houses were built on wooden posts. By the mid-1970s these were the oldest dwellings in the city and the timber foundations were rotting. To the great dismay of conservationists, virtually the whole street of half-timbered buildings was demolished. The only mitigating factor in the architecture of the blocks of flats that followed is that the 17C proportions and roof height were adhered to. At No. 38, on the east side, is the **Historische Museum**, with displays on the history of the region and the city (opening times: Tues–Sun 10.00–18.00). At the west end, near the popular fish café, **Gastmahl des Meeres**, is a ceramic column by Anni Jung of 1986 with 27 reliefs of highlights from 800 years of city history.

Bear right and north-west from the Grosser Moor into the SCHLACHTER-MARKT (Meat Market). At the heart of the market is a solid modern fountain of 1980 by Stephan Horota with a statue of a large and fearsome bull—the motif of Mecklenburg's coat of arms. The square was immaculately rebuilt in the 1980s, including the four red-gabled buildings that make up the rear of the town hall. A Glockenspiel plays at noon each day. Walk across the square to the north-west corner, passing the excellent but expensive Zum Goldenen Reiter where you might stop to sample some Mecklenburg specialities. Pass through the passage to the controversial and rusty modern statue *Der Runde Tisch* (The Round Table) intended to recall the days of 1989–90 when the various political parties met round a table to debate the future of the country. You have now returned to the main square and the end of the tour.

If you have time, do visit the small, cross-shaped **Church of St Nicholas** or **Schelfkirche** (1708–11 by Jakob Reutz) a gem of a small Baroque church in the centre of the most neglected quarter of the city, the Schelfstadt ('town on a shelf', i.e. above the level of the lake). The triple-tiered tower with its Baroque dome and slender steeple dominate the Baroque buildings of the square. Unusually for Mecklenburg, it is constructed partly of pale sandstone as well as brick and is one of the few examples of Baroque ecclesiastical architecture in Mecklenburg. The interior dates from 1858.

C. The environs of Schwerin

About 6km to the east of Schwerin, at Schwerin Muess, the next village along the B321 following the shore of Schweriner See from Zippendorf, is the **Mecklenburgisches Volkskundemuseum Schwerin-Muess**, also referred to as the Freilichtsmuseum (Open Air Museum) (opening times: May–Oct 10.00–18.00). Travel on the B321 towards Parchim, turning left at Muess, into Alter Crivitzer Landstrasse. Head north-east through the old village, then turn left, into Zum Alten Bauernhof, just past a thatched bus shelter, before the Post Office. After about 50m you will see the museum. This is one of most interesting museums in Mecklenburg-Pomerania, for both adults and children. You step back centuries into a lower German 17C Hallenhaus, with a herb garden, beehives and working bread oven; the large 18C barn is full of fascinating agricultural implements of bygone days. There is also a modest café at the museum.

23

From Schwerin to Güstrow

Schwerin—35km Sternberg—27km Güstrow.

The journey takes you east from Schwerin to the centre of Mecklenburg through rolling countryside, less intensively farmed as you travel eastwards. From Schwerin follow the A106, then the A104 signposted Güstrow and cross the Schweriner See.

Sternberg

5200 inhabitants.

The small town of **Sternberg** is set by a lake. The squat, square tower with the Baroque steeple is the parish church of Sts Mary and Nicholas. Built in early brick Gothic style, it was founded in 1322 and rebuilt in 1750. A detour here of some 5km north takes you to Gross Raden and the **Archaelogisches Freilichtsmuseum** (Archaeological Open Air Museum; opening times:

May–Oct, Tues–Sat 10.00–17.00), with its fascinating reconstruction of a Slav settlement and temple.

After Sternberg, as you continue eastwards, the countryside becomes wilder, characterised by lakes and beech woods. Some 22km from Sternberg, just beyond Bülow, the distinctive silhouette of Güstrow comes into sight. To the left is the Baroque spire of the Pfarrkirche St Marien, then the solid central mass of the Dom and on the right the more intricate outline of Schloss Güstrow.

Güstrow

38,000 inhabitants.

Tourist Information Office: 33 Glevinerstrasse, 18273 Güstrow. Tel. 61023.

Güstrow has been comparatively unaffected by the ravages of war, and with its main square is surrounded by the polychromatic gables of 17C burgher houses. It would be well worth stopping for the unspoilt townscape alone, but the grand Renaissance Schloss is of additional interest. Best of all is the chance to see the sculptures of Ernst Barlach, displayed at the Gertrudenkapelle and at his Atelierhaus (studio). This 20C German Expressionist painter and sculptor created some powerful work, with a good selection on display in Güstrow.

History. The town was founded in November 1228 by Heinrich Borwin II, the Wendish prince. Shortly afterwards a castle was built that became the seat of the von Werle princes. Sited at the intersection of important cross-country roads, including the one from Lübeck to Stettin, it soon became the main market town for the area.

Three major fires in the early decades of the 16C destroyed many of the medieval buildings, apart from the castle and the Dom. The town was rapidly rebuilt, retaining its original plan. In the midst of the Thirty Years War Güstrow enjoyed a fleeting Golden Age as Albrecht von Wallenstein's Residenz (Residential Town). Wallenstein had received the Duchy of Mecklenburg from the Kaiser as a contribution to his war expenses and moved into Schloss Güstrow (by then rebuilt in grand Renaissance style) in 1628. The town experienced a significant political, economic and cultural upturn as Wallenstein attracted leading figures from the fields of culture and science to his court in Güstrow. He re-organised the educational and judiciary systems, introduced care for the poor, wrote a book on agriculture and brought ice-cream to Mecklenburg. When Wallenstein left the town in 1629, he had instigated a number of reforms, which were revoked three years later.

The prosperity of the town continued, however, based on light industry and trade. The local wool market was the most important in Mecklenburg until well into the 19C, while trade in cloth, brewing beer and wrought-iron work were also staples of the economy. Around 1800 the façade of the Rathaus was rebuilt in Neo-Classical style, and many of the patrician houses followed suit. The interlacing of the Neo-Classical and medieval is a prominent feature of Güstrow.

In 1813 the town was the centre of anti-Napoleonic uprisings in Mecklenburg, during the Wars of Liberation. One of those closely involved was the early Romantic painter Georg Friedrich Kersting, born in Güstrow in 1785. Güstrow's most famous citizen, however, was the sculptor Ernst Barlach, who made the town his home between 1910 and 1938.

On 2 May 1945 the town was taken by the Red Army unharmed, but since then, due to general neglect, considerable restoration work has been necessary; Güstrow is now undergoing a comprehensive restoration programme and is one of the Models for Town Renovation (Modellstädte der Stadtsanierung) of the former East Germany.

For a tour of the town, start from the Tourist Information Office and turn left, heading east into the MARKTPLATZ, where the most important buildings of the town centre are situated: the Rathaus, the parish church and the gabled patrician houses, which are amongst the finest in Mecklenburg. The mansion façades date from the 17C and 18C, post-dating some of the Gothic gabled houses to be found in Wismar, Stralsund and Greifswald.

Houses in the Marktplatz worth looking at include Nos 10 and 12, much older than the others, and built in the 16C or 17C. On the green house, built in German Renaissance style, you can just make out the date of 1631. The distinguishing decorative elements of the time are clearly recognisable: the stepped gable, the volutes crowned by a figure at the top. In the red building the first floor is wider than the ground, another key feature of the period, which meant that despite a bigger living room (always on the upper floor), the width of the street could be maintained. In many of the houses, a German Renaissance or Neo-Classical style façade has been grafted onto a late medieval house, so that the house looked modern and impressive from the exterior, despite its dark and cramped interior.

Now head south down MÜHLENSTRASSE to find two of the oldest houses in Güstrow. No. 48, one of the most splendid merchant's houses, was built in 1535 as a late Gothic stepped gabled house. The façade on the courtyard side is just as decorative as that facing the street. The splendid Rococo front door is also of note (it was being restored at the time of writing). The board on the façade of Mühlenstrasse explains that Colonel St Julian and Albrecht von Wiengiersky, Wallenstein's commander in Güstrow, lived there from 1628 to 1630. A little further on is house No. 17, which stands out from its neighbours. It was built in 1607 with a high Renaissance gable and a distinctive oriel extension, and decorated with figures.

Continue west along Lange Strasse and then north into Hollstrasse, where No. 6 is the **Kerstinghaus Museum** (opening times: every day except Wed 10.00–12.00, 12.30–16.00). The house is the birthplace of Georg Friedrich Kersting (1785–1847) an important representative of the north German school of painting, and the display on the first floor is devoted to Kersting's life. Although nowhere near his stature as an artist, he was a friend of Caspar David Friedrich (1774–1840) and a third Romantic painter Gerhard von Kügelgen; they studied together in Copenhagen and then in Dresden. Unlike Friedrich, Kersting is known for his depictions of interior scenes, influenced by the Dutch masters Vermeer and de Hooch. The strong use of light and a figure placed near a window characterised his work. His most reproduced work is probably the portrait of his friend, *Caspar David Friedrich in his Studio* (1811). Kersting was active in the anti-Napoleonic movement in Mecklenburg. He joined the volunteer Jäger corps in 1813, the wealthier Friedrich supplying him with the uniform, and was mentioned in despatches. From 1813 to his death in 1847, Kersting was the artistic director at the Meissen porcelain factory, which he helped to revitalise.

The house itself is interesting as a good example of a medieval hall dwelling house (*Wohndielenhaus*). Amongst the ground floor exhibits is a model of the town as it would have looked in the early 19C, complete with the local regiment of soldiers on parade, which will delight children. The curator may also be persuaded to show you round the tiny reconstructed kitchen and down into the cellar.

Now return to the Marktplatz, heading north, to the **Rathaus**. Like the rest of the Marktplatz it was burnt down in 1503. The richly ornamented classical façade by D.A. Kuhfahl was added in 1798 onto the front of four earlier buildings, as can be seen clearly from the west elevation. The Güstrow town arms, showing a bull, appear in the gable.

Amongst the houses altered to Neo-Classical style at the same time as the Rathaus, No. 22 has a particularly splendid façade decorated with grotesques and typical classical motifs such as shell and palm frieze over the second floor. The angel door is a gem.

Now head west down DOMSTRASSE (Cathedral Street), first mentioned in 1313 as the street that linked the settlement round the market with a second settlement by the castle. On the building at the corner of Domstrasse and Burgstrasse look out for the Mecklenburg coat of arms dating from 1648, with the crowned bull's head, on the top left, indicating allegiance to Schwerin. Artisans and small-time burghers lived in the streets a little further from the town centre. In contrast to the lofty mansions round the Markt their houses were generally only two-storey, half-timbered and unembellished. The small house at Domstrasse 11 is typical. The wide entry could be used by a horse and cart. On the ground floor was the workshop and the first floor was used as a dwelling and for storage.

Continue west to the **Museum der Stadt Güstrow** at the end of the street, in the house with a wrought-iron balcony (opening times: Mon–Thur 10.00–12.00, 12.30–17.00, closed Fri, Sat. 13.00–17.00, Sun 11.00–16.00). It was founded in 1892 and has displays of archaeological finds, town history and crafts from the Middle Ages onwards. (The town history section was closed for redecoration at the time of writing.) There is an impressive collection of theatre programmes from 1741 to the present day. A small, tranquil garden behind the museum is a good place to pause.

Continue west into Franz-Parr-Platz. Immediately opposite is the **Barlach Theatre**, built in 1828, and the first of its kind in Mecklenburg. The simple, Neo-Classical building was designed by Schinkel's student, Adolph Demmler. Although the interior has been considerably altered (having once been used to store wool), the exterior has remained unchanged and is a fine example of the Schinkel school's restrained classicism. It quickly developed from a small provincial stage to a well-known theatre, and is now visited by touring companies. In 1957 it was re-named after Ernst Barlach, to honour his contribution to theatre. He wrote several plays, although they are seldom performed for technical reasons.

Walk west across Franz-Parr-Platz to reach the **Schloss Güstrow**. It comes as a surprise to find this grey, elegant château amidst the rather mundane red brick Gothic. As an important Renaissance castle, the Schloss is unique in Mecklenburg, indeed in north Germany. The south and west wings are the most interesting architecturally, and were designed between 1558 and 1566 by Franz Parr, one of a family of Italian architects. The Schloss is an extraordinary synthesis of different influences: the Italian, apparent in features such as the horizontal cornicing and the great stone stairwell; the French is seen in the chimneys, the pitch of the roof, and the turrets which would all look at home in the Loire; while the asymmetrical west façade and gable are motifs from local domestic architecture.

History. The site was originally the seat of the princes of Werle, who built a castle here in 13C. When their line died out, the land became part of the Duchy of Mecklenburg and Güstrow, like Schwerin, became a seat of the Dukes of Mecklenburg. During the rule of Ulrich III (1556–1603) part of the medieval castle burnt down. The duke had a new building designed, with a square four-winged layout. In 1558–66 Franz Parr built the west and south wings. After a second fire the Dutch architect and sculptor, Philipp Brandin, was commissioned to construct the north and east wings. The Schloss gatehouse and bridge were completed in the second half of the 17C by Charles Philippe Dieussart. During the Thirty Years War Wallenstein ruled Mecklenburg from here and his court was a cultural and intellectual centre.

The chequered history of the Schloss continued. In 1695, with the death of Duke Gustav Adolph, the Mecklenburg-Güstrow ducal line died out. The building was used as a dower house, but gradually fell into disrepair. In 1795 a large part of the dilapidated Schloss was pulled down, including the entire east wing.

In 1808 the French requisitioned the building for a barracks and hospital for Napoleon's army, after which it was used by the Freikorps Jäger. From 1817 to 1945 it was run by the Mecklenburg aristocracy as a notorious House of Correction (Besserungsanstalt) for the homeless and unemployed as well as for holding the politically suspect. After the end of World War II the building was used as an old people's home.

In 1963 comprehensive repair work began. By 1972 the Staatliches Museum in Schwerin was able to make use of the reconstructed rooms. The garden was also restored in Renaissance style, although it appears a little neglected at the moment.

Schloss Güstrow, built in the Renaissance style

The Schloss is constructed of brick, plastered to resemble stone. The west wing which faces the town is the most impressive, with its five storeys, steep roof and tall chimneys in French Renaissance style, and a gable that might have come from a wealthy German burgher's house added for good measure. Walk through the gatehouse and into the delightful courtyard, where, because of the lie of the land, there are only three storeys. The south wing has three open galleries, with a winding stairway at the east end. It is at the top that you find the entrance to the Heimatmuseum (opening times: Tues–Sun 09.00–17.00, but it is wise to enquire at the porter's lodge whether the museum is open, before climbing the stairs). Displays include the history of the feudal hunt and hunting weapons.

Of the interior rooms the grandest is the large assembly chamber, the **Jagdsaal** (Hunting Room), so-called because of the wonderful Baroque frieze decorated with red deer (1569–71, by Christoph Parr, brother of the architect) and the fantastic stuccoed ceiling (1620, Daniel Anckerman) with every possible variation on the theme of hunting.

Walk along to the end of the courtyard, and look down to the *parterres* of the Renaissance gardens, recreated over the last few years. You may be tempted to descend the flight of steps to stroll under the shady pleached hornbeam alley, and return the way you came.

In the middle of the square, originally a part of the palace grounds that was used for riding and exercise until the 18C, rises an iron monument dedicated to the Freikorps Jäger (the voluntary corps of freedom fighters formed in 1813, against French occupation), erected in 1863 to mark their 50th anniversary. The corner figures symbolise war, victory, peace and mourning. This monument is undergoing extensive restoration work.

Walk north along Philipp-Brandin-Strass to the DOMPLATZ. The brick Gothic **Dom**, dedicated to Mary, St John the Evangelist and St Cecilia, is the oldest surviving building in the town. On 3 June 1226 Heinrich Borwin II, on his death-bed, endowed a collegiate church and work on the church was probably begun in the same year. Over 100 years later, in 1335, the Dom was consecrated, though it was not finally completed until the late 15C. It is a brick basilica with nave and two aisles. The long choir area, typical of a Romanesque building, together with the transept, are the oldest parts. The two-bay nave was attached on to these (and not quite straight, as can be seen from the plan). In a further phase, towards end 14C, the massive west tower, 44m high, and the three south chapels were built.

After the Reformation reached Mecklenburg in 1549, the Dom stood empty. Thanks to the intervention of the Duchess Elisabeth (consort of Ulrich III) between 1565 and 1568, the Dom became the court church of the protestant Dukes of Mecklenburg-Güstrow. After their line died out in 1695 it acted as a second parish church. Between 1865 and 1869 the church was extensively restored and sombrely decorated.

The church furnishings are amongst the richest in Mecklenburg. The wonderful carved wooden altar (c 1500), from the workshop of Hinrick [sic] Bornemann, shows a turbulent crucifixion group flanked by apostles, the Early Fathers and martyrs. On the pillars of the main aisle are the oak carvings of the Twelve Apostles by Claus Berg, c 1530, all with expressive gestures. The figure of St John is believed to be the earliest.

The era as court church left its artistic legacy, in particular the wall tomb of Duke Ulrich III and his wives Elisabeth of Denmark and later Anna of Pomerania—life-size figures in a stately setting (1584–87, by Philipp Brandin). Historically interesting is the genealogy of the house of the Duchy of Mecklenburg on the north wall of the choir.

Ernst Barlach's famous war memorial *Der Schwebende* (The Hovering Angel) is in the north chapel. Originally commissioned in 1927 for the fallen of the First World War, it was Barlach's first great work in bronze and led to several public commissions, also in wood and stone, over the following five years, including war memorials for Kiel, Magdeburg and Hamburg. In 1937, under the Nazi regime, the *Schwebende*, who bears the features of Käthe Kollwitz, was removed, to Barlach's deep sorrow. After the end of the Second World War a second casting reached Cologne and was used to make this copy in 1953.

As you come out of the Dom, and look round the square, the gable house to be seen on the east side of the square (Domplatz 16) was built in 1583 by the Dutchman Philipp Brandin, the architect of the second stage of the Schloss. Rather interestingly, the top of the gable imitates the shape of a Dutch girl's cap. A plaque commemorates the years when Wallenstein's Court of Justice met here, 1629–31.

On the north-eastern corner of the square is the oldest school building in Mecklenburg, the former Domschule (1579). This Renaissance building was also designed by Philipp Brandin in 1579. Still surviving is the splendid entrance crowned by lions.

Leave the old town and walk east down the Schulstrasse to the **Grüne Winkel**. No. 10 is one of the few Baroque houses in the town, built in the mid 18C. A few years ago the plaster on the right side of the façade was removed to restore it to its original appearance, with its *trompe l'oeil* window and door frames.

You are now near the edge of the original medieval town, which by 1293 was enclosed by a strong wall with four double gates. The wall was kept in good repair until about 1800. With increasing industrialisation the need for a work force grew, and the town began to exceed its original limits, spreading into typical Gründerzeit (Founders' Years) suburbs. Now only fragments of the town wall can be seen. On the spot where you cross the town ditch there used to be a double gate.

Cross the busy road to the ***Ernst-Barlach-Gedenkstätte** in the Gertrudenkapelle (chapel with Ernst Barlach's sculptures; opening times: 1 Mar–31 Oct, 10.00–17.00, closed Mon; 1 Nov–28 Feb, 09.00–16.00, except Wed 10.00–1700, closed Mon; last entry 30 mins before closing). The Gertrudenkapelle is a small brick Gothic chapel (c 1430), set in a peaceful green churchyard. Since 1953 it has housed a collection of some of Barlach's most famous and powerful works, including the *Gefesselten Hexe* (Bound Witch) 1926, the *Wanderer im Wind* (Walker in the Wind) 1934, and the *Zweifler* (Despairer) 1937. The simple carved wooden figures convey the depths of emotion so typical of the Expressionists.

To return to the town centre cross opposite Wilhelm Wandschneider's 1908 memorial to the north German poet John Brinckman.

Walk south-west along the PFERDEMARKT, a main street first mentioned in 1270, and pedestrianised in 1972. The fountain designed in 1889 by Richard Thiele from Hamburg, once Barlach's teacher, was put up as a memorial to Heinrich Borwin II, Prince von Werle, the founder of the town. Return to the north side of the Marktplatz to visit the **Marienkirche**, which was first mentioned in the early 14C as the parish church. It too was a victim of the fire in 1503, but within five years a five-aisle brick Gothic church, with a massive tower built on the west end, was newly consecrated. It acquired its Baroque dome at the end of the 17C. By the late 19C, after extensive rebuilding, it became the present hall church with nave and two aisles.

The church is one of the most richly furnished of the inland town churches of Mecklenburg, reflecting both the piety and the wealth of Güstrow's citizens. The most striking piece is the large and wonderful Brüsseler Altar (1522), a double winged altarpiece; the wood carving is by Jan Borman of Brussels, and the oil painting on the reverse side by the Flemish court painter Bernaert van Orley. The central panel shows the Crucifixion and is flanked by scenes from the Passion on either side; note the *Noli mi tangere* at the bottom right. Above is the Man of Sorrows and Mary with 12 female saints. The predella, below, has carved figures of Christ and the Apostles. When it is half-closed you can see paintings of the Virgin Mary and Child, the Annunciation and the martyrdom of St Catherine. When the altar panels are folded over again, the figures of Sts Peter and Paul are revealed, depicted against landscapes in which their martyrdoms are represented in the background. You cannot get close to the altar but there is a helpful photomontage to the right. (The motif of St Catherine indicates the Brotherhood of St Catherine who commissioned the altar.)

Above the intersection of chancel and nave is a larger-than-life wooden Triumphkreuzgruppe (1516), with the unusual addition of Adam and Eve as outer figures. It was Barlach, with his intense interest in Gothic carving, who appreciated that for many years the rood had been incomplete, and thanks to him all the figures were restored to their original positions. Post-Reformation works include the carved sandstone pulpit of 1583 by Rudolph Stockmann (renovated 1883), and the carved Ratsgestühl (Council Pew) of 1599, by Michael Meyer from Rostock. The tower can be visited at certain times during July and August.

Before leaving Güstrow be sure to visit the ***Ernst-Barlach-Gedenstätte**, at the **Atelierhaus** (studio) am Heidberg, Heidberg 5, 18273 Güstrow (opening times: Nov–Feb Tues–Sun 09.00–16.00, Mar–Oct Tue–Sun 10.00–17.00. Closed Mon). The Atelier is a good half-hour's walk from the centre of Güstrow, in the midst of pine woods, overlooking Lake Inselsee. Here Barlach worked in splendid isolation until his death in 1938. Over 100 examples of his sculptures, models and drawings can be seen in this tranquil setting.

24

From Schwerin to Neustrelitz

Schwerin—143km Mirow—27km Neustrelitz—43km Waren.

The first part of the route is on the motorway, passing briefly through the province of Brandenburg, identified by its Prussian eagle. After the motorway the tour goes through the heart of the Mecklenburg Lake District with myriad lakes and lovely trees all along the route.

From Schwerin take the motorway A241/E26, travelling south. Be careful to leave the E26 at exit Pritzwalk (17km beyond the town itself) and after 3km join the E55/A19 at junction Wittstock, heading north towards Rostock. Exit at the next junction (Röbel) and head south-east on the 198 to Neustrelitz via Mirow.

The very open road between exit Röbel and Vipperow gives glimpses of **Lake Müritz** to the left and right. Müritz is the largest (115 sq km) of the Mecklenburg lakes, and second only to Lake Constance in the whole of Germany. Part of the route is along shady avenues. The avenues of trees (*Alleen*) restrict the width of the country roads and with the influx of traffic after unification this has created a conflict between the need to improve the roads and the desire to preserve the trees.

Pass through **Mirow**, a pleasant lakeside town, with a mid 18C Schloss, and a much altered 14C brick Gothic church. Continue through a countryside of open fields and mixed oak, birch, and conifer woods—an area that is good for walking and riding. The land becomes flat, marshy and rather poor after Wesenberg. Wesenberg has a 13C town layout, a parish church with chancel made of glacial boulders c 1300 and a brick Gothic nave built c 1400.

Neustrelitz

26,800 inhabitants.

Tourist Information Office: Am Markt 1, 17235 Neustrelitz. Tel. 4921). Opening times: May–Sept Mon–Fri 09.00–12.00, 13.00–17.00, Sat 10.00–14.30, Oct–April Mon–Fri 09.00–12.00, 13.00–17.00 (Fri 16.30).

Neustrelitz is a quiet lakeside town with an attractive park and Baroque buildings. Until now accommodation has been scarce; there are two new hotels, the luxury Park Hotel at the Fasanerie and the Hotel Haegart but chalets, bungalows, caravans and camping, are the most practical options. Neustrelitz, literally 'New Strelitz', is named after Strelitz (now Alt Strelitz), a few kilometres to the south east. (Strelizer was the Slav term for the archers who defended the original castle.)

History. The town was founded when the Residenzschloss of Duke Adolph-Friedrich of Mecklenburg-Strelitz burnt down at Strelitz in October 1712. The small hunting lodge on Lake Zierker was converted into a Baroque castle, Schloss Neustrelitz (1726–31). The court landscape gardener, Julius Löwe, was the architect and also laid out the park. When the Duke first moved into the Schloss the bureaucrats and courtiers still resided in Strelitz, but Julius Löwe was charged with planning a town near the court. The Marktplatz, rather than the Schloss, was the central point of the plan, with roads radiating in eight directions. A proclamation was published on 20 May 1733 and settlers soon arrived from various parts of Germany. The new town, however, remained part of the ducal domain and never really prospered. It was only in the 1880s that Neustrelitz began to expand to the east, and many of the Baroque houses in the centre were replaced by buildings from the Gründerzeit.

Schloss Neustrelitz was destroyed by fire in 1945, but the town still maintains many of its original features and an air of backwater charm.

Opposite the Tourist Information Office is a Baroque church of 1768–78, with a later four-storey tower (1828–31) by Friedrich Wilhelm Buttel and Karl Friedrich Schinkel. The ochre-coloured Rathaus (1841) is also by Buttel. Cross the square diagonally left and walk to No. 3 Schlossstrasse, which houses the **Museum der Stadt** (opening times: Tues–Fri 10.00–12.00 and 14.00–17.00, Sat 14.00–17.00). There is a good display, including interesting photographs of the town's history and the residences of the ducal family. The Hussars' uniforms and weapons from the Wars of Liberation 1813–14 are popular with children.

Continue until you reach the junction with An der Promenade, and across into the delightful **Schlosspark**, the high point of a visit to Neustrelitz. It is a pleasant place to stroll with its classical sculptures and over 40 species of trees, and is an excellent spot for a picnic. The park was laid out in 1731. It has been much altered since: in 1790 in the picturesque English style and landscaped again in 1852 by Peter Joseph Lenné—although the original main axis between the site of the former Schloss and the lake has been retained. The Hebetempel (1840, by F.W. Buttel) is the focal point at the northern end of the axis, with a copy of the statue of the Goddess Hebe (1856) by Antonio Canova (the original is in the Nationalgalerie Berlin). To the east of the main walk is the tree-lined Götter-Allee (avenue of the gods), with its copies of Baroque statues of the Four Seasons, gods, goddesses and other figures from classical mythology.

On the north-eastern edge of the park is the former **Orangery**, first built in 1755 by A. Seydel; the stucco work is by Carl Philipp Glume and Anton Vogel. Karl Friedrich Schinkel initiated alterations in 1840, when it was converted into a classic garden salon, the work being carried out by Friedrich Wilhelm Buttel and Christian Daniel Rauch. In the interior the wall and ceiling paintings in the salons are in Pompeian style, restored in the garish blue, yellow and red of Mecklenburg. In the wall niches are plaster casts of antique sculptures.

Continue west to the other side of the park to the **Landestheater Mecklenburg**, an orange-coloured edifice, built 1926–28 by Max Littman. Archduke Georg von Mecklenburg-Strelitz (1779–1860) decided to build a church near the Schloss and in 1846 the **Schlosskirche** was designed by Friedrich Wilhelm Buttel (1796–1869). The first plan was rather grandiose with a long nave and an imposing tower, but the church was finally built on a more modest scale as a romantic Gothic Revival cross-shaped church with a single nave and no aisles (*Saalkirche*). The foundation stone was laid on 12 August 1855 and consecrated exactly four years later. Constructed of yellowish brick, Neustrelitz Schlosskirche is one of Buttel's most beautiful works and is regarded as the high point of his almost 50-year career in the town (1821–69). The west façade, with the main entrance opposite the former parade ground in F.W. Buttel-Platz, is dominated by two slender towers, flanking two smaller turrets. The church has 12 turrets altogether. The centre of the façade is richly decorated with tracery. The rose window depicts Christ's head in the centre, surrounded by twelve circles representing the 12 Apostles. To the left and right of the rose window are the four Evangelists. The figures were fired whole in the workshop of Masch-Berlin. The church was restored in 1952–57, but at the time of writing the interior was closed for renovation.

From Neustrelitz either take the E96 north-east to Neubrandenburg (see Route 25) or return to Schwerin along the A193 and A192 via Waren.

Waren (25,000 inhabitants) rising fortress-like above Lake Müritz is a small, attractive, unspoilt lakeside town. Its silhouette across the water reveals the two churches of St Georg and St Marien. Near the Alter Markt, the core of the first of two medieval settlements, is the church of St Georg, a brick Gothic basilica from the early 13C, with its sturdy west tower (1414). Many Gothic Revival elements were introduced to the church in 1853–54. Near the Georgenkirche is the 15C brick Alte Rathaus. On the Neuer Markt is St Marien, an early Gothic brick 14C building, much changed in 1792 when the Baroque tower was added. The square is dominated by the Gothic Revival Neues Rathaus, built in 1850.

The **Müritz-Museum**, Friedenstrasse 5 (opening times: Oct–Apr, Tues–Fri 09.00–16.00, Sat and Sun 09.00–12.00, 14.00–16.00; May–Sept. Tues–Fri 09.00–18.00, Sat and Sun 09.00–12.00 and 13.00–17.00) is particularly strong on the natural history of the region.

25

From Neustrelitz to Neubrandenburg

Neustrelitz to—27km Neubrandenburg.

From Neustrelitz follow the road E251/A96; a pleasant rolling road with a view down to the left to Lake Tollensesee leads to an industrial area on the outskirts of Neubrandenburg. Passing a modern housing estate look ahead to the tower of the Marienkirche and then drive round the city wall with the park on your right.

Neubrandenburg

80,000 inhabitants.

Tourist Information Office: Turmstrasse 11, 17033 Neubrandenburg. Tel. 6187. Opening times: from 1 Apr–30 Sept, Mon–Fri 09.00–18.00, Sat 9.00–12.00; from 1Oct–31 Mar, Mon–Fri, Sat 10.00–17.00, closed Sun.

Set in lovely countryside chequered with unspoilt lakes, **Neubrandenburg** is a bustling, light industrial and market town with a good shopping centre. The modern town centre is surrounded by an ancient and stunning city wall with four superb Gothic Tore (City Gates) and half-timbered Wiekhäuser (Watchhouses). It is one of the most complete medieval brick-built fortification systems surviving in north-east Germany. Neubrandenburg was almost totally rebuilt in the 1960s to the original medieval street pattern, after rearguard fighting in 1945, followed by a ferocious fire, destroyed 80 per cent of the city.

History. Neubrandenburg was founded in 1248 at the instigation of the Margrave of Brandenburg, hence the name 'New Brandenburg'. The site on the banks of the Tollensesee was chosen as a favourable position where there was the only break in the 30km long barrier created by the lake and the River Tollense. This had been a crossing point on a north–south trade route to Stettin—a route with its origins in early history. Neubrandenburg is a textbook example of the German colonising scheme east of the Elbe: a circular groundplan, with the layout inside divided into square blocks by nine streets crossing at rectangles, and a large central market place. This pattern was retained during rebuilding.

Although the town was founded as part of the March of Brandenburg, scarcely five years later it was integrated into Mecklenburg, included in the dowry of the Margrave's daughter Beatrix on her marriage to Prince Heinrich II in 1292. In about 1300 a wall was built round the town. The 14C and 15C was a period of economic prosperity, based on weaving, hop-growing and brewing. It was, and still is, the chief market town for the area. It was during this period of growth that the Marienkirche was completed and the showy city gates were constructed.

In March 1631 Imperial troops under General Tilly attacked the town. The Neubrandenburgers resisted three days of cannonade and then were bloodily defeated. The city was stormed and sacked, and economic decline ensued. Fortunes began to revive with the building of the railway from Berlin to Stralsund in 1864. During the Nazi period, barracks and armaments factories were imposed on the town. On 29–30 April 1945, during the battles of retreat, the town was almost entirely reduced to rubble and ashes, though the city gates and walls survived largely unscathed.

It is possible to walk all round the wall, which is tree-lined along most of the outer side of the perimeter. However, bear in mind that the defence system is 2300m long and much of the path around is cobbled. A good solution for a short visit is to start at the Tourist Information Office, walk to one or two of the gates and see the walls at the same time (see below). For those who prefer minimum walking, there is a panoramic view from the top of the *Kulturfinger*, the 55m high **Haus der Kultur und Bildung** in the main square.

The city walls are interspersed at intervals by **Wiekhäuser**, small half-timbered houses set into the wall. There were 56 Wiekhäuser, originally used for safe cover, but as the town defences became less important, many were converted into dwellings and have survived. Restoration of the town wall began in 1970 and over 20 houses are now completed, but are no longer used for accommodation. Some of the houses were known as Kämpfhäuser (fighting-houses) and rose several metres above the wall, acting as look-out points in times of war and danger. Their ground floors were used to store weapons and fire-dousing equipment. Near the weekly market by the post office two such fighting-houses have been reconstructed in almost their original form.

The *•***Town Wall** is constructed of glacial boulders and is 7.50m high. The splendid *•***gates** (Tore) were added during 14C and 15C. They are stunning examples of brick Gothic architecture at its best.

To see parts of the wall and three Tore on a short tour, start from the Tourist Information Office. Walk south to the Stargarder Tor and turn left, walking east along the wall to the Neues Tor; then turn back and go in the opposite direction, west, to see the Treptower Tor. For the complete tour, start from the Tourist Information Office and begin by walking the same way.

The **Stargarder Tor** (1350) is a double gate in simple Gothic form, richly decorated. Particularly noteworthy are the nine female figures in stone on the town side; their origins and meaning are unknown and open to speculation. The field side, or outside, of the Stargarder Tor is particularly richly decorated, and takes its inspiration from the east gable of the Marienkirche. The gate is an architectural gem and reflects the civic pride of the town and its citizens.

Continuing to the left, heading east along the wall, the route takes you to the **Neues Tor**, built in 1450. It is the latest of the four town gates. During the Thirty Years War it was the focus of intense fighting, and only the inner gate remains, which is now home to the Fritz-Reuter Society. On the town side, at the base of the step gable, is a row of eight terracotta female figures, raising their arms as if in entreaty.

Following the wall north brings you next to the **Friedlander Tor**, the oldest and also the best preserved of the Tors. The inner gate, the outer gate and the semi-circular fighting-tower (*Kämpfturm*) in front, known as a Zingel, illustrate how when each of the four gates was closed, the town become virtually impregnable.

At the northernmost point of the wall the road leads out north to the station. In front of the station is a statue of Fritz Reuter (1810–74), a poet who wrote in Plattdeutsch ('low German'), the north German dialect. Reuter lived here from 1856–63, years he regarded as being amongst the happiest and most successful of his life. Opposite him is the Mudder-Schulten-Brunnen (Mother Scold's Fountain). The group of figures represent a scene from one of Reuter's novels and shows Mudder Schulten boldly presenting the improvident and impoverished young Duke Adolph Friedrich IV, who had a summer residence in Neubrandenburg, with his unpaid bread bill.

Continue round the wall, over a rough patch of cobbles, past the **Fangelturm** (medieval wall-tower), also known as **Mönchenturm** (monks' tower) because of the monastery lands behind it. It is the only remaining wall tower, with crenellations and steeple, restored in 1845.

The circle is almost complete when you head south to reach the **Treptower Tor** (c 1400) on the west side of the town. The Treptower Tor is a late Gothic building with double gates, joined by walls between them. On the town side the inner gate, at 32m high, is considerably higher than the other gates and is ornamented with blind tracery and a stepped gable. The field side of the outer gate deserves particular attention, and, like the **Stargarder Tor** echoes the tracery of the east gable of the Marienkirche. Since 1873 it has housed the **Regionalmuseum** (opening times: Tues–Fri 09.00–17.30, Sat and Sun 13.00–17.30) with a good pre- and early history department.

From the Treptower Tor you can return east, along Treptowerstrasse to the town centre and the large MARKTPLATZ. This is dominated by the 250 room Hotel Vier Tore (Four Gates Hotel) and by the 55m tower block **Haus der Kultur und Bildung** (House of Culture and Education) (1962–65) a monument to rebuilding during the socialist era. It has a splendid vista from the top.

Continue south from the square along the Stargarder Strasse to the ruined church of St Mary, the **Marienkirche** (1298). Formerly one of the great brick Gothic hall churches of northern Germany, the church was used as an arsenal during the Second World War, reduced to ruins by fire and fighting in 1945, and is now being rebuilt for use as a concert hall. It has a wonderful east gable (that shows parallels with the minster in Strasburg and the Marienkirche in Prenzlau) with its delicate early Gothic tracery of slender bars, circles, roses, gables and pinnacles.

Head south from the church to see the memorial stone for Pastor Franz Böll (father of the theologians and scientists Franz and Ernst Böll), designed by Caspar David Friedrich, whose parents came from Neubrandenburg. Friedrich produced numerous sketches and pictures of Neubrandenburg and the surrounding countryside on his frequent visits here.

To the south-west of the city the Tollensesee, whose name derives from the Slavic expression for low ground *doloniza ab*, comes close in to the town centre. It is a large lake, almost 11km long, and 32m deep in places. With its hilly, wooded banks it is ideal for sports and walking. It forms part of a 100 sq km area of protected countryside.

26

Wismar and the Island of Poel

From Schwerin take the A106 32km north to Wismar (the motorway alternative, E26, was not complete at the time of writing). In the high season, traffic may be a severe problem at the point where the 106 joins the E22 coastal road.

Wismar

58,000 inhabitants.

Tourist Information Office: Stadthaus am Markt, 23966 Wismar. Tel. 2958. Opening times: daily 09.00–18.00.

Wismar is a delightful introduction to the proud Hanseatic towns of the Baltic coast. Despite damage at the end of the Second World War, sensitive conservation has meant there are still plenty of well-preserved medieval houses, some with sensational decorative gabling. The large market square is certainly worth a detour and is a good place to pause on a journey along the coast.

History. Wismar's history may be divided into three main periods: the Golden Age of the Hanseatic era (*Hansezeit*); the long years under Swedish domination; and gradual recovery leading to industrialisation in the late 19C and 20C.

Wismar was founded on crossroads of the old east–west trading routes. The first settlement, dating from 1190 to 1203, was in the area around the Nikolaikirche, right on the coast, where the sheltered bay was perfect for a harbour. Its southern limit was the canal-like Grube, which was still a navigable outlet of the River Wismar-Aa that flowed from Lake Schwerin.

As for many of the settlements on the coast, in the early years the significance of the river was as great as that of the sea. The harbours were seldom integrated in the topography of these towns, and often lay outside the defences. In Wismar, the coastal settlement was joined to the much larger, planned chequer-board layout of the settlement around the large market place on the main road from Lübeck to Rostock and the parish church, the Marienkirche.

Between 1226 and 1229, at the request of Prince Heinrich Borwin, settlers came from Lübeck, Westphalia, Lower Saxony and Flanders, and the town received its charter from Prince Johann of Mecklenburg in 1266. The town quickly prospered as a trading base, and a growth in population meant that after 1250 the area around the Georgen-kirche, known as the Neustadt, was incorporated. By the mid 13C the layout of the town that we see today was already established and it has remained virtually un-changed.

In 1259 Wismar joined with Lübeck and Rostock for mutual protection of the sea trade routes from pirates. The Hansa of the Wendish towns (*Wendisches Quartier*) arose from this. Wismar was a leading participant and the 14C and 15C were centuries of great prosperity for Wismar, with feverish architectural activity that included rebuilding the churches of St Nicholas and St George. There were only 5000 inhabitants in the *Hansezeit* but three large churches, manifestations of patrician wealth and civic pride.

The power of the Hanseatic league had already waned by the time of the Thirty Years War. In 1648 at the Peace of Westphalia, Wismar was given to Sweden. Because of its strategically important position to the Swedes as a bridgehead to other German areas it became an important military base for Sweden and c 1680 the defences were dramatically extended so that Wismar became one of the most fortified cities in northern Europe. The cost of billeting up to 3000 troops, reparations and building the new defences drained the resources of the town and great hardship ensued. In 1804 the Swedish king needed money and mortgaged Wismar to the Duke of Mecklenburg for 99 years. The town became German territory again only in 1903. It had endured the longest period under Sweden of any town on the coast.

In the 19C industrialisation began slowly, encouraged by road and railway links. During the war there were 12 bombing raids, initially targeted at the Dornier aircraft factory. During the last three weeks of the war attacks on the historic centre and housing wrought considerable damage.

In GDR times shipbuilding was developed, concentrating on special orders from the Soviet Union. Wismar has been hit by the collapse of the eastern bloc as well as by the new market forces of unified Germany, with widespread redundancies. The excursion boats for a trip round the harbour or to the Island of Poel, formerly run by the state-owned *Weisse Flotte* are now private.

From the Bahnhof head south down Bahnhofstrasse turning right and west down Lübsche Strasse to the **Stadthaus am Markt** in the south-west corner of the marketplace. In medieval days this was the site of the stocks and pillory. The present building, 1858, was formerly the main guard house. It is now the local Tourist Information Office. Look across the spacious Marktplatz at the patrician houses opposite and then to the simple, Neo-Classical Rathaus, designed by Johann Georg Barca (the architect of Schloss Ludwigslust). The original Gothic town hall was rebuilt in Baroque style in 1780, but by 1807 had become so dilapidated that in 1819 it was replaced by the present Neo-Classical version. In April 1945 the right wing was destroyed, as were many historic buildings. Just before Christmas in 1960 a chimney fire wreaked further damage. The cellars are some of the loveliest in northern Germany with their early Gothic vaulting. They were part of the original 1350 building and, together with recently uncovered frescoes of religious and maritime scenes, should be open to the public by 1995.

Heading south across the square you pass the **Wasserkunst** (waterworks), which resembles a scaled-down bandstand. It was designed by Philip Brandin in the Dutch Renaissance style, and completed in 1601. The Wasserkunst acted as a pumping station for the town's piped water supply until 1897. Wooden pipes brought water from a spring 11km outside Wismar and it was then pumped round the town. The water basin is inside the wire guards surrounding the fountain. Spouts known as Adam and Eve used to play jets of water. About 15 years ago the 12-sided building with its copper dome was restored—the limestone figured pillars are not original. Looking closer you can see the gold inscriptions that tell the story of the town's water supply in Latin and Plattdeutsch (north German dialect or 'low German').

Continue east from the fountain to Wismar's oldest house with the most stunning brick Gothic gabling, the superbly restored **Alter Schwede**, built c 1380 for a wealthy member of the town council. The ground floor was used for business, the first floor for the family accommodation and the floors concealed behind the decorative gabling, for warehousing. The decorative effect of the three-tier stepped gable is enhanced by the skilful use of tracery and patterning with black-green glazed brick and five rows of windows and light openings. It first became a Gasthaus in 1878, when it was given the name Alte Schwede as a reminder of the years Wismar spent under Swedish rule, and is decked out with a carved Swedish head above the door—a copy of the one to be found at the harbour—and the wrought-iron sign of a knight with three Swedish crowns. Like all gabled houses, it was built with its narrow side to the street, because the price of a building plot was determined by its width. Inside it is once again a popular restaurant, full of weird and wonderful memorabilia of seafaring days.

Work on the **Reuterhaus**, to the right, was finished in 1991 although it was started before unification. Once a printer's house, it published the work of Fritz Reuter (1810–74), the famous low German poet (a sort of Mecklenburg Robert Burns). It has now been restored to its original appearance and, like its neighbour, is a restaurant serving good basic Mecklenburg dishes. To the left of the Alte Schwede is a gabled house recently restored to its original Art Nouveau style. Continuing down this side of the square you will see the Hotel Stadt Hamburg, which at the time of writing was being rebuilt by a West German consortium, retaining just the original façade. The most splendid of the buildings on the south side of the square, the double gabled house, once the seat of the Swedish Commander of the town, is now a bank.

Now cross the square diagonally north-west to go down one of the main shopping streets, the KRÄMERSTRASSE, named after the small traders who used to sell their wares here. It is now a broad pedestrian precinct. Continue north-west down the Krämerstrasse, crossing the HOPFEN-MARKT, named after the hops which were brought here by means of a narrow canal running down the centre of the street. Beer was an important export in Hanseatic times, when there were more than 180 breweries in a town of only 5000 inhabitants. The Hopfenmarkt has remained the hub of the city and its trading centre. In 1881 at No. 4, a Jugendstil building, Rudolph Karstadt founded the first of his string of chainstores, the German equivalent of Woolworths.

Turn right and immediately left past the Löwenapotheke (Lion Apothecary), crossing Breite Strasse and Bademutter Strasse into Bohrstrasse heading north. No. 5a, until recently the Tourist Information Office, is now the Registry Office. Nos 10–12, gabled houses, have protected building status, and are being converted into hotels. Look north down Scheuerstrasse to see the red building on the left that has been recently restored, one of the gabled attic or store houses that gave the street its name. Turn right into Kronhagenstrasse, noting Am Linden Garten at the end with the only remaining Wasserturm (Water Tower), part of the old town wall. To the right is the former Graukloster (Greyfriars), dissolved after the Reformation, which reached Wismar in 1541, and converted into a school which is still used today.

Turn left down a narrow alley, with medieval cobbles, for a superb view of the **Nikolaikirche** (Church of St Nicholas). Straight ahead is the remarkable south gable with its rose window. Below the window are rows of moulded figurines of Sts Nicholas and Mary. The flying buttresses that support the stupendously high nave can also be seen clearly; the lower part of the buttresses may be seen inside the church. Cross the bridge walking south over the Grube, the waterway that links the Baltic with Schwerin and the inland lakes, and was so important in medieval times, but which now is used only for leisure boats (see below).

Enter the church through the south portal with its tiled border of dragons and panthers. The Nikolaikirche (opening times: 10.30–12.30, 13.30–16.30 except Tues; Sun 13.00–16.00) is the church of seafarers and fishermen. On entering the impression is of breathtaking height—the nave soars to 37m—

the culmination of the Gothic heavenward surge. It is the fourth highest in Germany, just half a metre short of the Marienkirche in Lübeck. The church was built as a basilica in brick Gothic style with a high central nave, no distinction between the nave and the choir and an ambulatory with radiating chapels. It was modelled closely on the Church of St Nikolai in Stralsund, in its turn based on the Marienkirche in Lübeck, so strongly influenced by the cathedrals of northern France, and consecrated in 1380. The square tower, set into the west end of the church, lost its steeple during a storm in 1703 which also destroyed part of the medieval interior.

The church has been somewhat neglected during the 20C, both by the Nazis and by the GDR regime, but is slowly being renovated. The 62 windows are gradually being replaced at a cost of 40,000 DM each. At the west end of the south aisle is a large (10m high) late Gothic fresco of The Tree of the House of Jesse. In the tower hall is The Man of Sorrows (Schmerzensmann) with allegorical representation of the seven deadly sins and St Christopher. Although much of the original medieval furnishing has been lost, the Nikolaikirche is now home to some beautiful works saved from other Wismar churches. One of the best loved is the KRÄMERALTAR (Small Traders' Altar) from the Marienkirche; situated in the southern transept, it is gentle and sensitive, carved around first quarter 15C and restored in 1966. In the centre is The Virgin and Child, accompanied by an angel; to her left is St Maurice carrying a Roman legionary's shield, and on her right is St Michael. The side wings represent scenes from the life of Mary.

Other works of importance from the Marienkirche include a bronze font of 1335, with reliefs of biblical scenes including the Wise and Foolish Virgins and very similar to that in Lübeck cast by the same master, Johan Apengeter; and the bronze memorial showing the figure in relief of Duchess Sophie of Mecklenburg (d. 1504) in the second north side chapel. The Schifferaltar (Skippers' Altar) in the fourth north side chapel shows an early 16C Madonna with Crescent Moon (*Mondsichelmadonna*) flanked by the Sts James the Greater and Nicholas.

The former High Altar of the church of St George was stored in safety during the Second World War, and then placed here, where it may be found at the end of the north aisle. Dating from c 1430, it has one of the largest and best-preserved late Gothic altarpieces on the Baltic coast; when open it is 9.4m wide. The centre panel shows the Coronation of the Virgin.

The west end of the church has been separated by a glass partition to become a Winterkirche with underfloor heating. Several chapels may well be closed because of ongoing building work.

As you leave the church, immediately to the left, look out for one of the original statues from the Wasserkunst, moved here when it was restored. Turn right here to continue along the bank of the Grube. Created in 13C it is one of the oldest artificial water courses in the country. The council is intending to create a promenade from the station to the harbour along the canal side, passing in front of the Nikolaikirche. Opposite is the **Schabbel-haus**, a fine Dutch Renaissance house, built in 1569–71 by Philipp Brandin for the wealthy brewer Hinrich [sic] Schabbell, who later became mayor. The gable overlooking the canal is highly decorative with its stone scrolls and other details. The bricks used are smaller than usual, and were specially imported from Holland, acting as ballast on the trading ships. After many changes of hands and much renovation the Schabbelhaus is now the **Stadtgeschichtliches Museum**, with a good section on city history and local customs (opening times: Oct–Apr, Tues–Sat 10.00–16.00; May–Sept, Tues–Sun 10.00–18.00). The house itself has been restored to its original state, with a Diele (large hall), living area and attics.

Turn right along the canal and then right, heading north, into SCHEUER-STRASSE with its wealth of gabled houses. There were over 300 of these in Hanseatic days, their delightful gables concealing several tiers of lofts, used to warehouse goods awaiting shipment. Continue north into Spiegelberg, where again the houses all originally had lofts and gables in brick (note for example the fourth house on the right). The second house on the left was that of a sailmaker and ship's chandler, as can be seen from the text and decorations on the wall. Enter the harbour through the Wassertor, built c 1450 in late Gothic style. It was the last of five gates of the old town wall, 4m high, built in 1276. The wall was pulled down in the 1860s as the town expanded and traffic increased. Turn and look back at the brick gable with its decorative blind windows. Inside the passageway you can see another of the figures from the Wasserkunst and part of the iron-work used to close the heavy gates.

A short diversion along the quayside to the end of the old harbour takes you to the Baroque **Customs House** (1780), known as the *Baumhaus* (tree-trunk house) because a tree was put across the harbour at night as a customs control. During the Swedish period there were two Swedish figureheads here to show the port was Swedish, and these *Schwedenköpfe* now guard the front entrance to the house. Wismar was *Zollausland* (outside the customs zone of Mecklenburg) until 1866 so everything made here was subject to duty; this isolation from the natural trading hinterland caused great economic hardship. The new harbour was built in 1724. Grain, linen and flax, fish and beer were the main exports, while wood from Sweden was the most significant of the imports. The large warehouse with the green windows dates from c 1860, and to its right are 1930s warehouses that were used to store potash. Boat trips are available round the increasingly deserted shipyards.

Continue left along Am Lohberg and on the left at the corner of Kleine Hohe Strasse, is a half-timbered house that has had its plaster removed to expose the intricate patterns of brickwork—a brick sampler used by the bricklayers' apprentices to demonstrate their skills. Looking to the left on the gabled house you can see the Wismar coat of arms—an ox-head on one side and the Hanseatic red-and-white on the other. On the right is the Runde Grube—the half-timbered house over the canal that has been restored, although the poor quality paint hardly makes it appear so.

Continue south along the ZIEGEMARKT. On the right is the 1435 Schmiedehaus (Blacksmith's House). Turn right into Breitestrasse/Fischerreihe and then left into the Neustadt, so called because in 1250 the town needed to expand beyond the original walls. On the left is a green door in the wall—go through into the peaceful courtyard complex of the **Heiligen-Geist-Hospital**. Originally a hospice for those suffering from the plague, it was built just outside the old city walls as custom decreed.

To the right is the **Pfründner Haus** (Prebendiary House), also known as the **Lange Haus** (Long House) built c 1400 as part of the hospice and then for many years an old people's home. Note the oriel window and, looking carefully above the wooden tiles of its roof, you can make out the white dove, symbol of the Holy Ghost. The simple Gothic **Heiligen-Geist-Kirche** (Church of the Holy Spirit; opening times: Mon–Sat 10.00–12.00 and 14.00–16.00, Sun 14.00–16.00) was consecrated in 1324. It was built without a tower, but a small Baroque steeple added in 17C. Inside, the ceiling was painted with acanthus leaves, putti and Old Testament scenes in 1687. Parts of 14C and 15C frescoes can still be seen. The lovely stained glass north window is late Gothic and was salvaged from the Marienkirche in 1945. Most appealing are the three carved figures of the Adoration of the Magi—all that remains of a damaged early 15C altar from the Georgenkirche. Coming out of the yard and left up the street again notice once more the symbol of the Holy Ghost—the dove on the door handle on the left.

Cross over Lübschestrasse (Lubeck Street), looking down its gentle curve at the faded charm of the merchants' houses, and into the Grosse Hohe Strasse. Walking up the street you will come to the half-ruined **Georgen-kirche** (Church of St George). The Neustadt was built during 1238–50, and the Georgenkirche was begun as the parish church for this quarter, its site on the highest part of the Neustadt. Its beginnings in 1250 were quite modest—the original end of the nave remains—and it was enlarged in 1450. No longer a cross shape, the church was widened to be as large as the Marienkirche. However, Hanseatic prosperity was on the wane and it was never completed according to plan. The church is not open at the moment as it required extensive restoration after bomb damage and is being rebuilt through help from the Deutscher Denkmalschutz and much fundraising amongst the local people.

Continue left and south into Vor dem Fürstenhof where the **Fürstenhof** (the Prince's Court) stands, the most northerly Renaissance palace in Europe. Designed by Gabriel von Aken and Velentin von Lyra (inspired by the Palazzo Roverella at Ferrara), and built in 1553–54, it was intended as a summer palace for the Duke of Mecklenburg and was built by Duke Johann Albrecht I. It is the most important work of this kind in Germany. The limestone frieze depicts scenes from the Trojan Wars and the second-floor terracotta frieze, by the Lübeck master Statius von Düren, represents figures from the ancient world. Both were heavily restored and altered in 1877–78. The windows are framed by limestone or terracotta grotesque figures. The majestic portal has stone columns; the base of the one on the left shows Isaac's sacrifice while the one on the right shows Samson and the ass's jaw-bone. Above these are satyrs intertwined. The gryphons over the doorway support the arms of Duke Johann Albrecht I. Walk through, under late Gothic vaulting (part of the earlier building) to look at the reliefs on the inner side—the date-stone over the door and mouldings of David and Delilah flanking the larger figures of Samson and Goliath. Since 1653 the Palazzo has been used as the City Court.

Continue north into the **Marienkirchhof** (The Churchyard of St Mary's), where the tower of St Mary's rises forlorn from the car park. The church itself was irretrievably damaged by bombs in April 1945, and the ruins demolished in 1960. It was the oldest of Wismar's churches, begun in 1280, and probably took 300 years to build. The tower alone remained and in 1981 was restored, complete with new bells. After unification it was care-fully cleaned and the beauty of the stonework was revealed—the corners of the tower are particularly interesting as light limestone alternates with red brick. The four gables on the tower are quite ornate, with a tapestry of brick and dark glazed brick.

On the corner of the Marienhof, to the right, is the **Archdiakonatshaus** (Archdeacon's House) a text-book example of a north German late Gothic house (1450) that was badly damaged by bomb blast and has been recently restored. Different coloured brick has been used to great effect to create the stepped gable with crenellations, tracery and light openings. Turn this corner into Sargmacherstrasse which leads back to the Markt.

From the harbour in Wismar you can take an hour's ride round the docks, or further out to the **Island of Poel**. Poel is Germany's third largest island after Rügen and Usedom, 37 sq km and separated from the mainland by the narrow Breitling. The 3000 inhabitants live from fishing—excellent fresh fish can be tried in the many cafés—and increasingly from tourism (an estimated 450,000 visit annually). With its beaches on the Baltic it is busy in the summer, especially the resort of Timmendorf with its lighthouse. Schwarzer Busch and Gollwitz are popular too.

The ferry lands at **Kirchdorf**, the main village, which has an interesting 13C church, with remains of the 17C fortress close by. The Heimatsmuseum, at the entrance to Kirchdorf (opening times: May–Sept, Tues and Fri 09.00–12.00 and 14.00–16.00, Sat and Sun 09.30–11.30; Oct–Apr, Tues and Wed 09.00–12.00, Sat and Sun 09.30–11.30), displays the flora and fauna of the island, the history of the flax-growing and linen-weaving industries and a model of the 17C fortifications. Poel can also be reached by car over the causeway first constructed in 1760, heading north-east out of Wismar (9km) and turning left in the village of Gross Strömkendorf on the minor coast road.

27

The Baltic Coast: from Wismar to Rostock

Wismar—40km Kühlungsborn—10km Bad Heiligendamm—6km Bad Doberan.

From Wismar (see Route 26) take the E22/105, the main road heading east for Rostock. In high season it is essential to avoid peak times on this road. After 30km is Kröpelin with a 13C early brick Gothic church, with vaulted chancel, 14C nave, late Gothic 15C tower and 1885 steeple. Turn left here, continue through beautiful woods, and then straight ahead is the Baltic and in 10km Kühlungsborn.

Kühlungsborn

Tourist Information Office: Kurverwaltung, Strasse des Friedens 46, 18225 Ostseebad Kühlungsborn. Tel. 082 93284. Opening times: Mon–Sat 09.00–12.00 and 13.00–19.00; Sun 09.00–12.00 and 13.00–16.00.

Kühlungsborn is the largest of the Baltic coast resorts, with a wonderful wide sandy beach and a long promenade. The beach is clean, with trees stretching right down it. New development near the beach has been limited to some half-dozen thatched buildings in traditional Mecklenburg style, which include a good selection of well run cafés and restaurants. A high spot for steam enthusiasts is a trip inland to Bad Heiligendamm or Bad

Doberan on the **Molli**, the narrow-gauge railway that has been running since 1886 (the Tourist Office has a timetable). Kühlungsborn first became a well-known bathing resort around 1900, hence the large number of turn-of-the-century villas, whose glory is now faded.

From Kühlungsborn travel east along the coast on the Molli or drive through avenues of lime trees to Bad Heiligendamm.

Bad Heiligendamm

13,000 inhabitants.

Bad Heiligendamm is known as 'the white town by the sea' and is the oldest spa of its kind in Germany. It was founded in 1793 by the enterprising Duke Friedrich Franz I (1756–1837) at the suggestion of his doctor, Professor Dr Samuel Vogel, as a place for the wealthy to take a sea-bathing cure. The magnificent **Kurhaus** (1814–16), by Carl Theodor Severin, is one of the most important Neo-Classical buildings in northern Germany. Grand villas, hotels and elegant boarding houses such as the Maxim Gorky and Käthe Kollwitz dating from 1845, are succeeded further down the row by the Rosa Luxemburg and Karl Liebknecht, 1857–65—all with faded white stucco.

Bad Doberan

12,000 inhabitants

6km inland, or one more stop on the Molli, is **Bad Doberan**. Doberan was originally a Slavic settlement. Legend has it that Prince Heinrich Borwin, was hunting deer when swans flew by calling '*dobr, dobr*' (good, good), and this prompted him to found a monastery here. Swan and stag still feature on the town's coat of arms. The monastery church, now a minster, is one of the most beautiful brick Gothic buildings in northern Germany. At the end of 18C Duke Friedrich Franz I of Mecklenburg chose Doberan for the seat of his summer residence; a fashionable spa soon developed round the court with classical buildings to follow suit.

The *Münster (Minster) was founded by Cistercian monks who first settled here in 1171. After the destruction of the building during a Slav uprising in 1179, a new start was made in 1186. Richly endowed with lands, the monastery rapidly became one of the most powerful in north Germany. Between 1294 and 1299 work began on a monastery church on the site of an earlier Romanesque building destroyed by fire. The new church was built in high Gothic style, inspired by the cathedrals of northern France (which the builders knew through the Marienkirche in Lübeck), as a basilica with ambulatory and five radiating chapels. It retains, however, elements of Cistercian architecture. The exterior is plain and powerful with just a small steeple above the intersection of the nave (towers are precluded by Cistercian custom).

Proceed to the interior, noting the arcades of the nave which continue uninterrupted through the chancel. The addition of a triforium is a departure from the pure Gothic vertical. The rather bright colouring used to pick out the rib vaulting was added during heavy-handed Gothic Revival restoration. The church is wonderfully well preserved, largely because it was the family burial ground of the Dukes of Mecklenburg; 67 Dukes and Duchesses were laid to rest here, and the monument to Prince Pribislav himself is in the east of the north transept. The monastery exercised a tremendous artistic influence throughout Mecklenburg in the Middle Ages—many of the church furnishings in place for the consecration in 1368 may still be seen.

One of the most important of the many pieces is the richly carved *HIGH ALTAR of 1310, one of the earliest in Germany. On the wings are figures from the Old and New Testaments; in front and above is a blue and gold figure of the Madonna, surrounded by a sunburst, carved at the end of the 13C and placed in its lantern-like housing in the 15C. Showing the definite influence of Meister Bertram of Minden is the KREUZALTAR that divides the monks' area of the church from that used by the laity, a double sided triptych, probably dating from the consecration in 1368 with scenes from the Bible. Above it is the monumental rood cross, with scenes in relief on both sides. Looking west is the figure of Christ and looking east, the figure of Mary. In 1978 the pulpit in the chancel—given away in the 19C—was returned to its original position. Carved in the late 13C, its figurative reliefs include pelicans, eagles, wolves and lions.

The Minster is surrounded by a large park with well-preserved walls built in 1285. Of the monastery buildings, the granary (1270); brewery (1290) and ruined guesthouse (1285) may still be seen. Continue north from the east end of the Minster to see the small octagonal mid 13C brick Beinhaus, the ossiary where monks' bones were stored.

In contrast to the stately red Minster, are the pale late Baroque and Neo-Classical buildings of the spa. The most important of these are centred on the Kamp, the English-style park in the centre of the town. The **Logierhaus** (1793) is now the Kurhaus Hotel, a two-storey half-timbered building by J.C.H. von Seydewitz. Nearby is the Salongebäude (1802) built by Carl Theodor Severin, the chief architect of the town, for the guests of the spa. In 1957 it was restored to its original design. On the Kamp itself are two octagonal pavilions, also by Severin, the sole manifestation of chinoiserie in Mecklenburg. The larger, white building (1810–13) was built as a concert room and is now a café; the smaller red structure (1808–09) houses an art gallery.

The **Doberan Stadtmuseum** (opening times: Sept–May, Mon–Wed 10.00–12.00 and 14.00–16.00, Thurs–Sat 14.00–16.00, Jun–Aug, Mon–Wed 10.00–12.00 and 13.30–16.30, Thurs–Sun 14.00–16.30) in the Möckelhaus, Beethovenstrasse 8 (not far from the Münster) is worth a visit for exhibits on the early days of the sea cure with intriguing pictures of bathing machines.

From Bad Doberan continue east along the E22/A105 for 13km to Rostock.

28

Rostock

Bad Doberan—13km Rostock.

250,000 inhabitants.

Tourist Information Office: Schnickmannstrasse 13/14, 18055 Rostock. Tel. 34602/25260.

ROSTOCK is by far the largest city in Mecklenburg-Vorpommern (Pomerania). It has a superb site on the banks of the River Warnow, the best shops in the region and an excellent transport system. The beach at the colourful seaside resort of Warnemünde is 20 minutes away by train. Rostock has been a major seaport since Hanseatic days and, despite severe bombing during the Second World War, there is still much to see on a city walk and a good range of museums.

History. Medieval Rostock consisted of three earlier settlements. By the late 12C, on the right bank of the River Warnow, there was a Slav fortress and settlement. German settlers from Saxony and Westphalia drove a wedge into Slav lands in the wake of the founding of Schwerin in 1161 and by c 1200 the Slav trading post lost importance in favour of a German settlement on the higher, left bank. The site was advantageous as it was near the sea, elevated above the surrounding swamps within a semi-circular bend in the Warnow, making it easily defensible. It was within this stronghold that the Petrikirche (Church of St Peter) was founded; the church and the large market place formed the core of what is today known as the Altstadt. A town charter was granted on 24 June 1218, by Prince Heinrich Borwin I.

By 1232 the town had outgrown these boundaries and expanded into the area around the Marienkirche, which became known as the Mittelstadt, and into the square, the Neuer Markt, where a town hall was built in 1262 to administer the two fused settlements. In 1252, a little further west, the Neustadt was begun around what is now the University Square. Between 1262 and 1265 the three parts grew together, building city walls and a common defence system. The town soon became a great port, flourishing trade centre and a member of the Hanse of the Wendish towns, reaching its high point in the 14C. From the Hanseatic era stem the great brick Gothic churches and the gabled burgher houses.

In 1419 the first university in northern Europe was founded in Rostock, but by 1432 the city was so split between the bourgeoisie and the patrician council, that the Pope intervened and the university was temporarily transferred to Greifswald. By the late 15C the emphasis of shipping trade had shifted from the Baltic to the North Sea and the Atlantic so Rostock was no longer a major sea power although it would always remain a busy port. During the Thirty Years War the city was hit hard financially, having to make substantial contributions. Allegiance to Wallenstein meant quartering Imperial troops, and later being occupied by Sweden. A great fire in 1677 destroyed 700 houses and further impoverished the people. During the second half of the 18C the export of grain through the port of Rostock and a strong sailing fleet led to a resurgence in the economy. Napoleon's troops occupied the city, and it is hardly surprising that the statue of his conqueror, Blücher, a native of Rostock, has pride of place in Rostock today. In the 19C under the peaceful reigns of Archdukes Friedrich Franz I and II the town, the shipyards and industry gradually recovered. In 1830 the city expanded beyond its medieval site, but in 1942 much of the Altstadt was destroyed by bombing. After the Second World War new wharves and harbours were built and Rostock became once more a thriving port.

Adjusting to a market economy and loss of the pre-eminence the city enjoyed in the eastern bloc has not been easy for Rostock and the failure to become the capital of Mecklenburg-Vorpommern was disappointing for the town.

The Hauptbahnhof is situated in the south-west of the city. From here take the No. 11 or the No. 12 tram to the **Tourist Information Office**, housed in a beautifully restored gabled house, Schnickmannstrasse 13–14. This was built in 1795 as a granary—there are five floors for storing grain behind the gable. In 1984 it was reconstructed according to the original designs, including the wind-up lift. This pulley was usually operated by a type of treadmill in the cellar to haul the goods up to the high attic store rooms. This part of the city is the middle of the old harbour quarter that was imaginatively reconstructed during the 1980s along traditional lines, retaining the old street patterns and names. The new blocks of flats, using modern building methods, echo north German architectural motifs of red brick, gables and decorative bricks. The street slopes down towards the harbour and in the centre of the street runs an artificial watercourse.

Continue north to the bottom of the street where there is a good view over the old town harbour—Rostock's only harbour until 1960 and the pulse of the medieval Hanseatic city. The metal sculpture *Segel im Wind* (Sails in the Wind) is a reminder of the town's tradition of sailing ship journeys. A new leisure area with a marina is planned.

Turning right and right again you come into Wokrenterstrasse, again part of the reconstruction of the harbour quarter, devastated during the Second World War. Following the original plans, the houses were constructed in traditional building manner, with replicas of historic Rostock gables. The most interesting is No. 40, **The Architect's House**, built in 1490. It is the oldest remaining Gothic merchant's house in Rostock, and is a typical medieval two-storey brick gabled house with large hall (*Diele*) on the ground floor and living rooms above; the attic store rooms are concealed by a step gable with crenellations on top.

Continue south into the main town and the LANGE STRASSE, the showpiece of GDR 1950s architecture. It was almost totally destroyed during the war, as was most of this part of the city. Rebuilt in 1953, it is now classified as a conservation area by ICOMOS (International Council for Monuments and Sites). The details are intended to recall the north German tradition of brick Gothic, and the use of red brick, blind rose windows and the crenellation on the roofs are all typical.

Head east down Lange Strasse to the only building in this area to emerge virtually unscathed from the war, the **Marienkirche** (Church of St Mary). As the parish church of the council (Ratspfarrkirche) it is the largest and most important church in the city. It was finished in the mid 15C after nearly 200 years' building and has one of the most richly furnished interiors in Mecklenburg-Pomerania. No trace remains of the original church, which was founded in 1230. Of the early Gothic hall church, begun in 1260, part of the lower storey of the west tower with its Early Gothic portal can still be seen. Towards the end of 13C the transformation began into a Gothic basilica, with nave and two aisles, following the basic pattern of the Marienkirche in Lübeck, with an ambulatory and radiating chapels which embodied the prevailing French influence.

Unfortunately, in 1398 the half-finished nave collapsed. The work was recommenced, but with a change of plan. From the outside this can be observed in the change from red to yellow brick. The rebuilding of the nave and the projecting transept which was part of the new design reached

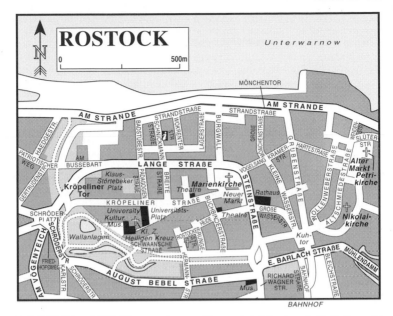

BAHNHOF

completion in c 1452. The massive west tower is intriguing. Initially thought of as a twin tower in the northern French style, like Lübeck and the Nikolaikirche in Stralsund, a change of plan meant the two parts were fused by the addition of a central intersection. The steeple dates from 1796.

Among the church furnishings worth seeing are: the bronze *FONT dating from 1290, which is the largest and most valuable medieval font in northern Europe, second only to that of Hildesheim. Cast in bronze in one piece, probably in Rostock by craftsmen from Lower Saxony, the font, with its conical lid, is supported by four kneeling figures—allegories of the elements—while the sides show reliefs from the life of Christ. The Rochus Altar (c 1530) is the altar of the guild of surgeons and barbers. A late Gothic triptych shows carved oak figures of Sts Rochus, Antony and Sebastian, possibly by Benedict Dreyer. In the centre is Rochus, a 14C French hermit, identified by his pilgrim's staff and the sore on his leg. St Sebastian is on the right, martyred by arrows; St Anthony on the left with his bell and pigs. All three are patron saints of the plague. The great 12m high astronomical clock behind the altar is a tremendous attraction. Originally made in 1472 by Hans Düringer from Nuremberg, it was renewed and enlarged 1641–43 by Andreas Brandenburg and Michael Grote. The figures of the apostles which move round at noon each day were carved by Laurentius Burchard. It is the only astrological clock in Europe to be kept in its original condition and is set to run until 2018. The pulpit carved in 1574 by Antwerp master Rudolph Stockmann is an important piece of Renaissance work. The pulpit canopy is high Baroque, dating from 1723. The High Altar of 1720–21 is by Berlin craftsmen. The vast organ (1770) reaches to the vaulting at the west end of the nave.

Continue south to the NEUER MARKT, with its coloured gabled houses; it lacks the tranquillity of other Mecklenburg market places, due perhaps to the cars parked in the middle and the main road. Tramlines on the east side pass in front of the Rathaus, making it hazardous to cross here, and the building is best appreciated by standing a little back.

The **Rathaus** is much changed in appearance since it was first built in 1230 as a twin-gabled house. After the mid 13C it was enlarged by building on one storey and adding a common façade, but only the early Gothic portal under the arcades on the market side is preserved. When a third house was built and finally the blind façade with seven brick pinnacles, it became a glorious Gothic building to match that in Stralsund. All this is now hidden, apart from the tops of the turrets which peep from above the rather incongruous addition of a Baroque building in front (1727–29). The Baroque council chamber inside dates from 1735. A visit to the medieval vaulted Ratskeller may be possible.

The oldest part of the city can be visited from here (see below). To continue on this route, turn right along the side of the Marienkirche into the ZIEGENMARKT, where a bronze statue of a goat on the fountain recalls the time when this was the Goat Market. Note No. 3, the **Alte Münze** (Old Mint), as indicated by the relief of a Münzschläger (a coin imprinter) of 1620–28 with a fine sandstone portal. Money was minted in Rostock for several centuries. This is a good moment to go into the Marienkirche by the main south portal.

Now turn south out of the Ziegenmarkt and right into KRÖPELINER STRASSE. This is the main boulevard of the city, pedestrianised since 1968 when it was extensively restored. It is lined by attractive gabled houses, mainly from the Renaissance and Baroque eras. The most splendid examples are of a later period than in other Mecklenburg Baltic towns, reflecting the prosperity of the corn trade. The oldest in the street is the most interesting: No. 82, now home to the public library, but once the Spitalpfarrhaus (Priest's house) of the Heiliger-Geist-Hospital (demolished in 1818). It is a brick building from the end of the 15C, with a five-storey stepped gable, decorated with friezes of shaped bricks and medallions with biblical reliefs. Note the bells on the modern gable of the last house on the right.

The Kröpeliner Strasse has a relaxed atmosphere and several pavement cafés. The street opens into the delightful UNIVERSITY SQUARE, in fact a triangle, once the Hopfenmarkt (Hop Market) of the medieval Neustadt, where the third German settlement of Rostock began c 1250. On the south side two stately Baroque palaces are the oldest survivors in the square. To the left of the fountain is the ochre-yellow **Barocksaal** of 1750 by Jean Laurent Legeay, the ducal palace used during sojourns in Rostock. The interior, now restored to its former glory, counts as one of the most beautiful ballrooms of northern Germany. To its right is the simpler Baroque Palais of 1714 by Leonhard Christoph Sturm.

At the western end of the square is the **University**, founded in 1419. This Neo-Renaissance building (1866–70), decorated with terracotta and sgraffito, was designed by the Schwerin court architect Hermann Willebrand in the style of Mecklenburg Renaissance buildings of the mid 16C. Statues of the Mecklenburg dukes Johann IV and Albrecht V, who were involved in founding the University, stand by the entrance. The relief above the entrance represents the first chancellor of the University, at that time Bishop Heinrich of Schwerin.

Under the trees you will see the monument to the first citizen of Rostock to receive the Freedom of the City, Gebhard Lebrecht von Blücher, hero of Waterloo, who was born in 1742 in a house not far from this square. The 3m

The Marienkirche, Rostock

high bronze statue, by Johann Schadow, was dedicated shortly before Blücher's death in 1819. On the granite plinth are allegorical reliefs of the defeats of Ligny and the victory of the Belle Alliance at Waterloo. (The inscription was composed by Goethe.) To the left of the University is the entrance to the tranquil site of the **Kloster zum Heiligen Kreuz** (Convent of the Holy Cross), a well-preserved complex of six buildings. The convent was originally founded as a penance by the Danish Queen Margarete in

1270; the queen spent the last years of her life here. Some of the legends from this period are depicted in the 9m long painting (16C) in the east cloisters. One tells how Queen Margarete, a superb horsewoman, was returning from Rome with her retinue, after a pilgrimage to atone for her late husband's sins. She paused in Rostock to visit her Cousin Waldemar. On trying to sail back to Denmark in stormy weather she was shipwrecked but was saved, founded the Cistercian convent and spent the rest of her days here. She was interred at Doberan in 1282. After the Reformation the convent was the only one in Mecklenburg not to be secularised, and it survived as a convent for the unmarried daughters of wealthy Rostock families until 1920. The desperate need for accommodation after the war led to the splitting up of the convent into small units. Restoration began in 1976, and in 1980 the Kulturhistorisches Museum was housed in the refectory, the dormitory and the north-west wing. A pretty garden reaches to the town wall, where in summer you can go through a gate to the ramparts.

The Klosterkirche is the only church of the mendicant orders remaining in Rostock. It is a plain brick Gothic, three-aisle hall church, with (in Cistercian tradition) no tower. It also houses valuable artistic treasures. Especially noteworthy are a mid-15C HIGH ALTAR with double wings depicting the Crucifixion and the apostles; and an early 16C altar, also with double wings: open, it shows the Crucifixion in the centre, with saints on the wings, while closed it displays interesting symbolic imagery. The outer wing depicts the betrothal of St Catherine, surrounded by semi-circular representations of the allegory of the Virgin (the Unicorn), the sacrifice of Christ's death (the pelican) and eternal life (the lion and the phoenix). Frescoes on the east wall of the south aisle are of the Mount of Olives (early 15C, restored) and those in the chancel are of the Last Judgement.

In the **Kulturhistorisches Museum** (opening times: Tues–Sun 10.00–18.00) amongst other fine exhibits are the Rostock coins and medallions going back to the early 14C—Rostock minted its own coins from 1325 to 1864. In 1300 there were 77 different crafts in Rostock; many of these are represented here by artefacts and tools. The important collection of pewter, household cutlery and kitchen tools derives mainly from the Rostock pewter works of the 15C and 16C; textiles are represented by standards of the city guilds, uniforms, clothes, ecclesiastical cloths and garments, some five hundred years old. Children will enjoy the toy collection. There are also Slavic weapons dating from the mid 6C to the high Middle Ages, including those found in the River Warnow at Schwaan in 1927–28. Also of note is the collection of minor Dutch paintings and work by 20C artists including Ernst Barlach and Käthe Kollwitz.

Directly behind the convent site runs part of the 13C town wall, which has recently been restored and is built of brick on a base of field stone. Ascend a flight of steps to a wooden platform, where there is a good view. Step through an enchanting the little archway and out onto a gravelled walk in the park at the top of the medieval ramparts. Along the wall small protrusions are all that remains of the former *Wiekhäuser*. The defences once had 22 town gates. The Kröpeliner Tor was the largest and most impressive of these and intended to demonstrate Rostock's wealth and might as a Hanseatic city.

The **Kröpeliner Tor**, the main west gate of town, was built in two stages to its present height of 54m. The lower part, of dark red brick, dates from 1280; a hundred years later five further storeys, in pale brown brick, were added. Until the mid 17C a wooden parapet ran round three sides of the tower. The exits onto the high-up parapet have now become windows. The four stepped gables, slender steeple, ornate tracery and decorative brick-work soften the military aspect of the building. On the town side of the gate are the colours of Mecklenburg on the left and on the right the town coat of arms: red and white are the hallmark of a Hanseatic city, and the golden gryphon on blue ground derives from the Slav princes.

If time permits, a walk through the oldest part of the town is repaid with the sight of the comparatively deserted streets of the former artisans' quarter. From Neuer Markt head north and look down Grosse Mönchen-strasse to see the last remaining example of the *Strandtore* (Shore Gates). There were once 13 in total which closed off all the roads which led to the harbour; this one is the **Mönchentor**, originally built in 16C and altered to Neo-Classical style in 1805 by the sculptor Gustav Schadelock.

Continue east down the Krämerstrasse and cross the Grubenstrasse, which once marked the boundary between the Altstadt and the Mittelstadt. It was originally an open canal, now vaulted over, and led from the Mühlendamm to the River Warnow. The former **Kloster St Katharinen** (Convent of St Catharine) was established in 1234 by the Franciscans. After secularisation in 1534 it became an old peoples' home and poorhouse. It was badly damaged in the town fire of 1677 and many alterations since have left a mixture of styles. However, traces of the original convent remain, such as part of the wall on the street with an arched portal, and columns on either side with early Gothic capitals, believed to be the oldest architectural details in Rostock. Since the Reformation it has served a variety of institutions; the town planners now envisage a college here.

Continue east up the Amberg and into the Alter Markt with the **Petri-kirche** (St Peter's church) straight ahead. This is the oldest part of the city, where the first German settlement was founded. It is also the highest point, 12m above sea level, where the river makes a semi-circular bend, offering the first settlers shelter and safety, surrounded by water and marsh.

The large ALTER MARKT measures 80m x 90m and was the earliest of Rostock's three market places. Cross the square, to the left of the church, and from the Petrischanze (St Peter's bulwark) look down to the River Warnow and the plains below, where the Slav settlement of Roztoc lay in the swampy area on the right river bank. A plaque in the wall records the granting of a town charter in 1218. Nearby is the monument to Lutheran reformer, Joachim Slüter, who, between 1525 and his death in 1532, preached in Plattdeutsch. The Petrikirche with its solid square tower was, until 1942, crowned with a steeple that rose to 117m. Its loss in the war was a double disaster, because with its exposed position the Petrikirche was an important landmark; the tower had been built to such a great height not only to glorify God, but also to help the sailors steer their ships—it was visible at sea from over 50km away. The original church was founded in the 12C and the present three-aisle brick Gothic basilica was begun in the 14C. The interior is much altered since the Second World War, when the nave and south aisle were burnt out and most of the Baroque furnishings destroyed. Exterior reconstruction is planned along with that of the steeple.

Continue south into the LOHGERBERSTRASSE and note house No.11 (18C) and No. 29 on the right, a restored brick gable house. Continue straight on to the second church of the Altstadt—the **Nikolaikirche**. It is not only the oldest church of Rostock, but also one of the oldest hall churches in the Baltic area. Begun around 1230, in what was then Wendish territory, it has been altered many times. By 1312 it was reconsecrated as a three aisle hall church. During an extension of the chancel and the tower in the early 15C, the street was tunnelled under the altar—the Schwibbogen (the route will take you under here). Rebuilding after serious damage in the Second World War featured a scheme unique to Germany: twenty flats were built into the roof. You can see their windows up amongst the tiles. The tower has been converted into ecclesiastical offices.

Cross the Grubenstrasse for a second time and leave the Altstadt heading west to reach the oldest town gate in Mecklenburg. It is first mentioned in 1262. From 14C onwards it was used only for the coming and going of cattle, so acquiring the nickname **Kuhtor** (Cow Gate). Continue along a section of the city wall to the Lagebusch Turm. This octagonal wall tower acquired its present form in 1575 and was used as a prison, powder chamber and site for artillery. Continue along the rather uneven path until you come back to the main road at the Steintor. A previous 13C building on the site was razed to the ground in 1566 because Rostock refused to swear an oath of alleg-iance to the reigning Mecklenburg duke, and it was replaced by this Dutch Renaissance style gate (16C). On the field side the cross-shaped stones which held the portcullis can be seen. Facing the town are reliefs of the three seals used by Rostock, from left to right: The Secret Seal, the town seal and the council's coat of arms.

From here you can see the **Schiffahrtmuseum** housed in a pale Neo-Clas-sical building on the corner of the square (Museum of Shipping; opening times: Sat–Thurs 09.00–17.00). The museum covers the history of seafaring and trade from the 8C to the present day. Particularly interesting is the section on the Hanseatic era, with the ship used by the merchants, the Kogge, taking pride of place. Diagonally opposite the Steintor is a large red building, the Ständehaus. Built in 1893 by Gotthilf Ludwig Möckel, it is a fine example of the late 19C Gothic Revival style, with its decorative brickwork, pointed arches and turrets. The four larger-than-life size bronze statues are of former dukes of Mecklenburg; from left to right they are: Duke Johann Albrecht, Archduke Friedrich Franz II, Archduke Georg and Duke Christian Ludwig. Inside the great staircase and the panelled council chamber are both impressive. A short detour here takes you to Hinter dem Rathaus No. 5, the **Kerkhofhaus**, with one of the most beautiful gables in Rostock. Built c 1530, for Mayor Kerkhof, it is in transitional style with a seven-part Gothic stepped gable, but there are indications of the Renais-sance in the terracotta decorative details and the rounded portal. The Stadtarchiv (City Archives) and the Standesamt (Registry Office) are located here. You now return to the main route and the Neuer Markt.

It is also worth visiting the **Kunsthalle**, Am Schwanenteich (opening times: Tues, Thurs, Sun 10.00–18.00; Weds 10.00–20.00) a modern museum with temporary exhibitions of work by 20C north German artists. The **Rostock-Warnemünde Heimatmuseum**, Alexandrinenstrasse 31, 18119 Warnemünde (opening times: Wed–Sun 09.00–12.30 and 13.00–17.30) con-centrates on local history.

Warnemünde lies at the River Warnow's outlet to the sea and is easily reached on the S-Bahn; tickets may be purchased from the Tourist Infor-mation Office or at the station. Displays concentrate on the history of the fishermen and sailors of the village, as well as exhibits of the attractive Warnemünde folk costumes.

29

The Baltic Coast from Rostock to Stralsund

Schwerin—83km Rostock—12km Rövershagen—8km Graal-Müritz—20km Ahrenshoop—10km Prerow—10km Barth—34km Stralsund.

To travel directly from Schwerin either take the A106 towards Wismar, and at Wismar take the coast road, the E22, via Rostock. However, this can be very congested, and another, slightly longer but enjoyable drive, is to take the A104 and head for Güstrow. You travel through rolling countryside with woods and huge fields until just after Bülow you see the skyline of Güstrow (see Route 2). Passing through Güstrow it is easy to stop at the *Gertrudenkapelle to look at Barlach's sculptures. This is quite well signed, on the left as you turn left into town. After Güstrow take the A103 motorway heading for Rostock.

Take the A105 heading north-east from Rostock towards Stralsund—this is a very busy road in summer so this route takes a diversion along minor roads to visit the **Fischland-Darss-Zingst peninsula**. After a windmill on the right, turn left and east, at Rövershagen. Drive through pine woods to arrive at Graal-Müritz, two linked resorts with a narrow but pleasant sandy beach backed by pine woods and the 275 hectare Grosser Moor nature reserve. The Grosser Moor (Great Bog) is a typical coastal wetland, where peat was cut until the early 1950s. The resort consists of little more than a cluster of cafés but may be convenient for a break.

Leave Graal-Müritz and after approximately 8km turn left and enter the **Nationalpark Vorpommersche Boddenlandschaft**, an area of strange and primitive beauty. The Baltic coastline from here to the island of Hiddensee and west Rügen is protected, as are the still lagoons, or Bodden, typical of this area. Woods, dunes, bogs of the hinterland are all part of the National Park, that covers an area of 805 sq km, of which 85 per cent is water. In the autumn more than 30,000 cranes rest here on their westwards migration. It is the most important resting place in Northern Europe.

The Fischland-Darss-Zingst peninsula combines this ecologically sensitive area with sandy beaches and old fishing villages that have become popular seaside resorts. At the turn of the century Berliners looking for a summer retreat began to spend their holidays here, and were warmly welcomed by the locals, glad to supplement an income dependent mainly on seafaring and fishing. The villages are now thriving resorts, but have avoided high rise development, and they still retain their quaint charm and sense of isolation.

Ahrenshoop (Tourist Information Office at the Kurverwaltung, Kirchnersgang 2, 18347; opening times: summer only, Mon–Fri 10.00–18.00, Sat–Sun 14.30–17.00), once a tiny fishing village, is now a sophisticated summer resort; during the GDR era it was greatly favoured by the party Prominenten. An artists' community was founded here in 1892 by the landscape painter Paul Müller-Kämpf, who built a house and started a painting school at a time when artists wanted to get out of the studio to paint in the open air. He organised a permanent exhibition hall, the Kunstkaten, which was also to serve as a model for new buildings in the area. The charming reed-thatched cottages down narrow lanes are usually holiday homes but built in the local idiom. Many of them have wooden crossed horses' heads surmounting the gable. Their origins and significance are uncertain, but they are traditional in rural architecture and are documented in Mecklenburg since 16C. The church in Ahrenshoop was designed in 1951 by Professor H.W. Hämer and is built from local material—wood and reed—in the shape of an upturned boat keel.

Continue east along the peninsula passing through the southern part of the Darss, with its ancient and inaccessible forest of beech, pine and alder; there are no roads, only footpaths and cycle ways. You then reach **Prerow** (Tourist Information Office, Kurverwaltung, Gemeindeplatz 1, 18375) once a fishing village and now a well-organised resort, famous for its naturist beaches. It still has rustic fishermen's cottages and a Seemannskirche (Sailors' Church) built 1726–28 when the village was a sea-faring centre, as is testified by the gravestones in the churchyard. The **Darssmuseum**, Waldstrasse 48 (opening times: May–Oct daily 09.00–17.00; Nov–Apr by appointment) draws on the cultural heritage of the seafarers of the village for its exhibits, and includes portraits of captains. The interesting flora and fauna of the peninsula is also represented.

Take the Barth road—in high season it is prudent to avoid continuing along to Zingst, because of traffic congestion returning to the mainland—and cross the Barther Bodden at the two-part bridge Grosse Meinigenbrücke, where you can see the beds of reeds used for thatching. Continue through **Barth** (12,000 inhabitants; Tourist Information Office, Lange Strasse 51, 18356). The stately parish church of St Marien is a Gothic hall church from the early 14C with an early (13C) Gothic chancel. The large, square tower was built in 15C, and the steeple in 1870. Barth is a small town that has expanded rapidly from its medieval centre.

From here travel south (8km) to rejoin the E22 at Löbnitz and then drive east about 25km to Stralsund.

30

Stralsund

75,000 inhabitants.

Tourist Information Office: Ossenreyerstrasse 1/2, Stralsund 18408. Tel. 2439. Opening times: May–Sept Mon–Fri 09.00–18.00, Sat–Sun 09.00–13.00, Oct–Apr Mon–Fri 10.00–17.00, Sat 10.00–13.00.

Stralsund's days of prosperity as part of the Hanseatic league lasted almost 300 years and have left a legacy of superb medieval brick Gothic architecture. The city has suffered a chequered history but its former status as a mercantile sea-power is immediately apparent. The town was less severely damaged during the Second World War than other great Baltic ports but was sadly neglected after 1945 and has lost 570 historic buildings. Attempts are being made to repair the medieval town centre, and the city's reconstruction to something approaching its once prosperous appearance is already under way.

It is well worth spending a few days based in Stralsund to explore the city and the neighbouring islands of Rügen and Hiddensee, both easily accessible from here. Accommodation is a problem, however. At the time of the *Wende* there were 150 hotel beds; there are now 1000 visitors a day coming through the tourist office in high season. The advent of a Swedish hotel ship, the *Astoria*, moored in the old harbour, and the half-completed transformation of a large workers' barracks, Haus am Rügendamm into a well-run budget priced hotel will ease the situation, but it is well worth booking ahead.

History. During the course of German expansion eastwards the town of Stralsund was founded at the site of the Slav fishing and ferry village of Stralow (the Slav word for arrow). It was at the crossroads of ancient trading routes, with a sheltered harbour and natural defences formed by the sea and large inland pools. Stralsund was granted a town charter in 1234 by Prince Witzlaw I of Rügen and streets were planned in regular pattern around the Alter Markt and the Nikolaikirche with the layout focused towards the sea. Trade prospered so quickly that the town was sacked in 1249 by Lübeck, wary of a potential rival. This prompted the building of a strong town wall to ward off further attacks. The city now looked like an impregnable island fortress. By 1256 a second settlement, the Neustadt, near the Neuer Markt and the Marienkirche, began to fuse with the Altstadt.

In 1293 Stralsund became part of the Hanseatic league, within a loose alliance of the Wendish towns on the Baltic coast with Lübeck, Rostock, Wismar and Greifswald. These cities joined together to defeat the Danes and in May 1370 the Peace of Stralsund (1370) heralded a new era of prosperity. As a leading member of Hanse, Stralsund flourished during the 14C and 15C. Its prosperity derived from overseas trade, particularly with Scandinavia and Russia, for which it was ideally sited. Trade was carried out as far afield as London, Flanders and Spain. The great monuments of Gothic architecture, the Nikolaikirche, the Marienkirche, the Jakobikirche and, of course, the Rathaus were all built during the Hanseatic heyday. Stralsund has been preserved as if in amber because of the town's rapid economic decline after 1500 as Hanse lost its sway with the rise of Holland and the gradual displacement of the main centre of shipping from the Baltic to the North Sea and Atlantic.

Stralsund embraced Protestantism as early as 1525, and was on the side of Sweden, against Wallenstein's imperial troops in the Thirty Years War, but the siege of Stralsund in 1628 was resisted. At the Peace of Westphalia of 1648, Stralsund came under Swedish rule, where it remained for the next 167 years.

Napoleon's troops occupied the city five times between 1806 and 1813, whilst freedom fighters, inspired by the poet Ernst Moritz Arndt and led by Ferdinand von Schill, made heroic attempts at resistance. At the Congress of Vienna in 1815 Stralsund became part of Prussia and a gradual economic revival began. Communications were helped by the train link with Berlin in 1863 and the construction of the Rügendamm in 1936. In 1944 the city was bombed and gaps where damaged buildings have been removed can still be seen. Under the GDR attempts at repair were made, and although much has been lost Stralsund remains one of the best preserved historic German towns, a monument of national importance.

From the railway station head north-east up Tribseer Damm and Tribseer Strasse to Neuer Markt then north up Mönchstrasse and east down Ravensberg Strasse to the Alter Markt. This is the **Altstadt** (Old Town) where the Tourist Information Office may be found on the west side of the Rathaus. The ***Rathaus**, with its ornate façade is one of the most impressive brick Gothic secular buildings in Europe. Its delicacy is balanced to the left by the bulk of the Nikolaikirche and together they form one of the finest groups of buildings in northern Germany.

The exact origins of the Rathaus are unclear, but it is believed to have been built in the late 13C with two north–south long wings, later joined at each end. The north decorative wall, which shows the influence of Lübeck town hall, is constructed of glazed and unglazed brick. Six ornate gable fronts, alternating with slender colonnettes, conceal the building behind. The elaborate design showed the world the town council had taste and the money to command the best architecture in the Baltic region. Each gable front is pierced by apertures in the form of rose windows with delicate tracery. Restoration in 1881 involved many alterations to the brickwork and the removal of a coat of plaster. Above the six large first-floor windows of the Löwensaal are the coats of arms of the Hanseatic towns of the Wendisches Quartier.

Inside, the vaulted ground floor, on either side of a narrow inner court, originally housed traders and their stalls. Elegant galleries on the first floor were added in 1686. The first floor assembly room or Löwensaal, is named after the Swedish Governor General Axel Graf von Löwen (1748–72) whose collection of objets d'art forms the basis of the city's museum (see below). Further links with Sweden are the bust of King Gustav II Adolphus (1594–1632) that was placed here in 1930 to commemorate the 300th anniversary of the king's visit to Stralsund in 1630, and, over the 18C Baroque portal leading out to Ossenreyerstrasse, the coat of arms of Stralsund under Swedish rule; the Swedish lion and Pomeranian gryphon support the Stralsund arrow motif on a bright Scandinavian blue background. Under the town hall is the huge and splendid Gothic vaulted Ratskeller measuring 60m x 30m. Until recently used as a restaurant it was undergoing refurbishment at the time of writing.

The ALTER MARKT has a special charm with the Nikolaikirche and Rathaus forming one side and the other three sides including some fine gabled houses, well restored after damage during bombing in 1945. Almost directly across from the Rathaus is No. 5, the Wulflamhaus whose ornate late Gothic gables echo those opposite. Regarded as one of the most beautiful Gothic houses in Stralsund, it was built c 1370 for the wealthy and dictatorial Mayor Bertram Wulflam, and reconstructed 1989–91 by a Polish firm of specialists. On the east side of the square the ochre-coloured Commandanten-Hus, a three-storey Baroque building, was built for the then Swedish Governor-General. A favourite spot for surveying the square is the balcony of the *Café Artushof*, No. 8, on the west side. Built as an hotel in 1912 it was re-opened after the *Wende*. The Alter Markt has little in the way of shops or traffic as strict regulations in Stralsund prohibit heavy vehicles in the old centre.

Before leaving the square look back towards the Nikolaikirche and to the right of the church notice a small wooden door which was traditionally used by brides entering the church. There is also a good view of the two towers—oddly mismatched. Turn right at the east end of the church, down Bechermacherstrasse, where No. 7, two-storeyed with a flat roof, is a rare example of a typical medieval artisan dwelling, where the family and apprentices lived above, with the workshop on the ground floor. Then turn right and enter the **Nikolaikirche** by the south portal (opening times: 10.00–12.00, 14.00–18.00 in summmber, but check with the Tourist Office).

This is the oldest parish church in Stralsund. Dedicated to the patron saint of seafarers, St Nicholas, it was also known as the Ratskirche, the church of the council, and it was used by the Rat for important gatherings as well as services. The building was begun as a hall church in 1270, but the fame of the Marienkirche in Lübeck had spread rapidly along the coast. The council, never willing to be outdone by Lübeck, altered plans and transformed the building into a brick Gothic basilica—a splendid demonstration of the burgeoning wealth and power of the city. The double towers, the flying buttresses and radiating chapels are all directly inspired by the Marienkirche of Lübeck, which in its turn reflected the Gothic cathedrals of northern France.

In 700 years the building has changed little outwardly, apart from the collapse of the original steeples, destroyed by fire in 1662. The south tower was replaced in Baroque style in 1662, but to the chagrin of succeeding generations of Stralsunders funds have never been available to replace the second. Following damage in the Second World War by bomb blast, the Roman Catholic Church (St Nicholas is Protestant) paid for the roof to be made watertight and work on the interior repairs is still being carried out. The church may be visited, although scaffolding is likely to be in place, masking the majestic dimensions: 85m x 70m x 29m.

As the church of the rich patrician council it was used to receive ambassadorial delegations as well as to read proclamations to crowds—the largest covered area in the town was put to practical use. Thus it was richly furnished, with 56 altars belonging to guilds and trade associations in various niches and chapels, and up to 200 masses were said a day by the numerous priests.

Many of the medieval furnishings were lost through outbursts of iconoclasm during the Reformation, but some noteworthy pieces remain. The late 15C High Altar was probably carved near Stralsund, although it shows Dutch influence. A triptych, with more than 100 figures, it depicts turbulent scenes from the life of Christ and the Passion. Of particular note is a very beautiful group of mourning women. Sadly, the central figure of the crucifix was stolen when in storage during the Second World War. A replacement is planned.

Five further altars from the Middle Ages are preserved: the outstanding late 15C **Schneider-Altar** (Tailors' Altar) with the figure of Mary and Jesus playing on her lap; the Junge-Altar (gift of the Junge family) from the early 15C with a beautiful Schöne Madonna; the Bergenfahrer-Altar (the altar of the Association of Traders to Bergen), c 1500, with scenes from the Passion and life of Mary, the Riemer-und-Beutler-Altar (a leather workers' guild), early 15C, a good quality piece from a Rostock workshop, with a crouching figure at the base of the Cross writing the inscription (an unusual feature sometimes to be found on Mecklenburg altars); and the Bürgermeister-Altar (the Mayor's Altar), endowed between 1500 and 1516, showing Sts George, Catherine and Martin.

The most distinguished of the single pieces is the 2.25m high plaster figure of the *Anna-Selbdritt-Gruppe* (St Anne with Mary and Jesus) dating from 1290, one of the most important works of its kind in the Baltic area. Perhaps the most fascinating object is the fragment of the Novgorodfahrer-Gestühl (the Association of Traders to Novgorod's pew). with graphic carved scenes of mink hunters catching their prey, then selling it to merchants outside the Russian city gates. The late 13C Swedish limestone font, with an ornate Baroque lid, is a reminder of early trading links with Sweden. The astronomical clock, 1394, by Nicholas Lilienfeld, is unfortunately not on view.

After visiting the church turn left into BADENSTRASSE, which leads from the south side of the Rathaus east to the harbour. Many of the administrative authorities had their seats here, and despite the grey façades and peeling plaster the street has some of Stralsund's grander houses, several in process of restoration. Look out for No. 12, a mid-16C Renaissance house with a richly decorated ogee gable. It was restored in 1956 and at the time a hoard of silver thalers from 1541–1626 was found, doubtless hidden in the cellar at the outbreak of the Thirty Years War, but not retrieved by the owner who probably died of the plague. No. 13 houses the town archives, in a Neo-Classical building with terracotta frieze above the ground floor. Virtually opposite are No. 44, a late German Renaissance double house with an unusual balcony on pillars and No. 45, the old Bärenapotheke (Bear Apothecary) of 1636 that has been reconstructed. Nos 40 and 42 are interesting examples of the differences between Renaissance and Gothic domestic architecture—the former, Renaissance, with the break in height in its attractive gable, the latter, Gothic, with its lines reaching ever higher. No. 39 is a late Baroque house, whose beautiful plaster ceilings should soon be restored to splendour, the crest over the rounded door recalls the use of the house by the Pomeranian Landstände (Provincial Diet). Look opposite, between Nos 39 and 40, for an excellent view of the Jakobikirche tower. No. 17, built 1736–40 by the famous Swedish architect Cornelius van Loos, as the palace for the Swedish Governor General, is a stately two-storey stucco building with wings, which was badly damaged in 1944.

Turn left opposite, through a passage, then past a playground in the midst of a group of modernised flats and turn around for a superb view of the Nikolaikirche with its flying buttresses and a clear profile of its basilica structure with the nave much higher than the aisles.

Continue north into SEMLOWERSTRASSE. No. 31/32, the early 18C big yellow house with the imposing gable, would once have been three houses. Keep on heading north over the street, and down a narrow alley with uneven, ancient cobblestones and a raised central path for ladies in the days of long skirts, before the introduction of street-cleaning. Coming out into Fährstrasse look right down to the Swedish hotel ship the *Astoria*. Purpose-built in just four months in 1991, the base was constructed in local shipyards and the rooms were made in Chile in containerised units that slotted on top, to be towed across the oceans completely kitted out with Scandinavian furnishings. It has made a significant difference to the accommodation capacity of Stralsund, is in a central position and offers good value accommodation.

FÄHRSTRASSE, dating from 1270, links the Alter Markt with the harbour and has a wealth of fine old gabled houses. An interesting feature of these houses is that often the courtyard side can be viewed from Bechermacher-strasse. No. 11, a brick gable house, has just been restored. In a paving stone in front of No. 21 is a plate commemorating the death of the freedom fighter Ferdinand von Schill (d. 1809).

Nos 23 and 24 are of particular interest. No. 23, the Scheelehaus, now a restaurant, is named after Carl Wilhelm Scheele (1742–86), an internationally famed scientist. You can enjoy a meal here featuring local specialities or glimpse inside to see the high-ceilinged hall or *Diele*, now beautifully restored. It is an excellent example of the layout of a patrician merchant's house, with its high front door, or portal, reaching almost to the first floor, to allow carts with wares to enter straight into the main room of the house. The merchant's goods were unloaded in the *Diele* and then hauled by pulley up to storage areas on the upper floors. The hall was used for much more than the transit of goods. With its two big windows and the only fireplace in the house it was the centre of both business negotiations and family life. Behind the hall was a smaller, narrower area, with kitchen and living room facing the courtyard at the back. Bedrooms were reached from first floor galleries—the gallery can be seen clearly here.

The merchants' homes also acted as warehouses, the goods stored in several floors of attics. Ornate gabling concealed their business activities as well as impressing colleagues with the wealth and status of a merchant and thus his credit-worthiness. The construction of gabled merchant houses hardly changed from the mid 13C to 17C Baroque times, that is the entire Hanseatic era.

Continue, turning right and then left, heading north-west into Schillstrasse and then to the remains of the **Johanniskloster** (Monastery of St John; check with the Tourist Office for opening times) one of the most atmospheric of the medieval monuments in Stralsund, with its ruined church, Barlach's sculpture of the Pietà, frescoes, and cells under the roof. The monastery was founded in 1254, by the poor order of the Franciscans. As was customary the monastery was built just within the city wall.

The hall church is 80m long, with one aisle. After a fire during a Christmas feast in 1624, only the chancel remained and the church was rebuilt in 1650. In 1944 it was bombed. The ruins have been restored and open air concerts are held—the acoustics are excellent. The Pietà (1932) in bronze, by Ernst Barlach, with Christ represented as a young soldier killed in the First World War, was rejected as a war memorial under Nazi rule, but was cast from a plaster model and placed here in 1988. Before leaving the monastery go through the gateway into the ruins for a closer look at the sculpture.

A tour of the monastery includes the glass-covered cloisters and the enchanting *Kapitelsaal* (Chapter Room), used for candle-lit concerts and until recently as a kindergarten. The redecoration of the Gothic vaulting was finished in 1992 in keeping with the original colours. The 15C frescoes depict a city wall with 12 towers with the Stigmatisation of St Francis opposite and the Crucifixion on the left. Up a narrow stairway is the archive room which leads to the most fascinating and cavernous area under the roof, carefully reconstructed to show the hutch-like original cells and chimney system—the Räucherboden (smoke attics). Just beyond the monastery is an idyllic second courtyard with pretty two-storey 17C almshouses.

Return to Schillstrasse, turning right at the end to head towards the **Kniepertor**, one of only two remaining town gates of the original 11 that were part of the town wall. First mentioned in 1304, the Kniepertor was altered in the early 15C to its present low, square shape with glazed brick friezes on both sides and blind windows. It has been used as a dwelling since the 1960s.

From the Kniepertor you can see part of the restored town walls along the Knieperwall. Only sections of the wall remain. It was begun in 1256 but took centuries to complete. The walls and the surrounding lakes Knieperteich and Frankenteich gave the impression of a fortified island and Stralsund was thus considered impregnable. During the siege of Stralsund (1628) even Wallenstein—who swore that he would take the city even if it were chained to Heaven—was resisted. This particular stretch of wall, built by the Franciscans 700 years ago, has been carefully restored to its original appearance, with crenellations and firing slits.

Cross and continue south-west along Schillstrasse. No. 6 is an unprepossessing church building, but conceals an ancient chapel behind, the

Kapelle St Annen and Brigitten, a small polygonal late Gothic brick building from the late 15C. No. 39, on the right, is a former Danish warehouse, the lower storeys dating from 1717. Finally turn left into Mönchstrasse and then continue back to the Rathaus and the Tourist Information Office on its west façade.

If time permits, the Marienkirche and the Heiligengeistkirche are worth visiting, as are the excellent museums in the Katharinenkloster.

The **Marienkirche**, entered from Bleistrasse, is just south of the Neuer Markt, the centre of the second town settlement. An early church was begun in 1298 but destroyed in 1382 by the tower falling in. As soon as the rubble was cleared away the existing building was begun and it is one of the most monumental achievements of German brick Gothic, not recognisably modelled on any other church. It was largely funded by the Guild of Tailors, with the express intention of surpassing the council's church, St Nicholas. This helps explain the transept with three aisles, creating a cathedral-like structure (in the Baltic area the only similar example is the cathedral in Schwerin), and the mighty west tower with extensions to the north and south, giving the impression of a west transept. The Tailors' Guild, for all their pretensions, kept to a simple, unified plan for the exterior walls, with little decorative detail and the chapels radiating off the ambulatory are not apparent from outside. All this is typical of late Gothic, north German taste. The tower rises in stages to 104m; you can ascend 349 steps for a superb view over Stralsund and Rügen. The square base with an octagonal tier on top lends a military aspect, despite the decorative blind tracery. The bulbous Baroque spire was added in 1708.

The interior is wonderfully light, with huge octagonal columns, quite unembellished, that fuse into the walls of the clerestory. The west end of the nave is dominated by the vast Baroque organ (1653–59) by Friedrich Stellwagen from Hamburg. Apart form three large carved figures (1430) of he Virgin Mary and Child, St Peter and St Paul, there is little left from the Middle Ages. Much was destroyed at the time of the Reformation and in 1807–10 French troops used the church as a barracks and barn. This prompted attempts at restoration during 1842–47 at a time of a new appreciation of Germany's Gothic past. Caspar David Friedrich and Karl Friedrich Schinkel were both involved in drawing up designs, although the work eventually went to local artist J.W. Brüggemann. Unfortunately, during the restoration work still more of the medieval furnishings were lost.

From the Marienkirche walk east along Frankenstrasse almost to the Langenkanal. There on a far smaller scale, is the charming **Heiligegeistkirche** (Church of the Holy Spirit, opening times: 10.00–12.00, 14.00–18.00, except Sun), the last of Stralsund's medieval churches. The Heilig-Geist-Hospital, a hospice for the poor and sick of Stralsund, was founded in 1256 by the town. The church was begun around 1400 as a hall church with nave and two aisles. It suffered badly during Wallenstein's siege (1628)—cannon balls can still be seen lodged in the outside walls—and even worse during the bombardment in the Nordic War (1715). Subsequently, repairs were made and the beautiful Baroque altar commissioned.

To the north-west of the Heiligegeistkirche is the **Jakobikirche**. Badly damaged during the Second World War, it cannot be visited. A brick Gothic basilica, it was originally a hall church but the nave was raised to alter the structure c 1400. The imposing west tower, on three levels, rises first above the main portal and large six-part window; then the main section is richly decorated with blind tracery windows, more so than the other Stralsund churches; the tower continues with four turrets and finally culminates in a Baroque helm which replaces the steeple lost by fire in 1662.

The Meeresmuseum and Kulturhistorisches Museum, have a superb setting in the former monastery building of the Katharinen-Kloster. Both are eminently worth a visit. The **Katharinen-Kloster** was founded in 1251 by the Dominicans. The monastery church is an early Gothic hall church with nave and two aisles, probably completed in 1317. In 1974 a three-floor free-standing steel structure was inserted into the church, which now houses the Meeresmuseum (Museum of the Sea). The cloisters, and the graceful vaulted former refectory are shared by both museums.

The **Kulturhistorisches Museum**, Mönchstrasse 25–27 (open daily 10.00–17.00, closed Mon) is strong on pre- and early history, including a wonderful find of gold Viking jewellery from the Island of Hiddensee. There is a delightful exhibition of toys and good displays of reconstructed interiors.

The **Meeresmuseum** (Museum of the Sea, opening times: daily May–Oct, 10.00–17.00; July and Aug, 09.00–18.00; Nov–Apr, Wed–Sun 10.00–17.00). Covering all aspects of fish and the sea, it is of international repute and the most popular museum in Mecklenburg-Pomerania, receiving over half a million visitors annually. Aquaria are displayed against the background of the ancient monastery. Highlights are the 16m skeleton of a Finnwal, and the 3m high coral reef in aquarium with exotic fish. The **Volkskunde Museum** in Bötcherstrasse is open Tue–Sun 10.00–17.00.

31

The Island of Rügen

*Rügen, in the north-east of Mecklenburg-Vorpommern is Germany's largest and most beautiful island. Covering an area of 926 sq km, it has a dramatic variety of landscape, from the soaring white cliffs of the Stubbenkammer and the windswept north cape at Arkona to long sandy beaches at Binz, the lagoon-like Bodden, the small coves at Lauterbach and the gentle hills of the isolated peninsula of the Mönchgut. Much of the island is protected, including the wonderful beech woods around Granitz and the ancient oak trees on the tiny island of Vilm. *The Adventures of Elizabeth on Rügen* (Virago, 1990) by Elizabeth von Arnim is a most amusing account of a tour of the island and well worth a read. Today tourism is the mainstay of the economy, but thanks to lack of development during the GDR years the island remains remarkably unspoilt. The most important sights can be seen in a day's tour, but this would certainly be rushed. It is absolutely essential to book, and to confirm, any accommodation on the island in high season. It may well be a better plan to stay in Stralsund and make leisurely excursions.

History. The earliest prehistoric finds are from the Old Stone Age, whilst those of the Middle Stone Age, 5000 years ago, are far more numerous. The first settlers were attracted by the quantities of flint and more than 20,000 stone tools and weapons have been discovered around Lietzow. The flints were a valuable commodity and traded over long distances by boat. Richly decorated ceramics from the New Stone Age

(2500–1700 BC) have been unearthed; also from this period are the big stone graves, Grossdolmen, with over 50 remaining on Rügen; the grave-field near Lancken-Granitz is worth visiting. From 1700 BC the people of the Bronze Age left tumuli of which the largest and most impressive is that of Dobberworth, south of Sagard. It is 10m high, with a circumference of 50m. The largest grave-field, with 13 tumuli, is at Wooke, north of Patzig.

Migration between 5C AD and 1168 brought the Slav Ranen from the east into the area. The Slav epoch spanned 500 years, and has been identified not only by archaeological finds but also by countless names of places and fields, those ending in -itz, -ow, and -in. Slavs constructed fortified sites that served as markets, refuges and temples, as in the reconstruction at Gross Raden, near Güstrow. Notable remains of the Slav fortresses are the Jaromarsburg on Kap Arkona, the Rugard by Bergen and the Hertaburg in the Stubnitz. For more information on the early history of Rügens visit the museum at Ralswiek, the Traditionstätte für Kulturgeschichte Rügens (opening times: May–Oct daily 09.00—17.00).

The Ranens worshipped the image of the God Swantewit, at the temple stronghold at Arkona on the north cape of Rügen. In 1168 the Danes, under King Waldemar I, stormed the fortress and destroyed the statue of the god. With the downfall of Arkona (1168), the region came under Danish sovereignty. The Slav Prince of Rügen agreed to be baptised and the earliest churches on Rügen—Schaprode, Altenkirchen and Sagard—show Danish influence in their architecture. The first German peasants began to settle the land in the 13C, encouraged by the princely house. Garz, in the centre of the island, remained the Slav capital and granted Stralsund a town charter, on 31 October 1234. In 1325 the line of Slav princes of Rügen died out and the island became part of the Dukedom of Pommern-Wohlgast.

Around the early 17C the subjugation of the peasants began, depriving them of any rights. In 1616 serfdom of peasants and shepherds was recognised by law. Neither the Pomeranian Dukes, who ruled the island stood until the line died out in 1637, nor the European power of Sweden, to whom the island belonged from 1648 to 1815, made any attempt at change. By the late 18C approximately 75 per cent of the population of the predominantly rural Rügen were serfs without rights or land and had to perform compulsory service (*Frondienst*) for the Junkers (landed aristocracy). It was the son of a former serf, Ernst Mortiz Arndt (b 1769 in Gross Schoritz), who publicised the serfs' plight in his book *An Essay on the History of Serfdom in Pomerania and on Rügen* (1803). Only in 1806 did the King of Sweden revoke serfdom.

After the Congress of Vienna, 1815, Rügen became part of Prussia. Nearly 200 years of Swedish rule had left hardly a trace. During the 19C tourism began to make a significant contribution to the economy. The first guests visited Rügen by the mid 18C, and a spa-type resort was started in Sagard in 1794. The Prince of Putbus had the Badehaus an der Goor built in 1816, modelled on Bad Doberan and Heiligendamm. Putbus was designed for the aristocratic guest, but like Sagard it soon lost its attraction, as it had no sea-bathing facilities.

Around 1860 the fishing and peasant village of Sassnitz was first discovered as a pleasing retreat for city-bound artists. Scientists, painters, poets and musicians spread the fame of the beauty of Rügen throughout the country and further afield. Wilhelm von Humboldt, Caspar David Friedrich, Philipp Otto Runge, Carl Gustav Carus, Adalbert von Chamisso, Theodor Fontane and Johannes Brahms were amongst the famous guests. Sassnitz in its turn was deserted in favour of the Baltic villages of Binz, Sellin, and Göhren, which became the leading resorts of the region. Fishermen's cottages and farmhouses lost their thatched roofs and were transformed into villas with several floors of wooden verandahs and balconies. Late 19C villas, pensions and hotels still remain from this era.

After the Second World War, older buildings were sadly neglected but seaside resorts were unspoilt by high rise development and the charm of both Rügen and the neighbouring island of Hiddensee was largely unaffected. There has been a steep rise in the number of visitors from 130,000 in 1957 to over 1 million in 1991.

It is fairly simple to reach Rügen by public transport from Stralsund, either by bus No. A417 or by train to Bergen, or by ferry to Altefähr. Travel around the island is considerably easier by car but there are train links on the eastern side of Rügen and intermittent buses serve the rest of the island. The road from Stralsund crosses the Rügendamm which was built in 1936. During peak times in summer this bridge can get very crowded, but check locally before setting out and there should be no problem. The village on the coast to the left of the bridge is **Altefähr**, with a late Gothic brick church. It is still linked by regular ferry services with Stralsund harbour. Turn right to head east, driving along a lime avenue, passing Gustow, and continue through open fields. This is a quiet road, traffic consisting largely of bicycles and agricultural lorries.

Garz (2400 inhabitants) is a small, attractive market town and the oldest on the island. Its wide main street is lined with plastered single-storey farmers' houses from the 18C and 19C. The parish **church of St Peter** was begun in the mid 14C and is a late Gothic brick building with a low, square tower. Until 1325 Garz was the seat of power of the Slav princes of Rügen, on the cross roads of two ancient trade routes. Now the rampart of a fortress is all that remains of the Slav princes' castles and temples. The town was given German civic rights in 1316. After a fire in 1765 the burgher houses were rebuilt, most with one storey in Neo-Classical style.

Garz was the home town of Ernst Moritz Arndt, author and poet of the Wars of Liberation, born in 1769 in the nearby Schloss Gross-Schoritz. The **Ernst-Moritz-Arndt-Museum** (opening times: Oct–Apr, Wed–Sat 10.00–12.00 and 14.00–17.00; May–Sept, Tues–Sat 10.00–12.00 and 14.00–17.00) was opened in his honour: displays and documentation on his life are prominent. There are also exhibitions on the history of the agricultural community and the Swedish occupation of Rügen.

Continue driving north-east along a road with wonderful old lime trees. After Kasneveitz you begin to travel through the *Biosphären-Schutzgebiet Sudost-Rügen* (Protected Biosphere of South East Rügen) covering the area from Putbus to the tip of the Mönchgut Peninsula and north up the coast to Binz). Continue for 10km to reach Putbus.

Putbus and Lauterbach

Tourist Information Office: In der Orangerie, Alleestrasse, 18581 Putbus. The opening times are complicated, but basically the office closes for lunch except on Friday, and is closed at the weekend.

Putbus is remarkable for the preservation of its original, Neo-Classical plan, and was the last of the northern German towns to be laid out (1808–23) as a Residenzestadt (ruler's residential town). The Prince of Putbus, conscious of his recent elevation (1807) from Graf, modelled his town on the fashionable Bad Doberan. A day could easily be spent in the town following the route below. Alternatively, if there is only time to cruise through, do not miss the Schlosspark on the right, the theatre to the left; drive round the Circus and continue towards Lauterbach.

Start at the **Theatre** (1819), its Neo-Classical façade embellished by four Tuscan columns and a pediment. The plaster frieze above the main portal facing Alleestrasse shows Apollo and the Muses. The writer Gerhard Hauptmann used to make occasional visits to the theatre from Hiddensee. Opposite the Theatre is the **Orangery**, built in 1824 to a design by Karl Friedrich Schinkel; it was remodelled in 1853, and now houses the Tourist

Information Office as well as being used for plays and exhibitions. Continue along Alleestrasse to the splendid **Circus**, with its white stucco buildings and eight roads radiating out. The left-hand (northern) side was carefully restored and repainted during the GDR period for use by the party establishment; the rest is still peeling. In the middle of the central gardens is an obelisk to Prince Wilhem Malte.

Turn down the Kastanienallee into the **Schlosspark**. The park was originally laid out as a Baroque pleasure garden in the 18C, then in 1805–25 Prince Wilhelm Malte of Putbus extended and re-modelled it in the picturesque landscape style which owes much to English influence. The ancient forest was cleared and new trees were planted, including rare and exotic species. The Giant Sequoias behind the Rosencafé now reach up to 35m. Tree planting was continued up to 1945. The Putbus park was not used by the Prince and his aristocratic bathing guests alone, but was also open to the local community. To the right you will see the monument (1869) to Prince Wilhelm Malte I. Behind it, overlooking the water, is the terrace where the Schloss once stood. The family seat, dating back to 1317, was remodelled into a Neo-Classical Schloss (1825) by the Berlin architect Johann Gottfried Steinmeyer, who worked on much of the town. Now there is nothing left but the terrace—in 1962, the Schloss was abruptly demolished. GDR chief Walter Ulbricht planned to visit the island, and it is believed that the local party officials had the Schloss removed to demonstrate to him that feudalism on Rügen was over.

From here walk round the Schwanenteich (Swan Lake) to the **Parkkirche** (Park Church), originally built as the Kursalon (1844–46), with a large ballroom. It was converted into a church in 1891. Turn right here up the Kirchallee and return to the Markt; or continue walking a little further through the park to the Wildgehege with its herd of deer. Walk round the high fencing and back to the Markt, to end the tour. The road leading from the far right-hand corner of the Markt is August-Bäbel-Strasse, an attractive street of two-storey, half-timbered houses built at the time the town was laid out to house the craftsmen.

Rügen's narrow-gauge (750mm) steam railway, the **Rasender Roland** (Raging Roland), runs from Putbus to Göhren and departs about five times a day, the journey taking just over an hour.

From the Circus take the road south-east for **Lauterbach**, a small fishing village. Boats sail from here round the Island of Vilm, known as the Regierungsinsel, a former holiday hideaway for the GDR establishment, now protected because of its delicate bio-structure.

On the promontory to the north of Lauterbach is the Doric-columned Neo-Classical **Badehaus in der Goor** (Bathing House on the Goor, 1817/1818). It was first used by guests of the Prince of Putbus, who took baths in 10 cabins with white marble tubs. The Badehaus was described by Elizabeth von Arnim as 'a long white building something like a Greek temple…conspicuous in its whiteness against a background of beech-woods'. Tracks lead through the woods, giving views over the sea to Vilm.

To Sellin and Sassnitz

Leaving Lauterbach take the road east to Sellin. Go first through the sleepy village of **Vilmnitz**, where the late Gothic brick church has a Romanesque choir c 1250. Continue along a very bad road, down an oak avenue and then into the forest. As you bear right onto the main road A196, look to your left above the trees and on top of the 107m Tempelberg you will see **Jagdschloss Granitz**. If you wish to visit the castle, turn left at the sign. It was built in 1837–46 by Prince Wilhelm Malte I of Putbus, as a hunting lodge, and is designed in Gothic Revival style to resemble a medieval fortress. The 38m high central tower is by the great Berlin architect Karl Friedrich Schinkel, and its dizzying central wrought-iron stairway takes you to a panoramic view from the top. The main body of the building is by his pupil, Johann Gottfried Steinmeyer. A museum is planned, but was not operating fully at the time of writing, so check before a visit.

Try to allow time to make a diversion towards Baabe, Göhren and the **Mönchgut Halbinsel** (peninsula). The Mönchgut (Monks' Estate) used to belong to the monastery of Eldena, across the Greiswalder Bodden—the limit of their lands was the Mönchgraben (monks' ditch), between Sellin and Baabe. The people were thus cut off both geographically and territorially from the rest of the island, and the sense of isolation has persisted through the centuries. For special occasions locals still don *Tracht*, the colourful traditional dress. At **Göhren** the excellent open-air **Mönchguter Museum** (opening times: May–Sept, Tues–Fri 09.00–17.00; Oct–Apr, Tues–Fri 09.00–12.00 and 13.00–17.00) has well-designed exhibitions devoted to the way of life, and folk customs and costumes of the peninsula.

At **Sellin** turn into the wide main street, lined with romantic turn-of-the-century villas. Like the whole town, these are well maintained, if of rather faded grandeur. A steep flight of steps beneath the former pier (removed in 1969 by the then Mayor, to the surprise and dismay of the locals) leads to a narrow sandy beach and shallow sea with good bathing. Wooded cliffs make a dramatic backdrop at either end of the sand.

Follow the road out of Sellin north towards **Binz**, travelling along avenues of beech and silver birch. Descend through beechwoods into Binz (Tourist Information Office, Kurverwaltung Binz, Heinrich-Heine-Strasse 7), the largest of the seaside resorts on Rügen. A long shallow sloping sandy beach curves round the bay. A promenade nearly 3.5km long follows the line of the shore. Pride of place goes to the massive red-roofed **Kurhaus** designed by Otto Spalding in 1908 and now one of the chain of Travel Hotels. The Kurhaus was built when the small fishing village of Binz became an internationally famous bathing resort at the end of the 19C. The turn-of-the-century origins are unmistakable in the numerous hotels and villas with wonderful carved wooden balconies and glass verandahs. A few, such as Pension Granitz, have been completely refurbished to show their intricate woodwork in all its former glory. Since the *Wende*, many have been dogged by legal wrangles over ownership, but will be restored once these are settled. The Rasender Roland runs to Binz, as well as mainline trains.

The road from Binz leads along a pine-clad narrow heath, with glimpses of the Baltic to the east and, to the west, the Kleiner Jasmunder Bodden, an ideal picnic spot. This is one of the places where large deposits of flints encouraged prehistoric settlers to Rügen.

Continue north to **Sassnitz** (Tourist Information Office: Rathaus 18546 Sassnitz, tel. 23131). By 1900 Sassnitz was a well established resort and far better known than Binz. Amongst many famous visitors was Johannes Brahms, who wrote his 1st Symphony here in 1876. With the advent of the international railway in 1892 it soon became a ferry terminal and small industrial town. Traffic to Sweden is still the mainstay of the economy, along with fishing and the production of writing chalk. At the station is the railway carriage that in 1917 took Lenin through Germany en route from Switzerland to St Petersburg.

The **Stubenkammer**, the famous chalk cliffs of Rügen, can be reached to the north uphill through beech woods. From the car park here buses run at frequent intervals to the clifftop. The cliffs are majestic and have inspired many painters and photographers, including Casper David Friedrich. Most famous is the white *****Königsstuhl** (King's Seat; 117m), named after Karl XIII of Sweden who is supposed to have watched a sea battle between Denmark and Sweden from this vantage point. It is possible to walk the 7km along the shore from Sassnitz, but check with the Tourist Office beforehand. Another good walk is along the clifftops from Sassnitz to the Wissower Klinken, where you can enjoy the same view that intrigued Caspar David Friedrich's young bride in his *Chalk Cliffs in Rügen*, c 1818. About 200m north west is a woodland café for a drink or light lunch.

To the right of the Königsstuhl coach park, a ten-minute walk south east leads to the quieter Viktoria-Sicht. Here a small platform is virtually suspended over the cliff to allow a dramatic view of the Königsstuhl. (The path down the cliff near here is not safe after rain.)

From the Stubenkammer you might continue to **Bergen**, where the Marienkirche has an extensive cycle of late Romanesque frescoes (very restored). Alternatively, follow the coast road north. There is a beautiful sandy beach (not very clean) between Glowe and Juliusruh. At Kap Arkona the old Neo-Classical lighthouse (1826–29) was designed by Schinkel. To the south, Jaromarsburg (Jaromar's fortress) dates from c 1000.

32

Hiddensee

Hiddensee is a small island only 17km long, 2km wide and 'absolutely flat, a mere sandbank, except the northern end where it swells up into hills' (Elizabeth von Arnim). Remote and inaccessible, it lies off the north-west coast of Rügen. It can be reached by ferry, crossing from Rügen at Schaprode or directly from Stralsund. It makes an ideal day trip from Stralsund and as the island is traffic free, has an unspoilt open landscape, 15km of good beaches, no large hotels or built up promenades, yet endless tracks and paths to explore on foot or by bike.

Hiddensee was discovered by writers and artists from Hamburg and Berlin in the 1880s; among the most famous of these were Albert Einstein, Thomas Mann and Max Reinhardt. The dramatist and poet Gerhart Hauptmann (1862–1946) spent his summers on the island from 1885 until his death. For the last 100 years tourism, along with fishing, has been the mainstay of the island's economy, with up to 250,000 visitors a year.

The boat from Stralsund calls at the island's three old villages. **Kloster**, in the north, is the most popular for a day's visit. It was founded as a monastery by Cistercian monks in 1296 (dissolved in 1534), hence its name. The tiny brick village church of St Nicholas is painted blue and white with roses on the ceiling. Built by the monks for the fishermen and farmers in 1332, it is a simple single nave building, in Cistercian style without a tower and has changed little in 600 years, apart from minor alterations. In the churchyard (behind the church to the left) is the grave of Gerhart Hauptmann, who was buried here at his request. Continuing a little further along the main street (a sandy track) of Kloster is Haus Seedorn, the holiday home of Gerhart Hauptmann, now known as the **Gerhart-Hauptmann-Gedenkstätte** (opening times: daily May–Oct 10.00–15.30, Nov–Apr by appointment). It is well worth a visit, even for those not familiar with Hauptmann's oeuvre, as it allows a glimpse of an unchanged 1920s interior.

Heading west towards the beach, at the shore side is the **Museum der Insel** (opening times: May–Oct daily 09.00–16.00), a converted lifeboat station. The main attraction of the museum is a copy of the 10C Hiddensee treasure; the greatest hoard of Viking gold jewellery found in Germany, it was discovered near here in 1872 and 1874. On the ground floor are displays of birdlife and of freshly-picked examples of the wild flowers to be found on the island. The long beach is protected from the worst of the wind by a barrier of stone blocks, with gaps for swimmers (many nude).

Kloster is also home of the **Vogelwarte**, a bird-watching station that is an outpost of the science department at Greifswald University.

Bicycles can be hired in the village (including ones with seats on for small children) to explore the heathlike area of the Dornbusch to the north of the village. Cyclists can take the concrete track leading up to the cliffs of the north of the island and the lighthouse; other paths should be explored on foot because of problems of erosion. **Vitte**, the village in the middle of the island, has a gallery for art exhibitions called the **Blaue Scheune**, a blue-painted former fisherman's house. The most southerly village is **Neuendorf**, an fishing village under conservation order. The sandy tip of the island, the Gellen peninsula, is closed to the public to allow birds to breed.

33

From Stralsund to Greifswald, Eldena and the Island of Usedom

Stralsund—31km Greifswald—3km Eldena—23km Wolgast—34km Ahlbeck.

From Stralsund take the E251 heading 31km south-east—note that on the return journey you may need to circumnavigate this direct road if there are traffic jams to the Rügendamm preventing access to Stralsund.

Greifswald

65,000 inhabitants.

Tourist Information Office: Schuhhagen 22, 17489 Greifswald. Tel. 3460).
Opening times: May–Sept 10.00–18.00, Sat 09.00–12.00, Oct–Apr 09.00–12.00.

Greifswald is well known as an historic university town, former Hanseatic trading port and birthplace of the Romantic artist Caspar David Friedrich.

Approaching the town from Stralsund, you are greeted by the silhouette of three churches: the Marienkirche, Nikolaikirche, and Jakobikirche—Dicke Marie, Lange Nikolaus and Kleine Jakob as they are known locally. Greifswald is a town that has more than doubled in size, if not in population, since 1945. Vast estates of blocks of flats do not, however, impinge on the medieval outline nor the attractive old town, which is centred round the market place with its multi-coloured gabled houses, amongst the finest in Mecklenburg-Pomerania.

History. The early history of Greifswald is linked to that of the nearby Eldena Monastery (see below), which was granted a town charter under Lübeck law in 1250 by Prince Witzlaw I of Rügen on the site of the monastery's market. Greifswald was in a favourable position on the Baltic—the hub of the Hanseatic world. The town quickly grew prosperous through long-distance trade and was an important second-tier member of the Hanseatic League from 1299. It belonged to the group of Baltic seaports known as the *Wendisches Quartier* (Wendish towns) after the Slav tribes who occupied the area before the influx of German settlers.

The pattern of the town layout, by the River Ryck, with its oval-shaped network of streets crossing at right-angles, is typical of 13C colonisation and remains virtually unchanged. The years of Hanseatic prosperity were followed by a period when the University was the most important influence in the town. Much of the medieval aspect of the town was destroyed by the ravages of the Thirty Years War when the town was besieged for more than four years by Wallenstein's troops. In 1648, at the Peace of Westphalia, Greifswald came under Swedish rule which was maintained until 1815. The ensuing decline in both town and university was relieved only when the building of the railway from Berlin to Stralsund in 1863 instigated a period of industrial expansion. The most significant industrial development was the building, from 1968, of the atomic power plant at Lubminer Heide (no longer in use); it was the first in the GDR and the associated electrotechnical industry brought about the greatest expansion of the town. The university also flourished and, at the time of the *Wende*, employed some 5000 staff for 4200 students. The university is now suffering cutbacks and the power plant has been closed down on grounds of safety. Although lucky enough to escape damage in the Second World War, when the town was handed over to the Red Army, Greifswald suffered from the policy in the late 1970s of replacing neglected historic buildings with new, prefabricated ones in the north part of the Altstadt. Much was lost before 1990, when the policy of replacing the Altstadt was changed to one of restoration and reconstruction.

To reach the Markt from the Hauptbahnhof take Bahnhofstrasse and Lange Strasse. The **Rathaus** is an elongated, free standing, two-storey building, with plastered walls and a steep roof. It was originally a brick Gothic building, first mentioned in 1349, but the medieval foundations go back to the founding of the town in 1250. In the 17C the outer appearance was changed and after two fires in 1713 and 1736 the town hall was rebuilt showing Baroque influence in its gables with volutes, the turret (1738), the octagonal lamp with a copper dome, and the weather vane. A bronze bell hung there until the Second World War. The interior has a stuccoed Ratssitzungszimmer (Council Chamber) designed in 1748 by Balthasar

Braun and carpets with mythological scenes dating from 1749. The arcades with their Gothic pointed arches were opened up again in 1936; the ceramic tile map of Greifswald is the work of Ilse Riedel (1959). The main door is decorated with two cast bronze reliefs by Joachim Jastram (1966). The Ratskeller retains its original medieval vaulting.

Next to the Rathaus is the **Ratsapotheke** (Council Apothecary), at first glance reminiscent of a scaled-down Doge's Palace, with its pale stucco exterior. It was, however, rebuilt in 1880 in Gothic Revival style with blind tracery, pinnacles and two oriel windows. The earlier, Renaissance building is recorded in a drawing by Caspar David Friedrich.

The main square, the original Markt, still has a thriving market today. The old square lies at the heart of the first settlement with its rectangular crossing streets. Eight streets lead onto it, with the Rathaus on the west side. None of the three large parish churches is positioned directly on the square; they were each the centre of a small settlement until the three combined into one, a common feature of newly-founded Hanseatic towns. In 1264 the Neustadt, which grew up from 1250 around the Jakobikirche, was united with the Altstadt, near the Markt and the Marienkirche. The square owes its character today to the gabled houses, dating from several periods, that surround it. Some of the best examples in Mecklenburg-Pomerania are to be found here, including **No. 11**. This outstanding example of brick Gothic architecture, built in 1425, in the heyday of the Hanse, was the residence and warehouse of a rich patrician family. The stepped gable overlooking the square is richly decorated, with six storeys composed of alternating light and dark glazed and unglazed brick, and fine tracery. Unfortunately, the general effect is rather spoilt by the 1856 ground floor. The gable on the courtyard side, where the wagons would have entered to load and unload goods, is half-timbered.

A little to the right is the rather more severe No. 13, a late Gothic gable house built about 1450, probably originally with a crenellated gable. Look out also for Nos 25, 26 and 27. No. 25 is a three-floored corner house, its earlier Baroque gable altered to Gothic Revival style in 1861; in 1976 it was converted into 18 flats. The round gable window is the last of the original Baroque features of No. 26. No. 27 is a two-storey house (1594) with a three-floor voluted gable; although the ground floor has been altered the portal retains its simple, late Renaissance shape.

Turn left into BADERSTRASSE to see more gabled houses. The rather shabby No. 2 is the oldest in the town, and is due for restoration. It was built in the 14C, but now has a Baroque gable, and its façade has been changed many times, most recently in 1927. No. 25 Baderstrasse is in a sorry state and is subject to temporary safety measures prior to reconstruction, but is an interesting shape, being built as an arsenal in 1650. It is a long, two-storey plastered brick building with two further attic floors under the pitched roof and a Baroque curved gable. Munitions were hauled to the storage floors by means of the protruding pulley. The gate to the left of the entrance, with its curved frame, allowed ready access from the street.

Heading east towards the cathedral church of St Nikolai, go down Dom-strasse, noting the classical façade of No. 29, built in 1802, and the late Baroque No. 24, finished in 1760, with its richly carved front door and fanlight showing the initials of the master joiner who owned it.

The oldest part of Greifswald is the area around the **Dom St Nikolai**. The Dom rose on the site of an earlier hall church (first mentioned in 1280), and was constructed between 1350 and 1375 as a triple-aisled brick basilica.

Externally its appearance has altered little. It has two significant features: the tower of Lange Nikolaus, much-loved landmark of Greifswald, and the Gothic Revival interior. The splendid, solid west tower combines elements from many periods. From the c 1300 square base rises a fortress-like middle storey with four watchtowers dating from 1350. Above that is a high Gothic octagon c 1400, with particularly rich blind tracery and a viewing platform at the top. This is capped by a delightful four-layered Baroque dome, then a soaring spire and weather vane, built in 1740 to replace a series of collapsed spires. The tower rises to 99.9m and is the centrepoint of Caspar David Friedrich's painting *Greifswald from the Meadows* (c 1820, Hamburg Kunsthalle). The exterior of the church was restored in 1978–81, and the interior owes its attractive light appearance to ongoing redecoration work begun in 1982.

The choir, altar, organ and pulpit, designed by Gottlieb Giese, were introduced during work on the church in 1824–33. A wave of enthusiasm for alterations to north German churches began after the Peace of Westphalia. Fortunately it was confined mainly to the interiors, and the exteriors mainly remained unchanged. During the French occupation (1806–10 and 1812–13) Napoleon's troops had used churches as hospitals, stores, stables, workshops and prisons, after which the buildings were in severe need of restoration. The recently restored Gothic frescoes, dating from 1420–50, in the south aisle were discovered during work in 1977. An interesting group picture shows Hans Rubenow and the six friends who helped him found the university, with the Virgin Mary in the background.

Leaving the Dom, continue along the Domstrasse, turning down the Rubenowstrasse to see the **Universitätsbibliotek**. The library was built between 1879 and 1881 and designed by Berlin architect Martin Gropius in typically ornate historicist style. It was enlarged in 1892 with the addition of another four windows. Further along the Domstrasse is the long, two-storey building of the **Ernst-Moritz-Arndt-Universität**. This building, on the site of the old university, was built between 1747 and 1750 and designed by the mathematics professor Andreas Mayer. The exterior was changed to Neo-Classical style in 1832, and few Baroque elements remain. Above the central gable are two figures holding the arms of the Swedish king and the Dukes of Pomerania. The interior has frequently been altered, but the stately **Aula** (Great Hall), used as part of the library until 1888, remains as one of the few late Baroque interiors on the Baltic coast. It extends through the two upper storeys of the central building; 12 wooden pairs of Ionic columns support a surrounding gallery and the balustrade is topped with putti and vases. Between the columns as 12 small free-standing wooden hermae of Apollo, Mercury, Minerva and the Muses. There is a fine Baroque painted ceiling.

The university is the second oldest in northern Europe; it received its charter in 1456 but had come into being rather earlier. The University of Rostock was founded in 1419, but under a papal inderdict was closed temporarily in 1432 because of internal disputes. Staff and students moved to Greifswald, and when the conflict was resolved six lecturers remained—it is these men who feature in the group picture in the Nikolaikirche (see above). The Council of Greifswald, at the peak of prosperous Hanseatic days and bursting with civic pride, seized the opportunity to found its own university.

During the university's 400th anniversary celebrations in 1856 the **Rubenowdenkmal** (Rubenow Memorial) was dedicated to the wealthy and dynamic Heinrich Rubenow, first rector of the university. His portrait in relief is in the middle of the 12m high Neo-Gothic column of bronzed zinc. In the niches are four of the dukes linked with the university, and on the corners are important representatives of the four classical faculties, including the professor of philosophy, Ernst Moritz Arndt (the opponent of serfdom and poet of the Wars of Liberation) after whom the university is named.

Just beyond the University is the **Jakobikirche**, the smallest of the three parish churches, a Gothic brick hall church with nave and two aisles, begun in the second half of 13C and altered around 1400, with a small square tower and pyramidal roof.

Turning back you can take the path through the gardens, past the Rubenowdenkmal and arrive at the back of the recently renewed **Hospital St Spiritus**, if the alley that leads through to Langestrasse is open. The Hospital was first mentioned as an old people's home in 1292, and now consists of a courtyard of half-timbered, single-storey houses, built in the second half of the 18C as almshouses. Today the complex is used for temporary exhibitions and has a café.

Turning right, return to the Markt. Continue straight along this street through the square and take the first left after leaving the square into Brüggstrasse. After some pretty vine-clad houses on the right you will see the solid mass of the Marienkirche.

If time permits the tour may be continued by turning left up Steinbeckerstrasse, past No. 31, a recently restored 1550s Renaissance brick gable house. To reach Brüggstrasse after Steinbeckerstrasse turn right into Friedrich-Loeffler-Strasse and take the third left. Immediately on your left you will see modern terraces described as an **Altstadt-Umstaltung** (Old Town Transformation) where, to quote the official guide of the GDR period: 'The historic town centre has been undergoing a programme of reconstruction to replace dilapidated buildings with modern constructions'. Continue along this street turning right at the top and right again to come to Brüggstrasse. No. 5 has been beautifully restored in its original style. Built c 1535 as a merchant's house for a councillor and his family, it has been reconstructed to include the original galleried hall as well as the decoratively gabled street façade. Continue along the street until you arrive at the Marienkirche.

The *Marienkirche is an outstanding example of a hall church. As in all hall churches, the nave and aisles are the same height, so the church is lit by windows in the aisles, making the aisles play a more central and integrated role in the church. Here the sense of spatial unity is still more dramatically emphasised by the lack of a chancel, and the interior plan is almost a square hall. This means there is no clear sense of direction, which results in a feeling of unity as there are no dividing barriers between priest and people and the church becomes one vast room. It is significant that the Marienkirche was Greifswald's first church, begun between 1250 and 1270 shortly after the town was founded, and was regarded as the church of the burghers. It took a hundred years to complete, the base of the tower being the first part to be finished. The west tower is short and stocky although four-storeyed. Its small roof with four turret towers was added in 1780 to replace a steeple destroyed in 1678. The simple shape reinforces the impact of the impressive but austere east gable (1360), the last part of the building to be completed. The gable is best viewed from near the university Mensa (Canteen) or across the River Ryk.

The interior is light and a powerful sense of space strikes you as you enter the nave, with its Gothic vaulting rising to 21m at its apex. The transition from early Gothic to High Gothic as the building work progressed can be seen by noting the changing shapes of the columns as you move from west to east. The small vaulted Annenkappelle was added to the south side of the church in 1321, and the long vestibule at the west entrance in 1450. A monument to Heinrich Rubenow records his murder in 1462; the 1587 pulpit by Joachim Meklenborg [sic] has intarsia figures and carved pillars. Above the altar hangs a 19C copy of Correggio's *Holy Night*. The 15C frescoes in the south chapel and the vestibule were discovered during restoration work. They were the clue that led to reinstating the church's original colour scheme during restoration between 1980 and 1984.

To visit the **Museum** walk left down Brüggstrasse to the end, turn right into Mühlenstrasse, then left into Theodor-Pyle-Strasse, and on round to No. 1, the Guardianhaus, a three-storey brick Gothic building. Originally the Prior's House, it is now the sole remnant of the Franciscan monastery. It was presented to the town on the dissolution of the monastery and since 1929 has been home to the museum. During restoration in 1978–81 the medieval clay figures, now seen on the stairwell, came to light. The museum has a fascinating second-floor exhibition based on the life of Caspar David Friedrich and Greifswald's artists of his time. The highlights are Friedrich's oil painting *Ruine im Riesengebirge* (Ruins in the Riesen Mountains) (1830–1835 and his watercolour of *Markt von Greifswald mit der Familie Friedrich* (The Market Place in Greifswald with the Friedrich Family), painted in 1818 when he returned to his hometown during his honeymoon. The ground floor is devoted to town history. Particularly interesting is the section on the nearby Eldena Monastery; on the walls are copies of Gaspar David Friedrich's famous sketches of the monastery ruins that so fired the German imagination. There is also a model of the monastery as it was in 1500. Finally, as you look at the street system on the 1-1000 scale model of 17C Greifswald, you realise how little the town has changed.

Eldena and Wieck

Eldena and Wieck, on the eastern outskirts of Griefswald, can be reached in a few minutes by car along the road towards Wolgast or by walking along the river bank. **Eldena** was the site of the former Cistercian monastery of St Hilda, which was instrumental in founding the town of Greifswald. The ruins feature in Caspar David Friedrich's paintings and sketches. In the early 19C, with the burgeoning of nationalism, Germans began to look to the past and under the influence of the Romantic movement began to appreciate the beauty of ruins. The ruins of Eldena were to become a *leitmotiv* for the German nation through Friedrich's work. They were often transposed into more dramatic landscapes, such as that in *Ruine im Riesengebirge* in the Greifswald Museum.

History. At the end of the 12C, monks from the Danish abbey at Estrom on Seeland, lured by a salt pan on the coast near Eldena and by the gift of land and revenue from Prince Jaromar I of Rügen, founded a monastery here in 1199. Salt was a precious commodity in medieval times and the only salt mines in east Germany were far away at Lüneberg, while the Baltic's low salinity made salt difficult to extract from the sea. However, Eldena was fortunate in its site on the edge of the Greifswalder Bodden.

Bodden is a Baltic term for a bay or inlet of the sea, where the water is very shallow, and the concentration of salt therefore much stronger.

Eldena was a powerful, prosperous and thriving abbey until its dissolution in 1535, when it became the property of the Dukes of Pomerania. In 1634 when the line died out, the abbey and its rich endowment of lands were given to the University of Greifswald. Sadly, it was plundered by Swedish troops in 1637 during the Thirty Years War, and then was used by them as a quarry, taking the bricks to build a bulwark at Ryck and reinforce the defences of Greifswald. Because of this the west and south wing of the monastery and a large part of the church were destroyed; only the east wing was spared as the estate manager used it as a barn and granary, but it then burnt down after being struck by lightning.

In 1827, thanks to Caspar David Friedrich's intense interest, the plight of the ruins was recognised, and at the instigation of the Crown Prince Friedrich Wilhelm, they became a national monument. In 1828 restoration began and the greatest landscape gardener of the time, Peter Joseph Lenné, planned the grounds. In 1968 the east wall was made safe and an open-air stage erected. Eldena jazz evenings have been popular for the last 10 years. Of the ruins that remain, the west wall with its mighty pointed arch window is the most impressive reminder of the early Gothic monastery church started in 1225.

Eldena is linked to **Wieck** by crossing the River Ryck via an extraordinary wooden **Klappbrücke** (swing bridge), built in 1886–87 following a Dutch pattern. It is the only one of its kind in Germany and is still used. Wieck is a picturesque, small fishing village, with cobbled streets and 18C and 19C thatched fishermen's cottages. Most of these are individually listed as historic buildings and the whole village is a conservation area.

If you have time to relax on the beaches of the **Island of Usedom**, drive north from Eldena through Wusterhusen 15km via the pleasant market town of **Wolgast** (16,000 inhabitants). In the Middle Ages Wolgast was a minor member of Hanse thanks to its sheltered harbour and easy access to the River Oder. The 14C Petrikirche, a brick Gothic hall church, is known for its Totentanzgemälde (cycle of the Dance of Death), painted in 1700 by C.S. Köppe after wood-carvings by Hans Holbein.

Continue north, crossing the Peene Strome on to the Island of Usedom, Germany's second largest island. It is 42km long, with approximately 12km of the south-east point belonging to Poland. The east coast of the island has long, sandy beaches that are crowded in the summer, and accommodation is hard to find. **Ahlbeck** is the largest and the most easterly of the chain of small resorts that line the coast and have been popular with holidaymakers since the mid 19C. Many of the turn-of-the-century buildings and promenades remain, in leafy beech wood settings, and the fine sand remains a constant attraction.

34

From Schwerin to Neustadt Glewe

From Schwerin—37km Ludwigslust—6km Grabow—10km Neustadt Glewe.

Schloss Ludwigslust makes a perfect half-day's outing from Schwerin. Follow the B106, 37km S from Schwerin to Ludwigslust. At Ludwigslust turn right towards the town centre and continue round the one-way system, following signs for Schloss Ludwigslust. There is ample (pay and display) parking directly in front of the house. At the far corner of the parking area is the Tourist Information Office.

Tourist Information: Schlossfreiheit 8, 19288. Ludwigslust. Tel. (03874) 28114.

Schloss Ludwigslust belongs to Schwerin City Museums (opening times: by guided tour only, Tue–Fri 09.00–17.00, Sat–Sun 10.00–17.00, last admission 16.30 (tel. 0852-28114/2 to organise an English-speaking guided tour). Schloss Ludwigslust is a Neo-Classical mansion set in a spacious park in the tradition of the English stately home. Originally built as a hunting lodge by Duke Christian Ludwig in 1742, his ambition to extend it to a Schloss was not realised until the reign of his son Duke Friedrich der Fromme. Friedrich moved the official residence of the Dukes of Mecklenburg from Schwerin to Ludwigdslust in 1764 and commissioned Johann Busch to build a relatively small but splendid late Baroque mansion (1772–76). The focus is on the prominent Baroque central section, where four Corinthian fluted pilasters are linked by stucco swags to the windows above and crowned by an elaborate coat of arms. This is flanked by two simpler wings with clean Neo-Classical lines—the east wing was the residence of the Duke, the west that of the Duchess. Forty larger-than-life-sized statues by Rudolf Kaplunger line the parapet: the figures represent allegories of the arts, sciences and virtues, reflecting Friedrich's interests. The walls of the building are clad with sandstone from Saxony.

In 1837 Duke Paul Friedrich moved the court back to Schwerin where he began to rebuild Schloss Schwerin, and Ludwigslust became marginalised. After the abdication of the ducal family following the November Revolution of 1918, Friedrich Franz IV and his family lived at Ludwigslust until 1945, when they fled from the Russians with the Allied Forces to Glucksburg on the Danish border to live. Christian Ludwig, the last of the line, returns here from time to time. After the Second World War, the Schloss was put to various uses, including the playing of badminton in the Goldener Saal, and almost all the interior furnishings were lost. The **Goldener Saal**, however, emerged surprisingly unscathed. Most of the rooms are unfurnished and rather forlorn, so this glorious room comes as a delightful surprise. The chamber is double height; the giant gilt Corinthian pilasters and much of the rest of the elaborate gilt-work are made of papier mâché. Although used initially for economy, this material has lasted better than others. It was produced locally to a secret formula that has never been de-coded. During the summer months concerts are held in the Goldener Saal.

Schloss Ludwigslust, the church and the town were conceived as a unified plan. The SCHLOSSSTRASSE, with its cobbled road and avenue of lime trees was built to house court officials. Two rows of charming two-storey red brick houses, with Dutch architectural details, lead west to the large Schloss square. The main north–south axis of the design at right angles to the Schlossstrasse has the Schloss at its centre. At the southern end of this axis is the Schlosskirche. **The Schlosskirche** (1765–70) was designed by Busch to resemble an antique temple. Above a classical Doric pillared portico is a pediment with a Latin inscription, and, on top, the large Greek letters X and R, a Christogram—the sign for Christ—to take the place of a steeple. Four figures of the Evangelists by Johann Eckstein stand guard.

Before setting off round the park, find time to visit the Schlosscafé (open 11.00–18.00; closed Tue), behind the Schloss, where you can sit in a huge antler-hung room, or outside on the terrace. The café also hires bikes, which is a good way of exploring the park, but you would be well advised to take a map of the paths which is on sale at the ticket office in the Schloss. In the mid 19C Peter Lenné transformed the Baroque palace gardens into an English style park, with groves of trees, winding streams, avenues and fountains. The canal with the Vierundzwanzig Brunnen (Twenty-Four Fountains) was restored in 1963. A good walk to the north-east corner of the park will bring you to the Schweizerhaus, a Swiss chalet built as a folly in 1789, where you may find refreshment.

If you have time to venture a little further continue south another 6km on the B5 (the continuation of the B106) to Grabow. **Grabow** is a bright, pleasant little town with a wealth of 18C half-timbered houses surrounding the market square, the Markt. In the 18C Grabow prospered by supplying the craftsmen for the nearby court, as up to 1800 they were not allowed to display their wares in Ludwigslust. From the mid 19C it was one of the first industrial centres of Mecklenburg. The serene, two-storey black-and-white **Rathaus** of 1726–27 has a Baroque clock tower. A cheerful crescent Man in the Moon, decorated with stars looks down from the pediment above the main door. Two flights of steps with wrought iron banisters lead up to the entrance. The church of St Georg is a brick Gothic hall church (14C) with an early Gothic choir, but the west tower dates from 1907. The small **Heimatmuseum**, Am Markt 2 just off market place has displays of local history (opening times: school holidays 09.00–11.00 Mon–Fri, otherwise Tues and Fri 09.00–11.00, Weds and Sun 14.00–16.00; closed Mon, Thurs, Sat). The most interesting are those on craftwork from the 17–20C, in particular the flax processing. It was dyeing flax that gave Grabow its reputation for being a 'colourful' town. The museum's most prized possession is the correspondence between a local doctor and Thomas Mann, whose ancestors came from Grabow.

From Grabow, return north towards Ludwigslust, by-pass the town and head 10km north-east, along the B191, about 10km to **Neustadt-Glewe**, for a stroll along the riverbank to see the medieval ruins of the 14C castle. The fortress overlooks the River Elde, and a walk on the grassy path around the walls shows the intricate brickwork. It was founded in 1250 by the Counts of Schwerin, and the main part of the present buildings is late medieval, on an almost square groundplan with a crenellated defence wall and parapet The top storey of the round keep is 16C. On the east side of the surrounding wall is the Neues Haus. During the 16C and 17C this was the ducal residence but it has been much altered over the years. On the west side of the site is the Altes Haus, with a 16C kernel, now a youth hostel and due for renovation.

Finish with a look at the faded glory of the **Neues Schloss**, a two-storey three-winged building, which was begun in 1619 in Dutch Renaissance style, by Ghert Evert Piloot, but interrupted by the Thirty Years War. Building resumed between 1711–17 in Neo-Classical style, by Leonhard Sturm. At the time of writing the exterior of the Schloss was in very bad condition, although inside there is good stucco work (1715) by the Italians Andrea Maiani and Giuseppe Mogia.

Now drive east about 2km to the E26, and head back north to Schwerin, either staying on the motorway and joining the A241, or taking the almost parallel B106, depending on which side of Schwerin you are aiming for.

35

Magdeburg

289,000 inhabitants.

Tourist Information: Alter Markt 9, 39104 Magdeburg. Tel. 35352. Opening times: Mon–Fri 10.00–18.00, Sat 10.00–12.00.

MAGDEBURG is the capital of the newly created Land of Sachsen-Anhalt. Situated in the centre of the state on the left bank of the Elbe it provides an ideal base for tours to the rest of the district, including the Harz mountains to the south. The city centre has a bustling, western European feel and is an important commercial centre. The city's restaurants and hotels are of a higher standard than normally found in eastern Germany and the medieval ambience of the great Cathedral and monastery have been preserved.

History. Founded as a trading settlement in the 9C and first mentioned in 805, Magdeburg's early prosperity was due to Emperor Otto the Great who founded a Benedictine monastery here in the 937 with an archbishop's see established in 968. Magdeburg became an important centre for the spread of Christianity eastward during the 10C and 11C. Magdeburg flourished as a commercial centre during the 13C to 15C, operating as a powerful member of the Hanseatic League. The Reformation was eagerly welcomed in 1524 and the clergy driven out to Halle. Like many towns in eastern Germany, Magdeburg suffered greatly during the Thirty Years War and was almost destroyed; only the Cathedral and Liebfrauenkloster escaped. The town soon recovered after the Peace of Westphalia with the erection of a splendid Baroque centre, destroyed by bombing in 1945. Magdeburg underwent rapid industrialisation in the 19C, establishing itself as an important rail intersection with the large Gurson Ironworks established in the Buckau suburbs to the south of the city centre in 1855. The factory was then bought by the powerful Essen based Krupp company in 1893. During GDR rule Magdeburg continued to be an important centre for heavy industry and the administrative capital of the Magdeburg district. In 1990 Magdeburg became the capital of the Sachsen-Anhalt Land, beating nearby Halle for the privilege. The region is made up of land forfeited by Saxony for supporting Napoleon in 1815 and the Anhalt from a duchy established by the Margraves of Brandenburg. The city is now attracting some major foreign investment and boasts not only a Macdonalds but also a C&A department store.

From the bustling 19C Hauptbahnhof cross the busy Bahnhofstrasse heading east towards the former Interhotel, now owned by Maritim Hotels. Continue south down the pleasant Otto Von Guericke Strasse to reach the **Kulturhistorisches Museum** at Nos 68–73 (opening times: Tues–Sun 10.00–18.00). Housed in an imperious, Neo-Renaissance building this was formerly the Kaiser Friedrich Museum, renamed after the war. The purpose-built Museum was designed by the Austrian architect, F. Ohmann in 1906 and boasts some interesting scientific, natural history, and design exhibits. The vestibule is dominated by the original version of the **Magdeburg Rider**. This fine Gothic sculpture is one of the earliest, post-Classical secular equestrian portraits in existence. The handsome, mounted rider is probably a portait of Emperor Otto the Great, created in 1240 in the cathedral workshops. On either side of the horse stands a female figure in

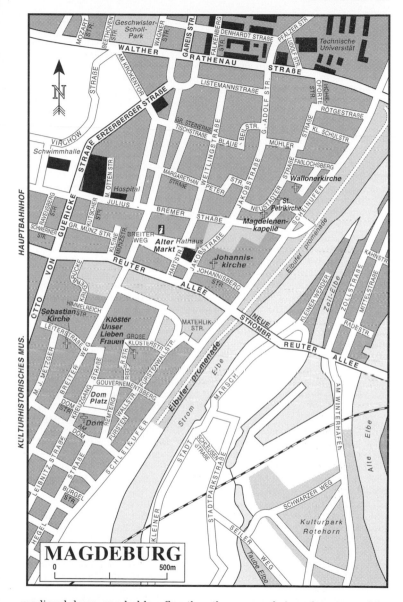

MAGDEBURG

0 ———————— 500m

medieval dress, one holds a flag the other a sword. A modern copy of the sculpture stands on top of a pillar in front of the Rathaus in the Alter Markt. On the ground floor is a display devoted to Otto von Guericke, the town's mayor during the mid 17C who also conducted the first demonstration of the vacuum in 1654 with the Magdeburg Spheres, demonstrated here with various interactive exhibits. There is a vast natural history display in the museum which includes a charming skeleton, many fossils and a moth-eaten stuffed wolf. On the landing leading to the first floor there are a series of 19C views of the Cathedral by Carl Hasenpfug. The first floor is occupied by a series of historic room settings from Baroque through to Jugendstil, complete with rare Otto Eckmann tapestry from 1897. There is also a cursory history of the computer which is, it has to be said, slightly dreary. The museum had an impressive collection of art before the war, which is now rather depleted.

It is a short walk from the museum to the *Dom St Mauritius und St Katharina east down Danz Strasse (opening times: daily 10.00–12.00 and 14.00–16.00). The great cathedral was built from 1208 onwards following the destruction by fire of the Benedictine Church of Otto the Great. Building work began in Romanesque style of the choir and nave. After 1230 the upper part of the choir was completed in early Gothic style and the aisles widened to make a Gothic basilica. From 1274 the transepts and nave were completed in purist High Gothic and the northern porch added in the mid 14C. The west towers, whose octagonal turrets crowned with spires are such a distinctive feature of the town's skyline, were added in 1520. This is the largest and most impressive cathedral in eastern Germany. Relatively unscathed by war it stands magnificently on the banks of the River Elbe, dominating the Domplatz behind.

Noted for its richness of sculpture both inside and out, look first at the Gothic PARADISE PORTAL on the north side. The porch was added in 1350 but the fine statues of the ten wise and foolish virgins date from 100 years earlier. The full-size statues fit rather clumsily between the canopy and base, indicating that they were not created for this site. The figures were originally polychromatic, but this has disappeared over the years.

The building is equally impressive inside, with excellent examples of sculpture through the ages. The sheer scale of the NAVE, 34m in height with soaring pillars and crossed ribbed vaulting is quite overwhelming. Proceed east through the late Gothic screen (1445) and into the CHOIR. The tomb of Otto the Great is situated in the middle of the choir and marked by a modest marble slab. The 12 marble columns which stand between the pointed Gothic arches in the choir originate from Otto the Great's earlier cathedral. They support painted figures of saints, skilfully crafted by the Magdeburg workshop in the mid 13C. The same workshop produced the splendid statue of St George, situated on the south side of the choir and a rare representation of a black figure from medieval times. Also note the richly carved, 14C stalls in the choir.

The chapels in the ambulatory have beautifully carved, capitals decorated with all manner of birds, beasts, foliage and human figures. Of special note are the two 12C bronze tombstones, commemorating a pair of archbishops and brought here from the original cathedral. An elaborate tomb for Otto the Great's English wife, Empress Edith, stands in the centre, erected belatedly c 1500. Also look out for the 13C sculpture of a crowned couple, thought to be Otto the Great and Editha, situated in the 16-sided chapel. There are more monuments dating from c 1600 in the nave and a splendid tomb dedicated to Archbishop Ernst of Saxony in the MEMORIAL CHAPEL between the two western towers. This was cast in bronze by Peter Vischer the Elder of Nuremberg in 1495 and is a masterpiece of Gothic craftsmanship. Clad in official dress and holding a cross and crozier, the bishop rests on a carved stone base, surrounded by statues of the 12 apostles with St Maurice at his head. More recent sculpture is situated in the north transept. A work by Expressionist artist, Ernst Barlach commemorates the victims of the First World War in carved wood (1929).

Cross the Domplatz to the smart Domcafé on the corner of Breiter Weg and Danzstrasse to the left, which offers quality refreshments and a good view of the west façade of the cathedral. Head north up Regierstrasse to reach the second medieval gem in Magdeburg, the *Kloster Unser Lieben Frauen (opening times: Tues–Sun 10.00–18.00). Badly damaged during the Second World War, the Romanesque monastery and church have been restored to create a museum, and cultural centre with café. Founded c 1070 as a cruciform basilica, the church was altered to Gothic style in 1230 and has acted as Magdeburg's main concert hall since 1977. The stone-built exterior is graced by two small, round towers at the west end whilst the interior has been heavily restored. The Romanesque cloisters are more impressive and house a national collection of Kleinplastik (small sculpture) in the Tonnergewölbe. The display includes early ecclesiastical work and more recent examples by Rodin and Barlach, set against the stark white walls and rounded arches of the cloisters.

En route to the Alter Markt it is possible to view the **Sebastiankirche** by heading back to the Domplatz, north up Kreuzgang Strasse and west across Breiter Weg. Founded in 1015 as a monastery church, the Sebastiankirche later underwent alterations in Gothic style including the interior of the hall church; the twin Baroque towers were added in 1631. Since 1949 the church has acted as the seat of the local Catholic bishop. Continue north up **Breiter Weg**, Magdeburg's principal commercial street since the turn of the century, linking the Dom with the Alter Markt. Once lined with 18C, gabled houses the street was badly damaged during the war. The splendid Hauptpostamt (Main Post Office) at Breiter Weg 203 beside Sebastiankirche is in German Renaissance Revival style and was fully restored during 1974–88.

Continue north to Nos 178–9, a magnificently restored Baroque mansion dating from 1728. Cross the busy Ernst Reuter Allee and, just past the Macdonald's fast food restaurant on the right is the Alter Markt, historic centre of Magdeburg. The Tourist Information Office is on the left, decorated with the remnants of the Baroque buildings which stood here before the war. The only building to have been restored is the **Rathaus** to the east of the square. A bronze copy of the Magdeburg Rider, made in 1966, stands on top of a pillar under the original, Baroque canopy making close inspection difficult. The Rathaus was built in confident, Baroque style in 1689–91 by H. Schmutze and enlarged in 1865. The carillon on the roof contains 48 bells. The Ratskeller behind dates from 1230–40. To the south of the square is the **Weinkeller Buttergasse** (Butter Alley Wine Cellar) which was discovered only in 1947. The 13C cellar, thought to be a meeting place for the tanners' guild, has been fully restored to create an atmospheric restaurant.

Continue north from the Rathaus to see the bronze statue of Otto von Guericke, erected in 1907 and, behind it, a bronze statue of 18C surgeon Andreas Eisenbart, erected in 1939. Beyond this stands the Neo-Baroque Magistrate's offices. Return to the Rathaus and continue east past a pleasant garden towards the river and Jakobstrasse. The burnt out **Johanniskirche** stands opposite: only the south tower and façade are still standing, and the remainder is in ruins. This late-Gothic hall church was left as a memorial to the destruction of war by the GDR authorities but is now being restored. A new door was added in 1982 with a serpent springing from it clumsily representing the evil of war. Two life-size figures stand either side, representing one woman collecting rubble and another protecting a child. Hopefully these less than appropriate 'improvements' will be dispensed with as part of the restoration. It is possible to climb the south tower for views of Magdeburg (opening times: Wed–Fri 13.00–17.00, Sat and Sun 10.00–17.00).

Head north up Jakobstrasse and then right into Neustädter Strasse. This brings you to the 14C **Magdalenenkapelle** (Magdalene Chapel) on the right, built as part of the Maria-Magdalenen-Klosters which were badly damaged both in 1631 and 1945. A little further north is the **Petrikirche**, also on the right. A stone Gothic hall church dating from 1380 with an earlier, Romanesque west tower, this has been a Catholic church since 1972. Further north is the **Wallonerkirche**: begun in 1285 as part of the Augustine Monastery and completed in 1366 it follows the hall church blueprint. Further north up Scheinufer behind the churches is the **Lukasturm**, part of the city's virtually impenetrable fortifications (opening times: Tues–Sun 10.00–18.00). Built from brick in the 15C it now houses a café and various temporary exhibitions of contemporary art.

Continue south down the Elbufer Promenade which skirts the banks of the River Elbe past the mooring point for boats which traverse the river during the summer months. If you follow the entire course of the Promenade, some 2.5km, you will reach the back of the Cathedral and the **Fürstenwall**, with two more remnants of the town fortifications: the Wehrturm and the Kiek in de Koken which may be admired to advantage from the opposite side of the river, near the ***Kulturpark Rotehorn**. To reach this eastern side of the city head north up Uferschlein then cross the Storm Elbe, the western branch of the Elbe which splits at the Grosser Werder island, by means of the Neue Strombrücke. Continue south down Kleiner Stadtmarsch to enjoy fine views of the Cathedral choir and the two towers. The park was laid out in 1871 with major additions in the 1920s. Just past the modern Hyparschale is the **Pferdetor** (Horse Gate), a series of six modern columns topped by rearing horses. This was designed by Albinmüller from Darmstadt (an important centre for early 20C German design), as an entrance to the exhibition park. Before continuing note the **Hubbrücke** to the right, a railway bridge over the river built in the 1840s with a turntable device to allow ships to pass either side. Through the Pferdetor is the **Stadthalle**, built as a theatre in 1926–27 in early modern style to designs by J. Göderitz. Further south is the 60m high **Aussichtsturm** (watchtower) in similar modern style which can be ascended by lift for panoramic views of Magdeburg (opening times: Tues–Sun 10.00–18.00) from the lofty café. To the east of the tower is a boating lake and to the west the *SS Württemberg*, an early 20C paddle-steamer with restaurant (opening times: Wed–Sun 10.00–19.00).

36

The Harz Mountains

From Magdeburg—46km Halberstadt—25km Wernigerode—29km Quedlinburg—63km Magdeburg.

The Harz Mountain range, the northernmost in Germany, was split in
two by an electrified barbed-wire fence after the Second World War,
with the most scenic and historic parts falling in the GDR. It stretches
from Halberstadt in the north to Stolberg in the south and rises
dramatically from the flat, agricultural planes of Saxony-Anhalt. A
popular tourist attraction during Communist times, the region is now
visited by smart western Germans, eager to absorb the medieval
atmosphere of preserved towns such as Quedlinburg which no longer
exist in the western part of the country.

From Magdeburg take the A81 south, being careful to follow the road
west when it branches off near Egen, to arrive after 46km in Halberstadt. Parking may be found near the cathedral. Trains run fairly
frequently from Magdeburg to Halberstadt with a journey time of just
over one hour. The train station is situated in the eastern part of the
town, and the Domplatz may be reached by tram No. 1 or 2.

A. Halberstadt

47,000 inhabitants.

Tourist Information: Düsterngraben 3, Halberstadt 38820 (tel. 3941 550). Opening times: Mon–Fri 09.00–13.00 and 14.00–18.00, Sat 10.00–13.00.

History. The town was first mentioned in documents in 780 and became a see in 989
under Charlemagne, receiving its town charter in 1100. During the 14C Halberstadt
grew as a trading centre, based mainly on textiles, and was a member of the Hanseatic
League. The town was a popular tourist destination even during the 1930s, when
visitors came to marvel at the rich stock of over 700 half-timbered houses from the 15C
to 18C. Few of these now remain, following an Anglo-American air raid in 1945, but
efforts are being made to restore the town with German state aid. The Dom was
virtually rebuilt after the War and the slender twin towers, which characterise the
skyline of Halberstadt, restored to their former glory.

The major attraction in **Halberstadt** is the Cathedral, with small museums
and the Romanesque Liebfrauenkirche situated in and around the Domplatz. Begin at the ***DOM ST STEPHANUS**, situated to the east of the
Domplatz. The magnificent, Gothic basilica was built during the 13C to 15C
on the site of a Romanesque church, dating from 1071, but heavily restored
during 1850–70. The two west towers were reconstructed in 1893–96. The
Dom is a rare example of French Gothic on German soil. The construction
of the west façade began in 1195 followed by the west part of the nave
which was completed in 1276 by stone masons also working on the Magdeburg Dom. The choir was completed in the 14C and the remainder of the

nave and the transepts in the 15C. The slender columns of the nave carry interesting carved figures—look out for two on the last columns of the transept. One represents St George and the Dragon, and the other St Jerome with a Lion. The most important work in the Dom is the **crucifixion group** in carved wood above the rood screen. Dating from c 1220. it was transferred here from the earlier cathedral. Mary and John the Baptist stand on either side of the cross, flanked by one angel on either side. The crossed, angular wings of the angels are quite incredible. Angels decorate the cross itself, to the left, right and at the top. Below is Adam, with his eyes and hands pointed upwards whilst the beam supporting the crucifix is beautifully carved and decorated. The entire group is lit from behind by the east windows. The choir contains richly carved stalls and the stained-glass is also of note, particularly that in the Marienkapelle dating from the early 14C.

Many of the Dom's treasures are on display in the ***Domschatz** (Cathedral Treasury) housed in the cloisters (opening times: by guided tour starting at the west portal, May–Oct, Mon–Fri at 10.00, 11.30, 14.00 and 15.30, Sat at 10.00 and 14.00, Sun at 11.30 and 14.30; Nov–April, Mon–Sat at 10.00 and 14.00, Sun at 11.30). Of special interest in this dazzling collection are the three tapestries dating from c 1150–70, some of the earliest examples in existence. They illustrate the Old Testament story of Abraham receiving the angels, the Apostles with scenes from the New Testament, and Charlemagne surrounded by Classical philosophers including Cato and Seneca, in simple, Romanesque style. They originally hung in the choir of the Dom, but were moved here for safekeeping. There are ecclesiastical sculptures from a slightly later period including the Halberstädter Sitzmadonna (Sitting Madonna), an early Gothic, serene Mary created c 1250. Also of note is the painted, Romanesque cupboard from 1235. Other treasures include silver gilt plates and early embroidery.

At the western end of the square is the **Liebfrauenkirche**, begun in Romanesque style in the 1005–20 and completed in the 12C following the model of the church at Hirsau in Wurtemburg (opening times: winter, daily 12.00–14.00 and daily 11.00–16.00 in the summer season). This erstwhile Augustinian monastery was built as a basilica with the later addition of two western towers in the 14C. Inside the most striking feature is the huge cross, the Triumphkreuz, hung from the roof. Carved in the early 13C this is another excellent example of late Romanesque German sculpture. Also of note is the choir screen, dating from 1200, which is decorated with rare painted, stucco reliefs of the Apostles, Jesus and Mary framed by an intricate band above and below. The cloisters in front of the church now house a small museum, the **Fachwerkarchitektur**, specialising in architectural antiques (opening times: Mon–Fri 09.00–16.00). The various fragments of bombed-out buildings have been preserved in the open passageways including complete door frames and capitals. Continue north to the Petershof: once the bishop's palace, and emblazoned with a magnificent Renaissance portal dating from the 16C, it now houses the town's archives.

Return to the Domplatz and the **Dompropstei** on the southern edge of the square with arcaded ground floor and half-timbered upper storey. This was built in 1592–1611 as a stately residence for Bishop Heinrich Julius von Braunschweig. Further round the Domplatz to the east, behind the Dom is the half-timbered **Gleimhaus** (opening times: Wed–Mon 09.00–12.00 and 13.00 16.00, Sun 09.00 12.00). This was the 18C home of writer and secretary to the Dom, Johann Wilhelm Ludwig Gleim (1719–1803). His remarkable collection of 150 portraits, the Freundschaftstempel (Temple of Friendship) is on display in the Museum, and includes portraits of such contemporary notables as Herder, Winckelmann and Lessing. Adjacent to the Gleimhaus is the Baroque Domdechanei, which now houses a medical school, and beside this the **Städtisches Museum**, recognisable by its fine Baroque façade, devoted to local history (opening times: Tues–Fri 09.00–17.00, Sat and Sun 10.00–17.00). Built in 1782 as the Domkurie, the museum was founded in 1905 and houses displays of furniture, including some interesting 17C examples, work by local painter Walter Gemm and more fine early German sculpture. The **Museum Heineanum** stands in the garden of the main museum and concentrates on natural history and ornithology in particular with a vast collection of stuffed birds from the region and further afield (opening times: Nov–April, Tues–Fri 09.00–14.00, Sat and Sun 10.00–16.00; May–Oct, Tues–Fri 0.00–17.00, Sat and Sun 10.00–16.00). The museum was founded on the 19C collection of Ferdinand Heine which comprises 16,000 stuffed birds and 5000 eggs.

If you want to escape the domination of the Dom and study the Halberstadt's past from a different perspective, take a walk north from the Domplatz to the Unterstadt (lower town). A labyrinth of run-down, timber framed 19C houses, this area looks like Dickens's London. The Unterstadt is now undergoing extensive restoration, funded by the German government. On Voigtei 48 is the fascinating **Museum Bürgerliche Wohnkulturum 1900** (Museum of middle-class life in 1900; opening times: Tues–Sat 09.00–12.00 and 13.00–16.00, Sun 09.00–12.00). Pass through the arched side entrance and cross the inner courtyard to the Museum. This was the home of the Schraube family until 1980 when the 73-year-old Margarete Schraube died; the house was then opened in 1984 as a museum devoted to early 20C bourgeois life. Everything has been left in its place, including an original kitchen complete with iron and other domestic appliances. Original greeting- and post-cards decorate the passageway including a New Year's Eve card for 1903 and examples of propaganda from the First World War. There is a grand dining room with the original furniture and wallpaper as well as the electrics. Upstairs on the second floor there are displays of domestic textiles and toys.

From Halberstadt you may wish to continue straight on to the UNESCO preserved town of Quedlinburg S via the A79 for 14km or continue your tour west on the A81 and A6 to 25km Wernigerode.

B. Wernigerode

36,000 inhabitants.

Tourist Information: Breite Strasse 12, 38855 Wernigerode. Tel. 330 35. Opening times: Mon–Fri 09.00–18.00, Sat 09.30–13.00.

Wernigerode is best known amongst tourists as the home of the narrow-gauge steam trains (the Harzquerbahn) which run south from here up and around the Harz mountains to the final destination of Nordhausen in Thuringia. The trains leave from the Hauptbahnhof, about 15 minutes on foot north of the town centre or the Bahnhof Wernigerode Westentor only 5 minutes west of the Rathaus.

History. Set picturesquely on the northern slopes of the Harz mountains, Wernigerode dates back to the 11C. Receiving its town charter in 1229, the small town flourished during the succeeding centuries, as the splendid town hall and burgher houses still standing today attest, its prosperity built on craft work. Wernigerode was a small principality, governed by the Counts of Wernigerode and then the family of Stolberg-Wernigerode, which became part of Prussia in 1714. The family lived in the magnificent, fairy-tale castle which dominates the town from a nearby wooded hill, until in 1930 bankruptcy struck and they had to abandon their residence which was opened to visitors. Escaping the war relatively unscathed, Wernigerode's chief attraction today, apart from the railway, is the well-preserved historic town centre and the Schloss.

There is central parking on the Ringstrasse, or trains run from Halberstadt with a journey time of 40 minutes. From the railway station head south then south-west down Breite Weg to the Marktplatz.

The amazing **Rathaus** stands to the south of the square, a brightly painted, half-timbered structure with high-pitched roof and two spindly turrets decorating its façade. It comes as no surprise to learn that this building was originally founded as a theatre in 1277 and was acquired by the town in the 15C to serve as a Rathaus. The main building work dates from 1492–98, with the façade added in the mid 16C. The Rathaus is decorated with sculptured ornament and the 33 figures which decorate the exterior are quite amusing, copied from figures which once embellished the long-gone Rathaus at Halberstadt; various musicians and jesters are represented. The Rathaus is crowned by a blue-and-gold clock and turret housing a bell, and is still called the Spielhaus today—plays are held in front of the Rathaus during the summer months. The decorative metal fountain in the centre of the Markplatz dates from 1848 and sports the local coats of arms.

To the right of the Rathaus stands the **Gothische Haus** (Gothic House) built in 1480 as the home of a wealthy merchant family—it has now been restored to its pre-war function as restaurant and hotel. More historic, half-timbered houses may be seen throughout the town centre, particularly on the pedestrianised Breite Strasse, north-east of the Marktplatz. At No. 72 is the **Krummelsches Haus**, dating from 1674 with chunky Baroque carving covering the entire façade. At No. 95 is the **Krellsche Schmiede**, built in 1678 with carving of horseshoes and horses' heads which indicate its function as a blacksmith's. Today this is a small museum specialising in the history of timber-framed buildings and the work of the blacksmith (opening times: Wed–Sun 13.00–17.00).

The Klintgasse leads off from the Marktplatz to the south-west between the Rathaus and the Gothic House. At No. 10 is the **Harzmuseum** (opening times: Mon–Fri 09.00–16.00, Sat 09.00–12.00). Contained in a Neo-Classical townhouse, the displays tell a comprehensive story of the local history of the region, concentrating mainly on natural history but including some material on the building of timber-framed houses. At No. 5 is the Schiefe Haus, dating from 1680 and originally a mill.

Continue south to reach the church of **St. Sylvester**, former parish church of the Altstadt. Built as a three-aisled early Gothic basilica and founded in the 13C, it underwent various alterations in 1500 and 1880–85. The interior is certainly worth a look, with a winged altar dating from the late 15C and tombs of local worthies from the 14C to 16C. So is the Oberkirchhof, a tranquil close of half-timbered houses dating from the 16C to 18C, surrounding the Church. Continue south down Teichdamm and turn left into Bachstrasse. On the second left in Kochstrasse is the smallest house in Wernigerode, the **Kleinstes Haus**, built in the late 18C to three storeys and only 3m wide.

It's a steep climb south up Burgstrasse, the second on your right, to reach the *Schloss (opening times: Tues–Sun 10.00–18.00, last admittance 17.30). During the summer it is possible to take a miniature train—the Bimmel-bahn—to the Schloss from the Marktplatz.

The knight Adalbert von Haimar built a Romanesque castle here on the Agnesberg in the 11C, thus establishing the seat of the family line of the Counts of Wernigerode. The building was substantially altered in the 17C and early 18C to become a Baroque castle. Count Otto of Stolberg-Wernig-erode then undertook the building of this Gothic Revival fantasy in 1862–85 with architect Karl Frühling. Otto's successor, Count Christian Ernst of Stolberg-Wernigerode was forced to give up the Castle in 1930 when he lost the family fortune as a result of the Wall Street Crash. From 1949 to 1990 the Schloss was home to a vulgar Marxist museum, the Museum of Feudalism, but is now the plain **Schlossmuseum**. Inside, apartments typical of the German nobility can be admired, furnished with fine antiques from the 13C to the 19C including examples of Louis Seize, Biedermeier and Empire furniture. It's easy to conjure up the heady days of Bismark's Germany as one stands in the Billiard Room, the Prince's living quarters and the Festsaal (Banqueting Room). The Chapel contains a mid-13C embroidery of Mary Magdalene and a carved, 15C altarpiece. Do not miss the splendid views from the terrace, of Wernigerode and the Harz Moun-tains including the Brocken, some 1142m in height. In the Schloss gardens is the Baroque **Orangery**, built 1713–19, which today houses the Schloss archives.

From Wernigerode head east on the A6 16km to **Blankenburg**, another pretty Harz town with its 17C Kleines Schloss Museum and ruined Burg Regenstein. The A6 then leads for 13km east to Quedlinburg, surely one of the best preserved towns in the Harz region. The train service takes roughly one hour from Wernigerode or 30 minutes from Halberstadt.

C. Quedlinburg

2900 inhabitants.

Tourist Information: Markt 12, 06484 Quedlinburg (tel. 2866 or 2633). Opening times: Mon–Fri 09.00–18.00, Sat and Sun 10.00–15.00.

The town of **Quedlinburg** is an absolute delight; if your time in the Harz mountains is limited, then a trip to Quedlinburg is a must. The town has been frozen in history, its winding narrow streets lined with half-timbered houses in the original medieval layout. Around 1600 of Quedlinburg's buildings are officially listed and UNESCO has earmarked it as a World Heritage Site. Many visitors from western Germany flock to the town to enjoy its special atmosphere, impressive Rathaus and high standard pave-ment cafés and restaurants.

History. Quedlinburg is a town of great historic importance. King Henry I (919–36), Germany's first monarch, founded the Schlossberg here in 925 and conducted meet-ings of the Imperial Diet in the town, while his wife, Mathilde, founded a college for women to train as abbesses; Henry and Mathilde were buried in an 11C crypt in the Collegiate Church. The powerful elite of royal protégées dominated the town until the Napoleonic Wars and trade did not flourish as in the neighbouring locations of Halberstadt or Wernigerode. During the 19C and 20C Quedlinburg enjoyed some measure of prosperity from its seed production. Only a few factories were built here in GDR times on the outskirts of town. The River Bode snakes through the town, with the Altstadt to the west of the river.

It is virtually impossible to navigate the narrow lanes by car and so parking out of the centre is recommended. From the A6 approach you enter Westerhäuser Strasse; at the end turn right and then first left into Altetopstrasse and parking can be found beside the Fachwerkmuseum on Carl Ritter Strasse, just to the south of the Markt. The main station is situated to the south-east of town—head up Bahnhofstrasse then bear left up Heiligegeiststrasse to reach the Markt.

In the Markt the most striking feature is the **Rathaus** in the centre. This Renaissance building has a beautiful columned portal, added in 1616–19. Note the Roland statue on the south-west corner, dating from 1427. The Markt is lined with timber-framed houses, including 16C guild houses at Nos 5 and 13/14. To the north of the Rathaus is the **Marktkirche St Benedikti**, a Transitional and late Gothic three-aisled hall church dating from the 14C and 15C. Enter via the northern Kalandskapelle to see the tombstones of local notables, the Mannerist pulpit, the Baroque altarpiece and the beamed ceiling. Continue to the southern edge of the Markt where the Tourist Information Office is situated adjacent to the virtually derelict **Blasiikirche**, a Baroque hall church dating from 1713–15 with an earlier Romanesque west tower.

Continue south down Wordgasse to reach the moderately interesting **Fachwerkmuseum Ständerbau**, which explains the history of timber-framed building (opening times: May–Sept, Mon–Wed and Fri–Sun 10.00–14.00). More interesting perhaps is No. 3 Wordgasse, where the Museum is housed, probably the oldest surviving house in Germany, dating as far back as the 14C. More rudimentary than the buildings seen so far in the Markt, its bulging white-washed sides are punctuated at irregular intervals by horizontal and vertical lengths of timber, with more regard for practicality than for visual appeal.

Continue east along Carl Ritter Strasse then south up Ritter Gasse to reach the Schlossberg. On the left, in the tiny close of Finkenherd, is the **Lyonel-Feininger-Galerie** (opening times: Daily 09.00–12.00 and 13.00–17.00). Feininger was an important Expressionist graphic artist who taught at the Bauhaus, designing the cover of the First Manifesto in 1919. Born in America to German parents he returned there in 1938 to be fêted as a great modern artist. The Gallery, built in 1901 as the Municipal Museum, contains fine examples of his watercolours, lithographs and drawings. Further on to the right is the **Klopstockmuseum** (opening times: May–Sept, Wed–Sun 10.00–17.00, Oct–April 09.00–16.00) childhood home of the classical poet, Friedrich Gottlieb Klopstock (1724–1803). His claim to fame is that his *Messiah* was set to music by Handel. The museum contains interesting relics from the period including furniture and paintings as well as information on two other contemporary Quedlinburg residents, Dorothea Christina Erxleben, the first German woman to earn the title of Doctor, and Johann Christoph Guts Muths who created gymnastics for young people.

Further north up Schlossberg is the **Schlossmuseum** (opening times: Tues–Sun, May–Sept 10.00–17.00, Oct–April 09.00–16.00), devoted to local history with medieval torture implements, folk-costume, fossils and the usual paraphernalia associated with these municipal museums. There are also 16C and 17C Italian and Dutch paintings of note plus interesting furniture from the 15–17C. Of great interest is the building itself: formerly

The Klopstock Museum in Quedlinburg

the Residenzbau of the schloss, and built in Renaissance style, it faces onto the main courtyard and forms part of the Schloss complex atop the Burgberg.

To the south-east is the **Stiftskirche St Servatius**, the 11C and 12C Romanesque Collegiate Abbey Church (opening times: by guided tour May–Oct, Sun and Mon 14.00–15.30, Tues–Sat 10.00, 11.30 and 13.00–15.30, Nov–April, Tues–Sat 11.00 and 14.00, Sun 14.00). The flat-roofed basilica is fittingly austere inside, the only decoration being the carved capitals with friezes above depicting various animals and plants amongst more abstract patterns. The church was built in 1070 following a fire which destroyed the original, note that the twin towers were rebuilt in 1882. Only the CRYPT remains from the 10C; built into the sandstone rock it contains the tombs of King Henry I and Mathilde. The rough floor and tunnel vaulting, supported by alternating round and square pillars, is truly atmospheric. On the south wall are the carved stone tombs of the powerful abbesses which stand in a upright position. On the vaulting are traces of wall-paintings from the early 12C and the richly carved capitals have been painted a deep red ochre. In the north transept of the church is the ZITTER (treasury) which contains some stunning early ecclesiastical objects. The *Adelheidevangeliar* (reliquary) of St Servatius is amazing. A central square of carved ivory depicting the apostles is set into a gilded mount studded with diamonds and coloured enamels. There is a bridal chest from the 13C and a tapestry, dating from c 1200.

It is well worth exploring the rest of the town at your leisure, meandering through the weaving lanes. Other historic buildings of note you may wish to make your way to are the **Gildehaus zur Rose** at No. 39 Breitestrasse (which leads north from the Markt) or the old tavern of **Zur Goldenen Sonne** at No. 11 Steinweg, east of the Marktkirche.

From Quedlinburg head north on Oststrasse and then Halbestädter Strasse to follow the A79 for 14km back to Halberstadt and the A81 to (37km) Magdeburg.

37

From Halle to Naumburg

From Halle—22km Merseburg—23km Naumburg.

Beginning from Halle, former capital of the land of Sachsen-Anhalt, the tour continues south to Merseburg and finishes at Naumburg with its famed cathedral containing the glorious sculptures of the medieval founders.

A. Halle

311,400 inhabitants.

Tourist Information: Roter Turm, Markplatz, 06108 Halle. Tel. 23340. Opening times: Mon, Tues, Thurs, Fri 09.00–18.00, Wed 10.00–18.00, Sat 09.00–13.00.

Even the tourist brochures concede that the charms of **Halle** are not immediately obvious. However, it is well worth persevering beyond initial impressions to discover some of the gems from Halle's distinguished past. Halle also makes a good centre for touring the southern tip of Sachsen-Anhalt as accommodation is certainly more plentiful here than in Merseburg or Naumburg.

History. This early settlement on the banks of the River Saale received its first documentary mention in 806. The production and trading of salt generated the wealth of the town from as far back as the Iron Age. The extraction of salt then a precious commodity, from brine guaranteed the prosperity of Halle from the 14C through to the 16C. Ownership of Halle was transferred to the San Moritz Cloister of Magdeburg by Otto I in 961 and Magdeburg has influenced the progression of Halle ever since. During the 16C the town was transformed into a prestigious Royal residence under Cardinal Albrecht von Brandenburg, with the building of the cathedral and the New Residence. From 1680 Halle formed part of the Brandenburg empire and in 1694 the University was founded. Halle was an important centre for pietism and then for the Enlightenment, focused around the University. In 1878 the German Academy of Nature Researchers, the Leopoldina, was established in the town. Halle was also swift to industrialise and lies at the heart of Germany's rail network, the first tracks being

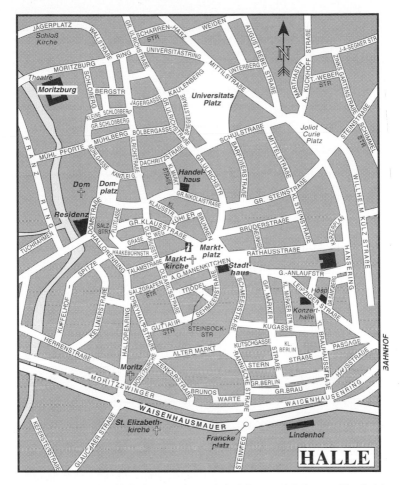

laid in 1840. In 1948 Halle became the capital of Saxony-Anhalt, a position lost to Halberstadt after the *Wende*.

The Tourist Information Office is situated in the modernist glass box built onto the 84m high **Roter Turm** (Red Tower) in the north of the Markplatz. Reach this central part of the town from the Hauptbahnhof by walking north-west for about 15 minutes up the pedestrianised Leipziger Strasse. Be careful crossing the Marktplatz as this is the main intersection for the tram network, and the lines criss-cross in front of the Rotes Turm. The tower was begun by the town's burghers in 1418 and completed in 1506 as a Gothic belfry and statement of civic independence. The four tiers and main spire, surrounded by four spindly turrets, were badly damaged during World War Two and the tower was extensively restored in 1975. A Roland dating from 1719 stands in front of the Tower, a rather blackened stone copy of the wooden original which dated from c 1250. The **Händeldenkmal**

(Handel Monument) stands in the centre of the Markplatz commemorating the centenary of the death of the town's greatest son, Friedrich Händel (1685–1759). Cast from bronze the monument, showing Handel in frock-coat and wig, hand on hip, was financed by both English and German subscriptions.

The **Marktkirche Unser Lieben Frauen** stands on the west side of the square (opening times: Mon and Wed–Fri 15.00–18.00, Thurs 16.00–17.00, Sat 09.00–12.00, Sun 11.00–12.00). The church is something of an anomaly with two pairs of towers from two different churches. It was built in 1529 on the site of two Romanesque churches, St Marien (1141) and St Gertrauden (1121). Under the orders of Cardinal Albrecht, who was anxious to establish Halle as a Catholic centre in opposition to the Reformation, the two were destroyed and one replacement Gothic hall church built linking the remaining towers. The pair facing directly onto the Marktplatz are linked by a bridge, added by master builder Nickel Hofmann when he extended them in the 16C. The church was eventually converted to Protestant worship. Inside the High Altar is of special note; painted by the Master of Annaberg from the Lucas Cranach school in 1529, it depicts Cardinal Albrecht surrounded by Sts Catherine, Mary and John the Evangelist. Above is the small Baroque organ, once played by Handel and built in 1663. In the centre of the south side of the nave is a beautifully carved Baroque pulpit and at the opposite end the Grosse Orgel (Great Organ), dating from 1713 decorated in Baroque style with playful cherubs. Note the stalls and galleries, which were carved and decorated by A. Pauwaert from Ypern during 1561–75.

The steel-framed **Ratshof** on the oppposite side of the square was built during 1928–30 with stone-clad exterior. The Stadthaus stands on the southern side of the Marktplatz. Built in 1891–93 to designs by Emil Schreiterer in Renaissance Revival style it houses the excellent Ratskeller. The red and white painted **Marktschlössen** with its pretty gabled roof stands on the north-west corner of the Marktplatz and Grosse Klausstrasse. Built c 1600 this late Renaissance palace now houses a display of musical instruments from the Händelhaus and temporary exhibitions of 20C art (opening times: Wed–Sun 13.30–17.30).

LEIPZIGERSTRASSE leads off from the south-east corner of the Marktplatz. A pedestrianised zone, lined with interesting 19C façades, this street also contains the **Konzerthalle in der ehemaligen Ulrichskirche** (Concert Hall in the former Ulrichs Church), half-way down on the right. A late Gothic hall church, it was converted to a concert hall in 1976, mainly for organ and choir recitals. Further south-east down Leipzigerstrasse is the **Leipziger Turm** (Leipzig Tower), an original part of the town's medieval fortifications which was rebuilt in 1573. Turn right just after the Concert Hall down Kleine Brauhausstrasse, then third right up Grosse Brauhaustrasse, then right up RANNISCES STRASSE which contains some of the best historic mansions in Halle. No. 17 has a lively Rococo façade and the 15C tavern of Zur Goldenen Rose, still a restaurant today, is at No. 19. Continue north to reach the ALTER MARKT, the old centre of the town where the original Rathaus was built in 1312 and important trade routes converged. The square is decorated with the whimsical Eselbrunnen (Donkey Fountain) which depicts a donkey treading on roses accompanied by a boy, apparently an old symbol of the town expressed in this recent sculpture. The square is also lined with historic townhouses including the 17C half-timbered example at No. 31 and the Goldenen Pflug (Golden

Plough) tavern at No. 27. Continue west down the Alter Markt to reach the **Moritzkirche**, the oldest parish church in Halle. Founded in 1121, with rebuilding from 1388 to 1411, it was finally completed in 1511 in Gothic style. Of particular note inside are the stone sculptures by Konrad von Einbeck, dating from 1411–20, to the right of the choir. The winged altar-piece showing Mary and the Crucifixion is by G. Jhener from Orlamünde and dates from the year when the church was completed, 1511. The star vaulting is also striking.

Continue north up Dreyhauptstrasse and Hallorenring to the **Dom**. A towerless hall church built originally for the Dominican monastery, it was rebuilt in 1520–23 for Cardinal Albrecht as his court church. Following the Reformation it was remodelled in Baroque style to become a Protestant church (opening times: Mon–Sat 15.00–16.00, Sun 11.30–12.30). The exterior is characterised by the strange upper storey with its arched gables, added to the top of the earlier hall church in 1520. The 17 massive statues of the apostles and saints, added during Albrecht's time and sculpted by the workshops of Peter Schroh, dominate the interior. Note also the 16C pulpit and the coat of arms of the all-powerful cardinal on the north wall. The organ and the high altar were added in the 17C, when Handel played here.

South of the Dom is the **Neue Residenz** (New Residence) founded by the Cardinal for the Archbishops of Magdeburg in 1529–31. The stone building hugs the eastern banks of the Mühlgraben river and was intended as a Catholic University to rival the Protestant University at Wittenburg. The building is now actually part of the latter, since Halle and Wittenburg merged in 1817. There is a chance to look inside the Renaissance buildings as the **Geiseltalmuseum** is housed in part of the Residenz (opening times: Mon–Fri 09.00–12.00 and 14.30–17.00). This is a museum, founded in 1934, specialising in the fossils found in the local brown coal. If you are interested in a visit to the **Technisches Halloren und Salinemuseum** (the Technical and Salt Museum of Halle) housed in the old salt works, it is a ten minute walk south-west from here down Mansfelder Strasse (opening times: Tues–Sun 10.00–16.00).

Continue north from the Domplatz up Mühlgasse to reach the **Moritzburg**, a fortress built by Archbishop Ernst in 1484–1503 and converted into a palace by Cardinal Albrecht in 1534–37. Although a fire in 1637 damaged much of the building it has been converted to house the student club and evening cabaret. The **Staatliche Galerie Moritzburg** (Moritz Castle Gallery) is housed in the south and west wings of the castle (opening times: Mon–Fri 10.00–17.30, Sat and Sun 10.00–18.00). The BRAUTZIMMER (Wedding Room) and GERICHTZIMMER (Court Room) from the Talamt (Salt Workers' Union) have been well preserved. The remainder of the gallery specialises in the decorative arts from medieval times to the 20C. Painting and the graphic arts are well represented in the gallery with Expressionist work by Paul Klee, Oskar Kokoschka, Emil Nolde and Franz Marc.

Continue east on the Moritzburg Ring to reach the pleasant **University sector**. The **Hauptgebäude** (Main Building) is a solid, white Neo-Classical building erected in 1832–34. The TREPPENHALLE (Stair Hall) inside is particularly striking, with decorative metal banisters and lights with murals depicting classical myths with windows above. The upper level is supported by Corinthian columns. South-east from here is the graceful

Robertinum, another Neo-Classical building erected in 1889–91; it contains the University's Archaeology Museum, not open to the public.

From the University make your way back to the Marktplatz south via Spegelstrasse and Grosse Ulrichstrasse, turning east into Grosse Nikolaistrasse to the **Händelhaus** (Handel's House) at Nos 5–6 (opening times: Mon–Sun 9.30–17.30, Thurs 09.30–18.30). The composer was born in this large Baroque mansion in 1685. Inside are all sorts of documentation relating to his life including portraits and rare musical instruments.

From Halle take the A91 to cover the short distance south to Merseburg. Trains and the tram No. 5 also link the two towns with a journey time of 15 minutes.

B. Merseburg

48,000 inhabitants.

Unfortunately set between the massive chemical plants of Leuna and Buna, **Merseburg** has certainly suffered from industrial pollution during the 20C. However, the town was an important religious centre in the Middle Ages with a bishopric established here in 968 which survived until 1561. Economic prosperity was enjoyed during the 13C and 14C through trade. The most important sites of cultural interest are the Dom and Schloss, situated on the Domberg hill overlooking the town. The **Dom**, with its four towers, was founded in 1015 and altered over the centuries with major restoration in the late 19C (opening times: Mon–Sat 09.00–12.00 and 13.00–16.00, 18.00 in the summer, Sun 13.00–17.00). The crypt is 11C Romanesque and the choir and transepts survive in Transitional style from the 13C, whilst the Gothic nave was added in the early 16C. Inside there is a 12C font but it is the tombstones which are of greatest interest. Rudolph of Swabia, who died in battle with rival Henry IV in 1080, has a splendid early bronze memorial dedicated to him in the choir. Also note the mid-13C memorial of Knight Hermann von Hagen in the chapel situated in the cloisters. The Dom LIBRARY contains an interesting collection of early manuscripts dating from as early as the 8C up to medieval times, including the Merseburger Zaubersprüche—a collection of pre-Christian spells.

On the north side of the Dom is the **Schloss**. Built to house the bishops in 1480–89, the palace was rebuilt in the 17C as a residence for Saxon princes. The styles span late Gothic to Renaissance with the powerful Renaissance portal and oriel being of special note. A caged raven hangs in the courtyard, condemned as part of the myth of Bishop Thilo Trotha whose ring was stolen and later found in a raven's nest following the execution of an innocent man accused of the theft. A small part of the Schloss is open to the public in the form of the Kreismuseum, dedicated to local history (opening times: Tues–Sun 09.00–17.00).

From Merseburg continue south to Naumburg by means of the A91 to Weissenfels, the A87 to Wethau and then the A180 W to Naumburg. The train journey from Halle takes about 30 minutes.

C. Naumburg

31,000 inhabitants.

Tourist Information: Lindenring 38, Naumburg 06618. Tel. 2514. Opening times: Mon, Tues, Thurs, Fri 08.30–17.00, Sat and Sun from 15 May–15 Sept, 09.00–12.00.

Naumburg was founded as a fortress town at the beginning of the 11C by Margrave Ekkehardt I from Meissen. It then existed as a bishopric from 1028 until 1564 with trade centring around the busy market place. The Dom was built in the 13C and has dominated the town ever since. The main reason for visiting Naumburg is to experience this magnificent cathedral, situated in the north-east of the town. Follow the Wenzelsring to the west then take Lindenring on the right and then turn left just before the Tourist Information Office. The railway station is situated on the northern outskirts of Naumburg and it is a ten-minute walk south down Bahnhofstrasse, Bergstrasse and Poststrasse to the Dom.

The **˙˙DOM ST PETER UND PAUL** (Cathedral of St Peter and St Paul) is a memorable high point of any trip to eastern Germany. Work began on the Dom in c 1220 and the bulk was completed by 1249. The Dom was consecrated in 1242 and is predominantly in Romanesque and transitional style. It is a two-choir basilica with transept and crypt in the eastern part. The early Gothic west choir was added in 1250–70 and the more refined east choir in c 1340 in Gothic style. The oldest part of the Cathedral in existence today is the crypt dating form 1170. The north-west tower is the earliest of the four, originating from 1249—the matching south-west tower was built as recently as 1894. The two east towers are Romanesque with Baroque spires and lanterns. Whilst examining the exterior look out for the fierce 13C gargoyles. (Opening times: Nov–Feb, Mon–Sat 09.00–16.00, Sun 12.00–16.00. March and Oct, Mon–Sat 09.00–17.00, Sun 12.00–17.00, April–Sept 09.00–18.00, Sun 12.00–18.00; guided tours in German on the hour, for other languages on the half-hour.)

On entering proceed west down the main nave, noting the bronze tombstones which adorn the pillars, to the west rood screen, which is decorated with scenes from the passion in painted high relief, dating from c 1270. From left to right the images represent the Last Supper, Judas Receiving the Thirty Pieces of Silver, Christ's Arrest, Peter's Denial of Christ, the Two Guards, and Pilate, who holds out his left hand to be washed. The two remaining reliefs are 18C copies, added when the originals were destroyed by fire. The captivating screen was carved by the unknown Master of Naumburg who was also responsible for the magnificent **Statues of the Founders** which stand in the west choir. The 12 lifelike figures represent the various margraves, counts and consorts who funded the building of the cathedral. They have a special place in the history of art due to the fineness of the carving and realism of the representation, and were created at the astonishingly early date of 1250. From left to right the figures represented are: Gerburg, Konrad, Hermann and Reglindis, Dietmar, Sizz von Kefernburg, Wilhelm von Camburg, Timo von Kistriz, Ekkhard and Uta, Gepa, Dietrich von Brehna. Most outstanding are the portraits of Margrave Ekkhard the founder of the town, and Uta his wife. Ekkhard stands masterfully holding his sword whilst Uta looks into the distance with her cloak wrapped around her entire body. The stained glass above is also of great interest, the first, fourth and fifth windows from the left are the 13C originals and show the apostles. Approach the east choir via the modern staircase,

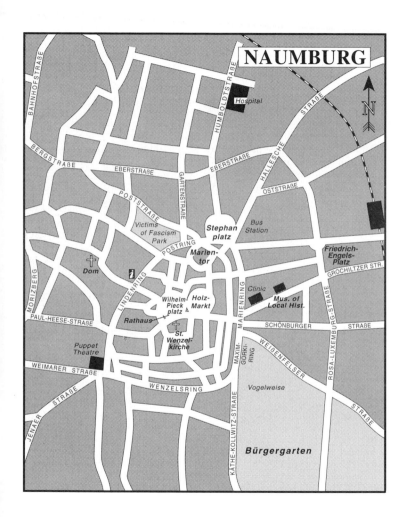

via the modern staircase, added in 1966 and decorated with various animals. The interior is far simpler, decorated with frescoes. Beyond is the high choir with choir pews which date from c 1500 and the sarcophagus of Bishop Dietrich II, also by the Naumburg Workshops and dating from 1270. The statue of a deacon in the west choir derives from the same workshops. He

Statues of the founders of the Cathedral, Margrave Ekkhard and his wife, Uta, by the Master of Naumburg, 1250

stands with a rather hang-dog expression with an open bible before him. It is possible to visit the 13C crypt; the 12C original is preserved in the centre with a Romanesque crucifix from 1170 standing on the altar. The Dom is also notable for the fine, naturalistic carving which decorates the capitals.

From the Dom proceed south-east, crossing Lindenring to reach the central **Markt**. You are greeted by the **Stadtkirche St Wenzel** (Town Church of St Wenzel), a late Gothic hall church completed in 1523 (opening times:

Mon–Sat 10.00–12.00 and 14.00–16.00, Sun 11.30–16.00). It contains two fine paintings by Lucas Cranach the Elder, *The Adoration of the Magi* and *Suffer the Little Children to Come Unto Me*. The interior was completely refurbished in the 17C and a splendid Hildebrand organ added. It is well worth climbing the tower of the church, which offers fine views of the town and the Saale valley beyond. (Opening times: April–Oct, Wed–Sun 10.00–18.00.) Also situated on the Markt is the late Gothic and Renaissance **Rathaus**. Completed in 1528 the arched gables are particularly striking. Note also the main portal, richly decorated with the local coats of arms. Historic houses line the square, most notably No. 6, the **Schlössen**, built for the Protestant bishop and No. 7, the **Alte Residenz** where Duke Moritz of Saxony lived before moving to the Schloss Moritzburg near Dresden.

The **Museum der Stadt Naumburg** (Museum of the Town of Naumburg) lies east from the Markt, down Jacobstrasse and Grochlitzer Strasse (opening times: Tues–Fri 08.00–13.00 and 14.00–17.00). Finally, to the north of the Markt and right down the Postring is the striking **Marientor** (St Mary's Gate). Dating from 1456, this is the only surviving town gate, built from rough stone with an arched entrance and tower which leads to an inner courtyard. During the summer concerts are given by the Puppentheater (Puppet Theatre; tel. 2764).

38

From Wittenberg to Dessau

From Wittenberg—21km Wörlitz Park—18km Dessau.

The tour encompasses two significant revolutionary centres which made an impact in different centuries and in different areas of human endeavour. Wittenberg was the 16C hub of the Reformation. It was here that Martin Luther nailed to the church door his 95 Theses which condemned the corrupt practices of the established church and laid the foundations of Protestantism. 35km away is Dessau, where the radical Bauhaus School of Art and Design flourished between 1926 and 1933. The spring of Modernist art and design was housed in one of the first International Style buildings in the world, and the impact of the Bauhaus was massive. The tour also stops off at Wörlitz Park, a German interpretation of the English picturesque landscape garden.

A. Lutherstadt Wittenberg

54,000 inhabitants.

Tourist Information: Collegienstrasse 8, 06886 Lutherstadt Wittenberg. Tel. 2239. Opening times: April–Oct, Mon–Fri 09.00–18.00, Sat and Sun 10.00–14.00; Nov–March, Mon–Fri 09.00–17.00.

History. The sleepy town of Wittenberg lies on the banks of the River Elbe and seems an unlikely location for the nerve centre of a radical, religious movement. Nevertheless, it was here that the Protestant Reformation began. Wittenberg was an important political centre before Luther. It was the capital of the Saxon Ernestine line from 1422, and the Elector Frederick the Wise, who came to the throne in 1486, founded the University here in 1502. The Augustinian monk, Martin Luther, lectured in Philosophy at the new seat of learning and developed his radical teachings whilst at the University. Frederick the Wise engaged the services of Lucas Cranach the Elder as court painter who perfectly expressed the solemn and earnest mood of the Reformation. The castle, castle church, new bridge, Rathaus and new town mansions gave Wittenberg a prestigious image during the 16C. Although Frederick did not agree entirely with Luther's doctrines he allowed him the freedom of speech so necessary to spread his subversive message. Preaching that people could reach salvation only through individual faith rather than ritual worship or empty 'good deeds', Luther was popular amongst ordinary folk as well as the German rulers, who saw an opportunity to eschew the dominance of Rome. Following Luther's death in 1546 the town's significance began to fade and in 1547 Dresden became the capital of Saxony. Devastated during the Thirty Years War, Wittenberg's University was to be merged with that of Halle. Wittenberg's fortunes were revived when the railway came here in the mid 19C, connecting it with Leipzig and Halle. The Communist government celebrated the achievements of Luther rather inappropriately as a great social revolutionary—he had in fact opposed the Peasants' Revolt—this meant that much of 16C Wittenberg has benefitted from thorough restoration. Since the *Wende*, the popularity of Wittenberg has greatly increased as a tourist destination, easily accessible by road or rail from Leipzig, Halle and Dessau.

From the train station its a short walk south to the illustrious street of COLLEGIENSTRASSE where Luther's steps can be traced. At No. 54 is the **Augusteum**, formerly part of the University, built during 1564–86 in Renaissance style and remodelled in Baroque mode in 1781–1802. It now houses a scientific library. In the courtyard is the *****Lutherhaus**, Luther's home from 1508–46, built as part of the Augustine monastery in 1502. The residence was presented to Luther in 1526 following the demise of the monastery and then bestowed on the University in 1564, being largely used as a student hall of residence. During the succeeding centuries the building fell into disrepair, and was not fully restored until 1844–83. Since then it has housed the **Reformationsgeschichtliches Museum** (Museum of the History of the Reformation) in the Luther Hall as well as the preserved apartments of Luther. (Opening times: Tues–Sun 09.00–17.00). Enter by means of the highly decorative Katharinenportal, a present to Luther from his wife Katharina von Bora in 1540. The ground floor contains material on the history of the building and the life and work of the great German Renaissance painter, Lucas Cranach the Elder. The chief works on display are *The Ten Commandments* and portraits of Luther and his parents. On the first floor are 11 rooms devoted to Luther's progress as a great reformer, with a wealth of contemporary documentation including paintings and prints. The Lutherstube (Luther Room) is particularly fascinating. This is where Luther and his family lived whilst in Wittenberg and it contains their original stove, trunk, seating and table. The walls and ceiling are decorated with 16C Renaissance painting. The second floor is devoted to the importance of Luther's translation of the Bible into German, with many fine examples of early printed books and original manuscripts from the period.

Continue west up Collegienstrasse to No. 60, the **Melanchthonhaus**, the original dwelling of Luther's closest colleague, Philipp Schwarzend (Melanchthon in Greek) who came to Wittenberg in 1519 as Professor of Greek. The Renaissance mansion, with its distinctive five-arched gable and 16C herb and spice garden at the rear, was built in 1536—look out for the stone table, dated 1551. The ground floor of the house is a local history museum and the first floor specialises in the work of Melanchthon who collaborated on Luther's most important works, including the Augsburg Confession (opening times: Mon–Thurs 09.00–17.00, Sat and Sun 10.00–12.00 and 14.00–17.00).

From the Melanchthonhaus follow the Collegienstrasse west to the Mark-platz. On the eastern side of the square is the **Stadtkirche St Marien** where Luther frequently preached, got married and had his children baptised. It was also from this church that Holy Communion was administered in both forms in 1522. The church houses one of the finest examples of Lucas Cranach the Elder's paintings, the triptych which stands at the altar. (Opening times: daily 09.00–12.00 and 14.00–16.00.)

The town Church of St Mary was founded in the 13C and the double-naved choir survives from this era. The main body of the church was rebuilt in 1411 and the octagonal towers added in 1555–58 with the addition of the connecting bridge in 1655. The church was extensively restored in the mid 1960s and is the oldest suriving building in Wittenberg. Inside, it is the works of art which are most arresting. The Cranach triptych known as the REFORMATION ALTAR, dating from 1547, depicts the Last Supper in the centre with the 12 apostles seated at a round table to avoid the construction of any hierarchy. Luther is daringly depicted as the twelfth disciple, receiv-ing the cup of holy communion wine. On the left wing, baptism is repre-sented and on the right, confession with a portrait of Melanchthon. On the predella Luther is depicted once more, this time preaching with the cruci-fied Christ before him. Also in the church is a fine memorial to Lucas Cranach the Younger dating from the early 17C and a bronze font by Hermann Vischer of Nuremberg from 1457.

To the south of the Stadtkirche is the Kapelle zum Heiligen Leichnam (Corpus Christi Chapel), a small church built in 1370 as part of the cemetery but now used for children's services.

The MARKTPLATZ is decorated with two statues which stand beneath ornate canopies outside the Rathaus. The first represents Luther and was created in bronze by Schadow in 1821 and the second commemorates Melanchthon by Friedrich Drake from 1865. The **Rathaus** was founded in Wittenberg's golden age during the 16C and was extensively restored in 1768. It is a solid, whitewashed Renaissance building with stepped gables and a decorative main portal, bedecked with various allegorical figures. Note also the historic burgher houses which line the Marktplatz. No. 3–4 was where Lucas Cranach the Younger was born in 1515 and Nos 5 and 6 also date from the 16C. Continue west down Schloss Strasse. At No. 1 is the house where Lucas Cranach the Elder lived, who was also mayor of Wittenberg during the 16C; he operated as an Apothecary from these premises. In the courtyard is an interesting stair tower. At the end of the street is the Schloss and Schlosskirche.

The *Schlosskirche** was built in 1489–1511 as part of Frederick the Wise's Renaissance Schloss complex on the site of Wittenberg's former fortress. The late Gothic, single-naved hall church was designed by Konrad Pflueger but was badly damaged during fighting in 1760 and 1813–14; it was fully restored in 1883–92 (opening times: Tues–Sat 09.00–12.00 and 14.00–16.45, Sun 10.30–12.00 and 14.00–16.45). The bronze door on the northern side of the church stands in place of the wooden door on which Luther nailed his 95 Theses. The original door was burnt down in 1760 and replaced by this bronze version which carries the text of the Theses and was cast in 1858. Appropriately the church hosted the first Protestant service ever to be held during 1521 when Luther was in hiding at Eisenach.

Inside, the church was extensively remodelled during the late 19C with the addition of buttresses in front of the gallery, new vaulting, altar and altar windows, statues and medallions of those associated with the Reformation. In 1982–83 the church exterior was replastered, giving it is pristine appearance, the mosaic featuring Luther's best known hymn 'A Mighty Fortress is our God' was renewed and new stained glass depicting various European reformers put in place. To the right of the entrance is a brass plate which marks the tomb of the Ascanian family, moved here in 1885 from the demolished Church of St Francis. The two stone tombstones on the south wall were removed from the same church and commemorate Prince Elector Rudolph II and his wife and daughter. Continue towards the altar and Luther's tomb may be seen on the right, just below the pulpit. A simple engraved brass plate marks the place where, 2m down, his body lies in a pewter coffin. A 1980s copy of Luther's original tomb plate can be seen nearby on the south wall. The original was cast in 1547 but failed to reach Wittenberg, due to war; it has remained in St Michael's Church, Jena ever since. The tomb of Frederick the Wise designed by Lucas Cranach the Elder is positioned in front of the altar, marked by a large bronze tablet alongside that of his brother, John the Steadfast to the right. On the left wall of the chancel is the bronze memorial to Frederick the Wise cast by Peter Vischer in Nuremberg in 1527. Note also the baptisimal font, designed by Schinkel in Gothic Revival style in 1832.

The **Schloss** itself, built in 1489–1525, is in worse repair; it has been repeatedly damaged by fire and war so little of the original remains. The west wing contains the **Museum für Natur und Völkerkunde** (opening times: Tues–Fri 09.00–17.00, Sat and Sun 09.00–12.30 and 14.00–16.00) with various natural history exhibits and material from Africa and Oceania. At Schlossplatz 1 is the pleasant restaurant, the Schlosskeller, just to the west of the Schloss itself.

From Wittenberg head W on the A187 to Coswig and then south on the A107 to Wörlitz. A car ferry will transport you across the broad River Elbe. Public transport consists of a bus from Wittenberg or by the Wörlitzer Eisenbahn from Dessau on Wednesday or the weekends during the summer.

B. Wörlitz

2000 inhabitants.

Tourist Information: Angergasse 131, 06786 Wörlitz. Tel. 216. Opening times: May–Oct, Mon–Wed and Fri 08.00–17.00, Thurs 08.00–18.00, Sat and Sun 09.00–12.00 and 12.30–17.00; Nov–April, Mon–Wed and Fri 08.00–16.00.

The suprising landscape park with its multitude of buildings stands to the north of the tiny village of Wörlitz. It covers 112.5 hectares with lakes, canals and islands. Built by Prince Leopold Friedrich Franz of Saxony-Anhalt in collaboration with architect Friedrich von Erdmannsdorff and landscape designer Johann Eyserbeck from 1765–1810, the *Wörlitzer Park is a popular tourist destination. Architect and Prince made a special journey to England before beginning work on the park and the Palladian influence is strikingly apparent. The **Schloss** stands to the north of the Markt, very near to the village. This was intentional, as from the beginning the Park was intended for the enjoyment of the villagers as well as royalty. (Opening times: by guided tour April and Oct Mon 13.00–16.00, Tues–Sun 10.00–16.00, May–Sept daily 10.00–17.00.) Constructed between 1769 and 1773 in imitation of the Palladian style then fashionable in England, the building has a splendid Roman portico with Corinthian columns. Inside there is a rare collection of porcelain, glass, painting and sculpture including *The Amazon of Wörlitz*, a Roman copy of a Greek original. The paintings are by Flemish, French, Italian and German artists from the 17C and 18C with the high points being Rubens, Ruysdael and Canaletto.

The Wörlitzer See to the north of the Schloss separates the village from the majority of the garden and buildings. To reach the other monument of architectural merit, the **Gotisches Haus**, head west from the Schloss following the banks of the lake. Pass the Gondel-Station where gondolas can be hired to cover the waterways of the grounds in roughly one hour. Cross the Friedrikenbrücke to reach the Neumarks Garten, the largest island of the complex, with its maze, pergola and library. Note the Rousseau Island to the west, named after the French Enlightenment philosopher. Cross to the Roseninsel (Rose Island) and the mainland beyond by ferry, then continue east by means of the Wolfsbrücke to reach the Gotisches Haus (opening times as for the Schloss). This cream-and-white Gothic fantasy was built in the romantic spirit of Strawberry Hill by Georg Christoph Hesekiel in 1773–1813, inspired by earlier English examples. The spindly turrets, windows with pointed arches and castellated walls and towers create a medieval fantasy. Inside there are interesting examples of Gothic Revival furnishings and displays of German, Dutch and Italian paintings including a good section on Lucas Cranach the Elder. Depending on available time you may wish to explore the garden further, taking in the various quasi-Classical garden statuary and temples. The east part of the gardens features the Eiserne Brücke, a petite model of the Ironbridge at Shropshire, and the Villa Hamilton, named after the British archaeologist, Sir William Hamilton. It would be possible to spend an entire day at the gardens, wandering along the winding paths and bijou bridges which link the various islands.

To reach Dessau from Wörlitz take the A107 5km south to Oranienbaum, with its 17C and 18C Dutch Baroque Schloss and Park, and continue west on the scenic A185 to Dessau.

Wörlitzer Park, built between 1769 und 1773 in Palladian style

C. Dessau

103,800 inhabitants.

Tourist Information: Friedrich-Naumann-Strasse 12, 06844 Dessau. Tel. 4661.
Opening times: Mon and Wed–Fri 10.00–12.00 and 14.00–18.00, Tues 10.00–18.00.

History. Dessau received its charter in the 13C and became the royal seat of the Anhalt-Dessau family in the 14C. The same family undertook important landscaping and building work in the 18C, creating some fine stately buildings. Dessau industrialised rapidly during the 19C and by the early 20C boasted an aircraft works and airfield. This factor, plus a sympathetic town mayor lured the Bauhaus School of Art and Design to the town from Weimar in 1926. However, the splendid modern building designed by Walter Gropius was closed down by the Nazis in 1933. The entire town was badly hit by Allied bombing in 1945, due to the aircraft works, and many historic buildings were lost. Dessau was rebuilt in ghastly Socialist modern style after the war, with its familiar windswept open spaces and multi-storey blocks of flats. However, the surviving Bauhaus building and 18C Mosigkau, Georgium and Luisium castles make it an attractive place to visit.

To reach the Bauhaus, the first stop on the town tour, follow the autobahn into Dessau from the Dessau Ost interchange. Continue east down Askanische Strasse past the Town Museum and turn right up Brauereistrasse and Öchelhäuser Strasse to the Bauhaus. The Bauhaus lies just behind the Hauptbahnhof. Leave by the rear exit and head west up Schwabestrasse, the building can be found at the end of Bauhaus strasse.

The **··Bauhaus building** is the highlight of a Dessau visit. This magnificent steel-framed building with flat roof and asymmetrical layout was designed by Bauhaus Director, Walter Gropius, in 1925. One of the first International Style buildings to be erected in the world, its reinforced concrete frame is clearly displayed on the workshop façade which faces onto the street. A complete curtain of glass, the corner of the rectangular block has no supporting pillar, a piece of technical virtuosity which Gropius had used at the Fagus factory at Alfeld in 1911. The building is lucidly divided into three main blocks: the workshops, the arts and crafts section and the administrative quarters which span the road running underneath. Continue round the back of the building to see the balconied student accommodation wing. The Bauhaus building was restored in 1977 after wartime damage by the GDR authorities who also installed a meagre display on the school's history. Harnessed into the state's Communist propaganda, the Bauhaus was celebrated in official literature as it '…sought to lead architecture and decorative art out of the crisis of late capitalist decadence'. Since the *Wende* the Bauhaus has operated as an adventurous art and design school once more with the focus on Green issues and the environment. Part of the building is now a museum (opening times: Wed–Fri 10.00–17.00, Sat and Sun 10.00–12.30 and 14.00–17.00) with Bauhaus furniture, photography and painting. It is also possible to see the theatre with tubular-steel seating by Marcel Breuer and the former office of Gropius on guided tours (contact the Bauhaus Dessau, Thälmannallee 38, PSF 160 Dessau to arrange a visit). Downstairs in the workshop block is a real treat: the newly restored café has excellent refreshments and bands playing late into the evening.

From the main Bauhaus building it is a short walk to the **Meistersiedlung** (Master's Houses) which Gropius designed for the various luminaries who taught at the school, including Russian abstract artist Wassily Kandinsky. Head north from the Bauhaus up Thälmannallee and left into Ebertallee. The seven compact houses were erected in 1926 with the detached Direktorenhaus completed first for Gropius. The building, which was destroyed during the war, was an elegant interplay of rectangular, white blocks which centre around a terrace. The remaining accommodation was situated in three pairs of semi-detached, flat-roofed buildings which the artists rented from the municipal authorities. The occupants did feel pangs of guilt at their luxurious new abodes and Walter Gropius directed the building of a working-class housing estate in the **Törten** suburb—reached via tram No. 1 (or drive south down Heide Strasse from the town centre). During 1926, 60 detached, Modernist houses were built on the estate using prefabricated building techniques. During 1927 a further 100 houses were added and, in the following year, another 156. In addition the *Konsumgebäude* (shopping centre) was built in 1928 with cafés and shops.

To explore the older parts of Dessau head north from the Hauptbahnhof and left down Friedrich Engels Strasse to the **Georgium**, an 18C park laid out beautifully by J. F. Eyserbeck with lakes and follies in the fashionable English style. In the centre stands the Schloss Georgium, designed by F. W.

The Bauhaus building, Dessau, designed by Walter Gropius in 1925

von Erdmannsdorff in crisp, Neo-Classical style in 1780–81. The building now houses a very good collection of painting in the Staatliche Galerie Schloss Georgium (opening times: Wed–Sun 10.00–18.00). Key artists shown in the gallery include Cranach, Rubens, Hals and Corot. The **Schloss Mosigkau** is situated c 9km south-west of the town centre, and may be reached by car via Altener Strasse, Junkers Strasse, Köthener Strasse and Orangerie Strasse where you turn right into J. von Liebig Strasse (parking may be found on the left). A train runs from the Hauptbahnhof to Mosigkau or buses D or L will take you there. The late Baroque palace was designed by Georg Wenzeslaus von Knobbelsdorff in 1754–56 and has housed a museum since 1951 (opening times: by guided tour, Tues–Sun 10.00–17.00). The Staatliches Museum contains work by Rubens and Van Dyck amongst some lovely Rococo interior decoration. There are summer exhibitions in the orangery which is situated in the pleasant grounds.

To the north-east of the town centre is a third park, the **Landschaftspark Luisium**, also laid out in the informal English style in the late 18C. It may be reached by bus line G or by car via August Bebel Strasse, then left just after crossing the River Mulde up Wasserstadt; bear left into Wilhelm Kreis strasse and the gardens are to the north up Am Luisium. Designed by J.F. Eyserbeck in 1780, the Schloss was built by F.W. van Erdmannsdorff in English Palladian style very closely related to that of the buildings at Wörlitz Park.

39

The Altmarkt region

From Magdeburg—56km Stendal—14km Tangermünde—9km Jerichow.

The cultural delights of the Altmarkt region which covers the north of Saxony Anhalt are relatively sparse. However, for those with a keen interest in brick Gothic architecture, it is well worth making the trip to see the UNESCO preserved Premonstratensian monastery at Jerichow, the town fortifications at Tangermünde and the Uenglinger gate tower and Cathedral at Stendal.

From Magdeburg take the A189 in a northerly direction to Stendal. This takes you through the sleepy town of Wolmirstedt (12,000 inhabitants) and across the heathland of Colbitz-Letzlinger. Frequent trains run from Magdeburg with a journey time of one hour.

A. Stendal

52,000 inhabitants.

Tourist Information: Kornmarkt 8, 39576 Stendal. Tel. 216186. Opening times: Mon–Wed and Fri 08.30–16.00, Thurs 09.00–17.00.

History. Stendal is the capital of the Altmarkt region which consists mainly of agricultural lowlands, bordered to the east by the River Elbe, Niedersachsen in former west Germany to the west and Brandenburg to the north. The town was founded in the mid 12C by Margrave Albrecht the Bear. From 1358 to 1518 Stendal was a member of the Hanseatic League. Stendal is most famous as the birthplace of leading German archaeologist and art historian, Johann Joachim Winckelmann (1717–68). Indeed, the French novelist Henri Beyle wrote under the pseudonym of Stendhal in homage to Winckelmann—the addition of the 'h' giving the French version of the town's name. Industry made an impact on Stendal during the 19C and a large nuclear power station was built here during GDR rule. A welcome stopping-off point on the route to the Baltic coast by rail or road, Stendal offers some interesting architectural sights, particularly from the town's medieval heyday.

From the railway station walk north up Bahnhofstrasse to reach the **Tangermünder Tor**. The granite base has survived from the 13C and the original town fortifications whilst the late Gothic upper section dates from 1440–60. Continue north to the **Pfarrkirche St Katharinen**, a late Gothic brick hall church founded in 1435. The **Almärkisches Museum** is situated in part of the old Katharinenkloster (opening times: Tues–Fri 10.00–12.00 and 14.00–

17.00, Sat and Sun 13.00–17.00) which specialises in the history of Stendal and the Altmarkt region. The **Dom St Nikolaus** is to the west of the cloisters, across Hall Strasse. Founded in 1188 with the majority of building taking place in 1423–67, this late Gothic hall church stands in the centre of a peaceful green (opening times: May–Sept daily 10.00–12.00 and 15.00–17.00; Oct–April, Mon–Fri 13.00–14.00). The western parts of the turret-like towers are in early Gothic style, dating from 1250. Inside the Dom look in particular at the 23 stained glass windows which date from 1425–70. They are possibly the best preserved, most complete set in Germany. There are also, in the choir, sculptures taken from the Romanesque church which once stood on this site, including 13 sandstone figures from 1240–50.

Continue north up Hall Strasse to reach the MARKT with the splendid grouping of the Renaissance, stepped gabled Rathaus and **Pfarrkirche St Marien** behind. The Roland statue in front of the brick Laubenflügel of the Rathaus is a 1974 copy of the 1525 original. The Ratskeller is a good place to stop off for refreshments and to enjoy the mid 16C vaulting of this former trade hall. The church of St Mary is a virtuoso piece of 15C brick architecture with its soaring twin towers and decorative detail (opening times: May–Oct daily 10.00–12.00 and 15.00–17.00). Inside, the late Gothic retable is of note, as is the bronze font dating from 1474. Look for the splendid 16C astronomical clock beneath the organ gallery on the west side. Behind the church is a Romantic statue of Winckelmann created by L. Wichmann in 1856. Continue north up Breite Strasse and on the right is the **Pfarrkirche St Jacobi**, built in 1340 with major alterations in 1470. The late Gothic building has some marvellous examples of 14C and 15C stained glass.

Continue north to the top of Breite Strasse and west down Altes Dorf to the most striking building in the town, the **Uenglinger Tor**. This brick-built 15C gateway is possibly the best town gate still existing in Saxony-Anhalt or Brandenburg. Erected in 1450–60, the square tower has one central turret framed by four corner towers. It is possible to climb this extraordinary building for sweeping views of the town (opening times: May–Sept, Sat and Sun 10.00–12.00 and 14.00–16.00). Head south from the Tower down Winckelmannstrasse where, at No. 36, is the **Winckelmann Museum** (opening times: Tues–Sun 10.00–12.00 amd 13.00–17.00). Situated in the half-timbered house which was his birthplace, this museum charts the life and seminal work of this 18C founder of archaeology and art history. The seven rooms contain relics pertaining to Winckelmann, whose academic study of Roman art laid the foundations for all future studies of the subject.

From Stendal follow the A188 SW to reach Tangermünde, there are also train and bus links between the two towns.

B. Tangermünde

11,800 inhabitants.

Stadtverwaltung (Local Council Offices, no Tourist Information): Lange Strasse 60, 39590 Tangermünde. Tel. 2971/973.

History. Situated picturesquely on the banks of the River Elbe at the mouth of the Tanger, the somewhat neglected town of Tangermünde was a long-time residence of the Margraves of Brandenburg. In 1373 Holy Roman Emperor Charles IV chose the fortress town of Tangermünde as his second residence after Prague and during

1373–78 it was capital of the Holy Roman Empire. It was well placed on the busy trade route between the Baltic coast and Central Europe and continued to flourish, even after the Emperor's death in 1378. The well-preserved town walls attest to the former glory of Tangermünde. In later years the town developed industrially, concentrating on foodstuff with an early sugar refinery built here, followed by other factories in the Communist era.

As you head south-west down Bahnhofstrasse from the station, the brick town fortifications immediately make an impact. The wall was begun in 1300 with the gates built during the 15C. Turn right down Karlstrasse, noting the Wassterturm dating from 1470 in the central square as you head towards Mauerstrasse, which skirts the inside of the western town wall. On the right can be seen the cylindrical Schrotturm, one of the town's fortifications. Continue south down Notpforte to Lange Strasse and the magnificent brick **Rathaus** stands in the central square. Built in 1430 and restored in 1846, the main façade has three pointed gables decorated with fanciful, mock rose windows and tiny turrets. In the basement is the **Heimatmuseum**, a collection pertaining to local history (opening times: April–Nov, Tues–Sun 10.00–12.00 and 14.00–17.00; Dec–March, Wed–Sun 10.00–12.00 and 14.00–16.00).

Head west down Lange Strasse to reach the former **Nikolaikirche**. Founded in the 12C, the church was extended in 1470 with the addition of a brick tower. Beside this is the **Neustädter Tor**, one of the town's most impressive gateways, dating from 1450. Built from decorative brick, it shares stylistic similarities with the Uenglinger Tor at Stendal. Continuing east back down Kirchstrasse, note the former Adler Apothecary at No. 53, a smart Neo-Classical building erected in 1816. At the eastern end of Lange Strasse is the brick **Stephanskirche** which was founded in 1184, with some rebuilding in the 14C and the addition of a Baroque northern tower in 1712. Inside this hall church there are interesting tombstones spanning the 15C to 19C, an early 16C font and a 17C organ made by Hans Scherer from Hamburg.

Continue north-east past the 15C Hühnerdorfer Torturm, the oldest of the town's gates, to the Burg. Little remains of the castle which Charles IV built in the 14C as it was occupied twice during the Thirty Years War. Some ruins still stand in the public park, including the main gateway or Burgtorturm and the Kanzlei, a former regal hall with beamed ceiling. Continue south down to the banks of the Tanger for an outsider's view of the town's fortifications. The **Elbtor** stands picturesquely in front of the Stephenskirche, built in brick with small arched entrance the upper part is half-timbered.

Retrace your steps back to the station, noting the plethora of half-timbered houses on Kirchstrasse which runs parallel to Lange Strasse.

To reach the next stop, Jerichow, by car take the A188 east across the Elbe and then the A107 south for 7km; Jerichow may also be reached by bus or train from Tangermünde.

JERICHOW is a tiny village with an impressive *Klosterkirche. An important medieval religious centre, the Premonstratensian monastery was founded here in 1144. The church is a late Romanesque, brick structure used over the years as farm buildings, schnapps distillery and warehouse before much needed restoration began in 1960. Now preserved under the auspices of UNESCO this stunningly simple church has twin towers, added in the mid 14C in Gothic style. It is well worth visiting the interior for a sight of the amazing crypt dating from 1178 (opening times: by guided tour

April–June, Sept and Oct, Mon–Fri at 14.00, Sat and Sun at 11.00 and 14.00). The capitals are skilfully carved with naturalistic patterns in stone, supporting the groin vaulting. On the south side of the church is the Kloster which nowadays houses a museum focusing on the history of this early religious settlement. The Romanesque monastery buildings are grouped in three wings around a central courtyard (opening times: April–Oct, daily 10.00–17.00; Nov–March, Tues–Fri 10.00–12.00 and 13.00–16.00).

Return to Magdeburg by means of the A107 south to Genthin, 27km south-west on the A1 to Burg, south of which connect with the E30 for Magdeburg. By train, return via Stendal from Tangermünde.

The late Romanesque Klosterkirche of Jerichow

VI THÜRINGEN

40

From western Germany to the Thüringian Forest

Bad Hersfeld—45km Eisenach—40km Schmalkalden—30km Suhl—10km Ilmenau—20km Arnstadt—18km Erfurt.

This route crosses the old east–west German border three times and then traverses a major portion of the picturesque **Thüringian Wald** (Thüringian Forest) which stretches over 100km in length and covers most of the south-west of the Land of Thuringia. Heading south from Eisenach (see Route 41) this semi-circular journey presents an opportunity to visit some of the most scenic villages and castles in eastern Germany. The landscape is not particularly mountainous, but the woods lie on gently sloping hills, the highest point being the Grosser Berberg (Great Berry Mountain) which reaches 982m above sea level.

Take the E40 from **Bad Hersfeld**. This is not a road of motorways standards, but a slow moving dual carriageway with average speeds of c 60mph. The popularity of travel to the eastern parts of Germany can be seen in the sheer volume of traffic heading east. Heavy traffic heading west is notable for the sheer volume of Polish vehicles. The E40 crosses the border with Thuringia three times in all as it snakes through the gentle slopes. Deserted border posts and striking views of sleepy towns, including Berka, make a fascinating contrast. It is chilling to think that it was not until 1989 that traffic could move freely along this stretch of road.

Take the first junction off the E40 once you enter Thuringia proper, heading south on the A7 to Eisenach. Take the A19 south out of Eisenach which passes the main road to Schloss Wartburg Castle. On the right after 5km is the **Hohe Sonne**, a wooden ridge 435m high with a pleasant café and beer garden. The **Rennsteig**—an ancient hill track which connects Horschel near Eisenach to Blankenstein by the Czech border—cuts across the A19 at this point. The complete route takes six days to cover and is 168km long, however, it was laid out as a path in the 19C with signs and so it is simple to cover only small sections. There are magnificent views of the Wartburg from this vantage point. A further 3km south is the **Wilhelmstal**, where the yellow building on the right, a hunting-lodge built in the 17C and altered by Duke Charles Augustus in the 18C stands by a lake, fed by the River Elte. 3km south on the right is the international campsite, Altenburger See, situated in the woods surrounding a pleasant lake with facilities for safe swimming and boating. There is also a good café open from 10.00 to 22.00. Continue south through the picturesque villages of Etterwinder, Waldfisch and Barchfeld. Follow the signs from Schmalkalden heading east on a minor road.

A. Schmalkalden

17,000 inhabitants.

Tourist Office: Mohrengasse 2, 98574 Schmalkalden. Tel. (0037 670) 3182, Mon–Fri 09.00–12.00 and 13.00–17.00

This charming and picturesque town, with its atmospheric narrow streets and half-timbered houses has an interesting range of museums and historic architecture.

History. Schmalkalden occupies an important place in the history of the Reformation and industrial archaeology. The town was first mentioned in 874 with the founding of the monastery of Fulda. The town flourished in medieval times, with fortifications built in 1315, and in the 15C it became an established centre for the manufacture of iron hand tools, made from iron ore mined near the town. Schmalkalden is best known as the home of the Union of Schmalkalden, made between Protestant German princes and leaders of the Free Imperial Cities, who wished to remain independent of any centralised control, in 1530. The Union ended in 1546 with the War of Schmalkalden. By the 16C Schmalkalden was the second largest town in Hessen and the local aristocrat, Wilhelm IV of Hessen, built a hunting and summer residence here, the Wilhelmsburg Castle, which still stands as the most important cultural edifice in the town and one of the best examples of Renaissance building in Germany. The village itself is well preserved and was a popular tourist attraction from Russians during GDR times. Now Schmalkalden attracts visitors from western Germany and funds are being poured into an extensive renovation programme. Its popularity seems set to continue with over 100,000 visitors in 1991 and virtually double this in 1992.

The information office is situated in bijou premises in the ALTMARKT. To the west is the **Stadtkirche St Georg**: the south tower is Romanesque and the remainder late Gothic, dating from 15C. The architect for the later building was Meyer of Erfurt and his image is immortalised on the exterior of the northern part of the church. Organ recitals may be heard in the church during the summer months. Situated behind the church and opposite the southern tower are two historic houses: straight ahead is a half-timbered dwelling dating from 1669; and to the left a school for reformers dating from 1658 (formerly a soup kitchen, the building now stands empty awaiting a decision about its fate). Return to the Altmarkt and the 15C **Rathaus**, situated on the south-west of the square. The exterior has an interesting stepped gabled roof and inside are wall-paintings dating from the 19C. The Ratskeller offers good refreshments, indoors and out.

Cross the Altmarkt, passing the information office, and head north-east up the STEINGASSE, the oldest extant street in Schmalkalden. No. 11 was built in 1545; formerly the post office, it has been a chemists since the 17C and is now the Risenapotheke. Straight ahead on the Lutherplatz at No. 7 is the **Lutherhause** where the famous reformer lived in 1537; it is recognisable by the carved swan, a symbol of Luther, which graces the exterior. Luther lodged here on the second floor and also preached at the Stadtkirche. Pass by the Lutherhaus and north-east up the Schlossberg to reach the **Schloss Wilhelmsburg** (open Feb–Oct, daily 09.00–17.00, last admission 16.30); Nov–Jan 10.00–16.00, last admission 15.30).

Enter through an archway and then turn right onto a terrace which affords wonderful views of the red-roofed town sloping beneath. The building straight ahead is the law courts—formerly the stables for the palace—and the curious Neo-Classical building to the left is the town's cinema which is currently closed. Also on view to the south is the only remaining tower which formed part of the old town wall. The whole district is known as the 'priest' district as so many clergy lived here at one time. Back up the steps from the terrace you face the castle, a largely 19C reconstruction of the 15C original. The sole remaining portion is the tower which houses the Lutheranian church to the right. Enter the courtyard, where a pleasant café is situated, take the door labelled 'Museum' and head up the stairs. There are 50 rooms here, many of which are on show with some interesting exhibits. In the first room of the tour, thought to be the dining room, are wall-paintings claimed to be 400 years old. They were carried out by artists from Kassel working under the Dutch artist Wilhelm Vermukken, whose inspiration came from the Italian Renaissance. There are classical representations of Justice and Prudence, Charity and Temperance framing the windows. The furniture on view is authentic to the 15C, but did not originally belong to the castle. Original to the castle, however, are five stoves, one of which is on show the first room with iron-plate base and ceramic upper made in Hessen and depicting scenes from the Bible. Displays concerning the history of Schmalkalden, the iron-works, the Schmalkalden Unity and a Luther Bible printed by Hans Luft in Wittenburg in 1548, fill the succeeding rooms. The heavy handed restoration work of the 19C and 1960s are much in evidence. Temporary exhibitions of contemporary art are on view in three of the rooms, including the work of Berlin sculptor Wieland Forster.

The tour's second last stop is at the **Riesensaal** (Hall of Giants), a large hall built for concerts and still used for that purpose today. There is some interesting wall and ceiling painting in naïve style, depicting mythological heroes and Old Testament figures. A 17C portrait of the castle's founder, Wilhelm IV, is painted over the door. The last room is the most splendid and the only truly original part of the castle—the **Schlosskirche**. This magnificent white and gold, three storey church is quite stunning with altar, pulpit and organ arranged on one, central axis. It is the earliest surviving church built for Protestant worship. The ground floor was where the townsfolk worshipped, while the officers of the castle were to be found on the first and the Landgraves on the second. There is a marble table altar, a pulpit projecting from the first floor above and wooden organ dating from 1590 wonderfully preserved and used frequently for summer concerts above this. Built by Daniel Meyer, an organmaker from Gottinger, it is the oldest working example in central Europe. The organ shutters are beautifully painted with Biblical scenes, and the workings consist of six rows of 42 pipes, making 252 in total. The wooden construction of the organ gives it a distinctive tone, particularly suitable for Baroque music. The organ was painstakingly restored during the 1970s using the organ in Frederiksborg near Copenhagen as a model. The reconstructed 19C kitchen can also be visited with a lovely display of wooden and metal utensils where meals for over 100 of the guests who would return from a hunting trip would be prepared. The comprehensive collection of 50 cast-iron stove plates can also be viewed.

Other attractions in the town include the Hessenhof, situated near the Neumarkt on Klostergasse. Built c 1551 on earlier foundations, this was originally the Landgrabe's Court where the land lying to the south of the Thurinigan forest was administered. The present cellar was originally the first floor and contains some stunning 13C frescoes. These wall paintings are based on the epic poem *Iwein* by Hartmann von Aue (1203) and were painted in Romanesque style c 1220.30. The old iron works, the **Hockofenanlage Neue Hutte** (open April–Oct, Wed–Sun 10.00–17.00) at Gothaer

Strasse to the north of the town in the suburbs of Weidesrunn can also be visited. Here the 19C forge, blast furnace and metalwork shops can be seen as relics from the town's industrial past. The old iron ore mine is now also a museum, situated 5km north-east in Asback. **Schaubergwerk Finstertal**, with a display of mining equipment, is open April–Oct, Wed–Sun 10.00–17.00.

Head south-east out of Schmalkalden on Recklinghauser Strasse to join the A19. Head south at the junction to Wasungen, just past Welkerhausen join the B280 to Zella-Mehlis and the A247 to Suhl.

B. Suhl

57,000 inhabitants.

Tourist Information: Steinweg 1, 98527 Suhl. Tel. 5605.

Lying in the valley formed by the Lauter and Hasel rivers, **Suhl** is an important skiing resort as it lies on the south-west fringe of the Thüringian Forest. Although major rebuilding work took place in the post-war era, including the usual blocks of flats and anonymous Hall of Friendship, some older parts, dating as far back as the 17C are well preserved and house interesting museums.

History. The first mention of Suhl dates back to 1318 as a small settlement in the country of Henneberg-Schleusingen. Early trade took place on the extraction of salt in the town and the mining or iron ore in the nearby Dollberg and Domberg mountains from 1300 onwards. In the 16C the production of small arms began, for which Suhl is still known today. The first gunsmiths came here from Augsburg and Nuremburg in 1535 and this tradition is celebrated in the town's Weapons Museum. During the industrial revolution a weaving mill and porcelain factory were opened here and the town was connected to Erfurt by railway in 1884. During the 20C the small arms manufacturing industry continued to flourish and tourism also became an important industry.

In the town centre the most important port of call is the **Weapons Museum**, located in Wilhelm-Pieck-Strasse. The museum contains examples of weapons dating from the 16C onwards. The museum is housed in a splendid half-timbered malthouse dating from 1663. Other historic half-timbered buildings still standing include the former Municipal Home for Orphans and the Poor (1687) in Neuendorfer Strasse and the Golden Stagg Inn in Suhl-Neuendorf (1616). The Rathaus on Suhl-Heinrichs is also halftimbered and well restored, the original structure dating back to 1657 with the stone ground floor dating from 1551. Suhl also boasts two important churches, the 18C **St Marien** and Baroque **Kreuzkirche** (1731–39) with stucco ceiling, original organ casing and richly decorated pulpit and altar. To the north-west of Suhl lies the Domberg mountain which reaches 676m above sea level and is crowned by the 19C Ottilienstein and Ottilien chapels, also providing magnificent views of the town.

Take the Ilmenauer Strasse east out of Suhl in the direction of Schmiedefeld. Just after Schmiedefeld join the B4 north to Ilmenau. In Stützerbach, 10km south of Ilmenau, is a small museum devoted to local glass and to the town's former inhabitant, Goethe.

C. Ilmenau

26,000 inhabitants.

Tourist Information: Linderstrasse 12, 98693 Illmenau. Tel. 3677 62132.

Ilmenau is best known through its connection with Goethe. In his capacity as minister of state in Weimar he visited the town several times between 1776 and 1831. His mission was to revive the fluorspar mining industry which had generated the wealth of the town since the Middle Ages. Goethe also carried out natural science investigations in Ilmenau and the surrounding district. The town's history is celebrated in the local museum, situated on the Market Place in a former Baliff's House dating from 1736 with examples of Ilmenau glassware, porcelain and souvenirs of Goethe's time here. The 861m high mountain, **Kickelhahn**, lies just south of Ilmenau and the Goethe-hauschen is situated here near the summit. On the occasion of his last visit to Ilmenau in 1831 with his two grandchildren he made a pilgrimage to this secluded hut, where he had written the words of a poem devoted to the town on the walls. Unfortunately, the hut was burned down in 1870; a reproduction now stands in its place.

Take the Erfurter Strasse north-west out of Ilmenau to connect with the B4 once again towards Plaue. On the right just past Plaue is the Reinsberge; Arnstadt is then entered from the south, on Plauesche Strasse.

D. Arnstadt

30,000 inhabitants.

Tourist Information: 3 Markt, 99310 Arnstadt, tel. 20 49, open Mon–Fri 09.00–12.00, 12.30–18.00, Sat 09.00–12.00.

Arnstadt is a particularly well preserved Thüringian town with a rich diversity of museums, churches and castles. The town was first mentioned in 704 and is thought to be the oldest in Thuringia. The town walls were erected in the 12C and in 1266 Arnstadt was granted a town charter, its 3000 inhabitants being mainly employed in farming, crafts and trade. The **Liebrauen Church** equals Naumburg in importance. Built between 1215 and 1235, it is in the Transitional style, marking the change from Romanesque to Gothic. The town is particularly linked with Johann Sebastian Bach, who embarked upon his career as organist at the Boniface Church (now the Bachkirche) from 1703–07. The town grew in commercial importance during the 19C with the construction of the three railway lines which intersected here. A pleasant afternoon can be spent strolling through the cobbled streets, relaxing in the cafés and visiting the impressive sights of cultural interest.

The **Rathaus** on the corner of the main square, the Markt, is a three-storey building which differs from most of the town halls to be seen in Thuringia in that it is in Dutch Renaissance style, designed by Christopher Junghans and built between 1583–85. Note the two richly ornamented, scrolled gables and magnificent portal surmounted by the town's coat of arms—an eagle with outspread wings crowned by the arms of the then members of the town council. The symbols of Justice, Bravery, Faith and Love as well as rich ornamentation complete the decoration. Between the Rathaus and the Bachkirche to the east of the Markt stands a fountain dating from 1708, with the small stone figure, a knight by the sculptor Heinrich Christoph Meil added in 1737.

The modest **Bachkirche** (open Mon–Fri 08.00–12.00 and 14.00–16.00) stands in the centre of the Markt. A Baroque building, it was designed by Andreas Rudolph and erected during 1676–83 as Bonifatiuskirche (Boniface church). A basic hall church, it has a straight east end and neither choir nor bell tower to the west. The original church was burnt down in 1581 and only the annexe on the south side remains from the earlier structure, having been built in 1477. Inside can be seen a carved tombstone of Georg von Schonberg dating from 1570 and a crucifixion scene with three carved figures by Christoph Meil in Baroque style (c 1700).

Head south to the **Galerie**, a pretty row of shops with an arcade built in 17C. On the south-east corner of the Markt stands the **Haus 'Zum guldenen Greif'** at No. 11. This building the frontage of which dates from 1586 and the rear from 1624, was substantially renovated in 1971 and is now an inn. On the north-east corner, the bay window on the ground floor has interesting Renaissance ornament and a small hall in the interior has plaster decoration dating from 1780–90. In the south-west of the Markt stands a modern bronze statue commemorating Bach, by Bernd Gobel, a local sculptor. Behind this at No. 8 is the **Haus 'Zum bunten Lowen'** (Brightly Coloured Lion) built in 1765 and a chemists since 1860.

North-west across the Markt at No. 3 is the **Haus 'Zum Palmbaum'** (Palm tree house) (opening times: Mon–Fri 08.00–12.30 and 13.00–17.00, last Sat in month 08.00–13.00). It derives its name from the exotic stone palm tree which stands over the main entrance, dating from 1740. Formerly a Burgherhaus this is now the Bachmuseum which opened in 1985 and houses various exhibits devoted to the composer. The Tourist Information can be found to the left in the same building.

Continue west to the magnificent **Liebfauenkirche**, one of the most important churches in Thuringia (opening times: Mon, Tues, Thurs and Fri 14.00–16.00, Wed and Sat 10.00–12.00).

A twin-towered basilica built between 1215 and 1235 it is notable as an example of the transition from Romanesque to Gothic style. The church was first designed by the Abbots of Hersfeld as a flat-roofed basilica. The plans were changed shortly before the mid 13C to include a nave and rib vaulting. The most striking aspect of the church is the pair of towers on the west front, which closely resembles those at Naumburg. The south tower of the west front and both upper storeys of the north tower date from the 13C. The south tower of the west front and both upper storeys of the north tower date from c 1270. The nave and three-aisled choir are in the high Gothic style, as building work eventually finished c 1307. The Benedictine Monastery of St Walburgis was established here with the Liebfrauenkirche but the monastery was dissolved as a result of the Reformation. The church has undergone various alterations during the succeeding years: the Nuns' Gallery was removed in 1880 and restoration took place in 1912 and 1956. Inside, situated in the choir, there is a triptych dating from 1498—and the work of a north Thüringian workshop of painters and carpenters. The centre panel shows the crowning of Mary and the wings are decorated with reliefs illustrating the life of Mary as well as the cycle of the Passion. In the north side choir there are several memorials to the Counts of Schwarzburg. The tomb of Gunther XXV who died in 1368 and his wife Elisabeth from 1381 are in the early Gothic style of the noted Prague-based studio of Peter Parler. Many other monuments in the church celebrate local notables from 13C to 18C including Gunther the Quarrelsome (1590).

Continue south-east down Schulplan and then Pfarrhof to reach the **Oberkirche** (Upper church) to the left. This is a single-nave Gothic church dating from the early to mid 14C with altar, pulpit and font dating from 17C and designed by Burkard Furstenstand. Head north up Markstrasse to reach the Bachkirche once more and continue east down Zimmer Strasse then north up Schlossstrasse to reach the Neues Palais which contains the impressive **Schlossmuseum** (opening times: April–Oct 08.30–12.00, 13.00–16.30, Oct–April 09.30–16.00; closed Mon). This Baroque palace was built between 1728 and 1732 by Prince Gunther I as a Dower House for his wife Princess Elisabeth Albertine von Schwarzburg-Sondershausen. There is a display of period rooms, including the Grosser Spiesesaal with fine 18C plasterwork on the ceiling and a small part of the valuable Dresden and Oriental porcelain collection on show. More than 100 pieces of oriental porcelain are on display in the sumptuous Porzellankabinett, custom-built for the collection in 1735 with intricate shelving and console tables created by Heinrich Christoph Meil.

The key attraction at the Neues Palais is the 'Mon Plaisir' collection of 400 dolls dating from 1690 to 1750 and displayed in 82 miniature period rooms. The collection was made for the princess Augusta Dorothea, wife of Anton Gunthers II von Schwartzburg-Arnstadt, and is a positive delight. A detailed *Hofkuche* shows five dolls in period dress as servants and chefs in a tiled kitchen, complete with miniature wooden furniture, ceramics, brass plates and utensils hanging from the walls. The *Apotheke* is beautifully made, with tiny sets of drawers, scales and bottles and the recreation of an *Audienz* shows a princess seated on her throne complete with monkey on a chain, interviewing a grandly dressed gentleman. The walls are decorated with fashionable Chinoiserie silk with matching chairs. Also on view at the neues Palais are 11 16C Brussels tapestries illustrating scenes from the Old and New Testaments, Rococo wood carvings and 18C paintings.

To the north of the Palais is the Neptungrotte, created in 1736 with a marvellous statue of Neptune created by Heinrich Christoph Meil. The ruin of the Schloss Neideck stands to the right of the Neptungrotte in the Schlossgarten. The Schloss collapsed in 1779 and only parts of the east wing and the 65m tower remain, with its distinctive Baroque cupola. On the east side of the Schlossgarten is the Fischtor, one of the remaining three town gates, built in the 16C with half-timbered upper storey.

From Arnstadt it is possible to make the popular trip north-west to the **Drei Gleichen** (Three Alike), a trio of castles which dominate the surrounding landscape. The first, **Wachsenburg**, lies just north of the village of Holzhausen and was founded in the 12C. Perched on top of a wooded hill, it was once the base for a robber knight, Apel Vitstum, who ambushed Erfurt traders. The castle then became the property of the Dukes of Gotha in 1641 and now houses a restaurant, hotel and small museum. The second castle is the **Mühlburg**, adjacent to the village of the same name, and the oldest of the three. Built in 704 it was given by Duke Heden II to the Bishop of Utrecht as a base for the dissemination of the Christian faith in the 12C. The castle was then occupied by the town of Erfurt to protect their trade routes. However, its military significance declined in the 17C and the

Mühlburg now stands as a ruin as does the 11C **Burg Gleichen** though the latter still has its Renaissance residence intact. The last of the three castles, it stands just north of the E43 motorway.

From Arnstadt it is a short drive to the main town of Erfurt, north on the A4 leading from Ichterhauser Strasse.

41

Eisenach and the Wartburg Castle

47,000 inhabitants.

Tourist Office: 3–5 Bahnhofstrasse, 99817 Eisenach. Tel. 76162, 4895, 2284. Opening hours: Mon 10.00–18.00, Tue–Fri 09.00–18.00, Sat 09.00–15.00.

Railway station: Bahnhofstrasse.

EISENACH has a wealth of museums and architectural jewels to visit. Situated near the former border with West Germany, it has a comparatively international atmosphere. This is partly due to the location just outside the town of the **Wartburg Castle**, which attracts visitors from all over Europe during the summer months; indeed, over two million are claimed to visit the town annually. There is the faded elegance so familiar in eastern Germany, from the cobbled streets to the amazing, crumbling buildings. In the days of the GDR Eisenach was best known as the home of Wartburg car production. Now the massive factory complex lies idle as a testament to the old regime. New BMW and Opel plants have been built here since 1989 but do not employ the same massive numbers. At present the charming narrow streets are relatively quiet but this will soon change, as restoration work and an adjustment to Western economics will surely attract many more tourists.

History. The history of Eisenach is closely related to the building and inhabitants of the Wartburg Castle. Situated on the north-west fringe of the Thüringian forest, the town was founded in the 11C at the same time as the Castle. It is still overlooked by this mighty medieval stronghold, perched on a rock some 412m above the town and founded in 1067 by Ludwig the Springer as a defence against Emperor Henry IV of Saxony. The castle became an important cultural centre in medieval times as the residence of the Landgraves of Thuringia, playing host to the famous Sangerkrieg or Wartburgkrieg, a minstrels' contest, in 1207. This was the subject of a medieval poem and an opera by Richard Wagner, *Tannhäuser*, which he wrote after staying in the castle in 1842. The Wartburg Castle earned a different sort of renown through the daughter of Andreas II of Hungary, Elisabeth, who married Ludwig IV of Thuringia, nursed the sick and poor at the Castle and was canonised four years after she died in 1235. The stronghold was inhabited by the Landgraves until 1440, when the line died out. The castle also boasts historical associations with Martin Luther. Proclaimed a heretic by the Diet of Worms, he stayed there from 4 May 1521 to 6 March 1522, as a fugitive from the authorities, and translated the New Testament from Greek into German. He was protected by the Elector Frederick the Wise, and assumed the identity of Junker Jörg ('Farmer George'), a minor nobleman. There are further links between Eisenach and Luther as the house in Georgenstrasse was the home of the Cotta family with whom Luther lodged when he was 16. Eisenach is also well known as the birthplace of Johann Sebastian Bach, and this fact is commemorated by a museum and an annual music festival in March. Excelling as a cultural centre during the 17C and 18C, Eisenach developed industrially during the 19C in the production of textiles and cars.

A. Eisenach Town Centre

Begin at the **main railway station**, a fine Jugendstil building with a stained glass window over the main entrance celebrating 70 years of car building. Cross the main road after leaving the building and head west up Bahnhofstrasse where the main **Tourist Office** can be found on the right. The Korso Café at No. 7 offers delightful food and drink, including an English breakfast! Straight ahead is the massive 12C Romanesque town gate or **Nikolaitor**, the only one remaining of four originals. The two sculptures above the arch represent Ludwig I, founder of the Ludowingian dynasty who first ruled Thuringia, and the other is the district's heraldic symbol, a lion. Built onto this is the **Nikolaikirche**, a later Romanesque structure of c 1200. The octagonal tower was restored in 1887 and painted decoration added in 1894. In front of the church in Karlsplatz is a statue of Luther by Donndorf dating from 1895, commemorating one of the town's most famous inhabitants. Four panels around the base celebrate aspects of Luther's life: one shows Luther at work translating in the Wartburg, another Luther singing as a boy, the third Luther disguised as Junker Jörg and the last a hymn by Luther 'Solid Castles'. The statue was built to commemorate the 375th anniversary of Luther arriving in Eisenach.

Diagonally across the square, in the direction of Sophienstrasse, is the **Monument to Medicine**, erected in 1926 in a Modernist style. Continue west down Sophienstrasse, to the right is the THEATERPLATZ with the town's fine Renaissance revival theatre, built in 1879. Continue west and the 19C **Elisabethkirche** is on the left. Built in 1888 as a copy of the larger Magdeburg original for the town's small Catholic population, it has a simple interior with fine rib vaulting. Across the street are new flats, built in the 1970s in bland, modern style. On the corner, partly obscured by bushes, is a plaque commemorating Professor Ernst Abbe who was born here in 1840 and founded the famous Zeiss factories in nearby Jena for the production of optical equipment. Further down Sophienstrasse is an abstract fountain, its design supposedly based on the cones of the eye. Just beyond this piece of Socialist sculpture in the Jakobsplan is the 18C residence of the Bechol family, where the great philosopher Goethe stayed in 1774–1780. Behind this pleasant 18C villa is the former garden of the house which is now the Goethe Park, flanked on one side by remains of the town wall and tower. A new fountain has been built in the garden, surmounted by a donkey symbolising the role these animals played in carrying people and supplies up to the Wartburg Castle.

Continue to the end of Sophienstrasse and turn left down Hospital Strasse, heading south to Georgenstrasse. On the corner a plaque marks the site of the old Georgentor, another of the city gates. Across the street is an interesting contemporary monument, celebrating the town's new start after the *Wende*. Suprisingly, it consists of five eggs, symbolising rebirth, two pretzels, symbolising eternity and a crowing rooster, heralding a new dawn.

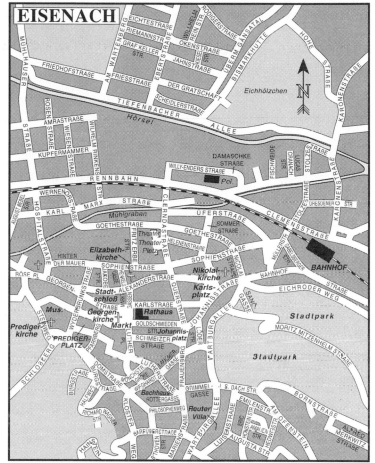

WARTBURG CASTLE

Created by local sculptor, Josef Laufer, the monument encapsulates the tremendous optimism felt by East Germans during the days of re-unification. To the west is the RÖSEPLATZ, site of the Annenkircke founded by St Elizabeth in 1226. Behind the Laufer sculpture is the oldest existing dwelling in Eisenach, a tumbledown timber-framed house. Down an alleyway past the house is the 17C Crest Church and tower from the old town wall, reconstructed in the 18C and used to imprison religious radical Fritz Erbe.

Continue south into the Schlossberg where the Wartburg Information Office is situated (opening hours: Mon 10.00–18.00, Tues–Fri 09.00–18.00, Sat 09.00–15.00). In Predigerplatz is the **Predigerkirche**, which has functioned as a Museum for nearly one hundred years (opening hours: Tues–Fri 09.00–12.30, Sat and Sun 09.00–16.00). The museum consists of a display of Thüringian church sculpture carved in wood. There are examples from as early as the 12C, with Gothic Crucifixions, Pietàs and Madonnas as well as altarpieces from the 16C. The last of the Landgraves of Thuringia, Heinrich Raspe, is also represented here, by a sculpture in amazing realist form, partly inspired by the Naumburg School.

Continue east down Untere Predigergasse to the splendid MARKTPLATZ where stands the late Gothic **Georgenkirche**, marked outside by a statue of St George and the Dragon dating from 1708. In the entrance to the Georgenkirche on the right is a fearsome statue of Bach, installed in 1939 and a typical example of Nazi art.

The church was founded in 1180–88 by Ludwig IV, husband of the future St Elisabeth. The church was rebuilt just before the reformation in late Gothic style and became a major Protestant place of worship, with Luther preaching here in 1521. The upper galleries were added at this date. Bach was baptised here in 1685 and the original stone font still stands, dating from 1503. Many of Bach's family played here but not the great composer himself, who left the town at the age of ten. The organ mechanisms themselves are fairly recent but the beautiful wooden carving dates from the 18C. The crucifixion group of sculptures behind the altar is the only artefact which dates from before 1525; it was created in local workshops in c 1500. On the north wall beside the altar is a large painting, made up of two parts, which Duke Johann Ernst I donated to mark the centenary of the Reformation. On the left the delivery of the Augsburg Confession to Emperor Charles V is depicted, and on the right Luther and Huss. Luther is represented giving Johann Ernst I the chalice, while Huss is offering Frederick the piece of bread. The painting has a wonderful carved frame with figures symbolising Christian virtues. In the centre the Saxon arms dominate the frame; on the right a pelican is shown giving its young its heart's blood to drink, symbolising Christ's Crucifixion. This is countered on the left by a phoenix which dramatically rises from the ashes as a symbol of the resurrection. There is an interesting exhibition in the church which documents its history, including the damage suffered during the Second World War. The Georgenkirche was the focal point for candle-lit demonstrations and meetings during 1989 in Eisenach; and organ concerts, mainly of Bach's music, are held here during the summer.

The Marktplatz has other buildings of architectural and historical merit well worth visiting. Opposite the church is the post-office, 18C residence of local burgher, Thalman. To the right, on the north side of the square is the **Stadtschloss** (April–Oct, Tues–Sun 10.00–17.00, Nov–March, Mon–Sat 10.00–17.00) which houses The Thüringian Museum, a fascinating display of decorative arts, prints and paintings from 18C to the present day. The Schloss was built between 1741 and 1745 as a Rococo palace and second residence for the House of Saxe-Weimar-Eisenach which had just been united. Some of the original 18C decoration can be seen in the museum's interior. To the right, on the east of the Marktplatz is the **Rathaus**, complete with original measure on the wall for market traders to size lengths of cloth. The Rathaus, built in 1638, has been painted in a rather gaudy red. Proceed east down Karlstrasse, a pedestrian zone, created during the days of the GDR to impress the town's many tourists, which now boasts seven shoe shops! Turn right down Querstrasse where you will find the narrowest house in eastern Germany, measuring only 1m 98cm across with four rooms. The house, built by a struggling merchant who could not afford anything larger, is now privately owned and is open as a museum during festivals.

Proceed south to Johannisplatz and west down Schmelzerstrasse to the Lutherplatz. On the left is the **Lutherhaus Museum**, the place where Luther is said to have lodged with the Cotta family during 1498–1501 (open Oct–April, Mon–Sat 09.00–13.00, 14.00–17.00, Sun 14.00–17.00; May–Sept, Mon–Sun 09.00–13.00, 14.00–17.00). This 15C, half-timbered house was damaged during the Second World War and has been fully restored, containing an archive of Luther's works and publications dating from the Reformation. Continue south down Lutherstrasse and the yellow painted **Bachhaus** stands at the bottom of the street on the Frauenplan. This is now a museum devoted to the life of Bach (open Mon 13.30–16.30, Tues–Fri 09.00–16.30, Sat and Sun 09.00–12.00, 13.30–16.30). Although it was not his actual birthplace, Bach lived in Eisenach until he was 10 years old and then moved to Ohrdruf to live with his brother, Johann Christoph, when his parents died. The museum's main interest lies in the valuable collection of musical instruments, including a Swiss chamber organ c 1745 and a Silbermann spinet dating from 1760 on which the staff occasionally demonstrate short pieces by Bach.

Turn right into the Marienstrasse and south past the Karthaus-Garten on the left until you reach the Reuterweg, leading to the 19C **Reuter Villa**. Designed by Ludwig Bolustedl in Renaissance Revival style for the writer Fritz Reuter, who lived there from 1863 to 1874, it now houses a display devoted to his work and that of Richard Wagner (open Tues–Sun, 10.00–17.00). The display on the ground floor maps out Wagner's life whilst the collection of over 6000 volumes and 200 Wagner letters is housed on the second floor, normally open only to specialist researchers. The Reuter display is situated on the first floor with original furnishings and wallpaper in the bedroom and study. The drawing room, with its fine balcony overlooking the Helltal valley, and original Pompeiian-style painted decoration is also delightful. (The steps which begin at the Reuter Villa offer a picturesque route on foot to the Wartburg Castle.)

Retrace your steps and on the corner of Marienstrasse and Waisenstrasse is the former, grand headquarters of the hated GDR's secret police, the Stasi. The many fine, turn of the century villas in this southern area of the town acted as luxury homes for Stasi staff and their families. They are now mainly occupied by professors and doctors and are worth a closer look for their intricate, exterior ironwork and stone carving depicting *femmes fatales* and strange beasts.

Further north, down the Wartburg-Allee is the former mineral water spa, built at the turn of the century in Roman style. Further north still is the purpose-built **Automobile Museum** (open Mon–Sun 09.00–16.00).

Until recently the museum was used to exhibit an historic display of cars from the last 90 years, culminating with the Wartburg, the GDR's highly desirable saloon car. It had a four-stroke engine, was built from metal and was far superior to the Trabant with its noisy two-stroke engine and plastic body. Since the Wende the scenario has obviously changed with the addition of brand new Opels and BMWs. Early examples on show in the museum include the Dixi, manufactured in Eisenach during the early 20C, and BMW sports-cars from the 1930s. In Eisenach the inhabitants are obviously proud of their historic links with car manufacturing and attempts are being made to reap the benifits of re-unification. The Wartburg factory employed over 10,000 workers but is now in the hands of the receiver and lies empty. The word *Freiden* (Freedom) has been daubed on the side of one of the tall, redundant chimneys. Opel and BMW have built new factories to the north of the town, but BMW, for example, employs only 1200 and the citizens are naturally perturbed by the 15 per cent unemployment rate. Continue north down Wartburg Allee, back to the Tourist Information office and Railway Station.

B. The Wartburg Castle

A full day should be put aside to visit the magnificent **Wartburg Castle** (open daily April–Oct 08.30–18.00, Nov–March 09.00–17.00). This must be one of the highlights of any tour of the Thüringian region. Positioned high above the town of Eisenach, it rises out of the heavily wooded slopes. It is advisable to begin your visit as early as possible because this is such a popular tourist attraction. The Wartburg was originally founded as a fort by Count Ludwig I in 1067, and it became the seat of his descendants, the Landgraves, with a medieval court entertained by epic poets and troubadours. The residential part of the castle was founded in 1170, built from sandstone quarried at nearby Seeburg. The Saxon rulers were forced to surrender their symbol of power in 1918 when the Weimar Republic was declared.

There are various methods of reaching the castle. It may be reached by car up the narrow winding road from the end of the Marienstrasse where you may park for a small fee and walk up the many steps to the top or take a donkey, the traditional form of transport to the castle. Alternatively, cars may be left at the bottom car park and a miniature train or mini-bus taken to the castle. The hardy may enjoy the 30-minute walk up the hillside, which affords the best views; the path is signposted just beside the Reutervilla.

After crossing the drawbridge and paying a small admission fee at the gate the first courtyard is entered. This is known as the **Vorburg** and includes the Lutherstube on the right connected to the Gothic Ritterhaus (house of the knights); to the left is the Elisabethgang, a battlemented passage. Pass through the Vorburg and head for the second courtyard, known as the Haptburg with the 12C Palace on the east side. It is important to realise that the Torhalle which separates the two courtyards, the Bergfried (Keep) and Neue Kementie were all added in the 19C in rather unconvincing Romanesque style. The same is true of the interior, which bears the mark of 19C Romantic decoration and furnishing. To visit the interior of the Palace it is necessary to join the German guided tour (an English translation of the guide's words may be borrowed).

The tour begins in the **Knight's Hall**. This north facing room was restored during 1978–82, when the rough stone floor was uncovered. The high-point is the central, loadbearing pillar with eagles carved on the capital. This is one of 200 original carved capitals in the Palace. On leaving the room on the left is a barrel-vaulted staircase leading to the Minstrels' Gallery on the first floor. The simple Dining Room comes next, with an oak beamed ceiling—apparently dating from 1168. There is another of the enchanting carved, central columns here, as well as pieces of furniture and furnishings from the Wartburg collection which was begun in 1815 when Goethe, a frequent visitor, suggested that a museum should be founded in the castle. Proceed down an exterior passageway with stunning views of the Thüringian forest to the impressive Elisabeth Room, decorated entirely with mosaics composed of over one million pieces of glass, gold leaf and mother-of-pearl to designs (1902–06) by August Ötken, showing scenes from the life of St Elizabeth. Two low ceiling lamps in green and yellow glass housed in a metal frame add to the exotic atmosphere. The stylised flowers on the ceiling show the Celtic influence on Jugendstil. The first floor is reached via a wooden spiral staircase, leading to the **Chapel**, built in 1320 with a faint fresco showing the six apostles; there is also a Romanesque font and capital. Adjacent is the **Hall of Song**, famous for its inclusion in Wagner's opera *Tannhäuser*. In 1855 the Romantic artist, Moritzvon Schwind, painted the large-scale mural of the mythical singers' contest, described in a 13C epic poem. According to legend, in 1206 six *Minnesängers* (German troubadours) were in competition to entertain the Landgrave Hermann I and his family, with the loser forfeiting his life. One of the contestants, Heinrich von Ofterdingen, did not pay homage to Hermann I but to the Duke of Austria. This bad form meant that Ofterdingen was declared the loser. He appealed to the Countess and the competition was postponed for one year whilst Ofterdingen visited Hungary and brought back the wizard Klingsar, who magically concluded the whole affair. The legendary contest was the inspiration for Wagner's opera, which he began writing in 1842 when staying at the castle. Other points of interest in the room include a 19C Gothic Revival cabinet and minstrels' gallery.

The tour then proceeds through a carved wooden door to the **Landgrave's Room**. Originally an audience chamber, it has the family symbol, a lion, on the base of the central pillar. The chief point of interest in the room however, is the mural running round the top of the walls by Moritz von Schwind (1854), depicting scenes from the mythical history of the castle including Count Ludwig I in Robin Hood attire, hunting a white stag. It is said that he came to the top of the hill where the Wartburg presently stands and declared '*Warte Berg, du sollst mir eine Burg Werden*' (Wait, mountain, you shall be my castle) thus creating a name for his fortress. The mural is part of the heavy-handed restoration of 1838–67 instigated by Charles Alexander, heir to the Grand Duchy of Saxe-Weimar-Eisenach, who commissioned architect Hugo von Ritger to supervise the work. The **Festival Hall** is the last room of the tour and is an entirely 19C creation. Taking up the whole of the second floor it has an elaborate coffered ceiling and wall painting in Romantic style depicting the triumph of Christianity over Paganism. Concerts are held here which, before re-unification, were broadcast on radio as '*Stimme der DDR*' (The voice of the GDR).

After the tour it is well worth walking along the **Wehrgang** (Sentry Walk) and looking around the museum in the Neue Kemante, back in the north Courtyard, which contains works by Lucas Cranach including *Hans und Margarete Luther* (mother and father of the great religious reformer), as well as weapons, tapestries, furniture and sculpture from the time of the Restoration. One of the Wartburg's greatest claims to fame is that Martin Luther lived here during 1521–22; the very room in which he laboured to translate the New Testament from Greek to vernacular German is well preserved as the **Lutherstube** and may also be visited. With its simple oak panelled walls, table, bookcase and copy of the original *Lutherbibel* it is evocative of the 16C. Legend has it that Luther threw an inkpot at the wall in a rage when he saw an apparition of the devil and this splash of black ink remained on the white plaster. However, souvenir hunters have chipped this away and there is now a hole reaching right back to the stone. Fine views of the Thüringian forest can be glimpsed from the window here. There is also a shop in the northern courtyard selling a comprehensive range of publications and visual reference material. Down the steps below the Wartburg Castle is the hotel which has four good restaurants and cafés, including a terrace bar. Bear in mind that food is not served until 11.00.

If time permits, there are several interesting walks from the Wartburg. On foot the Anna Tal, a pretty wooded ravine 3km south of Eisenach, can be reached in 45 minutes. Follow the signs which begin under the drawbridge. The path continues past the Anna Tal to the Hohe Sonne, which lies 5.5km south of Eisenach. This is a wooded ridge with a popular inn, affording dramatic views of the Wartburg.

42

Erfurt

220,000 inhabitants.

Tourist Information: 37 Bahnhofstrasse, 99084 Erfurt. Tel. 2 62 67.

ERFURT is the regional capital of Thuringia, the largest town in the Land and its Altstadt, which escaped destruction in the Second World War. It is well worth a day's visit. The spectacular Cathedral and Severikirche stand together as fine examples of medieval architecture. Burgher houses from the 15C to 18C are well preserved and the 15C Krämerbrücke spanning the River Gera, lined with 33 timber-framed and gabled houses used by traders, is a high point of the town tour.

History. The earliest record of Erfurt's existence dates from 742 when the town was established as a Bishopric by St Boniface and was then incorporated into the Bishopric of Mainz. The early economic growth of Erfurt depended on agriculture and the cultivation of woad plants, the only source of precious blue dye before the re-introduction of indigo in the 16C. Because of its geographic position on the River Gera and the existence of a ford, from which the name of the town derives (*furt* meaning ford), Erfurt also developed into an important trading centre. It was positioned on the Via Regia (Royal Road) which ran right across Europe from west to east. Town fortifications were begun in 1168 and in 1392 a university was founded here, second only to that in Prague. During 1501–05 Luther was a student in Erfurt, gaining the qualification of Master in Philosophy. He entered St Augustine monastery in Erfurt to be ordained in 1507. In 1511 Luther returned to Wittenberg but came to Erfurt en route to Worms. He was welcomed enthusiastically; the town became predominantly Protestant and the University became an important centre for Humanist scholarship.

Erfurt suffered economic decline after medieval times with the replacement of woad by indigo and the growth of nearby Leipzig as a trading centre. The town was occupied by the Swedish army during the Thirty Years War; the Swedish king Gustavus Adolphus stayed here during his advance into Germany and his Queen heard the news of his death at the Battle of Lutzen whilst still in Erfurt. Economic recovery began only in the late 18C when horticultural production, particularly seed cultivation and market gardening, flourished. The town was under French rule during 1808–14 and it was here that Napoleon summoned Goethe for an audience. Following French defeat

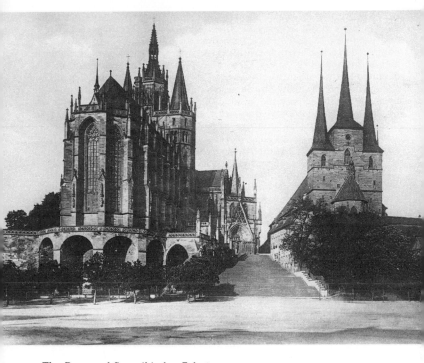

The Dom und Severikirche, Erfurt

Erfurt came under Prussian rule and the university was closed in 1816. Growth continued after the impact of the industrial revolution and in 1906 Erfurt, boasting a population of over 100,000, qualified to become a city. The town was known as an agricultural centre during the post-war years, with the permanent Internationale Gartenbauaustellung (International Horticultural Exhibition) held here 1961. The city is now establishing itself energetically on the academic scene with the reopening of the University and a great effort to attract more tourist trade to the city.

The first stop of any visit to Erfurt must be the *DOMBERG (Cathedral Hill), where the Cathedral and Severikirche stand, dominating the skyline of the town centre. These two splendid structures were built onto a rocky plateau, reached by five flights of steps from the magnificent square below.

The **Mariendom** (Cathedral, opening hours May–Oct, Mon–Fri 09.00–11.30, 12.30–17.00, Sat 09.00–11.30, 12.30–16.30, Sun 14.00–16.00; Nov–April, Mon–Fri 10.00–11.30, 12.30–16.00, Sat 10.00–11.30, 12.30–16.00, Sun 14.00–16.00) was originally founded as a wooden structure at the time of the creation of the diocese of Erfurt by St Boniface in 742. A stone replacement was built in 1154 with numerous alterations and extensions made over the succeeding years. In 1349 the High Altar was added, making the creation of an enormous sub-structure, the *Cavaten* necessary to support the building beyond the rock. The choir faces you as you ascend the broadstairs, known locally as the Graden, with lofty, slim lancet windows reaching the roof, which was restored in 1967–69. The three spires were renewed in the 18C and 19C and the central tower contains the Maria Gloriosa, one of the largest church bells in Europe, cast in bronze in 1497 and weighing 12 tons. A relic from the earliest period of the Cathedral's construction is the 'Triangle Portal', the main entrance situated on the north side at the top of the stairs. Created c 1330, the north-east entrance is decorated with sculptures of the Apostles; above the door is a Crucifixion group and St Mary with baby Jesus is situated on the middle pillar. On the north-west entrance are the Wise and Foolish Virgins, and an enthroned figure of Jesus stands above them with St Mary and St John the Baptist next to him. The door pillar, decorated with Archangel Michael, is a 19C addition.

On entering the Cathedral the overall impression is one of spaciousness and lightness, partly created by 12 magnificent windows in the choir measuring 12m in height; they were made during 1370–1410 and painted with scenes of the Creation and St Hubert with a yellow stag with purple horns. The oak choir stalls date from 1350 and are beautiful examples of skilful carving. The outer panels of the south stalls are decorated with harvest scenes framed by richly-ornamented scrolls with grapes hanging from them. On the north panels are angels playing musical instruments. The altar is Baroque, dating from 1697. To the south-east corner of the nave stands a bronze figure with outstretched arms known as Wolfram. Dating from 1160 this piece of Romanesque sculpture is now used to carry candles. Beside this on the south aisle is bronze monument to Henning Goden, Provost of Wittenberg and Prebendary of Erfurt, created in 1522 by Peter Vischer. Further along the south aisle is a sandstone monument to Count Ernst II of Gleichen and his two wives, dating from 1250. On the north aisle, to the left of the main entrance is 'The Engagement of St Catherine' by Lucas Cranach the Elder c 1520. Further down the south aisle is a baptismal font by artist Hans Friedemann the Elder, dating from 1587 and reaching 18m into the vault.

Also perched above the Domplatz to the north-west of the cathedral is the **Severikirche**, distinguished from the Mariendom by its three graceful spires (opening times: May–Oct, Mon–Fri 09.00–12.30, 13.00–17.00; Nov–April, Mon–Fri 10.00–12.30, 13.30–16.00). The church was begun in 1278 and completed c 1360 and is one of the earliest Gothic hall churches in Erfurt, consisting of five naves of almost equal height. Inside is the beautiful St Severus sarcophagus, c 1365, with side reliefs telling the story of the wool weaver Severus who became the Bishop of Ravenna. In the south-west corner is the magnificent font dating from 1467 with an elaborate and lofty canopy on which stands a figure of the Virgin and Child surrounded by rays of glory. An alabaster relief showing St Michael slaying the dragon is located on the southern wall of the nave, with the fearsome monster biting and clawing the spear in quite an alarming manner. The high altar and elaborate organ front are Baroque in style, dating from 1670–1714.

Behind the Domberg is the **Petersberg**, which was important during medieval times as the site of a monastery and the town's fortifications. It is a rocky plateau measuring 640m by 440m. Little evidence of its former glory remain as the Peterskirche, originally built in 1103–47 as a Romanesque basilica, was incorporated into the town's fortifications in 1664–1726. Artillery fire destroyed the monastery in 1813 and the church was burnt out. The Prussian authorities then pulled down the church towers and changed it into a military store and it now stands largely derelict. Parts of the 17C citadel remain, including the original entrance. It was built in 1664–1702 with eight bastions designed by A. Petrini; the extant Baroque doorway dates from this period and is decorated with the coats of arms of Philip of Mainz.

Return to the DOMPLATZ (Cathedral Square), where several houses stand dating back to the 16C, having survived the 1813 bombardment. Zur Hohen Lilie is situated on the south-west corner and is a fine Renaissance building, dating from 1538 when it was built for the goldsmith Johannes Ludolf on the site of a Gothic house. During the 14C to 19C it was used as a guesthouse and eminent visitors included Luther, Gustav Adolph II of Sweden and, from 1817, the Prussian town commander. The building now houses a pleasant restaurant.

Continue east down MARKTSTRASSE which once formed part of the Via Regia and is where the prosperous merchants and traders lived. Pass the **Allerheilgenkirche** (All Saints Church) on the left with its 53m tower, the highest in Erfurt, to the FISCHMARKT. One of Erfurt's oldest squares, dating back at least to 1248, this formed an important trading centre in the town. The square is dominated by the magnificent **Rathaus**, built in Gothic Revival style between 1868–75 with interesting frescoes by Kampfer inside on the walls of the stairs, passages and great hall depicting the myths and history of Erfurt and surrounding Thuringia. The 1930s building to the south is a savings bank.

In the centre of the Fischmarkt stands a statue of Roland (1591) disguised as a Roman soldier; the north-east of the square is lined with Renaissance Burger houses. At No. 6 is the Goldene Krone (1488–1564), and No. 7 is the **Haus zum roten Ochsen** (1562), a three-storey Renaissance building first occupied by a wealthy woad trader. Most interesting is the frieze which decorates the exterior of the house with various mythical figures. From left to right these are Saturn, Mars, Jupiter and Venus followed by the house sign, an ox and then the figures of Mercury and Luna. There are also eight Greek Muses represented and the gable above is decorated with ornamental satyrs and putti, topped with a soldier on top carrying a flag. The building was converted into an art gallery, Galerie am Fischmarkt, in 1977–78 (opening times: Wed–Sun 10.00–18.00, Thurs 10.00–22.00, admission free 18.00–22.00 on Thurs). At No. 13 is **Zum Breiten Herd** (1584) again beautifully preserved with stepped gables and figures decorating its brightly painted façade. At No. 11 is Zum Roten Storn.

Continue east past the Rathaus to the KRÄMERBRÜCKE. A detour north up Michaelstrasse brings you to the old university district. At No. 39 is the Collegium Majus, main site of the university between 1392 and 1816. Although damaged during World War II, the building now houses the Amploniana, a specialist archive of manuscripts with a 19C technical library beyond. Opposite is the Gothic Michaeliskirche which contains a Renaissance altarpiece and 16C Dreifaltgkeitskapelle with tranquil courtyard. An arched stone bridge spanning the River Gera, it was first founded in the 11C on the site of the legendary ford, but the present version dates from 1472. Like the Ponte Vecchio in Florence the bridge is lined with shops, in this case 32 and it is the only such example to survive in Europe north of the Alps. The shops are mainly timber-framed and devoted now to selling antiques, flowers and souvenirs.

Originally there was a church at each end of the bridge but now only **Ägidienkirche** (St Aegidus) remains at the east side. Completed in 1325 in Gothic style it was used by the traders for accommodation. Protestant services are now held in the room above the gateway leading from the Krämerbrücke.

On entering Wenigemarkt the Gothardtsttrasse heading north may be taken to the **Augustinerkirche** and **Kloster** where Luther spent time as an Augustine monk in the community which had settled in Erfurt in 1266. (Guided tours only, April–Oct (closed Mon), Tues–Sat on the hour 09.00–16.00; Nov–Mar (closed Mon) Tues–Sat 10.00–12.00 and 14.00, Sun at 10.30 after the main service, other times possible by arrangement (tel. 23603).) A great deal of damage to the 16C church and cloisters was suffered during the Second World War and the woadhouses and library were completely destroyed. The colourful St Augustine window survived in the church, as did various gravestones dating back to 13C, and a former monk's cell is on show as Martin Luther's cell.

Continuing east from the Wenigemarkt, Futterstrasse leads to Johannesstrasse. Immediately opposite at No. 169 is the **Museum für Stadtgeschichte** (Museum of Local History) housed in the 17C Haus 'Zum Stockfisch' (opening times Sun–Thurs 10.00–18.00). In 13 rooms the history of the town has been told through various displays from the Middle Ages to 1815. Other fine examples of merchant dwelling stand in this street including 'Zum Grunen Sittich und Gekronten Hecht' (House of the Greenfinch and the Crowned Pike) at No. 178 and, at No. 168, 'Zum Mohrenkopf' (Negro's Head House) both dating from the 17C. From the Museum für Stadtgeschichte it is possible to take a quick detour west back down the street opposite, Futterstrasse, to see at No. 15–16 the city's former ballroom and theatre, now called the **Kongresssale**. During the Congress of Erfurt in 1808 the Comédie Français performed here with Goethe in the audience. The theatre was rebuilt in 1831–32 and in 1891 was the venue for the German Socialist Labour Party which adopted the Erfurt Programme here. It is also possible to walk east up Krämpferstrasse and then north up the JuriGagarin-Ring to the **Museum für Thuringer Volkskunde** (Thüringian Folklore Museum) at No. 140 (opening times: Wed–Sun 10.00–18.00). Housed in the 16C former hospital building, the permanent display includes ancient and modern craftwork, living on the land and the interesting folk customs of Thuringia. Many of the exhibits are displayed in recreated, period dwellings.

South of Krämpferstrasse is what is called ANGER, the town's main shopping street and not a name easily forgotten by English speaking visitors! This broad vista is especially notable for its fine Jugendstil and Art Deco buildings as well as pleasant pavement cafés. At the top of the street is the **Kaufmannskirche** (Merchant's Church), Erfurt's oldest parish church where Bach's parents were married. It is basically Romanesque in plan with rebuilding taking place in the 14C. The interior is simple, embellished with paintings by a family of local artists called Friedmann dating from 17C. Continue south down Anger noting the range of historic façades including the Renaissance Revival Post Office (1892–95), the Art Deco shop at No. 59, Art Nouveau Café Gydor at No. 23 and 16C Burgher houses at the southeast end. At No. 18, about half-way down is the **Angermuseum**. This is a Baroque house built by the town governor, the Elector of Mainz Philip Wilhelm von Boyneburg, during 1706–12 as a Packhof or customs and weights and measures house. At the Packhof all goods coming into or leaving Erfurt were charged a duty by the Elector. The highly decorative façade includes the figure of St Martin, the patron saint of the town and four statues of Justice, Charity, Prudence and Vigilance by Gottfried

Gröningen from Münster. The museum contains exhibits of medieval works of art including sculptures and panel paintings. There are also examples of later German art including Lucas Cranach the Elder, Liebermann, Feininger and Corinth. (Open Wed–Sun 10.00–18.00.)

Further south on the right at No. 53 is the **Bartholomäusturm** (St Bartholomew's Tower), once part of the family church of the Counts of Gleichen, which houses one of the biggest carillons in Germany, consisting of 60 bells which are played on Wednesdays and Sundays at 17.00 and are well worth hearing. At No. 37–8 Anger is the impressive Haus Dacheroden, orignally the Haus Zum Goldenen Hecht and the Haus Zum Grossen und Neuen Schiff which were brought together as the Dacherodensches Haus for the Dacheroden family in 1833. The Renaissance façade dates from 1557 and is the most elegant in the town with a beautifully decorated doorway and a slender turret gracing the roof. At the southern end of the Anger is a fountain dating from 1889/90 which celebrates Erfurt trade. To the right is the **Wigbertikirche**, the court church for governors sent from Mainz to Erfurt. Named after the Benedictine friar Wigbert, who was one of St Boniface's chief assistants, the church was founded in 1223 but was burnt down 70 years later. It was rebuilt in 1409–72 in its present later Gothic form. Inside there are the remains of a tabernacle from the early 17C by Hans Friedemann the Elder and gravestones for the governors from Mainz who were buried here.

Near the Wigbertkirche is the **Stadthalterei** (Governor's Palace), built as the municipal palace during 1711–20 on the site of two older houses. Designed by the Mainz court architect Maximilian von Welsch aus Franken in Baroque style it has a massive festival hall measuring 200 square metres.

From the bottom of the Anger head north up Meister Eckehart Strasse and east up Barfüsserstrasse to the **Barfüsserkirche** (Wed–Sun 10.00–18.00). This 15C church was founded by Franciscan friars but their monastery buildings were demolished by the Swedes in the 1600s. The church was badly damaged by bombing in 1944 and has been left in ruins apart from the choir, which has been restored and since 1977 has housed part of the municipal art collection concentrating on the medieval period. The original high altar can be seen as part of the exhibition, dating from 1445. There is a moving tombstone made for noblewoman Cinna von Vargula, carved in stone in 1370.

Return along Barfüsserstrasse to Meister Eckehart Strasse and continue north to the **Predigerkirche** (Preachers' Church). Completed in 1370, it was built for the friars of the orders of Dominicans or Preachers, who settled in the town in 1229. The Dominicans left during the Reformation and since then the Predigerkirche has acted as the main Protestant church in Erfurt. This fine Gothic structure contains many examples of 14C works of art including *Madonna with Child* (1350); the stunningly ornate high altar was created by Linhardt Koenberg in 1492. From here it is a short walk west up Paulstrasse and Kettenstrasse to return to the Domberg.

The town of Erfurt also has a zoo, the Thuringer Zoopark (approximately 4km north of the town centre), and the Stadtpark behind the main railway station which is a pleasant spot for a rest and a picnic. The **Internationale Gartenbauaustellung** (IGA for short) is situated on the south-west fringe of Erfurt. Founded in 1961 as the International Horticultural Exhibition it is open all year round complete with Gartenbaumuseum (Easter–Oct daily 10.00–17.00) which is housed in the old Cyriaksburg. If time permits it is also worth visiting the **Schloss Molsdorf**, a small Rococo palace in beautiful parkland built during 1736–45, 10km south-west of Erfurt (guided tours Wed–Sun hourly from 14.00; other times by arrangement, tel. Neudieten-dorf 0292 505).

From Erfurt it is possible to reach Weimar quickly on the B7 heading east.

43

Eisenach to Weimar via Gotha

Eisenach—31km Gotha—55km Weimar

This route takes in Gotha, a lovely Thuringian town with splendid Baroque castle, and traces the north-eastern fringe of the forest, cul-minating with the historic town of Weimar.

Follow the A7 out of Eisenach (see Route 41), signposted to Gotha, through the crumbling suburbs of the town with its uneven road surfaces, a mixture of cobbled streets with patches of tarmac. The road follows the main railway line between Eisenach and Gotha for 15km, traversing it at a slow level crossing just outside Wutha, with its interesting half-timbered houses. Pass through Schonau and then Kalberfeld with its 16C, stepped gabled village church to Sattelstadt and then Mechterstadt. The road then passes under the motorway, the E40, and continues to Teutleben with its pretty tree-lined road and 17C church with soaring steeple. Pass through Aspach as the road and villages come to resemble those of rural France with areas of arable farmland. From Trugleben it is a further 5km into Gotha but the skyline, dominated by the towers of the Schloss Friedenstein, comes into view.

Gotha

54,000 inhabitants.

Tourist Information: Blumenbachstrasse 1–3, 99867 Gotha. Tel. 54036). Opening times: Mon–Fri 09.00–17.00, Sat 09.00–12.00.

GOTHA is a comparatively well preserved town whose chief attraction, the Schloss Friedenstein, escaped damaged during the Second World War. The Castle is of particular interest to British visitors as it was the capital of the former duchy of Saxe-Coburg-Gotha, the British Royal family name until it was changed to Windsor during the First World War. A pleasant day can be spent in Gotha, taking in the castle and its many attractions, the town square and castle park. The surrounding countryside can be explored on the Thüringerwaldbahn (Thuringian Forest Railway, tel. 52402) which leaves from Gotha's main station and travels 21km south to Friedrichroda, Tabarz and Walterhausen up steep inclines and through picturesque forest.

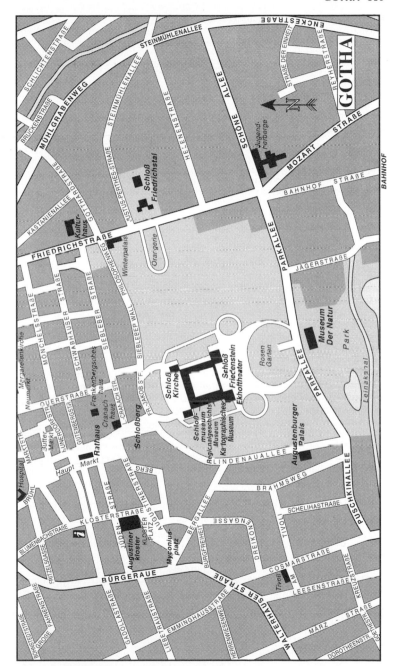

GOTHA

ENCKESTRAßE

SCHLICHTENSTRAßE

STEINMÜHLENALLEE

MÜHLGRABENWEG

BRÜCKENSTRAßE

STEINMÜHLENALLEE

STRAßE DER EINHEIT

REYHERSTRAßE

SCHÖNE ALLEE

HELENENSTRAßE

JUSTUS-PERTHES-STRAßE

Schloß
Friedrichstal

Jugend-
herberge

MOZART STRAßE

BAHNHOF STRAßE

BAHNHOF

KASTANIENALLEE

GOTHARDSTRAßE

Kultur-
haus

PARKALLEE

FRIEDRICHSTRAßE

PHILOSOPHENWEG

Winterpalais

Orangerie

JÄGERSTRAßE

MÖNCHELSSTRAßE

SCHWABHÄUSER STRAßE

SIEBLEBER STRAßE

SIEBLEBER WALL

Park

Margaretenkirche
Neumarkt

QUERSTRAßE

GUTENBERGSTR.

Frankenbergsches
Haus
Cranach-
haus
CRANACH STR.

Museum
Der Natur

Rosen
Garten

PARKALLEE

Leinakanal

Butter
Markt

HÜNERDORFSTR.

Rathaus

Schloßberg

Schloß
Kirche

Schloß
Friedenstein
Ekhoftheater

Leinaktal

FR.-JAKOB STR.

Schloß-
museum
Regionalgeschichtes
Museum

Kartographisches
Museum

Augustenburger
Palais

BERG STRAßE

MARKTSTR.

Hospital

BRÜHL

Haupt
Markt

LINDENAUALLEE

Augustenburger
Palais

BLUMENBACHSTRAßE

KLOSTERSTRAßE

JUDEN STRAßE

KLOSTERSTRAßE

AUGUSTINERSTRAßE

Augustiner
Kloster

KLOSTER
PLATZ

AUGUST
PLATZ

Myconius-
platz

BERGALLEE

BRAHMSWEG

SCHELIHASTRAßE

PUSCHKINALLEE

TIVOLI

FRITZELSGASSE

FRIEDRICHSTRAßE

BÜRGERAUE

BÜRGERAUE

AUGUSTINERSTRAßE

BURGFREIHEIT

ENGGASSE

DREIKON

COSMARSTRAßE

LEESENSTRAßE

TIVOLI

AM

GRÖDLLSTRAßE

BONSTEDTSTRAßE

GROßE FAHNENSTRAßE

HERRENWIESENWEG

LIEBETRAUSTRAßE

EMMINGHAUSSTRAßE

HERRENWIESENWEG

KREUZSTRAßE

WALTERHÄUSER STRAßE

MÄRZ STRAßE

DOROTHEENSTR.

GOETHESTR.

History. Gotha was first mentioned in a document by Emperor Karl dem Grossen in 775. The town grew as an important trading centre and a market settlement was established here on the site of the present Hauptmarkt in 12C. The town flourished in the 15C and 16C through trade in cereals, timber and woad. The first Duke of Saxe-Gotha, Ernest the Pious decided that Gotha should be his capital in 1640 and began work on the Schloss. His descendants made various alterations to the Schloss, including the redecoration of the guest wing in Neo-Classical style during the reigns of Duke Ernst II (1772–1804) and Duke August (1804–22). In the 18C Gotha was part of the intellectual movement inspired by the French Enlightenment and centred in nearby Weimar. The first German edition of the works of Voltaire were published here and the French philosopher stayed as a guest at the palace in 1753. The first theatre in Germany was built at the Palace by Conrad Ekhof during 1774 to 1778. In 1817 E.W. Arnold founded the first technical school here and in 1821 the first fire insurance office in Germany was opened followed in 1827 by a life insurance office. In the 19C Gotha played host to the congress of the Social Democratic Workers' Party and the All-German Workers' Union, which amalgamated in 1875. The town also has an important history of publishing, notably the maps and atlases produced by Hermann Haack Geographisch-Kartiographische Anstalt since the 19C and still in production today. The town now enjoys a lively tourist trade.

A. Town Centre

From the station cross into Bahnhofstrasse and continue north into Fried-richstrasse. On the right is the two storey, Baroque **Schloss Friedrichstal** (1712) currently occupied by government officials and a technical school. On the left is the Orangery with two pavilions, one a café and one the town library, begun in 1744 by G.H. Krohne and finished in 1774 by D. Weidner. Turn left into Philosophenweg and proceed west to Friedrich Jacob Strasse where a fine view of the Palace with fountain in the foreground can be enjoyed.

Proceed right down Schlossberg to the HAUPTMARKT where a market selling fresh fruit and flowers trades every morning. Built on a slope, the sweeping market place was the original centre of the town. Standing in the middle is the fine, red-painted **Rathaus**, built in 1567 and restored in 1898. The northern façade is in early Renaissance style, with stepped gables decorated with carved stone, a clock and statues of medieval knights. Above the door is the coat of arms of the Ernestiner dukes, former rulers of this district. The southern tower has a rounded cupola and is topped by a lantern. The Rathaus was used as a covered market until 1665 when it became the town hall. Lining the picturesque Hauptmarkt are several historic dwellings including, west of the Rathaus, the green-fronted Thum und Taxissches Posthaus which, from 1845 provided a stopping-off point and resting place for horses in the 19C, before the advent of the railway. On the east side of the Hauptmarkt at No. 3 is the **Ratskeller** (Mon–Fri 11.00–22.00, Sun 11.00–15.00) built c 1900 in a sturdy Jugendstil style. Closed throughout the 1980s for restoration it was opened on 3 October 1990 to celebrate reunification. Further south on the left is a chemist, originally founded in 1578. On the next corner is the Lucas Cranach house at No. 17, which once belonged to the painter. This building dates from 18C apart from the cellar (which contains the 100 hundred year old workings of the **Liene Fountain** on the Schlossberg) and the portal, which are earlier. A brief detour down Lucas Cranach Strasse reveals the Rococo Franken-bergsches Gartenhaus, standing in a courtyard down the alley. Proceeding south to the Schloss Friedenstein on the right is Zum Fuhrsfursthe, built in 1711 specifically as a place for the Dukes to dine, with a fine Baroque façade.

Continue west down Augustinerstrasse to the Klosterplatz where the Augustine Monastery, with splendid 14C Gothic cloisters, it closed presently for restoration but is due to open again shortly. Beside the Monastery is Augustinerkirche. A single-naved, Gothic church, it dates originally from 1366; the Baroque alterations were carried out in the 17C under the direction of Duke Ernst the Pious. Martin Luther stayed here during 1515–16 and preached at the church during 1521 and 1529. Meetings of discontented east Germans took place here weekly during 1989 and provided the local focus for demonstrations. South is Myconiusplatz which leads onto Bürgeraue and then Cosmarstrasse where the former museum 'Tivoli', dedicated to the history of the working class movement stands on the corner with Am Tivoli. The famous congress of the Social Democratic Workers Party (Eisenacher) and the All German Workers Union (Lassalleaner) was held here in 1875. In the days of the GDR this was open as a museum as no opportunity to celebrate the achievements of the left was neglected, but is now closed awaiting a decision about its future. Return to Klosterplatz and continue north up Klosterstrasse which leads into Blumenbachstrasse and the new Tourist Information Office. The decrepit 19C houses which stood until recently in this area have been replaced by modern flats with central heating and bathrooms, much sought after by local residents. The housing to the east of the main square is now undergoing restoration rather than demolition. Just past the tourist office on the right is the Gretengasse alley where an original woad house stands, dating from 1576. Originally built onto No. 36 Hauptmarkt, the valuable woad plants were stored here and the trade in this blue dye conducted from these premises.

Rejoin the Hauptmarkt where reviving drinks and snacks can be enjoyed at No. 31, Bäckerei Bonsack. The street leading north west from the Hauptmarkt is the BRÜHL, dating from the 14C with its half-timbered houses including at No. 7 the 'Königs-Sahl' house (1580). Return to the Hauptmarkt and continue east down Marktstrasse to the NEUMARKT. This is a new shopping precinct dominated by the 15C Margaretenkirche, a three-naved, late Gothic hall church built in 1494 on the original foundations of a Romanesque basilica. The entrance to the west, facing onto the Neumarkt, is called the Brautportal (Bride Portal). The church was seriously damaged during the Second World War and rebuilt, complete with 65m high steeple. Other buildings destroyed during the last war include the beautiful Renaissance Revival theatre and nearby viaduct. From the church return to the Hauptmarkt, then head south to the Schloss Friedenstein.

B.   Schloss Friedenstein and grounds

Walking up the Schlossberg you will pass a fountain, built in 1895 at the same time as the rest of the terrace, to commemorate the completion of the Leina canal in 1369. This had been built to provide extra drinking water for the town's expanding population when the wells proved insufficient. On the terrace is a statue of Duke Ernst the Pious, the first duke of the house of Saxe-Gotha who chose Gotha as the capital of his new domain in 1640.

The castle which Duke Ernst I erected during 1643–44 stands on the 311m high hill on the site of the former fortress-like Grimmenstein Castle, which had been destroyed in 1567. From the terrace, stunning views of the town can be enjoyed with the tall spire of St Margaret's church dominating the skyline.

Duke Ernst I aimed to create a residency which symbolised his power as a liberal statesman. The sheer size of the three-winged structure is impressive, measuring 140 x 100m with 365 rooms and 2000 windows. The two distinctive towers which crown the two wings of the palace differ in shape—one has straight eaves, while the other is curved beneath the grey slate. Each is crowned by a Baroque cupola and lantern. The building of the castle is interesting in that it began during the Thirty Years War, symbolising the desire for peace. Indeed, the name Friedenstein derives from 'Peace Stone' as opposed to the earlier 'Grim Stone'. Andreas Rudolph supervised the building work. Apart from the magnificently preserved interiors, the castle contains four important collections: the Palace Museum, Local History and Folklore Museum, Cartographic Museum and Public Record Office (Opening times: daily 09.00–17.00).

Enter through the centrally placed main gate in the north wing with its double set of Corinthian pillars forming an impressive portal. Note the so-called '*Friedensküss*' (peace kiss) over the door (1646) a carved and painted sandstone shield bearing the embracing figures of Genien Pax and Justitia, with the words '*Friede ernehret, Unfriede versehret*' surrounding them in Gothic script. Further celebrations of peace crown the '*Friedensküss*' with a long motto carved into stone, drawing attention to the fortress of Grimmenstein which had stood on this spot for 500 years. Inside, the courtyard is impressive not only for its massive scale but also for the arcading which lines all four sides of the building. The ticket office for the **Schlossmuseum** is to the right and well worth a visit as some quite exceptional items are on show, the collection have been built up since the days of the first duke to rival that of neighbouring duchies, particularly that of Dresden. The first duke, Ernst the Pious, established a chamber of arts when building on the castle began and the oldest inventory of the castle's collection, dating from 1656, mentions a small collection of German and Dutch paintings.

ROOM 1 (Kirchgalerie) contains a fine collection of altarpieces and stone carvings from local churches dating from the early 16C including a splendid triptych known as the *Gotha Table Altar* dating from 1539–41 which illustrates 160 separate Biblical scenes. The succeeding rooms on this floor house a magnificent collection of paintings, including Lucas Cranach the Elder's *Christ and Mary* (1512–14) a stunning double portrait in comparatively naturalistic style for the time. Other Cranachs include *Madonna and Child with the young John the Baptist* (1534) and *Betrayal of the King* (1514). One of the best known pictures in the collection is the *Lovers of Gotha* painted in 1484 by the mysterious Meister des Hausbuches, a tender portrait in representational style which pre-dates Dürer. This was added to the collection by Duke Ernst II (1772–1804).

On the OBERGESCHOSS (upper floor) is the collection of Dutch and Flemish paintings, on show in three consecutive rooms interesting for their decoration in themselves. They were built as part of the Corps de Logis for the prince who would become Duke Friedrich II in 1691. ROOM 1 has a marvellous marble floor and coffered ceiling, highlights include Abraham van Beyren *Still Life With Flowers and Crab* and Jan I Davidsz de Heem

Schloss Friedenstein, built by Duke Ernst I in 1643–44

Still Life with Wine Glass (1628) both from the golden age of Dutch painting. ROOM 2 has a wonderfully ornate wooden floor and plastcrwork and ceiling painting dating from c 1730. On the walls hang two stunning Rubens sketches, *St Athanasius* (1620) and *St Basilius* (1620) for the ceiling of the Jesuit church at Antwerp and works by other Flemish masters including Cornelis de Vos. ROOM 3 is also decorated in late Baroque style with further gems of 17C Dutch art including Emanuel de Witte's *The Interior of a Gothic Church* (1650). Pass back through the three rooms to the anteroom for the Prince's apartments, where there is a fascinating display of the original wooden models made when deciding on the design of the castle, dating from 1643 onwards. This leads to the FESTSAAL (Celebration Hall) an amazing, Baroque banqueting hall some 42m long and two storeys high. Created in 1687–89, it was even larger at that time, before space was taken for the Prince's lodgings. The most striking aspect of this room is the luscious plasterwork, created by Samuel and Johann Peter Rust. Huge garlands of fruit and flowers as well as nymphs hang from the ceiling. Pairs of Hermes frame portraits of the Saxe-Weimar ancestors which flank the throne area, indicated by the two shields which hang over the entrance. The throne no longer stands here, but an interesting display of the table silver and porcelain is on show.

Through the exit to the right is the KLEINES KABINETT with plasterwork by the Rust brothers; this leads to the SCHWARTZE GALERIE (Black

Gallery) created as the ante-chamber for the Duchess's rooms with more plasterwork by the Rust brothers on the ceiling, in Baroque style, dating from 1695 and 19C Renaissance Revival oak panelling. Beyond the Galeriesaal and Braune Galerie the GROSSER GOBELINRAUM is reached, so called because of the impressive Brussels tapestry, dating from 1690 and depicting the coat of arms of the Dukes of Saxe-Gotha against a classical background, commissioned by Duke Friedrich I. A cabinet standing in the centre of the room contains some remarkable curiosities. There is a drinking vessel in the form of a silver rabbit with detachable head (1700) and a portrait of Duke Ernst I minutely carved from a cherry stone. The AUDIENZZIMMER, the political nerve centre of the Corps de Logis, has Baroque plasterwork on the ceiling and walls, created by Giovanni Cariveri in 1683. The grey marbled pilasters were inspired by the French style of decoration as exemplified at Versailles. On the ceiling are four medallions with different initials: F stands for Duke Friedrich I, ES for Elisabeth Sophie his mother, MS for Magdalene Sybille his first wife and C for Christina his second. Next is the small Arbeitskabinett with 18C, French-inspired décor with embossed leather wall hangings, followed by the ANKLEIDE- und BETTKABINETT, with special raised platform for the bed of Duchess Christina, second wife of Duke Friedrich I. A portrait of the Duchess hangs above the alcove, supported by two plaster putti by Caroveri. More work by Caroveri can be seen in the FÜRSTLICHES SCHAFGEMACH where the interlocking initials of F (Friedrich I) and C (Christina) can be seen over the ornate doorway. The GROSSER ROKOKOSAAL was created in 1751 and is far more delicate in comparison to the 17C interiors seen so far. The ceiling, sconces and wall mirrors are in the asymmetrical style which typifies the Rococo. In the following ROKOKOKABINETT and KLEINES ROKOKOKABINETT, also decorated in 1751, some pleasing Rococo furniture is on display including a chest of drawers made in 1770 by the workshop of Abraham Röntgen. The SPIEGELKABINETT was specially created as a porcelain display room in 1730–33 by Friedrich Joachim Stengel after Daniel Marot. Pass back through the Festaal and into the west wing to view the fascinating Weimar Galleries.

The WEIMAR GALLERIES were redecorated in Neo-Classical style during the late 18C and early 19C under the reign of the Duke Ernst II (1772–1804), Duke August (1804–22) and Duke Friedrich IV (1822–25). The Weimar Gallery itself is a long passageway which lies directly over the Kirchgalerie below. There is an important collection of the work of French Neo-Classical sculptor Jean-Antoine Houdon (1741–1828) here, which rivals that of the Louvre. Such was the fascination of the Saxe-Weimar court with Enlightenment ideals and culture that the entire west wing of the castle was redecorated in a Neo-Classical style with French art works. Friedrich Melchior Grimm was a German agent resident in Paris who purchased most of the Houdon sculptures for the castle. There is a bust of Benjamin Franklin who was the first ambassador to Paris from America during 1776–85. There is also a bust of French philosopher Voltaire, complete with toga, by Houdon dating from 1778. Voltaire actually visited this sophisticated court and conducted a lifelong correspondence with Princess Elisabeth; the letters are in the collection in the library and attract a number of international scholars. Further down the passage is an interesting collection of ancient Egyptian artefacts founded by Duke August of Saxon-Gotha in 1831. The first room off to the right of the Weimar Gallery is the MARMORZIMMER (Marble Room) decorated from 1797–99 by the Gotha court sculptor Friedrich Wilhelm Eugen Döll with green and black marbling on the walls and simple, white plaster ceiling. The Blaues Zimmer has elegant powder-blue and yellow silk decorating the walls and again features delicate plasterwork by Döll on the ceiling with blue and white, Wedgwood-inspired decoration. The aptly named POMPEIANISCHES ZIMMER (Pompeiian Room) has wall paintings inspired by its Roman namesake. The EMPIRS-SCHLAFGEMACH (Empire Bedroom) contains some gems of Empire style. There are chairs designed by Schinkel and a beautiful cabinet in the shape of a globe with many tiny compartments, made for Duke August by local cabinet-maker Munk in 1800. Created at the same time was the splendid clock, 'Oracle d'Amour' which was made in France in gilt bronze with fashionable Roman decoration. The walls of the bedroom are painted with signs of the zodiac and feature Emperor Napoleon as the sun and Duke August as the moon. The charming DICHTER-ZIMMER is decorated with purple taffeta, and contains a copper urn in Roman style which stands on a column made in Jena in 1799. Romantic works of art decorate the walls, including one version of Casper David Friedrich's *Cross in the Mountains*. The Weimar Galleries conclude with the Neo-Classical style ELIEDERZIMMER and LAUBENZIMMER.

The **Ekhof-Theatre** (opening times: Mon 09.00–12.00, 12.30–16.00, Tues–09.00–12.00, 12.30–17.00, Sat 09.00–12.00, 13.00–17.00, closed Sun) is situated in the south-west tower and should not be missed. This was the first purpose-built theatre in Thuringia and now is the oldest example still extant in Europe. Built in 1683 the auditorium has been altered on numerous occasions but the stage and its workings are authentic. Duke Friedrich I converted the ballroom into a 'Comedy House' during 1681–83 and the first opera was performed there in 1683. The theatre is named after Konrad Ekhof, one of the leading German actors of the 18C who founded the first permanent company of actors in Germany at the theatre in 1775. Ekhof managed the company of actors until his death in 1778. The company then disbanded and the theatre was used only periodically by touring companies. The tradition of a permanent company was re-established in 1826 when the houses of Coburg and Gotha united, the ensemble performing alternately in the two towns. Prestigious performances continued throughout the 19C but the theatre was badly damaged in the Second World War. Restoration work carried out between 1966 and 1968 ensured that the theatre could once more be used for performances with its 300 seats and authentic, 17C stage.

The **Regionalmuseum** is situated upstairs and includes some material on the history of the theatre. Unfortunately the **Schlosskirche** in the east wing is open to the public only for actual services; it has a fine Baroque plasterwork ceiling by the Rust brothers, executed between 1695 and 1697. Just in front of the east wing in the **Pagenhaus** (Page's House) is the Museum für Kartographie (opening times: Mon–Wed and Fri 09.00–12.00, 12.30–17.00, Thurs 10.00–12.00, 12.30–19.00, Sat and Sun closed) which is of specialist interest.

Continue through the southern gateway to the restful Rose Garden where the 19C, Renaissance Revival **Museum der Natur** (Natural History Museum) can be seen south across the Parkallee (opening times: Mon–Wed 09.00–12.00 and 12.30–17.00, Thurs 10.00–12.00 and 12.30–19.00, Fri 09.00–12.00 and 13.00–17.00). The Museum was purpose-built to house the Kunstkammer in 1879 but now houses a display of minerals and stuffed animals which certainly delight children. Antique dioramas which set animals like tigers and bears in realistic settings are screened from the light by curtains. A part of the Leinakanal can be seen behind the Museum as can the Dorischer Temple, on an 18C folly by Friedrich Wilhelm von Erdmannsdorff which stands on the edge of a boating lake. The 50 acres of grounds were landscaped during the 18C, and included the Teeschlossen, a folly built in the style of a small, Gothic church which also stands in the grounds.

From Gotha it is a short drive (20km) to **Walterhausen**; travel west down the E40 until the next intersection, then follow the signs. This small town boasts the 16C Tenneberg Palace, now a museum of local history, and the Baroque Stadtkirche (1719–23). 4km south is Friedrichroda; best known as a centre for walking and skiing, it also has a 19C Schloss. Alternatively, from Gotha it is an easy drive straight to Weimar (see Route 44), heading south out of Gotha on the A247 to connect with the E40 heading east. The Drei Gleichen can be spotted as the road nears Arnstadt. From the E40 it is only 6km north to Weimar, a route which cuts through the lovely 19C suburbs of this straightlaced but historic town.

44

Weimar

61,375 inhabitants.

Tourist Information: 4 Marktstrasse, 99423 Weimar. Tel. 2173. Opening times: Mon 10.00–18.00, Tues–Fri 09.00–18.00, Sat 09.00–16.00. For information on guided tours, which leave the office on Mon and Sat 10.00 and 14.00, Sun and Bank Holidays, 10.00, tel. 6 12 40.

There is no other town in eastern Germany so evocative of the 18C and the golden age of German classicism as **WEIMAR**. This exceedingly picturesque town, which was comparatively well cared for during Communist rule, is now attracting substantial funding for renovation. The town, with lovely buildings, parks and museums to enjoy, deserves a visit of one full day at the very least. Weimar now buzzes with Western tourists and building work, with optimism about the future in evidence on every street corner.

History. Weimar's early development was the result of its geographical features. The Ettersberg rises to the north and the Ilm river traverses the town from north-west to south-east. Weimar was the seat of the local rulers from at least AD 531 and the Counts of Weimar resided in the Hornstein, now the site of the Schloss. The settlement received its first documentary mention in 975 and was designated a town in 1254. Economic activity centred on craft and farming rather than trade, as Weimar did not lie on any important trade routes. During the 16C the town's fortifications were built with its four gates, 10 towers and double wall. The Reformation reached Weimar as early as 1510 when Martin Luther preached to the local Franciscan monks. They were to leave the monastery, founded in 1453, in 1533. Weimar enjoyed a resurgence of political power in the late 16C when it became the residential town of the Dukes of Thuringia, beginning with Elector John Frederick the Generous in 1547. New palatial

WEIMAR

0   200m

Map labels:

BAHNHOF · FRIEDENSSTRAßE · WEIMARHALLEN PARK · Weimar halle · Stadtmuseum · SCHWANSEESTRAßE · K.-LIEBKNECHTSTRAßE · ROLLGASSE · FRIEDENSGASSE · Kinder-Krankenhaus · Jakobs-kirche · AM JAKOBSKIRCHHOF · JAKOB STR · FERD FREILIGRATH STR · WAGNER GASSE · BRÜHL GASSE · N · Goethe-u.Schiller-Archiv · JENAER STR · TIEFURT · Altenburg · Rollplatz · Kabinett · GR KIRCHE GASSE · UNTERGRABEN · GERBER-STR · HANS-WAHL-STRAßE · KEGEL BRÜCKE · GEHR-HAUPTMANN-STRAßE · GRABEN · Goethe Platz · Kasse-turm · KARL · KL. TEICH GASSE · St. Peter und Paul Stadtkirche · JAKOBS STR · MARSTALL STRAßE · Albert Schweitzer Gedenkstätte · Kirms-Krackow Haus · Kegel-platz · HEINRICH-HEINE STRAßE · WIELAND STRAßE · Geleitschenke Jugendzentrum · GELEITSTRAßE · Herder-platz · Schloß · BÖTTCHER GASSE · RITTER GASSE · WINTISCHEN STR · KAUF STRAßE · SCHLOßGASSE · STERNBRÜCKE · AN HORN · Kunsthalle · Deutsches Nationaltheater · Theater platz · MARKT STR · Rathaus · Grüner Markt · Stern · DINGELSTEDTSTR · Wittums-palais · HUMMELSTRAßE · SCHILLER STRAßE · Markt-Schiller platz · haus · Stadthaus Cranachhaus · GROPIUS-STRAßE · SCHÜTZENGASSE · BRAUHAUSGASSE · STRAßE · Hochschule für Musik · PUSCHKINSTRAßE · FRAUENTOR STR · Frauen plan · Goethe Wohnhaus/Goethe museum · Haus der Frau von Stein · HEGEL STRAßE · LEUBENSTRAßE · Wieland-platz · ACKERWAND · Beethoven-platz · Goethes Gartenhaus · SCHUBERT STRAßE · Naturbrücke · Borkenhäuschen · Staatsarchiv · Shakespeare-Denkmal · Sophien Krankenhaus · Museum für Ur- u frühgeschichte · MARTENSTRAßE · AMALIENSTRAßE · Liszt-haus · Ruine Tempel-herrenhaus · PARK AN DER ILM · HUMBOLDT · AM POSECKSCHEN GARTEN · GESCHW · SCHOLL-STRAßE · Liszt-Denkmal · CRANACH STRAßE · Rüssich-orthodoxe Kirche · R.BREITSCHEID-STR · KARL-HAUBKNECHT-STRAßE · BAUHAUSSTRAßE · Hochschule für Architetur und Bauwesen · BELVEDERALLEE · HAGEN-WEG · Goethe-und Schiller-Gruft · ECKER-MANN-STR · BERKAER STRAßE · HAECKELSTR · Römisches Haus · Ilm · SCHLOß BELVEDERE

buildings were erected including the Grunes Schloss (Green Palace) and Rathaus. In the early 17C the Ducal printworks, art collection, orchestra and opera company were founded in Weimar. The excellent cultural life of the town received a further boost in 1708–17 when Bach was in residence as the court organist and Kapellmeister. In 1775 Johann Wolfgang von Goethe settled in Weimar as the advisor and close friend of Duke Carl August (1757–1828), staying there until his death 56 years later. The town earned the reputation for being the centre of German classicism. By this time the rulers were from the Duchy of Saxony-Weimar which became the Grand Duchy of Saxony-Weimar-Eisenach in 1815. Great writers such as Johann Gottfried Herder and Friedrich Schiller were attracted to the lively cultural scene of Weimar. In 1781 the Free School of Drawing opened, followed by the Comedy Theatre in 1779. After a fire in 1774 the Schloss was rebuilt during 1790–1803. Weimar was given its classical appearance by Clemens Wenzeslaus Coudray who rebuilt the centre, creating pleasant squares and boulevards. From 1846 the town enjoyed rail links with Weissenfels and cosmopolitan Erfurt in 1847 with a line opening to Gera in 1876.

The cultural life of Weimar continued to flourish and in 1848 Franz Liszt settled here as the director of the court orchestra, living with Princess Carolyne von Sayn-Wittgenstein until 1861. The Franz Liszt Association was based here as was the German Schiller Society, founded in 1859, the German Shakespeare Society of 1864, the German Dante Society 1865 and the German Goethe Society from 1885. Weimar sustained modest industrial growth in the 19C and early 20C with a piano factory and agricultural machinery plant opening in the north. The town earned an important place in history when the parliament, which replaced the German monarchy after the First World War, met in the Deutsches Nationaltheater in 1919 where the new constitution was agreed. In the same year the Bauhaus was founded in Weimar with architect Walter Gropius appointed as its head. Weimar then became the new capital of Thuringia in 1920, to be replaced by Erfurt in 1950. The Buchenwald Concentration Camp was built to the north of the town from 1937 with an accompanying estate of housing for SS officers. Weimar was badly damaged by bombing early in 1945 and the area was handed over to the Soviets in July. Reconstruction began in earnest and the town is now seizing the opportunity to attract tourists and enhance its profile as a centre for classical culture.

A. Town Tour

From the Hauptbahnhof, in the north of the town, cross the Schopenhauer-strasse heading south down Carl-August-Allee to a statue dedicated to the revolutionary Ernst Thalman who died in Buchenwald. Cross Carl-von-Ossitezky-Strasse and head south down Kohlstrasse to join Ernst Thalmann Strasse. This links to the Weimarhallen Park on the right where the **Stadtmuseum** is situated (opening times: Sun–Thurs, 09.00–13.00, 14.00–17.00, closed Fri and Sat). This unremarkable museum, with a collection pertaining to the natural history of the town, is housed in the Neo-Classical Bertuchhaus, built between 1802–6 for the prosperous merchant, Friedrich Justin Bertuch. Cross the K-Liebknechtstrasse east to reach the **Jacobskirche**, placed on the north-eastern corner of the Rollplatz. This Baroque church was erected during 1712–13 and served as the court and garrison church from 1778. The graveyard is of particular interest, as it includes the tombs of Goethe's wife, Christiane, Lucas Cranach the Elder and a vault, the Kassen, created for Schiller before his remains were taken to the Goethe-Schiller Crypt.

On the corner of Karl-Liebknecht Strasse and Graben is the modest **Kunstkabinett** (opening times: Mon–Thurs 09.00–13.00, 14.00–17.00, Sun 10.00–13.00, 14.00–17.00, closed Fri and Sat). Head south into GOETHE-PLATZ, one of the focal points of the town, created 150 years ago from farmland. On the north-east corner stands the main Post Office, built 1887–88, and opposite is the **Kasseturm**. This round tower was reconstructed in the 18C and was originally one of the corner towers of the medieval town walls; it now houses a student club. Bearing south-east at the bottom of Goetheplatz brings you to the picturesque THEATERPLATZ. In the centre stands Ernst Rietschel's powerful Goethe-Schiller Monument, erected in 1857, the bronze statue of the poet-friends has become the symbol of the town. Gracing every tourist publication about Weimar, the pair jointly hold a laurel wreath whilst sternly looking in different directions. Behind the monument is the graceful **Deutsches Nationaltheater**.

Built in pared-down Neo-Classical style during 1906–8, the Theatre occupies the site of the Baroque court theatre, built in 1779, where Goethe worked as artistic director during 1791–1817 and where Schiller's *Wilhelm Tell* was first performed. The present theatre was built when the town was replanned following the removal of the medieval fortifications. The German National Assembly met here in 1919, when it was proclaimed as the Deutsches Nationaltheater (German National Theatre). Sadly, the building was extensively damaged during the Second World War bombing but it has been largely rebuilt, keeping the original façade. It reopened triumphantly in 1948 with a performance of Goethe's *Faust*.

Opposite the Nationaltheater is the **Kunsthalle** (opening times: Tues–Sun 10.00–18.00 in the summer, 09.00ö17.00 in the winter; closed Mon). Originally built as a coach house by C.W. Coudray in the same style as the Theatre it was used as a store and then converted into an Art Gallery in 1955; it now houses temporary exhibitions. Beside the Kunsthalle is the **Wittumspalais** which contains the **Wieland Museum** (opening times: Tues–Sun, 09.00–12.00 and 13.00–17.00, closed Mon, Nov–March, closed Mon and Tues). This two-storey, Baroque residence was built in 1767 on the site of a Franciscan monastery. Between 1774–1807 it was the home of the widow Duchess Anna Amalia, mother of Karl August, who regularly held soirées for important members of the court, artists, writers and philosophers in the TAFELRUNDE room. Although badly damaged during the last War, the rooms where discussion on the Enlightenment took place have been lovingly restored, including the FESTSAAL, POET'S ROOM MUSIC ROOM and the Tafelrunde interior. The latter is a small, wood-panelled room decorated with portraits from Weimar's classic period and Empire style furniture including the cherrywood, round table. In 1963 five of the rooms in the east wing were converted into a museum devoted to Enlightenment theorist, Christoph Martin Wieland (1733–1813), who was a frequent guest at the Wittumspalais. This Humanist philosopher came to Weimar in 1772 at the invitation of Anna Amalia to coach her son in the latest Enlightenment thinking.

Continue south-west from Theaterplatz down Schillerstrasse, a curved street—now a pedestrian zone—which follows the former line of the town fortifications, to reach the **Schillerhaus** at No. 12 (opening times: Wed–Mon, 09.00–17.00, closed Tues). Built in 1777, this was home for Schiller from 1802 until his death in 1805. The building was purchased by the town of Weimar in 1847 to be preserved as a memorial to the great writer. During his twilight years, after resigning from his University post at Jena, he wrote William Tell and the Maid of Orleans here. The top floor has been preserved just as Schiller knew it, with a simple study complete with wooden desk and authentic writing implements. There is the small ante-room, where visitors would wait before being conducted into the classical drawing room. Beside the Schillerhaus is the Schillermuseum, built in 1989 to display contemporary documents on the writer's life.

From the Schillerhaus it is a short walk south down Schillerstrasse to the Frauenplan, where the intriguing **Goethe-wohnhaus und Goethe-museum** can be found (opening times: Tues–Sun 09.00–17.00, closed Mon). This is where Goethe lived for 47 years, having been made a present of the splendid Baroque mansion in 1792 by Duke Charles Augustus. The house was bequeathed to the State in 1885 by the poet's grandson, Walter von Goethe. It was then restored to its 18C state to open to the public in 1908, the annexe to the right was built in 1914 to house his special collection.

Originally built in 1709, Goethe extensively altered the building in 1794 to his own designs, following his rubric of 'highest utility in beauty'. The classical staircase which must be climbed to reach the first floor rooms was designed by Goethe himself. The rooms which look out over the Frauenplan to the north are the more public reception and display rooms whilst the more austere work rooms of Goethe lie to the back. At the top of the staircase is the GELBER SAAL (Yellow Room or Dining Room) which contains casts of antique sculptures and paintings which were souvenirs of Goethe's journey to Italy. Leading off the Gelber Saal is the JUNOZIMMER, named after the stately cast of the Juno Ludovisi which dominates the room. Used as a reception room by Goethe it also contains a copy of the *Aldobrandine Nuptials* by H. Meyer, portrait of Zelter by K. Begas and a piano said to have been played by the young Mendelssohn and by Clara Schumann. Leading from the Jonozimmer is the URBINOZIMMER, so-called because a portrait of the Duke of Urbino hangs here amongst other items from Goethe's art collection. Crossing by the spiral staircase the more modest BIBLIOTHEK (Library) is entered, containing Goethe's personal collection of some 5000 volumes. Adjacent is the ARBEITZIMMER (Work room or study), which was open only to close friends, with simple wooden furniture, bare floorboards and plain blue walls. His desk is placed by the window, which looks out over the well-tended garden, complete with his own writing paraphernalia. Adjacent to the Arbeitzimmer is the SCHLAF-ZIMMER (bedroom), an equally spartan room where the poet died whilst seated in the armchair on 22 March 1832 at the grand old age of 82. The simple bed with its washed-out red quilt, small rug on the bare floorboards and the two humble tables attest to the basic comforts Goethe allowed himself in his working life.

On the eastern side of the first floor, beside the Gelber Saal, is the DECKENZIMMER (Stucco Ceiling Room) which contains drawings by Angelica Kauffmann, Rubens, Bloemaert and P. Vischer the Younger with some lovely Biedermeier furniture. This leads into the MAJOLIKAZIMMER (Majolica Room) with white painted, glazed cabinets containing Goethe's collection, and the GROSSE WOHNSTUBE (Large Living Room) which contains a portrait of Goethe's patron, Carl August, by Kolbe (1822). The **Goethe National Museum** stands next door and has, since 1914, contained the extensive scientific and art collections of Goethe in its 24 rooms. Goethe's broad range of interests, from minerology to majolica can be appreciated on a visit to the Museum.

On the eastern side of the Frauenplan is **Zum weissen Schwan** (The White Swan) an inn frequented by Goethe when he tired of his studies. The hostelry was first mentioned in 1533 and its entrance is decorated with a white swan and the inscription: *Der weisse Schwan begrüsst dich jederzeit mit offenen Flügeln* (the white swan will always welcome you with open wings). Embedded into the gable wall is a cannon ball, reminder of the Napoleonic Wars and the Battle of Jena of 1806 when Weimar was shelled and subsequently occupied. Inside, the White Swan is just as welcoming as in Goethe's day, serving traditional German food and drink.

The **Gänsemännchen-Brunnen** (Gooseherd Fountain) in the centre of the Frauenplan was made in cast-iron by Clemens C. Coudray in 1822 and depicts a nonchalant farmworker, one goose tucked under each arm with water trickling from their beaks. To the east of the Frauenplan, down Seiengasse is the **Haus der Frau von Stein** (Frau Stein was the love of Goethe's life for ten years when he first arrived in Weimar). This stately,

The Goethe-Schiller Monument by Ernst Rietschel, 1857

symmetrical building was formerly the royal stables and was converted into the home of the Stein family in 1770 by Frau Stein's husband, Baron Friedrich von Stein. It is now only a short walk north up Frauentorstrasse to the centre of Weimar at the MARKT. Here stands the large and efficent Tourist Information Office and the Gothic Revival **Rathaus**, built in 1841 on the west side of the square. Opposite is a striking Renaissance building, the **Stadthaus** and **Ratskeller**, built during 1526–47 by Nicol Gromann. It was used as a trading centre and then, in the 19C, a ballroom and theatre. The New Weimar Club, founded by Franz Liszt in 1854, met at the Stadthaus. Damaged during the Second World War, it was substantially rebuilt in the late 1960s to the original designs and now houses the Ratskeller and various apartments.

Beside the Stadthaus is the **Cranachhaus**, where the famous Renaissance artist lived from 1552 until his death the following year at the age of 80. It was originally built by Nicol Gromann during 1547–49 for the Royal Chancellor, Christian Brück, the son-in-law of Lucas Cranach the Elder. The famous artist worked here on the altarpiece for the Stadtkirche. Weimar's first bookshop was opened in these premises in 1725. Substantially restored in 1972 to mark the 500th anniversary of Cranach's birth, the façade has been authentically reproduced with its four, richly decorated arches. The coat of arms of the Cranach family, the winged serpent, can be seen above the right-hand arch.

On the south side of the Markt is an inn dating back to the 16C—**Zum Schwartzen Bären** (The Black Bear), complete with carved bear above the main arch. Beside Zum Schwartzen Bären is the town's best hotel, Hotel Elephant. A hotel has been situated here since the 16C with major rebuilding work taking place in 1938. This explains the fairly stern façade, which is in the tradition of German modernism. The Elephant became an Inter-hotel in 1965 and was the only place that Western visitors could stay on a visit to Weimar. It is now a four-star hotel and still the premier place to stay (despite competition from the Hilton in the park by the Ilm); Thomas Mann immortalised it in his novel, *Lotte in Weimar*. The northern side of the Markt is lined with four, reconstructed Renaissance buildings including the **Hofapotheke** (Court Pharmacy) with the **Neptunbrunnen** (Neptune Fountain) standing before it.

Continue north up Kaufstrasse to reach HERDERPLATZ, the oldest market square in Weimar, which was superseded by the Markt in c 1300, and is dominated by the most important ecclesiastical building in the town, the **St Peter und Paul Stadtkirche** (opening times: Mon–Fri 10.30–12.00 and 14.00–15.30, Sat and Sun 14.00–15.00). The St Peter und Paul Stadtkirche dates from 1498–1500 and is also known as the Herderkirche as Johann Gottfried Herder was minister here from 1776–1803. It is a splendid triple-naved, late Gothic hall church which was altered in Baroque style in 1726 and 1734–45 by Johann Adolf Richter and disastrously damaged in 1945. Restoration work began in 1948 with novelist Thomas Mann donating prize money from the Goethe award to the costs. Inside, the large, winged altarpiece, begun by Lucas Cranach the Elder in 1522 and completed by his son after his death in 1555 is particularly noteworthy. The Crucifixion is depicted in the centre panel with portraits of Luther and Cranach included to the right of the cross. Lucas Cranach the Elder's original gravestone, with its life-size portrait of the artist, was transferred here from St Jacob's cemetery and lies beneath the chancel. Other important tombs include those of members of the Royal family in ornate marble and brass, amongst them Duke Bernard (d. 1639) the leader in the Thirty Years War, Duchess Anna Amalia (d. 1807) and Elector John Frederick the Generous (d. 1554). Herder is also entombed here, beneath the organ with a cast iron slab bearing the motto '*Licht, Liebe, Leben*' (Light, Love, Life). A statue of Herder stands outside the church, erected in 1850 and designed by Ludwig Schaller.

Set back from the Herderplatz, standing beside the church, is the former **Gymnasium** (Grammar School) built during 1712–16 with the **Herderdenkmal** (Herder Memorial Fountain), dating from 1832, before it. Behind the Stadtkirche is the Baroque Herderhaus, where the poet and philosopher lived whilst working at the Stadtkirche during 1776 until his death in 1803. Continuing north a short distance up Jacobstrasse will bring you to the **Kirms-Krackow-Haus/Herdermuseum** (presently closed for restoration). A well preserved Renaissance building, originally the dwelling of a wealthy town official in the 16C, it was occupied during Goethe's time by the Kirms family. After the death of Charlotte Krackow in 1915 it was bought by the town and opened as a museum devoted to 19C, middle-class life with its authentic interiors. The Herder Museum was then opened here on the second floor in 1963 with a strong Marxist bias, currently being erased as part of the renovation.

The tour ends with the **Schloss**, which houses the town's impressive Weimar Art Collection (opening times: Tues–Sun 10.00–18.00, closed Mon). To reach the Schloss complex take the Mostgasse east from Herderplatz and enter via the Burgplatz. The huge building, which backs onto the River Ilm, originated in a moated castle erected in the 10C, which burnt down. The Schloss was rebuilt in 1439 with the lower, stone portion of the castle tower and gateway which make up the Bastille still extant today. Under the supervision of Nicol Gromann the Schloss was converted into a residential palace during the 16C, but another fire in 1618 destroyed much of the work. The palace was then totally redesigned by Johann Moritz Richter (1620–67) during the mid 17C. With the exception of the upper portion of the tower, added in 1730, the present-day appearance of the Schloss dates from the time of Goethe, who also participated in the redesign of the building following another fire in 1774. Under the supervision of leading Berlin architect Heinrich Gentz, work was finally completed on the Schloss in 1803, with fine Neo-Classical detail, particularly in the interiors. The southern side of the building was added in 1914, very much in the Neo-Classical style of the remainder. The Schloss has housed the **Kunstsammlungen** (Weimar Art Collection) since 1923 as well as the

The house in Weimar where Goethe lived for forty-seven years

Nationale Forschungs und Gedenkstatten (National Research and Memorial Centre of the Classical Writers of German Literature in Weimar).

Enter through the archway in the centre of the south wing, noting the Bastille to the right which includes the tower and east portal dating from 1439 and west portal from c 1550. This leads into a huge, rectangular, cobbled courtyard outside the entrance to the Kunstsammlungen. This is a first class collection of paintings, displayed in over 70 rooms, with those dating from before and during the Reformation of particular note. The present collection was founded by the Duke in the late 17C and was augmented by the art museum which Goethe founded in 1809.

The first part of the display concentrates on German art from the Middle Ages to the Reformation with the work of Lucas Cranach the Elder highlighted. This includes the tender wedding portraits of Elector John Frederick I and Sybille von Cleve of 1526, a marvellous *Luther as Junker Jörg* and a rather mind-boggling *Age of Silver*, which illustrates an allegorical battle. Work by Cranach's less talented son is also on display, with the rather uncouth *Hercules Asleep* and *Hercules Awake* as representative examples. There is fine work by Dürer including the double portrait, *Hans and Elspeth Tucker* (1499) and in the Italian gallery work by Tintoretto and Veronese. On the first floor, Dutch and Flemish masters are also well represented with work by Ostade, Reubens and Brouwer as well as a comprehensive collection of Russian icons from the 15C to 19C. There is German 19C Romantic painting and sculpture in the collection, with work by Friedrich, Runge, Kersting and Tischbein. Work by the local Weimarer Malerschule are also of interest. This group of artists were committed to painting domestic scenes and landscapes from a realist or symbolic as opposed to Romantic perspective. Centred around the Grand-Ducal Art School between 1875 and 1890, the group, led by Arnold Böcklin and Franz von Lenbach with followers such as Karl Buchholz and Christian Rohlfs, whose work is on show here, paved the way for German Impressionism. Work from the 20C comes mainly from the Bauhaus projects by masters such as Feininger, Muche, Kandinsky, Itten and Klee. There is also a comprehensive collection of graphic work numbering over 65,000 items.

On the first floor there is also a good selection of the original interiors dating back to the 18C and 19C in the east wing, occupied by the former Grand-Ducal family until the Second World War. The FALKENGALERIE (Falcon Gallery) designed by Gentz is a masterpiece of Neo-Classical interior decoration. The inlaid, wood floor and plaster ceiling are decorated with abstract, symmetrical patterns and the walls are ornamented with painted glass panels depicting graceful, classical goddesses. The tops of the four walls are decorated with plaster friezes featuring putti and garlands, finished with a Greek key border. The WEISSEHSAAL (White Hall), also by Gentz, has a striking coffered, barrel-vaulted ceiling painted in white with beautiful chandeliers and wall sconces.

From the Schloss it is a short walk to the charming Park an der Ilm (Park on the Ilm), the subject of the next tour.

B. Park an der Ilm and the Schloss Belvedere

Cross the River Ilm by means of the STERNBRÜCKE (Star Bridge) from the Schloss, noting the remains of the castle mill which was destroyed by fire in 1882. Walk south to reach the **Stern** (Star) itself. The present grounds were planned under the patronage of Duke Carl August, who had grown tired of gardens designed in the formal, French style. Inspired by his visit to Wörlitz Park, Goethe instigated the informal layout of the meadow area in a more English style, with follies and statues. The work was enhanced by the meandering path of the River Ilm and trees planted individually or in groups. The Stern dates back to the more formal, 17C Royal Park, when the main paths through the landscape converged here. Take the path east from the bottom of the Stern and then the Corona-Schroter-Weg to reach **Goethes Gartenhaus** (opening times: Tues–Sun 09.00–12.00 and 13.00– 17.00). This simple building with sloping, red-tiled roof was Goethe's first home when he came to Weimar in 1776 at the age of 27. Bought at an auction by Goethe, it was a derelict vineyard house with unkept garden, which was renovated by the poet who also planned its grounds. This was his main Weimar residence until 1782, when he moved to the house on the Frauenplan, although he continued to use it as a retreat until his death. Here, Goethe could escape his professional obligations and the formalities of court life to commune with nature. The rooms are small, with furniture and works of art dating from Goethe's time.

From the Gartenhaus cross the river over the NATURBRÜCKE to reach the **Nadelöhr** (Eye of a Needle), consisting of stone steps leading from the bridge, through an archway and up the bank to reach the remarkable **Borkenhäuschen** (Bark Cottage). This was built in three days by Goethe in 1778 for Princess Carl August as a retreat. To the south is the **Shakespeare-Denkmal** (Shakespeare Memorial Statue) by Otto Lessing, erected in 1904, and the first monument to the English writer to be erected on the Continent. Carved from Carrara marble it shows a seated, young Shakespeare casually surveying the park with one hand on his hip. To the west of the Shakespeare-Denkmal is the **Ruine Tempelherrenhaus**. This was a tea salon, converted from a conservatory in 1786 and decorated with four lifesize statues of Templars by Martin Gottlieb Klauer. Demolished in 1811 it was recreated in 1823 with the Templar knights carved in sandstone only to be ruined by bombing in the Second World War. Just a few remains of this once charming folly are now in evidence.

Further south is the **Liszt-Denkmal**, a marble statue of Liszt, created by Hermann Hahn in strict, classical style and erected in 1902. To the west of this is the **Liszthaus**, bordering on the park (opening times: Tues–Sun 09.00–13.00 and 14.00–17.00). The composer lived in this house, originally built for the court gardeners, during the summer months of 1869–86. Liszt had been appointed Royal Conductor for Extraordinary Services in 1842, directing Weimar's orchestra and opera company. However, artistic differences had prompted his resignation in 1859 but he returned to Weimar and to this house every summer for the rest of his life. Following his death in 1886 the house was used to hold Liszt's estate and the Liszt Museum was created in 1891. Inside, the rooms on the first floor are all furnished in authentic 19C style as Liszt would have known it, with a small museum devoted to his life and work on the ground floor.

Continue south through the Park to the **Römisches Haus** (Roman House) built as a summer retreat for Duke Carl August in the style of a Roman dwelling (opening times: April–Oct, Wed–Sun 09.00–12.00 and 13.00–17.00). Designed by Goethe, it was built in 1797 at the bottom of a wooded slope. The rustic ground floor, best seen at the rear, supports the classical upper floor. The west facing portico has four Ionic columns and pediment and the interior is characteristically severe with various side rooms, a vestibule, salon and study.

If time permits, the walk may be continued c 8km south to the **Schloss Belvedere**, through the park past the Bienenmuseum (Bee Museum, currently closed for renovation) and the Ehringsdorf area. Alternatively, a bus may be caught from Belvederer Allee to the Schloss Belvedere. In the Ehringsdorf area important Ice Age human remains, including the top of a female skull, have been found; this discovery has been commemorated with a special plaque. The Schloss Belvedere is then reached; set in its own parkland, it was built as a hunting lodge during 1724–32 and was the main summer residence of Duke Ernst August (opening times: April–Oct, Wed–Sun 10.00–13.00 and 14.00–18.00). The white and yellow façade of this Baroque palace dominates the broad vista leading to the entrance. This central block and the four 'Cavaliers' Houses' (now the home of the Special School of Music) were designed by Johann Adolf Richter with later alterations by Gottfried Heinrich Krohne. The park was originally set out in formal, French style but was redesigned in the English, picturesque manner in the 18C. There are various follies in the grounds dating from this time including the KUNSTLICHE RUINE (Artificial Ruin), IRRGARTEN (Maze) and HECKENTHEATER (Hedge Theatre). The palace itself was turned into a splendid **Museum** devoted to the Rococo in 1925. The high point of the collection is porcelain dating from 17C and 18C in predominantly Rococo style. The Belvederer Allee is an historic avenue which leads north back to Weimar from where a bus can be caught.

C.   From the Marktplatz to the Goethe-Schiller Crypt

This walk should take only half a day and incorporates some sights not included on the main Town Tour, most notably the former Bauhaus and Central Library for German Classicism. From the Marktplatz head southeast past the Cranachhaus to the PLATZ DER DEMOKRATIE. Formerly known as the Furstenplatz (Princes' Square) as many of the palace buildings backed onto it, it was renamed Platz der Demokratie in 1945. On the north side of the square is the **Rotes Schloss** (Red Palace), built between 1574 and 1576 as a home for the widow of Duke Johann Wilhelm, the Duchess Dorothea Susanna (1544–92). The façade is graced by the original, Renaissance portal complete with coat of arms and three gables with a staircase tower at the rear. During 1781–1807 the Rotes Schloss housed the important Free School of Drawing but has since been used for state administrative offices.

Beside the Rotes Schloss is the smaller **Gelbes Schloss** (Yellow Palace) built for Duchess Charlotte Dorothea Sophie in 1702–04. On the east side of the Platz der Demokratie is the **Grünes Schloss** (Green Palace); built during 1562–65 by Nicol Gromann it was converted into a library in 1861. The Grünes Schloss now houses three libraries and contains 800,000 volumes in all: the national collection of German Classical Literature, the Thuringian State Library and the collection of the German Shakespeare Society—the largest in Europe. The main feature of the building is the splendid reading room, designed by Johann Schmidt, which may be visited on application to the reception desk. The Rococo room is two storeys high and oval shaped. Painted in white and gold it is decorated with busts of the great writers and thinkers who have worked in Weimar, including Goethe, Schiller and Herder. The upper floor consists of a balcony with smaller galleries leading off it, giving access to the special collections.

On the south side of the Platz is the Franz Liszt **Hochschule für Musik** (College of Music), housed in the former **Fürstenhaus** (Prince's House). Built between 1770 and 1774 to house the local administration offices by Anton Georg Hauptmann (1735–1803), it also played host to the Free School of Drawing from 1808–16. The front façade was substantially altered in 1899 with the addition of formal columns. In front of the Hochschule für Musik stands an equestrian statue of Duke Charles Augustus by Adolf Donndorf, erected in 1875. Pass between the Hochschule and the Library south-west to join the **Ackerwand**, a road laid out in 1800 with interesting 19C, classical houses at Nos 9, 15–17 and 19–21. The Ackerwand passes behind Goethe's garden to join the WIELANDPLATZ, with a bronze statue of the poet, Christoph Martin Wieland erected in 1857 by Gasser. (Wieland resided at No. 1 Marienstrasse, which leads south-east from Wielandplatz, during 1777–92.) Also note the Jugendstil **Hansa House** on Wielandplatz, built in 1905. Continue south-west down AMALIENSTRASSE and on the right is the **Museum für Ur und Frühreschichte Thüringens** (Museum of Thuringian Primeval and Early History; opening times: Tue–Fri 09.00–17.00, Sat and Sun 10.00–13.00, 14.00–17.00). This museum contains a collection of artefacts charting the history of the area from the Stone Age to Medieval times with a superb display of Neolithic pottery.

Continue south down Amalienstrasse and take the next left into Geschwister-Scholl-Strasse to find the **Hochschule für Architektur und Bauwesen** (College of Architecture, Building and Construction, closed to the public). The two buildings were designed in 1904 by the Belgian Art Nouveau architect and design theorist, Henry van der Velde (1863–1957) who was also its Director from 1911 when it opened, until 1915 when the War forced its closure. There had been an art school of some description here since 1860, when the Weimar Academy of Fine Art was founded in a building which stood on this site. With the appointment of Van der Velde the Grand-Ducal Saxon School of Arts and Crafts was founded with the Grand-Ducal Saxon Academy in Fine Art in the building opposite. The School has earned a leading place in the history of 20C design as it was here that Walter Gropius, who succeeded Van der Velde as Director, opened the famous Bauhaus in 1919. The font of all modern architecture and design, the school survived in Weimar for only six years before being forced to move to the more industrial Dessau in 1925. The students, with their wild behaviour and strange dress, offended the conservative Weimar inhabitants and the tradition of fostering cultural experiment in the town came to an end. The building itself is typical of Van de Velde's work, which blends Art Nouveau and Modernism to produce simple but stylish designs. The School for Arts and Crafts has a series of regular, sturdy pilasters which give the building a weighty appearance. The Academy of Fine Art's studios are lit by massive windows which cut into the roof on the southern façade. The general appearance is one of elegant functionalism which was to be taken further by Gropius when he designed the new Bauhaus buildings in 1925 at Dessau.

From the Hochschule, cross Marienstrasse west and enter the **Alter Friedhof** (Old Cemetery). Founded in 1818, the cemetery covers an area of 36 hectares and contains the graves of some 100 people associated with the golden age of classical Weimar. Most notable are Charlotte von Stein, C.W. Coudray and Walter and Wolfgang von Goethe. Most important is the **Goethe-Schiller-Gruft** (Goethe-Schiller Crypt, opening times: 09.00–13.00 and 14.00–17.00, closed Tues). This Neo-Classical mausoleum was commissioned by Duke Carl Augustus and built by C.W. Coudray during 1825–26. It was originally intended to be the exclusive royal family crypt—26 family coffins were transferred here from the Palace church in 1825—but the Duke decided that the two leading lights of his court should also be laid to rest here. Enter the Crypt by means of the broad flight of stairs and classical portico which lead to the domed Hall of Honour from where stone steps lead down to the burial chamber. The tombs of the former rulers can be seen, beginning with Duke William (d. 1662) and including Duke Charles Augusutus (d. 1828) and his wife Luise (d. 1830). At the northern side of the Crypt is the small **Russisch-orthodoxe** Kirche, built for Duchess Maria Pavlova, the wife of Duke Charles Augustus's son, who refused to renounce the Russian Orthodox faith of her family.

D. From the Kegelplatz to the Tierfurt Park and Schloss

The Tierfurt district lies c 5km to the north-east of Weimar and can be reached by bus from the Goetheplatz. Alternatively, the distance may be walked taking in the Goethe-Schiller-Archiv and the Altenburg.

The KEGELPLATZ was the site of the Kegeltor, one of the fortified town gates. The Marstall stands on the square, a Neo-Renaissance building by Ferdinand Streichhan, built during 1873–78. Used as the administrative centre for the Thuringian state from 1922, it now houses the Weimar State Archives. The **Albert-Schweitzer-Gedenkstätte** (Albert Schweitzer Memorial; opening times: Tues–Fri 09.00–17.00, Sat and Sun 10.00–13.00, 14.00–17.00) lies on the north side of the Kegelplatz. This mildly interesting display of the great doctor's life and work, opened in 1984, is housed in a late Baroque town house. The author and creator of fairy tales, Johann Carl August Musäus (1735–87) lived here whilst working as a teacher in the grammar school. A rather sentimental statue of Schweitzer by Gerhard Geyer, erected in 1968, stands in the Kegelplatz. A brief detour down the Graben to the north-west of Kegelplatz is rewarded by the sight of some superb Jugendstil house façades, now thankfully being fully restored. The Graben follows the curve of the former town wall, which was demolished in the late 18C.

From the Kegelplatz cross the river Ilm by means of the KEGEL-BRÜCKE—the 18C stone original was largely reconstructed in 1950 following war damage. Take the Hans-Wahl-Strasse north to the **Goethe-Schiller-Archiv**. This is, without doubt, the most important collection of literary manuscripts in Germany. The archive began in 1885 when

Walther Wolfgang von Goethe, the poet's last grandson, bequeathed the family collection of manuscripts to Grand Duchess Sophie. Schiller's papers were presented in 1889 by his grandson, Baron Ludwig von Gleichen-Russworm. A building was then specially designed by Otto Minkert (1845–1900) and finished in 1896 to house the collection. Presently it contains manuscripts pertaining to over 130 German authors, artists and philosophers including Herder, Wieland, Nietsche and Fritz Reuter. The building was modelled on the small, summer palace at Versailles and a splendid view of Weimar can been enjoyed from the terrace. From the Archiv cross Janaer Strasse east to the **Altenburg**. This pleasant, 18C building was given to Princess Carolyne von Sayn-Wittgenstein (1819–87) when she came to Weimar in 1848. Franz Liszt also lived here between 1850 and 1861, when the house was a famous meeting place for artists and musicians. It is now the home of local author, Jutto Hecker as well as the Weimar Franz Liszt Centre.

Continue north up Jenaer Strasse and take Tierfurter Alle to the east, which leads to the **Schloss and Park Tierfurt**. Note to the right the Webicht, a steep sloping forest of deciduous trees and the massive railway viaduct of some 138m in length and 37m in height which opened in 1876, connecting Weimar to Gera.

The Schloss Tierfurt lies on the banks of the river Ilm and was originally leased out until 1775, when the Duchess Anna Amalia had it refurbished for her son Constantin and his tutor, Carl Ludwig von Knebel. (Opening times: Wed–Sun 09.00–13.00 and 14.00–17.00.) The Duchess then used the Schloss herself, as a summer residence between 1781 to 1806, where many of the famous Round Table discussions took place. The interiors of this comparatively modest Schloss have been well preserved, with superb examples of Rococo, Neo-Classical and Biedermeier furnishing and decoration. There are also fine paintings by G.M. Kraus and F.A. Oeser as well as sculpture by M. Klauer.

The grounds provided a charming backdrop for summer festivities and were layed out in 1786 in the informal, English style in sympathy with the extreme bend of the River Ilm. By the river stands the most famous of the park's follies, the MUSENTEMPEL (Temple of Muses), consisting of a small, classical pavillion set in a formal garden. The MOZART MONUMENT, the first to be erected in Europe in 1799, is in marble with the masks of the two muses surmounting the inscription *'Mozart und Den Musen'*. The TEE-SALON (Tea Salon) was built in 1805 from red brick and is now, sadly, boarded up. Of the memorials in the park, that devoted to Herder, a pyramid, and to the Duchesses's son, Constantin, are the most striking. The TEMPLE OF FRIENDSHIP on the left bank of the river houses a statue of Polyhymnia, Muse of singing.

45

From Weimar to Mühlhausen via Ettersberg, Sonderhausen and Nordhausen

Weimar to—8km Ettersberg—48km Sonderhausen—20km Nordhausen—45km Mühlhausen.

This route explores the north-western corner of Thüringen, taking in the chilling Buchenwald Memorial, the Ettersberg Palace and onto the Kyffhauser hills and the medieval city-states of Nordhausen and Mulhausen.

A. Ettersberg

Ettersberg dominates the northern suburbs of Weimar, towering 240m above the town. Near the highest point is the poignant Buchenwald Memorial and to the north is the Ettersburg Palais, royal summer residence during the 18C hosting a glittering, international court. Leave Weimar heading north on the A85 and then branch off left after the Hauptbahnhof to the village of Ettersburg. The village was first recorded in 1089 and now consists of a handful of modest dwellings and the Ettersburg Palace itself. There are remains of 13C and 14C fortifications but the main body of the Palace was built during 1706–12 to designs by Johann Mutzer. It was originally intended to be used as a hunting lodge for the Weimar Duke Wilhelm Ernst. During the 18C it was used as a summer residence with plays and concerts taking place there; visitors included Goethe, Napoleon and Tsar Alexander I. To the south of the Palace are the 10C ruins of the old palace and landscaped gardens, laid out by Prince Puckler and Eduard Petzold during 1844–46 in the existing forest.

Return to the Palace heading north then take the narrow road west through the forest. This leads to the **Konzentrationslager Buchenwald** (Buchenwald Concentration Camp; opening times: Tues–Sun 08.45–16.30). Built in 1937 the Camp held 239,000 prisoners with 56,000 meeting their death here through maltreatment. The harrowing remains of this dreadful place have been preserved, complemented by a memorial erected in 1958 in memory of the dead. Great political capital was made of the site during former GDR times and now that Germany is undergoing a total reassessment of its past, chilling reminders of the extremities of Naziism such as this are vital. There is now a museum and one can visit the original prisoners' compound, gate, assembly square and canteen.

Return to the A85 and continue north through Buttelstedt, Olbersleben and Kolleda. The A85 then crosses the River Unstrut and continues through the undulating scenery of the Schrecke range of hills before passing through **Bad Frankenhausen**, a town of 10,000 inhabitants with a Baroque Schloss of 1689, largely reconstructed during the 1970s. To the north lies the picturesque **Kyffhauser** range of wooded, sandstone hills where the Barbarossahohle is situated (open daily May–Sept 09.00–18.00; Oct–April 09.00–17.00) a massive gypsum cave with stalactites and a lake, discovered in 1865 and linked with the myth of the warlike king Barbarossa. Legend has it that he is buried beneath the Kyffhauser and will burst back to life from his slumbers when Germany regains its former might. From Bad Frankenhausen head west on the minor road to Sonderhausen.

B.   Sondershausen

24,000 inhabitants.

Tourist Information: 20 Ferdinand-Schlufter-Strasse, 99706 Sondershausen. Tel. 8111. Opening times: Mon–Fri 09.00–12.30 and 13.30–17.00, Sat 09.00–11.00.

Sondershausen was orignally the capital of Schwarzburg and later of Schwarzburg-Sondershausen. This modest town boasts a 16C Schloss with many Baroque additions which now functions as a Museum (opening times: Tues–Sun by guided tour at 09.00, 10.00, 11.00, 14.00, 15.00 and 16.00). From the Markt ascend the steps beside the Alte Wache. Built during 1534–76, the Schloss was greatly extended when the two sons of the family were honoured as Princes of the Holy Roman Empire in the late 17C. During the tour the richly decorated, 17C HOFAPOTHEKE (Court Apothecary), Baroque RIESENSAAL (Hall of Giants) and Rococo WEISSEM SAAL can be seen. The plasterwork is perhaps the most striking aspect of the Schloss interior, with high Baroque creations on the Riesensaal coffered ceiling and the Wendelstein. There is also a small, 19C theatre in the Schloss. Court entertainment also took place in the Karussel, a large, 18C pavilion situated in the Schloss grounds to the west. The local orchestra, Loh-Orchester, founded in 1801, often perform here.

Continue of the A4 north out of Sonderhausen, noting the Windleite hills to the right and Hainleite to the left. Passing through Marionhall and over the River Helme, the larger town of Nordhausen is reached.

C.   Nordhausen

48,000 inhabitants.

Tourist Information: 42 Rautenstrasse, 99734 Nordhausen. Tel. 4938. Opening times: Mon, Thurs and Fri, 09.30–12.00 and 13.30–16.30, Tues, 09.30–12.00 and 13.30–17.30, Wed 09.30–12.00 and 13.30–15.30.

Nordhausen stands on the south-east fringe of the Harz mountain range in a region which is named Goldene Aue (Golden Meadow) due to the mild climate and fertile soil, served by the River Helme. Nordhausen was the site of a castle as early as 874 and a convent was founded here by Empress Mathilde in 962. After the town was virtually destroyed by Henry the Lion in 1180 it was rebuilt to become a Free Imperial City in 1253. Many remains of this auspicious past have survived, despite Nordhausen being one of the Thuringian towns most badly bombed during the Second World War, sustaining 75 per cent total damage.

Architecturally most important is the **Dom**, founded in 961 as a church for the Convent and rebuilt as a Gothic hall church in the mid 14C. Beneath the late Gothic choir is an impressive Romanesque crypt with simple, carved capitals. Many of the furnishings, including the carved choir-stalls, date from the 14C; the memorial stones date from the 14C to the 16C, whilst the Baroque high altar dates from 1726. Beside the Dom to the east is the **Pfarrkirche St Blasii**. Founded in the 15C this late Gothic hall with curved rib vaulting contains *The Raising of Lazarus* by Lucas Cranach the Younger with portraits of Luther and Melanchton amongst the mourners. The two octagonal towers were added in the 18C and the pulpit dates from 1592. Up to the north of Pfarrkirche St Blasii is BARFUSSER STRASSE which boasts several half-timbered houses dating back to the 17C. One of the most famous of Nordhausen's landmarks is the statue of **Roland** on the west side of the Rathaus in the Markt. Dating from 1717 many leading Germany towns erected a statue of Roland, the nephew of Charlemagne, as a symbol of civic justice from the Middle Ages onwards. The most important of these statues stands in the Markt at Bremen, nearly 6m high and carved in sandstone. The Nordhausen version is a merry gentleman with long curls and moustache. Badly damaged during the Second World War he has been painstakingly restored and is now protected by a canopy. The Rathaus was similarly damaged and subsequently rebuilt to resemble closely the 1610, German Renaissance original in 1952.

On the northern outskirts of Nordhausen is another memorial to the victims of Nazi atrocities at the **Konzentratsion-lager Dora**, a part of the main Buchenwald concentration camp, where 18,000 of the 60,000 prisoners died. They were engaged in making missiles in underground caves and tunnels. The memorial can be visited Tues–Sun 09.00–15.15.

Return to Sonderhausen on the A4, which lies in a valley between the Hainleite and Windleite range of hills. To the south, in the Hainleite woods is a hunting palace, **Zum Possen**, built in 1732–38; its attractions today are a restaurant, a wildlife park and the 18C AUSSICHTSTURM (watch-tower), which can be climbed to gain a fine view of the surrounding hills and trees. (open daily, 10.00–18.00.) Take the A249 south through Ebeleben to Mühlhausen.

D. Mühlhausen

44,000 inhabitants.

Tourist Information: 57 Gomarstrasse, 99974 Mühlhausen. Tel. 2912. Opening times: Mon–Fri 09.00–12.00 and 13.00–17.00.

History. Nestled near the foot of the Hainich hills on the River Unstrut, Mühlhausen was first mentioned in 775 and a schloss was built which became an important regal seat. Mühlhausen was to join the Hanseatic League after becoming a free town in 1348; trade was based on textiles and leather goods. The most famous event in Mühlhausen's history, and one that was celebrated to the hilt by the GDR, was the flight of revolutionary Thomas Muntzer there from Allstedt in 1524, when he was expelled by the Saxon authorities. Mühlhausen then became the centre for a peasant uprising with the Communists marking the 450th anniversary of this event in 1975 by renaming the town Thomas-Muntzer-Stadt, a name which now looks unlikely to stick. Muntzer attempted to create an egalitarian theocracy in Mühlhausen but was defeated in battle at Frankenhausen. He was taken as prisoner back to Mühlhausen to be tortured and executed. Many memorials and exhibitions to Muntzer were created by the Communist authorities but the town can be enjoyed for its great medieval atmosphere, with narrow winding streets, Gothic churches and half-timbered houses.

From the Tourist Information Office on Gomarstrasse head north to the Rundturm, one of the towers which formed part of the medieval town walls which still stand. The **town wall** was built in 13C and measures 2700m in total length. It encircles the town and most of the original can still be seen, including six towers and two gateways. Follow the wall west and take the next left down Hauptmannstrasse past the Allerheiligenkirche (All Saints' Church), then continue south to Gormarstrasse and Roblingstrasse and west to Untermarkt.

The parish church of **Divi-Blasii** dominates the square. Founded in 1260, the cross-ribbed vault with round pillars was completed in 1270 with all building work finished by 14C; the church has barely been touched since. The interior features many valuable furnishings and the stained glass windows date back to the 14C. It is also worth mentioning that Bach was briefly resident organist here—from 1707–08. To the south of the Divi-Blasii-Kirche stands the 13C **Annenkapelle**, an early Gothic structure, and nearby are two early 17C burgher houses. The **Burenhof** dates from 1607 and the **Altes Backhaus** from 1631. To the west of the Annenkapelle, built into the town walls, is the Heimatmuseum. This museum of local history features interesting displays on handicrafts of the area, natural history and the general development of the town.

Continue north across the Johann-Sebastian-Bach-Platz, up Linsen-strasse to reach the Kornmarkt on the left. Here stands the **Barfusser-klosterkirche**, a Gothic hall church dating from the 13C and 14C, which formerly served the Franciscan monastery; it is now a museum of the German Peasants' Revolt (opening times: Tues–Sun 10.00–16.30). The church was unfortunately converted into a piece of propaganda in 1975 to mark the 450th anniversary celebrations with a dry exhibition of weapons, prints and other documents on the history of this local revolt.

The **Rathaus** to the north of the Barfusserklosterkirche is the splendid *pièce de résistance* of Nordhausen. Founded in 1300, but with many subsequent additions and alterations, the key parts are in Gothic and German Renaissance styles. The building is now situated on two sides of the street, connected by a covered walkway. Inside is the ornate RATS-STUBE (Council Chamber) where Muntzer held the Ewige Rat (Eternal Council), with decorative wall painting dating back to 1571 and the richly decorated Ratssaal. In the southern wing is the Archiv, with exhibitions of local history. In the courtyard is a fountain dating from 1747.

Directly north from the Rathaus, up Ratstrasse, is the OBERMARKT. In this area are a number of well-preserved, historic dwellings. At No. 8 Obermarkt is the old tavern of the **Goldener Stern** (Golden Star) dating from 1542. At Nos 21–3 Obermarkt is the 18C Brotlaube where a series of medieval shops once stood. To the west of the Brotlaube is the **Marien-kirche** (opening times: 10.00–12.00 and 14.00–16.00, closed Fri). Founded in the 14C it is the largest of the Thuringian churches after that of Erfurt. It is a Gothic hall church whose central, 86m high Gothic tower with 19C steeple is framed by one Romanesque and one early Gothic tower. Also worth seeing is the south façade which is decorated with sculptures by the Parler School of Prague and features Kaiser Karl IV, his wife Elizabeth and two companions placed on a balcony. Inside, the church was converted into the Thomas Munzter Gedenkstätte (Thomas Munzter Memorial) in 1975 as the fanatic preached here during his three months based in the town. Noteworthy are the late Gothic altar (15C and 16C), devoted to Mary, and the 14C and 15C stained glass.

Continue west down Herrenstrasse where, at No. 1, stands the halftimbered house on the site of the house where Muntzer lived during 1525. At the end of Herrenstrasse is the stone Frauentor, the main west entrance to the town in times gone by. It is possible to enter the **Rabenturm**, just to the north, climb to the top and walk along the top of the wall (opening times: July and Aug 10.00–12.,00 and 13.00–16.30, closed Fri; May, June and Sept, Wed and Sat 14.00–17.00, Sun 10.00–12.00 and 13.00–16.30).

46

Weimar to Gera via Dornburg, Tautenburg and Jena

Weimar—34km Dornburg—5km Tautenburg—20km Jena—32km Gera.

This picturesque route reveals some of the more out-of-the-way castles to be found in east Thuringia. The tour concludes with Jena, a bustling city with intersting Gothic Stadtkirche, Rathaus and renowned university.

Leave Weimar on the B7 heading east signposted for Jena, a slow but scenic road into the softer landscape of the eastern part of Thuringia with the forest now well behind to the south-east. Just past the main intersection at Umpferstedt, where the B87 crosses the B7, on the left the ruins of the **Kapellendorf** are visible. Turn off left at Frankendt for a short detour to the castle. This was originally built as a fortress, protected by surrounding swampland, and the 12C structure forms the central core of the moated castle as it stands today. Further alterations in 1508, when the castle was sold to the town of Erfurt for 300 pieces of silver by Burgrave Hartman van Kirchberg, give the castle its present day appearance. The castle now contains a modest museum of weapons, household utensils and clothing from 14C to 17C as well as a café.

Rejoin the B7 east to Jena and here take the B88 north, running alongside the river Saale to reach **Dornburg**. The silhouette of the three castles which make up this small complex greets you on the horizon as you approach. Take the next road to the left, signposted Dornburg, and head up the steep, winding road. The castles, Ratskeller and church are on the first left; next left is a pleasant tavern 'Am Brauhaus' where drinks, meals and snacks can be enjoyed in a small terraced area. The main square or Markt is oddly situated on the top of this 90m high rock with splendid views across the

Saale valley below. It is somehow caught in a time warp: its 17C and 18C buildings seem strangely disengaged from the 20C. The Ratskeller is placed on the north of the square. To the west is the **Stadtkirche St Jacob**, founded in 971 and rebuilt in 1777, with a full restoration carried out in 1978. The 18C interior is well worth a look.

To the south of the square is the entrance to the **Renaissanceschloss** (opening times: Tues–Sun 10.00–12.00 and 13.00–16.00). Built as a two-storey castle in 1539 by a court official from the Saxe-Weimar Duchy, the staircase in the tower with its richly decorated portal was added in 1608. The building is constructed in solid, whitewashed stone topped with a grey slate roof. It is known locally as the Goethe Palace as the great poet and philosopher stayed here on over 20 occasions from 1776 onwards. The tower now houses a museum devoted to him, with three rooms furnished in 18C style. This building and the neighbouring Rokokoschloss are owned by the National Institute of Research and Commemoration of Classical German Literature in Weimar.

The **Rokokoschloss** is delicate by contrast with the Renaissanceschloss, decorated with graceful stucco-work. It was built by J.A. Richter and G.H. Krohne from 1736 to 1747 as a summer residence for the Dukes of Weimar. The exterior is currently undergoing restoration but inside the collection of 18C porcelain and furniture can be viewed. The beautiful gardens are also worthy of a leisurely stroll. To the north is the third of the palaces, the **Altes Schloss**, now an old people's home but formerly an imperial palace. In 1691 Dornburg became the property of Weimar and Duke Wilhelm Ernst swore his oath of allegiance at the castle. Some Romanesque remains can be seen, but the majority of the building dates from 15C.

Return to the B88 and continue north to Steudnitz, then turn right to reach the small village of **Tautenburg** (400 inhabitants) whose spectacular ruined castle is visible for miles around. The castle was founded by a family of knights, the Tuto von Tutenberc, in the 13C. The family vault can be seen at Frauenpriessnitz, 5km north. Also situated near Tautenburg is the Karl-Schwarzschild observatory, built in 1960 by the GDR Academy of Science, housing a 2m reflecting telescope made in nearby Jena.

Rejoin the B88 and head south again for the city of Jena, travelling through the faded but charming Jugendstil suburbs which would have been demolished many years ago in the West, to reach the massive car park in the town centre at the Eichplatz.

Jena

105,000 inhabitants.

Tourist Information: 35 Ernst-Thalmann-Ring, 07747 Jena. Tel. 2 46 71. Opening times: Mon–Fri, 09.00–18.00, Sat 09.00–14.00.

Jena is worthy of at least one afternoon's visit and really deserves one full day. Apart from monuments of architectural interest, particularly the Rathaus and Johanniskirche, there is a wide selection of museums which make much of the town's associations with Goethe and Schiller, and an early planetarium, built in 1925–26.

History. The town was first mentioned in documents in 9C, growing as an important market town in the medieval era. Prosperity hinged on the town's vineyards and wine-making; indeed, coins struck at Jena's mint bore the symbol of a grape. From 1331 to 1485 it came under the rule of the Wettien dukes, who lost control in 1485 to the Ernstine dukes. The University was founded in 1558 at the former Dominican monastery in the south-west of the town. The University expanded during the 16C and opened its own brewery in 1565, the Rosenschenke. It was also an important centre during the Reformation. After suffering during the Thirty Years War the University gained prestige during the later 17C, with publishing houses, printers and bookshops blossoming in Jena. During the 18C the University was promoted by Goethe, then minister of state based at Weimar. A galaxy of names associated with the German enlightenment and the Romantic movement—Friedrich Schiller, Gottlieb Fichte and Georg Friedrich Wilhelm Hegel—were all professors at the University and it grew in size until it was the second largest in Germany.

Jena suffered badly during the Napoleonic Wars, with the Battle of Jena just to the north of the town on 14 October 1806, in which the Prussians and Saxons were defeated. The town recovered and became an important administrative centre, as it still is today, with the Oberappellationsgericht (High Court of Appeal) being founded here in 1817. Industrial expansion was closely allied to technological advances: Carl Zeiss established the manufacture of microscopes here in 1846, moving from small workshops to factory in 1880. In 1884 Zeiss along with University professor Ernst Abbe and Otto Schott, a glass chemist, established a laboratory for producing technical glass, now the Jenaer Glass factory. Thus Jena became an early centre for the production of high quality glass for optical precision tools such as microscopes and telescopes. After Zeiss's death Abbe created the Carl-Zeiss-Foundation in 1890 as a trust to prompt further technical advances in the manufacturing of glass and to fund social programmes, such as the building of the Volkshaus (Cultural Centre) and Volksbad (Indoor Swimming Pool). Jena grew in size and importance in the early 20C with various outlying villages becoming part of the conurbation. The town suffered more than most from Anglo-American bombing in the Second World War and great efforts have been made to re-establish Jena as a centre for culture, academic achievement and technology.

Parking can be found in the Eichplatz, just north of the efficient Tourist Information Office. On the south-east corner of the Eichplatz stands the square, stone-built **Rathaus**. Erected originally in 1377–80 with sloping, red-tiled roofs in late Gothic style. The whitewashed Baroque turret was added between the two hipped roofs in 1755, embellished by a late Gothic clock with the figures of Schnapphans—angels and pilgrims which strike the hours. In the centre of the Markt stands a stately bronze statue of Johann Friedrich der Grossmütige, the founder of the University. It was created by Johann Friedrich Drake in 1858 to commemorate the 300th anniversary of the University. Behind the statue, which is also known as Hanfried, is one of the most interesting and attractive buildings in Jena, the **Göhre**. Named after its proprietor it now houses the Town Museum, and it is a useful starting point for the town tour because it places the town in its historical context (opening times: Tues–Sun, 10.00–13.00, 14.00–17.00, Weds 10.00–18.00). The town's mill originally stood here in the 14C and the present building, with its steep pitched roof and half-timbered frontage, was built c 1500. Inside, local crafts are displayed but the main focus of the museum is the history of the town of Jena, which is retold in exhibits which cover four storeys. Beginning in the 9C and continuing to the 19C the story of Jena as a wine-producing town is unfolded, the Thirty Years War and the founding of the University forming a central part of the display. There is also a pleasant café in the museum, decorated in 19C style (opening times: Wed–Fri, 14.00–18.00, Sat and Sun 10.00–13.00 and 14.00–17.00).

Behind the Göhre to the north is the **Stadtkirche St Michael** (May–Sep, Mon–Fri 10.00–17.30, Sat 10.00–14.00). A massive hall church of the late Gothic period, it was under construction during the 12C. Most striking on the southern exterior is the Brauportal (Bridal Doorway), a feature of many churches of this region. Inside there is one of the 'Seven Wonders of Jena', a passage which runs under the chancel and a beautiful Romanesque wooden statue of St Michael and a dragon, created by the Bamberg School. On the north wall there is also a bronze memorial plate dating from 1549 dedicated to Martin Luther, designed by Lucas Cranach the Elder, bearing a full length portrait of the religious reformer. This was originally installed at Wittenburg but was brought to Jena for safekeeping. The interior of the church is painted white and yellow which accentuates the stone ribs of the vault.

Continue east down Kirchplatz and turn first right into the OBERLAUEN-GASSE where the 17C Am Breiten Stein building with the Löwenbrunnen (lion fountain) can be seen. Beside this is the Honigmann House and the tavern, Zur Noll. At the southern end of Oberlauengasse is Unterm Markt and at No. 12a is the **Romantikerhaus**, a green painted 18C town house with a small museum celebrating early Romanticism. It is officially known as the **Jenaer Kunstsammlung und Gedankstatte der deutschen Früh-romantiik** (opening times: Tues–Sat 10.00–13.00 and 14.00–17.00, Wed open until 18.00). This was the residence of philosopher Johann Gottlieb Fichte between 1795 and 1799. He greatly admired the philosophical ideals linked with the French Revolution and was an early exponent of Romanti-cism in Germany, gathering a côterie of poets and writers around him for regular meetings at his home. Fichte is commemorated with a series of rooms furnished in authentic period style including some fine Empire furniture. The small art collection on display shows German paintings from 17C to 20C, including work by Erich Heckels and Carl Crodels.

Just beside the Romantikerhaus to the east is the **Roter Turm** (Red Tower) which marks the southern end of the old town fortifications. These were built c 1300 and of the four original towers the Roter Turm and the Pulverturm (Powder Tower), to the north-east are in well-preserved condi-tion whilst the Anatomieturm (Anatomy Tower) to the south-west now lies in ruins. Continue north up the Unterlauengasse where the Haus am Stack, the former home of a prosperous wine-grower dating from 1596 with a fine example of a Renaissance portal can be seen and the Platanenhaus with its four storey-turret.

At the top of Unterlauengasse turn right into the Saalstrasse where the Griesbach Auditorium stands. It was here that Schiller delivered his in-augural lecture as a young history professor. Head north to the Lutherplatz where the Student Fraternity Memorial stands. It was created by Adolf Donndorf in 1883 and celebrates Jena as the site for the founding of this important student movement in 1815. Behind is the **Third University**, one of the University buildings erected on the site of the old castle in 1905–08 and designed by Theodor Fischer. The four figures on the façade symbolise the faculties of philosophy, medicine, law and theology. The building is open to the public and houses the university library which contains impor-tant archives including the library of the Wittenberg electorate and the Dominican monastery library. Opposite is the Schwarzer Bar with a plaque and oil painting commemorating Luther's first stay in Jena in 1522.

Continue west down FÜRSTENGRABEN where a vast array of monu-ments commemorate figures such as Fritz-Reuter-Denkmal. On the right, at No. 18 is the Frommannsches Haus (Frommann House). This was the home and publishing house of the bookseller Carl Friedrich Ernst Fromman and a meeting place for Jena intellectuals during the early 18C. Continue west down Fürstengrassen and on the left at No. 23 is the Wucherey, named after its 18C owner; this was a student hostel and from 1861 to 1908 it was in use as the Second University.

Retrace your steps to the crossing between Fürstengraben and Am Planetarium where you will find the entrance to the University's **Botanical Gardens**, in use for research but also open to the public (opening times: Tues–Sun 09.00–16.00). There are over 12,000 different kinds of plants growing in the gardens which include a fascinating Palm House and impressive Alpine rock garden. On the southern side of the garden adjacent to the Fürstengrassen is the **Inspektorenhaus** (opening times: Tues–Sun 09.00–13.00), a modest garden study which Goethe designed for himself and where he wrote many of his works including *The Theory of Colours*. A portion of the house is now a museum dedicated to the writer, the Goethe Gedenkstatte.

The famous **Zeiss Planetarium** is situated to the north of the gardens, in the Griesbachgarten (opening times: closed Mon, times vary on other days). Built in 1925–26 in classical style, this is the oldest planetarium in the world. Just behind the Planetarium is the Prinzessinnenschlösschen, the summer retreat of the theologian Johann Jacob Griesbach. Built in 1784 in Neo-Classical style, it was the hub of intellectual life in the late 18C.

Returning to Fürstengraben, turn left at the end into Johannisplatz and Leutragraben to continue south. To the west can be seen the cylindrical, multi-storey tower of the University, built during 1972 and soaring 120m above the rest of the town. On the left is the **Pulverturm**, the former north-eastern tower of the town wall. It is possible to climb the tower for fine views of the Fürstengraben. Adjoining the Pulverturm is a small section of the former town wall which links to the Johannistor, a well preserved, medieval town gate with an interesting steeple. Turn next left into Johannisstrasse to see the former University tavern Zur Rosen, a fine Baroque building. Continue south down Leutragraben and take the next left into Kollegieng where the most important historical building in Jena, the **Collegium Jenense**, can be seen. Now a listed building, under the protection of UNESCO, it housed the University. Founded in 1286 as a monastery by the Dominican order it was closed down as a result of the Reformation. The University moved here in 1558, and the building, with numerous additions made over the centuries, now houses various parts of the Friedrich Schiller University. In the cobbled courtyard, carved in stone on the wall, is the coat of arms of the Ernestine line of the house of Wettin. It is now a short walk back to the Eichplatz.

If time permits, a tour further south into the suburbs is also of interest. From Eichplatz take Leutragraben and continue south to Schillerstrasse, and into Schillergässchen. On the right at No. 2 is the **Schiller Gedenkstatte** (Schiller Memorial) formerly the home of the famous dramatist and poet, Friedrich Schiller (opening times: Tues–Fri 10.00–12.00 and 13.00–16.00, Sat 11.00–16.00). Schiller lived in the house from 1797 to 1802 whilst Professor of History at the University, now named after him. Of particular interest is the study in the garden house where Schiller did much of his writing, preserved as it was c 1800 with his bookcases and writing desk. Continue south down Schillergässchen and on the left on Am Paradiesbahnhof is the **Phyletisches Museum** (open Mon–Fri 09.00–16,00, Sat and Sun 09.00–14.00) which consists of a display of the evolution of certain species of animals. The Museum was founded by Darwinian zoologist Ernst Haeckel in 1907 and contains rooms full of stuffed foxes, goats and rabbits. Bearing north it is a short distance to the museum devoted to Haeckel, the **Ernst-Haeckel Haus**, to the left on Berggasse (opening times guided tour: Mon–Fri 08.30. 10.00, 11.30, 14.00 amd 15.30, Sat 08.30, 10.00, 11.00 and 14.00). The zoologist lived and worked here during most of his life (1834–1919) and the rooms of the 'Villa Medusa' are furnished in 19C style with splendid glass-fronted bookcases crowned by busts of eminent scientists along with the equipment he used for experiments. There is also a display of Haeckel's watercolours.

To the north-west, crossing Ernst-Haeckel Platz will take you to the **Optisches Museum** on the Carl-Zeiss Platz (opening times: Tues–Fri 09.00–17.30, Sat 09.00–16.00). This is a technical museum with examples of historic precision instruments made largely by the local firm of Carl Zeiss. Of interest is the Zeiss Workshop, dating from 1866. Outside the museum is a large memorial dedicated to Ernst Abbe, created by Constantin Meunier, Henry van de Velde and Max Klinger in 1911. Walk east down Goethestrasse to rejoin the Teichgraben, and from here it is a short walk north past the Tourist Information to the Eichplatz.

Take the dual carriageway south for 7km to join the E40, then head east to Gera.

47

Gera

131,000 inhabitants.

Tourist Information: Main office at 1 Filiale Breitscheidstrasse, 07545 Gera. Tel. 26432 and 26433. Opening times: Mon–Fri 10.00–17.00, Sat 09.00–12.00; Branch office at the Hauptbahnhof (tel. 24430); opening times. Mon–Fri 12.00–19.00.

Situated to the east of Weimar and Jena, **GERA** is the second largest town in Thuringia after Erfurt. Often overshadowed by its more famous neighbours, particularly Weimar, the town warrants a visit because of its fine Renaissance and Jugendstil architecture. Gera was modernised in the post-war era, but this was carried out with proper regard for the town's historic architecture. A fascinating guide, *Gera: Gestern and Heute* (Gera: Yesterday and Today) published in 1986 and available from Tourist Information contrasts 19C and 20C images of the main parts of the town.

History. Gera sits in the valley of the river Weisse Elster, at the foot of gently rolling hills. The town earned an early mention in 999 when Kaiser Otto III gave the land to his sister, the Abbess of Quedlinburg. The mountain castle of Osterstein was founded at this time, and from there the Knights of Gera ruled the small state. From 1180 the area was ruled by the Vogts of Weida and an independent House of Vogts existed from 1209, from where the autonomous principality of Gera emerged. In 1237 Gera was officially designated as a town and, from 1532 to 1918, the Princes of Reuss governed what was one of the smallest German states from here, generating lively intellectual activity around the court with a Grammar School, library and theatre opening in the

17C. This was the lesser Reuss line, or *Reuss jüngere Linie*; the senior part of the family, the *Reuss ältere Linie*, merged in 1918 to form the Freistaat Thüringen (Thuringian Free State) with Weimar as the capital. Gera also developed from 15C onwards into a prosperous production and trading centre, particularly in the wool and textile making trades. Industrialisation took place comparatively early with a steam-powered spinning machine installed in 1833. Industry continued to flourish in the 20C, particularly under the GDR.

Beginning from the rear of the Hauptbahnhof on Ernst-Toller-Strasse, cross this main road to the **Küchengarten**, a lovely municipal park area. The **Bühnen der Stadt** dominates the eastern part of the park. A splendid example of Jugenstil, the Reuss state theatre was built during 1900–02 and designed by Heinrich Seeling. Largely reconstructed during 1977 following war damage, the green-and-white building's symmetrical façade has a staircase tower at either side with an statue of an angel watching over the main entrance. The phrase 'MUSIS. SACRUM' is emblazoned below here, picked out in gold. A central dome dominates the entire structure which now houses the municipal theatre and concert hall, with a programme of ballet and opera.

To the west of the Bühnen der Stadt is the **Kunstgalerie** (opening times: Tues, Wed and Fri–Sun 10.00–18.00, Thurs 12.00–20.00). Housed in a charming, Baroque orangery in what were the palace kitchen gardens, the building is semicircular in layout (earning it the local nickname of 'Bratwurst') and was built between 1729 and 1732 to designs by G.H. Krone, the central pavilion being added in 1748–49. There are temporary exhibitions of art held here as well as the permanent display with work dating from medieval times to the present day. Most noteworthy was the Otto Dix exhibition, celebrating the town's most famous artist who was born in a house on Mohrenplatz, not too far from the west crossing over the Weisse Elster. The artist's birthplace was restored to mark the centenary of his birth and a new **Otto Dix Museum** opened in 1991 to house the town's collection of his early and Neue Sachlichkeit work. Also on the pleasant Mohrenplatz, beside the Otto Dix Museum, is the late Gothic hall church of **Kirche St Marien**. Dating from c 1400–40, the church tower is a squat, stone structure from the top of which rises an incongruous, slender steeple.

To the south, just across Mohrenplatz, is the **Schloss Osterstein**, so badly damaged during Allied bombing on 6 April 1945 that no effort was made at restoration and the remains of the once awesome Baroque castle were removed apart from the 12C Romanesque Keep. A terrace café, built on the foundations of the upper palace court in 1964 with good views over the town, offers little compensation for the loss of such an important historic building.

Retrace your steps back over the river Weisse Elster and the Küchengarten and take Ernst-Toller-Strasse south-east through Puschkin Platz and souht-east down Schlossstrasse. Note the modern **Haus der Kultur** (House of Culture) on the right, pride of the Communist authorities when it was built between 1977–81 with its 1700 seater auditorium. Further south in the centre of the massive Zentraler Platz is the **Stadtmuseum** (opening times: Sat–Thurs, 10.00–17.00) housed in the former town prison and orphanage. The red-and-white Baroque building stands in splendid isolation amongst the anonymous concrete and glass of this part of Gera. Built between 1732–38, the building no longer houses prisoners and children but interesting furniture from the Osterstein Castle, historic prints and displays mapping out the history of the town.

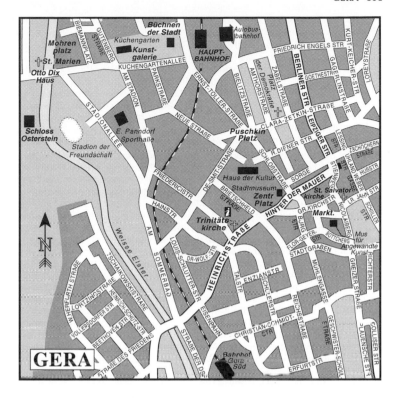

Cross Heinrichstrasse south to Burgstrasse and east to the highlight of any visit to Gera—the MARKT. Surrounded by Renaissance buildings, this modest square is supremely evocative of the Renaissance past. The **Rathaus**, designed by Nicol Gromann and built during 1573–76, is situated in the south-eastern corner and dominates the square. It is the 56m high staircase tower on the front of the building which is particularly striking. Built in an octagonal form, it is placed asymmetrically and surmounted by a slender bell-tower with clocks. The main entrance portal stands at the base of the tower and is richly decorated with coats of arms and mythological figures, dating from 1576. In the basement of the Rathaus is a good restaurant and the satirical cabaret act, Fettnäppchen, performs here regularly.

In the centre of the Markt is the **Simsonbrunnen** (Simson Fountain) originally by Caspar Junghans the Elder and constructed in 1685–86. This is a contemporary replica, dating from 1979, which shows the Biblical Samson standing astride a lion, the open jaws of which spout water. Next-door-but-one to the Rathaus there is a comprehensive bookshop, particularly good for travel literature, and on the south-western corner is the impressive **Apotheke am Markt**. Built in the 17C, it has a superb oriel window dating from 1606. The rich carving shows the Apostles, the Four

Seasons and the coats of arms of the Solms, Reuss, Schwartzburg and Hohenlohe families, surmounted by a weather vane.

From the Markt head uphill east up Grosse Kirchstrasse, noting the fine Burgher houses at No. 7, which dates from 1712, and No. 17 dating from 1765, to reach the **St Salvatorkirche**. This triple-naved, Baroque church was built between 1717–20 with the addition of a tower in 1781–82 on the west side. The church interior is reached by means of a sweeping staircase and a visit is certainly recommended because of the suprising Jugendstil interior. The church was totally refurbished during 1903 and many of the interior fittings are in the then fashionable Art Nouveau style. The pulpit, for example, is decorated with undulating lines and exotic fruit and flowers.

To the north of the St Salvatorkirche is the **Museum für Naturkunde** (Museum of Natural History; opening times: Tues–Sun 10.00–17.00). It is interesting not so much for its dusty display of local geology and natural history, as for its location in the **Schreiberhaus**. Built during 1687–88 for this wealthy, merchant family, it is the oldest dwelling to be preserved in Gera. The museum is worthy of a visit to see the original richly ornamented Baroque hall. At the rear of the Museum für Naturkunde are the **Geraer Höhle** (caves, guided tours Mon–Thurs 11.00 and 15.00, Sat 14.00 and 15.00, Sun 10,00, 11.00, 14.00 and 15.00). Not for the faint-hearted, this tour of underground caverns reveals the working conditions of the 17C and 18C, when these underground caverns were used as workshops. Continue south down Steinweg, noting the Baroque Burgher house at No. 15, dating from 1706, to reach the **Museum für angewandte Kunst** at Nos 37–39 Greizer Strasse. This is located in the historically important **Ferbschen Haus**, the largest house dating from the 18C left in Gera and contains an interesting display of local arts and crafts. Head west down Stadtgraben, north-west up Reichstrasse and then south-west down Heinrichstrasse, passing the hideous and expensive Hotel Gera to reach the last architectural sight on the tour, the **Trinitätiskirche** (Trinity church). This Gothic church was founded in the 14C and further extended in 1611. Inside there is a splendid, Baroque altarpiece, a good late Renaissance pulpit and a fine painted ceiling. The late Gothic, exterior pulpit dating from c 1500 on the north side of the church was originally part of the Wolfgang Chapel—no longer in existence.

48

From Gera to Kohren-Sahlis via Altenburg and Windischleuba

Gera—47km Altenburg—7km Windischleuba—4km Gnadstein—3km Kohren-Sahlis.

This tour takes in the north-eastern corner of Thuringia and a little of Freistat Sachsen with some of the lesser-known sights of eastern Germany. Off the beaten track, it features a fine Museum in Altenburg and some out-of-the-way German castles.

Leave **Gera** on the B7 headed east through the wooded landscape of north-east Thüringen. The road slants to a more north-east direction after the main intersection with the E4. The leisurely drive passes alongside the river Pleisse before heading directly north to Altenburg. The town is approached from the south on Schmollrische Landstrasse and plentiful parking can be found by continuing north to Puschkin- strasse.

Regular trains also run from Gera to Altenburg.

A. Altenburg

52,500 inhabitants.

Tourist Information: Weibermarkt 17, 04600 Altenburg. Tel. 31 11 45). Opening times: Mon 09.00–16.00, Tues 09.00–17.00, Wed 09.00–18.00, Thurs and Fri 09.00– 16.00.

Altenburg is a moderately sized town with a certain Renaissance ambience. It is best known in Germany as the home of the card game, Skat. But visitors will be disappointed if they buy a souvenir pack here, as they only begin from number six! (the game does not involve numbers 1 to 5). There are impressive museums in the town as well as an early 15C Schlosskirche (Castle Church), 10C Schloss and the Lindenau Museum. The latter is of international quality with brilliant examples of pre-Renaissance Italian art. It is little known as Altenburg has been off the tourist beat for so long. It deserves to be on the itinerary of any visitor with an interest in art.

History. Altenburg was the capital of the Duchy of Sachsen-Gotha-Altenburg until 1918 when the eight Thüringian states joined to make the new Freistat Thüringen with Weimar as the capital. There are many traces of this regal ancestory in Altenburg, which was first mentioned in 976 AD as an important intersection between trade routes. The Schloss began life as a fortress in the 10C when Altenburg was the ruling town of the surrounding Pleissland. Friedrich I (nicknamed Barbarossa after his red beard) lived in the Schloss during 1152–90 and the town was officially recognised in 1256. The Schloss developed from a fortress to a Royal Residence from the 15C onwards. In 1455 a famous event in German history took place at the Castle; the two young princes, 14-year-old Ernst and 12-year-old Albrecht were abducted from their bedroom in the Schloss by the knight, Kunz von Kauffungen, to found the royal family of Saxony. Prince Albrecht was to give his name to the Albrechtsburg at Meissen, built as the new family seat in 1471–85. From 1603–72 Altenburg was the capital of the Duchy of Sachsen-Altenburg and the seat of the Sachsen-Gotha-Altenburg line from 1826 to 1918.

Altenburg also flourished as a trading centre over the centuries, with streets devel- oping around the commercial centre of the Markt. From 1832 playing cards were manufactured here for the card game of Skat, with the national body based in the town from 1927. Arguments over certain games which cannot be resolved are brought to the Skat Court at Altenburg for a final verdict. Altenburg has been rather overshad- owed by Leipzig, which lies only 45km to the north, and was part of the Leipzig district under GDR rule from 1952 to 1990. It now lies within the state of Thüringen. Its great royal heritage, impressive collections and proximity to two other Länder will surely guarantee more growth in the future as a centre for tourism.

From Puschkinstrasse take the Neubauerstrasse east and continue in the same direction down Nansenstrasse to bring you into the MARKT. The distinctive church facing onto the Markt is the **Brüderkirche**, an odd mix of stepped gabled nave with towering, slender spire in earthy red. The Tourist Information Office can be found here and the Renaissance glory of the town centre is on full display.

The **Rathaus** stands to the south of the Markt beside Moritzstrasse. This imposing building was erected in 1562–64 to designs by N. Grohmann, with a fine octagonal tower complete with decorative clock, stepped gables and Ratskeller, the doorway of which is decorated with German Renaissance ornament. The corner bay window has fine 16C stone carving illustrating the ruling Saxon princes. During the week the Markt thrives as a lively centre for trade, and is now fully pedestrianised.

From the Markt continue east to Wallstrasse and down Frauenfelstrasse to the **Rote Spitzen** (Red Points), a strange-looking church with one pointed steeple and one round tower. Built in characteristic red brick, it was founded as part of an Augustine Monastery in the 13C. Return to Wallstrasse and continue north to the **Schloss**, which stands at the summit of a towering, porphyry rock. A winding driveway leading to the castle is flanked by two obelisks built in the early 18C. Most of the Schloss dates from between the late 17C and the 19C but there are 11C remains on the north side in the form of the Flasche, a tower built into the defence walls. To the south-west stands the late Gothic **Schlosskirche**, rebuilt during 1645–48. Inside, amongst the rich decoration and star-vaulting, is a fine 18C organ, built by Heinrich Gottfried Trost in 1735–38 and played by Bach during his visit here in 1739. Inside the courtyard is a lively Baroque statue of Neptune dating from c 1602. In the Schloss itself is the **Schloss und Spielkartenmuseum** (opening times: Tues–Sun 09.00–17.00, last admission 16.30). Guided tours of the Schloss interior run from the museum (Tues–Sun 10.00–16.00) and offer views of the splendid **Festsaal** with its marble columns, gilded capitals and painted ceiling by Karl Mossdorf illustrating the legend of Cupid and Psyche. The smaller 20C **Bachsaal**, with equally lavish painted ceiling, is also included in the tour. Both rooms are used occasionally for concerts. Also within the museum is a display devoted to the history of Altenburg, with examples of Meissen and oriental porcelain and weaponry; the history of card-playing since the 17C is well represented.

The **Schlosspark** in which the Schloss is situated is a pleasant location for a stroll or a picnic. Planned by Peter Joseph Lenné in the 19C, the Teehaus and Orangery to the east of the Schloss were built in 1712 and designed as garden follies by Johann Heinrich Gengenbach in fashionable, Neo-Classical style. Take the path north past the Teehaus to the **Lindenau Museum** which is surely the high point of any visit to Altenburg (opening times: daily 09.00–12.00 and 13.00–17.00). Housed in an Italian Renaissance Revival building dating from 1873–75, the collection was founded by Bernhard August von Lindenau (1779–1854) a high-ranking civil servant. The main attraction is the 180 Italian works of art dating from the 13C to 16C—one of the most extensive in Europe outside Italy itself. Part of this collection is on display on the first floor. Most striking is the *Throned Madonna* by Lippo Memmi of c 1340 which shimmers with gold leaf. The dedicated expressions of mother and child are quite moving. There are other works of equal quality by Simone Martini, Fra Angelico, Filippo Lippi, Giovanni Santi, Masaccio and Signorelli. On the ground floor is an amazing collection of over 300 Greek, Roman and Etruscan vases. There is also a display of 19C and 20C fine art and graphics on this floor.

To the east is the **Mauritianum** of **Naturkundemuseum** (Natural History Museum, Mon–Fri, 08.00–12.00, 13.00–17.00 and Sun 10.00–17.00) housed in a modest pavilion built in 1908 with the usual displays of fossils, stuffed animals with startled expressions and preserved insects. Return to the Schloss complex and continue south-west across Theaterplatz to view the **Landestheater**, built in 1869–71 as the court theatre. The building was designed in Italian Renaissance style by Julius Richard Enger and largely inspired by Semper's opera house in Dresden. A diverse range of concerts are staged here (Box Office opening times: Tues–Fri, 09.00–17.00, tel. 31 12 12).

Behind the Landestheater to the west is the Brühl and Alter Markt, the oldest marketplace in Altenburg. On the south side stands the **Seckendorffsche Palais**, a Baroque town house built 1724–25. Behind this is the **Skatbrunnen** (Skat Well) of 1903 showing four arguing jacks carved in stone. To the west of the Well is the main parish church, the grey stone **Bartholomaikirche** dating from the late 15C with a noble octagonal tower in four tiers crowned by a cupola. Inside is evidence of earlier building—the Romanesque crypt, dating from 12C. To the north of the Bartholomaikirche is the **Botanischer Garten**, reached by taking the Burgstrasse west and then Haeckelstrasse and Spalatinpromenade north.

South of the Markt, down Schmöllnsche Landstrasse then left and east down Riegenstrasse is the Nikolaikirchturm, a 12C structure originally built as part of the town's fortifications. It stands in the dilapidated area known as the Nikolaiviertel (Nicholas Quarter) with rundown, deserted housing which is ripe for restoration as an historic district of the town. Further south is the massive Volkspark with boating lake complete with small zoo situated on an island in the centre.

B. Windischleuba

Head north out of Altenburg on the B93 up Leipzigerstrasse signposted to Borna. After c 5km take the B7 right to **Windischleuba**, a tiny village which stands on the southern shores of the massive lake, Stausee Windischleuba (camping on the north side). Here stands the **Schloss Windischleuba** where the lyricist Borries von Munchhausen lived (1874–1945). The 19C Schloss was built on the foundations of a 14C Wasserburg or fort.

From Windischleuba continue on the B7 over the border into Freistat Sachsen. Take the next major turning right onto the B95 to Dolsenhain then the minor road east to Gnadstein. In this small village is the **Burg Gnadstein**. Founded in the 10C with a Palace added later, it stands romantically perched on top of the 33m high Bergfried. There is a museum in the Burg and three altarpieces by P. Breuer dating from 1502–03 in the Burgkapelle. Continue east to **Kohren-Sahlis** (2000 inhabitants; Tourist Information, tel. 40494 258) where a charming fountain, the Töpferbrunnen (Potter's Fountain), can be seen in the main square. Built in red brick, with craftsmen depicted on its eight sides, it quite rightly features in much of the tourist literature of the region. There is also a museum devoted to pottery and crafts in the village, the Töpfermuseum.

From Kohnen-Sahlis head north to Roda where the B7 is joined then left and west back to Altenburg on the B7 and B93. Alternatively it is possible to turn north when you join the B93 and then follow the B95 and E2 north to Leipzig.

49

From Weimar to Grosskochberg, Rudolstadt, Saalfeld and the Schloss Schwarzburg

Weimar—40km Grosskochberg—7km Rudolstadt—13km Saalfeld—17km Schwarzburg.

This route covers the south-eastern pocket of Thuringia, following the River Saale downstream with its numerous historic castles and picturesque, wooded scenery. The tour finishes in the Schwarza Valley, popular amongst Germans for outdoor holidays, the area also boasts many ruined castles including the Schloss Schwarzburg.

Head south by means of R. Breitscheid-Strasse and the A85 out of Weimar, passing through Gelmeroda and noting the Schloss Belvedere to the left. After crossing the E40 motorway the A85 leads to Bad Berka, through Blankenhain and onto Teichel. The next turning right leads to the village of **Grosskochberg** with the Renaissance **Schloss Kochberg**. Once a fortified castle, founded in the 12C, it had a moat supplied by natural springs. Little of the Romanesque original remains, and the present building dates from the 16C and 17C. The four-winged Renaissance palace was refurbished in Baroque style in the 1730s. The palace was owned by the Stein family and the great love of Goethe's life, Charlotte von Stein, occasionally stayed here during the late 18C. Goethe was a frequent visitor during 1775–88 and the castle is now a memorial to the poet with a special Goethe Museum which includes the Stein family writing desk on which Goethe recklessly carved his name on the occasion of his first visit. The Schloss, with its whitewashed walls and sloping gables, picked out in ochre, is controlled by the National Institute of Research and Commemoration of Classical German Literature and is regarded as an important site by academics. The building itself stands in a landscaped park, the Baroque garden house beside the palace was converted into a small theatre for amateur productions during 1796–99.

Return to the A85 and continue south to Rudolstadt.

situated high above the water on a wooded rock. Founded in 14C as a border fort, the present Schloss dates back in parts to 1403. During the 17C, when the defensive role no longer existed, conversions were made in the Baroque style. In the 18C more rebuilding took place to make the Schloss into a hunting lodge in the Rococo style. The exterior consists of splendid towers, some half-timbered, and a cobbled courtyard. Inside there are a variety of rooms from different historic periods including the SCHLOSSKAPELLE, dating from 1624–25, which houses a magnificent Silbermann organ (1743) and the RITTERSAAL (Knight's Hall) which has a fine painted Renaissance ceiling. The grounds of the Schloss were created during 1749–53 when earth was moved there by local peasants to cover the rock. The pretty Sophienhaus pavilion was built in the grounds at the same time in Rococo style.

To reach the **Schwarza Valley** and Schwartzburg itself, take the A88 south out of Rudolstadt, staying on that road when it forks off to the right (towards Bad Blankenburg). After Schwarza take the next turning right to **BAD BLANKENBURG** (8500 inhabitants; Tourist Information: Am Bahnhof, 07422 Bad Blankenburg (tel. 22 19 or 26 66), a small town with a big 12C ruined castle. Covering an area of 250 x 100m the **Schloss Greifenstein** was one of Germany's most substantial, feudal castles. It was also the birthplace of the tragic figure of King Günther von Schwarzburg who attempted to rival Emperor Charles IV for his position but was poisoned in 1349.

Continuing south-west on a more minor road into the beautiful Schwarza Valley, the village of **Schwarzburg** is reached. Here, to the south-west of the village, stands another Schloss, ruined since 1940 with a restored Baroque KAISERSAAL (Imperial Hall). The castle dates back to 11C and was renovated and restored many times subsequently, with the last version dating from 1724. The ruin stands perched on a wooded rock high above the village, and acted as the ancestral home of the princes of Schwarzburg. There is a small museum here, devoted to a display of weaponry and craft. For good views of the Schwarza Valley, Schwarzburg and its castle the **Trippstein**—a rocky crag north-west of the town, is ascended by means of a well signposted path (taking c 1 hour). For railway enthusiasts there is a precarious mountain railway which runs from **Oberweissbach**, 8km south-west of Schwarzburg, a distance of 1400m on a gradient of 1:4 to the mountain station of **Lichtenhain**. Covering a climb of 323m, it is claimed to be the steepest railway line for standard gauge carriages in the world.

A. Rudolstadt

32,000 inhabitants.

Tourist Information: 32a Ernst-Thalmann Strasse, 07407 Rudolstadt. Tel. 23633). Opening times: Mon 13.30–17.00, Tues and Fri 09.00–12.30 and 13.30–17.00, Wed 09.00–12.30 and 13.30–16.00, Thurs 09.00–12.30 and 13.30–18.00, Sat 10.00–13.00.

Rudolstadt has two focal points, the Schloss Heidecksburg which dominates the town from a north-western hill and the town centre, with its Baroque buildings and Folklore Museum. The town stands on the banks of the River Saale, just north of its intersection with the River Schwarza.

History. The existence of Rudolstadt as a town goes back at least to the 9C, with its first documentary mention. From the 14C onwards the town was governed by the Schwarzenburg family, who owned two castles unfortunately destroyed during the battles of 1345. The present castle was built in the 18C by the Princes of Schwarzburg-Rudolstadt, as the ruling family was then known. The town earned the reputation for being a 'Klein-Weimar' (Little Weimar) in the 18C and it was here that Schiller met his wife-to-be Charlotte von Lengefald and where he first met Goethe. A china factory opened here in 1762 with other, small businesses following. The state of Schwarzburg-Rudolstadt became part of the Free State of Thuringia following the First World War. In GDR times, Rudolstadt was celebrated as a centre for the production of synthetic fibres but now its cultural significance has come to the fore once more.

Behind the Bahnhof and across the River Saale is the Heinrich-Heine-Park, location of the **Volkskundemueum Thüringer Bauernhäuser** (Folklore Museum of Thuringian Farmhouses; opening times: Wed–Sun 09.00–11.30 and 13.00–16.30) a fascinating museum of everyday, rural life of the region. There are two original, half-timbered houses dating from the late 17C; complete with wooden shutters they look like something from a Grimm's fairy tale. Inside authentic furniture, household utensils and tools can be seen.

Heading north from the Bahnhof the main MARKTPLATZ is reached, with the 16C **Rathaus** complete with later Baroque decorated oriel window, roof turrets and good Ratskeller. Behind the Marktplatz rises the magnificent **Schloss Heidecksburg**. This is the only example of Rococo architecture in northern Germany except Sanssouci at Potsdam. It was begun in 1735 when the old Renaissance palace was razed by fire, and Prince Friedrich Anton, having recently been promoted to a prince of the Holy Roman Empire, aspired to the Baroque splendour of Dresden. The Schloss was designed by Johann Christoph Knöffel (1686–1752) the leading Dresden architect, who had been appointed Oberlandbaumeister of the city in 1734. The only building work by Knöffel to survive the Second World War in Dresden is the Hofkirche, which he completed following Chiaveri's departure for Rome in 1748. The Schloss at Rudolstadt is therefore Knöffel's most important surviving piece of architecture.

The building has three wings and elegant tower; the double Renaissance portal on the northern wing is the sole reminder of the former palace. The **Schlossmuseum** is housed here (opening times: 09.00–17.00, closed Fri) with a moderately interesting display of various weaponry and local history, housed on two floors. Entrance to the main state appartments is gained through taking a guided tour from the Chapel in the west wing (Tues–Sun 09.00–17.00). The Chapel itself contains a good display of locally produced porcelain. Inside the Schloss the most striking room is the double height FESTSAAL. Built by Krohne during 1743–46, the upper level has delicate bowed balconies which alternate with painted panels. Beneath the balconies on the lower floor are concave niches which contain ornamental porcelain. The walls are decorated with marbled stucco by Italian craftsman Johann Baptist Pedrozzi (1710–78) who also worked in Potsdam. There are many splendid examples of ceiling painting by Deisinger in the palace, not least here with the massive representation of Mount Olympus. There are further examples of such rich, Rococo decoration and furniture throughout the Schloss, including the Spiegelkabinett and Bänderzimmer, with their beautifully inlaid floors. The tour concludes with the Art Gallery which contains a collection of 17C–20C paintings including an impressive work by Caspar David Friedrich, *Morning Mist on the Mountains* (1808). Through skilful use of stippling, Friedrich perfectly evokes the haunting qualities of a mountain summit, swathed in mist.

From Rudolstadt take the A85 south, then turn off to the right 4km out of the main town, to the suburb of Volkstedt where Schiller stayed on his second visit to Rudolstadt in 1788. Continue south for 9km to reach Saalfeld.

B. Saalfeld

33,400 inhabitants.

Tourist Information: 4 Blankenburger Strasse, 99996 Saalfeld. Tel. 3950. Opening times: Mon and Sat 09.00–13.00, Tues–Fri 09.00–13.00 and 14.00–15.00.

Saalfeld is situated on the northern fringe of the Thüringian slate mountains on the banks of the River Saale. Best known for its Feengrotten (Fairy Grottoes) the town also boasts a secular, Romanesque building, a former Franciscan Monastery and three original town gates.

History. In 1071 a Benedictine monastery was founded on Petersberg hill and the town grew during the ensuing 12C. Trade routes from Nuremberg to Leipzig triggered the expansion of Saalfeld and the town walls, castle of Hoher Schwarm and the Franciscan monastery were built. The development of mining during the 14C and 15C instigated further growth. A flourishing middle class meant that some fine Renaissance houses were built, some of which still stand today. From 1680 to 1735 the town was the seat of the Saxe-Saalfeld line but Saalfeld suffered decline as a commercial centre from the 16C until the 19C when industrialisation breathed new life into the economy. Steelworks were built here as well as paint and machinery being produced in new factories. During the Second World War a substantial part of the historic town centre was destroyed but the town prospered during GDR rule with the continuation of steel production. Traditionally a resort for water sports, walking and climbing, Saalfeld's historic features and geographic location should guarantee future prosperity.

From the Hauptbahnhof cross the River Saale on the Bahnhofstrasse and head west. This brings you to the 16C **Saaltor**, one of the surviving town gates which gave access to Saalfeld in former times. Continue south-west down Saalstrasse, noting the examples of 17C building at No. 11, the Stadtapotheke, and at No. 17, Höhn House, to reach the MARKTPLATZ, the central public space of Saalfeld which has existed in some form since 1180. The **Rathaus** on the south-eastern side was built between 1529 and 1537 in late Gothic and Renaissance style, its most notable aspect being the staircase tower which protudes from the centre of the main façade capped by a slender spire. One rectangular and one rounded, corner oriel windows

flank the tower; they are both richly decorated and deserve close inspection. Opposite is the remarkable **Markapotheke** (Court Pharmacy) a secular building in the Romanesque style dating back to the 12C with many subsequent alterations. Note the arched windows with stone mullions.

Continue north to the splendid Gothic hall church, the **Stadtkirche S Johannis**. Founded in 1380 and completed in the 16C, the church has two graceful steeples which flank the chancel and three naves. The exterior is decorated with sandstone carving dating back to the time of the church's foundation and influenced by the School of Parler; the west portal is particularly noteworthy. Inside there are some remarkable works of art including a life-size statue of John the Baptist, carved c 1514 by H. Gottwalt, and a winged altarpiece dating from 1480.

Continue north up Brudergasse to the former Franciscan Monastery situated at No. 5 Münzplatz (opening times: Tues–Fri 08.00–12.00 and 13.00–16.00, Sat and Sun 09.30–12.00 and 13.00–17.00). This now houses the **Thüringer Museum** with a good display of medieval carving in wood created in local workshops. There are also local coins, examples of Thuringian craft and displays concerned with the history of mining in the museum. Also of note is the interior, the plaster ceilings on the upper floor were created by J.H. Ritter c 1725. Some of the late Gothic monastery remains including the two chapels and a portion of the cloisters. Further north of the Altstadt, up Schloss Strasse, is the Baroque Schloss dating from 1677, now used by local government for administration purposes.

Return to the Marktplatz and the Saaltor, then take the road left, Am Hügel, south to reach the **Schlösschen Kitzerstein**. Now a Music School, this small palace was built in the 16C and is crowned by two magnificently shaped gables. Beside the Schlösschen is the former **Kirche St Nikolai**, the oldest church in Saalfeld. Founded in 13C as the castle church, it was converted into living quarters in the 19C. Beside the Kirche St Nikolai stands the romantic ruin of the **Hoher Schwarm**. This stone edifice was built for Count von Schwartzburg in the late 13C and early 14C and still has two slim, castellated turrets.

The jewel in Saalfeld's crown however, has to be the **Feengrotten**, reached by heading south-west from the Marktplatz, down Obere Strasse and Sonnenberger Strasse. The walk takes about 30 minutes. The caves were mined for their rich deposits of vitriol and alum from 16C until supplies were exhausted and the mine closed in 1846. Interest in the caves was resurrected in 1910 when water seeping from the closed mine was found to be rich in minerals. The caves were once again opened up and it was found that the interaction of water and the natural minerals present had led to the formation of fantastic stalactites and stalagmites. The walls of the caverns are covered with various minerals producing an amazing, multicoloured effect. The Feengrotten are entered through a 500m gallery which leads through three floors (guided tours, Feb–Nov 09.00–17.00). Most stunning is the Märchendom mit Gralsburg (Fairytale Cathedral with Holy Grail Castle). The natural wonder of the caves is heightened by the use of coloured lighting.

From Saalfeld it is a short drive (c 10km) south on the A85 to **Hohenwarte Stausee**, a huge reservoir created by damming the River Saale. There is a profusion of camp sites around this expanse of water and it is possible to take a boat trip around Hohenwarte. The views are quite spectacular such as trip, as the wooded hills which surround the water rise to between 500m and 700m in height. To the south of Hohenwarte is the **Schloss**

INDEX

Ahrenshoop 243
Altenburg 353
Arnstadt 302
August I, (Augustus the Strong)
143,144, 154, 158, 160, 162
Augustusburg 202

Bad Blankenburg 360
Bad Doberan 233
Bad Heiligendamm 233
Barth 244
Bauhaus 20, 89, 292
Bautzen 188
Behrens, Peter 20, 48
Berlin 31
Ägyptisches Museum 72
Akademie der Wissenschaften
52
Alexanderplatz 56
Alte Königliche Bibliotek 51
Alte National Galerie 59
Altes Museum 58
Anhalter Bahnhof 86
Annenkirche 81
Antikenmuseum 73
Bauhaus-Archiv-Museum für
Gestaltung 89
Bebelplatz 50
Belvedere 70
Berlin Museum 87
Berliner Dom 55
Berlinische Galerie: Museum
für Moderne Kunst,
Photographie und
Architektur 86
Bode 62
Botanischer Garten 80
Botanisches Museum 81
Brandenburger Tor 15, 47
Brecht, house of Bertolt 84
Breitscheidplatz 39
Bröhan Museum 72
Brücke Museum 81
Brüder Strasse 88
Budapester Strasse 46
Charlottenburg Palace 67
Charlottenburg Palace Grounds
70
Dahlem 73

Berlin cont'd
Deutsche Staatsbibliothek 50
Deutsche Staatsoper 52
Deutscher Dom 52
Deutscher Theater 83
Dorotheenstädtischer un
Friedrichswerdersche Friedhof
84
Ephraimpalais on Mühlendaum
56
Fernsehturm 57
Französischer Dom 52
Freie Universität Berlin 82
Friedrichstadt-Palast 84
Friedrichstrasse 49
Friedrichstrasse station 83
Friedrichwerdersche Kirche 53
Friseurmuseum 85
Funkturm 73
Gemäldergalerie 76
Georg Kolbe Museum 73
Glockenturm 73
Grosser Müggelsee 92
Grunewald 81
Gutshaus Dahlem 81
Handwerkmuseum 56
Hardenbergplatz 39
Hedwigskirche 51
Heimat Museum 72
Hitler's Bunker 47
Humboldt University 50
Husemannstrasse 85
Jagdschloss Grunewald 81
Jüdisches Gemeindehaus 90
Kaiser-Wilhelm-
Gedächtniskirche 39
Käthe-Kollwitz-Museum 90
Kietz 92
Knoblauchhaus 56
Kollwitz Platz 85
Köpenick 90
Köpenick Local History
Museum 91
Kreuzberg 85
Kulturforum 47, 64
Kunstgewerbemuseum 66, 92
Kupferstichkabinett 80
Landwehrkanal 46
Lustgarten 58
Marienkirche 56

Berlin cont'd
  Märkisches Museum 88
  Martin-Gropius-Bau 86
  Marx-Engels-Platz 58
  Matthäikirche 66
  Mausoleum 71
  Museum Berliner
    Arbeiterleben um 1990 85
  Museum für Deutsche
    Geschichte 54
  Museum für Deutsche
    Volkskunde 80
  Museum für Indische Kunst 74
  Museum für Islamische Kunst
    79
  Museum für Naturkunde 85
  Museum für Ostasiatische
    Kunst 79
  Museum für Verkehr und
    Technik 87
  Museum für Völkerkunde 75
  Museum Haus am Checkpoint
    Charlie 85
  Museum Island 58
  Musikinstrumenten Museum
    64
  Nazi Air Ministry 86
  Neue Nationalgalerie 65
  Neue Wache 54
  Neues Museum 60
  Nikolaikirche 56
  Nikolaiviertal 55
  Olympic Stadium 73
  Otto Nagel Haus Gallery 89
  Palast der Republik 55
  Pariser Platz 48
  Pergamon Museum 60
  Philharmonie 64
  Pioneerpark Ernst Thälmann
    91
  Platz der Akademie 51
  Potsdamer Platz 47
  Prenzlauer Berg 85
  Prinzessinnenpalais 52
  Reichstagsgebäude 48
  Rotes Rathaus 56
  S-Bahn 32
  Savignyplatz 90
  Schauspielhaus 51
  Schinkel Pavilion 70
  Schloss Bellevue 89
  Schloss Köpenick 91

Berlin cont'd
  Schlossbrücke 54
  Siegessäule 46
  Skulpturengalerie 75
  Soviet Embassy 49
  Staatsbibliothek 65
  Synagogue 84
  Tegel Airport 31
  The Tiergarten 64
  Theater am Schiffbauerbamm
    83
  Tiergarten 46, 64
  Topographie des Terrors 86
  U-Bahn 32
  University district 82
  Unter den Linden 49
  Zeughaus 54
  Zoo Station 32
  Zoologischer Garten 39
Binz 255
Bismarck, Otto von 13, 36
Bodt, Jean de 54
Brandenburg 135

Charles V, Emperor 12, 13
Chemnitz 198
Chorin 120
Colditz 195
Cottbus 114
Cranach, Lucas the Elder 18, 149

Dessau 291
Dix, Otto 20, 350
Dornburg 344
Dresden 143
  Akademie des Bildenden
    Kunste 153
  Albertinum 148
  Alstadter Wache 156
  Alte Meister 148, 149
  Altmarkt (Old Market) 145
  Augustusbrücke 160
  Blaues Wunder 161
  Blockhaus 160
  Brühlsche Terrasse 156
  Dreikönigskirche 160
  Frauenkirche 148
  Georgentor 154
  German Hygiene Museum 145
  Goldener Reiter 160
  Grünes Gewölbe 148, 151
  Hauptstrasse 160

Dresden cont'd
  Historisches Museum 157, 159
  Hofkirche 154
  Italienisches Dorfchen 155
  Jägerhaus 161
  Japanisches Palais 160
  Kreuzkirche (Church of the
    Cross 145
  Landhaus 148
  Landtag 154
  Mathematisch-
    physikalischer Salon 157, 159
  Munzkabinett 152
  Museum der Fruhromantik 160
  Museum für Volkskunst 161
  Museum of Pre-history and the
    Museum of Ethnology 161
  Museum of the Town of
    Dresden 148
  Neue Meister 150
  Neumarkt 148
  Neustadt Market 160
  New Town Hall 145
  Porzellansammlung 157, 158
  Residenzchloss 154
  Schillerhaus 161
  Schloss Albrechtsberg 161
  Schloss Eckberg 161
  Schloss Lingner 161
  Schlossplatz 154
  Semper Opera House 155
  Sistine Madonna by Raphael
    149
  Spiegelzimmern 154
  Stallhof (Royal Mews) 153
  The Palace Quarter 153
  Theaterplatz 155
  Tierkundemusuem 157
  Verkehrsmuseum (Transport
    Museum) 153
  Weisser Hirsch 161
  Zwinger, The 157
Dürer, Albrecht 18, 149

Eberswalde 118
Eisenach 298, 305
Elbe, River 143, 162
Eldena 262
Erfurt 312
Erzgebirge (Ore Mountains) 143,
  201
Ettersberg 326, 340

Finow, river 118
Frankfurt an der Oder 123
Frauenstein 204
Frederick I (Barbarossa) 11
Frederick I 18, 34
Frederick II, the Great 13, 34, 35,
  50, 94
Freiberg 202
Friedrich, Caspar David 19, 69,
  215, 225
Garz 253
Gera 349
Goethe, Johann Wolfgang von 19,
  302, 310, 327, 329
Göhren 255
Görlitz 191
Gotha 318
Grabow 265
Greifswald 258
Grosskockberg 356
Güstrow 214

Halberstadt 271
Halle 278
Harz Mountain 271
Havel 106
Hiddensee 256
Hitler, Adolf 14, 20, 37
Hohe Sonne 298
Hohenzollern, Albrecht von 12

Illmenau 302
Ilm river 326

Jena 345
Jerichow 296

Kapellendorf 344
Knobelsdorff, Georg Wenzeslaus
  von 50, 51, 52, 68, 69, 98, 103
Kollwitz, Käthe 60, 85, 90, 172
Kühlungsborn 232
Kuort Oybin 193

Langhans, Carl Gotthard 47, 52,
  56, 68, 70
Lauterbach 254
Lehde 113
Leipzig 177
  Ägyptisches Museum 184
  Alte Borse, Die 182
  Alte Rathaus 181

Leipzig cont'd
  Alte Waage, Die 182
  Altstadt 180
  Auerbachs Keller 181
  Bachmuseum 183
  Deutsche Bucherei 187
  Deutsches Buch und Schrift
    museum 187
  Grassaimuseum 186
  Hauptbahnhof 180
  Hochschule für Graphik und
    Buchkunst 186
  Königshaus 182
  Museum für Bildene Kunst 185
  Museum für
    Kunsthandwerks 186
  Museum für Völkerkunde 186
  Musikinstrumenten-
    museum 186
  Neues Gewandshaus 184
  Neues Rathaus 184
  Nikolaikirche 181
  Nikolaischule 181
  Oper 184
  Russische Kirche 187
  Stadtgeschichtliche Museum
    182
  Thomaskirche 183
  University 184
  Volkerschlachtdenkmal 187
  Zum Kaffeebaum 182
Lenné, Peter Joseph 46
Lübben 111
Lübbenau 113
Ludwigslust, Schloss 264
Luther, Martin 12
Lutherstadt Wittenberg 286

Magdeburg 266
Meissen 173
Mengs, Anton Raphael 154
Merseburg 282
Mirow 221
Moritzburg, Schloss 170
Mühlhausen 342
Müritz, Lake 221

Nationalpark Vorpommersche
  Boddenlandschaft 243
Naumberg 283
Nering, Johann Arnold 18, 54, 67
Neubrandenburg 223
Neustadt-Glewe 265

Neustrelitz 221
Neuzelle 130
Niederfinow 123
Nordhausen 341

Oder, River 129
Otto I 11

Permoser, Balthasar 144, 152, 154,
  158
Pillnitz 162
Pirna 166
Poel, Island of 232
Pöppelmann, Matthaeus Daniel
  19, 144, 158, 163
Potsdam 101
Potsdam, Park Sanssouci 93
Prenzlau 132
Putbus 253
Quedlinburg 275

Radebeul 169
Rauch, Daniel Christian 50, 72, 84
Rennsteig 298
Reuter, Fritz 225, 309
Rostock 235
Rudolstadt 357
Rügen 251

Saale, River 356
Saalfeld 358
Sassnitz 256
Schadow, Gottfried 47, 54, 60, 84
Schadow, William 19
Schiller, Friedrich 348
Schinkel, Karl Friedrich 19, 49, 51,
  53, 54, 58, 59, 69, 70, 84, 95, 101,
  107, 108, 156, 184, 189,193, 194
Schinkel, Karl Friedrich 19, 156
Schlüter, Andreas 18, 19, 54, 55,
  56, 68
Schmalkalden 299
Schwerin 205
Sellin 255
Semper, Gottfied 155
Semper, Gottfried 144
Sonderhausen 341
Spreewald 110
Stendal 294
Sternberg 213
Stralsund 244
Suhl 301

Tangermünde 295
Tautenburg 345
Thuringian Wald 298
Tieck, Frederick 51, 53

Usedom, Island of 263

Vilmnitz 255

Waren 222
Wartburg Castle 305, 310

Weimar 326
Wernigerode 273
Wieck 263
Wilhelm II, Kaiser 13, 14, 36, 55
Windischleuba 355
Wismar 226
Wolgast 263
Wörlitz 289

Zittau 193
Zwickau 200

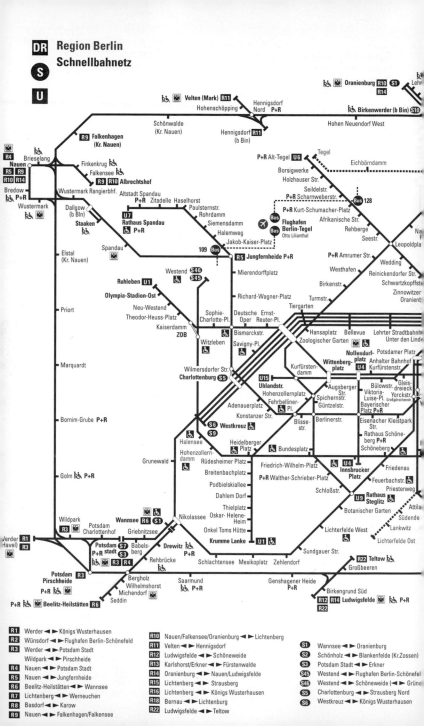

Region Berlin
Schnellbahnetz

DR S U

Legend of lines:

R1	Werder ◄ ► Königs Wusterhausen	
R2	Wünsdorf ◄ ► Flughafen Berlin-Schönefeld	
R3	Werder ◄ ► Potsdam Stadt	
	Wildpark ◄ ► Pirschheide	
R4	Nauen ◄ ► Potsdam Stadt	
R5	Nauen ◄ ► Jungfernheide	
R6	Beelitz-Heilstätten ◄ ► Wannsee	
R7	Lichtenberg ◄ ► Werneuchen	
R8	Basdorf ◄ ► Karow	
R9	Nauen ◄ ► Falkenhagen/Falkensee	

R10	Nauen/Falkensee/Oranienburg ◄ ► Lichtenberg
R11	Velten ◄ ► Hennigsdorf
R12	Ludwigsfelde ◄ ► Schöneweide
R13	Karlshorst/Erkner ◄ ► Fürstenwalde
R14	Oranienburg ◄ ► Nauen/Ludwigsfelde
R15	Lichtenberg ◄ ► Strausberg
R16	Lichtenberg ◄ ► Königs Wusterhausen
R18	Bernau ◄ ► Lichtenburg
R22	Ludwigsfelde ◄ ► Teltow

S1	Wannsee ◄ ► Oranienburg
S2	Schönholz ◄ ► Blankenfelde (Kr.Zossen)
S3	Potsdam Stadt ◄ ► Erkner
S45	Westend ◄ ► Flughafen Berlin-Schönefeld
S46	Westend ◄ ► Schöneweide (◄ ► Grüna
S5	Charlottenburg ◄ ► Strausberg Nord
S6	Westkreuz ◄ ► Königs Wusterhausen

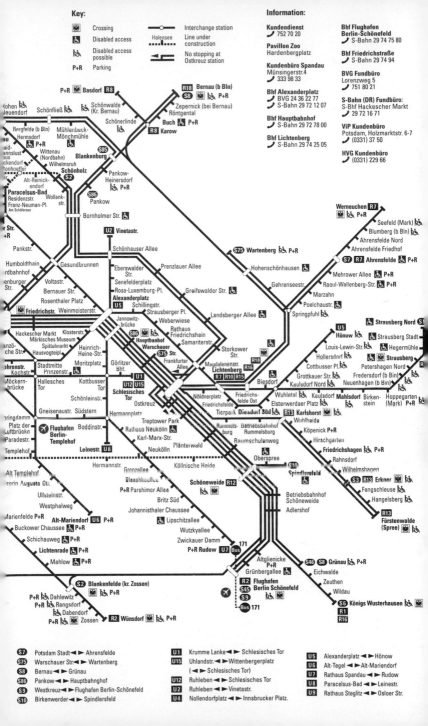

A. Rudolstadt

32,000 inhabitants.

Tourist Information: 32a Ernst-Thalmann Strasse, 07407 Rudolstadt. Tel.
Opening times: Mon 13.30–17.00, Tues and Fri 09.00–12.30 and 13.30–17.00,
09.00–12.30 and 13.30–16.00, Thurs 09.00–12.30 and 13.30–18.00, Sat 10.00–1

Rudolstadt has two focal points, the Schloss Heidecksburg which do
nates the town from a north-western hill and the town centre, with
Baroque buildings and Folklore Museum. The town stands on the banks o
the River Saale, just north of its intersection with the River Schwarza.

History. The existence of Rudolstadt as a town goes back at least to the 9C, with its
first documentary mention. From the 14C onwards the town was governed by the
Schwarzenburg family, who owned two castles unfortunately destroyed during the
battles of 1345. The present castle was built in the 18C by the Princes of Schwarzburg-
Rudolstadt, as the ruling family was then known. The town earned the reputation for
being a 'Klein-Weimar' (Little Weimar) in the 18C and it was here that Schiller met his
wife-to-be Charlotte von Lengefald and where he first met Goethe. A china factory
opened here in 1762 with other, small businesses following. The state of Schwarzburg-
Rudolstadt became part of the Free State of Thuringia following the First World War.
In GDR times, Rudolstadt was celebrated as a centre for the production of synthetic
fibres but now its cultural significance has come to the fore once more.

Behind the Bahnhof and across the River Saale is the Heinrich-Heine-Park,
location of the **Volkskundemueum Thüringer Bauernhäuser** (Folklore
Museum of Thuringian Farmhouses; opening times: Wed–Sun 09.00–11.30
and 13.00–16.30) a fascinating museum of everyday, rural life of the region.
There are two original, half-timbered houses dating from the late 17C;
complete with wooden shutters they look like something from a Grimm's
fairy tale. Inside authentic furniture, household utensils and tools can be
seen.

Heading north from the Bahnhof the main MARKTPLATZ is reached, with
the 16C **Rathaus** complete with later Baroque decorated oriel window, roof
turrets and good Ratskeller. Behind the Marktplatz rises the magnificent
Schloss Heidecksburg. This is the only example of Rococo architecture in
northern Germany except Sanssouci at Potsdam. It was begun in 1735 when
the old Renaissance palace was razed by fire, and Prince Friedrich Anton,
having recently been promoted to a prince of the Holy Roman Empire
aspired to the Baroque splendour of Dresden. The Schloss was designed
by Johann Christoph Knöffel (1686–1752) the leading Dresden architect
who had been appointed Oberlandbaumeister of the city in 1734. The only
building work by Knöffel to survive the Second World War in Dresden is
the Hofkirche, which he completed following Knöffel's departure for
Rome in 1748. The Schloss at Rudolstadt is therefore Knöffel's most important surviving piece of architecture and the double Renaissance

The building has three wings, the main chapel in the west wing is gained
portal on the northern wing. The
Schlossmuseum is housed striking room is the double height
with a moderately in 1743–46, the upper level has delicate
housed on two
through taking
09.00–17.00). Th
porcelain. Insid
FESTSAAL. Bui

es which alternate with painted panels. Beneath the balco-
ower floor are concave niches which contain ornamental
e walls are decorated with marbled stucco by Italian craftsman
ptist Pedrozzi (1710–78) who also worked in Potsdam. There are
endid examples of ceiling painting by Deisinger in the palace, not
re with the massive representation of Mount Olympus. There are
examples of such rich, Rococo decoration and furniture throughout
chloss, including the Spiegelkabinett and Bänderzimmer, with their
utifully inlaid floors. The tour concludes with the Art Gallery which
ntains a collection of 17C–20C paintings including an impressive work
y Caspar David Friedrich, *Morning Mist on the Mountains* (1808).
Through skilful use of stippling, Friedrich perfectly evokes the haunting
qualities of a mountain summit, swathed in mist.

From Rudolstadt take the A85 south, then turn off to the right 4km out of
the main town, to the suburb of Volkstedt where Schiller stayed on his
second visit to Rudolstadt in 1788. Continue south for 9km to reach Saalfeld.

B.   Saalfeld

33,400 inhabitants.

Tourist Information: 4 Blankenburger Strasse, 99996 Saalfeld. Tel. 3950. Opening
times: Mon and Sat 09.00–13.00, Tues–Fri 09.00–13.00 and 14.00–15.00.

Saalfeld is situated on the northern fringe of the Thüringian slate mountains
on the banks of the River Saale. Best known for its Feengrotten (Fairy
Grottoes) the town also boasts a secular, Romanesque building, a former
Franciscan Monastery and three original town gates.

History. In 1071 a Benedictine monastery was founded on Petersberg hill and the town
grew during the ensuing 12C. Trade routes from Nuremberg to Leipzig triggered the
expansion of Saalfeld and the town walls, castle of Hoher Schwarm and the Franciscan
monastery were built. The development of mining during the 14C and 15C instigated
further growth. A flourishing middle class meant that some fine Renaissance houses
wer   me of which still stand today. From 1680 to 1735 the town was the seat
             d line but Saalfeld suffered decline as a commercial centre from the
             hen industrialisation breathed new life into the economy. Steel-
             as well as paint and machinery being produced in new factories.
             orld War a substantial part of the historic town centre was
             prospered during GDR rule with the continuation of steel
             esort for water sports, walking and climbing, Saalfeld's
             ic location should guarantee future prosperity.

             the River Saale on the Bahnhofstrasse and
             16C **Saaltor**, one of the surviving town
             in former times. Continue south-west
             les of 17C building at No. 11, the
             use, to reach the MARKTPLATZ,
             has existed in some form since
             was built between 1529 and
             st notable aspect being the
             the main façade capped
             corner oriel windows

flank the tower; they are both richly decorated and deserve close in:
tion. Opposite is the remarkable **Markapotheke** (Court Pharmacy) a 1
secular building in the Romanesque style dating back to the 12C with m:
subsequent alterations. Note the arched windows with stone mullions.

Continue north to the splendid Gothic hall church, the **Stadtkirche S**
Johannis. Founded in 1380 and completed in the 16C, the church has two
graceful steeples which flank the chancel and three naves. The exterior is
decorated with sandstone carving dating back to the time of the church's
foundation and influenced by the School of Parler; the west portal is
particularly noteworthy. Inside there are some remarkable works of art
including a life-size statue of John the Baptist, carved c 1514 by H. Gottwalt,
and a winged altarpiece dating from 1480.

Continue north up Brudergasse to the former Franciscan Monastery
situated at No. 5 Münzplatz (opening times: Tues–Fri 08.00–12.00 and
13.00–16.00, Sat and Sun 09.30–12.00 and 13.00–17.00). This now houses
the **Thüringer Museum** with a good display of medieval carving in wood
created in local workshops. There are also local coins, examples of Thuringian craft and displays concerned with the history of mining in the
museum. Also of note is the interior, the plaster ceilings on the upper floor
were created by J.H. Ritter c 1725. Some of the late Gothic monastery
remains including the two chapels and a portion of the cloisters. Further
north of the Altstadt, up Schloss Strasse, is the Baroque Schloss dating from
1677, now used by local government for administration purposes.

Return to the Marktplatz and the Saaltor, then take the road left, Am
Hügel, south to reach the **Schlösschen Kitzerstein**. Now a Music School,
this small palace was built in the 16C and is crowned by two magnificently
shaped gables. Beside the Schlösschen is the former **Kirche St Nikolai**, the
oldest church in Saalfeld. Founded in 13C as the castle church, it was
converted into living quarters in the 19C. Beside the Kirche St Nikolai
stands the romantic ruin of the **Hoher Schwarm**. This stone edifice was built
for Count von Schwartzburg in the late 13C and early 14C and still has two
slim, castellated turrets.

The jewel in Saalfeld's crown however, has to be the **Feengrotten**,
reached by heading south-west from the Marktplatz, down Obere Strasse
and Sonnenberger Strasse. The walk takes about 30 minutes. The caves
were mined for their rich deposits of vitriol and alum from 16C until supplies
were exhausted and the mine closed in 1846. Interest in the caves was
resurrected in 1910 when water seeping from the closed mine was found
to be rich in minerals. The caves were once again opened up and it was
found that the interaction of water and the natural minerals present had led
to the formation of fantastic stalactites and stalagmites. The walls of the
caverns are covered with various minerals producing an amazing, multi-
coloured effect. The Feengrotten are entered through a 500m gallery which
leads through three floors (guided tours, Feb–Nov 09.00–17.00). Most
stunning is the Märchendom mit Gralsburg (Fairytale Cathedral with Holy
Grail Castle). The natural wonder of the caves is heightened by the use of
coloured lighting.

From Saalfeld it is a short drive (c 10km) south on the A85 to **Hohenwarte**
Stausee, a huge reservoir created by damming the River Saale. There is
profusion of camp sites around this expanse of water and it is possible
take a boat trip around Hohenwarte. The views are quite spectacula
such as trip, as the wooded hills which surround the water rise to bet
500m and 700m in height. To the south of Hohenwarte is the **Schloss**

situated high above the water on a wooded rock. Founded in 14C as a border fort, the present Schloss dates back in parts to 1403. During the 17C, when the defensive role no longer existed, conversions were made in the Baroque style. In the 18C more rebuilding took place to make the Schloss into a hunting lodge in the Rococo style. The exterior consists of splendid towers, some half-timbered, and a cobbled courtyard. Inside there are a variety of rooms from different historic periods including the SCHLOSSKAPELLE, dating from 1624–25, which houses a magnificent Silbermann organ (1743) and the RITTERSAAL (Knight's Hall) which has a fine painted Renaissance ceiling. The grounds of the Schloss were created during 1749–53 when earth was moved there by local peasants to cover the rock. The pretty Sophienhaus pavilion was built in the grounds at the same time in Rococo style.

To reach the **Schwarza Valley** and Schwartzburg itself, take the A88 south out of Rudolstadt, staying on that road when it forks off to the right (towards Bad Blankenburg). After Schwarza take the next turning right to **BAD BLANKENBURG** (8500 inhabitants; Tourist Information: Am Bahnhof, 07422 Bad Blankenburg (tel. 22 19 or 26 66), a small town with a big 12C ruined castle. Covering an area of 250 x 100m the **Schloss Greifenstein** was one of Germany's most substantial, feudal castles. It was also the birthplace of the tragic figure of King Günther von Schwarzburg who attempted to rival Emperor Charles IV for his position but was poisoned in 1349.

Continuing south-west on a more minor road into the beautiful Schwarza Valley, the village of **Schwarzburg** is reached. Here, to the south-west of the village, stands another Schloss, ruined since 1940 with a restored Baroque KAISERSAAL (Imperial Hall). The castle dates back to 11C and was renovated and restored many times subsequently, with the last version dating from 1724. The ruin stands perched on a wooded rock high above the village, and acted as the ancestral home of the princes of Schwarzburg. There is a small museum here, devoted to a display of weaponry and craft. For good views of the Schwarza Valley, Schwarzburg and its castle the **Trippstein**—a rocky crag north-west of the town, is ascended by means of a well signposted path (taking c 1 hour). For railway enthusiasts there is a precarious mountain railway which runs from **Oberweissbach**, 8km south-west of Schwarzburg, a distance of 1400m on a gradient of 1:4 to the mountain station of **Lichtenhain**. Covering a climb of 323m, it is claimed to be the steepest railway line for standard gauge carriages in the world.